Praise for Robert C

"Robert Christgau is not just the self-proclaimed Dean of American Rock Critics, he is the thinking man's rock fan, a tirelessly leftist boho thinker whose dense thicket of prose in praise of pop has influenced a generation of rock writers." —Roy Trakin, *Hits*

"Christgau is one of the three writers who have shaped the language, perspective, and values of virtually all rock criticism. . . . While Marcus's view of rock is metaphoric and Bangs' was psychodramatic, Christgau's is empirical. Christgau's hundred words on an album . . . have often been the first and last on the subject, rendering more long-winded analyses superfluous. . . . Christgau has managed to remain conspicuously undated and relevant in a medium that almost immediately renders everything else dated and irrelevant. He's as well-positioned to view and analyze the '90s as he was the '60s, '70s, and '80s. . . . Christgau is in fact one of the fairest and least predictable critics, always making an effort to see beyond his biases and acknowledge the worth of artists who aren't really his cup of tea. . . . He constantly inspires his readers, by sheer force of argument, to re-evaluate their opinions, which is ultimately the truest measure of a critic's value." —Steve Erickson, *LA Weekly*

"His pungent, often pithy reviews balance pointed remarks against letter grades, a combination that can give his readers a surprisingly detailed sense of what a record is like." —Joel Selvin, *San Francisco Chronicle & Examiner*

"[Christgau] was already writing mature, intelligent rock criticism in the mid-'60s, when rock writing was almost entirely confined to teen magazines. He is certainly the dean of the zingy one-liner." —Robert Palmer, *The New York Times*

"The best record guide money can buy." —Chuck Eddy, *Request*

"Robert Christgau understands rock 'n' roll. When he's on—when his knotty thought processes and compacted prose connect—no other rock critic can touch him." —Mark Coleman, *Rolling Stone*

CHRISTGAU'S CONSUMER GUIDE: ALBUMS OF THE '90s

ALSO BY ROBERT CHRISTGAU

Grown Up All Wrong: 75 Great Rock and Pop
Artists from Vaudeville to Techno

Christgau's Record Guide: The '80s

Rock Albums of the '70s: A Critical Guide

Any Old Way You Choose It:
Rock and Other Pop Music, 1967–1973

CHRISTGAU'S CONSUMER GUIDE: ALBUMS OF THE '90s

ROBERT CHRISTGAU

ST. MARTIN'S GRIFFIN ⚏ NEW YORK

About 15 percent of the full and capsule reviews in this book are previously unpublished, as are the two introductions and all of the appendices. Most of the remainder is based (sometimes verbatim, although many hundreds of reviews have been slightly or drastically revised) on Consumer Guides and other pieces written for *The Village Voice* between 1990 and 2000, plus auxiliary material—in all but a few cases sentences or phrases—written for *Playboy, Rolling Stone, Spin,* and *Details.* Citing the source for each of approximately 3,800 reviews and listings would obviously be impossibly unwieldy. But I would like to gratefully acknowledge permission from the *Voice, Playboy, Rolling Stone,* and *Spin* for material that originally appeared in their pages. A portion of the review for Clint Black's *The Hard Way* was originally published in a different form in *Details* magazine.

www.stmartins.com

Library of Congress Cataloging-in-Publication Data

Christgau, Robert.
    Christgau's consumer guide : albums of the ' 90s / Robert Christgau.
      p. cm.
  ISBN 0-312-24560-2
    1. Sound recordings—Reviews. 2. Rock music—1991–2000—Discography. I. Title.

ML156.9.C52 2000
016.78164'0266—dc21   00-031731

First Edition: October 2000

10 9 8 7 6 5 4 3 2 1

This book is dedicated to everyone
who's ever written to thank me
for turning him or her on to a record.
If I haven't responded, I'm sorry.
It always means a lot—in fact,
it helps keep me going.

INTRODUCTION

This isn't supposed to be where I tell you how I wrote this book. This is supposed to be where I tell you how I conceive the '90s. Only, how I wrote this book dovetails with how I conceive that decade. So let me outline my method of business.

The time-consuming work of engaging a multiplicity of recordings—of learning how they sound and discovering how they feel—has been standard in my life since the summer of 1969, when as a fledgling *Village Voice* rock columnist I thought up the Consumer Guide. For the next two decades, I dispatched 20 LPs a month with a brief review and a letter grade from A plus to E minus (A to C minus, practically speaking). But after I transformed my '80s columns into a book worthy of its ISBN, a task that involved double listening for a year or two, something had to give. I wanted to hear as much music as ever, from 10 to 18 hours a day of it. I just wanted to enjoy it more.

As long as you prefer compact cars and have never understood why people burden themselves with country houses, rock criticism is a peachy job. It would be graceless to complain about a life whose chief drawback is a shortage of shelf space. But one thing has always bothered me. I probably take active pleasure in more records than any critic out there—and not casually, either. By the time I parcel out an A or an A minus, I've heard the CD 5 or 10 times, concentrated hard at least once or twice, perused the credits and the lyric sheet if there is one, and ascertained that it gives me a charge I can't resist. If it doesn't, it's not worth an A or A minus—that's the main way I tell. My other secret is that I count cuts, avoiding the temptation to listen through the humdrum songs that interlard or trail off from the galvanizing few, which is how critics itching to announce their latest discovery fool themselves. But once the judgment is rendered and the review written, the record sometimes leaves my life forever. Looking over my A list from 1992, say, I can pick out half a dozen titles I don't remember playing since I wrote about them—records I wish I could play right now. Only I can't, because I'm listening to something newer that I want to know about.

I started working this way out of ethics (the label gave me this, I should use it) and hubris (the crude desire to know more about my subject than *anyone else in the world*). For quite a while I tried to sample at least a cut or two of every record that came my way, and got to 80 or 85 percent. But by 1980, when I finished my '70s book, I'd accepted the imperfection that my .800 average quantified—there were things I was never gonna dribble past the pitcher, much less slam out of the park. A decade later my BA was down to .400, and that's only counting the pitches I actually saw—plenty were never delivered. Being on all the major-label lists was no longer enough.

Independents were a factor in the '70s—in just the S's from that decade I count 20-odd, including traditional r&b, rock, and jazz companies, a few folk start-ups, and a stirring of the fan and DIY labels soon to mushroom into the postpunk underground. The *Voice* being the original alternative weekly, many such labels mailed me stuff. But one reason indies put out interesting music is that they're unrationalized, and since that extends to hit-or-miss PR, just keeping track of what was available soon became almost impossible. Moreover, not since the early-'80s heyday of Rough Trade, Twin/Tone, and SST has an indie imprimatur been anything to get excited about. The majors play it safe, supporting established artists, well-connected nonentities, imitations of whatever's selling, gifted young musos who color inside the lines, and occasionally some undeniable talent or genius. Even the good music they underwrite is too predictable. By serving specialist markets whose enthusiasms can be shared by generalists with open ears, indies underwrite an outsized share of rewarding music. But they have their own problems, usually starting with myopia of genre, scene, or—since most express the tastes of one or two impresarios—sensibility, with boosterism, aestheticism, obscurantism, and self-righteousness just down the track. Convinced of the justice of their cause, everyone in the indie world—owners, publicists, clerks, fans, fellow musicians, and what pass for critics—waxes ecstatic over music no one outside the circle need care about. By 1990, the predictive value of postpunk word-of-mouth was approaching zero.

I bring this up mainly because the Amerindie aesthetic has been keeping me busy for two decades now. In point of fact, the independent label explosion—itself just one aspect of the boutiquing of America, which in a direct response to the malling of America created a boom for all manner of workshop-crafted goods in the '80s—was hardly limited to rock. Even as the big boys conglomerated, there were folk and world and blues and jazz and soul and reggae and Latin and house and techno and rap and Christian companies all over the place. Though many indies released only a few records a year, others were prolific, and their total output was overwhelming, especially combined with expanded production at the majors and their shifting web of affiliates, farm clubs, vanity imprints, and distributees. So the decision not to listen to everything, which began as a straightforward piece of time management that formalized my limitations as a music processor, was by the end of the decade a physical inevitability. That wasn't my conscious motivation for adjusting my methods again. But I'm sure I sensed it.

In September of 1990, then, I overhauled the Consumer Guide. The hardest part of the job I'd set myself was telling a B minus from a C plus, and then finding language to say yet again that there weren't enough good songs on a record either way. So I decided to give B minuses and C pluses short shrift. Most of my readers—not critics and bizzers, but real-life consumers—used my primary critical outlet for its putative purpose. They wanted to know what to buy. So thenceforward—with time out for a November Turkey Shoot consisting entirely of pans—I'd review only A records, meaning anything from A minus, which would greatly predominate, to A plus. The bad ones I'd just list ungraded, as Duds. When a good song set me on the spoor of an otherwise negligible album, I'd give the song credit, as a Choice Cut. And, let's be realistic, there'd always be things on the cusp; it would be efficient to review those too, doling out the occasional B plus, formerly my commonest grade. As for the lower B pluses, well, the solid ones would get 10 words in a section called Honorable Mention. Wouldn't want to waste all that ear time, would I?

Not wasting ear time is a weakness of mine. Not cheating is another. So just to prove I'd given Honorable Mentions a fair shake, I thought it only proper to recommend cuts from them, a piece of fussbudgetry that's cost me hundreds of hours. But the Honorable Mention was the fatal flaw in this schema in any case. For the first year or two I wasn't too good at it—saying something meaningful in a phrase can be tough. But by 1994 or so the category, which initially added just three or four records a month, was up to 10 or 15, an extra job in itself. Other categories evolved as well. Early on I told myself I had to listen one final time before declaring anything a Dud, a scruple I eventually abandoned; some of the Duds in this book (meet and greet Ned's Atomic Dustbin) are records I specifically recall being unable to stomach again back when. In 1992 I initiated an unpublished file called Neither ("neither here nor there") for records that weren't good enough for Honorable Mention or bad enough for Duds. And in early 1993 I succumbed to the arguments of future *Voice* music editor Eric Weisbard and began reviewing and grading a Dud of the Month in each column. Where the highest grade for a Turkey was B minus, Duds included a fair number of dull, disappointing, or overhyped B's; for book purposes, the two categories have been combined. I trust my negative gradations are of critical interest. For consumption purposes, however, read everything from B on down as a flunk.

At some gross level the revamping worked as planned—I found about 20 more A records per year than in the '80s, and had more fun as a result. But I'm not certain this wouldn't have happened anyway. The reason I can't be sure is that in the '90s, musical production stopped expanding and started exploding. Supposedly the decade's biggest story is digital sound, which began by making the compact disc a commercial standard and ended by threatening to render the CD and the album itself obsolete via the Internet. But as of January 1, 2000, digital's main practical effects had been to encourage self-expression (aka bloat) by accommodating 75 minutes of music per disc where vinyl held 50, and to spur bizzers to deplete their archives in a deluge of reissues, reconfigured best-ofs, "rarity"-stuffed boxes, proudly unearthed old concert tapes, genre surveys of varyingly encyclopedic expediency, concept compilations that included series keyed to golf, cigars, and chicken soup, and newly canonized schlock, cheese, treacle, kitsch, and crap. Moreover, catalogue exploitation wasn't even the main reason production went through the roof. There were simply more artists making music and more hustlers financing it, in America and all over the world. The factoid I latched onto, a possible fabrication that's très poetic regardless, was that between 1988 and 1998 the number of recordings released annually increased *tenfold,* to something like 35,000. Even if the 35,000 included a whole lot of singles, which as near as I could tell it didn't, this would mean that there was more music recorded than there were hours in a year—quite possibly twice as much. I'd escaped completism in the nick of time.

Many bemoan this state of affairs. Artists record too soon, charge old DIY'ers belatedly smitten with the aesthetic efficiency of quality controls. It's impossible to rack everything, bitch retailers who once lured big spenders to best-sellers with one-stop shopping. We don't have time to prescreen anymore, snivel college radio jocks who've been conflating different with good since they discovered Mouse on Mars. And it's daunting for me too—I regularly contract vertigo contemplating all the records I'll never hear. But if I remain up-beat about the future of rock 45 years after its estimated birthdate, it's primarily because I've always believed the distinction between quantity and quality was 50 percent elitist jive.

The standard whine among my contemporaries concerns what I long ago dubbed The Mattering. Music doesn't "make a difference" anymore, 'tis said. Once we thought it would change the world; now we're lucky if it can change its socks. Who can possibly believe that Madonna and the Wu-Tang Clan mean as much to the Culture at Large as the Beatles and Aretha Franklin? These objections obviously reflect the strictly subjective reality of listeners who've heard far more music now than they had in 1969—listeners whose lives have accrued so much experiential bulk that nothing budges them much anymore. But they're real nevertheless. Much as I detest '60s nostalgia—and punk nostalgia, which sickens me less only because it isn't my fault—the popular music we call rock did once galvanize social forces in a way it hasn't since, not even if you regard the cripplingly site-specific U.K. rave/acid house/techno phenomenon as "revolutionary." As an unrepentant leftist, I'm distressed by this. In the tradition of Emma Goldman, who never had much use for rave either, I want a revolution I can pat my feet to. I wish rock and roll could spark or catalyze or at least provide the soundtrack to a drastic restructuring of the class system that ended racism, sexism, and homophobia in the bargain. But I never really expected that in the first place, which never stopped me from conceiving rock politically. So if it seems just about impossible now, don't put it past me to see a bright side.

To state it plainly, popular music in the year 2000 is a democratic cornucopia. Nothing else compares. Forget TV, which too readily induces the passivity envious elitists too readily blame on it. Forget movies, beyond the means of freelancers at their most low-budget. Forget sports, capitalist tools whether you love 'em (baseball, basketball) or hate 'em (football, hockey). Forget zine and Net and comix and fan-fantasy culture, all so atomized they hold out no promise or metaphor of broad-based communion. Music is the great equalizer. Created by a worldwide virtual community comprising hundreds of thousands of artisans of vastly disparate technical training, general education, and raw intelligence, milking hundreds of promiscuously disseminated styles and genres whose mixed pedigrees make nonsense of any notion of the pure or authentic, music puts us face to face with one of democracy's first principles, which is that people with nothing to say to you have plenty to say for themselves. You may not want to listen to all of them—a third of a century on, I'm still taking potshots at whiners, mooners, swooners, wimps, simps, snobs, thugs, back-slappers, breast-beaters, cunthounds, bigots, universalists, damn fools, pretentious wankers, and seekers after mystical enlightenment. But with the possible exception of damn fools (regular fools we obviously need), not a one of these objectionable personality types has proven incapable of skill, wit, joy, imagination, individuality, or musicality. Which means representatives of every one have had something to say to me after all.

Especially if you noticed how I set up this pronouncement by slipping from the warmly inclusive "rock and roll" to the impossibly general "popular music," you may think I'm some kind of universalist myself. But I'm not—I'm just a pluralist, into many-is-many, not all-is-one. Because I follow many genres without devoting my life to any of them, I understand the chronic disgruntlement of pop monists—aging alt-rockers, techno exutopians, roots loyalists, jammers, jazzers, citizens of the world, the Serbs, Croats, Bosnians, and Slovenians manqué of the hip hop community. Objectively, there's not enough going on in their worlds to keep any of them running at full capacity. And although many hip hoppers and a few armchair ethnomusicologists enthuse madly anyway, they'll never convince the rest of us. The reason ordinary consumers can't figure out what's going on with most raves in the flagship hip hop mag *The Source,* or for that matter its tiny world music counterpart *The Beat,* isn't just that ordinary consumers are square, or that superfans can't write, or that specialists are to formal wrinkles as princesses are to peas. It's that the reviewers in question are kidding themselves. I don't kid myself, and you don't have to either. There's just too much out there.

That's what I mean when I say that how I wrote this book dovetails with how I conceive the decade. Spread your net wide, experiment without slipping into self-improvement mode, and the way things are currently set up you'll never run out of new music. But while we're not kidding ourselves, let's not kid ourselves about boutique capitalism (which in this millennium is often online capitalism; though I reside in the retail paradise of Manhattan, I end up purchasing half the obscurities no one's sent me on the Internet anyway). People fret about The Mattering because most of the best popular music is what I've long called semipopular music. Semipopular music fuels subcultures without number, but its relation to any bigger social entity is a metaphor, not a promise; in fact, a cardinal value of most such subcultures is that bigger is worse. How anyone can believe this is altogether a good thing is beyond the ken of an old-fashioned humanist like me.

Yet though my style of eclecticism commits me to both pop and change, my nominees for the happening musics of the '90s are all subcultural, and also, give or take a few shifts in jargon and attitude, all the same as my nominees for the happening musics of the '80s. What once was rap now is hip hop, an endlessly various mass phenomenon that continues to polarize older rock and rollers, although it's finally convinced some gatekeeping generalists that it may be of enduring artistic value—a discovery to which they were beaten by millions of young consumers, black and white. The Amerindie of the early '80s became known as alternative or alt-rock, ascendant from Nirvana until 1996 or so but currently very unfashionable, never mind that the music is still there. And although I found well over 100 terrific new-in-America African albums in the '90s, I don't pretend they'll make you the life of the party. Its hip moment long over, Afropop is now clearly an eccentric taste unless you happen to be one of 500 million black Africans—I would guesstimate its non-African following in the 100,000 range.

Supposedly, an arthritic boomer like me shouldn't enjoy such things at all. Even Afropop, much of which gets here 10 or 15 or 40 years late and attracts an audience as aged as John Fogerty's, is seen as an affectation. But I swear the old-fashioned humanist in me craves all three styles, a hunger that proceeds directly from the taste epiphanies of my teens—the Alan Freed–style rock and roll of Chuck Berry, the Coasters, and "In the Still of the Night," with a touch of the Bird-Monk-Miles-Ornette-'Trane(-Brubeck) that filled my college years. It would be racially politic to cite in addition Jerry Lee Lewis, the Crickets, and "At the Hop," all favorites of mine, but in fact r&b crossing over hit me deepest. What I heard in '50s rock and roll, I believe (the formula undergoes perpetual modification), was pop music quite distinct from the pop music that preceded it, but pop music nonetheless. I heard good songs with a good beat. Although they foregrounded rhythm—in part because they had a more compelling beat, in part because that beat didn't have as much to compete with—the simple melodic resources of these songs were no less winsome than those of their Tin Pan Alley rivals. They were best sung by the unsophisticated—teenagers and their admirers, JDs and hillbilly cats, African Americans of modest pretension. Direct, compact, energetic, meant to move your body and create a disturbance in your mind, they were the province of a young, urban/suburban variant on what interested slummers since Herder had referred to as the folk.

Note, however, that when stuck on a New Hampshire campus far from WINS, I passed up "folk music" for jazz. This was a minority option—folkies transformed American rock in the '60s, not jazzbos. So rather than explain it—something about pulse and dissonance and hating Joan Baez—I will merely point out, in the way of a consumer advisory, that it bears on my enthusiasms to this day. I'm not musically schooled enough to follow jazz changes, but I get my charge from them anyway, because bebop and its progeny signify on a more vulgar level than connoisseurs of "America's classical music" might prefer. In fact, I access punk with much the same part of myself that loves Thelonious Monk, who (like punk) buzzes the synapses while stimulating gross motor function, a metaphor and catharsis designed for the modern city. In the '90s, avant-punks like Sonic Youth and Pavement made this convergence explicit as hip hop propagandists pumped jazz analogies—earning them best, I've always thought, in the screeching beats the Bomb Squad dropped on Public Enemy, not the literally jazz-inflected swang of A Tribe Called Quest. As for Afropop, it's considerably more jazzlike than Ameripop to this day.

But jazz is for shading—what I still value most is good songs with a good beat. The problem is that even for adepts of neoprimitivism, the preferred aesthetic of fine rock and rollers everywhere, good songs have gotten more complicated. Pop formulas that were liberating in the Brill Building's glory days are now often as deadening as snobs always charged. Beyond the international ballad of Celine Dion and Diane Warren—beyond the schlock that is always with us—two bigger-is-better genres made impressive passes at revitalizing the formularistic in the '90s: country and teenpop. But neither succeeded. The onset of Garth Brooks, a major artist despised by most critics, inspired much wild talk of a Nashville takeover. But Garth was Garth and Vince Gill wasn't, ditto Shania and Faith Hill; anyway, well before Brooks achieved self-parody it was clear that Nashville didn't address all of America any more undeniably than Newt Gingrich did. With teenpop, rampant for a year as I write, I don't have the benefit of hindsight. As with Nashville, however, the quality call is a no-brainer. Although there's genuine genius there, as is usually the case when entertainers fill a yawning need, most of it is pap. In the age of Internet boutiquing, I can imagine economic models in which teenpop and similarly mass-cultural strategies would dominate corporate rock, which has always idealized the passive consumer. But most of the best songs would be elsewhere, in subcultural interstices maintained by self-supporting artisans and small entrepreneurs.

Although I see the undaunted if segmented alt-indie world as the prime source, great songs are everywhere, from Shania and the Backstreet Boys to Le Tigre and Imperial Teen. Folkies write plenty, r&b revisionists quite a few. Forget lyrics-not-singing-or-meaning and Afropop is full of 'em; forget melody-not-hook-or-cadence and hip hop is fuller. But gradually, the good beat part of the rock and roll mantra has become more prominent, a development addressed in rather different ways by Afropop, where intricate polyrhythms flow and mesh, and hip hop, where rugged polyrhythms jerk and clash. The complexity of both musics (which sometimes exchange m.o.'s, natch) would have been unimaginable and probably intolerable in the '50s. But as far as partisans of the third significant '90s movement are concerned, the crucial action was elsewhere, in the dance movement Americans call techno, although Brits who've lived through their island's rave and/or acid house upheavals barely recognize the term.

Until they realized they weren't taking over the world, techno's prophets were the most utopian futurists rock has ever known. Much too much is made of the political bent of '60s rock; it was "nihilistic" punk that produced the great radical bands—Clash, Gang of Four, Minutemen, Mekons. But at least acidheads knew there was a war on. Beyond some antiauthority/antimilitary rant, the '60s that rave reinvented were a totally cultural affair in which drug-fueled dances and technological extensions of man were all the justice and equality a passion for change required. This illusion wasn't necessarily fatal—fond of much naive folk-rock for its naked postadolescent lyricism alone, I was fully prepared to get close to the high-tech textures and artificial energy of mindless electrodisco. In a few cases I did, too: Utah Saints! Utah Saints! But soon I realized that techno just wasn't for home consumption. Inextricable from massive sound systems, mixed in the live moment by the DJs who were its true auteurs, heightened by communal ecstasy and the chemical Ecstasy that made it feel real, it was designed to be accessed exclusively by its subculture. And it was also designed to kid itself—to leave its claims to magic immune to empirical verification.

Due in part to its disdain for vocals and song form, techno's subculture never got as massive as projected, never became bigger and better—certainly not in the U.S., and really not in Europe either. I like Big Beat, the poppest of its uncountable subgenres, and faithfully check out its *succès d'estimes,* most of which are overrated—although the very best, by Tricky and Moby and DJ Shadow, rank among the decade's truly brilliant albums. I also test-drive likely-looking compilations, the most accessible of which show up in my columns sporadically, if only as Honorable Mentions or Choice Cuts. But I don't want to kid you—my techno recommendations are for dabblers. Worse, I'm convinced dabbling is what the music deserves. Good songs with a good beat have been the essence of popular music for as far back as we can guess. They aren't used up, and they aren't going away. Any futurism that counts them out is no futurism at all.

And there in a nutshell is how I conceive that decade—richly chaotic, unknowable and that's good, thus highly subject to vagaries of individual preference, but nevertheless conducive to some manageable degree of general comprehension and enjoyment by any rock and roller. The main purpose of this book is to help you join in no matter where or when your tastes took shape—like it says, it's a consumer guide. Above all I'm urging you to please shake your groove thing or climb out your window. But I have another stake in this writing—a writer's stake, a commitment to language and ideas that assumes the best about who's shaking or climbing. I intend my paragraphs and one-liners to be informative, entertaining, and, uh-oh, original; at best I hope they say something new, even difficult, and at worst I insist that they take truisms a half-step further. Since this is rock and roll, I do joke around when possible—years of loud guitars have convinced me that ideas are best expressed rudely. Nevertheless, my reviews are often densely tex-tured—written for readers who may not catch all the references, but are willing and per-haps even eager to infer their context. In theory, precisely this sort of curiosity is what gets people to try out strange-looking records in the first place.

So I hope you read this book for fun and edification as well as buying tips. But since it's fine with me if buying tips are your prime concern, I ought to explain more about how it was put together before I direct you toward Jewel Ackah and away from Adamski. Ap-proximately 3,800 records released in the '90s are reviewed or listed herein. More than 500 of these were never Consumer Guided in the *Voice,* and many hundreds of the pre-viously published capsules have been tweaked, revised, or totally rewritten. Every A record I could find by May 2000 is reviewed herein. But where in 1990 I allowed as how I must have missed some B pluses, now I'm sure I've missed A minuses. For starters, there are imports, and not just by Brits—dozens if not hundreds of African records I've never heard would certainly make the cut. And despite the unreliability of subcultural word-of-mouth, I'm sure there's more '90s hip hop in my future. With alt-rock, where the ethos is closer to home, I'm more confident even if my disdain for lo-fi shoegazers makes me uncool forever. And with mainstream pop I believe I've gotten all of what not much there is to get, though I may have missed some country. Beyond a few young acoustic players, blues records were mostly bar fodder and journeymen repeating themselves in the '90s. But though the dancehall strain that dominated reggae proved as specialized as techno, it must have more to offer those who feel its groove and affect than I could find.

Yet with all these musics and a good many others I kept my antenna up and hit the high spots—most of the Duds, Neithers, and Choice Cuts you never heard of are records that somebody worth taking seriously pumped pretty hard. In fact, I deleted about 100 published Duds and unpublished Neithers from the book because only some tiny cabal ever gave them support—Sexpod, Linoleum, Drugstore, goodbye forever. I may have missed a few early records by artists I discovered late (I've yet to hear Destiny's Child's debut, the Dismember-ment Plan's either), but usually I've checked back and usually they're inferior. If an artist gets a good grade early in the decade and then vanishes, chances are excellent that I sampled a few later cuts and moved on—and that neither sales nor press impelled me to reconsider.

Criteria for inclusion and grading of best-ofs and archival music also merit explana-tion. I automatically consider any old material that's never been available on album in the U.S., whether newly unearthed live tapes or newly collected singles and vault exhuma-tions. With African and Latin American artists who've never enjoyed the U.S. hearing they deserve, old music is brand new. But in the pompous box-set rip-off, so-called rarities are customarily preferred as bait to consumers who already own the core music in an-other form. Except in the very few instances when the bait redefines a canon—James Brown's *Star Time* and Janis Joplin's *Janis* are shining examples—you can assume I rec-ommend single albums by the artist in question, not the box. With all compilations, utility and redundancy as well as listenability are relevant critical considerations, which is why some best-ofs (XTC's *Upsy Daisy Assortment,* say) that draw heavily on albums worth owning in themselves have been downgraded, and others have been ignored altogether. For the most part, excellent new best-ofs on artists who were already icons in 1990 have been left for some other book—a simple call with Lefty Frizzell or the Marvellettes, tougher with Woody Guthrie or Captain Beefheart. Since compilation itself is a quintes-sentially CD-era craft, I've honored the amazing likes of *Closer Than a Kiss* and *Ameri-can Pop: An Audio History,* and the rediscovery of *Anthology of American Folk Music* was such a pop event I couldn't ignore it. But if in the end any of my decisions in this area seems arbitrary, what can I say? Someone had to make them, so I did.

Alphabetization protocols are unchanged: by surname, nickname, or group's first word. Numbers and abbreviations are ordered as if spelled out; English articles are ignored, foreign articles treated as words. Especially thorny cases have been cross-referenced. Those familiar with earlier Consumer Guide books may wonder why I dispensed with the original grades I used to provide when a record got knocked up or down a notch or two. Because I decided the book's subject should be your albums rather than my opinions, that's why. (For the record, the biggest rise was accorded Shania Twain's *The Woman in Me,* C to Honorable Mention; the biggest dip was by the Kronos Quartet's *Pieces of Africa,* A minus to Neither. Ten or so titles lost an A, and as many Honorable Mentions picked one up.) Label designations are as they originally appeared, and although these shift with the corporate tides (which is why updating is useless), pursue artist-and-title and you'll find what you want. Multiartist compilations are now separated out at the end of each letter-chapter as well as cross-indexed in an appendix. Some Choice Cuts are marked [comp] or [ST] to indicate compilation or soundtrack in the confusing cases when the artist who recorded the song isn't credited with the album. Note also that Hon-orable Mentions, which in the *Voice* are listed in order of preference, have been divided into three-star, two-star, and one-star categories that reflect a similar gradation.

Those Honorable Mentions are all pretty good records—I'm rarely sorry to hear them again. So since tastes differ, you may want to avail yourself of a few, especially if you've figured out that your feeling for an artist or genre is warmer than mine. But since you could go broke just buying the nearly 900 albums that fill the A Lists in back, you should probably start there. In fact, I recommend that if you have your doubts about this book you perform a test. Go up toward the top of one of the A lists, where the true A's as opposed to high A minuses are found. Check out a few corresponding reviews, purchase the album that seems coolest, and—this is important—play it more than once when you get home. If you like it, buy the book; if you don't, move on.

Forgive me for believing I could sell a lot of copies that way.

KEY TO ICONS

An **A+** is a record of sustained beauty, power, insight, groove, and/or googlefritz that has invited and repaid repeated listenings in the daily life of someone with 500 other CDs to get to.

An **A** is a record that rarely flags for more than two or three tracks. Not every listener will feel what it's trying to do, but anyone with ears will agree that it's doing it.

An **A–** is the kind of garden-variety good record that is the great luxury of musical micromarketing and overproduction. Anyone open to its aesthetic will enjoy more than half its tracks.

A **B+** is remarkable one way or another, yet also flirts with the humdrum or the half-assed.

A ★★★ Honorable Mention is an enjoyable effort that consumers attuned to its overriding aesthetic or individual vision may well treasure.

A ★★ Honorable Mention is an likable effort that consumers attuned to its overriding aesthetic or individual vision may well enjoy.

A ★ Honorable Mention is a worthy effort that consumers attuned to its overriding aesthetic or individual vision may well like.

A ⓝ Neither may impress once or twice with consistent craft or an arresting track or two. Then it won't.

A 🍬 Choice Cut is a good song on an album that isn't worth your time or money— sometimes a ⓝ, more often a 🦃. Some 🍬s are arbitarily personal, others inescapably social. Sometimes one is so wondrous you'll be tempted to spring for the package anyway. More often it would fit sweetly onto a compilation you can only pray will include it.

A 🦃 is a bad record whose details rarely merit further thought. At the upper level it may merely be overrated, disappointing, or dull. Down below it may be contemptible.

A 🦃 is a bad record of some general import, though no artist should be saddled with more than two in a decade. What distinguishes a 🦃 from a 🦃 is that it's reviewed and graded. I'm aware of no 🦃 lower than D, and a few even get a B, a grade reserved for the *Voice* Dud of the Month, whereas the annual Turkey Shoot works down from B–. But such distinctions are, as the saying goes, academic. In this age of grade inflation, all of 'em flunk.

ACKNOWLEDGMENTS

I always end these things with her, so let's get this party started quickly: Carola Dibbell, Carola Dibbell, Carola Dibbell. She's my wife, my lover, my domestic partner. She's a great critic who writes better fiction. Her love of music is exceeded only by her tolerance for it. And on this book she did the dirty work, brainstorming structure and overseeing details of organization and manuscript prep as well as editing the newly written stuff, some 15 percent of the text.

Many others have also critiqued this material, of course, most prominently six *Voice* music editors: Doug Simmons, Joe Levy, Ann Powers, Evelyn McDonnell, Eric Weisbard, and Chuck Eddy. Tiny bits of it have been cribbed piecemeal from freelance work that originally appeared elsewhere: *Playboy* (Barbara Nellis, Helen Frangoulis), *Rolling Stone* (Nathan Brackett), *Spin* (Eric Weisbard, Charles Aaron, Craig Marks), and *Details* (James Truman).

Obtaining old records is always a pain with CG books, so I'm grateful I could call upon Vince Aletti, Nina Christgau, Chuck Eddy, Jason Gross, Tom Hull, Mark Jacobson, Joe Levy, Evelyn McDonnell, Ann Powers, Tom Smucker, and Eric Weisbard for personal loans. Rob Sheffield, who mailed me a bunch early, deserves special tribute, as does Will Hermes, who burned me five late. Together with the great Milo Miles, some of these guys also constituted my e-mail council on deletions. Levy, Powers, Weisbard, Tom Carson, Greil Marcus, Kit Rachlis, and John Rockwell weighed in on title variations. And in a time when many labels have made back catalogue virtually off limits to journalists, I'd like to thank Ken Braun, Alan Brown, Charlie Burton, Cindy Byram, Dan Cohen, Tom Cording, Stacey Earley, Kira Florita, Bobbie Gale, Michelle Gutenstein, Jessica Hopper, Jodi Levy, Sonia Muckle, Liz Rosenberg, Heidi Schuessler, Rick Steiger, Amy Wan, Karen Weissen, and Sandy Zolotka for raiding vaults on my behalf.

We've been overrun with record guides and rock encyclopedias since 1990, and I've consulted every one I got free. Rarely did this make me wonder whether I should quit while I was ahead, because most of them are aggressively mediocre. Four major and useful exceptions are Eric Weisbard and Rob Sheffield's *Spin Alternative Record Guide* (sharpest writing), Ira Robbins's *Trouser Press Guide to '90s Rock* (highest accuracy), Martin C. Strong's *Great Rock Discography* (maddest completism), and Patricia Romanowski and Holly George-Warren's *New Rolling Stone Encyclopedia of Rock & Roll*.

And though its facts cry out for double-checking (change that Will to Power date, guys), the online All-Music Guide (www.allmusic.com) is a resource no music journalist does without anymore. The same has gone for Joel Whitburn's always reliable *Billboard* books, since the early '70s.

My agent, Sarah Lazin, gladly took on the burden of peddling this book in a midlist-hostile time, and has provided needed support throughout its preparation. It's a good thing for us that the editor she found was Elizabeth Beier, whose enthusiasm, appreciativeness, flexibility, and all-around good judgment have minimized every potential difficulty. I thank both of them for being pleasures to work with as a matter of principle.

Joe Yanosik, who for reasons best known to himself catalogues my every published opinion in his computer, provided an invaluable fail-safe for Carola and me. He also scrutinized the A lists we prepared, and, wouldn't you know, found a dozen or so titles we'd missed despite all our triple-checking.

Last but not least (or truly last) is my daughter, Nina Christgau, who just last night heard Taana Gardner's "Heartbeat" for the first time and, after inventing a dance for it, immediately discerned what I'd never noticed—it was the source of Ini Kamoze's greatest bassline. Nina knows music through and through, and more than makes up for playing Z-100 too loud with endless insight and info. Also, she turned me on to the Backstreet Boys (although not, so far, Mariah Carey or 'N Sync).

The reason Nina's not last is that I wanted to end where I began and always begin, with her mom. Carola Dibbell, Carola Dibbell, Carola Dibbell. Thanks, darling. This year I promise we'll fix up the alcove.

Aaliyah: "Got to Give It Up" (*One in a Million,* Blackground/Atlantic '96)
Aaliyah: "Are You That Somebody" (*Dr. Dolittle: The Album,* [ST], Atlantic '98) ⬥

Abana Ba Nasery: *¡Nursery Boys Go Home!* (Green Linnet '92) "the guitar and bottle kings of Kenya"—sometimes charming, sometimes too charming ("Esiesi Siolle," "Elira Yesu Ndayanza") ★

ABC: *Absolutely* (Mercury '90) a career downhill—hear Martin Fry turn into the disco whore he begins by parodying so lovingly ("The Look of Love," "S.O.S.") ★

Paula Abdul: *Spellbound* (Virgin '91) 💣

Safi Abdullah: "Afrika Is Burning '89," "Another One Gone" (*Another One Gone,* Shanachie '90) ⬥

Ace of Base: *The Sign* (Arista '93) simple music for a perfect world ("All That She Wants," "Happy Nation") ★★★

Aceyalone: *All Balls Don't Bounce* (Capitol '95) ⓝ

Achanak: "Nukhe Chakhee Javana" (*What Is Bhangra?* [comp], I.R.S. '94) ⬥

Jewel Ackah: *Me Dear* (Highlife World import '90) A onetime soccer pro who's been singing 25 years, long enough to watch highlife sink from top of the Afropops to regional specialty, he's not down, no sir. Talking tradition here and synthesis there, based in Ghana but happy to service the Anglophone diaspora, he goes with what he knows, including blues licks, reggae beats, and pop-funk basslines. From Accra to Toronto, he's making it in his own little world, and he's here to tell you you can too. A–

Adam & the Ants: *Peel Sessions* (Strange Fruit '91) ⓝ

Bryan Adams: *Waking Up the Neighbors* (A&M '91) 💣

Adamski: *Liveandirect* (MCA '90) Acid house isn't stupid music; it isn't even bad music. It's music for some other species—with the Other, as always, relative to where one's Self happens to hang out. Singerless and virtually wordless, undeviating in its "textless" functionalism, it's impervious to consumer guidance: nobody who doesn't dance to it knows it exists, and nobody who does is gonna believe an alien like me. Nevertheless, it does exist, so say this: the best analogy isn't disco (though cf. MFSB and the Salsoul Orchestra) or dub or new age. It's fusion—beyond virtuosity, yet hopelessly in love with the almighty keyb. Though this guy isn't as weird and tricky as 808 State or A Guy Called Gerald at their fleeting best, his bottom seems suited to survival in an oxygenated environment, and once in a while he surges into something resembling life. There's the review. Now you can talk about it at parties. C+ 🦃

C.C. Adcock: "Done Most Everything," "Do Right Lil' Lady" (*C.C. Adcock,* Island '94) ⬥

Add N to X: *Avant Hard* (Mute '99) 💣

King Sunny Ade and the New African Beats: *Live at the Hollywood Palace* (I.R.S. '94) Ⓝ

King Sunny Ade: *E Dide/Get Up* (Mesa '95) Can't claim this sustains the promise he had going for him on both sides of the Atlantic in the early '80s—that sense of limitless possibility betrayed by chaos in Nigeria, parochialism in Gaia, and the failure of *Aura* to move up the charts. But it's possible to applaud his development of Lagos's recording facilities and still be glad he's cut another studio album outside of Africa. A nickel short on both hook and flow, it nevertheless achieves an internationally suitable balance of detonation and quietude—and of voice, percussion, and guitar. B+

King Sunny Ade: *Odù* (Atlantic/Mesa '98) Ade is no longer a signifier of polyrhythmic African mystery—he's a lesson learned and absorbed. Recorded almost live in a Louisiana studio, this is a convincing statement by an individual titan who dominates juju the way Joseph Shabalala does mbube. Ade's slightly roughened pipes subtract less than Jonah Samuel's piano and organ add to an almost jazzlike synthesis of studio-imposed concision and party-time expandability. And the lyrics are translated and transliterated, situating the music in its culture for anyone who cares. A−

Adventures of Stevie V: *Adventures of Stevie V* (Mercury '90) 💣

Aerosmith: *Get a Grip* (Geffen '93) There are no rules. Obscene megabucks, boring rehab, song doctors, turning 40, minuscule interest in doing something new—nothing stands between the world's greatest hard rock band and their best album since *Rocks*. The drugs long gone, they show a strong professional commitment to rebellion and an undiminished relish for the fleshpots. If the song doctors prescribed "I'd rather be O.D.in' on the/Crack of her ass," not to mention "It's like gettin' head from a guillotine," they were worth every point. And though at first you may miss the killer cut, the "My Fist Your Face" or "Janie's Got a Gun," in fact the midtempo, classic-rock, love-as-pain "Cryin'" should prove irresistible to anyone who doesn't equate good art with doing something new. A−

Aerosmith: *Big Ones* (Geffen '94) "Janie's Got a Gun" yes, "My Fist Your Face" no, two expert Michael Beinhorn add-ons yes, *Get a Grip* no ("Janie's Got a Gun," "Blind Man") ★★

Aerosmith: *Nine Lives* (Columbia '97) Ⓝ

The Affected: *A Fate Worse Than a Fate Worse Than Death* (Frontier '94) raised-on-AOR guitar with punk attitude—thousands try it, these particular Australians get it right ("Wilt," "Mind") ★★★

The Afghan Whigs: *Gentlemen* (Elektra '93) No Butch Vig or Steve Albini tidying or toughening up this sucker—those conflicted guitars are a direct function of the singer-writer-producer-guitarist's agonized self-exposure/-examination. If the album wears down into covers and instrumentals, that's only to signify its spiritual exhaustion. No reason to trust Greg Dulli—just his brain selling his ass at a higher convolution. But anyone susceptible to simpler lines, as fisherman or prey, can learn plenty. And the jaded can appreciate the clean, snakelike trajectory of the cast. A−

The Afghan Whigs: "My World Is Empty Without You/I Hear a Symphony," "Mr. Superlove" (*What Jail Is Like,* Elektra '94) 👁

The Afghan Whigs: *Black Love* (Elektra '96) doesn't know the Prince of Darkness as well as he thinks he does ("Double Day," "Going to Town") ★

The Afghan Whigs: *1965* (Columbia '98) Ⓝ

Africando: *Vol. 1: Trovador* (Stern's Africa '93) Ⓝ

Africando: *Vol. 2: Tierra Tradicional* (Stern's Africa '94) Ⓝ

Afro-Cuban All Stars: *A Toda Cuba le Gusta* (World Circuit '97) lots of soneros, lots of salseros, and Ry doesn't get in the way ("Habana Del Este," "Alto Songo") ★★★

After 7: *The Very Best of After 7* (Virgin '97) ⓝ

Christina Aguilera: *Christina Aguilera* (RCA '99) "Genie in a Bottle" was such a dazzlingly clever piece of teen self-exploration cum sexploitation that it seems the better part of valor to hope it was a fluke. But this was avoidance—like Leann and unlike Britney, Christina already has "adult" grit and phrasing down pat, and so threatens to join Gloria, Mariah, Celine, and Leann herself in the endless parade of Diane Warren–fueled divas-by-fiat hitting high notes and signifying less than nothing. "What a Girl Wants" is clever too, but in a far less ingratiating way—like its two-hour promotional video writ small, it raises the question of how this ruthlessly atypical young careerist can presume to advise girls not cursed with her ambition, and the fear that some of them will make her a role model regardless. Give me Left Eye any day. **C+**

Eric Agyeman: *Highlife Safari* (Stern's Africa '92) Guitarist Agyeman composed three of these six songs and sings only one—the one that wasn't on this classic LP in 1978, which is no ringer unless you resent its echoes of the unforgettable "Abenaa Na Aden?," in which case move on to something more Euro right now. If Ghanaians warmed to the palm-wine antecedents and Ashanti flavor of his musicianship, what Euros hear is his innate, acculturated gift for rhythm-melody and his conviction that scaling postcolonial highlife down to size doesn't mean traditionalizing it altogether. Catchy not cute, charming not picturesque. **A–**

Ahmad: *Ahmad* (Giant '94) Masterminded by Kendal Gordy, the scion turned hip hop pop-pup said to have discovered this South Central youth after he was bused to high school in Pacific Palisades, *Ahmad* proves yet again how meaningless a concept "commercial" is. If it weren't for the one about the lad who holds up a minimart so he won't get slammed by the neighborhood bad guys, you'd think Gordy still believes Kid 'n Play represent a viable sales strategy—still believes there are rap fans out there who *want* to look soft. Maybe he just believes they deserve "Freak," jammed with vocal parts that articulate, embroider, and tangle the beat—breakneck rap, dancehall impression, girls going "She did the freak," girls going "doo-doo-dada" further down, cries, murmurs, and cross-comments below that. Ahmad's long, excitable, word-stuffed phrases bespeak a kid who always colored outside the lines—they're about desire rather than control, so eager to get over you hate to think what will become of him if they don't. With too much integrity, naiveté, and offhand sass to disguise a self-starter's ambition as a thug's greed, he likes to call himself a "niggaroe." He turns 19 in October. **A–**

Mahmoud Ahmed: *Soul of Addis* (Stern's/Earthworks '97) ⓝ

Air: *Moon Safari* (Source/Caroline '98) As a rock yeoman in good standing, I direct postrock chauvinists to Simon Jeffes's Brian Eno–sponsored Penguin Cafe Orchestra, whose similar (albeit unamplified) hipster kitsch can now be found in the New Age bin. For the nonce, however, the comfy-funk bass, space-age sound effects, and moments of cool femme treacle on this moist piece of patisserie are good-humored enough to win over even an old-ager who remembers when easy listening was worth hating. **A–**

Air: *Premiers Symptomes* (Astralwerks '99) 💣

Aisha Kandisha's Jarring Effects: *Shabeesation* (Rykodisc '96) defying the dread hand of Moroccan tradition by reinventing it—or maybe just recapitulating it ("A Muey A Muey," "Dunya") ★★★

Akinyele: *Put It in Your Mouth* (Stress/BMG '96) 💣

Albita: *Dicen Que . . .* (Crescent Moon/ Epic '96) ⓝ

Dennis Alcapone: *Forever Version* (Heartbeat '91) In the dawn of toasting, well before dancehall or rap, Alcapone played Hammer to U-Roy's PE, stealing pop hooks for the fun of it rather than constructing remixes as deep as his ideological posture. And he's a lot wittier than Hammer. Expostulating, cheerleading, butting in, fabricating duets with local heroes who have worse to worry about, he acts like the best parts of his favorite hits belong to him. And even if that's only because entertainment law hasn't hit Kingston, it's a truth for the ages. **A–**

Ali: *Crucial* (Island Black Music '98) That's short for Alistair, he's English— Jamaican English, with a flair for the pan-African and a feeling for the African American. Not only has he mastered a vocal style half Al Green and a quarter each Ronnie Isley and Luther Vandross, he writes songs worthy of his musicality, even if that means throwing some publishing to a collaborator. Untouched by reggae, funk, hip hop, or the spindrift impressionism of the postmodern love man, this kind of blindered formal command can only be learned from records—from aural data free of inhibiting social complications. After years of overrated Seals and Caron Wheelers, I wish we could be certain he'll be rewarded for it. **A–**

Alice in Chains: *Dirt* (Columbia '92) A heroin album, take it or leave it— "Junkhead" certainly isn't "ironic" and probably isn't "fictional" either. Crunch crunch crunch, riff riff riff—way harder, louder, and more metallic than Soundgarden ever will be. But the price of this power is that it's also uglier and stupider—the sound of hopeless craving. Sitting here with my "books and degrees" (well, degree), I very much doubt that if I "opened my mind," as resident sickman Layne Staley suggests, I'd be "doing" like him (er, the narrator of the song). I'll wait for my own man, thank you. **B** 🐸

Alice in Chains: *Jar of Flies* (Columbia '94) ⓝ

Terry Allen & the Panhandle Mystery Band: "Gimme a Ride to Heaven Boy" (*Bloodlines,* Fate '93) 🐟

Terry Allen: *Human Remains* (Sugar Hill '96) autumnal Austin ("Peggy Legg," "Crisis Site 13") ★

Terry Allen: *Salvation* (Sugar Hill '99) for an artist (visual division) a pretty good songwriter and a fine village atheist ("X-Mas on the Isthmus," "Salivation") ★★★

All-4-One: *All-4-One* (Blitzz/Atlantic '94) color them goodd ("I Swear," "The Bomb") ★

All-4-One: "We Dedicate," "I Could Love You Like That" (*And the Music Speaks,* Blitzz/Atlantic '95) 🐟

All-4-One: *An All-4-One Christmas* (Blitzz/Atlantic '95) always they should have such good material ("Silent Night," "Frosty the Snowman"/"Rudolph the Red-Nosed Reindeer") ★★

The Allman Brothers Band: *Hell & High Water* (Arista '94) ⓝ

The Allman Brothers: *Mycology: An Anthology* (Epic '98) that's Warren Haynes, rhymes with Duane's ("End of the Line," "Nobody Knows") ★★

All Saints: *All Saints* (London '98) selves-made prefab ("Trapped," "If You Want to Party") ★

All Saints: "Lady Marmalade (Timbaland Remix)" (*Dr. Dolittle: The Album* [ST], Atlantic '98) 🐟

The Almighty RSO: "One in the Chamba" (*Revenge Ov Da Badd Boyz,* RCA '94) 🐟

Dave Alvin: *Blue Blvd* (HighTone '91) voice a little better, corn a little worse ("Guilty Man," "Haley's Comet," "Wanda and Duane") ★★★

Dave Alvin: *Museum of Heart* (High-Tone '93) ⓝ

Dave Alvin: *King of California* (High-Tone '94) A closet folkie since the Knitters were the Unravelers, Brother Dave isn't just marking time with this unplugged job, he's figuring out how to sing—quietly, like maybe John Prine, who croaked as a rockabilly himself. Yes his own songs top the covers, only there's a Tom Russell vignette you'd swear he made up; yes the old songs top the new ones, only check the Nashville-simple Rosie Flores duet. As for the old ones, his gravelly sprechgesang conjures more from most of them than Brother Phil or John & Exene ever did. If words are his gift, empathy is their secret, and empathy blooms in the stillest moments. **A–**

Dave Alvin and the Guilty Men: "Interstate City" (*Interstate City,* HighTone '96) 🕭

Dave Alvin: *Blackjack David* (HighTone '98) Fronting an acoustic band that gives his voice the breathing room it needs, Alvin brings off the quiet despair of "Evening Blues" and "From a Kitchen Table." But making the personal historical is still his metier—the border patrolman of "California Snow," the Vietnam casualty of "1968." He also knows how to make rootlessness historical. But I say he just likes the road. **B+**

Phil Alvin: *County Fair 2000* (HighTone '94) Ⓝ

Bud Alzir: "Morocco" (*Macro Dub Infection Volume One* [comp], Caroline '95) 🕭

Amadou et Mariam: *Se Te Djon Ye* (Tinder '99) "blind couple of Mali"—reassuring melodies, two voices, one acoustic guitar ("Se Te Djon Ye," "Kelen la Seben") ★★

Ambassadeurs: See Les Ambassadeurs

Ambitious Lovers: *Lust* (Elektra '91) normal don't suit him ("Tuck It In," "Umbabarauma") ★

American Music Club: *Everclear* (Alias '91) misery as state of grace, and give him credit—he has a sense of humor about it ("Crabwalk," "Why Won't You Stay") ★★★

American Music Club: *Mercury* (Reprise '93) Unable to resist the excessive eloquence of new producer Mitchell Froom and the slam-bang fills of new drummer Tim Mooney, or else in a really crummy mood, Doyen of Depression Mark Eitzel wallows in it. The much admired epitome is "Apology for an Accident," where, among other things, he emotes the excellent lines "I've been praying a lot lately/It's because I no longer have a TV" as if nothing so horrible had ever befallen a drunk with too much time to kill. Unsurprisingly (although it was a bitter pill at first), "What Godzilla Said to God When His Name Wasn't Found in the Book of Life" isn't funny either. Oversinging and all, "Johnny Mathis' Feet" is. It's also the wisest thing on the record, which isn't to say it's wise in any absolute sense. That comes later, we hope—but don't necessarily expect. **B–** 🦃

American Music Club: *San Francisco* (Geffen '94) 💣

Amina: *Yalil* (Mango '90) 💣

Doctor Ammondt: *The Legend Lives Forever in Latin* (K-Tel Latin '95) For the prelate who has everything, a Finnish (naturally) musicologist sings all of seven Elvis songs, including the oft-requested "Wooden Heart (Cor ligneum)," in what sounds from here like Eye-talian, but nobody's asking me. The style is Eurovision, the orchestration boilerplate, the voice tender and mild. Just thought you should know. **D** 🦃

Tori Amos: *Little Earthquakes* (Atlantic '91) She's been raped, and she wrote a great song about it: the quietly insane "Me and a Gun." It's easily the most gripping piece of music here, and it's a cappella. This means she's not Kate Bush. And though I'm sure she's her own person and all, Kate Bush she'd settle for. **C+**

Tori Amos: *Crucify* (Atlantic '92) 💣
Tori Amos: *Boys for Pele* (Atlantic '96) 💣

Tori Amos: *From the Choirgirl Hotel* (Atlantic '98) 💣

The Amps: *Pacer* (4AD/Elektra '95) Definitely slight and probably a one-off, which is what we said about the Breeders, this collection of songs for workaday buddy-band is as uneven as the vocal charms it showcases. But showcase them it does—speedy or dreamy, Kim Deal sounds so sane, so unpretentious, so goddamn nice that you want to take her home and give her a shampoo. **B+**

John Anderson: *Seminole Wind* (RCA '91) it's no secret you feel better when you try ("Straight Tequila Night," "Who Got Our Love") ★★★

John Anderson: *You Can't Keep a Good Memory Down* (MCA '94) but you can keep a good man in check, as these lesser hits prove ("Lower on the Hog," "Down in the Orange Grove," "Lying in Her Arms") ★★★

John Anderson: *Paradise* (BNA '95) Ⓝ

John Anderson: *Greatest Hits* (BNA '96) By now his irreverent working-stiff warmth is both likable shtick and a precondition of his specialty, happy love songs whose notion of permanent fun combines conjugal self-sufficiency and downhome raunch. The best thing here is a rocking Georgia Satellites remake. The most surprising comes when he cops to his own careerism with a sad, loving song about a family that's functional but not altogether together. **B+**

John Anderson: *Takin' the Country Back* (Mercury '97) Minding his market, Anderson announces his commitment to quality with the hilarious male chauvinist love song "Somebody Slap Me" ("She's into football, she likes my chili"), then slips off to the orange grove to pitch woo for a few tracks. That pleasant chore done, it's one exemplary piece of Nashville after another, many with his name on them. He sketches a generic small town, reclaims the eponymous country, rings changes on autumn and "I Used to Love Her," and ends up in one of his white-trash paradises bouncing on a trampoline. "Jump on It," that one's called—belongs right up there with Aretha, Van Halen, and the Pointer Sisters. **A–**

Laurie Anderson: *Bright Red* (Warner Bros. '94) Ⓝ

Laurie Anderson: *The Ugly One with the Jewels* (Warner Bros. '95) The difference isn't between "spoken word" and "music." The difference is that this is stories and the dull *Bright Red* is songs—and that right now she can better justify her obsession with the limits of American sense by recounting her travels than by devising metaphors for her displacement. Anyway, *Bright Red*'s music retreats so far downtown from *Strange Angels* that it's reprised (minimally, of course) in the portentous swells and eerie punctuation here—which showcase her most striking musical talent, for recitative, even if the clipped phrases and drawn-out final consonants do get predictable. Not something you'll play a lot. But broadening. **B+**

Thomas Anderson: *"Alright It Was Frank . . . And He's Risen from the Dead and Gone Off with His Truck"* (Out There '90) Just this frail-voiced songwriter in an Oklahoma college town, where Botticelli rubs souls with Belle Starr and Chaucer specialists give up tenure for love. His drummer can play, his bassist likes "Sweet Jane," the tunes his songs share are good ones, and though he's slightly word-drunk, he's too smart and funny and unassuming to waste many. You'd enjoy getting to know him. And feel proud you're American when the visit ended. **A–**

Thomas Anderson: *Blues for the Flying Dutchman* (Blue Million Miles import '93) Like most iambic story-songs, Anderson's yarns, plaints, and fables improve when they rock out a little. The putdowns of classy ex-girlfriends get annoying, but his old lit prof Larissa would seem to deserve every word, and from petroleum to Nash the Slash his historical conundrums make sense or no sense as the case may be. Most important, he rocks out like somebody who expected more than he got from Nash the Slash—and remembered it when he founded Angry Young Grad Student Music and opted for singer-songwriting. **A–**

Thomas Anderson: *"Jerry's Kids"* (*Moon Going Down*, Marilyn '96) 🕭

Thomas Anderson: *Bolide* (Red River import '98) weird tales from many badlands ("Come Back to America," "Theremin Cider") ★★★

Horace Andy: *Skylarking* (Melankolic '96) the humble history of one weird tenor ("One Love," "Skylarking") ★★

Anggun: *Snow on the Sahara* (Epic '98) 💣

Angry Samoans: *Angry Samoans* (Triple X/Bad Trip '98) Ⓝ

Animaniacs: "U.N. Me" (*Yakko's World*, Kid Rhino '94) 🎧
Animaniacs: The Animaniacs Faboo! Collection (Kid Rhino '95) At the far end of a trajectory determined by Noel Coward and Shel Silverstein, we come upon Steven Spielberg's answer to *Aladdin* and the Archies, where three actors I never heard of—Jess Hornell as acutely all-American Wakko, Rob Paulsen as thickly Liverpudlian Yakko, and Tress MacNeille as precocious little Dot—warble a significant body of new nonsense songs. The music is "Turkey in the Straw," Gilbert & Sullivan, Offenbach, and lesser clichés, all rendered in loungecore-ready registers. But three writers with suspiciously similar surnames (Rogel, Rugg, Ruegger) furnish lyrics that are suitable for children (which makes the mildly risqué moments more fun), occasionally educational ("Yakko's World" lists U.N. members, "The Presidents" mentions Nixon's ignoble end and says Jefferson wrote the Constitution), and always clever fun, especially on the reissued debut that fills out this two-CD, one-hour box. Maybe you can live without the cannily self-referential "I Am the Very Model of a Cartoon Individual." But don't you have something to learn from "All the Words in the English Language"? **A–**

Another Bad Creation: *Coolin' at the Playground Ya Know!* (Motown '91) The lead kiddies have more trouble making the notes than Michael Jackson or Ralph Tresvant ever did. So I figure they'll wear off before they grow on me. But nonsexist

Bell Biv Devoe is my idea of great concept—who cares whether their two best songs are "Poison" in disguise as long as neither beats up on the object of its terrified affections? Svengali Michael Bivens's juxtaposition of boy sopranos against dissonant jackbeats is pedagogy at its finest. "Spydermann," which also sounds kind of like "Poison," is in the great tradition of Mother Earth's "Marvel Group." And sampling their parents is a cute idea. **B+**

Anthrax: *Attack of the Killer B's* (Island '91) 💣
Anthrax: *Attack of the Killer A's* (Beyond '99) 💣

Antietam: *Rope-a-Dope* (Homestead '95) at long last rock-a-roll—by which I mainly mean a handful of decent songs, honest ("Hands Down," "Graveyard") ★

Anttex: *Suburban Etiquette* (Tuff City '91) Ⓝ

Apache: *Apache Ain't Shit* (Tommy Boy '93) 💣

Aphex Twin: *Selected Ambient Works Volume II* (Sire '94) "Veering between an eerie beauty and an almost nightmarish desolation," intoneth Frank Owen. "Imbuing machine music with spirituality," saith Simon Reynolds. And, most incredibly, "Always a groove going on," quoth J. D. Considine. I mean, what are these dudes *talking* about? Not that ambient-techno wunderkind Richard James is offensive—when I played all two-and-a-half hours of this at a quiet thermal spring in Puerto Rico, the worst any of the attendant pensioners could say about James's nightmarish desolation was "interesting." And smack dab against Eno's instrumental box—well, if James really gets "physically ill if [his] music sounds like anybody else's," that's one consumer object he'd best not sully his expanded consciousness with. Thing is, James is rarely as rich as good Eno, not to mention good Eno-Hassell or Eno-Budd. One piece here does the trick (no titles or track listings—too Western, y'know—but it is, how crass, the lead cut) by folding in a child's voice (or is that one of his electronic friends?). In general, however, these experiments are considerably thinner ("purer," Owen wishes) and more static ("pulse dreamily," Considine dreams) than the overpriced juvenilia on the import-only Volume I. Anyway, a lot of Eno's "ambient" music could also be described as bland wallpaper. When Kyle Gann or (please God) Tom Johnson pumps a minimalist, I wonder whether I'm missing something. Otherwise I believe my own ears—and pull out David Berhman's *On the Other Ocean/Music from a Clearing* when I need deep background. **B-** 🐌

Aphex Twin: *Richard D. James Album* (Sire/Warp '96) Jungle sure has livelied up this prematurely ambient postdance snoozemeister. His latest syntheses are infested with hypertime electrobeats that compel the tunes themselves to get a move on. And where once he settled for austere classical aura, now he cuts big whiffs of 19th-century cheese. He even sings. Hey, fella—I hear Martha Wash needs work. **B+**

Aphex Twin: *Come to Daddy* (Warp/Sire '97) 💣

Aphrodite: *Aphrodite* (Gee Street/V2 '99) junglism simplified—at their most brazen, beats to jack your soul ("B.M. Funkster," "Woman That Rolls") ★★★

Aphrohead: "In the Dark We Live" (*Journeys by DJ: DJ Duke* [comp], Moonshine Music '94) 🐞

Fiona Apple: *Tidal* (Work '96) Ⓝ
Fiona Apple: *When the Pawn . . .* (Clean Slate/Epic '99) For any showbiz kid from the Upper West Side, musical comedy is mother's milk, more "natural" than the rude attack of rock or the polite confessional of folk. And having gone mega, Fiona was autonomous enough to want it that way. With crucial help from Jon Brion, she's got the Richard Rodgers/Kurt Weill part down, and will surely tackle the Dorothy Fields/Lorenz Hart part later. Meanwhile, confessional attacks like "A

Mistake" and "Get Gone" will do. Webber & Sondheim, watch out. **A−**

The Apples in Stereo: *Fun Trick Noisemaker* (SpinArt '95) 💣
The Apples in Stereo: *Tone Soul Evolution* (Sire/Warp '96) Robert Schneider's second pass at homemade Beatles conquers his embarrassment over how much he adores this stuff. Stripped of sonic camouflage, the songs are consistently pretty, fanciful, and slight, as clear as existential questions can be. Half a dozen ways he wonders whether he can lose himself forever in this music—and by so doing, find himself. You don't have to believe in harmony to grant him the right to try. **A−**

The Apples in Stereo: "Ruby," "Questions and Answers" (*The Wallpaper Reveries*, SpinArt '99) 🐞

Aqua: *Aquarium* (MCA '97) 💣

Arcana: *Arc of the Testimony* (Axiom/Island '97) Expecting some avant-ambient acid jazz venture, you put it on and wonder why the other guys can't be this smart. Then you check the personnel and decide it's because these aren't actually avant-ambient acid jazz guys—just Bill Laswell indulging his fondness for post-Coltrane saxophone and post-Hendrix guitar. But since Laswell has long explored these tastes with depressingly competent results, you transfer credit to the late Tony Williams. Unfortunately, Williams hadn't been making such focused records either. So, with Buckethead and Nicky Skopelitis ruled out as decisive variables, the secret comes down to this: Pharoah Sanders doing his thing, Graham Haynes being told what his is. **A−**

Arc Angels: *Arc Angels* (DGC '92) 💣

Archers of Loaf: *Icky Mettle* (Alias '93) Guitars screeching every which way, beats speeding and hesitating and slamming chaos back into the box, twentysomething boyvoices whining and arguing and drawling and straining, it's the world according to indie rock: a tantrum set to music as sharp and self-contained as a comedy routine. Aurally, this is now—one now, anyway. If it has zero to say about tomorrow, why don't you worry about that then? **A**

Archers of Loaf: *Archers of Loaf vs The Greatest of All Time* (Alias '94) Even when they fuck around—half a minute of silence to open, two minutes of scales to whet or ruin your appetite for their catchiest tune—they sound like a live band ready to service a living audience, their gleeful anger felt rather than assumed. And with a new album coming down the chute, this abrasively aestheticized little EP could be your last chance to one-up the madding crowd. **A–**

Archers of Loaf: *Vee Vee* (Alias '95) Eric Bachmann's pissed-off, speechlike yowl-to-croak isn't as callow or pop as Stephen Malkmus's demented, speechlike croon-to-whine, but their bands share an aural gestalt: tuneful two-guitar breaks that set off unkempt explosions before recombining in brief climaxes soon interrupted by more disarray. The Archers trace the agitated melodies and off guitar to the Replacements, as if the clamor Bob Stinson unloosed by accident and spirit possession was instead planned out by former sax major Bachmann and axe-wielding bad boy Eric Johnson. With Paul Westerberg an adept of the realistic pop-song and the Archers' titles so gnomic they forget them themselves, I resisted this notion until the show where I caught myself shouting out a whole utterly comprehensible stanza: "They caught and drowned the front man/Of the world's worst rock and roll band/He was out of luck/Because nobody gave a fuck/The jury gathered all around the aqueduct/Drinking and laughing and lighting up/Reminiscing just how bad he sucked/Singin' throw him in the river/Throw him in the river/Throw him in the river/Throw the bastard in the river." **A**

Archers of Loaf: *The Speed of Cattle* (Alias '96) The usual outtake flotsam—singles, B sides, flexis, compilation cuts, alternate versions, John Peel instrumentals, long-intro thing that would have fit onto *Vee Vee,* seven-minute opus that thank God wouldn't have. All punky, all dissonant, all yet to be melded into one of them seamless wholes. But I say the bits and pieces of the most musical band in Alternia beat the fully realized works of art of mortal road heroes. In fact, I say they *are* fully realized works of art. **A–**

Archers of Loaf: *All the Nation's Airports* (Alias '96) What verbal content you can parse might be sardonic if it carried any emotional weight at all—conned customers, security from LAX to JFK, assassination on Christmas Eve. Yet it's too hoarse and wild to seem detached or even deadpan; basically what it gives off is intelligence, as a given you live with rather than a goal you achieve. The import's in hoarse, wild, intelligent music that's also virtuosic, especially up against the myriad alt bands who fancy themselves players these days. The controlled discord of the four instrumentals recalls the compositional smarts of Eric Bachmann's sax-based Barry Black, the nasty little guitar lines have Eric Johnson all over them, and bass and drums put in their two bits as well. True, their WEA debut could be more songful. But don't blame them for making the most of the cognitive dissonance that is their lot. **A–**

Archers of Loaf: *Vitus Tinnitus* (Alias '97) buy the EP, then see the show ("Nostalgia," "Audio Whore") ★

Archers of Loaf: *White Trash Heroes* (Alias '98) Hey, we all have our personal alt-rock standbys—campaigners who've stuck out a sound that rings our chimes dead center. So if I tell you mine are the Voidoids revisited, will I maybe make a sale? Two guitars, one choppy and one fleet, rip up bebop-worthy dissonances over punk forcebeats, and if the frontman seems less than charismatic, well, Richard Hell types never hold their bands together for six years. Seeker that he is, Eric Bachmann varies croak with tweetle, massages some keybs, even samples. Minor details, I insist. This is their sound, there is none higher, other indie bands should just retire. **A–**

Joan Armatrading: *Square the Circle* (A&M '92) in her search for love may she record forever ("True Love," "Weak Woman") ★

Arrested Development: "Tennessee" (*3 Years, 5 Months and 2 Days in the Life of . . .* , Chrysalis '92) 🐝
Arrested Development: *Unplugged* (Chrysalis '93) Let the record show that they loved the people so much that with all deliberate greed they "rearranged" half of their biggest and only album for quick resale. Let the record show that to stretch the material to full-price length they basted on a fashion sermon and seven as-I-would-say "versions." And let the record show that the people understood their spiritual needs so poorly that the resulting live and MTV-approved product lingered a mere 12 weeks on the charts, never rising above 60. The revolution will be hard, brothers and sisters. **C** 🐝
Arrested Development: *Zingalamaduni* (Chrysalis/ERG '94) Will someone in the chart department tell us the last time the follow-up to a number-one album endured only eight weeks on the *Billboard* 200, topping out at 55? Although it's still alive on the r&b list, which they can claim proves a racial militance that was never in doubt or the point, this looks like a stiff of historical proportions, more evidence that their short-term commercial success was a long-term musical fraud—limp, sententious rap feel-goodism quickly forgotten once it failed to drive the scary stuff away. Maybe in another three years, five months, and two days they'll come up with another slice of life like "Tennessee"—or another guilt trip like "Mr. Wendal." But they don't have that long. **C+** 🐝

Arsonists: *As the World Burns* (Matador '99) Ⓝ

Asiandubfoundation: *Rafi's Revenge* (Slash '98) Ⓝ

Ass Ponys: *Mr. Superlove* (OKra '90) clearly too smart for graduate school ("Ford Madox Ford," "[We All Love] Peanut Butter") ★★
Ass Ponys: *Grim* (Safe House '93) also dim—aurally, not intellectually ("Not Since Superman Died," "I Love Bob," "High Heaven") ★★
Ass Ponys: *Electric Rock Music* (A&M '94) Before lo-fi liars convince you to put out a search on *Grim,* remember that where concept bands are designed to blow up on impact, song bands have a way of, well, *improving.* Preserved on tape by Afghan Whig John Curley, the music of their normal Middle American freak show—tunes, beat, Chuck Cleaver's anxious falsetto—has gained decisive aural legibility on their major-label sellout, which cost a whopping $2,500 to record. And the folk-rock lyrics are firmly grounded in literalist local color from Sherwood Anderson to Tom T. Hall. **A–**
Ass Ponys: *The Known Universe* (A&M '96) existential despair in 75 words or less—also in Ohio ("It's Summer Here," "Redway") ★★

Asylum Street Spankers: "Startin' to Hate Country," "Funny Cigarette" (*Spanks for the Memories,* Watermelon '96) 🐝
Asylum Street Spankers: *The Asylum Street Spankers* (Watermelon '97) like the Squirrel Nut Zippers only older, funnier, and named after a Texan Candy Barr ("Mama Don't Allow," "Chinatown") ★
Asylum Street Spankers: *Hot Lunch* (Cold Spring '99) Ⓝ

Atari Teenage Riot: *60 Second Wipe Out* (DHR '99) 💣

Chet Atkins/Mark Knopfler: "There'll Be Some Changes Made" (*Neck and Neck,* Columbia '90) 🐝

Juan Atkins: *Wax Trax! MasterMix Volume 1* (Wax Trax/TVT '99) 💣

Natacha Atlas: *Halim* (Beggars Banquet '97) 💣

Natacha Atlas: *Gedida* (Beggars Banquet '99) Although production is credited as usual to Transglobal Underground, bassist Count Dubulah has departed, and so has keybman Alex Kasiek—unless he also goes by the name Tim Whelan, as some suggest. In any case, the music has morphed so that it now bears in on the always dominant Middle Eastern pop aspect of Atlas's mystery-laden Belgian-Arab-Asian-Jewish persona. It's good riddance to the multicultural kitchen sink—bhangra rappers, hyped-up electropercussion, metaphysical atmospherics, long slow Arabic meditations on I could never care what. Instead we get a probably shallow and definitely delightful piece of exotica—ouds and hand drums and Cairo strings, tunes that hold your ear until the next one begins, perky tempos that always convey good cheer as they reduce passion to a trope. Unless your idea of magic is switching to English and presto change-o turning into Björk, Atlas is one of thousands who prove that a terrific voice doesn't guarantee great singing. But as the icing on this cake, she could make belly dancing look like a lesson in self-determination. **A–**

Atomic Dog: "Natural Born Killaz" (*Jungle: The Sound of the Underground* [comp], Sour/Columbia '96) 🐟

Lee Atwater: *Red Hot & Blue: Lee Atwater & Friends* (Curb '90) 💣

Auntie Christ: *Life Could Be a Dream* (Lookout '97) Ⓝ

The Auteurs: *New Wave* (Caroline '93) Deeply cynical, deeply tuneful, lead everything Luke Haines reconceives the Pet Shop Boys as a guitar band, writing about what he knows—the bedsit-bohemian fringe. He housesits, he parks cars, he goes to the library, he disses astrology and thrift shops and his low-rent showbiz family. All that's missing is a temp job in word processing. He ain't heavy, he's your brother. **A–**

The Auteurs: *Now I'm a Cowboy* (Vernon Yard '94) only one auteur here, and his success has gone to his songs ("Chinese Bakery," "Lenny Valentino") ★

Avtograf: *Tear Down the Border* (Bizarre/Straight '91) 💣

Aster Aweke: "Yedi Gosh" (*Kabu,* Columbia '92) 🐟

Axiom Funk: *Funkcronomicon* (Axiom '95) P-Funk with Bill Laswell's sense of humor, God help us ("Free-Bass [Godzillatron Cush]," "Orbitron Attack") ★

Adewale Ayuba: *"Mr. Johnson" Play for Me* (Sony import '92) Ⓝ

Abed Azrié: *Aromates* (Elektra Nonesuch '90) A Paris-based Syrian sets poems to Arab psaltery, Arab flute, Arab percussion, and Arab-style synthesizer. They'll stop you short the minute they come on, but translations or no they background better than they foreground: at its grandest, the music's world-exotic aura is not without faint echoes of Vangelis. Because it's text-driven, however, it never accrues the emotional mass of true schlock. With a culture being devastated, heightened emotion seems not only permissible but just. **A–**

Aztec Camera: *Stray* (Sire/Reprise '90) This virtually unnoticed album is Roddy Frame's fourth in eight or nine years as a prodigy, which I guess makes him a failure. Sounding like Harold Arlen one minute and the Clash the next is no way to convince the world of your unique genius, especially if you hint at Scritti Politti in between. But I say he gets it all, and wish the pomo crowd would pump his pastiche. **B+**

Aztec Camera: *Frestonia* (Reprise '95) 💣

A/COMPILATIONS

Adventures in Afropea 3: Telling Stories to the Sea (Luaka Bop/Warner Bros. '95) Like Nonesuch's lavishly praised and quite possibly worthy Cesaria Evora project, David Byrne's compilations have been lyric-heavy in a world where only saints and singers enjoy interpretive nuance in a foreign tongue. Here the slow ones, including Evora's classic morna "Sodade," are so choice they get across before they're swept away by a panoply of Caribbean-tinged Afro-Lusophone dance styles at their most hookily universal. I know it's crass of me, but I find that dirty little catch in Jacinta Sanchos's throat more alluring than all Evora's incomprehensibly earthy wisdom. **A–**

The Adventures of Priscilla: Queen of the Desert (Mother '94) **Ⓝ**

African Ambience (Shanachie '99) Skipping all over the continent, raiding definitive albums by King Sunny Ade and Franco & Rochereau, this is not the kind of Afrocomp that ordinarily gets my seal of approval. But does it ever do what it sets out to do, and what competitors on Music Club, Mango, Putumayo, and others too crappy to remember don't: segue the incongruous vocal attacks and rhythmic gestalts of, for instance, Youssou N'Dour's "Immigres" and Thomas Mapfumo's "Nyoka Musango" into the kind of danceable mix tape world beat's venture capitalists once imagined we'd all be partying to by now. An ideal introduction for the neophyte, who might then branch out to Ade, Franco, Rochereau, and Loketo's *Extra Ball* too. Me, I hope I can find that album by Cameroon's Masao for less than the $26 it'll set me back at CDNow. **A**

A*F*R*I*C*A*N E*L*E*G*A*N*T (Original Sound '92) **Ⓝ**

African Salsa (Stern's/Earthworks '98) in Wolof, both the consonants and the clave are harsher (Pape Fall, "African Salsa"; Super Cayor de Dakar, "Xamsa Bopp") ★★★

Afro-Latino (Putumayo World Music '98) African salsa derivatives tend toward a relaxed retro, guitar-dappled with a charanga feel, avoiding merengue hyperdrive and reducing hectic horns to a synth wash or solo obbligato. And while it wouldn't be Putumayo without the Peruvian-American subway musicians who write as flat as they groove or the conceptually slack if musically deft Cuban son selections, this opens the niche nicely, expertly promoting label debuts by Sam Mangwana and Ricardo Lemvo and locating an ace lead by the obscure Tam-Tam 2000 as well as picture-card filler by the overpraised Africando. **A–**

Afro-Peruvian Classics: The Soul of Black Peru (Luaka Bop/Warner Bros. '95) Andean salsa, say (Susana Baca, "Maria Lando"; Lucila Campos, "Toro Mata"'; Peru Negro, "Lando") ★★★

Ain't Nuthin' but a She Thing (London '95) 💣

All the King's Men: Scotty Moore & D.J. Fontana (Sweetwater '97) There's no rationalizing the success ratio of this tribute comp—I mean, gosh, Elvis Presley's original sidemen collaborate with *artists who like them*. I'd like to credit Scotty and D.J.'s groove, but with second drummers powering the two rockingest cuts and extra guitarists everywhere, let's just call it serendipity. Plus maybe—since Joe Ely, Steve Earle, and Raul Malo all benefit from not trying too hard—the kind of affable discretion that stays out of talent's way. The knockout rockouts are Cheap Trick's "Bad Little Girl," which sounds like great John Lennon, and Keith Richards and the Band's "Deuce and a Quarter," which sounds like great old roots-rock and also like nothing I've ever heard. And then there's Ronnie McDowell with that essential soupçon of Memphis-to-Vegas schmaltz. **A–**

American Pop: An Audio History (West Hill Audio Archives '98) Nine CDs spanning 1893–1946, it'll set you back a hundred bucks, and it's not really what it says it is, cheating Tin Pan Alley, John Philip Sousa, George M. Cohan, Ruth Etting, Broadway, Northerners, Ukulele Ike, Gene Austin, humor, Hollywood, Fred Astaire, Glen Gray, Glenn Miller, the Andrews Sisters, and anybody who doesn't sing-a de English, among others. Nevertheless, it's an endless delight, almost 11 hours where Harry Smith's *Anthology* is four-something, and a powerful illustration of the antibiz aesthetic in which the best popular music derives from and is aimed back at subcultural audiences the artist can smell and touch. Play any disc and you'll soon be rummaging around for the first booklet, where all the track listings are. So *that*'s James Reese Europe! Ella Mae Morse! Geeshie Wiley! Only isn't it Geechie? And who the hell are Polk Miller and His Old South Quartette? **A**

Amp (Astralwerks '97) Working for the MTV dollar, Caroline wipes out 1996's *Wipeout XL*—the two repeats, Fluke's "Atom Bomb" and Future Sound of London's "We Have Explosive," are the two killers, and Chem Bros, Prodigy, Orbital, Photek, and the accursed Underworld check in on each. But though I miss the disaster-movie conceit (and Orbital's "Petrol" to go with it), this is an EZ-duz-it tour to sit still for. Before you're good and sick of Tranquility Bass's groovy psychedelica, it's daring you to upchuck at Goldie's pop kitsch instead. Take two Dramamines and hate yourself in the morning. **A–**

Anokha: Soundz of the Asian Underground (Quango '97) With zip to do with bhangra, and no commitment to drum 'n' bass, here's a travelogue designed to remind us that tabla players (presenter Talvin Singh, for instance!) have been hand-producing something like breakbeats for years. Not exactly like breakbeats, though. Anyway, who buys records solely for breakbeats? (Wait, I don't want to know.) **C+** 🐞

Anthology of American Folk Music (Smithsonian Folkways '97) Harry Smith's act of history—three two-record sets originally released by Folkways in 1952, now digitally remastered into a gorgeously appointed six-CD box—aces two very '90s concepts: the canon that accrues as rock

gathers commentary, and the compilations that multiply as labels recycle catalogue. In its time, it wrested the idea of the folk from ideologues and ethnomusicologists by imagining a commercial music of everyday pleasure and alienation—which might as well have been conceived to merge with a rock and roll that didn't yet exist. What enabled Smith to bring off this coup was his preternatural ability to hear unknown songs that were irresistible to his own people—the bohemians and collectors who have been inflecting pop ever since. Somebody you know is worth the 60 bucks it'll run you. So are you. **A+**

Antone's Women (Antone's '92) Eight gals whose natural habitat is the blues bar in all its beery, bedenimed isolation—the malest enclave this side of the men's locker room. Individually they're not immune to the rowdy conservatism that shackles all so-called house-rockin' music, but together they constitute a singular sisterhood: tough and independent, yet—with guidance from the label's cofounder, unflappable Austin old-timer Angela Strehli—willing to help each other hoe that hard row. The songwriting is high generic, which in bar blues takes effort, and this sampler isn't just a wheat-from-chaff job. It highlights facets of a collective sensibility—earnest or cynical or sluttish or loving or proud, it's always of its world. **B+**

Asia Classics 1: The South Indian Film Music of Vijaya Anand: Dance Raja Dance (Luaka Bop/Warner Bros. '92) I get my kicks on Globestyle's *Golden Voices of the Silver Screen,* but I'm too much a creature of my own culture and counterculture to enjoy the strings. Anand's synthesizers, on the other hand, are obviously world music, and this very rock-era composer, dubbed Jude Matthew by his Catholic schoolteacher father and Victory Ecstasy by himself, is a pomo dream. Does he have no shame? The usual amount, probably; the usual amount of taste too, given his unusual amount of formal training. But in a classic pop meld of artistic innovation and audience appetite, he'll try anything. He doesn't exploit a Vegas-soul horn chart or Indian mode or bluegrass run or Eurodisco beat or the anonymous ur-soprano of a thousand previous sound-tracks or any of countless other distinct usages, strings included, because it'd make a cool juxtaposition. He just thinks it'd *sound good there,* and most of the time he's right. Makes you wonder why John Zorn bothers. **A–**

Aural Ecstasy: The Best of Techno (Relativity '93) blaring rave comp so obvious even I knew three cuts (Holy Noise, "James Brown Is Still Alive"; Pornotanz, "Cysex") ★

Austin Powers—The Spy Who Shagged Me (Maverick '99) genuine simulated psychedoolic Velveeta (Madonna, "Beautiful Stranger"; Dr. Evil, "Just the Two of Us") ★

Azagas and Archibogs (Original Music '91) Most of these 22 pre-Biafran War dance-band highlifes are just 45s with names on them from the Decca West Africa vaults in Lagos—only three decades later, almost nothing is known of the multilingual Charles Iwegbue & His Archibogs beyond the band intro on "Okibo," or of the raucous Aigbe Lebarty & His Lebartone Aces except that he seemed to be from around Benin. There's not even a consistent style to grab on to, and the overall effect is a lot less suave than that of stars like E. T. Mensah or Sir Victor Uwaifo. They take a long time to sink in. But in the end I get a kick from every one. The will to fun that's palpable in this music isn't anonymous. It's—and I don't give a fuck if this is a naughty word in these anti-essentialist times—universal. **A–**

b

Eric B. & Rakim: *Let the Rhythm Hit 'Em* (MCA '90) Like every rapper, Rakim boasts: "I'm pushin' power that's punishin'/Prepare to be a prisoner/The hit man is the/Brother with the charisma." But he never brags. Even at warp speed, as in the title track, where the four seconds just quoted can be found if you listen up, he's always calm, confident, clear. On their third album, as on their phase-shifting 1986 debut, Eric B.'s samples truly are beats, designed to accentuate the natural music of an idealized black man's voice: it's Rakim's rhythm that hits us. Whether we find that disquieting or reassuring depends on what we were scared of going in. **A–**

Eric B. & Rakim: *Don't Sweat the Technique* (MCA '92) Rakim didn't really frag that general in Iraq—wasn't even there. He's just trafficking in the metaphors nightmares are made of, exploiting the interface between horror movies and the postmodern imagination. Putting it literally: "My intellect wrecks and disconnects/Your cerebral cortex/Your cerebellum is next." And metaphorically: "I took a kid and cut off his eyelids/Killing him slow so he could see what I did/And if he don't understood what I said/I push in his eyeballs way to the back of his head/So he could see what he's getting into/A part of the mind that he's never been to." As for the star of the show, Rakim calls Eric B.'s new groove—a jazzy minimalist funk trailing uncentered horn hooks—relaxing with pep. When he hits it right, it's like the mouth you love doing the spot you forgot. **A–**

Heather B.: "Don't Hold Us Back" (*H.E.A.L.: Civilization Vs. Technology* [comp], Elektra '91) 🥢

Howie B.: *Music for Babies* (Island '96) On a major label yet, the Skylab instructor and U2 pet takes the aimless vapidity of ambient another step toward total stasis. Lullabies are universal. Crib death needn't be. **D** 🦃

Melanie B.: "I Want You Back" (*Why Do Fools Fall in Love* [ST], EastWest/Warner Sunset '98) 🥢

Baader Meinhof: *Baader Meinhof* (VC import '97) that's right, auteur two-times-over Luke Haines's song cycle about the West German terrorists, and at 30 minutes not half bad or too long ("Baader Meinhof," "There's a Gonna Be an Accident") ★★

Babes in Toyland: *Spanking Machine* (Twin/Tone '90) Three daring women who decided that if Mudhoney could do it, they could too. And made rock feminists all over zineland darn proud. **C+** 🦃

Babes in Toyland: *To Mother* (Twin/Tone '91) 🗡️

Babes in Toyland: "More . . . More . . . More (Pt. 1)" (*Spirit of '73: Rock for Choice* [comp], 550 Music/Epic '95) 🥢

Baby Bird: *The Greatest Hits* (Baby Bird '97) needs a whole lot less of Jesus and a lot more rock and roll ("Man's Tight Vest," "In the Morning") ★

★★★, ★★, ★ Honorable Mention   🥢 Choice Cut   Ⓝ Neither   🗡️ Dud   🦃 Turkey

Babybird: *Ugly Beautiful* (Atlantic '97) tunes are not enough ("I Didn't Want to Wake You Up," "Cornershop") ★★

Babyface: *The Day* (Epic '96) Softly, cornily, oh so subtly, Kenny Edmonds hangs real songs off the big pop statement new jack pretenders pretend to. Playing a woman-loving, male-proud guy with ordinary domestic problems, pressing romantic emotions, and infinite sexual patience, he remains alive to black achievement and black pain—you think he doesn't know what it signifies when he runs the elegant "All Day Thinkin'" off hip hop shading and the Ebonic "be"? Deploying Eric Clapton, L. L. Cool J, Mariah Carey, Stevie Wonder, and Kenny G, dipping his well-mannered falsetto into a growl on "I will be down," or marshalling dulcet studio rats for a tribute to the golden age of postdoowop, the man is in such command it may take you half a dozen plays to notice. **A−**

Baby Gramps: *Same Ol' Timeously* (Grampophone '99) This long-overdue CD from a post-Luddite codger who prefers 78s features a unique guitar style only other folkies can hear and not a one of his endless supply of Dylan covers. Instead we get blatant blues and welcome Wobbly songs, cartoon heroes, throat-singing techniques learned from Popeye or a pet frog, and loving versions of "Teddy Bears' Picnic," "Let's All Be Fairies," and "I'm Gonna Eat Some Worms." Also eight minutes of palindromes (damned if I can make the "Margy" in his sobriquet do such tricks) and a recitation utilizing but a single vowel (not counting—can't fool me, Bearded Wonder—"Don Juans" and "ironical"). Inspirational uncontrovertible (sic) facts: "Rooks do not roost on spoons nor woodcocks snort/No dog on snowdrop rolls/Nor common frogs concoct long protocols." **A−**

Susana Baca: *Susana Baca* (Luaka Bop/Warner Bros. '97) 💣

Backstreet Boys: *Backstreet Boys* (Jive '97) I'm not claiming I would have gotten the message without a 13-year-old I know broadcasting it from her boombox. But keynoted by two guaranteed pop classics, one dance and one heart, this is genius teensploitation. I give half credit to songwriter-svengali Max Martin, who's put in time with Ace of Base. But as someone who still suspects Abba were androids, I award the other half to the Boys, without whose sincere if not soulful simulations of soul and sincerity Martin's slow ones would be as sickening as any other promise that's made to be broken. Together the team manufactures a juicy sexual fantasy for virgins who get nervous when performers grab their dicks and think it's gross when teenage ignoramuses copy the move. They deserve one. After all, it is gross. **A−**

Backstreet Boys: **"That's the Way I Like It"** (*Backstreet's Back,* Jive import '97) 👁️

Backstreet Boys: *Millennium* (Jive '99) softening it a little up for their younger demographic, sexing it up a little for their own peace of mind ("I Want It That Way," "Larger Than Life") ★★

Bad Brains: *The Youth Are Getting Restless* (Caroline '90) live 1987, when skank-wise hyperkinesis was still a cultural mission ("Day Tripper/She's a Rainbow," "At the Movies") ★

Bad Brains: *Rise* (Epic '93) 💣

Bad Religion: *Against the Grain* (Epitaph '90) life still sucks ("21st Century (Digital Boy)") ★

Bad Religion: *80–85* (Epitaph '91) Ⓝ

Bad Religion: *Generator* (Epitaph '92) in lieu of the future, they'll accept nice neighbors and the occasional stroll ("Too Much to Ask," "Generator") ★

Bad Religion: *Recipe for Hate* (Epitaph '93) Ⓝ

Bad Religion: *Stranger Than Fiction* (Atlantic '94) keeping the bad faith ("Incomplete," "Hooray for Me") ★

Bad Religion: *All Ages* (Epitaph '95) Maintaining a sonic constancy that makes the retirees in the Ramones seem chameleonic by comparison, these Valley boys are monotonous enough to benefit from a best-of, but don't think they've ever settled for a duff album—they're too focused, and too brainy. No doubt a better writer would find a simpler, more eloquent way to say, for instance, "Culture was the seed of proliferation/but it has gotten melded/into an inharmonic whole." But (a) the song bashes like a mother anyway. And (b) the big words are a hook. If their antipolitical ecopessimism isn't spreading like wildfire, which is just as well anyway, give them credit for aiming to challenge, not convince. And believe that where most bands with a message for the masses wind up looking like bigger fools than they already are, Ph.D. candidate Greg Graffin and departed homeboy Brett Gurewitz aren't just better informed than their fans—they're probably better informed than you. **A–**

Bad Religion: *The Gray Race* (Atlantic '96) now the Greg Graffin Group, as you can tell with a scorecard ("Punk Rock Song," "One in Twenty Ten") ★

Bad Religion: *No Substance* (Atlantic '98) ✇

Erykah Badu: *Baduizm* (Universal '97) for one thing, Billie didn't write her own material ("Rimshot," "Afro") ★

Erykah Badu: *Live* (Universal '97) knew about the technique, glad about the personality, waiting on the content ("Tyrone," "Stay") ★★

David Baerwald: *Bedtime Stories* (A&M '90) ✇

David Baerwald: *Triage* (A&M '93) ⓝ

Issa Bagayogo: *Sya* (Cobalt import '99) Mali's great circle, described with the help of a drum machine ("Sya," "Gnangran") ★★

Bahamadia: *Kollage* (Chrysalis/EMI '96) word-mad proof that real has a softness and tough can flow ("UNKNOWHOW-WEDU," "Spontaneity") ★★★

Dan Baird: *Love Songs for the Hearing Impaired* (Def American '92) macho token of the year ("I Love You Period," "Dixie Beauxderant") ★★★

Anita Baker: *Compositions* (Elektra '90) ✇

Anita Baker: *Rhythm of Love* (Elektra '94) ✇

David Ball: *Thinkin' Problem* (Warner Bros. '94) ⓝ

Marcia Ball: "Let Me Play with Your Poodle" (*Let Me Play with Your Poodle,* Rounder '97) ☻

Marcia Ball / Tracy Nelson / Irma Thomas: *Sing It!* (Rounder '98) ✇

Sékouba Bambino: *Kassa* (Stern's Africa '97) ⓝ

Banco de Gaia: *Last Train to Lhasa* (Mammoth '95) ⓝ

The Band: *The Best of Volume II* (Paradox '99) pretty fair country bar group/cover band ("Blind Willie McTell," "Atlantic City") ★

Robson Banda and the New Black Eagles: *Greatest Hits Vol. 1* (Zimbob '95) If Thomas Mapfumo is a genius, his biggest fan is a pro, reassuring of voice and steadfast of mind. There's no prophet in him—he's a singing moralizer who knows that when a Zimbabwean commandeers three guitars, two have learned something from the thumb piano. Reprocessing the little melodies in which southern Africa abounds, Banda leads two Earthworks compilations with standouts this showcase couldn't do without. Here are some more. **B+**

Bangles: *Greatest Hits* (Columbia '90) Catchier cut for cut than *All Over the Place,* this is also the sad testament of good-girls-gone-bad in the El Lay money-pits. Launched by Susanna Hoffs and Vicki Peterson's "Hero Takes a Fall," "Going Down to Liverpool" to "Manic Monday" to "If She Knew What She Wants" to "Walk Like an Egyptian" is one of those euphoric pop sequences that makes you believe this can go on forever—this happiness, this knowledge, this being 26, this crest of the wave. Problem is, they didn't write a one of those songs. Culled for dross, the self-penned stuff that follows reaches with some success for the mature self-awareness that is the current El Lay currency. And not a one sounds as fresh or as wise as Paul Simon's "Hazy Shade of Winter." **A–**

Bang on a Can: *Music for Airports: Brian Eno* (Point Music '98) The problem with the original was that it had a bit too much going on melodically and structurally to minimalize down into a synthesizer, especially one that wasn't pretending to be anything else. Here the piano-clarinet-cello-guitar-bass-percussion ensemble pretends to be a synthesizer. And although I pray postdance knob-twisters don't fall for the Gregorian goo goo girls who douse "1/2" with blancmange, the lovely textures will make them drool. Or anyway, sweat. Perspire. Exude. **A–**

Buju Banton: *Voice of Jamaica* (Mercury '93) praise Jah—neither "Wicked Act" nor "If Loving Was a Crime" has anything to do with batty boys ("Wicked Act," "Deportees [Things Change]") ★

Buju Banton: *'Til Shiloh* (Loose Cannon '95) Even if you find the male voice dancehall has unleashed on the world as incomprehensible in its brawny macho as in its machine-gun patois, the way it embraces contradictions of pride and arrogance, class and gender, strength and menace ends up being more original, powerful, and distinctive than the beats it rode in on. Banton's gay-bashing "Boom Bye-Bye" remains one of that voice's vilest moments. But nobody out there commands a huger growl—Buju could whisper sweet nothings to the World Bank and be a hero by force of physical endowment alone. So I'm grateful for the maturity he vaunts at 23. There is one about the size of his other physical endowment, which he hooks to Maurice Williams's "Stay" just in case. But let the guy have his fun. He can carry a tune, pick a hook, choose a collaborator (a few more cameos like this and the whole world will mourn Garnett Silk). And everywhere else here he articu-

lates empathy, vulnerability, and concern, personalizing and politicizing a style of conscience that comes naturally to the 15th child of a Maroon family. The most fully accomplished reggae album since the prime of Black Uhuru. **A–**

Buju Banton: *Inna Heights* (VP '97) This starts out in the heights of "Hills and Valleys," an affirmation of Rasta community which adds to the deep soul of "'Til Shiloh" a melody that is hope itself. After that shoo-in for the reggae canon, the album can only descend, and while Banton's voice remains the essence of dancehall and the tracks are well conceived—strong rhythms, welcome guests, thought-through principles, the nice touch of "Small Axe"—it soon appears that PolyGram 86ed the flagship act of banished troublemaker Lisa Cortes on practical grounds: by pop standards the vehicle seems high-generic. But the last five songs suggest that spite was at work. Suddenly the music zooms upward from its pleasant plateau, spooky bouncing bass and twisty guitar stile and intense Toots remake with the man himself chanting "I say yeah" and "54–46" like prison was yesterday, all culminating in the voice-only social-determinism tract "Circumstances," a heartening bit of analysis from a man who 45 minutes earlier was claiming his "Destiny" far less convincingly. **A–**

Baobab: See Orchestra Baobab

Mandy Barnett: "Planet of Love" (*Mandy Barnett,* Asylum '96) 🕭

Mandy Barnett: *I've Got a Right to Cry* (Sire '99) The main thing her critics'-choice debut proved was that when you put a good young singer up against a bunch of Kostas songs, the Kostas songs win. Not that this 23-year-old Patsy Cline fan is any less produced or conceptualized here—more so, actually. But the conceptualization is so bold, and so perfectly suited to her timbre and swing, that it's more fun than what it rips off, by which I mean countrypolitan. The strings, the prefab licks, the rinky-dink beats, the hooks with exclamation points on them, the background singers going woo-oo-oo and whoa-oh—everything the late Owen Bradley did for and to country music is here, with Owen himself overseeing four tracks and his brother-partner following his notes on the rest. Yet Barnett has these wonderful pipes, and not only does she sing as if she loves these songs, she sings as if she can scarcely contain her warm fuzzy feelings for the style itself. My fave is "Trademark," originally a c&w No. 2 for the forgotten hit machine Carl Smith in 1952. But the new-growth corn tastes just as good with a coating of caramel. **A–**

Barry Black: *Barry Black* (Alias '95) Headman of nifty young almost-punk group studies sax in college, organizes sax-led instrumental side project that evokes marching bands, Dixie Dregs/ Love Tractor/Pell Mell, klezmer, Henry Mancini for pinheads, a quieter jauntier Beefheart. "Interesting" but boring, you might expect, and it could just be that I share some weird somatic bond with fellow German American Eric Bachmann. Nevertheless, I usually think side projects are pathetic, and I say this one is funny, lyrical, a gas. It shoots a Zen arrow in the air. **A–**

Barry Black: *Tragic Animal Stories* (Alias '97) 🎸

Basehead: *Play with Toys* (Emigré '91) laid-back Howard minimalists outart and outjosh the Native Tongues ("Not over You," "Ode to My Favorite Beer") ★★★

Basehead: *Not in Kansas Anymore* (Imago '93) 🎸

Basement Jaxx: *Remedy* (Astralwerks '99) like so much good house, more fun than reading the newspaper and less fun than advertised ("Red Alert," "Rendez-Vu") ★★

Bash & Pop: *Friday Night Is Killing Me* (Sire/Reprise '93) where the Replacements were antiintellectual, they're just unintellectual—as opposed to untalented, or even uninspired ("Fast & Hard," "Loose Ends") ★★

Bass Is Base: *Memories of the Soul-shack Survivors* (Loose Cannon '96) Ⓝ

Bass Kittens: "Heartbreak Factory" (*Spin Control* [comp], Imix '96) 🔵

Bass Kittens: *Sweaty Planet* (OMW '98) Ⓝ

Waldemar Bastos: *Blacklight (Pretaluz)* (Luaka Bop/Warner Bros. '97) crystalline vision of pan-African bliss ("Morro do Kussava," "Kuribôta") ★★★

The Bats: *Compiletely Bats* (Communion '91) Up against the Clean and the Chills, to whom they bear a strong, witting family resemblance, these New Zealanders are lightweights, which is saying something. Their mild anxieties, while explicit enough if you listen with care, provide only subliminal content, serving mainly as insurance that they don't turn into anyone's new Beach Boys. Some differentiate their albums by rhythmic intensity, but this career selection homes in on their essence: wispy tune buoying flat drone. **A–**

The Bats: *Fear of God* (Mammoth '92) jangle clarion, melodies well-defined, beat clear, lyrics intelligible, meaning murky ("Dancing as the Boat Goes Down," "The Looming Past") ★★

The Bats: *Silverbeet* (Mammoth/Flying Nun '93) Ⓝ

Les Baxter: *The Exotic Moods of Les Baxter* (Capitol '96) Not so terrible, I caught myself thinking first time I played these imaginary soundtracks, and they're not—not by the standard of the early-'50s radio mush preserved on the companion *Baxter's Best* ("Unchained Melody," "I Love Paris," oy). Here, selections from *Ritual of the Savage* and its many successors exploit mallet instruments with some verve and tickle those nostalgic for their grandparents' fantasies of benign imperialism. But even in the same dubious vein, Esquivel has more razzmatazz and Martin Denny is crucially sparer. The strings and occasional brass are de trop enough—if you can abide the choruses doo-dooing and ahh-ahhing away, start monitoring your insulin levels. **C+** 🐢

Beastie Boys: *Check Your Head* (Grand Royal '92) Ⓝ

Beastie Boys: *Some Old Bullshit* (Grand Royal '94) Ⓝ

Beastie Boys: *Ill Communication* (Grand Royal '94) Another you-gotta-believe record, just like *Check Your Head*—only less so, thank God, whose appearances herein are frequent and auspicious. Short on dynamite yet again, at least it starts with a bang. Two bangs, actually, one hip hop and one hardcore—their loyalty to their roots closely resembles an enlightened acceptance of their limitations. With each boy having evolved into his own particular man, the rhymes are rich and the synthesis is complex. You-gotta-love the way the ecological paean/threnody emits from a machine that crosses a vocoder and a Taco Bell drive-through, but their collective spiritual gains peak in the instrumentals, which instead of tripping up the Meters evoke the unschooled funk of a prerap garage band. If they've never run across Mer-Da's *Long Burn the Fire,* on Janus, maybe I could tape them one? **A–**

Beastie Boys: *The In Sound from Way Out!* (Capitol/Grand Royal '96) 💣

Beastie Boys: *Hello Nasty* (Grand Royal/Capitol '98) Rap is their heritage, and having wasted years proving they can't play their instruments while enrapturing MTV fans who loved them for trying, they come home not an album too soon—flowing prose to cons and cons to pros, scheming rhymes against reason like flow against know. Old-school in their spare breakbeats, skilled back scratching, and heavy-breathing beatbox, they also remember how to lay on the guitar, and dance like Juba through missteps from planet-rock vocoder to Roy Ayers carioca to good old Hammond B-3. And of course they rhyme, wise and wise-ass, humanitarian without ever getting sappy about it—and without mentioning the Dalai Lama once. **A**

The Beastie Boys: *Beastie Boys Anthology: The Sound of Science* (Grand Royal/Capitol '99) Simultaneously over-confident and generous as usual, this asynchronously omnivorous package has all the hits, only there aren't that many, so 16 of 42 tracks are "rarities." In their opinion, that doesn't include the revelating early single "She's Got It" or the fine late B side "Skills to Pay the Bills." It does include Fatboy Slim's "Body Movin'" remix, which is as much fun as "Fight for Your Right," which they apologize for, although they're proud to debut "Boomin' Granny," which puts moves on a "sassy, sophisticated, sexy" 80-year-old in the checkout line (hey, that's my mama—and the song's nice in an offensive sort of way, their calling card). Of course, their rarities can be as flat as anybody else's, as can their showcases, like the Latin-funk "Sabrosa" on its third go-round. Still rappers and rockers, still wise guys seeking wisdom, they'll try anything twice and convince half their many fans to like it, usually to the benefit of said fans if not musical history. This double-CD is their claim on said history. They've earned it. **A–**

The Beatles: *Live at the BBC* (Capitol '94) Only a grinch would deny the intrinsic entertainment value of this significant-by-definition package. For one thing, these are the first known radio tapes where the talk is more precious than the music—in addition to everything else, they were the funniest rock stars ever. A few of the covers—"A Shot of Rhythm and Blues," "Soldier of Love," "Lucille," and a "Baby It's You" that proves once and for all that John was the cute one—are among their greatest. But a number of the odder songs (Ann-Margret? the Jodimars?) never reached vinyl for the simple reason that they were too lame, and I bet most of the seven Chuck Berrys were vetoed for redundancy. What's more, these drop-in sessions give off none of the adrenaline rush of the screaming meemies at the Hollywood Bowl or the amphetamine intensity that breaks out of the dim Hamburg tapes—the audience is missing, and nothing else is powerful enough to take its place. So in the end the chief historical beneficiary is George Martin, who may just have driven his lads to heights they were too relaxed to scale on their own. **B+**

The Beatles: *Anthology* (Apple '95) after the hype has cleared, this—their inalienable right to juvenilia, historical context, and live ones where you can hear the words ("Money [That's What I Want]," "Can't Buy Me Love," "Shout," "Moonlight Bay") ★★★

The Beatles: *Anthology 2* (Capitol/Apple '95) 💣

The Beatles: "I've Got a Feeling," "What's the New Mary Jane" (*Anthology 3,* Capitol/Apple '96) 👜

Beats International: *Let Them Eat Bingo* (Elektra '90) Norman Cook has gone too far—the samples in his kitchen sink are just too blatant, too eclectic. Which is why this is the mixing record Coldcut only talk to interviewers about. Whether he's constructing a new rock and roll subgenre from blues, Burundi, and some kind of jump band or embellishing Herman Kelly's "Dance to the Drummer's Beat" with who knows what horns and African huzzahs or revivifying pleasant little tunes you can't quite place and are sort of surprised to hear again, Cook's music is perfect for people who like more stuff than they have time to listen to. When I play two records at the same time I just get chaos. But here nothing is forbidden and everything fits. The only people immune to music this all-embracing are copyright lawyers. **A−**

Beats International: "Brand New Beat" (*Excursion on the Version,* Polydor '92) 👜

The Beautiful South: *Welcome to the Beautiful South* (Elektra '90) They're to the Housemartins as General Public was to the English Beat, only General Public stunk up the joint. And though the first two cuts do last 12 minutes, this album isn't soft, sweet, or dead on its feet—it's a killer. Its surface is even more feckless and dulcet than the old guys': drummer-turned-vocalist Dave Hemingway trades

sugarlumps with Paul Heaton, who sheathes his political edge. The tempos, the keybs, snazzy new guitarist David Rotheray and his sneaky-catchy tunes—all are camouflage for Heaton's righteous self-righteousness and radical unease. Personally, I miss the Marxian animus he's abandoned for attacks on the pop power structure and sarcastic relationship songs. But I'm knocked out that he can progress so naturally from subverting garage-pop to subverting the real thing. He's a sweet, soft force to be reckoned with, and if he wants to camouflage his politics, hey, the pop power structure is worth taking on—as long as you do it right. **A−**

The Beautiful South: *Choke* (Elektra '90) cute but deadly, pop but not, fussy but that can change ("I've Come for My Award," "I Think the Answer's Yes") ★★★

The Beautiful South: *0898 Beautiful South* (Elektra '92) Even more obscure Stateside since he got lusher, songsmith Paul Heaton does his endangered species proud. The tunes stick, and the lyrics transcend their sarcastic shtick—predictably idiosyncratic though "You do English/I'll do sums/You break fingers/I'll break thumbs" may be, it brings you up short. Peter Gabriel–Kate Bush hand Jon Kelly adds musical authenticity, and third vocalist Briana Corrigan sings lines like "This is the woman you laid" with just the right undertone of icy remorse. Introduce them to a decent drum programmer and they could be a threat. **A−**

The Beautiful South: *Miaow* (Go! Discs import '94) too pissed for their own good ("Prettiest Eyes," "Mini-Correct") ★★★

The Beautiful South: *Carry On up the Charts: The Best of the Beautiful South* (Mercury '95) Though Paul Heaton isn't the first or last pop aesthete to tense dark lyrics against lite music, not many have (a) set up disparities as stark as "I love you from the bottom of my pencil case" or (b) gone so literally pop with them. I don't want to make too much of his common touch, which is limited to England, where his extreme Englishness seems (somewhat) less exotic—not many Stateside have sampled the three albums that yield 10 of these tracks, and no one has heard them on the radio. But from Randy Newman's liberal elitism to Stephin Merritt's camp, American practitioners of this strategy like to pretend they're putting something over. So maybe Heaton's pop credibility is a reward for his sincere belief that the same people who suck up sweet music have an appetite for bitter sentiments. And maybe he seems so much deeper than Ben Folds because he's never snide. Sarcastic, bloody well right. Fond of his own cleverness, he'll drink to that. Tuneful, that's his fookin job. But pissed off to the heart. **A–**

The Beautiful South: *Blue Is the Color* (Ark 21 '97) Guitars vestigial, jokes brittle sometimes but no less funny, Paul Heaton's finest album evolves toward the calling he was born too late for: music hall. Like such northern stars as Dan Leno and George Formby Sr., he voices the sharp-witted resentments of working stiffs resigned to their lot. Or maybe not: from "Don't marry her, fuck me" to "Imagine a mirror/Bigger than the room it was placed in," a few women here see beyond the repressive depression of English suburban life, where one of two husbands drinks as much as Heaton and the other is as boring as Phil Collins—and the loners are tedious souses. The triumph in this vein is "Liars Bar," the greatest in a long line of drinking songs by the man who's said: "I consider myself a workaholic, it's just that I like to have a drink while I'm working." It comes with a video in which a disheveled Heaton leads a chorus of homeless drunks through a lurching soft shoe like a born variety artist. "I'm a stand-up comedian," he sings, and it sounds like a job application. **A**

The Beautiful South: *Quench* (Mercury '99) next stop AA ("Dumb," "Your Father and I") ★

Francis Bebey: *Nandolo/With Love: Francis Bebey Works: 1963–1994* (Original Music '95) Ⓝ

Beck: *Loser* (DGC '94) his greatest hit, an album demo, and two-for-three prime odds and ends ("Fume," "Alcohol") ★

Beck: *Mellow Gold* (Bong Load/DGC '94) His clip file is home to a bigheaded kid who's memorized Bob Dylan's *Playboy* interview, a slacker version of the Pretentious Asshole—here a folkie there a punk everywhere an image slinger (with absurdist tendencies, *mais oui*). But his album barely contains an exuberant experimenter whose verbiage coheres on record—either because he knows records are history or because repetition tamps down the loose ends. He's a folkie-punk version of, well, the Young Bob Dylan, except that he also loves hooks enough to cast his net wider than the Young David Johansen, finding them everywhere from an electric sitar to an illicitly taped tirade from a "Vietnam vet playin' air guitar" downstairs. Full of fun and loaded with 'tude, he doesn't care what you think of him and makes you love it, right down to the nose-thumbing bummer dirges that close each side. Proving how cool you are by making an album that sounds like shit is easy. Proving how cool you are by making an album that comes this close to sounding like shit is damn hard—unless you're damn talented. **A**

Beck: *Stereopathetic Soul Manure* (Flipside '94) The absurdist neofolkie as goofball abuser, most strikingly in ("ironic"?) rural guise—hick hermit, acoustic bluesman, wallower in honky-tonk lamentation. Satan, tacos, and aphids make multiple appearances, as does a crazy alien's unnatural falsetto. Cultish, and less than the sum of its inconsistent parts. But the offhand dazzle of these odds and sods is the stuff cults are made of. **B+**

Beck: *One Foot in the Grave* (K '94) his one-offs top Calvin Johnston's keepers ("He's a Mighty Good Leader," "Asshole") ★

Beck: "Got No Mind" (*Beercan*, DGC '94) ☎

Beck: *Odelay* (DGC '96) Hipsters are wary of "Loser." It was a "novelty," they fret; frat boys liked it. So one reason they swear by this entry pass for denizens of the Club Club is that except for a touch of hip hop retro there's nothing so easy to swallow here. Not quite forbidding, it embeds its lyricism in soundscape; only prolonged, well-intentioned exposure will enable squares to get inside its skilled flow and ramshackle sonic architecture. Worth the effort, absolutely. But for me, its unpretentious aural array, which shares an aesthetic with contemporary hip hop from Tricky to Wu-Tang, doesn't evoke any more specifically than its lyrics do. What's more, I doubt it signifies for anybody else either—except in the personal-to-arbitrary unreadability of its individual sound choices. When fragmentation is your cultural condition, heroism means trying to make it sing. **A–**

Beck: "The Little Drum Machine Boy" (*Just Say Noël* [comp], DGC '96) 🎧

Beck: *Mutations* (DGC '98) *Mellow Gold*'s loser thumbed his nose at the world; *Odelay*'s winner put his mark on it. On this adjustment to musical fashion, a success story discovers what he already knew but hadn't seen up close—eventually, winners lose. No longer immersed in failure, which you joke about (and then beat), he takes on decay, which you hold at bay (for a while). Although he hones his insults when the occasion arises, forget jokes—he's in mourning for dead relationships and the bodily passing they prefigure, and he sounds it. But because he's kept up with the times, he also sounds lyrical and elegiac, evoking the soft nostalgia of folk-rock without falling into it. Embracing the new directness, he feints and sidesteps just like always, exploiting a fad's expressive potential like the shapeshifter he remains. **A–**

Beck: *Midnite Vultures* (DGC '99) does eventually get funky, if anybody cares but me ("Pressure Zone," "Peaches & Cream," "Debra") ★

Jeff Beck: *Who Else!* (Epic '99) 💣

Walter Becker: *11 Tracks of Whack* (Giant '94) rich junkie's gimlet-voiced lament ("Junkie Girl," "Down in the Bottom") ★★★

Beenie Man: *Many Moods of Moses* (VP '98) Ⓝ

Lou Bega: "Mambo No. 5 (A Little Bit of . . .)" (*A Little Bit of Mambo,* RCA '99) 🎧

M'Bilia Bel: *Bameli Soy* (Shanachie '91) Rochereau's breathy ex hangs with some players ("Faux Pas") ★★

The Believers: "Who Dares to Believe" (*Journeys by DJ: DJ Duke* [comp], Moonshine Music '94) 🎧

Bell Biv Devoe: *Poison* (MCA '90) Because their new jack thing is supposed to be a "pop" move, softening rap's male-bonded "rock" ethos with sweet beats and romantic lies, their misogyny is more alarming than usual. Scared shitless of how much they need the one thing on their minds, they dis the girls who give it to them. "I had to prove my manhood/Show her that the B-I-V was damn good," but he's sure it isn't just him who makes her hot: "She's like that every day." You might say they'd have a shot at a decent sex life if they'd stop obsessing on every "sexy X-rated video queen." But that's the symptom, not the cure—a cure the slick, juicy polyrhythms of Dr. Freeze and the Shocklee-Sadler crew make me wish they'd find. Sure it's possible they're just shaking off their New Edition image. It's also possible they're mean bastards. **B+**

Bell Biv Devoe: *Hootie Mack* (MCA '93) Fame is fleeting in the mack daddy bizness, which is why they rushed out their remix rip, and why this long-awaited-by-their-accountants follow-up barely eked out its 500 thou before going south. To prove they're still down with the profitable, they lead off with a simulated toke, and instead of slandering honeydips behind their backs, they insult them to their faces—or their butts, if it makes any difference. To no avail. They've been outflanked smooth and nasty, and they don't have a clue how to reposition themselves. Which until they trip over another "Poison"—in their dreams, if they're real good to their mommies and daddies—will be no loss to anyone. Except their account-ants. **C+** 🦃

Chris Bell: *I Am the Cosmos* (Rykodisc '92) Protopomo chameleon Alex Chilton had so much Anglophile in him he didn't need this full-fledged Beatle obsessive to create Big Star's world-historic *Radio City* and suicidal *Third*. And where Chilton evolved toward bent cabaret-rock, Bell's secret vice was folkiedom. But it's clear from Bell's very posthumous solo al-bum—recorded mostly in 1975, three years before he slammed his TR-6 into a telephone pole—that Big Star was his idea. Stuck inside of Memphis with the Liverpool blues again, so pop-against-them he never fully grasped the function of the rhythm section, he was every bed-room bohemian who ever drove 300 miles to see the Kinks. Yet at the same time his spiritual yearnings are hippie on "I Am the Cosmos" (adolescent self-absorption at its most sex-starved), Southern on "Bet-ter Save Yourself" (in Jesus' name, amen), and both on "There Was a Light" (God meets gurl as if Bell's truly secret vice was Al Green). **A−**

Lurrie Bell: *Mercurial Son* (Delmark '95) Ⓝ

Belle and Sebastian: *If You're Feeling Sinister* (The Enclave '97) Sly guys, sub-tler gals. Straight out the stereo, they didn't have enough oomph to open my clip drawer—they go for dim where corporate pop favors hot, their lo-fi more *Exile on Main Street* than Sebadoh. So I assumed they were two or three twee public-school snobs just smart enough to mock their own privilege, with stray art-buddies chip-ping in. Instead, it appears (although they are coy about it) that they comprise seven popwise Scots in the same general record-collector tradition as Orange Juice, Teenage Fanclub, and Bis, none of whom sound like Belle and Sebastian or each other. And while younger folks debate the intellectual content of Stuart Murdoch's mild-mannered cynicism, for me his clever affect is there to test the strength of his third-power catchiness. You don't just recognize these tunes. You don't just hum snatches in tranquility. You sing along, ir-resistibly, sometimes with verse and cho-rus both. Just be glad Murdoch is into bemused sex rather than the glories of E or attacks on the culture industry. **A−**

Belle and Sebastian: *The Boy with the Arab Strap* (Matador '98) Rather than singing the anxieties of suspended post-adolescence in lyrics that dissolve upon contact with the mind, Stuart Murdoch pins his themes down one scenario at a time. Rather than tracing his uncertainties in music that wanders hill and dale, he erects song structures and rounds their corners with wispy vocals. With his little gang helping him, the music comes out beautiful and fragile. When their childhood ends, as it must, they'll be happier than they are now—or else much sadder. **A−**

Belle and Sebastian: *Tigermilk* (Mata-dor '99) It's their U.K. debut, done cheap back when school was the main thing they knew. So they made up songs ideal-izing the yearnings of every sexually con-fused young person who ever sat alone in a lunchroom humming a Chills song. Soaring wistfully above a misery recol-lected from something like last week, Stu-art Murdoch clearly believes these kids are superior beings. But he's so noncon-frontational in his elitism that only a jock wouldn't root for them. **A−**

Belly: "Slow Dog," "Feed the Tree" (*Star,* Sire/Reprise '93) 👁
Belly: "Are You Experienced?" (*Stone Free: A Tribute to Jimi Hendrix* [comp], Reprise '93) 👁
Belly: *King* (Sire/Reprise '95) Pigeonhol-ing Belly as just another pop band is a fa-tuity if not an insult. The signature shape of these songs for two guitars, bass, and drums—apparently aimless prologue veer-ing into stronger, squarer verse and then, when all goes well, slamming home on a fast, hooky chorus that glints gold later than the usual paydirt—duplicates no-body else's. Just as decisive is the be-mused contour of Tanya Donelly's voice—

slanted and enchanted, as some clever soul put it. And if the lyrics are a little soft, they're tailored to the mystofemme aura she naturalizes so modestly. Anyway, they're also generous. Not to mention nicely rounded. **A–**

The Beloved: *Happiness* (Atlantic '90) ⓝ

Eric Benét: *A Day in the Life* (Warner Bros. '99) ⓝ

Tony Bennett: *MTV Unplugged* (Columbia '94) ⓝ

Bentley Rhythm Ace: *Bentley Rhythm Ace* (Astralwerks '97) busy busy busy ("Bentley's Gonna Sort You Out!" "Whoosh") ★★★

Tsèhaytu Bèraki: "Aminèy" (*Éthiopiques 5* [comp], Buda Musique import '99) 🕳

Matraca Berg: "Back in the Saddle" (*Lying to the Moon and Other Stories*, RCA '99) 🕳

Dan Bern: *Dog Boy Van* (Work '97) 💣
Dan Bern: *Dan Bern* (Work '97) Messiah one song and king of the world the next, this absurdist upstart isn't above flat-out imitating the young Dylan, although he'll settle for a more general resemblance. Whether he's strumming to beat the band, flattening guitar-bass-drums into deep background, joking around with throat singing, or stealing the spoken melody of "Brownsville Girl," his metier is folk music of the culturally retrograde antihoot variety. If he didn't make me laugh where his fellow wannabes make me wince (while trying to make me laugh), I might even figure him for one of those losers who claims Beck got his best shit from Paleface. So right, he's not an innovator—just drunk on words, like the young Dylan. And the young Beck. Deny yourself this pleasure if you think that makes you an aesthete. I enjoy it because I think it makes me an egg cream. **A–**
Dan Bern: *Fifty Eggs* (Work '98) when you joke around, perfect aim is all ("Chick Singers," "Monica") ★

Dan Bern: "Talkin' Woody, Bob, Bruce & Dan Blues," "True Revolutionaries," "Cocaine/Blue Jay Way" (*Smartie Mine*, DBHQ '99) 🕳

The Beta Band: *The Three E.P.'s* (Astralwerks '99) 💣
The Beta Band: *The Beta Band* (Astralwerks '99) still lost in sound, but oriented enough to make tunes out of it ("The Hard One," "Round the Bend") ★★★

Better Than Ezra: *Deluxe* (Elektra '95) 💣

Bettie Serveert: *Palomine* (Matador '92) by the time the tunes grow on you, you'll be wondering why the songs never get where they're going ("Brain-Tag," "Palomine") ★★
Bettie Serveert: *Kid's Alright* (Matador '93) ⓝ
Bettie Serveert: *Lamprey* (Matador '95) ⓝ
Bettie Serveert: "I'll Keep It with Mine" (*I Shot Andy Warhol* [ST], Tag Recordings '96) 🕳
Bettie Serveert: *Dust Bunnies* (Matador '97) simpler, cuter, sexier, and, need I add, less hep ("Geek," "Sugar the Pill," "Heaven") ★★

B*witched: *B*witched* (Epic '99) In teen pop as in world music, Gaelic signifies untouched by the tarbrush—Van Morrison, Phil Lynott, and *The Commitments* notwithstanding. And despite the saucy bits in "C'est La Vie" (first a "You show me yours," then an "I'll blow you [away]"!), this bid to whiten the Spice Girls is so clean you'll be hard-pressed to remember it's there—unless, like me, you get sick to your stomach at Uileann hooks, mid-Atlantic brogues, and Enya lite. The obligatory rhythmic recitation, yclept "Freak Out" and declared "too hot for hip hop," has less bottom than Audrey Hepburn and is over in two minutes. "Like the Rose," unfortunately, takes four. **C–** 🦃

Beyond Three: "The Positive Step" (*Return of the D.J. Vol. II* [comp], Bomb '98) 🕳

The B-52's: "Is That You Mo-Dean?," **"Hot Pants"** (*Good Stuff,* Reprise '92) 🐚
The B-52's: *Time Capsule: Songs for a Future Generation* (Warner Bros. '98) The B-52's I bonded with at Max's and CBGB were an art band who epitomized the lost bohemian ideal of camp as love—embodied it so fully that after unspeakable adversity they became the thing they took off on and from. But while I could cavil about edgier song choices and '90s shortfall and their firstest was their bestest, I know that their chosen legacy honors the band that belongs to the ages and the masses—the pop band that still launches keg parties on Myrtle Beach and sells khakis at the Gap. From "Private Idaho" to "Good Stuff," songs I've never cared for are pure fun here. So are songs I've always adored. And the main thing wrong with the two new ones is that they're not fit to shine the spaceship of 1992's visionary "Is That You Mo-Dean." Personal to all tailgaters: the debut's really *cool.* Er, *hot.* What you said. **A**

B.G.: "Intro (Big Tymers)" (*Chopper City in the Ghetto,* Cash Money/Universal '99) 🐚

The Bicycle Thief: *You Come and Go Like a Pop Song* (Goldenvoice '99) Thelonious Monster's feckless leader explains what happened to his teeth ("Cereal Song," "Boy at a Bus Stop") ★★★

Big Dipper: *Slam* (Epic '90) Marginally more lyrical on Epic than on Homestead (less like the Embarrassment, which I take as evolution rather than compromise), their one great new postpunk moment is called "Monsters of Jazz" (about music, natch). They exemplify Amerindie's throw-it-up-against-the-wall phase—ordinary bands granted their arbitrary shot, stiffing, and diluting the credibility and capital available to inspired music. No tragedy, because it isn't important enough. Just sad. **C+** 🥀

Big Punisher: *Capital Punishment* (Loud/RCA '98) fastest mouth in the East ("Still Not a Player," "Beware," "Super Lyrical") ★★★

Big Star: *Live* (Rykodisc '92) *Radio City,* loose and in person ("O My Soul") ★★★
Big Star: *Columbia: Live at Missouri University 4/25/93* (Zoo '93) Nostalgia has nothing to do with it. For Alex Chilton, redefining garage pop with Chris Bell, Jody Stephens, and Andy Hummel was but a single obscure step on a pilgrim's progress toward eternal oblivion, and that they came up with one of the great catalogues in the process merely constituted one of life's little ups and downs. Here he and Stephens and a couple of Posies, who play loud even if they sing wimpy, remake that catalogue as a rock and roll noisier and more impolite than anything he would have tried at the time. Or anything he's especially inclined toward now, either—last time I caught him he covered Johnny Lee, Chet Baker, Frank Sinatra, and the Vancouvers (the Spanish ones, how did you miss them?). **A–**

Big Stick: *Hoochie Koo Time* (Blast First import '91) This duo is so mysterious I've never read anything about them I believed or heard anything by them I didn't play again. And without benefit of a "Crack Attack" or "Shoot the President," here's 10 inches of ugly introduction to their politically incorrect punk-industrial. The guy processes his voice down deep and then talk-sings like a demented trucker, drag racer, or metal animal, leaving a sexy Kim Gordon tribute/parody to the gal, who also shines in groupie and waitress cameos. Yes, Virginia, there is an underground. **B+**

Big Youth: *Isaiah—First Prophet of Old* (Caroline '97) Mr. Sunshine Meets the End of the World—in 1978 ("World in Confusion") ★

Bikini Kill: *Bikini Kill* (Kill Rock Stars '92) As usual when a punk band does the trick, the secret isn't just magic. It's ideas, like the way Kathleen Hanna slips into the cockney "roights" on "Double Dare Ya," or the weary "Fine fine Fine fine Fine fine Fine fine" that ends "Suck My Left One," which I'd say is about learning to make something of sexual victimization and then learning that it's still no fun, but I could be wrong, which is why we need this band even if we don't believe racism and eating meat are, and I quote, "the same thing." Poly Styrene discovers ideology. Ideology discovers Poly Styrene. **A−**

Bikini Kill: *Yeah, Yeah, Yeah, Yeah*/Huggybear: *Our Troubled Youth* (Kill Rock Stars '93) Ⓝ

Bikini Kill: *Pussy Whipped* (Kill Rock Stars '93) The inspired amateur caterwaul of a thousand zine dreams, more convincing than the boys' version even if it isn't as good as it ought to be or as right on as it thinks it is. By now male hardcore bands feel obliged to at least master the fast four-four, which has its advantages but ends up formulaic. This music scorns all rules—there's no way to prepare for it. The primitive tunes stick like peanut butter to the barbed-wire sound, and while Kathleen Hanna stays calm on her love song "For Tammy Rae," she prefers to break her lyrics down into preverbal emotion—the big-dick grunts of "Sugar," the can't-come screams of "Star Bellied Boy," the scratch-your-eyes-out ululations of "Li'l Red." Ideological though their rage may be, it comes off rooted rather than received or rote, so they scare people. If I were young enough to have girlfriend problems, I might scrounge around for ad feminam putdowns myself. **A−**

Bikini Kill: *Reject All American* (Kill Rock Stars '96) I define punk so that it includes the Replacements and Nirvana and Sleater-Kinney and any other short-fast guitar unit that gives me a thrill. These gals-and-guy are less broad-minded. So here's a '70s punk album as classic as, say, Green Day's—more so if, like these gals-and-guy, you think those guys-and-more-guys are way too fucking broad themselves. The first album got over on spirit. Here Kathleen Hanna's vocals and Bill Karren's guitar add definition, confi-

dence, (let's bite the bullet and call it) technical skill. Also, right, tunes. Plus I always listen up when they get to the slow one about a dead boy genius. **A−**

Bikini Kill: *The Singles* (Kill Rock Stars '98) Nine songs in 18 minutes—one bunch of three entrusted to Joan Jett in 1993 and keyed to the unforgettable anthem "Rebel Girl," the rest vented by the band in 1995 and keyed to the unforgettable title "I Like Fucking." It's striking and impressive the way they ratcheted their popcraft down. With this band, incoherence was always a way of knowledge, imbuing their spew of ideas and feelings with a conviction that made one's confusion about whether they liked sex or not irrelevant. After all, it was probably a little of both—given their intensity level, a lot of both. **A−**

Tony Bird: *Sorry Africa* (Philo '90) Ⓝ

Bis: *This Is Teen-C Power!* (Grand Royal '97) Teensy power, they mean—six teensy songs on a teensy 15-minute CD. But if lines like "We all want the system to fail" seem wishful, "Kill Yr Boyfriend" and "This Is Fake D.I.Y." are minusculely magnificent. In a world full of rote bands who thought riot grrrl would be easy, these boys-and-girl perpetuate the illusion. **B+**

Bis: *The New Transistor Heroes* (Grand Royal '97) I'd take their rhetoric more seriously if it wasn't so embedded in their aesthetic. The main function of their anti-biz antisexism is clearly to drive grownups nuts, just like their high voices and their chanted choruses and their keyby guitars and their jingly catchiness, one song after another after another 18 strong until you feel like you can't stand to recognize another. Only you can; in the right frame of mind, in fact, you get off on it. Cheek, the English call such annoying charm. What the Scots call it is for Bis to know and us to find out. **A−**

Bis: *Intendo* (Grand Royal '98) cute, and not just the way demos are cute ("Girl Star," "Statement of Intent") ★★

Bis: *Social Dancing* (Grand Royal '99) from a punk band on top of the world to a disco band who want to stay there ("I'm a Slut," "Making People Normal") ★★

Elvin Bishop: *Don't Let the Bossman Get You Down* (Alligator '91) Mr. Entertainment ("My Whiskey Head Buddies," "Soul Food") ★

Elvin Bishop: "Another Mule Kickin' in Your Stall" (*Ace in the Hole,* Alligator '95) 🕶

The Bis-Quits: *The Bis-Quits* (Oh Boy '93) Ⓝ

Biz Markie: *I Need a Haircut* (Cold Chillin' '91) Everyrapper as Everynerd—his manageable tribulations, his modest progress, his magniloquent doody jokes ("T.S.R. [Toilet Stool Rap]," "Busy Doin' Nothing") ★★★

Biz Markie: *All Samples Cleared* (Cold Chillin'/Warner Bros. '93) Singin' in the rain 'cause he got the audacity, Biz returns from legal limbo to mumble, spritz, fart around, cop a hit from McFadden & Whitehead, ride four different versions of "Get out My Life Woman," and rhyme "audacity" with "Butch Cassidy." From "Family Tree," which builds off 20 first names, to "The Gator," which cuts to the beat in the interests of asthma prevention, he never tries harder than is absolutely necessary, and seldom comes up less than beguiling and hilarious. Masterstrokes: the positive "I'm a Ugly Nigger (So What)," in the great tradition of *Huckleberry Finn,* and "I'm Singin'," in which he does for Gene Kelly what he tried to do for Gilbert O'Sullivan—and nobody is thin-skinned enough to stop him. **A–**

Björk: *Post* (Elektra '95) This well-regarded little item rekindles my primeval suspicion of Europeans who presume to "improve" on rock and roll (or for that matter Betty Hutton, originator of the best song here). I don't miss the Sugarcubes' guitars so much as their commitment to the groove, which—sporadic though it would remain, Iceland not being a blues hotbed—might shore up the real intrinsic

interest of her eccentric instrumentation, electronic timbres, etc. Then there's her, how shall I say it, self-involved vocal devices. Which brings us to, right, her lyrics, which might hit home if she'd grown up speaking the English she'll die singing, but probably wouldn't. Anybody out there remember Dagmar Krause? German, Henry Cow, artsong and proud of it? She was no great shakes either. But at least she had politics. **C+** 🦃

Björk: *Homogenic* (Elektra '97) she organizes freedom—how Scandinavian of her ("Joga," "Bachelorette") ★★

Clint Black: *The Hard Way* (RCA '92) Country music is for those old or repressed enough to care deeply about monogamy—one-on-one love in all its passion, comfort, consternation, impossibility, and routine. That's why I doubt the Nashville hunks have siphoned much support from Nirvana, Madonna, or Public Enemy—their targets are Richard Marx and Bryan Adams. Still, this is a sad one. Spoiled by fame or his own manly profile—he looks so craggy up against his *Knots Landing* wifey on the cover of *People*—a guy who got Nashville to notice him with terse neoclassicist regrets gets Hollywood to bank him with soggy pseudoromantic homilies. Imagine how tritely condescending "A Woman Has Her Way" could be and you'll know what sentiments Clint considers suitable to a matinee idol. **C** 🦃

Clint Black: *The Greatest Hits* (RCA '96) Ⓝ

Blackbird: *Blackbird* (Scotti Bros. '92) 💣

Black Box: *Dreamland* (Deconstruction '90) program the singles ("Everybody Everybody," "Hold On," "Ride on Time") ★★

Black Box Recorder: *England Made Me* (Jetset '99) Terrorism behind him, Auteur auteur Luke Haines (plus a Jesus and Mary Chain guy, bet he had a lot of ideas) sets himself to limning the kind of g-i-r-l indie-poppers can't resist: rich, delicate, contained, and so neurotic that to expect her to give of herself would be meaningless. In her pretty little voice, Sarah Nixey convinces the world that rich English girls have every right to hate their rich English parents and covers the happy ragga-reggae "Up Town Top Ranking" and the morbid teen-chanson "Seasons of the Sun" as if they reflect the identical sensibility, which now they do. **A–**

The Black Crowes: *Shake Your Moneymaker* (Def American '90) 💣
The Black Crowes: *The Southern Harmony and Musical Companion* (Def American '92) Nothing wrong with mixing up a blues-based mush of Stones and Faces and Allmans and whoever, especially when you come by your influences naturally and don't imitate any of them. So of course these youngsters are "original" enough. What they're not is good enough. After all, the Faces and the Allmans weren't such hot songwriters either, and their heirs don't exactly have a Young Rod or a Gregg-and-Dickey to compensate. With seven of *Southern Harmony*'s 10 live-in-the-studio cuts going on longer than 17 of *Exile on Main Street*'s thick-mixed 18, call them the new Humble Pie and put out a search on DFX2's *Emotion*. Now there was a Stones rip. **B–** 🐦
The Black Crowes: *Amorica* (American '94) 💣

Black Eyed Peas: *Behind the Front* (Interscope '98) Ⓝ

Black 47: *Home of the Brave* (SBK '94) As he'll be happy to tell you if only you ask and probably if you don't—at great length, all the gory details, plenty of asides, with bells on—Larry Kirwan has been around. The Major Thinkers, Turner & Kirwan of Wexford, God knows and I've forgotten what and who else—failure after failure, always with Kirwan struggling against the injustice of his continued obscurity. And though he's finally landed a major-label contract and three pounds of clippings, he's still struggling, for in truth now, Black 47 hasn't exactly eaten Sound-

Scan for breakfast. Kirwan has plenty of brains and the gift of gab, but he's always overdone it, and these 16 songs last 70 minutes, the better to undergird their hefty arrangements—guitar-bass-drums, pipes and whistles, horn section, arena-jig beat, colleens, gad. Worst of all are Kirwan's vocals, soul-as-overstatement rockism-with-a-brogue. The Irish immigrant underground is a great subject, and Kirwan knows its stories even if he overdoes those too. Maybe some laconic guy with an acoustic guitar will cover a few when the smoke clears. **B–** 🐦

Black Grape: *It's Great When You're Straight . . . Yeah* (Radioactive '95) frat-rock for the apocalypse (what apocalypse?) ("Reverend Black Grape," "Kelly's Heroes") ★

The Black Heart Processions: *The Black Heart Procession* (Up '99) three clattering dissonant songs (or tracks) establishing their right to record yet more clattering dissonant songs (or tracks)—not that anything could stop them ("Song About a . . . ," "A Truth Quietly Told") ★

Black Sabbath: "Psycho Man (Danny Saber Remix)" (*No Boundaries: A Benefit for the Kosovar Refugees,* Epic '99) 🔊

Black Sheep: "The Choice Is Yours," "U Mean I'm Not" (*A Wolf in Sheep's Clothing,* Mercury '91) 🔊

Black Stalin: *Roots Rock Soca* (Rounder '91) There's more fun, which means room for choice, in Buster Poindexter's novelty "Hot Hot Hot" than in the coercive carnivalesque of Arrow's soca original. So what first attracted me to this Trinbago Rasta wasn't his antiparty politics, as in "Wait Dorothy Wait," whose verses list the injustices that will have to go before he can write verses to match the "smutty" chorus. It was the slackness of his music—his sun-warmed arrangements and smoker's baritone. Anyone resourceful enough to own his 1982 *Caribbean Man* will balk at repurchasing its seven best tracks. But the lyrics, notes, and remixes are all improvements, and so are the four later songs. Even "Dorothy" is eclipsed by "Burn Dem," in which he begs Saint Peter to let him throw down Christopher Columbus, Cecil Rhodes, and Margaret Thatcher himself. **A–**

Black Stalin: *Rebellion* (Ice '94) democratic opinion inna bacchanal style ("All Saints Road," "Nation of Importers") ★

Black Star: *Mos Def & Talib Kweli Are Black Star* (Rawkus '98) As "underground" freestylers, they like their beats stark, claiming old school and achieving arty like so many neoclassicists before them. Even saluting Slick Rick (in a tale where the bad kid jacks beats instead of grandmas) or the Funky Four Plus One (and neoclassicist break dancers), they're never "raw," no matter what they think. On the contrary, they're cooked as hell. Making hard lyrical as they drop "black like the perception of who on welfare" and "you must be history because you keep repeating yourself," they devise a hip hop imaginary where hater players lose their girls-not-bitches to MCs so disinterested they give 'em right back. The rhymes are the selling point. But the subculture that cares most about these words is what you'll come back to. **A–**

Blackstreet: *Another Level* (Interscope '96) Ⓝ

Black Tape for a Blue Girl: *As One Aflame Laid Bare by Desire* (Projekt '98) 💣

Black Umfolosi: *Festival—Undlalo* (World Circuit '93) Ⓝ

Blake Babies: *Sunburn* (Mammoth '90) Sure this trio has its own sound, kind of—jagged, perky, sprung. And more important, songs. But so many indie bands have sound and songs that they flop or fly on content anyway, and here content means Juliana Hatfield. For their varying gender-based reasons, some men and some women find her too cute, but I say she's a former girl who's willing to be winsome and has her gender-based beefs

regardless, e.g., "I'm not your mother." Later, probably with a different guy, she pops the big question: "If I called on you from far away / Would you say the things I want you to say?" I would, Juliana, I would, whisper a million (or anyway a couple thousand) lonely fellows. But when it came down to cases they probably wouldn't. **A–**

Blake Babies: *Rosy Jack World* (Mammoth '91) 💣

Blake Babies: *Innocence and Experience* (Mammoth '93) Who would have figured that the quintessential indie babe would make something of one of those preband-, demo-, live-, and 45-strewn overview comps where other slackers hide their dirty laundry? She's actually impressive covering, duh, a Neil Young song—and, oh wow, a Grass Roots trifle that hit before she was out of diapers. Thank punk and the Berklee Music School she isn't the folkie she would have been in an earlier counterculture. Cutting her upper-middle-class enunciation with open-tuned pitch, strange chords she can just barely play, and enough guitar noise to get the circulation going, she earns the right to steal her namesake's title. But remember, Julia: "Those who restrain desire; do so because theirs is weak enough to be restrained." **A–**

Bobby Bland: *Blue Sad Street* (Malaco '95) Ⓝ

The Blasters: *The Blasters Collection* (Slash/Warner Bros. '91) The remains of a great catalogue, baited with three rockin' previously unreleaseds that can't hold a candle to the *Non Fiction* gems now put down the memory hole (a moment of silence for "It Must Be Love," "Bus Station," "Leaving"), this nevertheless makes its commercially viable case for the matchless titans of "American Music," rockin' style. Dave Alvin and his singing brother Phil you know, kind of. So introduce yourself to the rhythm section—Gene Taylor's panboogie piano, John Bazz's fast-stepping bass, and especially Bill Bateman's whipcrack drums. And tell the world about the songbook they all share. **A–**

The Blazers: *Short Fuse* (Rounder '94) Ⓝ

Peter Blegvad: "Daughter" (*Just Woke Up,* ESD '96) 🕭

Mary J. Blige: *What's the 411?* (Uptown/MCA '92) real is not enough, but attached to the right voice it's something to build on ("Sweet Thing," "Real Love") ★

Mary J. Blige: *My Life* (Uptown/MCA '94) an around-the-way girl's recipe for happiness ("Mary Jane," "I'm Goin' Down") ★★★

Mary J. Blige: *Share My World* (MCA '97) Her song sense rooted in slow jams not soul, her soul rooted in radio not the church, Blige is a diva for her own time. As befits her hip hop ethos, she's never soft if often vulnerable, and as befits her hip hop aesthetic, she plays her natural vocal cadences for melodic signature and sometimes hook. Too strong to talk dirty, she leaves not the slightest doubt of her sexual prowess. She redefines the New York accent for the '90s. And she's taken two straight follow-ups to the next level. **A–**

Mary J. Blige: *The Tour* (MCA '98) If "street" seems fake and "real" stupid, try an older cliché: "down-to-earth," a corny compliment no one in the '90s earns more completely. Because she cultivates youth-center loose rather than arena big, Blige's de facto best-of is more than an enlargement. If her raucous tone and sour pitch aren't deliberate, they aren't unwitting either—she believes, correctly, that her fans will relish them as tokens of honesty. And to go out she covers Aretha's "Day Dreaming," which made clear long ago just how street soul sisters on both sides of the monitors really want to be. **A–**

Mary J. Blige: *Mary* (MCA '99) Rather than hating playas, she's bored with them. Between Aretha and Lauryn and the sister who knocked on the door and just by being sincere convinced Mary she'd had Mary's man's baby, all that she can say is that she's ready to love someone serious and walk away from anyone who isn't. Beyond Bennie and the Jets, her pop allies don't do much for her song sense, which is why her live album is still where to begin. But two more like this and she'll be ready for another. A girl who can come out of a Diane Warren composition with no symptoms of soul death has performed a miracle that defied Al Green. **A–**

Blind Melon: *Blind Melon* (Capitol '93) The biggest assholes yet to go alternative platinum share management with Guns 'N Roses and woodshedded in El Lay before moving to North Carolina to research their image. Musically they're kind of a cross between Rhinoceros and Savage Resurrection, although without the steamroller drive of the former or the messy idealism of the latter. They do boast better chops, however. A quarter-century down the line, that's what bizzers call progress—chops, and MTV. **C+** 🦃

Blind Pigs: *Sao Paulo Chaos* (Grita! '97) no samba, no ska, 14 songs, 26 minutes ("No Pistols Reunion," "In Love with a Junkie") ★

Blink 182: "Dammit" (*Can't Hardly Wait* [ST], Elektra '98) 🕭

Blink 182: *Enema of the State* (MCA '99) Ignore the porn-movie cover except insofar as it conveys terror. These guys are so frightened of females that they turn down sure sex from one hussy on grounds of name-dropping and reject another for being too quick with the zipper. There's no macho camouflage—girlophobia is their great subject. And boy, have they worked up some terrific defenses. If preemptive jealousy doesn't do the trick, there's always suicide, or abduction by aliens. Yet note it well—because they're out front about their little problem, "Going Away to College" is the love song the Descendents put Green Day on earth to inspire. **A–**

Blinky and the Roadmasters: *Crucian Scratch Band Music* (Rounder '90) Ⓝ

Blondie: *Essential Blondie: Picture This Live* (EMI/Capitol '97) Repeating nine songs from the perfect slickpopdiscosellout *Parallel Lines,* this piece of brass welds two sections of a 1980 show around one from 1978 into memento mori for fans who loved them to the bone and forensic evidence against fools who mistook their flesh for plastic. It laughs at polish all the way to a 15-minute "Bang a Gong"/"Funtime." Punk? Who knows? Garage? Wake up and smell the carbon monoxide. **A–**

Blondie: *No Exit* (Beyond '99) Forms lose their spring; social configurations fissure and disintegrate. But what usually wears out first is the commitments they inspire, and here the commitment is as palpable as such ironic formalists can make it. Chris Stein is still a great listener, and Debbie Harry never stopped growing. She sings with a force and technical command unimaginable in 1980, and producer Craig Leon comes back at her resonance for resonance. No new song will equal your very favorites. But as a "Rapture"/"One Way or Another" guy, I'll trade the sexo-mystico "My Skin" for "Heart of Glass," the Euro-friendly "Maria" for "Call Me," and *No Exit* for, oh, *Eat to the Beat.* **A–**

Blondie: "Rapture" (*Blondie Live,* Beyond '99) 🌀

Alpha Blondy: *The Best of Alpha Blondy* (Shanachie '90) Unless some dancehall visionary has escaped notice, this cosmopolitan Rasta is the great reggae hope. Forget Majek Fashek, Lucky Dube—the African skank of the Ivoirian's Solar System Band makes the Wailers themselves sound a trifle straight. And on half these gloriously hypnotic tracks they get their chance—though because he's an equal-opportunity Africanist, he allots them their fair share of weird sound effects and polyglot righteousness. Marcus Garvey words come to pass. **A**

Alpha Blondy: *Live au Zenith (Paris)* (World Pacific '94) ⓝ

Alpha Blondy and the Solar System: *Dieu* (World Pacific '95) ⓝ

Bloodhound Gang: *One Fierce Beer Coaster* (Geffen '96) fighting for their right to show you their underpants ("Lift Your Head Up [And Blow Your Brains Out]," "Going Nowhere Slow") ★★

Blood Oranges: *The Crying Tree* (ESD '94) ⓝ

Bloque: *Bloque* (Luaka Bop '98) worldbeat en español ("Daño en el Baño," "Majaná") ★★

The Blue Chieftains: "Punk Rockin' Honky Tonk Girl" (*Rig Rock Jukebox: A Collection of Diesel Only Records* [comp], First Warning '92) 🌀

Blues Traveler: *Travelers and Thieves* (A&M '91) They sure can play their axes— might even be tolerable as a boogie band. But "All in the Groove" is just a classic-rock line. John Popper's interest in fun is strictly rhetorical, and his rhetoric is so prolix I bet they only play three-hour sets so he can get all the words in. I also bet that as a Jack Bruce fan he thinks it's groovy when his rhythm section hustles out more notes than a good groove needs. **C–** 🦃

Blur: "Girls & Boys" (*Parklife,* SBK/ERG '94) 🌀
Blur: *The Great Escape* (Virgin '95) ⓝ
Blur: "Song 2" (*Blur,* Virgin '97) 🌀
Blur: *13* (Virgin '99) halfway there, it sits down in the middle of the road and won't budge ("Tender," "B.L.U.R.E.M.I.") ★★★

Body Count: *Body Count* (Sire/Warner Bros. '92) Exploiting and burlesquing the style's whiteskin privilege from "Smoked Pork" to "Cop Killer," Ice-T's metal album takes rap's art-ain't-life defense over the top. Not only does he off pigs, he murders his mom—because she taught him to hate white people. Then he cuts her up, sticks her well-catalogued body parts in Hefty bags, deposits same all over this great land of ours, and suggests that listeners with parents on the racist tip follow his example. For Satanism he tangles with a voodoo queen and enters the "Bowels of the Devil," aka the state pen. He wilds with Tipper's 12-year-old nieces, fucks his "KKK Bitch" in the ass when a rally gets his dick hard, and fakes an orgasm for good measure. And like any long-haired frontman worth his chart position, he sings a tender ballad—in which a coke fiend steals enough money to buy the best product, then goes cardiac when he smokes it. **A–**

Body Count: "Hey Joe" (*Stone Free: A Tribute to Jimi Hendrix* [comp], Reprise '93) 👝

Body Count: *Born Dead* (Virgin '94) ⓝ
Body Count: *Violent Demise: The Last Days* (Virgin '97) ⓝ

Suzy Bogguss: "She Said, He Heard" (*Give Me Some Wheels,* Capitol '96) 👝

Michael Bolton: *Soul Provider* (Columbia '90) His imitation of Joe Cocker's Ray Charles imitation is almost OK, but usually he's indistinguishable from pop metal except in the wattage of his guitar parts and the shamelessness of his song doctors. Name to remember: Diane Warren. Give her a composition credit and she'll give you a hit—and a bad record. **C–** 🦃

Bone Thugs-N-Harmony: *E. 1999 Eternal* (Ruthless '95) If the popular songs you love are gunslinging tales recited over a faux Bernie Worrell tootle, of course this wordy quintet will sound like some kind of change. Unison chants, schoolyard tunes, and goopy slow jams may not be how to rock anybody else's world, but gangstawise they add up to a new flava, kinda. Anyone musical enough to hum good, however, will find the concoction unfathomably dull even if they don't notice the cold hand of Eazy-E deadening beats from beyond the grave. **C+** 🦃

Bone Thugs-N-Harmony: "F——tha Police" (*In Tha Beginning . . . There Was Rap* [comp], Priority '97) 👝

Bone Thugs-N-Harmony: *The Collection Volume One* (Ruthless '98) ⓝ

Betty Boo: *Boomania* (Rhythm King/ Sire/Reprise '90) true, disposable, pop deeelite ("Doin' the Do," "Where Are You Baby?") ★

Boogie Down Productions: *Edutainment* (Jive '90) insufficiently scientific ("Love's Gonna Getcha [Material Love]," "100 Guns") ★★★

Boogie Down Productions: *Sex and Violence* (Jive '92) Brother Kris: "I think some of these journalists need to start getting punched in they face." Brother Kenny: "I got a big fist." Which just goes to show that you don't love KRS-One because you think he's right—you love him because *he* thinks he's right. Of course his ideas are dangerous—if they weren't, they'd be inconsequential. In words and music as tactless as a battering ram, he praises "humanism," names capitalism as the enemy, calls out fake Muslims, and, well, urges drug dealers to get into the education game. Definitive: "13 and Good," like "100 Guns" before it a morality-tale-sans-moral that makes me wonder whether he's studied Roger Abrahams's anthology of African folk tales or comes by the tone naturally—and yes, I'm sure I know what he thinks about that one. **A–**

Boogie Down Productions: See also KRS-One

Boogiemonsters: *Riders of the Storm: The Underwater Album* (Pendulum/EMI '94) ⓝ

James Booker: *Resurrection of the Bayou Maharajah* (Rounder '93) live fantasias and self-indulgences ("Medley: Slow Down/Bony Maronie/Knock on Wood/I Heard It Through the Grapevine/ Classified," "Medley: Tico Tico/Papa Was a Rascal") ★★★

Pat Boone: "Smoke on the Water" (*In a Metal Mood: No More Mr. Nice Guy,* Hip-O '97) 👝

The Boo Radleys: *Giant Steps* (Creation/Columbia '93) ℕ

Bootsy's New Rubber Band: *Blasters of the Universe* (Rykodisc '94) ℕ

Boss: "I Don't Give a Fuck" (*Born Gangstaz*, DJ West/Chaos/Columbia '93) 🎩

Bottle Rockets: *Bottle Rockets* (ESD '93) roadies' band, blunter and rockinger than their bosses in Uncle Tupelo would stoop to ("Kerosene," "Got What I Wanted") ★★★

The Bottle Rockets: *The Brooklyn Side* (ESD '94) More raucous and pointed than such fellow Midwestern alternacountry-rockers as the Jayhawks, Uncle Tupelo, and Blood Oranges, these citizens of Festus, Missouri, will hit you where you live when they lay out other people's pains and foibles—the welfare mom on Saturday night, the Sunday sports abuser, the constable with his radar gun, the local Dinosaur Jr. fan. They also speak plain truth when they criticize their car. And if they seem to relive clichés when they confess their many romantic errors, how do you think clichés get that way? (Including this one.) **A–**

The Bottle Rockets: *24 Hours a Day* (Atlantic '97) Like Wilco, only not so generically or formalistically, this is a rock band. They love Lynyrd Skynyrd; they love the Ramones. Their country leanings merely ground their commitment to content—Brian Henneman's savory sense of character and place, the every-word-counts delivery that lends his singing its specific gravity. Going for simple, they pay a price in detail this time out. But the likes of "Smokin' 100's Alone" and "Perfect Far Away" would be pretty damn rough for Nashville. And "Indianapolis" is the sequel all us "1000 Dollar Car" fans were waiting for even if it was written first. **A–**

Bottle Rockets: *Leftovers* (Doolittle '98) honky-tonk romance, laborious dirge, and caffeinated double-time the quality outtakes you'd expect, dining-car praise song and Chattanooga chantey the lost

oddities you'd hope ("Dinner Train to Dutchtown," "Coffee Monkey") ★★★

Bottle Rockets: *Brand New Year* (Doolittle/Mercury '99) bitchin rock move, but any band that boasts about not using a calculator cares less about history than it believes ("Gotta Get Up," "Headed for the Ditch") ★★★

Boukman Eksperyans: *Kalfou Danjere/ Dangerous Crossroads* (Mango '92) conscious, fluent, liberal-ready pan-Africanism, Haitian-Congo style ("Zansèt Nou Yo") ★★

Boukman Eksperyans: *Libète (Pran Pou Pran'l!)/Freedom (Let's Take It)* (Mango '95) utopian militance, Haitian worldbeats, soulful vocalizing, near-pop song sense ("Ganga," "Zan'j Yo") ★

Boukman Eksperyans: *Revolution* (Tuff Gong '98) These righteous Haitians are thought of as a pan-African party machine, but in the aural fact they're devotional. Well past their new flavor moment, they turn out to be one of those bands that develops its craft rather than one of those bands that hits you over the head with an idea they proceed to wear out. Something like soulful, drenched with synthesizers because synthesizers seem natural, their impassioned trance recalls Nyabinghi chants more than Holiness hymns and is closely related to both. **B+**

Boukman Eksperyans: *Live at Red Rocks* (Tuff Gong '99) ℕ

Jean-Paul Bourelly & the BluWave Bandits: *Fade to Cacophony Live!* (Evidence '96) Bootsy meets Hendrix meets Watson meets Blood, and let us not forget Dru Lombar ("Toxic Your Love") ★

Jean-Paul Bourelly & the BluWave Bandits: *Rock the Cathartic Spirits: Vibe Music and the Blues!* (Koch '97) ℕ

Jean-Paul Bourelly: *Tribute to Jimi* (Koch '97) splitting the difference between jazz-rock and rock-jazz ("Electric Lady-land," "Who Knows/Talkin' Bout My Baby") ★★★

Henri Bowane: *Double Take—Tala Kaka* (RetroAfric '94) By the time it reaches our tight little backwater, Afropop has generally been winnowed down to some kind of essence—famous tracks by famous artists. The rare albums that originally signified as such tend to be acknowledged masterpieces, rarely dating much earlier than 1980 and often not even recorded in Africa. By comparison, this one could be some lost Brit obscurity—by the Move, the Soft Boys, you know. Back when Kinshasa was still Leopoldville, Bowane is said to have named Franco and invented a crucial rumba guitar move, but his hit years were over by independence, and when he cut his only album—in 1976, in Ghana, heretofore unreleased due to vinyl crisis—he was just a bizzer. If you didn't wonder briefly what a Francophone big man was doing in an Anglophone studio, perhaps you won't hear the brash yet modest cross-cultural claims of this simple yet polyrhythmic dance music—soukous guitar over highlife beats until the improvs come in. A–

David Bowie: *Black Tie White Noise* (Savage '93) Having erected a whole label around this piece of history, the legendary artiste and his new management returned triumphantly to the corporate scene of the artiste's salad days. But within a few months it had stiffed irretrievably, whereupon BMG-né-RCA dumped both artiste and label for a comeback as spectacularly ignominious as any rock and roll has known. Oddly enough, the music is the artiste's most arresting in many years; the dancebeats and electrotextures make you prick up your ears and wonder where they'll lead. Then the artiste begins to sing—often lyrics of his own devising, as in the title tune, a metaphor for race relations. B– 🐝
David Bowie: *Outside* (Virgin '95) 🐦
David Bowie: *Earthling* (Virgin '97) 🐦
David Bowie: "All the Young Dudes" (*Essential David Bowie: Best of 1969–1974,* EMI/Capitol '97) 👁
David Bowie: "Hours . . ." (Virgin '99) 🐦

Boyz II Men: *Cooleyhighharmony* (Motown '91) new kids on the jack ("Motownphilly," "Please Don't Go") ★★

Boyz II Men: *II* (Motown '94) watch out America—polite four-part harmonizers are coming to fuck your daughters ("U Know," "I'll Make Love to You") ★★★
Boyz II Men: "The Girl in the Life Magazine" (*Evolution,* Motown '97) 👁

Ruby Braff and Ellis Larkins: *Calling Berlin, Vol. 1* (Arbors '95) So imagine you walk into this, well, lounge in Miami. Or Atlantic City, say. Maybe Chicago. Two old guys are playing, one black and one white, piano and trumpet (cornet, actually, but why quibble?). It's jazz, all right, but not the arty kind—mostly you can follow the melodies, some identifiable ("Alexander's Ragtime Band," "Easter Parade," even you know those) and many vaguely familiar. The tunes are a little corny, and so's the playing now and then, yet the playing also has an attitude—jaunty or humorous or gently sarcastic or just damn pleased with the whole situation. Not campy at all, and never bad even when it seems generic. In short, it embodies the sophisticated spiritual ideal toward which lounge aspires while remaining too serious and self-possessed to tickle the young twits who claim to have rediscovered the stuff. If you're no twit yourself, two first-rate players and one major 20th-century composer may have something to offer you. A–

Billy Bragg: *The Internationale* (Elektra '90) 🐦
Billy Bragg: *Don't Try This at Home* (Elektra '91) Ⓝ
Billy Bragg & Wilco: *Mermaid Avenue* (Elektra '98) Here's this Brit folksinger, a punk by heritage and a pop star by ambition whose most salient talent is how guiltlessly he mixes up the three. And here's this middle-American alt band, folkies by sensibility and pop pros by ambition whose most salient talent is a musicality they don't know what to do with. With the wisdom of half a century's ripoffs behind them, both are more resourceful melodically than the icon whose thousands of unpublished lyrics they were chosen to make something of. So be glad

he kept the tunes in his head. Because while the words are wonderful and unexpected—author of several published books and reams of journalism, Woody Guthrie could have made his mark in any literary calling—it's the music, especially Wilco's music, that transfigures the enterprise. Projecting the present back on the past in an attempt to make the past signify as future, they create an old-time rock and roll that never could have existed. Finally—folk-rock! **A**

Brand Nubian: *One for All* (Elektra '90) Constricted by rage, sanctimony, and defensive rationalization from Movement Ex to King Sun, most black-supremacist rap sags under the burden of its belief system just like any other ideological music. This Five Percenter daisy-age is warm, good-humored, intricately interactive—popping rhymes every sixth or eighth syllable, softening the male chauvinism and devil-made-me-do-it with soulful grooves and jokes fit for a couch potato. They sound so kind and confident and fun-filled you almost believe that someday they'll throw away their crutches. But just because they were feeling irie when they made their record, don't bet they'll have the good sense or fortune to grab the chance. **A–**
Brand Nubian: *In God We Trust* (Elektra '93) 🎸
Brand Nubian: *Everything Is Everything* (Elektra '94) Ⓝ
Brand Nubian: *Foundation* (Arista '98) funk lite to improve the race ("Probable Cause," "Let's Dance") ★★★

Brandy: *Brandy* (Atlantic '94) Ⓝ
Brandy: *Never Say Never* (Atlantic '98) America's sweetheart, and why not? ("The Boy Is Mine," "U Don't Know Me," "Almost Doesn't Count") ★★

Bran Van 3000: *Glee* (Capitol '98) This song-filled genre trip is best enjoyed as a totality, like *Endtroducing . . . DJ Shadow.* Whether it's constructed or just strung together, its flat moments are spritzed by its highs, which include sexy pomo new jack hip hop, girl-pop Slade/Quiet Riot cover, faux-country faux-fable, numerous humorous middle-class layabouts, several minibricolages, and a sarcastic indictment of capitalism. How eclecticism should work—even if it almost never does. **A–**

Bratmobile: *Pottymouth* (Kill Rock Stars '93) adolescent petulance, tingling clits, no bass player ("Throway," "No You Don't") ★★★
Bratmobile: *The Real Janelle* (Kill Rock Stars '94) Ⓝ

Brave Combo: "A Night on Earth" (*A Night on Earth,* Rounder '90) 🐚

Toni Braxton: *Toni Braxton* (LaFace '93) Ⓝ
Toni Braxton: *Secrets* (LaFace '96) Front-loaded with five pieces of sexy rocket fuel, including a miraculous Diane Warren ballad you'll want to hear again—the miracle being that it's by Diane Warren and you want to hear it again. Soon the air whooshes out except for the *Waiting to Exhale* hit and "Love Me Some Him" with its overdubbed *yes,* but by then her pop presence is established. The apprentice diva of the debut was demure, composed, virtually anonymous. I'll take the right It Girl anytime—especially one who insists on getting her props. **A–**

Breakbeat Era: *Ultra-Obscene* (XL/1500/A&M '99) Ⓝ

The Breeders: *Pod* (4AD '90) Ⓝ
The Breeders: *Safari* (4AD/Elektra '92) Now posing as a major-label debut, Kim Deal and Tanya Donelly's 1990 one-off still sounds like the art project it was, but although Donnelly is otherwise occupied, this EP sounds like a band. Postamateur Raincoats, say. They substitute the Who's "So Sad About Us" for the Kinks' "Lola" because they're less arch and less soft. But they're lovers not fighters nonetheless. **A–**
The Breeders: *Last Splash* (4AD/Elektra '93) Kim Deal can't sing and neither can Kelley—not with force, anyway. But what the hey. Unabashed models of fem-

inine weakness, they murmur, they chant, they make a pass at harmonizing, thus revealing the once-ominous tunings of sonic youths everywhere for the benign art-school move they are. No way are these songs "pop"—they won't make little children smile or Mom pat her foot. But their sweetness is no less certain for that, and considerably rarer. **A–**

BR5-49: *BR5-49* (Arista '96) not Hank or Gram or Jeff Tweedy either—vintage Asleep at the Wheel? ("Little Ramona [Gone Hillbilly Nuts]," "Even If It's Wrong") ★★

Dee Dee Bridgewater: *Live at Yoshi's* (Verve '99) After fruitlessly sampling whatever Bridgewater albums came my way for 25 years, I harbored few hopes that this one would escape decorum, delusions of grandeur, and/or commercial confusion just because it was live. But it does, and then it keeps on going. It's funny, it's sexy, it swings like crazy. Long workouts on "Slow Boat to China" and "Love for Sale" show off her fabled chops without dwelling on them. The many extended scats are worthy of Ella herself. Even the gaffe proves her heart is in the right place when she's out there working the crowd—James Brown's "Sex Machine." **A–**

B-Rock & the Bizz: "MyBabyDaddy" (*And Then There Was Bass* [comp], Tony Mercedes/LaFace '97) 👁

Brokin English Klik: *Brokin English Klik* (Wild Pitch '93) they aim their hostility where it belongs—at cops, you, me, and the next fella ("Who's Da Gangsta?," "Youth Gone Mad") ★

Garth Brooks: *No Fences* (Capitol '90) free-range country ("Friends in Low Places," "Two of a Kind, Workin' on a Full House") ★★

Garth Brooks: *Ropin' the Wind* (Capitol '91) As El Lay song doctors process NutraSweet, textured cellulose, and natural fruit flavors through a web of synthbites, a Nashville neotraditionalist thrice-removed wins a nation's heart standing up for the studio-pop verities. After scoring one of those songfests Nashville sneaks past us urbanites in 1989, he bet the farm on the follow-up and won over a country audience in the market for its own style of schlock. Here, backed by apparently living session men as he imitates now Merle, now George (Strait), now Charlie (Daniels), he picks sure-shots from the if-you-say-so rebellious "Against the Grain" to the if-you-say-so soulful Billy Joel cover, and now and then he helps write one: the light-hearted death-to-cheaters yarn "Papa Loved Mama," or the marriage counselor's theme "We Bury the Hatchet" ("And leave the handle stickin' out"). Last album he landed only three or four; this time there are maybe six, plus a couple of marginals. Ergo, this one's twice as good. Resist him at your elitist peril. **A–**

Garth Brooks: *The Chase* (Capitol '92) Burdened by the responsibilities he believes come with success, Brooks leads with the first song in Nashville history to inveigh, however discreetly, against not just racism but homophobia. There's nothing as wicked as "Papa Loved Mama," which didn't bat an eye when mama fucked around or papa ran her over with his truck. But "Somewhere Other Than the Night," about sex on the farm, and "Learning to Live Again," about a divorcé's blind date, typify the smarts of a guy who knows not all suburbanites are as stupid as Michael Bolton believes. Having mastered the kind of nice-guy aura that has escaped pop superstars since the days of Como and Cole, Brooks could yet get away with being a liberal. **B+**

Garth Brooks: *Beyond the Season* (Liberty '92) 💣

Garth Brooks: *In Pieces* (Liberty '93) His crusade against the used-CD scourge puts him up there with Rudy Giuliani on the ever-growing list of public figures who could have gone either way and promptly went that, and like Rudy, he wants the world to know that he has no use for the welfare crowd. Nor is his music getting any purer. But it is getting Garther, which means it may soon approach wonder-of-nature status—if there's anybody trying to stuff bigger emotions into a song, he or she is a lot crazier than this professional entertainer. As garish as their titles, "Standing Outside the Fire" and "The Red Strokes" won't convert skeptics. But that kind of middle-class heat is what he's about. When he calls his Baton Rouge honey every hundred miles, you can feel his dick throbbing—probably even if you don't have one yourself, which is of course the idea. And when he constructs a soap-opera plot about how an adultery connects to a random suicide, he enters passion's twilight zone. **A–**

Garth Brooks: *The Hits* (Liberty '94) Ahh, get over it. For one simple reason: if you shut him out, if you *let it bother you* that he's full of shit, your sex life will suffer. Especially compared to Garth's, which last time the *Enquirer* checked was still with one woman, although songs like "Last Summer" (cowritten by his wife, who must do her share of fantasy work) keep him in touch with his urges. He enjoyed his amazing run, summed up for the cynical set by this 18-track stocking stuffer, because he has the most voracious emotional appetite of anyone to hit pop music since Aretha Franklin, and because he's such a perfectionist that he always threads his big feelings through the eye of a succinct narrative or sentiment. I just wish he'd announced for the Senate when David Boren retired. **A**

Garth Brooks: *Fresh Horses* (Capitol '95) A little heavy-handed (all right, a little *more* heavy-handed), with three rodeo songs and a big fat Irish anthem that won't be to everyone's taste (all right, *your* taste). Don't matter, because he's so far from the schlock phony he's taken for—so open-hearted, so extreme, so sui generis—that all but a couple of tracks do his thing even when he's protesting too much (which, all right, may *be* his thing). Cute trick: the two about marriage explain his weakness for bucking broncos. **B+**

Garth Brooks: *Sevens* (Capitol '97) Hyped into what may be the least label-profitable quintuple-platinum album of all time, this is the confirmation of everything Garth-haters believe. But for those with the heart for his avid ways, what happens is an old alchemical switch—where before he channeled his drive to succeed into the emotion of the song, transmuting his ambition as he intensified his music, now his loony need to maintain his unreal numbers distorts material that would be better off without him, or at least it. Not counting "Two Pina Coladas" (Jimmy Buffett, get outta his way), the songs are exceptional, but hearing past the gulping self-parody of his "interpretations" takes so much out of you that it's hard to tell. If that means the perfect divorce song "She's Gonna Make It" is lost to history, NOW should lodge a protest—or work out some kind of cross-promotion. I don't understand these things. **B** 🦃

Garth Brooks: *Chris Gaines' Greatest Hits* (Capitol '99) 🎸

Meredith Brooks: *Blurring the Edges* (Capitol '97) Ⓝ

Brooks & Dunn: *The Greatest Hits Collection* (Arista '97) "Hard Workin' M[e]n" tell "Honky Tonk Truth" inna Nashville-songsmith-with-big-drum-sound stylee ("She's Not the Cheatin' Kind," "Boot Scootin' Boogie," "Lost and Found") ★

Bobby Brown: "That's the Way Love Is" (*Bobby,* MCA '92) 😎

Bobby Brown, Bell Biv Devoe, Ralph Tresvant: *New Edition Solo Hits* (MCA '97) Laid out conveniently on one info-pack, the best of lesser half A and group B, with every track uptempo if not contempo (those electrothwocks are already over), and microstar C on board primarily to slow it down a little right here. In sum, new jack swing nostalgia—not a moment too soon. **A–**

Charles Brown: *All My Life* (Bullseye Blues '91) 🎸

Foxy Brown: *Ill Na Na* (Def Jam Music Group '96) 💣

Foxy Brown: *Chyna Doll* (Violator/Def Jam '99) if bomb-ass pussy could talk ("Hot Spot," "My Life") ★★★

Greg Brown: *The Poet's Game* (Red House '94) Ⓝ

James Brown: *Star Time* (Polydor '91) Canonizing as they commodify, CD boxes sever individual works from history. They obscure how albums as much as singles reflect cultural moments as well as formal imperatives and personal impulses, and rarely are their remixes, B sides, and previously unreleaseds more enlightening or entertaining than the album tracks they supplant. Redefining as it compiles, this is the great exception. The "songs" are all familiar, but with Brown, songs are only an excuse. Though his catalogue conceals a ballad album that could scare the shades off Ray Charles, with "Papa's Got a Brand New Bag" he discovered the deepest of his many callings, which was putting rhythm on top of American pop. Hence there's no excess in the many extended performances compilers Harry Weinger and Cliff White extract from the vault. Except perhaps on the first disc, which strains to provide the originals of songs known to most of us from their once-overs on *"Live" at the Apollo,* the five hours of music never falter. Only one question remains. If James Brown is the greatest popular musician of the era, how come he's never put out an album this convincing himself—not even *Sex Machine?* Does he know something about records that we don't? Is it possible they're not so important after all? **A+**

James Brown: "Teardrops on Your Letter" (*Love Over-Due,* Scotti Bros. '91) 👁

James Brown: *The Greatest Hits of the Fourth Decade* (Scotti Bros. '92) yes, he did have a synth-funk phase ("Get up Offa That Thing/Dr. Detroit") ★

James Brown: *Universal James* (Scotti Bros. '92) 💣

James Brown: *Live at the Apollo 1995* (Scotti Bros. '95) tempos up a notch, vocal pitch down a notch, he puts out like he has something to prove ("It's a Man's World," "Make It Funky") ★★★

James Brown: *I'm Back* (Georgia Lina/Mercury '98) it was like you never left ("Funk on Ah Roll [S-Class Mix]," "James on the Loose") ★★

James Brown: *Say It Live and Loud: Live in Dallas 08.26.68* (Polydor '98) Counting the half-studio *Sex Machine,* this makes Brown's fifth live album from the crucial 1967–1971 period—and except for *Sex Machine,* it's the best. Its chief competition, *Live at the Apollo Volume II,* was released a few weeks after it was recorded, but Brown moved so fast in those years that the Apollo record is radically different, a soul envoi at a moment when the funked-over "Cold Sweat" was his centerpiece and the daring "Say It Loud—I'm Black and I'm Proud" his pride and joy. From touchstone to newborn, from bop-inflected Maceo on the piss-break instrumental to born-again JB on the climax medley, breakneck intensity for the ages. **A–**

Junior Brown: *Semi Crazy* (MCA/Curb '96) the essence of Western swing—jazzy picking, lousy singing, and a light heart ("Gotta Get Up Every Morning," "Venom Wearin' Denim") ★★

Junior Brown: *Long Walk Back* (Curb '98) virtuosity as novelty act, meaning virtuosity that knows itself ("Stupid Blues," "Peelin' Taters") ★★

Marty Brown: *High and Dry* (MCA '91) His wailing purist intensity closer to Hank than to any of the proud Hank fans who made him a gamble worth taking, Brown damn near gets across on sound alone. Just before you've had it with "I'll Climb Any Mountain" (guess what he'll swim any), you realize he was astute enough to expend one of his few decent tunes on it. But soon you also notice that the chorus of "Every Now and Then," which you went along with because it was fast, does actually go: "Like a thief in the night/It cuts like a knife." Imagine Hank without hits. Pray Brown gets the knack, or buys himself a few. **B+**

Marty Brown: *Wild Kentucky Skies* (MCA '93) 🎸

Marty Brown: *Cryin', Lovin', Leavin'* (MCA '94) ⓝ

Shirley Brown: *The Soul of a Woman* (Malaco '97) ⓝ

Tanya Rae Brown: *Meet the Mrs.* (TRB '99) ⓝ

brute.: *Nine High a Pallet* (Capricorn '95) The songs on Vic Chesnutt's albums are so good he sometimes puts them across, which is more than anybody can do for the songs on Widespread Panic's albums. But that doesn't stop the latter from touring or the former from wishing he could eat his reviews, and so this cross-inspirational fluke will probably never be anything more than the ace Athens oddball-mainstream one-off it is. Chesnutt provides the cocked eyebrow and fancy dreamwork, the band turns his strums into tunes, and who the hell is going to notice? Sure "Good Morning Mister Hard On" is really about his matins, but that won't boost it into heavy rotation. These days, the path of commercial expedience would be to make it about his banana. **A–**

Gavin Bryars: *Jesus' Blood Never Failed Me Yet* (Point Music '93) It's 1971 in the streets around London's Waterloo Station. With halting certainty an old homeless man—"tramp," the term was—sings one stanza of a hymn a cappella. Takes about 25 seconds. The stanza is looped, with "classical" accompaniment that grows gradually grander. In the original 25-minute version it repeated some 50 times; this CD lasts 74 minutes, so make that 150 or so. Doesn't matter—if you're like me, you never get tired of it. You hum it to yourself, murmur the words, eventually sing it aloud, unable to resist a show of expression that reveals only your own banality. Some complain that at this length the piece is overblown, but as a

devotee of ordinary voices, I much prefer it to Bryars's 1995 expansion of the B side, the "classical" documentary *The Sinking of the Titanic.* I'm ready to swear the "composer"'s—really arranger's—writing never once obtrudes on the voice or the conviction it embodies. Even Tom Waits bellowing along in a star-time cameo does the tramp's song not the slightest violence. My only regret is that we never get to hear the whole hymn. The tramp is the true star, and he deserves his say. **A–**

Buckcherry: "Lit Up" (*Buckcherry,* DreamWorks '99) 👁

Lindsey Buckingham: *Out of the Cradle* (Reprise '92) 🎸

Jeff Buckley: *Live at Sin-é* (Columbia '93) 🎸

Jeff Buckley: *Grace* (Columbia '94) Although Tim's vocal traces are in his genes as surely as John's are in Julian's, it's wrong to peg him as the unwelcome ghost of his overwrought dad. Young Jeff is a *syncretic* asshole, beholden to Zeppelin and Nina Simone and Chris Whitley and the Cocteau Twins and his mama—your mama too if you don't watch out. "Sensitivity isn't being wimpy," he avers. "It's about being so painfully aware that a flea landing on a dog is like a sonic boom." So let us pray the force of hype blows him all the way to Uranus. **C** 🌀

Richard Buckner: *Bloomed* (DejaDisc '95) ⓝ

Richard Buckner: *Devotion and Doubt* (MCA '97) "So after all those months we're splitting up, and it had to happen but I'm feeling like shit. We pack the U-Haul, and of course everything in the kitchen is hers except these big jars of oregano and garlic powder I bought in a dollar store to spice up my pizza. It's so late she stays over, and I watch her sleep, you know? God. But she wakes up pretty early and we kiss good-bye and she gets in the car and then what do you think happens? The U-Haul breaks free and there's dishes all over the road. It seemed awful at the time, the mess and the delay had me stressing, but I gotta laugh about it now. And you know the funniest part? Without her noticing I kept some of those dishes—you're eating your pizza off one right now. More oregano?" Well, that's how I'd replot the best song here—in Buckner's version, it's *ditches* all over the road. He still thinks the whole thing was awful. And of course, he has just the sensitive baritone to make awful seem awful romantic to sad sacks and the women who love them. **B–** 🦃

Buckshot Le Fonque: *Buckshot Le Fonque* (Columbia '94) 💣

Harold Budd & Hector Zazou: *Glyph* (Made to Measure/Freezone import '98) downtown minimalism meets ambient techno meets the Algerian half of (how could you forget?) Zazou Bikaye ("The Aperture," "As Fast As I Could Look Away She Was Still There") ★★

Buena Vista Social Club: *Buena Vista Social Club* (World Circuit '97) guitarist-producer intrusive, son worse, music mild, geezers grand ("Chan Chan," "Candela") ★

Buffalo Daughter: *New Rock* (Grand Royal '98) 💣

Buffalo Tom: *Big Red Letter Day* (Beggars Banquet '93) In which the purely horrendous Dinosaur Jr. clones of *Birdbrain* enlist the aid of reputed pop producers to reconfigure themselves as virtually mediocre Soul Asylum drones. Don't despair, children, the attempted J Mascis roar is still with us—augmented, as they say, by jangle, harmony, and the occasional tunelessly rendered tune. Does college radio really believe this is art and Janet Jackson isn't? **C** 🦃

Bugs & Friends: *Bugs & Friends Sing the Beatles* (Kid Rhino '95) beats the Rutles—or as Elmer would put it, Wutles ("Hello Goodbye," "The Fool on the Hill") ★★

Buick MacKane: *The Pawn Shop Years* (Rykodisc '97) 💣

Built to Spill: *Ultimate Alternative Wavers* (C/Z '92) ah sweet mystery of youth, extracting form from chaos and candy from dirt ("Nowhere Nothin' Fuckup," "Three Years Ago Today") ★

Built to Spill: *There's Nothing Wrong with Love* (Up '94) Biz big boys of both sexes are besieging Doug Martsch, and why not? Guy's yoked his fully realized guitar style to material even more mature than that—how rare it is for a rock and roll dad to write songs about childhood that don't trade self-pitying adolescent sentimentality for self-congratulatory adult sentimentality. So you know what Doug Martsch tells the big boys? That he likes Idaho—and his family—too much to hit the rock and roll road. Here's hoping he can turn a modest profit while sticking to the essence of this decision, one of the sanest antistar biases in all indiedom. And here's hoping he keeps writing those songs and playing that guitar. **A–**

Built to Spill: *Perfect from Now On* (Warner Bros. '97) "In a world that's not so bad," Doug Martsch builds a hideout worth visiting—more tree house than basement or cave, with hooks for footholds and misty guitar vistas when you finish the climb. Not a loner, just a small-town kind of guy, he derives his idea of the social from his experience of the musical. So when he says, "You won't help anyone/cause you're unusable," he can't possibly be talking about himself. I hope. **B+**

Built to Spill: *Keep It Like a Secret* (Warner Bros. '99) like grunge never unhappened ("You Were Right," "Center of the Universe") ★★

L.T.J. Bukem: *Logical Progression* (FFRR '96) Ⓝ

Sonny Burgess with Dave Alvin: *Tennessee Border* (HighTone '92) 💣

Burn Barrel: *Reviled!* (Heathen '99) neo-realism Columbus style—via Far Rockaway, but Winesburg is proud anyway ("Scratch," "Mrs. Tubbs") ★★

Burning Spear: *Jah Kingdom* (Mango '91) Ⓝ

Burning Spear: *The World Should Know* (Heartbeat '93) ◐

Burning Spear: *Rasta Business* (Heartbeat '95) 💣

R. L. Burnside: *A Ass Pocket of Whiskey* (Matador '96) ◐

R. L. Burnside: *Mr. Wizard* (Fat Possum/Epitaph '97) they don't explode, they just pound, and pretty hard too ("Alice Mae") ★

R. L. Burnside: *Sound Machine Groove* (High Water/HMG '97) 💣

William S. Burroughs: *Dead City Radio* (Island '90) ◐

William S. Burroughs: *Spare Ass Annie and Other Tales* (Island '93) the Disposable Heroes meet shtick from the crypt ("The Junky's Christmas," "Words of Advice for Young People") ★★

William Burroughs: "What Keeps Mankind Alive?" (*September Songs: The Music of Kurt Weill* [comp], Sony Classics '97) 🍱

William Burroughs: See also Material.

Charlie Burton and the Hiccups: *Green Cheese* (Wild '90): mooning his love life, mooning the world ("Without My Woman . . . ," "Anyone I Know?") ★

Charlie Burton & the Hiccups: *Puke Point at the Juke Joint* (Wild '91) ◐

Charlie Burton and the Texas Twelve Steppers: *Rustic Fixer-Upper* (Lazy SOB '97) "She's the sugar in my gastank" and other funny lines ("Baby Let's Play God," "Livin' on Borrowed Time [Livin' on Borrowed Money]") ★★★

Charlie Burton: *One Man's Trash: The Charlie Burton Story: '77–'99* (Bulldog '99) Since the dawn of the Sex Pistols, it's been art-for-art's-sake for this poet of song, whose evocations of succubi, coronary thrombosis, garbage, manners and morals, dead chickens in the middle of the road, and the varieties of romantic disaster have thrilled and enlightened music lovers in university towns cum state capitals from Lincoln, Nebraska, all the way to Austin, Texas. 'Tis oft claimed he can't sing a lick, but he's learned to croon a slurp, not to mention rock a bite in the ass. And lest anyone whine about perpetual adolescence, this well-culled collection goes out proving how much he's grown in human understanding: "Without my woman," he intones gravely, "I'd be a hopeless sack of shit." **A–**

Bush: *Sixteen Stone* (Trauma/Interscope '94) You think the million-plus American rockers who've purchased Gavin Rossdale's not altogether unmusical howl of male pain are this far gone? For that matter, you think Rossdale is? Nah. It's an idealization—a level of despair to aspire toward rather than shared pain requiring collective catharsis. In other words, things could get worse. **B–** 🦃

Kate Bush: *The Red Shoes* (Columbia '93) ◐

Bushwick Bill: *Little Big Man* (Rap-a-Lot '92) Of course you have a big one, Bill. It goes with your minority-group status—dwarves are famous for their big ones. And when you cut it off, you'll probably write something as scary as "Ever So Clear." Scarier than your mind-of-a-skitso shtick, that's for sure. **C+** 🦃

Chris Butler: *The Devil Glitch* (Future Fossil '96) one song with a shitload of choruses, or, "Sometimes you can fix something 550 times/there's special grace in repetition" ("*Track 3:* Mars Williams—sax player from the Waitresses"; "*Track 15:* Christopher D. Butler—computer music wiz") ★★

Butthole Surfers: *Pioughd* (Rough Trade '91) beyond noisome ("Lonesome Bulldog") ★

Butthole Surfers: *Independent Worm Saloon* (Capitol, '93) With closet M.B.A. Gibby Haynes t.c.b., their freak show has always had more P. T. Barnum than Salvador Dali in it, and more Salvador Dali than Swamp Dogg. All John Paul Jones does is improve their entertainment value. Channeling horrible noise into runaway power riffs, they maintain a style of momentum reminiscent of Gibby's sometime collaborators in Ministry—messier, which is their calling card, but not that much messier, and with more blatant guitar. With nuttier jokes, too. A fun-loving guy, Gibby. **A–**

Butthole Surfers: *Electriclarryland* (Capitol '96) Ⓝ

Butt Trumpet: *Primitive Enema* (Chrysalis/EMI '95) 💣

Buzzcocks: "Palm of Your Hand" (*Trade Test Transmissions,* Caroline '93) 🕭

Buzzcocks: *All Set* (I.R.S. '96) love life much smoother, music summat ("Totally from the Heart," "Point of No Return") ★★★

Buzzcocks: *Modern* (Go-Kart '99) looking for the same new love with the same new tunes ("Thunder of Hearts," "Why Compromise?") ★★★

BWP: *"Two Minute Brother"* (*The Bytches,* No Face '91) 🕭

David Byrne: *The Forest* (Warner Bros./Sire/Luaka Bop '91) 💣
David Byrne: *Uh-Oh* (Luaka Bop/ Warner Bros. '92) 💣
David Byrne: *David Byrne* (Luaka Bop/Sire/Warn Bros. '94) over a gawky world-groove, basic singer-songwriter stuff—the biological mystery at the core of technological life ("Lilies of the Valley," "Buck Naked") ★★
David Byrne: *Feelings* (Luaka Bop/ Warner Bros. '97) 💣

Don Byron: *Nu Blaxploitation* (Blue Note '98) 💣

B/COMPILATIONS

Baby Sounds (Kid Rhino '98) ambient bio ("Baby Sounds [Part Two: Toddlers]," "Baby Sounds [Part One: Babies]") ★★★

Backbeat (Virgin '94) Not to blame the staunchly soul-effacing Greg Dulli and Dave Pirner for bodies they don't have, but all that stops this experiment in multiconscious neoprimitivism from approxi- mating the freedom to which it aspires is that the lead voices don't fly high enough—Pirner's McCartney is too gravelly, Dulli's Lennon devoid of falsetto. Instrumentally, soundtrack honcho Don Was has detonated a miracle of postmodernist disguise, inducing a supergroup cum pickup band comprising Sonic Youth's Thurston Moore, Nirvana's Dave Grohl, R.E.M.'s Mike Mills, and Gumball's Don Fleming to enter the spirits of the Beatles in Hamburg, where they made their living covering Motown and Chuck Berry before anyone thought the '60s needed heralding. To the puny alternative mind-set, the Beatles have long seemed too pop and the rock and roll that "preceded" them too quaint, but forced to confront history, these present-day musicians play both halves of the synthesis as raw, fast, and unscientific as they actually were. At 12 songs in 27 minutes, the formal result is the great punk album *Live! at the StarClub* never was—and yes, technical sophistication matters, sonically and musically. Meaningwise, of course, it's a Chinese box. Talk about constructing a subject—what would Lacan make of this? **A–**

Bad Boy Greatest Hits Volume 1 (Bad Boy '98) Ⓝ

Batman Forever (Atlantic '95) the class of cross-promotional new wave songbooks (PJ Harvey, "One Time Too Many"; Massive Attack with Tracey Thorn, "The Hunter Gets Captured by the Game") ★

Beats & Rhymes: Hip Hop of the '90s, Part I (Rhino, '97) Between 1990, when old school went emeritus, and 1992, when gangsta stuck daisy age's pistil up its stamen, came a nondescript downtime that Rhino maps without recourse to rap crossovers, which meant less than nothing to the loyalists who were just then insisting that what they loved was called "hip hop." But though all three volumes are pretty subtle for nonloyalists, only here are the high points obvious—hits from key Jungle Brothers and Tribe Called Quest albums, BDP's "Love's Gonna Get'cha"—and the selections from minor figures like Special Ed, Def Jef, and K-Solo open to challenge from the likes of me (I nominate "Taxin'," "Fa Sho Shot," and "Tales from the Crack Side"). Even so I love the YZ, Poor Righteous Teachers, and D.O.C. tracks, not to mention the BDP radio edit with sound effects where the bleeps should be. I also love Cold Chillin''s "Erase Racism." **B+**

Beats & Rhymes: Hip Hop of the '90s Part II (Rhino '97) Meet and greet such subculturally certified rhymesmiths as Leaders of the New School, Organized Konfusion, Main Source, the UMC's, and the oft-odious DJ Quik. Plus, for some reason, three predictably solid Chubb Rock tracks. Plus minor hits from Rakim, Lyte, and Run-D.M.C. Think wordplay not signification. Think beats not hooks. Go with their flows. **A–**

Beats & Rhymes: Hip Hop of the '90s Part III (Rhino '97) This bumps along for eight tracks distinguished by two new to me—Lord Finesse's "Return of the Funky Man" ("you're softer than baby shit") and Double X Posse's "Not Gonna Be Able to Do It" ("I'm not gonna be able to do")—before vaulting off Naughty by Nature and Quest into four consecutive guaranteed great, hilarious records: Del Tha Funkee Homosapien's Three Stooges bit, Humpty Hump's nose, the Pharcyde's dozens, and FU-Schnickens' advertisement for Jive Records, which has steadfastly kept their catalogue in print. Then Romy-Dee expands the legend of funky Kingston. **A–**

Beat the Retreat: Songs by Richard Thompson (Capitol '94) I hate tribute albums. They're patchwork by definition—even when the oeuvre is worth reprising, no way will all the contributors hit it right or the producer hear any way to segue the results if they do. But this one peaks early and often, with double side-closers by balladic Britons June Tabor and Maddy Prior wiping out the creamy off-taste left by Bonnie Raitt and Shaun Colvin. The honoree's chronic inability to sing as good

as he writes adds use value, and the two tours de force are vocal—the Five Blind Boys of Alabama's autumnal "Dimming of the Day" and R.E.M.'s joyous "Wall of Death." Since the honoree has also been known to play guitar, Mould, Gilkyson, et al. make like it's a cutting contest. And then there's the oeuvre. **A–**

The Beavis and Butt-Head Experience (Geffen '93) 💣

Before Benga Vol. 2: The Nairobi Sound (Original Music '93) We all know African music is meant to be apprehended rhythm foremost—except for the oddballs who think maybe it actually comes tunes first. Early electric pop from a high-set city too temperate for open-air dance halls, these lovingly collected Kenyan singles lilt and sway beguilingly, and the lyrics mix timeless courtship and dated topicality with an earnest smile I'm sure will charm Swahili speakers. But the collective genius is in the tunes. Play it a dozen times, then attend as each melody makes a modest entrance, and you'll swear you've been hearing every one for years. And I guess it's possible you have. But not in the same place. **A**

Bergville Stories (Columbia import '97) As a South Africa–only release, the original-cast album to this drop-dead entry in Lincoln Center's South African theater series will be sought out only by those who already dig mbube/iscathimiya. Stateside that means Ladysmith, period—almost nothing else is in the racks. Yet mbube is the heritage of one of the most voice-crazy peoples on the planet—every Zulu is taught to sing, damn well if field recordings from labor congresses and informal competitions mean anything. So in this play, set in a besieged Soweto hostel, the actors break into song every few minutes. Not primarily singers, they aren't pure amateurs either. They know how to project and present, and writer-director Duma kaNdlovu orchestrates their flow—home pitch fluctuates from chant to chant, call-and-response patterns shift, sound effects and catchy choruses kick in just when you need them. The result is a vivid representation of the mbube I've always read about, a rougher and more male-chauvinist domain than the elegant Christians of Ladysmith ever hint. **A–**

The Best of Reggae Dancehall Vol. 1 (Profile '90) As disco habitués learn to perceive its marginal distinctions, tolerate its generic repetitions, and crave its pulse, Jamaican post-toasting becomes less accessible to simple curiosity seekers like yours truly. I'm sure every song on this assiduous compilation was a special favorite in context, and appreciate all the little touches—the late-breaking piano hook on "This Feeling Inside," the lilting Sunday School promise of "Prophecy," the multiple interjections of "Nah Go Switch," the aggressively incredulous "Wha-at"s of "Bun and Cheese" and then "Life," the squeaky echo of "Life." But excepting three or four—Tiger's "Ram Dance Hall" (he roars), Gregory Peck's "Oversized Mumpie" (blue patois), and Derrick Parker's "Cool It Off" (sounds like "coup d'etat"), with Shelly Thunder's "Kuff" a dark horse—I still could stand some more big touches. **A–**

The Best Punk Album in the World . . . Ever! (Virgin import '95) I can just see the ad scrolling down the late-night screen: "Anarchy in the U.K."!/"2-4-6-8 Motorway"! /"Alternative Ulster"!/"Teenage Kicks"!/ "Psycho Killer"!/"Blank Generation"!/"Sex & Drugs & Rock & Roll"!/"Milk and Alcohol"! Images of leather and shirtless Iggy and pogoing and skinny-tied Joe and safety pins and Siouxsie and her tits jutting out (hey, get rid of that swastika fer Chrissake). But even with the Clash MIA, this stupid two-CD hodgepodge is how punk or new wave or whatever the fuck it was hit U.K. rock and rollers—with strong, fast songs by white people suffering from attention deficit disorder—and it's also how most impressionables will absorb it now. It ignores L.A., which London didn't know existed ("I Hate the Rich"!), and preserves some tracks you

can't stand (Tubes, Adam and the Ants) as well as unearthing a few you missed (Skids, Jilted John). Collectors of a certain age don't need it, especially at import prices, and volume two is less surefire. But the title sells it like it is. **A**

Big Beat Conspiracy: BBC 1 (Pagan '98) as much fun as a new chemistry set (Laidback, "International"; J Knights, "Catch a Break"; Surreal Madrid, "Insanity Sauce") ★★★

Big Phat Ones of Hip-Hop Volume 1 (BOXtunes '95) "Press play on remote at the Playaz Club"—a mythic realm of unknowable pleasure (Rappin' 4-Tay, "Playaz Club"; Scarface, "I Seen a Man Die") ★★★

Big Rock'n Beats (Wax Trax!/TVT '97) Funny and shameless, whomping where artier types now skitter and not too futuristic for harmonicas or choo-choo trains, the 13 acts from five nations who here define what some dubiously dub "big beat" cohere more generically than does the high-buzz *Amp*. But in a compilation that claims to lay out a genre, that's a mark of honor. **A–**

Bombay the Hard Way (Motel '99) slightly hyped-up (and camped-up) Bollywood orchestrations by Kalyanji and Anandji V. Shah ("The Good, the Bad and the Chutney," "Swami Safari") ★★

Boomerang (LaFace '92) Ⓝ

Born to Choose (Rykodisc '93) Granting the thematic animus of the Mekons' brazen "Born to Choose" and Soundgarden's ball-busting "HIV Baby," this charity comp has less in common with *No Alternative* than with *A Very Special Christmas*. The secret is consistency: quality artists (11 of the 12 have finished Pazz & Jop top 50, six top 10) doing quality material (perceptive enough to get involved, they cared enough to do it right). Kudos, then, to organizers Craig Marks and Karen Glauber, both of whom happen to be journalists—even, dare I say it, rock critics. Inspirational Verse, from John Lennon via

Matthew Sweet: „She said/I know what it's like to be dead." **A–**

Bring in 'Da Noize, Bring in 'Da Funk (RCA Victor '96) No matter how many of the owners have *been in bands,* the voices of *Rent* epitomize that anonymous synthesis of "talk 'street'" and "pro*ject,* my dear, e-*nun*-ci-ate" with which Broadway has fended off "rock" since *Hair.* But the second time I braved the two-CD original-cast monster, I noticed something strange—not only did I remember half the songs a month later, some of them made me feel something. That the singing is better on its African American counterpart is no surprise, but the catch sure is: for all practical purposes, there is none. This is an album of people banging their feet on the floor while a PBS narrator talks about oppression. No noize, no funk, OK—what do you expect of the musical theayter? But no songs? Call 'da po-lice. **D+** 🦃

Brother's Gonna Work It Out: A DJ Mix Album by the Chemical Brothers (Astralwerks '98) **Ⓝ**

Buddhist Liturgy of Tibet (World Music Library import '93) Fourteen monks climax a Tantric meditation by chanting the Sutra. Unison readings are augmented and sometimes driven by precise percussion, patches of multivoiced murmur (like the prelude to a Kiwanis luncheon) are less predictably accompanied, and maybe the coughs are on purpose too. Whatever else goes down, though, the voices are interrupted every four or five minutes by a din out of Wynton Marsalis's nightmares. Handbells and cymbals, rattles and boom-booms, deafening oboes and monster trumpets unite in music that at this distance evokes nothing so much as a four-car accident—and that over there connects to the divine. Meaning notwithstanding, it's an astonishing *sound*—and I've yet to play it for anyone who's reported back unimproved by the experience. Rock and roll! **B+**

Bulworth: The Soundtrack (Interscope '98) This makes room for too much mere soundtrack, I suppose—only that means not just honorable filler but utterly infectious party-scene beatbombs like "Zoom" and "Freak Out" and album picks and outtakes from B-Real, Cappadonna, Witchdoctor, Public Enemy. Canibus's "How Come" is a quizzical billow in the millenarian tidal wave. And Ol' Dirty Bastard's girly backup bits on Pras's "Ghetto Supastar" are pure Dennis Rodman postmacho. **B+**

Chris Cacavas: *Junkyard Love* (Heyday '92) raw, sweet, and gawky—too bad Neil himself didn't play guitar ("Did You Hear What She Said?" "Many Splintered Thing") ★★★

Cachao: *Master Sessions Volume 1* (Crescent Moon/Epic '94) Israel Lopez is a 76-year-old contrabassist credited with bringing the jam to Cuba and the mambo to the world. He has lived in the U.S. since 1962. Yet this is his first major-label album. So thank Emilio Estefan and Andy Garcia for capturing a genius even a salsa agnostic like me can't ignore. Working with Paquito D'Rivera, Néstor Torres, Chocolate Armenteros, et al., Cachao cut 30 tunes one week last May, and these 12 alone run over 76 minutes. Far less hectic than New York salsa, often with a stately charanga feel, they respect Cachao's roots in the old danzón tradition, but the youngbloods' heat and surface motion stimulate a veteran of more Miami weddings and bar mitzvahs than he can count. The notes claim that all the tunes are stone classics, and this agnostic believes. **A–**

Cachao: *Dos* (Salsoul '95) Having fallen at first for Sony's fib that *Master Sessions* was Israel Lopez's U.S. debut and then been set straight by a savvier fan's lengthy computerized list of the now 78-year-old bassist's specialty-label output, I went down to Bate Records on Delancey Street and selected two classic-looking items. The way I feel it, the perfectly lis-

tenable 1959 and 1974 sessions recycled on Kubaney's *La Leyenda Vol. 1* overdo the ballroom politesse. And though it's true and crucial that politesse has never been disrespected by this vigorous old man, not even when he was revolutionizing danzón at 21, I prefer this five-track, 30-minute sample of a mid-'70s attempt to cement his legacy. The ballroom's here for sure. But so are the Havana street, the African village, the dockside joint in Anyport, Terra. The ensemble emphasis assures smooth progression from güiro to danzón to descarga to congafest as famous sidemen come and go. **A–**

Cachao: *Master Sessions Volume II* (Crescent Moon/Epic '95) As an instant fan of its predecessor, I find this too hyperactive and choppy to listen easy. Cut by cut, however, it seldom slips to acceptable. Discerning no serious letdown between the showpiece that sets veteran sonero Rolando Laserie to "stalking the melody" of "El Guapachoso" and a coro-hooked jam off the top of Cachao's head, I choose not to quibble. **A–**

Cadallaca: *Introducing Cadallaca* (K '98) There's a Cadallaca interview where Corin Tucker confuses the Ronettes with the Shirelles, and even if it was a "put-on," as young people say, that's all you need know about how much this side project has to do with classic girl groups and the rest of that rot. It's just a song sluice for an irrepressible talent—somewhat gentler and less conflict-purging, with Sarah

---

★★★, ★★, ★ Honorable Mention   Choice Cut   Ⓝ Neither   🎣 Dud   🦃 Turkey

Dougher's organ replacing Carrie Brownstein's guitar. The one noir period piece is the one misstep; elsewhere they imagine 1942 and dis a booker and invent new romance tropes the way they would in any other band. I love Brownstein. But Tucker could end up eclipsing Polly Jean Harvey herself if that was the way she thought about the world. And one of her strengths is that it isn't. **A**

Cagney and Lacee: *Six Feet of Chain* (No. 6 '97) 💣

Cake: *Motorcade of Generosity* (Capricorn '95) unambiguity from the near side of cool ("Rock'N'Roll Lifestyle," "Jesus Wrote a Blank Check") ★
Cake: *Fashion Nugget* (Capricorn, '96) the ridiculous pathos of everyday life ("I Will Survive," "Frank Sinatra") ★★
Cake: *Prolonging the Magic* (Capricorn '98) Ⓝ

Cake Like: *Delicious* (Avant import '94) MTV cheerleaders make art-punk as angular as they look and as angry as they feel ("Bum Leg," "Suck") ★★★
Cake Like: *Bruiser Queen* (Vapor '97) 💣
Cake Like: *Goodbye, So What* (Vapor '99) 💣

John Cale: *Walking on Locusts* (Hannibal '96) 💣
John Cale: See also Eno/Cale, Lou Reed/John Cale

John Campbell: *Howlin Mercy* (Elektra '93) This white bluesman paid his dues on the Gulf Coast circuit, then moved to New York and went electric. Shortly after he released his second album, his fatal heart attack attracted as much attention as his music ever had. Given his loose talk of teaching hellhounds to sit and keeping the devil in his hole, some wondered piously whether he'd made a pact with the unnameable. More likely he just drank too much. **C** 🦃

Stacy Dean Campbell: *Lonesome Wins Again* (Columbia '92) No strings, no metaphors, no shows of soul. Fast ones medium fast, slow ones medium slow. Backup singers, but they make the Jordanaires sound like the Harry Simeone Chorale. Music Row tunes, but never clever and always indelible. Voice pure, quiet, serious, deeply unpretentious. In short, a country album so austere it's like a Platonic ideal. Or anyway, like Chris Isaak rockabilly minus the arty pose—this guy's alternate career was with the sheriff's department. **A–**

Stacy Dean Campbell: *Hurt City* (Columbia '95) more is less ("Pop a Top," "Mind over Matter") ★

Stacy Dean Campbell: *Ashes of Old Love* (Paladin '99) Ⓝ

Cam'ron: *Confessions of Fire* (Untertainment/Epic '98) cheap sensationalism has its own rewards ("Feels Good," "Me, My Moms & Jimmy," "The Wrong Ones") ★

Can: *Soon over Babaluma* (Spoon import '96) A basically instrumental excursion that aficionados rank with the sprawling *Tago Mago,* this 1974 Kraut-rock opus is to the Miles Davis of the era as acid jazz is to real jazz. It's never pompous, discernibly smart, playful, even goofy. If you give it your all you can make out a few shards of internal logic. But the light tone avoids texture, density, or pain. The jazzy pulse is innocent of swing, funk, or sex. And if it generates any intrinsic interest, as opposed to the conceptual kick of being so singularly European, after half a dozen plays I should have some inkling what that interest is. **B–** 🦃

C + C Music Factory: *Gonna Make You Sweat* (Columbia '90) shameless ripoffs to be proud of ("Things That Make You Go Hmmm . . . ," "Here We Go, Let's Rock & Roll") ★★★

Candlebox: *Candlebox* (Maverick/Sire/ Warner Bros. '93) These postgrunge scene-suckers aren't total pop-metal conformists—they're a tad more intense, with sharper drumming. Their chief distinction is that at 2.5 mill they'll probably outsell the artist-cum-label-owner who set siege to Seattle to sign them—the one we hoped would next re-create herself as a visionary entrepreneur. **C** 🦃

Canibus: *Can-I-Bus* (Universal '98) So what exactly is supposed to be wrong here? His bragging, tsk-tsk? His retrograde reliance on "bitch" and such? His fealty to the Betrayer of Lauryn Hill? His voice, all gritty and ugly and clear and New York? His "flow," Lord help us? He doesn't flow, he overflows, spouting extra verbiage when any normal logorrheic would shut the eff up, and that form-fucking illusion of distended stanza *is* his flow. Unfettered after the manner of Kool Moe Dee, uncanny after the manner of Fox Mulder, and uproarious either way, he makes sure his gangsta tropes stay that way because he believes language supersedes reality. And all this I pinned down after being sucked in by the chamber orchestra, Hawaiian guitar, mixed-down Wagner, Claudine Longet parody, Wonder Mike parody, and Roxanne Shanté sample. You'll gasp. You'll chortle. You'll wonder what exactly is supposed to be wrong here. **A**

Capital Tax: *The Swoll Package* (MCA '93) joy riding, hustling quarters, getting hard the next time, and other modest street skills ("Mista Wonka," "I Can't Believe It") ★★

Cappadonna: *The Pillage* (Razor Sharp/Epic Street '98) as it is written, "Wu-Tang Productions Presents" ("Milk the Cow," "Run") ★

Captain Beefheart & His Magic Band: *Grow Fins: Rarities (1965–1982)* (Revenant '99) If you have any doubts about needing this handsome $94-list package, you don't. If you're moved to ask pop-friendly me, you don't. Every CD box is larded with marginalia, but the good folks at Revenant—who last year reckoned that Charlie Feathers cut 42 "essential" tracks between 1954 and 1969—live for it. They believe consumers should share the thrill of digging through the crates, palpitating as the voice of genius emanates from a dusty reel. So instead of winnowing out an hour or so of lost songs, jelled jams, and unjust outtakes, they throw in a 13-minute CD of dim studio chatter, a minute of Don Van Vliet playing the harmonica over the telephone, etc. Take it from pop-friendly me—if you've spent more time with the Captain's free sessions than with Ornette Coleman's, you need to get your priorities in order. **C+** 🎹

The Cardigans: "Hey! Get Out of My Way," "Daddy's Car," "Sabbath Bloody Sabbath" (*Life,* Minty Fresh '96) 🎸

The Cardigans: *First Band on the Moon* (Mercury '96) Popper-than-thou aggregation backs cute blonde for fun and profit. Think Blondie. They're Swedish. Think Abba. They're Euroalt-by-default. Think, er, Bettie Serveert. Only nowadays, anythinger-than-thou commits you to that extra mile, so that these reformed metalheads make their Beatle move à la Black Velvet Flag. And since metalheads can really, how you say it, play their axes, they also score some funny Black Sabbath covers. As for the blonde, alt types were calling her dark even back when she was imitating a love doll. Me, I prefer her now that she's imitating a cynical young woman—especially since the metalheads provide dissonances suitable to her self-critical rhetoric, which greatly smartens their flute and tinkle. **B+**

The Cardigans: *Gran Turismo* (Stockholm/Mercury '98) with a hit on their résumé, they're free to be the depressed Swedes they always were ("Paralyzed," "Do You Believe") ★

Mariah Carey: *Mariah Carey* (Columbia '90) I swear I didn't know her mama was an opera singer, but I'm embarrassed that I didn't guess. She gets too political in her brave, young, idealistic attack on "war, destitution and sorrow": "Couldn't we accept each other/Can't we make ourselves aware." Elsewhere she sticks to what she doesn't know—love. Debbie Gibson, all is forgiven. **C** 🎹

Mariah Carey: *Emotions* (Columbia '91) 🎸

Mariah Carey: *Music Box* (Columbia '93) 🎸

Mariah Carey: *Butterfly* (Columbia '97) 💣

Mariah Carey: "Fantasy [Featuring ODB]" (#1's, Columbia '98) 👁

Mariah Carey: *Rainbow* (Columbia '99) not a "real" r&b thrush, but good enough to fake it ("Heartbreaker," "Crybaby") ★★

Bob Carlisle: *Butterfly Kisses (Shades of Grace)* (Diadem '97) I don't hate the single like I'm supposed to—I think it's healthy for Christians to acknowedge the erotic subtext of parental love, and anyway, I choke up a little when she gets married (stop smirking unless you have a pubescent daughter). I note that as pop oversingers go he's on the human side of Celine and Hanson. And I like the professed humility of lines like, "I'm not tryin' to preach to ya/and tell you that I've found all the easy answers/when half the time I can't even find my keys." But the problem isn't just that this promise keeper is lying—music is his ministry, and damn straight he uses it to preach. It's that only on his fluke hit does he have the grace to universalize his beliefs even as much as Kirk Franklin, who makes *his* song about "mustard seed faith" signify even though it's far more God-proud. Carlisle is a niche evangelist, addressing the men's-movement generation of alienated suburban husbands, white and Protestant assumed. He's pretty good at it. But he's so short on true proseytizing zeal that no one else will remember he exists once his smash crashes. **B–** 🦃

Ralph Carney: *I Like You (a Lot)* (Akron Cracker '99) Ⓝ

Mary Chapin Carpenter: *A Place in the World* (Columbia '96) Why do I believe this Nashville liberal showers three times a day and doesn't think sex is the right place to get your face wet? Is it the Stones riff that marches by as neatly as the quaint mandolin-and-harpsichord figure? The voice that never doubts its own clarity? Creative writing like "The sepia tones of a lost afternoon/Cradle a curio storefront"? As dull as Al Gore and Ralph Nader put together. **B–** 🦃

Mary Chapin Carpenter: *Party Doll and Other Favorites* (Columbia '99) 💣

James Carr: *Take Me to the Limit* (Goldwax '91) Most of Carr's legend is in his voice, a great grave thing that doesn't so much interpret his best material as haunt it, and for as long as the songs on this album hold out, the voice holds out too—even on the light-hearted "Sugar Shock." I think that's how it works, anyway—all I can swear is that somewhere around cut seven the proceedings thicken uncomfortably and then grind to a near halt. Since the rest of Carr's legend revolves around his long periods of seclusion, I attributed the undistanced commitment of his rare, recent live show to the fact that he'd never sung his great songs into the ground. Having since located this record, I now suspect that some of those I thought I'd forgotten were new. "Take Me to the Limit" and "She's Already Gone" are squarely in the obsessive tradition of "Dark End of the Street," which belonged to him first. **B+**

Joe "King" Carrasco & the Crowns: *Royal, Loyal and Live* (Royal Texicali '90) acceding to local custom, they beef up their party with horns, guitar solos, and the appropriate frat-rock faves ("Hey Joe," "96 Tears (Every Woman I Know)") ★

Deana Carter: *Did I Shave My Legs for This?* (Capitol '96) for the catch in her throat as well as her well-schooled indifference to anybody's purist niceties ("I've Loved Enough to Know," "Before We Ever Heard Goodbye") ★★

Deana Carter: *Everything's Gonna Be Alright* (Capitol '98) Ⓝ

James Carter: *The Real Quietstorm* (Atlantic '95) I don't see the point of comparing the most prodigious young jazzman since David Murray if not Ornette to anyone less titanic than Sonny Rollins. He can play anything, with a giant sound on all four saxes plus bass flute and bass clarinet. I greatly enjoy and highly recommend his two blowing sessions for DIW, *JC on the Set* and *Jurassic Classics,* with the latter slightly favored for its classic heads—Monk, Ellington, Rollins, Coltrane, Clifford Brown. Still, neither suggests much reason for the playing beyond the playing itself, however sufficient a cause that may be. This romantic set has some concept. Two unfazed Carter originals complement a surprising selection of make-out music by Monk, Ellington, Sun Ra, Bill Doggett, Carter's main man Don Byas. Not only is it more unified, it's more pop, which intensifies the aesthetic charge. And Carter lets Byas's "1944 Stomp" rip so fast and hard you'll order up a blowing session immediately. **A**

James Carter: *Conversin' with the Elders* (Atlantic '96) Say his Wynton Marsalis side provides technique, ambition, maybe focus. Plus, OK, respect for his elders—for sure he's not mocking or upstaging Buddy Tate and Sweets Edison. But it's his Lester Bowie side that inclines him to adore their melodiousness, and their melodies. It's his Bowie side that covers a march by elder Anthony Braxton, consorts with Coltrane via elder Hamiet Bluiett, revs his own waltz into a flag-waver and reduces it to a cartoon. It's his Bowie side that covers the Lester Bowie reggae, defining the grooveful, comic, demotic tone of everything that follows. A jazz album, absolutely. But one any rock and roller who can abide a saxophone could love. **A**

James Carter: *In Carterian Fashion* (Atlantic '98) I could call the organ a pop concept, but fact is I enjoy this as a jazz record. Just by blowing so lustily and swinging so edgily, Carter puts out more personality and pleasure than all but a few musical word-slingers. Deep meanings? I dunno. Aren't we in this for the pizzazz? **A–**

Carter the Unstoppable Sex Machine: *30 Something* (Chrysalis '91) 💣

Eric Cartman: "Come Sail Away" (*Chef Aid: The South Park Album* [comp], American '98) 👁‍🗨

Lionel Cartwright: "30 Nothin'," "Waiting for the Sun to Shine" (*Chasin' the Sun*, MCA '91) 👁‍🗨

Johnny Cash: "Delia's Gone" (*American Recordings,* American '94) 👁‍🗨
Johnny Cash: *Unchained* (American '96) "If I can't make these songs my own, they don't belong," say the notes, which belong ("Mean Eyed Cat," "I Never Picked Cotton") ★

Rosanne Cash: *Interiors* (Columbia '90) With husband-producer Rodney Crowell down to "guest vocal," she's on her own. Not only is this the first time she's produced herself, it's the first time she wrote all the songs—only once before has she even come close. Musically it's singer-songwriter rock, though as always Cash redeems tasteful arrangements with high-quality melodies and intense vocal focus. But lyrically this prolonged meditation on a marriage in pain is country at its best, because country is marriage music and Cash knows the territory. Anger, fear, separation, transcendence, change—this woman has thought about the tough stuff. Most of the time she has as much to say as, to choose a random example, Woody Allen girding himself up for a big statement. And even when she's corny, her seriousness is so palpable that the emotional effort carries the songs. **A–**

Rosanne Cash: *The Wheel* (Columbia '93) Cash's literary ambitions would be hard on any singing songwriter, not just a country star with New York on her mind. So while these evocations, explorations, and other -ations of life and love a-borning are prim by good American-music standards of process and groove, give her credit for evoking and exploring like she means it, which has always been her strength. "I'm changing like a girl/On the threshold of her life/In love with the whole world," this thirtysomething sings, and you can feel it. **A–**

Rosanne Cash: *10 Song Demo* (Capitol, '96) sin, sex, beauty, God—if she doesn't sing them all, she comes close ("The Summer I Read Colette," "Take My Body") ★★

Cassius: *1999* (Astralwerks '99) 💣

Tommy Castro: *Right as Rain* (Blind Pig '99) 💣

Cat Power: *Moon Pix* (Matador '98) At least Chan Marshall's not trying to fool anybody. From "she plays the difficult parts and I play difficult" to "the music is boring me to death," she's an honest heroine of the new indie staple—not noise-tune and certainly not irony, both as passé as the guilty pop dreams they kept at bay, but sadness. Slow sadness. Slow sadness about one's inability to relate. And not to audiences. Hell is other people. **C+** 🦃

Nick Cave & the Bad Seeds: *Henry's Dream* (Mute/Elektra '92) Cave's admirers crow about his literary virtues—a rock musician who's actually published a novel! and scripted a film! about John Henry Abbott, how highbrow! Then they proffer dismal examples like "I am the captain of my pain," or the bordello containing—what an eye the man has—a whalebone corset! (Whalebone is *very* literary—it hasn't been used in underwear since well before Nick was born.) If this is your idea of great writing, you may be ripe for his cult. Otherwise, forget it—the voice alone definitely won't do the trick. **C** 🦃

Nick Cave & the Bad Seeds: *The Best of Nick Cave and the Bad Seeds* (Reprise '98) 💣

Sheila Chandra: *The Zen Kiss* (RealWorld, '94) The mysterious young beauty who once fronted U.K. Indipop hitmakers Monsoon has long since become a woman, and a drone-backed or a cappella mélange of cross-cultural vocalisms is how she expresses the universality accruing to that exalted state. Although I hope her tabla impressions get sampled and guess that her so-called ragas are as Zen as any, she's a paternalist's dream, slaking RealWorld's endless thirst for dark-skinned people willing to exoticize progressive opinions. Nothing too vulgar or entertaining, please—we must mind our manners. **C+** 🦃

Changing Faces: *Changing Faces* (Big Beat '94) Ⓝ

Changing Faces: All Day, All Night (Big Beat/Atlantic '97) 💣

Marshall Chapman: *Inside Job* (Tall Girl '91) real smart gal ("Real Smart Man," "Come Up and See Me") ★★

Marshall Chapman: *It's About Time ... Recorded Live at the Tennessee State Prison for Women* (Margaritaville '95) She was raised to be a lady, and how she ended up in this godforsaken venue connects to the prison doctor she settled down with after a lost decade-plus of sleeping with guitarists and four years of sleeping alone. His love song is the only soggy moment on this half-retrospective half-showcase. Some of her references—jet sets, self-help books, money-making machines—seem beyond her captive audience's ken. But old charges like "Booze in Your Blood" and "Bad Debt" stick. And new ones like "Good-Bye Forever" and "Alabama Bad" leave no doubt that she still understands her great subject: why she didn't grow up to be a lady. **A–**

Marshall Chapman: *Love Slave* (Margaritaville '96) Ⓝ

Tracy Chapman: "Bang Bang Bang" (*Matters of the Heart,* Elektra '92) 🐚

Tracy Chapman: *New Beginning* (Elektra '95) Beyond thrilling to "Bang Bang Bang" and the inescapable "Fast Car," my only felt insight into Chapman's aura came at a Nelson Mandela tribute where her voice filled the venue, which happened to be Yankee Stadium. Maybe it's a positive that her recordings never convey that kind of size—means she's less pompous than her foremothers, Joan Baez and Odetta. But what's left is a joylessly self-sufficient gravity that makes her "heaven's here on earth" sound a lot more pro forma, not to say phonier, than her "The whole world's broke/And it ain't worth fixing." **B–** 🦃

The Charlatans U.K.: *Some Friendly* (Beggars Banquet '90) Historically, children, the organ has occasion vague-outs and one-shots. Unless you count the Animals, which I don't advise, or the Zombies, where Rod Argent favored piano, the only '60s pop legends to feature one were the Small Faces, and not as a "trademark." When you record your "96 Tears," or even your "Itchycoo Park," call. "The Only One I Know" ain't bad and ain't it. **C** 🧨

Charles & Eddie: *Duophonic* (Capitol '92) if Sade could sing, or at least emote . . . ("Would I Lie to You?," "House Is Not a Home") ★★
Charles & Eddie: "24-7-365," "Keep on Smilin'," "Jealousy" (*Chocolate Milk,* Capitol '95) 👁

Ray Charles: *My World* (Warner Bros. '93) 🎸
Ray Charles: *Berlin, 1962* (Pablo '96) first live recording with his big band, which gets in the way ("Alexander's Ragtime Band," "Bye Bye Love") ★

Boozoo Chavis: *Boozoo Chavis* (Elektra Nonesuch '91) Ⓝ

Doc Cheatham: *The Eighty-Seven Years of Doc Cheatham* (Columbia '93) memoirs of a nice old man ("I Guess I'll Get the Papers and Go Home," "Blues in My Heart") ★★
Doc Cheatham & Nicholas Payton: *Doc Cheatham & Nicholas Payton* (Verve '97) Our lesson for today concerns the persistence of culture. Or perhaps the inadequacy of the organic model in matters of style and genre. Or perhaps we should start with the relativity of age. At the time of recording, the session's driving force, trumpeter Payton, was 23. Its star, trumpeter-vocalist Cheatham (now deceased, and not a damn thing relative about that), was 91. One trombonist was barely 40, the other pushing 80. Clarinetist Jack Maheu—next to the trumpeters, the pacesetter here—was almost 70, the others in their fifties. Given his softer embouchure, Cheatham's solos are a little less forthright than Payton's, but both leaders are so immersed in New Orleans style that you rarely register the difference. As rendered here by tourist-circuit revivalists, working scholars, one original, and one pomo phenom, that style isn't dead, decadent, or ironically self-conscious, retaining its spry life and interactive unpredictability even though its revolutionary irreverence is lost to history. Payton keeps his song choices on the novelty side of Tin Pan Alley, where taste-mongers are too good to travel unless Berlin or Mercer leads the way, and Cheatham, who only began singing professionally in his late fifties, breathes gentle humor into everything from "Stardust" and "I Gotta Right to Sing the Blues" to "Jada" and "Save It Pretty Mama." Somebody tell Neil Young about this. He's not fool enough to try it, and it'll make him feel good. **A**

Sam Chege: *Kickin' Kikuyu-Style* (Original Music '96) A Kenyan music journalist whose shopkeeper parents struggled to send him to college, Chege recorded these 12 unassuming songs in Nairobi with session men off the street and backup singers from the university. Although he reports significant sales, his profits haven't cut his straight career off at the pass—he's now studying at Iowa. So this collection is more Afropop in intent than in fact, and while we can't call it Afrosemipop, its self-consciously recombinant formalism—mixing, Chege reports, Swahili taarab, South African kwela, and Congolese soukous over Kenyan benga, tingeing Kikuyu vocal technique with "the poetic intonations of North Africa"—is more Neal Tennant than Sam Mangwana. Credit its irresistible tune appeal to the liquid tonal patterns of the underrecorded Kikuyu language. Fleshed out with a brightness, quickness, and rhythmic complexity absent from the classic folkish Afropop it superficially recalls, this appeal isn't just rare, it's unique. Sweet, cheerful, full of fun—at times almost a dream of happy happy. Yeah sure. Song subjects include suicide, domestic violence, and trading love in on money. **A–**

The Chemical Brothers: *Exit Planet Dust* (Astralwerks '95) They won't convert you because their main interest is pleasing you—pleasing anybody who's both open-minded enough to conceive techno as a bright sun in the rock cosmos and well-adjusted enough not to start star wars over it. Starts out whomping irrepressibly, ends up schlocking imperturbably, and either way provides the noise, beats, and basslines us earthlings like in our eletrically enhanced popular music. Means nothing—except that pleasure is a function of somatic and cultural givens less malleable than mutants have always claimed. **A–**

The Chemical Brothers: *Loops of Fury EP* (Astralwerks '96) "a little early but thanks anyway" (I think) ("Get Up on It Like This") ★

The Chemical Brothers: *Dig Your Own Hole* (Astralwerks '97) Their secret isn't technowizardry, formal daring, or Lord help us eclecticism. As with so many pop wunderkinds, it's spirit—generous, jubilant, unfazed by industrial doom, in love with energy and sound. Noel Gallagher only wishes he had their heart; they say more with a borrowed catchphrase—"Who is this doin' this type of alphabetapsychedelic funkin'?"—than he can with a whole album of verse-chorus-verse. Of course it matters that they're not retro. But it matters even more that their futurism is neither exclusionary nor puritanical. **A–**

The Chemical Brothers: *Surrender* (Astralwerks '99) nostalgic—for futurism past, yet—at, what, 27? ("Hey Boy Hey Girl," "Let Forever Be") ★

Cher: "Believe" (*Believe,* Warner Bros. '98) 👁

Eagle-Eye Cherry: *Desireless* (Work '98) Watch out for this mild-mannered simp: underneath his lite croon, refabricated truisms, and avant-garde pedigree, he's got the tunes. The title track, an instrumental-with-chant composed by his trumpeter dad, points up how flimsy they are. **B–** 🦃

Neneh Cherry: *Homebrew* (Virgin '92) She's marked out a meaningfuil piece of turf: sophisticated secondhand homegirl, personally decent and artistically accessible, a friend to rely on. But where the lithe beats and uncorny sonics flesh out the concept and jolt every track, the lyrics settle for honest. "The choice is mine/With my ordinary joy and pain inside" is up toward the high end, with "Money talks love is for real" and "How long can we be this way" too typical. Personal to Yo Yo: consider a career in rhyme medicine. **B+**

Cherry Poppin' Daddies: *Zoot Suit Riot* (Mojo '97) 💣

Mark Chesnutt: *Longnecks and Short Stories* (MCA '92) the clichés tuneful, the jokes better, it was ever thus ("Bubba Shot the Jukebox," "Old Flames Have New Names") ★

Mark Chesnutt: *Greatest Hits* (Decca '95) Chesnutt's claim to authenticity is that he grew up in Beaumont like George Jones and cut a lot of dud 45s like his daddy before him—not that he came out of the East Texas that produced the music, but that he came out of the music East Texas produced. Forget it, Mark—you're Nashville. On your breakthrough single you hang out in the honky tonk as an alternative to playing golf. On your breakthrough tearjerkers you only wish you could wilt as many bouffants as that fat wimp Garth. And on your best-of you put on your hits one at a time and see if they stand up. The tearjerkers deserve more juice, but somebody up there knows how to pick 'em. And when it comes to working-class hell-raisers like "It Sure Is Monday" and the immortal "Bubba Shot the Jukebox," you're the bully of the town. **A–**

Vic Chesnutt: "Little Vacation" (*About to Choke,* Capitol '96) 👁

Vic Chesnutt: *The Salesman and Bernadette* (Capricorn, '98) Ⓝ

Chic: *Chic-ism* (Warner Bros. '92) once upon a time there was a drummer named Tony Thompson . . . ("Chic Mystique") ★★

Chic: *Live at the Budokan* (Sumthing Else '99) featuring Sister Sledge,

Slash&Winwood DoJimi, and the great Bernard Edwards on the night he died ("Good Times/Rapper's Delight," "We Are Family") ★★

The Chills: *Submarine Bells* (Slash/ Warner Bros. '90) I might never have known without the printed lyrics, but there's no evidence here that Martin Phillipps is in love with death. He just sees too much of it. So don't dismiss the printed Greenpeace propaganda as gratuitous—for the Chills it's an antidote. What distinguishes them from so many politically well-meaning popsters is that neither cheery music nor dour message is one-dimensional or pro forma—this bravely wistful album generates plenty of punk gall and a surprising complement of bliss. Maybe "Heavenly Pop Hit" is about waking up as an angel, but I say Phillipps believes there can be a heaven before he's dead, and if his vision of transcendence is a bit nature-bound for my tastes, it's the thought that counts. Anway, his true theme song is "Singing in My Sleep," about all the other theme songs—"a word from the wise for the mindless," "a stinging reproach against violence," etc.—he can't remember in the morning. **A**

The Chills: *Soft Bomb* (Slash/Reprise '92) As with so many formal coups, one of the pleasures of *Submarine Bells* was how incorrigibly it challenged unwritten rules (about brightness, concreteness, pretension, keyboards) while adhering to the ones you really can't break (about tunefulness, concision, savvy, guitars). This is just the opposite: adventurous on a surface that accommodates depressive codas and Van Dyke Parks strings, but produced with Martin Phillipps's new acquired phalanx of L.A. sidemen in mind. Though most garage-pop improves when the beat gets solider, the hooks get clearer, the singer moves up in the mix, and Peter Holsapple adds a guitar, these devices are misconceived for the evanescent Chills. Even when they're all 20 seconds too long, however, Phillipps's tunes stay with you. Reordered to close on

"Song for Randy Newman Etc.," a living metaphor for the difficulty of his craft, and to surround the personal songs with the social context Phillipps captures so much more vividly than he thinks he does, this would be a worthy follow-up. I suggest a tape that goes 1-2-3-11-8-6-12-10-13-14-4-9. Skip the fragments, and the long dead metaphor for the shallowness of his craft that implicates a defenseless cab driver. Continue to foreground "Male Monster from the Id," a Greenpeace supporter's bleeding-heart analysis of the sexual power play. **A–**

Martin Phillipps & the Chills: *Sunburnt* (Flying Nun '96) fading tunefully to wan ("Lost in Future Ruins," "Surrounded") ★

Alex Chilton: *19 Years: A Collection of Alex Chilton* (Rhino '91) Even if Chilton approved the selections himself, his retrospective isn't what it ought to be—we get half of *Third* (with "Thank You Friends," "Jesus Christ," and other goodies left to the spiffy new Rykodisc reissue), the Lust/Unlust seven-inch (no Ork seven-inch), bits of the eminently excerptable *Like Flies on Sherbert* (no *Bach's Bottom*), dollops of mid-'80s spurt (no "Under Class" or "Dalai Lama"). So you were expecting maybe *Exile on Main Street*? If Chilton had ever figured out his calling, he would have made a living at it; he's the EP king because coherence and endurance mean less to him than quantum physics (which he no doubt studied on his own when that dishwashing job dried up). You can't excerpt such an eccentric to anybody's satisfaction but your own, and even then you couldn't build an hour's momentum. But listen to any three cuts in any order and I guarantee you'll get off on two and a half. A money-saving introduction to his self-abusing pop and Southern-hipster r&b. **A–**

Alex Chilton: *Blacklist* (New Rose import '92) the Shakespeare, or Gregory Corso, of the EP ("Little GTO," "Guantanamerika") ★★

Alex Chilton: *Clichés* (Ardent '94) recorded performance art—rock hipster misprises classic pop as acoustic folk ("My Baby Just Cares for Me," "Time After Time") ★★★

Alex Chilton: "What's Your Sign Girl" (*A Man Called Destruction,* Ardent '95) 🐝

Alex Chilton: "Sugar Sugar"/"I Got the Feelin'" (*1970,* Ardent '96) 🐝

Stella Rambisi Chiweshe: *Chisi* (Piranha import '91) Ⓝ
Stella Rambisi Chiweshe: *Kumusha* (Piranha import '92) Ⓝ
Stella Chiweshe: *The Healing Tree* (Shanachie '98) healing don't make humming, especially on a thumb piano ("Huya Uzoona," "Mudzimu Dzoka") ★★★

Chocolate Genius: "My Mom" (*Black Music,* V2 '98) 🐝

Chumbawamba: *Anarchy* (Ten Little Indians import '94) transient punk-style agitprop with announcements ("Timebomb," "Mouthful of Shit") ★★
Chumbawamba: *Tubthumper* (Republic/Universal '97) tub as platform, tub as cornucopia, tub as slop bucket ("Tubthumping," "Amnesia") ★★★
Chumbawamba: *Uneasy Listening* (EMI import '98) This "Collection of Stuff From 1986–1998" establishes that their sloganeering gift for the catchy long preceded "Tubthumping," and also that it's not in them to write apolitically—"This Girl," described as one of "a series of jangly love songs" they tried because they weren't supposed to, concerns a nonconformist who throws bricks from the top of a parking garage. Their music and their anarchism combine the programmatic and the quirky. Despite the trumpets, many arrangements reduce to rock readymades with a march pulse, yet despite the guitar chords and drumbeats the enunciated lyrics evoke music hall. Really, they're that funny. You say that when they barf to cap each infinitely repeated "Your ugly houses look so . . ." there's no way to know they were inspired by Sting's country mansion as opposed to row-house ticky-tacky? I say the notes are worth reading. **A–**

Cibo Matto: *Viva! La Woman* (Warner Bros. '96) Ⓝ

Kaouding Cissoko: *Kora Revolution* (Palm Pictures '99) Ⓝ

Eric Clapton: *24 Nights* (Reprise '91) Ⓝ
Eric Clapton: *Unplugged* (Reprise '92) Laid-back doesn't equal dead—*461 Ocean Boulevard* is laid-back. What's wrong with this stopgap is it means to be inoffensive. Relegating Clapton-the-electric-guitarist to the mists of memory and capturing Clapton-the-pop-vocalist in a staid mood only an adrenaline junkie could confuse with the sly somnolence of "I Shot the Sheriff" and "Willie and the Hand Jive," it turns "Layla" into a whispery greeting card. No wonder the pop star he most closely resembles on television is James Galway. **B–** 🦃
Eric Clapton: *From the Cradle* (Reprise '94) cf. Son Seals, Otis Rush—plays better, sings worse ("Motherless Child," "Blues Before Sunrise") ★★
Eric Clapton: *Pilgrim* (Reprise '98) Actually, Lord, there's been a misunderstanding. Remember when we said it was OK for You to sing? What we meant was . . . well, first we just wanted You to get rid of Jack Bruce. Then it was more like, Don't be shy, Sonny Boy Williamson didn't have that much range either. But never, never, never did we say, You have the right if George Benson does. Or, You could be the next Phil Collins. Or, Guitars are for sound effects anyway. Really. That wasn't the idea at all. **C+** 🦃

Guy Clark: *Boats to Build* (Asylum '92) Ⓝ
Guy Clark: *Keepers: A Live Recording* (Sugar Hill '97) making the most of a legacy and an ad hoc band ("Homegrown Tomatoes," "Let Him Roll") ★

The Clash: *From Here to Eternity Live* (Epic '99) "I'd like to hear 'Wooly Bully,' by Sam the Sham and the Pharoahs—yes, not Sham 69, but Sam the Sham" ("Capital Radio," "Know Your Rights") ★★★

Otis Clay: "Thanks a Lot" (*I'll Treat You Right,* Bullseye Blues '92) 🐝

The Clean: *Vehicle* (Rough Trade '90) Sporadic semipros in an Anglo enclave so remote it evades ordinary patterns of formal exhaustion, these three New Zealanders are garage Velvets—even their "eclectic" folk-rock delicacy and speed-pop buzz make the connection. Fortunately, they're too tasteful to pretend they're jaded when they're not—10 years after their first burst there's still a boyish strain about them. And if I remain utterly suspicious of garage exotica, I'm a proud sucker for this quick, hard, flat, lyrical sound—professional no, clean and how. **A−**

The Clean: *Unknown Country* (Flying Nun '96) 💣

Clem Snide: *You Were a Diamond* (Tractor Beam '97) deadpan country-folk, nasty when you turn your back ("Nick Drake Tape," "Chinese Baby") ★★

Patsy Cline: *Live at the Cimarron Ballroom* (MCA '97) Cline's current iconicity (which for all I know could signal a heroic surge that will leave her as fixed a star as Aretha Franklin or Edith Piaf) is bound up in the vogue for pre/nonrock pop (which for all I know could prove permanent). Her Virginia twang mere seasoning in an unusually robust pop voice, she's Patti Page with guts. But the main reason she's remembered as the most credible of the countrypolitans is that countrypolitan was invented for her, by producer Owen Bradley. Entertaining the Southern folks who were her bread and butter—at maybe $500 a show, pickup backup provided—she was and remains something else. And this 1961 Tulsa gig with Leon McAuliffe's Cimarron Boys establishes that the spare physicality and exquisite timing of her Grand Old Opry transcriptions are only a starting point. She could have used more rehearsal here. But the Western swing maestro led a group who were ready for anything, and Cline rose to their challenge as they did to hers: hard high-plains dance music, with her amazing trademark yowl at the end of "Lovesick Blues" a promise of the

"Shake Rattle and Roll" she has all set to follow. **A−**

George Clinton: *Hey Man . . . Smell My Finger* (Paisley Park '93) Half rap album the way so many rap albums these days are half P-Funk albums, it's never stronger musically than when one of a galaxy of rapping starchildren, most forcefully Humpty Hump and Ice Cube, is adding his or Yo Yo's natural rhythms to those of Uncle George, whose original-rapping was long ago extended technically by his extended family. For all their shows of militance, though, the kids' minds still haven't followed their asses as intrepidly as the old man's. And on "Dis Beat Disrupts" and "Get Satisfied," among others, his own beats beat all. **A−**

George Clinton and the P-Funk All-stars: *T.A.P.O.A.F.O.M.* (550 Music/Epic '96) authenticated gangsta grooves for the sample factory ("If Anybody Gets Funked Up [It's Gonna Be You]," "Funky Kind [Gonna Knock It Down]") ★★★

George Clinton: *Greatest Funkin' Hits* (Capitol '96) A remix album, not a best-of, and one that avoids the promotional overkill and commercial double jeopardy of its half-assed demigenre. The live track, the previously unreleased, the remakes from the unnoteworthy *R&B Skeletons* and the unnoticed Jimmy G., the woofing bookends, the recycled P-Funk classics—all are renewed and of a piece. One secret weapon is youngbloods who owe him, including the Miss America he saved from the bluenoses and a typically non-judgmental range of excellent rappers—Ice Cube and Q-Tip, Coolio and Busta Rhymes, Humpty Hump and Ol' Dirty Bastard. Another is Clinton's perpetually renewable tracks, which are always of a piece. **A**

George Clinton & the P-Funk All Stars: *Live and Kickin'* (Intersound '97) more funky than fresh, their best live one withal ("Flashlight," "Cosmic Slop") ★★★

George Clinton & the P-Funk All Stars: *Dope Dogs* (Dogone '98) The God-uncle hasn't made a bad record since the band broke up or an exciting one since *Computer Games.* Until now. Don't try this at home, kids, but the secret is that instead of adapting to youthcult fashion, a trick he manages like no other fiftysomething can, he indulges an idée fixe. For years he's been fascinated by the involvement of Old Mac Uncle's C.I.A. ("I-O") in contraband—meaning weapons, ultimately, but more enjoyable threats to human life first. So he starts by assuming dogs sniff dope because they gotta have it and takes off. Just about every song has both dogs and dope in it, with variations as comical as Mr. Wiggles the Worm and considerably darker. The funk is long on guitar and capable of anything. Is that bebop? You know, behind the elementary-school rappers and the pill-popping poodle? **A**

Roger Clinton: *Nothing Good Comes Easy* (Pyramid '94) 💣

Coupé Cloué: *Maximum Compas from Haiti* (Earthworks '92) Now almost 70, Gesner Henry is a master of Creole double entendre who chose his stage name (literally Cut Nailed) to signify Cut and Score in soccer and Fucking Fucking in sex. Yet the puns that are lost in translations-provided aren't missed, because Henry is also a master of the same Cuban guitar style that spawned Zairian rumba in the '50s. By the time these tracks were recorded circa 1980, his large, simple band—three male singers, three guitarists, three percussionists, bass, drums—had perfected a beguiling lilt free of Kinshasa's far-off fashion wars. I wish I understood the words, but I'm not greedy—the music may well be sweeter without them. **A**

C-Murder: *Life or Death* (No Limit '98) 💣

Arnett Cobb: *Arnett Blows for 1300* (Delmark '94) circa 1947—honking jump blues on the big-band side ("Cobb's Idea," "Big League Blues") ★★

Cobra Verde: *Nightlife* (Motel '99) if Bryan Ferry was a theoretical dandy,

which was hard, then John Petkovic is a theoretical theoretical dandy, which is harder—and he's also John Petkovic ("Conflict," "One Step Away from Myself") ★

Joe Cocker: *The Best of Joe Cocker* (Capitol '93) Ⓝ

The Cocktails: *Long Sound* (Carrot Top '93) 💣

Adam Cohen: *Adam Cohen* (Columbia '98) 💣

Leonard Cohen: *The Future* (Columbia '92) Sometime between ages 54 and 58, Cohen appears to have lost his voice. Where once his whisper was the essence of intimacy, now he's singing loud and saying less for longer. Which ends up not mattering because the music is his best since John Lissauer split in 1979. Even the instrumental is satisfying minor Cohen, kind of like the sexy stuff. The political stuff—the horror-stricken "The Future," the hope-stricken "Democracy"—is major. And the eight-minute send-up of Irving Berlin's 10-line "Always" is a pomo triumph: the hoarsely pitchless singing, the soul-on-demand of the backup girls, and the thudding beat are all travesties, all acts of love. At first you think, Sure, Lenny—"Always." Endless love, just your style. But as the minutes wear on you begin to think he may mean it, and then you begin to worry. Holy shit—is this old drunk going to be on my case for the rest of his unnatural life? Would he settle for a lost weekend? **A–**
Leonard Cohen: *Cohen Live!* (Columbia '94) Ⓝ

Marc Cohn: *Marc Cohn* (Atlantic '91) Cohn sings like a sentimental Warren Zevon—an exclusively sentimental Warren Zevon, I mean. He's got some tunes. But his lyrics are sticky with decaying Americana, and he shows no grasp of his limitations. A folkie with a piano is dreaming concert hall—a level of signification higher than folkie talent generally reaches. **C+** 🐢

Lloyd Cole: "Don't Look Back," "No Blue Skies" (*Lloyd Cole,* Capitol '90) 🐚

Lloyd Cole: *Don't Get Weird on Me Babe* (Capitol '91) ⓝ

Natalie Cole: *Unforgettable* (Elektra '91) 🎺

Paula Cole: *This Fire* (Imago/Warner Bros. '96) Before anyone knew she'd go platinum, Netcrit Glenn McDonald presciently declared Cole the new queenpin of a female tradition he traced from Kate Bush through Peter Gabriel, Melissa Etheridge, and Sarah McLachlan. Although McDonald sanely declared this genre the obverse of male-identified metal, a skeptic with no tolerance for subpeaks in either would like to note that each is beholden to "classical" precepts of musical dexterity and genitalia-to-the-wall expression. Where Kate Bush overwhelms petty biases as inexorably as Led Zep, Cole is just a romantic egotist who can't resist turning ordinary human problems into three-act dramas. Kate Bush fans will love her. **C+** 🦃

Ornette Coleman: *Tone Dialing* (Harmolodic/Verve '95) After a spate of productivity in the late '80s, this genius hasn't released an album in seven years. But the layoff hasn't affected his m.o.— through 16 cuts that go on about as long as the double-LP *In All Languages,* he's neither stale nor overflowing. As is his practice, he leads with dynamite: an opening charge, a poetry-with-jazz rap that fits together so well the words don't matter, a restful West Indian ditty, some rearranged Bach, and a gloriously oversampled collage that orchestrates "unmusical" sound into improvisatory ground. After which he spends 40 minutes demonstrating his undiminished ability to create beauty out of what would have been called chaos before he changed the world's ears. I don't claim to love it all. But I take exception only to the tabla thing. **A–**

Ornette Coleman: *Sound Museum: Hidden Man* (Verve '96) not the ideal place to get to know him ("Macho Woman," "City Living") ★★

Ornette Coleman: *Sound Museum: Three Women* (Verve '96) nor to continue your acquaintance—or is it the other way around? ("City Living," "Macho Woman") ★★

Ornette + Joachim Kühn: *Colors* (Harmolodic/Verve '97) Having divided his career between better-than-average fusion records that still weren't anything to write reviews about and explorations of his moderately prodigious classical chops, Kühn proves a serviceable helpmeet to genius. On this live-in-Leipzig duet album his pianistics comprise an exotically European environment for Ornette's transcultural sound and melody—a bracing change and a damn fine handle whether crashingly atonal or liltingly romantic. **A–**

Collective Soul: *Hints Allegations and Things Left Unsaid* (Atlantic '94) I swear these tuneful blandos were hands-down winners of the REO Speedwagon eight-track earmarked for the Least Alternative "Alternative" of 1994 *before* I ever read their bio. I swear I didn't know the frontman studied guitar at Berklee and took his band name from *The Fountainhead.* **C–** 🦃

College Boyz: *Radio Fusion Radio* (Virgin '92) 🎺

Mark Collie: "She's Never Comin' Back" (*Born and Raised in Black and White,* MCA '91) 💿

Color Me Badd: *C.M.B.* (Giant '91) "We just stick to what you want to hear" ("I Wanna Sex You Up," "All 4 Love") ★

Shawn Colvin: *Fat City* (Columbia '92) This ambitious sophomore wins the prize—the female postfolkie you're too bored to hate. The digitalized Suzanne Vega is wisely popwise and the bionic Joan Baez positively swangin' by comparison. Matching strong, undistinguished voice to literate, undistinguished verse, Colvin is like a young Joni Mitchell without swoops or self-invention. And lest you riposte that young Joni Mitchell beats old Joni Mitchell, Columbia doles out production chores to old Joni Mitchell's bass-playing husband, who drags the ordinary down toward an offensively well-groomed studio folk-rock that combines the smugness of '70s El Lay with the overstatement of '80s Megapop—and later for the '90s. **C** 🦃

Combustible Edison: *I, Swinger* (Sub Pop '94) Finally, recorded evidence of the more-cited-than-sighted lounge-music wave, including Nino Rota cover, stereo panning, Canadian Club vocals, and of course a vibraphone. In today's anything-goes environment, they might conceivably make music hepper than Liz Phair's or Pearl Jam's and more enduring than Leon Redbone's or Dan Hicks and His Hot Licks', only they're not talented enough. "Nothing coy here, no sly indie-rock wink, and never say 'novelty.'" Right. **D+**

Come: *Eleven: Eleven* (Matador '93) Already a veteran of three bands that meant a great deal to their tiny complement of fans and bubkes to everyone else (Dangerous Birds, Uzi, and Live Skull—how could you forget?), Thalia Zedek is now an established cult heroine. Read her notices and you'll learn that Come is both her song move and her blues move; listen to the music and you'll notice a few flatly projected melodies and some slide guitar. Since her lyrics range from unintelligible to incomprehensible and a groove would be too kind, we're left with a sound—the raw stylization of one woman's alienation. Those who happen to have been captivated by her "dark," "androgynous" live shtick can read into this alienation what they will—most likely some parallel to or complement of their own, which is most likely different. Those who haven't needn't worry their heads about it. **C+** 🦃

The Comedian Harmonists: *The Comedian Harmonists* (Hannibal '99) About 10 years ago I fell for these Weimar pop phenoms in a five-hour documentary at the Public, in which they performed American standards and trombone imitations in the vocal and sartorial regalia of the finest lieder singers. The effect is somewhat less vivid on this, their first-ever U.S. release—although their harmonies pene-trate, their comedy sometimes doesn't. But listen to them gurgle in tune before breaking into perfect German gibberish on "Kannst du pfeifen, Johanna?" and you'll get the idea. Beautywise they lived off the tenor of restaurant singer Ari Leschnikoff, likened by archivist Joe Boyd to Edith Piaf and Oum Kalsoum, though the Klezmatics' Lorin Sklamberg may be more the point. A Bulgarian, he was one of the "Aryans" who got to stay in Germany when Goering deported the Jewish founder and his two fellow mongrelizers in 1935—they were too famous to kill, at least in 1935. In the film, he's a thin old man in a dreary Sofia housing project. He hasn't heard his own records in decades. He listens and weeps. **A–**

Come On: *New York City 1976–80* (Heliocentric '99) Who are these guys? There were five of them, including a female guitarist—neatniks all, favoring white shirts, black pants, and short hair. Half of this belated testament was recorded CBGB 1978, a final track Hurrah 1980. But I'd never heard of them, and when I checked with *New York Rocker*'s Andy Schwartz, he remembered only the name. On the evidence of these 16 homages to first-growth Talking Heads, from long before it was determined that the world moved on a woman's hips, we were missing something: the halting yet propulsive, arty yet catchy ejaculations of the uptight nerd as subversive geek. A five-year-old sex fiend joins suburban tennis players exposing their underthings join two straight songs about kitchens join the incendiary "Old People": "Get out in the streets/Turn over cars/Elbow young people/Set garbage on fire." Not important, obviously. Funny, though. **B+**

Common Sense: *Resurrection* (Relativity '94) the hip hop of daily life—a rare yet too ordinary thing ("I Use to Love H.E.R.," "Pop's Rap," "Resurrection") ★★
Common: *One Day It'll All Make Sense* (Relativity '97) With no notable penchant for ear candy or mass ass appeal, this Chicago rhymer carves out an unpreten-

tious artistic space that couldn't have existed before hip hop—no singer-songwriter's everyday ruminations come near such social content or physical form. Common raps about black life as most black people live it and black manhood as most young black men grow into it, and while his flow isn't primed for the dance floor, it's complex and full-bodied in a way few, you know, white artists could imitate, much less make up. Nor is that the only way he's complex—guy spends considerable time dancing in his head. **B+**

Company Flow: *Funcrusher Plus* (Rawkus '97) 💣
Company Flow: *Little Johnny from the Hospital* (Rawkus '99) 💣

Ray Condo and His Ricochets: *Swing Brother Swing!* (Joaquin '96) Mining catalogues known and unknown (Count Basie, Carl Perkins, Ruth Brown, Red Allen, maybe Stuff Smith—but Larry Darnell? Glenn Barber? *Lew* Williams?), this Vancouver combo converts swing, jump blues, and rockabilly nonoriginals into fiddleless Western swing chocked with newly unearthed references to getting laid and pissing ice and Jerry Lee's taste in teenagers and romantic despair vanquished with a simple "Come the revolution for me." They take over the material so completely that it's hard to tell whether the songs were this good to begin with, and beside the point to care. Singer Condo has a rubber mouth to go with his brain, both of which he sometimes stretches around a saxophone reed. Drummer Steve Taylor could rock the beer joint with takeout chopsticks and a wastepaper basket. **A–**

The Congos: *Heart of the Congos* (Blood & Fire import '95) Lee Perry's falsetto-and-tenor duo revived for our dubwise era ("Row Fisherman," "Children Crying") ★★★

Conjunto Céspedes: *Flores* (Xenophile '98) Ⓝ

Harry Connick, Jr.: *"He Is They Are"* (*Blue Light, Red Light*, Columbia '91) 🪰

Harry Connick, Jr.: *She* (Columbia '94) Junior calls this career move funk to avoid conceding that the antirock rhetoric of his swang thang was pure micromarketing guff. But no matter how many beats he cops or Meters he runs, his New Orleans band plays with all the elasticity and panache of the Billy Joel aggregation. With lyricist Ramsey McLean dumbing up for the occasion, here's hoping (and predicting) Harry will sell back in once he accepts that there's an upper limit on how many units he can move. **C+** 🦃

Consolidated: *The Myth of Rock* (Nettwerk '90) industrial for the oppressed masses ("This Is a Collective," "Dysfunctional Relationship") ★

Consolidated: *Friendly Fascism* (Nettwerk '91) White males freaked by the mess of change, these rappers quickly transmute what little science they do drop—about the megapathology of late capitalism, say, or the economy of meat consumption—into purer-than-thou rhetoric. Repulsed by "deceptively complex" contradiction, hyping the cruel ultraleft fallacy that no oppression can end until all oppression ends, they obsess on meat-is-sexism and await the millennium with their "career going down the toilet"—not because people don't agree with them, of course, but because "the culture industry" has brainwashed us all. I predict that within five years at least one of them will sell out, find religion, or both. And can't resist quoting their fellow San Fran assholes the Residents: "Hitler was a vegetarian." **B–** 🦃

Paolo Conte: *The Best of Paolo Conte* (Nonesuch '98) As befits the cosmopolitan roué this old Italian guy is already pigeonholed as, he writes lyrics worth translating. How about "Maybe by now I have forgottten my colleagues/Locked in the bathroom"? Except that "I sing everything and nothing/Music without music" is the point. Assuming he isn't apologizing for his operatic shortcomings (Italians are weird), I assume this refers to the pidgin English "'swunnerful" and "happy feet," to the harelip scat of "Come di," to the half-stifled laughter that actually gets him laid. And to his music. Steering his piano closer to vaudeville vamp than fancy-pants boogie-woogie, commandeering trad-jazz, world-pop, and Euroschlock colors with pananche (not to mention brio), he's a modernist middlebrow and a natural wit who enjoys cynicism too much to let it go to his heart. **A–**

Continental Drifters: *Continental Drifters* (Monkey Hill '94) two women singers/songwriters—why didn't the Band think of this after Robbie left? (wait, don't tell me) ("Get Over It," "Mixed Messages") ★
Continental Drifters: *Vermilion* (Razor & Tie '99) The lyrics resolve on home truisms, earned and learned but predictable nonetheless, just like the alt-pop songforms and country-rock groove. So Concerned Citizens Against Teenpop should note that this consistently expert supergroup material has a secret weapon, and it's not the ex-dB, the ex-Bangle, or the ex-Dream Syndicate. It's the ex-Cowsill, little Susan, who before she was 10 knew Top 40 fame on some awful songs and one for the books: "Indian Lake," which said more about vacations than was dreamt of in Connie Francis's philosophy. These days Susan sings with a flat generosity whose ever so slightly sour and serrated relation to pitch renders to the truisms their portion of truth while never suggesting that she doesn't enjoy getting away. **A–**

Cool Breeze: *East Point's Greatest Hit* (Organized Noize/A&M '99) Ⓝ

Coolio: *It Takes a Thief* (Tommy Boy '94) the confessions of everygangsta swallow the boasts ("Mama I'm in Love with a Gangsta," "In Da Closet") ★★★
Coolio: *Gangsta's Paradise* (Tommy Boy '95) Hip hop intellectuals hype the aesthetic of the new like Harold Rosenberg gone funky, so of course they snort at this dumb loser. It's not that he was sent up for check passing rather than some manly crime like assault (I hope), but that he favors samples everyone recognizes—especially everyone who's memorized the complete works of Tom Browne, either back in the day or by ingesting every rap record in the universe. Me, I'm glad Coolio did that job for me. Nor does it hurt that his smile is friendlier than Sly Stone's. Great black music past to the present. This must be paradise. **A–**
Coolio: *My Soul* (Tommy Boy '97) voice of reason ("C U When U Get There," "Homeboy") ★★

Julian Cope: *Peggy Suicide* (Island '91) 💣

Cornelius: *Fantasma* (Matador '98) Ⓝ

Chris Cornell: *Euphoria Morning* (A&M '99) For years Cornell struggled to claim the class rage and overgrown-adolescent angst that is every metalman's birthright—only in Soundgarden's last years did he find the macho muscle to fully inhabit that role. Now, as if to prove he can't be satisfied, he sets his solo sights on the manly empathy and world-weary remorse of the big-rock balladeer. Here's hoping he never gets there. **C+** 🦃

Cornershop: *Woman's Gotta Have It* (Luaka Bop/Warner Bros. '95) There are only so many places you can take the Velvet Underground at this late date, and after an overly indie indie debut, this cheeky Anglo-Punjabi consortium has found one. Sometimes the signature trick of spicing up the art-punk drones with Indian ones is self-evident because the sitar or tamboura gives it away; other times you sit there wondering where exactly they stole that rough yet perfect chord. Also included are found sound, lo-fi textures, various keyb cheats, and the casually irresistible Punjabi street tune of "6 A.M. Jullandar Shere," all mixed in with just the right edge of false naiveté. **A–**
Cornershop: *When I Was Born for the 7th Time* (Luaka Bop/Warner Bros. '97) What's so disarming, and confusing, about Tjinder Singh is that he doesn't have a lot to say. Here he is realizing a historical inevitability a decade or three in the making—

namely, an international pop so seamless that its fusion of Anglo-American alt-rock, Indian melody, international hip hop, and what-all is subsumed into its own song-based catchiness right up to the time Singh reclaims "Norwegian Wood" for the land of the sitar. And indeed, his lyrics vaguely express the proper liberal attitudes toward the weighty social issues his achievement implies. But there's no sense of mission—just a handsome dilettante enjoying his easy tunes and found beats. He's not even trying to go pop, especially. Which is why he has at least the potential to become a naturalizing force. **A**

Jayne Cortez & the Firespitters: *Taking the Blues Back Home* (Verve '96) the band articulates complexities the words gloss over ("Mojo 96," "Taking the Blues Back Home") ★

Elvis Costello: *Mighty Like a Rose* (Warner Bros. '91) Too often his pessimism sounds like not just bitterness but spite. He didn't take over the world, and is he mad—not only can't he make the personal political, he can't even make it popular. The Mitchell Froom–produced arrangements here are stuck between Tom Waits as Kurt Weill and Tom Waits as Jackson Browne—Randy Newman is beyond them. So as performed, the good songs are overblown tragedies, the bad ones overblown trifles. The best is the simplest because it's the simplest—"Playboy to a Man," love to hear John Hiatt rockabilly it. The most tragic is the chiliastic "Other Side of Summer," recommended to punk bands in the market for a song with a lot of words in it. And I admit "Invasion Hit Parade" almost makes the spiteful political. Its theory of life is that fascism has a great deal in common with songs you don't like on the radio. **C+** 🐛

Elvis Costello and the Brodsky Quartet: *The Juliet Letters* (Warner Bros. '93) 💣

Elvis Costello: *Brutal Youth* (Warner Bros. '94) fussy as Streisand, ugly as sin, touched with grace ("London's Brilliant Parade," "My Science Fiction Twin") ★

Elvis Costello: "Strange," "Payday" (*Kojak Variety*, Warner Bros. '95) 🎧

Elvis Costello & the Attractions: *All This Useless Beauty* (Warner Bros. '96) 💣

Elvis Costello: "Tramp the Dirt Down," "Hurry Down Doomsday" (*Extreme Honey: The Very Best of the Warner Bros. Years*, Warner Bros. '97) 🎧

Elvis Costello with Burt Bacharach: *Painted from Memory* (Mercury '98) sings Burt's chewy music lots better than Burt, not to mention Hal, who proves a healthy influence on his poesy ("Such Unlikely Lovers," "The Long Division") ★★★

Mary Coughlan: "Sunburn" (*After the Fall*, Big Cat '97) 🎧

Counting Crows: *August and Everything After* (DGC '93) Adam Duritz sings like the dutiful son of permissive parents I hope don't sit next to me at Woodstock. He went to good summer camps; he doesn't eat junk food; he's confused about all the right things. And he's not going away anytime soon—so starved are his peers for a show of musical emotion more learned than Mariah Carey's that some even compare him to Van Morrison, as if all sodden self-pity were the same. It doesn't end with Duritz either—"Mr. Jones" and "Anna Begins" might live up to the songs in them if the band conceived the tracks as music first and songs second. Folk-rockers never do. **B−** 🐛

Counting Crows: "Hanginaround" (*This Desert Life*, DGC '99) 🎧

The Coup: *Kill My Landlord* (Wild Pitch '93) collegiate revolutionary cliché equals gangsta revolutionary revelation ("Dig It!," "I Know You") ★★

The Coup: *Genocide and Juice* (Wild Pitch '94) gangstas never, criminals when they deem it necessary ("Fat Cats, Bigger Fish," "Takin' These") ★

The Coup: *Steal This Album* (Dogday '98) Even in the wake of albums called *Kill Your Landlord* and *Genocide and Juice*, it's a shock to hear anyone working in a pop form come out and say flatly: "See,

I'm a communist." But the Coup are pure Oakland, a cross between Too Short, whose deep-bumping beats presaged a live-in-the-studio funk that would have sounded old school when the Bomb Squad was def, and David Hilliard, the Panther whose autobiography tops a reading list that also recommends Manning Marable and Saul Alinsky. Boots Riley's tour de force, which climaxes by flipping a surprisingly street Microsoft-Macintosh metaphor, is a corny, well-plotted tale where a 24-year-old kills the pimp and surrogate father who long ago murdered his mom. But every track impresses, including the music-as-dope opener, the revolutionary call to arms, the brutal medical exposé ("It seems that he's lost the will to pay"), the repo-man burlesque, funny stories about sneaking into the movies and driving broken-down hoopties, and "Underdogs," which translates Manning Marable into terms any ghetto struggler can recognize. Ideologues believe communist artists are never this humorous, this balanced, this concrete. They're wrong. **A**

Courtney & Western: "Go to Blazes" (*Rig Rock Jukebox: A Collection of Diesel Only Records* [comp], First Warning '92) 🐢

Coverdale/Page: *Coverdale/Page* (Geffen '93) 💣

Cracker: *Cracker* (Virgin '92) ⓝ
Cracker: *Kerosene Hat* (Virgin '93) 💣

The Cranberries: *Everybody Else Is Doing It, So Why Can't We?* (Island '93) Dream-pop as techno-folk-rock. Lissome Limerick lass Dolores O'Riordan injects spiritual lilt, Smiths/Furs producer Stephen Street applies commercial grease, and like a good dance comp with one set of tonsils, it never quits. Every song diddles your beauty spot by hook or by slick, and with O'Riordan swooping, moaning, and emoting, the worst you feel is a bit of a softy. Believe in the dream. **A–**
The Cranberries: *No Need to Argue* (Island '94) soulful things to say, tuneful

ways to say them, way too long getting there ("Ode to My Family," "Zombie") ★★
The Cranberries: *To the Faithful Departed* (Island '96) In which the deserving pop stars discover noise and politics simultaneously, and nuts to any part-of-the-problem who preferred them when they knew their dreamy place, right? Wrong. Tragically but also irritatingly, Dolores O'Riordan indulges all the vices people too stupid for Woody Guthrie or Linton Kwesi Johnson say politics bring out in music: she's strident, moralistic, simple-minded, full of herself. Not only is she shocked to discover that wars are caused by, I would never have guessed, "political pride" and "territorial greed," but she thinks she's a better person for telling Tchaikovsky the news. Better than you. Better than me. Better than Tchaikovsky. And much, much better than Alanis Morissette. **C+** 🦃
The Cranberries: *Bury the Hatchet* (Island '99) lucky for her music she's been unlucky in love ("You and Me," "Loud and Clear") ★★

Cranes: *Forever* (Dedicated '93) eerie, stately, cosmic, minor, cute, beautiful, full of shit ("Everywhere," "Clear") ★★
Cranes: *Loved* (Dedicated/Arista '94) ⓝ

Crash Test Dummies: *God Shuffled His Feet* (Arista '93) ⓝ

Crash Vegas: "You and Me" (*Stone,* London '93) 🐢

The Robert Cray Band Featuring the Memphis Horns: *Midnight Stroll* (Mercury '90) few if any soul men play better, not many write better, plenty arrange better, almost all sing better—a formula for the blues ("These Things," "My Problem") ★★
The Robert Cray Band: *I Was Warned* (Mercury '92) Where the misguided soul strategy of *Midnight Stroll* emphasized undigested horn arrangements and vocals Cray couldn't handle, this aims for AOR guitar hooks—every solo stings, and with producer Dennis Walker foregrounded again, every song catches. But

the biggest difference is that the two have abandoned their evil ways—the part of the mean mistreater is invariably played by one of the women traditionally handed that role in blues culture. There's no point calling this a sexist sellout when it makes sense developmentally—the pain and cruelty of Cray's and Walker's songs always made you fear for their personal lives, and I bet their lovers (and ex-lovers) think it's about time they dealt in straightforward bull like "I'm a Good Man." The mood is penitent, full of pleas for time to work things out and summed up by "A Whole Lotta Pride"'s "Do you have to leave me baby/Just to even up the score?" There's room for Walker's Nashvillian expertise in tragic marriage too. But connoisseurs may well prefer the perverse kick of the band-written "Our Last Time," in which an impassively disconsolate Cray watches his latest conquest dress after "the sweat begins to dry," certain without a word from her that she'll never come back for seconds. **A–**

The Robert Cray Band: *Shame and a Sin* (Mercury '93) Out from under Dennis Walker, Cray sounds less twisted, his thwarted-love compulsions a species of old-fashioned blues suffering. He shuffles and slides like he's been studying up on his Chess reissues, and the directness carries over into his old-fashioned soul exhortations. He even fools around a little, as if finally convinced that his guitar ain't no joke. **A–**

The Robert Cray Band: *Some Rainy Morning* (Mercury '95) ♂

The Robert Cray Band: *Sweet Potato Pie* (Mercury '97) Ⓝ

The Robert Cray Band: *Take Your Shoes Off* (Rykodisc '99) T-Bone Walker as Jerry Butler, only not as good ("There's Nothing Wrong," "What About Me") ★

The Robert Cray Band: *Heavy Picks—The Robert Cray Band Collection* (Mercury '99) You want proof of greatness, stick with *Strong Persuader.* You couldn't care less, this expedient survey documents his staying power as a songman. The lead literally cuts to the

chase: he's just gotten to Chicago with a dime to his name, which he invests in a number on a phone booth wall. **A–**

Crazy Horse: *Left for Dead* (Sisapa '90) Anyone mind-damaged by *Ragged Glory* should note that the essential Crazy Horse is a rhythm section, as the kind-hearted designate Billy Talbot and Ralph Molina. The chief vocalist-songwriter here is a fellow named Sonny Mone, who misses 1969. "Once there was a rose in a fisted glove," he pines—and also real metal, dammit, not MTV shit. **C** 🦃

Creed: *Human Clay* (Wind-Up '99) In the year rock died again, what should come storming back but metal—dba "hard" or "loud" rock and, as Syracuse demonstrated, uglier than ever. Yet these God-fearing grunge babies sound falser than rape-inciting Limp Bizkit, abuse-tripping Static-X, party animals Buckcherry, or even world-dance Days of the New. Because their songs address universals they don't debase women, a plus. But their spirituality is as sodden as their sonics. I mean, it's not as if familial oppression isn't real. It's the main thing that turns the hard and loud into truth-seekers and revenge-seekers both. So after years of Marilyn Manson lies, young bands seem to have found a psychic space where such themes open up the musical imagination. By contrast, these guys are still in denial, bellowing regressive circumlocutions to drown out the truth inside. Which is what? Maybe lust. **C** 🦃

Creeper Lagoon: *I Become Small and Go* (Nickel Bag '98) ♂

Marshall Crenshaw: *Life's Too Short* (Paradox/MCA '91) By now there's comfort in his surprising little modulations as well as his plain-spoken prosody, and it's nigh on 10 years since he collected so many strong songs; heard live, "Better Back Off" and "Don't Disappear Now" seem no less inevitable than "Cynical Girl" or "Whenever You're on My Mind." But even if he finally gets his just market share, the new converts won't sing the same praises as the original faithful, because by now his feeling for his craft runs to weary wisdom rather than brimming delight. Marshall's compact solos and Kenny Aronoff's firm beat reinforce his resolve without hinting at his grace. **B+**

Marshall Crenshaw: *Marshall Crenshaw Live . . . My Truck Is My Home* (Razor & Tie '94) You know the Iron Law of Live Albums: "They all suck." And you also know the Great Exception: "Unless you're a big big fan." Which, all right, I am—not least because his intelligence, integrity, and passion for the great song always show up in his music. As for instance here: 14 titles recorded at eleven separate engagements, most of '90s provenance but two dating back to '82, including fabulous covers of Dave Alvin and Alvin Cash, Bobby Fuller and the Byrds, Abba and the MC 5. And even the ones he wrote himself will remind those who never fell for that wimp nonsense about his passion for great guitar. The man can play. **A−**

Marshall Crenshaw: *Miracle of Science* (Razor & Tie '96) picking 'em better than he writes 'em ("Twenty-five Forty-One," "The 'In' Crowd," "Theme from 'Flaregun'") ★★★

Marshall Crenshaw: *The 9-Volt Years* (Razor & Tie '98) Ⓝ

Marshall Crenshaw: *Number 447* (Razor & Tie '99) Although Crenshaw likes to call his g-b-d trio rockabilly, he's not above keybs, gives a fiddler one, and weaves in three instrumentals that are anything but filler—rock and roll mood music, melodic and contemplative. On an album that negotiates the awkward transition from superannuated teen to balding homebody, the two well-crafted infidelity songs don't altogether mesh with the two well-crafted I-should-have-loved-you-better songs. The masterstroke is "Glad Goodbye," which passes for the world's millionth breakup song while addressing a much rarer theme: a couple, both of 'em, dumping a home and a physical history they no longer love. **A−**

Crooked Fingers: *Crooked Fingers* (Warm '99) Eric Bachmann describes degradation as if he wants you to avoid it like a plague ("Broken Man," "She Spread Her Legs and Flew Away") ★

David Crosby: *Thousand Roads* (Atlantic '93) Crosby adds new meaning to the word "survivor"—something on the order of "If you can't kill the motherfucker, at least make sure he doesn't breed"—and until VH-1 got on the revolting "Heroes" video, I'd hoped never to sample this make-work project for his rich, underemployed friends. Oh well. The only thing that could render it more self-congratulatory would be a CD bonus cover of Jefferson Black Hole's "We Built This City." **C−** 🦃

Crosby Stills Nash & Young: *Looking Forward* (Reprise '99) Right, you knew already. But though I pray I hear solo Y render the title song hopeful instead of smug, I know that in my head I'll still hear N harmonizing insipidly behind. And when S explains how when he was young old people were wrong and now that he's old young people are wrong and then disses "overfed talking heads" without ever once acknowledging overfed singing ex-head C to his immediate left, I imagine some computer nerd with more brains than sense joining the arms race just to get even. Still a menace—and still conceited about it. **C** 🦃

Sheryl Crow: *Tuesday Night Music Club* (A&M '93) Ⓝ

Sheryl Crow: *Sheryl Crow* (A&M '96) thank not just Alanis but Tchad ("The Book," "Home") ★

Sheryl Crow: *The Globe Sessions* (A&M '98) the most sensible tunes in pop today ("It Don't Hurt," "My Favorite Mistake") ★

Sheryl Crow and Friends: *Live from Central Park* (A&M '99) Boy did this look like some rock-star bullshit when it happened—Clapton, McLachlan, Richards, Hynde, Nicks, Chicks, oy. All that was missing was Carlos Santana. Only it

uates for years, have just now
d their biggest album ever, a redo-
13 years after they didn't actually kill
at Arab. I ask you, where were the
Moody Blues after 13 years? (Riding their
second—and final—No. 1 album, since
you didn't know.) **C+**

The Cure: *Galore: The Singles 1987–1997* (Elektra/Fiction '97) Ⓝ

The Customers: *Green Bottle Thursday* (Vapor '96) imagine a band whose formative philosophical experience was Ralph Molina's drums ("All Your Money," "Drinking Again") ★

Cybotron: *Empathy* (Fantasy '93) Ⓝ
Cybotron: *Cyber Ghetto* (Fantasy '95) 💣

Cypress Hill: *Cypress Hill* (Ruffhouse/Columbia '91) "How I Could Just Kill a Man" is about what it says it's about, anger rather than advocacy, but that doesn't mean I buy their this-is-reality we-don't-glorify-it any more than anybody else's—putting a hole in someone's head because he's trying to steal your car is foul, not to mention bad for your health, and I wish they'd cop to that. Still, shit happens, and from their Beasties-Spanglish accents to their guitar-hip samples, it sounds different when these guys make music out of it—funny, for one thing, which in hard guys amounts to a new vision. They like hemp, hate cops ("pigs"), use the word "fag" in vain, and celebrate their neighborhood rather than their dicks. I like their music—plenty. **A–**
Cypress Hill: "Insane in the Brain," "When the Sh-- Goes Down" (*Black Sunday,* Ruffhouse/Columbia '93) 🔊
Cypress Hill: *III (Temples of Boom)* (Ruffhouse/Columbia '95) 💣
Cypress Hill: "Looking Through the Eye of a Pig" (*Cypress Hill IV,* Ruffhouse '98) 🔊

Billy Ray Cyrus: *Some Gave All* (Mercury '92) With Cyrus oversinging like Michael Bolton at a Perot rally, this album revolted me well before I got to its climac-
tic title cut, about how brave guys help their fellow man by killing other men, presumably not fellow and most likely gooks or something. Only it turns out Michael Bolton was on the same side as Michael Stipe, and it also turns out that Cyrus manages a nice macho self-mockery on both that achy-breaky thing and the likes of "Wher'm I Gonna Live?" and "I'm So Miserable." Give him a few years of ups and downs, and he could be the 21st-century Waylon Jennings. Can't wait, can you? **C+** 🐦

C\COMPILATIONS

Cape Verde (Putumayo World Music '99) Trust the escape merchants at the world's softest world label to put a happy face on saudade—the tempos a little quicker, the melodies a little brighter. Still, it's not like these musicians are trying to get the party started, increase efficiency in the workplace, or reduce sales resistance to clothing bought cheap and sold dear—not that they know of, anyway. They're just confronting the sense of loneliness and loss built into "the romance of these remote and exotic islands." And maybe because they're beginning to feel it's too easy to hold their cultural heritage at bay by correctly pronouncing one of its many names, they're beating it, honestly if temporarily. Good for them. **A–**

Casa de la Trova (Detour '99) Even when the musicians have a drop taken, there's nothing bacchanalian about this survey of the poetic, composed Cuban folk songs it designates *trova*. Their clave subsumed in guitars and the occasional chamber orchestra, they're formal, precise, intensely romantic, old-fashioned, crotchety. All the singers are stylists, and sticklers for harmonic detail, and though only the 70-ish sisters Faez, tart as grand-aunts and weird as widows in a haunted house, command one-of-a-kind deliveries, the vocal variety keeps you alert. Call it the

Buenas Vozes Hearts Club Band and hire a film crew. **A–**

CB4 (MCA '93) the rap rainbow from goof-off to off-whitey (Public Enemy, "Livin' in a Zoo"; Boogie Down Productions, "Black Cop"; CB4, "Straight out of Locash") ★★★

Christmas Party with Eddie G. (Strikin' It Rich/Columbia '90) novelty pretty paper cut to ribbons (Detroit Junior, "Christmas Day"; Bobby Lloyd and the Skeletons, "Do You Hear What I Hear/You Really Got Me"; Rufus Thomas, "I'll Be Your Santa Baby") ★

City of Industry (Quango '97) pop noir turns soundtrack noir (Bomb the Bass Featuring Justin Warfield, "Bug Powder Dust [UK Album Version]"; Lush, "Last Night [Darkest Hour Mix]"; Massive Attack, "Three") ★

The Civil War (Elektra Nonesuch '90) A panorama of American melody circa 1865, when all manner of minstrels and semiclassically trained composers were melding hymns and folk airs into an American popular style. Modest execution guards against dated fussiness, forced projection, and parlor gentility—on its own terms it's a quiet classic. But its elegiac reflectiveness calls out for gruesome pictures that aren't there—because it conceives music as a respite from war, never as a weapon, it's more sentimental than the music deserves. Did you know that North Carolina's Salem Brass Band used to play in the midst of battle to spur the boys on, or that at a post-Appomattox concert a Southern major told his Yankee hosts, "Gentlemen, if we had had your songs, we'd have licked you out of your boots"? Not from this you didn't. **A–**

Closer Than a Kiss: Crooner Classics (Rhino '97) Vanilla sex—yum. Eighteen white guys of yesteryear, six black but only Al Hibbler and Johnny Hartman hinting at difference, show their voices the way peacocks present their tails and rent boys display their ivory hard-ons. Their creamy grain and relaxed, well-groomed flow promise smooth sailing all the way to sweet, gradual, uncomplicated orgasm. **A**

Cole Porter: A Centennial Celebration (RCA '91) Capitol's swinging *Anything Goes* survives incursions from the likes of Gordon MacRae. But any solon who disses *Red Hot + Blue* had better not try and tell me schlock kings like Andre Previn, Skitch Henderson, Robert Shaw, Norman Luboff, and Arthur Fiedler—none of whom even bother with lyrics, for God's sake—do him justice. At least Al Hirt's "I Love Paris" is a travesty, not unlike Les Negresses Vertes'. And then there are the vocalists. Better Arthur Fiedler than opera dropout Mario Lanza, and if Dinah Shore or Alfred Drake understand the material as well as Sinéad O'Connor or Jimmy Somerville, they don't let us in on the secret. From Mary Martin to Patti Lupone, actresses let the songs do the talking, and the two convincing male singers here have the "worst" voices. One is Fred Astaire. The other is Cole Porter, whose three demo-style vocals-with-piano are so alive that I'm praying some solon exhumes a whole album's worth. If Porter found them insufficiently musical, he was wrong. Now he belongs to the ages. **B–** 🦃

The Commitments (MCA '91) Just as it's impossible to make a credible flick about a rock star because no mere actor can play the role, it's impossible to make a credible flick about a bar band because no mere movie fan will sit through the music. So director Alan Parker had to cheat where novelist Roddy Doyle didn't. Aided by L.A. studio simulacra Dean Parks, Mitchell Froom, and Alex Acuna, his home-grown white-soul cover specialists sacrifice idiosyncrasy for competence—they don't even risk the Dublin version of "Night Train" the novel turns on. Now that's what I call soulful—a cross between *The Big Chill* and *The Blues Brothers*. **C+** 🦃

Concept in Dance: The Digital Alchemy of Goa Trance Dance (Moonshine Music '94) 💣

The Corruptor (Jive '99) Obsessed with death, declaring 1985 the Golden Age, counterbalancing two pieces of pimp shit with two pieces of ho fuck you, these tough, articulate third-generation voices document a gangsta myth innocent of all hope. Nostalgic credo: "When niggaz keep their weapons concealed it's all real." Guys, that much could happen. Maybe it's already started. **B+**

Crooklyn (MCA '94) the young person's guide to '70s soul (the Chi-Lites, "Oh Girl"; Joe Cuba, "El Pito [I'll Never Go Back to Georgia]") ★★★

Cuba Classics 2: Dancing with the Enemy (Luaka Bop/Warner Bros. '91) **Ⓝ**

Cuba: Fully Charged (Earthworks/Caroline '92) **Ⓝ**

Cuban Dance Party: Routes of Rhythm Volume 2 (Rounder '90) Though the companion *A Carnival of Cuban Music* is half field recording, Rounder's folkloric bias finally does a pop compilation some good. Most of the seven bands on this live tour of vintage Cuban dance rhythms date to before Fidel; one features an 82-year-old trumpeter, another a 92-year-old bongo player (who takes a solo). And all of them—including the post-Fidel Irakere and Los Van Van, whose signature "Muevete" is the longest and strongest of the three versions I know—thrive on the loose-limbed ethos of the dance-concert contexts. There's space in this music, odd touches—it feels freer than modern dance hits from Trinidad or the Dominican or Cuba itself. Freest of all is the old mambo "Here Come the Millionaires," which is what one group of pre-Fidel dockworkers decided to call themselves when they got jobs. **A–**

Cuba Now (Hemisphere '98) I prefer son to other salsa cousins because horn arrangements annoy me even when they have more jam than the Cherry Poppin' Daddies'. I work on this prejudice, primarily to accommodate my clave-loving in-house adviser, who plucked this item out of the confusion of Cuban comps we've sampled during the current fad. Sucked in, as who wouldn't be, by the off-kilter montuno of NG La Banda's lead "El Tragico," she ignored the blare and voted with her hips. Grooves struggle against surface clutter throughout. Usually they win. **A–**

Cumbia Cumbia (World Circuit import '91) Hits back to the '50s from Colombia's Disco Fuentes label, with history sweeping consistency aside—any gringo can tell Conjunto Tipico Vallenato's accordion side-closers are country and Rodolfo's coffee commercial isn't. But even if the accordion stuff belongs on a vallenata comp, it passes muster on a collecton where at least half the songs bristle with the *exigente* hooks that sell classic pop the world over. And the unmistakable beat runs down a consummate South American groove, halfway between Euro clomp and Afro hipshake. **A–**

Cumbia Cumbia 2 (World Circuit '94) Where the first volume was an all-subsuming best-of that ignored details of stylistic and historical development, this one focuses on the '60s, "la epoca dorada de cumbias Colombianas," and what it sacrifices in hooks it more than gives back in consistency and gestalt. Horn-dominated with plenty of accordion, far more playful and unpretentious than competing salsa or merengue, it's infectious rather than inescapable, lively rather than driving. I'd dance to it. I'd also give it to Scrooge for Christmas. **A–**

d

Chuck D: *Autobiography of Mistachuck* (Mercury '96) If rap, now hip hop, is the black CNN, the coiner of that historic phrase has gone public access—his disappearing solo debut topped out at 190 pop and broke "r&b" well south of House of Pain. So his claim to righteousness has to stand as music, or if he's lucky the kind of rumor that kept Amerindie going—like Spearhead and Gil Scott-Heron, not Wu-Tang or Buju Banton. And until he gets winded half an hour in, he slam-dunks. Over a muscular bottom of unsampled funk—"NO contracts NO tracks with NO mechanicals"—the proud Chevy owner pounds home the plain, intricately rhymed truth about black folks dreaming of Jenny Jones, about hip hop going to hell in an armored limo. Sure helped me get straight after I spent an hour with the law one afternoon. I can only hope it'll do the same for people who really need it. **A–**

Da Brat: *Funkdafied* (So So Def/Chaos/Columbia '94) **Ⓝ**

Daft Punk: "Da Funk" (*Homework,* Virgin '97) 🕭

I. K. Dairo, M.B.E.: *Juju Master* (Original Music '90) Ibadan circa 1963—a quiet revolution in a language you don't understand ("Omo Lanke") ★
I. K. Dairo M.B.E. and His Blue Spots: *I Remember* (Music of the World '91) Two Nigerian album sides and four new six-minute moments by the 60-year-old singer-guitarist-accordionist, who in the '60s ruled Yoruba pop with innovations that made King Sunny and the rest of modern juju possible—whereupon modern juju nearly ended his career. Then, in 1985, after a decade of mixed success as a hotelier and Christian preacher, Dairo returned. Inspired and chastened, he's learned to adapt, and though his arrangements aren't quite as intricate as the younger guys', some may prefer his old-fashioned songfulness. The two English-language market ploys remember his darling and "George Washington, Marcus Garvey/Booker Washington, Abraham Lincoln/John Kennedy, Dr. Martin Luther King." The Yoruba titles get the best tunes. And the album side "F'eso J'aiye" is modern juju at its most intricately delightful. **A–**
I. K. Dairo M.B.E. and His Blue Spots: *Ashiko* (Xenophile '94) **Ⓝ**
I. K. Dairo: *Definitive Dairo* (Xenophile '96) 1971—the juju patriarch still undefined ("Okin Omo Ni," "Labondo") ★★

Da Lench Mob: *Guerillas in the Mist* (Street Knowledge '92) 💣

Ya Ntesa Dalienst & Le Maquisard: *Belalo* (Sango Music import '92) Franco's main tenor leads a large portion of Franco's immense band through five endlessly seductive cuts, all in the 10-minute range, which those who find Afropop too atmospheric to begin with will consider a bit much. I hear the tunes shift beguilingly and think the real star of the show—which includes alternate tenor Lassa Carlito, ace

---

★★★, ★★, ★ Honorable Mention   🕭 Choice Cut   Ⓝ Neither   💣 Dud   🦃 Turkey

guitarist Dizzy Mandjeku, and a battery of casually tuned horns—is bassist J-Baptiste Nsamela, whose snake the music rides till the river reaches the sea. **A**

Dama & D'Gary: *The Long Way Home* (Shanachie '94) Dama is a classic folkie, a cosmopolitan leftist credited with inventing Malagasy nueva cancion, an elected legislator as renowned in Madagascar as Victor Jara was in Chile. D'Gary is a classic find, a prodigy-protégé from cattle country where the main road is an 11-hour walk away. Though their rainbow rhythms are formally unique and patently pleasurable, not even producer Henry Kaiser claims to apprehend them fully. The hook is D'Gary's distinctively Malagasy way with his recently acquired guitar, and even more, since that wasn't enough to put his solo album over, Dama's calm, good-humored, deeply assured vocal presence—a politician's gift from a place and time where oratory is still entertainment. Despite excellent notes, the satisfactions remain fairly general for the English speaker. But Kaiser and friends' understated filigrees remind me that said satisfactions far exceed those of similar projects—Ry Cooder's Ali Farka Toure soundtrack, say. **B+**

The Dambuilders: *Encendedor* (East-West '94) sound punk, structures art-rock, violin bi ("Copsucker," "Idaho") ★★★
The Dambuilders: *Ruby Red* (East-West '95) they don't like what they see and they know how to sound that way ("Teenage Loser Anthem," "Drive-By Kiss") ★★
The Dambuilders: "Break Up with Your Boyfriend," "Itch It" (*Against the Stars*, Atlantic '97) 👁️

Dance Hall Crashers: *Honey I'm Homely* (MCA '97) 💣

D'Angelo: *Brown Sugar* (EMI '95) OK, OK, but Marvin did write songs ("Brown Sugar," "Sh*t, Damn, Motherf*cker") ★★

Danzig II: *Lucifuge* (Def American '90) I'm sure Glenn Danzig is right about Jim Morrison. If he hadn't given up the ghost, the fourth Door would have stepped up his flirtation with Satan and adjusted his music to a metallic pitch of precision preening. But then, I already knew Morrison was a putz. Misfits fans had convinced me to hold out some hope for Glenn. **B–** 🦃

Olu Dara: *In the World: From Natchez to New York* (Atlantic '98) 💣

Terence Trent D'Arby: "She Kissed Me" (*Symphony or Damn,* Columbia '93) 👁️

Terence Trent D'Arby: *TTD's Vibrator* (Work '95) Ⓝ

Dark City Sisters/Flying Jazz Queens: *Dark City Sisters and Flying Jazz Queens* (Earthworks '94) Lumped with the Mahotella Queens when recalled by Afropop historians at all, Joyce Mogatusi's close-harmony Dark City Sisters are far less raucous—more girl-group than big-mama. They offer the best clue yet as to just exactly what the mysterious "marabi" sounded like. Recall if you can the pop-jazz shadings of Dorothy Masuka, and note the three inevitable and excellent Mahlathini tracks—where the Queens compete with the witch doctor, the Sisters stay as sweet as they are. Also, be glad of this: no fewer than seven songs adduce dances—some new, some traditional, some just themselves. **A–**

The Darling Buds: *Erotica* (Chaos/Columbia '92) Ⓝ

Das Efx: *Dead Serious* (EastWest '92) deep funk versus jibber-jabber, dick versus diarrhea ("They Want Efx," "Looseys") ★

Dave's True Story: *Sex Without Bodies* (Chesky '98) lounge as Jackie Cain and Roy Kral, not Martin Denny, and why don't you know the reference? ("I'll Never Read Trollope Again," "Once Had a Woman") ★

Gail Davies: "Unwed Fathers" (*The Best of Gail Davies,* Capitol '91) 👁️

Richard Davies: *Telegraph* (Flydaddy '97) 💣

CeDell Davis: *The Best of CeDell Davis* (Fat Possum/Capricorn '94) slide is beautiful ("Rock," "CeDell's Boogie") ★

Guy Davis: *You Don't Know My Mind* (Red House '98) blues his heritage, his politics, his craft ("Best I Can," "If You Love Somebody") ★★

Miles Davis: *Pangaea* (Columbia '90) can the flute and add track listings ("Zimbabwe") ★★

Miles Davis: *Live Around the World* (Warner Bros. '96) 🎯

Miles Davis: *Black Beauty* (Columbia/Legacy '97) Live at the Fillmore West, 1970. April 1970, that is—things moved fast in those days. Soloists' music, and hence the corniest electric Miles on record, this double-CD preserves an inkling of why the jazz-rock idea seemed so auspicious before it found form in fusion's flash and filigree. Wailing through "Directions" or blasting the blues from out "Miles Runs the Voodoo Down," Chick Corea's keybs sound more audacious and grounded than they ever will again, with an uncommonly muscular Miles challenging his facility and fledgling soprano whiz Steve Grossman mimicking it. Beyond a few dollops of needless noodle, Jack DeJohnette keeps the troops in order, injecting more notes and accents than Ginger Baker on double amphetamines into a beat that rocks. A−

Miles Davis: *Dark Magus* (Columbia/Legacy '97) The guru-manipulator shifted gears at will in his early '70s music, orchestrating moods and settings to subjugate the individual musical inspirations of his young close-enough-for-funk subgeniuses to the life of a single palpitating organism that would have perished without them—no arrangements, little composition, and not many solos either, although at any moment a player could find himself left to fly off on his own. Harsher and dreamier than *In Concert,* louder and sweeter than *Agharta* or *Pangaea,* this well-tweaked 1974 concert culminates the aesthetic. Where pure funk subsumes jazz and rock in a new conception, albeit one that privileges rock, Miles leaves the two elements distinct and recognizable. Dave Liebman is good for wild-to-mellow jazz input that's solidified by a Coltrane-esque house call from Azar Lawrence, and for rock there are three guitarists: Reggie Lucas and Dominique Gaumont wah-riffing the rhythm as Chess session man turned cult hero Pete Cosey launches wah-wah-inflected noise into the arena-rock stratosphere. The beat belongs jointly to Michael Henderson and Al Foster. And Miles is Miles whether blasting out clarion notes or letting his Yamaha drench the scene. A

Miles Davis: *Panthalassa: The Music of Miles Davis 1969–1974* (Columbia '98) Tapes of these Bill Laswell remixes have been around almost a year, and for the longest time I didn't get the point. When the original albums were edited down for release by Teo Macero, that was Davis's choice; alive, he was free to object should Macero's forays into formlessness strike him as too discursive or commercial. Anyway, learning to distinguish among the author-authorized variants was tricky enough. Hand them over to the ambient-techno brigade and the tide would never stop rising. But one night I listened with a first-timer and got the message. Metastructures condensed, themes highlighted, beats punched up by a master tinkerer who's loved them forever, the transcendent buzz of electric Miles nevertheless remains undulant, unpredictable, perverse—and so relaxed about getting where it's not actually going that newcomers will find it hard to imagine how much more unhurriedly it might arrive. For me this will get played like *In a Silent Way* and *Jack Johnson* before it. It's a passport to provisional utopia. A

Miles Davis/Various DJs: *Panthalassa: The Remixes* (Columbia '99) ambient techno goes to heaven, or hell—anyway, steals trumpeter ("On the Corner [Subterranean Channel Mix]," "Shhh [Sea4 Miles Remix]") ★★

Days of the New: *Days of the New* (Outpost '97) As marketing, pure genius.

Looks like alt-country, no electric guitars even, yet is actually America's answer to Silverchair. And hey, it's sincere—17-year-old heartland frontman Travis Meeks really is depressed, really has immersed in Soundgarden, really does think it's deep to hook your single to the all-purpose trope "abuse." This is why grownups need Hanson. It's also why they need Radish. **C** 🦃

DC Talk: *Supernatural* (Virgin '98) If the scruffy yokels of Jars of Clay are tent preachers, these hunky moderns are tele-vangelists, their well-riffed Queen homage the musical equivalent of Tammy Faye Bakker's false eyelashes—considered sinful excess in an earlier era, claimed for Christ now that it is known not to herald the end time. Reports that they have something—anything—to do with rap are apparently based on the presence of a certified Black Person in the group. Instead, they do up a jolly ska tune whose love object is, shall we say, not female, and address a generically whiny-sarcastic selling-out putdown to Collective Soul, trumping their assertion of spiritual superiority by insisting that they still "love" their backsliding brothers. They should remember I Corinthians 13:4: "Charity suffereth long, and is kind; charity envieth not; charity vaunteth not itself, is not puffed up." **C** 🦃

Dead Can Dance: *Into the Labyrinth* (4AD '93) Any doubt that pop medieval-ism equals pop exoticism and both are worse for it is put to rest by trance-dance's answer to Enya, who cheapen ideas that heretofore were merely shite with tunes to uplift or gull the unenlightened masses. Since this will give said masses the wrong idea—something about anything you don't understand being mysterious so long as it's geographically or historically remote (hence not your own self-deluded life)—that just makes the music worse. **D** 🦃

Chico DeBarge: *Long Time No See* (Kedar/Universal '97) Marvin Gaye gets

out of jail ("Love Still Good," "Love Jones") ★★

Chico DeBarge: "The Game" (*The Game*, Motown '99) 💿

El DeBarge: *Heart, Mind and Soul* (Reprise '94) The great lost love man enlists Babyface (five songs, four jumpy), Jerome Dupri (one trick groove), various siblings (backing up his ballads), and the shade of Marvin Gaye (self-penned title finale) in an overdue quest for his own genius. The incomparable *In a Special Way* was 1984, and those hung up on the irretrievable innocence and naturalness of the past may take offense at the digital aesthetic, not to mention El's occasional descent into a manly tenor. Me, I applaud his appetite for the freaky, and note fondly that he adores her for it in the morning, as dogged as ever in his helpless devotion. I urge him to find more harmony work for Bunny and the others. But this is his second-best album. **A–**

Deee-Lite: "Good Beat" (*World Clique*, Elektra '90) 💿

Deee-Lite: *Infinity Within* (Elektra '92) New Age disco in the musical biosphere of Bootsy, Bernie, Catfish, and the Horny Horns ("Rubber Lover," "Electric Shock") ★★★

Deee-Lite: *Dewdrops in the Garden* (Elektra '94) Ⓝ

Deep Forest: *Deep Forest* (550 Music/Epic '93) Ⓝ

Le Général Defao: *"Ambiance Plus" (Bana Congo Vol. 2 Dance Mix)* (Roma Productions import '99) Well after soukous supposedly withered away, a second-tier crowd pleaser with a willingness to throw his big body into a dance he named puts out his 17th or 18th album, something like that. Vocally he's no Wemba or Rochereau, but Manda Chante (of Wenge Musica, how did you miss him?) caramelizes one track, and Le Jeune Makuta, Likanga Mangenza, and others I've never heard of take guest turns. Vocal colors shift as leads come and go; the chorus expands and contracts. Rhythms converge, thin out, flow horizonward. A saxophone comes in to garnish the guitars. Songs segue for easier dancing, or divide into parts the dancers better be ready for. The jollity is general, audible. A generic good time is had by all. **B+**

Def Jef: *Soul Food* (Delicious Vinyl '91) self-appointed griot ("Fa Sho Shot," "God Complex") ★

Def Leppard: *Vault 1980–1995: Def Leppard Greatest Hits* (Mercury '95) 💣

Carmaig de Forest: *Carmaig de Forest's DeathGrooveLoveParty* (Knitting Factory Works '93) if the Femmes had never gotten famous . . . ("Bend Down Low," "So Happy Together") ★★★

Carmaig de Forest: *El Camino Real* (Saint Francis '97) sharp narrative eye, cocky nerd attitude, too smart for folk and his own good ("Coldwater Park," "Sexy/Scary") ★★

Def Squad: "Rhymin' Wit' Biz Markie," **"Def Squad Delite"** (*El Niño*, Def Jam/Jive '98) 💣

Deftones: *Around the Fur* (Maverick/Warner Bros. '97) 💣

The Deighton Family: *Mama Was Right* (Philo '90) Basically this is an English folk band doing lots of "trad. arr."—"Soldiers Joy," "Bonaparte's Retreat," "Farther Along," "Freight Train." But though the instrumentation is pretty conventional right down to the electric guitar, the sound is unique, probably because Mama Josie brings a little bit of South Molucca (in Indonesia, where she grew up) to her guitar (and bodhran), and the kids learned at both parents' knees. Papa Dave arrs., gives history lessons, defines folk to include "When You're Smiling," "Taxman," and "Wonderful Tonight," and sings like a busker who's found his place in the world. **A−**

The Deighton Family: *Rolling Home* (Green Linnet '91) **𝟎**

De La Soul: *De La Soul Is Dead* (Tommy Boy '91) studio obscurantism as street credibility ("Millie Pulled a Pistol on Santa," "Fanatic of the B Word," "Keepin' the Faith") ★★★

De La Soul: *Buhloone Mindstate* (Tommy Boy '93) They end their dark night as funny and unpredictable as when they were kids, and a lot looser. With grease from Maceo and friends, the mostly jazzy beats have penetrated like liniment—for all its quick turns and fancy wordplay, at bottom this feels like a groove record. Guest MCs SDP and Tagaki Kan take pig Latin to the land of the ideogram, and battling sexism is De La's own Ladybug, the effervescent (and short) Shortie No Mass. Inspirational Credo Sure to Be Quoted in Non-Family Newspapers Everywhere: "Fuck being hard, Posdnous is complicated." **A**

De La Soul: *Stakes Is High* (Tommy Boy '96) After almost four years, Posdnuos and company emerge from the ether like the long-lost friends they are. Their wordplay assured in its subtle smarts, their delivery unassuming in its quick, unmacho mumble, their cultural awareness never smug about its balance, they bind up an identifiable feeling in an identifiable sound, and just about every one of the 17 tracks comes equipped with a solid beat and a likable hook or chorus. It's a relief to have them back. But it's never a revelation. **B+**

The Del-Lords: *Lovers Who Wander* (Enigma '90) 💣

The Del-Lords: *Get Tough: The Best of the Del-Lords* (Restless '99) If 15 years later the anthem that goes "I believe that there's a heaven before I'm dead" seems almost as naive as the anti-imperialist title song, well, these guys were more a straw to be grasped than a future to be seized even at the time—an American version of the Clash just as the Clash was headed for the shredder, substituting for rootsy punk formalism a full embrace of rock and roll and its sources. Leader Scott Kempner and believer Eric Ambel were never dead-on songwriters or overwhelming singers, so this distillation is the perfect place to recall just how humanistic the straight stuff can be. Slightly out of time in their time, today they're just as likely to make you ask why the hell it couldn't happen again. **A–**

Del Tha Funkee Homosapien: *I Wish My Brother George Was Here* (Elektra '91) funkentelechy vs. hoodz and Hammer ("The Wacky World of Rapid Transit," "Mistadobalina") ★★★

Iris DeMent: *Infamous Angel* (Philo '92) Because it leads with the miraculous "Let the Mystery Be"—an agnostic's declaration of faith so homespun it makes the word "agnostic" seem absurdly hoity-toity and severe, so unfaltering it conceals the tremendous intellectual effort her decision not to know self-evidently required—this Kansas City 31-year-old's debut has authenticity hounds in a lather. But she never gets so near perfection again—the catchy "Our Town" seems contrived by comparison, the signature "Infamous Angel" obscure. Also, she worries more about her sins than an agnostic should. It's hard to believe she's ever done anything *that* bad. **B+**

Iris DeMent: *My Life* (Warner Bros. '94) Although her attack is more austere, DeMent's voice is as country as Kitty Wells's or Loretta Lynn's, and her writing defines the directness sophisticates prize in traditional folk songs—she has something she wants to say, and so she proceeds from Point A to Point B in the straightest line she can draw without a ruler. She doesn't get lost not just because she knows where Point B is, which is rare enough in this ambivalent time, but because she knows where Point A is—she knows that who she is begins with where she comes from, and she's made her peace with that. Unlike so many American artists who outgrow fundamentalism, she's not wracked by rage or guilt; at worst, she's sad about her distance from forebears she loves and admires despite their strict morality—a morality she'll never return to even though it's the bedrock of her personality and ultimately her work. The only change her

major-label move means is a firmer commitment to pleasure—that is, to melody. Her dad, who gave up the fiddle when he got saved, would surely understand. **A+**

Iris DeMent: *The Way I Should* (Warner Bros. '96) Ooh, ick—four *protest songs*. One about *sexual abuse*—isn't that a little old? And what right does she have to put down upwardly mobiles with that "Quality Time" cliché? Only maybe she does have the right—maybe she's a better person than you, me, or the striver next door. Anyway, intellectual originality isn't her stock in trade. She's just a singer with the God-given ability to convey commonplace feelings as if they belong to her, as they do to all of us. And that these feelings should now include righteous indignation only proves that she's alive in history. Who else could intimate raging obscenity by putting the words "ass," "crap," and "damn" in the same song? Only the woman who still adduces home, marriage, and spiritual struggle with the unaffected simplicity you loved before she belonged to the world. **A**

Demolition Doll Rods: *Demolition Doll Rods* (Matador '99) two girls, one guy, no pants—sex and more sex and rock and roll ("Married for the Weekend," "U Look Good") ★

Depeche Mode: *Violator* (Sire/Reprise '90) Fearing the loss of their silly grip on America's angst-ridden teens, who they're old enough to know are a fickle lot, they forge on toward the rap market by rhyming "drug" and "thug." And for the U.K.'s ecstasy-riding teens, who God knows are even more fickle, there's the techno-perfect synth/guitar sigh/moan that punctuates the easily rescinded "Policy of Truth." **C–**

Depeche Mode: *Songs of Faith and Devotion* (Sire/Reprise '93) 💣

Derek and the Dominos: *The Layla Sessions* (Polydor '90) Sloughing off the myth of the album as artistic unit and denying proven spendthrifts a face-saving shred of consumerly discrimination, CD boxes are invariably about marketing rather than music. But this triple smells. Supposedly necessitated by the slovenliness of *Layla*'s first digital remix, still for sale as a "special-price" double-CD even though the same material squeezes onto one disc here, it pretends that Eric Clapton's finest pickup band—which as the notes inadvertently remind us begat George Harrison's endless *All Things Must Pass* (you remember "Apple Jam," now don't you?)—deserves the kind of genius treatment that's dubious even with great jazz improvisers. And since it unearths not much Duane Allman (no surprise, since he barely met the band), it cheats on the dueling-guitars fireworks that made *Layla* explode. This is pop, gang—arrangements matter. Outtakes are outtakes because the keepers are better. Jams take too long to get anywhere worth going. And when a mix trades raunch for definition, the exchange is usually moot. **B–** 🐦

Descendents: *Somery* (SST '91) Now dba All, these unprivileged Orange County punks had two great moments, *The Fat EP* and *Milo Goes to College*—both half cannibalized here, both now fully comprised by the *Two Things at Once* CD. Begin there. But anyone beguiled, enthralled, or smacked between the eyes by how nakedly these guys don't quite understand their class rage and love-hungry sexual anxiety will hear through their bouts of misogyny and sophomoric humor for the 19 more tuneful if less inspired selections from three later and lesser albums, as in the tortured break-up song/metaphor "Dirty Sheets" and the fuckup/square's confession "Coolidge." **A–**

The Descendents: *Everything Sucks* (Epitaph '96) Ⓝ

Ignace de Souza: *Ignace de Souza* (Original Music '94) Migrating to Ghana from Dahomey in 1955 to become a highlife star in the '60s, the trumpeter's selling point was his Francophone roots, which gave him a leg up on those newfangled

Congolese rhythms. He wasn't above the occasional twist or cha-cha either. Initially these 19 cuts sound pleasingly familiar but not all that distinctive, on the cusp between the generic-elemental and the generic-clichéd. Yet although my highlife comp of choice remains the same label's more obscure, more exacting *Azagas and Archibogs,* slowly the pleasure wins out. **B+**

Des'ree: *Mind Adventures* (Epic '92) 🎯
Des'ree: *I Ain't Movin'* (550 Music/Epic '94) Ⓝ
Des'ree: *Supernatural* (550 Music '98) 🎯

Destiny's Child: *The Writing's on the Wall* (Columbia '99) I like teenpop fine, but please, one song at a time. And since teenpop likes this glamorous femme quartet, individual songs are all a reasonable grownup would expect. Uh-uh. Lyrics are the usual problem—if there's a quotable quote here, I haven't noticed it. But that may just be because the multivalent harmonies, suavely irregular beats, and, not incidentally, deep-seated self-respect have been keeping me busy ever since I heard through the visuals. **B+**

Deus: *In a Bar, Under the Sea* (Island '96) 🎯

Devo: *Smooth Noodle Maps* (Enigma '90) 🎯
Devo: *Hardcore Devo Vol. 1* (Rykodisc '90) 🎯
Devo: *Greatest Hits* (Warner Bros. '90) Just when everybody agreed this new wave novelty act was full of poot, here came *Pee-Wee's Playhouse,* which was dreamt of in their "philosophy" but not mine. So OK, they were an Important Band, fabricating a minimalist funk of blatant entertainment value and covert sexuality. "Whip It" aside, what "hits" they had are the U.K. singles on the accompanying *Greatest Misses,* and the socialist cheapskate in me wishes they'd prepared a more economical tour—even if it would mean leaving off, say, the interlocking mechanisms of the ironically entitled "Gut

Feeling," which missed me altogether on their first album. Nevertheless, its peaks prove higher and more numerous than I'd have figured. Doody now for the future. **A–**

Devo: *Greatest Misses* (Warner Bros. '90) marginalia rools ("Be Stiff," "[I Can't Get No] Satisfaction," "Mongoloid," "Penetration in the Centrefold") ★★

Devo: *Hardcore Devo Vol. 2* (Rykodisc '91) 💣

D'Gary: *Malagasy Guitar* (Shanachie '93) Ⓝ

D'Gary & Jihé: *Horombe* (Stern's Africa '95) the master autodidact of Madagascar guitar figures out a band ("Mbo Hahita Avao," "Mihasy Lonaky") ★★

D'Gary: See also Dama & D'Gary

D-Generation: *No Lunch* (Columbia '96) 💣

D-Generation: "Helpless," "Rise and Fall" (*Through the Darkness,* C2/Columbia '99) 🍬

Adama Diabate: *Jako Baye* (Stern's Africa '95) Ⓝ

Djanka Diabate: *Djanka* (Sound Wave '91) she sings Sahel and grooves Afro-Parisian ("Malaka") ★★

Sona Diabaté: *Girls of Guinea* (Shanachie '90) Rather than romanticizing a righteous African sister, take her for a griot who's good at her job. In a nation where preserving musical treasure has been a point of socialist pride, her adept, folky elaborations avoid the appearance of self-consciousness—the closely related guitar figures underlying these songs are graceful, welcome, inevitable. But she's a trifle too dutiful to put much passion into her righteousness. And when we call music righteous, passionate is usually what we mean. **B+**

Toumani Diabate with Balaka Sissoko: *New Ancient Strings* (Rykodisc '99) 💣

Toumani Diabate: See also Taj Mahal & Toumani Diabate

Ramata Diakité: *Na* (Cobalt import '99) hews so close to girl-of-Wassoulou verities she's lucky her musicians don't ("Na," "Aye Yafama") ★★★

Alpha Yaya Diallo: *Aduna "The World"* (Tinder '98) Guinéean doctor's son learns guitar in Malinke, botany in college, and pan-Africanism in Vancouver, British Columbia ("Yéké Yéké," "Aduna") ★

Alpha Yaya Diallo: *The Message* (Wicklow '99) Canadians—presumably white Canadians, although with all the slave names up there one can't be sure—in an Afrowhatever band? A guarantee of New Age blandness if ever I've patted my foot, and every time the Celtic fiddle comes in on one track I get the urge to slaughter a whale. Yet somehow this Guinéean guitarist-vocalist parses the link between pan-African beatsmanship and world-music eternal return, evoking now soukous, now chimurenga, now the circularities if not the koras of Sahel griots and hunters. Soothing, mostly—yet provocative enough to make you ejaculate when you least expect it. **A–**

Jali Musa Jawara [Djeli Moussa Diawasa]: *Yasimika* (Hannibal '90) A 1983 French release picked up by U.K. Oval in 1986, this is the renowned album that made Mango's 1989 *Soubindoor* inevitable. Though only vocalist–kora master Jawara plays on both, the bands—each featuring balafon, two guitars, and two women singers—achieve an identical sound. Yet though I heard this one second, it grabbed me where Mango's entry rewarded my dutiful attention. I swear the emotion is higher here, the interaction a quantum more intense. And of such quanta are world-music classics made. **A–**

Djeli Moussa Diawara: *Sobindo* (Mélodie import '96) As Jali Musa Jawara, the Guinéean conceived two earlier landmarks of Manding neotraditionalism, *Yasimika* and *Soubindoor,* and here once again he flirts with the escapist spirituality of "world music." There's a flute and a piano and a telltale tabla; at times the kora could almost be Italian or (another give-away) Andean. Yet once again his confident weave and powerfully West African (Guinéean?) vocal feel (technique?) overwhelm secular skepticism. Right, this kind of Beauty is an ideological construct. Don't we all deserve a vacation once in a while? **A–**

Djeli Moussa Diawara: *FlamenKora* (Mélodie import '99) **Ⓝ**

Diblo Dibala & Matchatcha: *Laissez Passer* (Afric Music import '92) The master of speed soukous succumbs to traditionalist tastemakers or repetitive stress injury and waxes (almost) lyrical (almost) half the time. Just because it isn't him doesn't mean he can't fake it—he changes pace a lot more hummably than his old boss Kanda Bongo Man. Check out the mandolin imitation on "Merci Papa." **A–**

Diblo Dibala: *My Love* (Atoll Music import '96) the kind of genre move you miss when the well runs dry ("Radi," "Reconnaissance") ★★

Manu Dibango: *Wakafrika* (Giant '94) all your Afropop faves, with extra added attractions ("Soul Makossa," "Diarabi") ★★

Bo Diddley: *A Man Amongst Men* (Atlantic '96) **Ⓝ**

Die Toten Hosen: *Learning English: Lesson One* (Atlantic '94) 🎸

Diferenz Featuring Jazz Con Bazz: "Face" (*More Noize Please* [comp], Shadow '96) 🍬

Joe Diffie: "Startin' Over Blues" (*Regular Joe,* Columbia '92) 🍬

Ani DiFranco: *Imperfectly* (Righteous Babe '92) In which woman love becomes a vividly attractive life option rather than a cause. Does she advise her friend in the bad relationship, the one who "sits there like America suffering through slow reform," to come out? Nope, she tells her "there's plenty of great men out

there." Linguistic craft as a means to character—a barely drinking-age performer-entrepreneur's own headstrong, mercurial, sensual, edgy, alert, pissed off, affectionate, waggish, empowered, needy, indomitable, fierce, left-wing, hyperemotional, super-competent persona. **A–**

Ani DiFranco: *Puddle Dive* (Righteous Babe '93) or is that puddle diva? ("Names and Dates and Times," "Pick Yer Nose") ★★

Ani DiFranco: *Like I Said* (Righteous Babe '93) cherry-picking the skillfully turned-out nakedness of (her first) two self-released tapes/CDs ("Lost Woman Song," "Both Hands," "Anticipate") ★★

Ani DiFranco: *Out of Range* (Righteous Babe '94) distracted by piano, accordion, even horns from her lithe sound, self-starting folk-punk remains a tough broad who aims to figure it all out ("The Diner," "Letter to a John," "Face Up and Sing") ★★★

Ani DiFranco: *Not a Pretty Girl* (Righteous Babe '95) Although her girlcult loves her madly, the guys I know smell trouble every time she opens her mouth. This has nothing to do with her face, body, or sense of style. It's her words, the sheer volume of them, jetting out as if she feels free to say any goddamn thing that comes into her head. But give DiFranco the chance and she'll make you like her ancient formula for self-indulgent song-poetry. Augmented only by a drummer this time, her acoustic guitar and electric bass produce a one-of-a-kind sound, and those torrents take shape as literal accounts of a mercurial inner life with more love than anger in it. So if she's not my type and maybe not yours, big deal. At 24, she already has seven albums hanging from her nose ring, and they're getting good enough that we need her more than she needs us. **A–**

Ani DiFranco: *Dilate* (Righteous Babe '96) On an album loaded with quotable quotes, my favorite is the refrain (well, she says it twice) of the six-and-a-half-minute "Adam and Eve": "i am truly sorry about all this." I mean, she *knows*—knows what a pain in the ass she is, knows how much space her emotions take up, knows she once banged a power line with her stickball bat and blacked out the entire Eastern seaboard. She boasts about her integrity, her vulnerability, her joy. She jokes about them too. She has a friend's mom phone in obscure verses of "Amazing Grace." She utters, I kid you not, the most vituperative "fuck you" in the history of the music. She is herself, and for once that's more than enough. **A–**

Ani DiFranco: *Living in Clip* (Righteous Babe '97) DiFranco has always been beat-happy. From the beginning you can catch her speed-strumming just for the rush, but in general her guitar figures and her sense of rhythm are both much quirkier; older folkies would have diagnosed them as symptoms of some awful nervous disorder. In the spare and agile Andy Stochansky, who isn't averse to powering up but more characteristically states and embellishes a single eccentric line with brushes or mallets or lightly wielded sticks, she may have found the best folk-rock drummer who's ever lived, and this live double-CD, which draws liberally on her formative folk-punk years for those who only caught on with *Dilate,* is his showcase. Joined as well by the supplest of her several bassists, Gang of Four stalwart Sara Lee, DiFranco proves herself not just arch and sisterly and sexy and effervescent, but a bandleader who has wiggled free of deadening acoustic-with-backup commonplaces—and evolved from the truth of "Smile pretty and watch your back" to that of "We lose sight of everything when we have to keep checking our backs." **A–**

Ani DiFranco: *Little Plastic Castle* (Righteous Babe '98) Here's hoping she gets used to fame, a theme the coolest new-famous are now hip enough to sidestep or caricature. But DiFranco doesn't have much use for ordinary standards of cool, which is one reason she's new-famous, and for the nonce she can do no wrong. Always underlying her bull-session eloquence, a hook no matter the message, is the supple, seductive, self-amused musicality that puts her records across. A typical touch here is her choice of world-jazz-ambient trumpeter Jon Hassell to decorate the 14-minute spoken-word finale "Pulse": "you crawled into my bed/like some sort of giant insect/and i found myself spellbound/at the sight of you there/beautiful and grotesque/and all the rest of that bug stuff." "That bug stuff"—who else would dare it? **A–**

Ani DiFranco: *Up Up Up Up Up Up* (Righteous Babe '99) Reports that she's fallen in love with the mirror are rank last-big-thingism. She's still the girl who ran away with the circus because bearded ladies do honest work, and far from going too far, her 13 climactic minutes of poetry-with-jazz attest to her unflagging esprit. She should let her junkie jones be for a while. But not her class jones. The rich are always with us. **A–**

Ani DiFranco: *To the Teeth* (Righteous Babe '99) overreaching? her? just demonstrating her integrity is all ("Cloud Blood," "Freakshow") ★

Ani DiFranco: See also Utah Phillips

Digable Planets: *Reachin' (A New Refutation of Time and Space)* (Pendulum '93) The title's about escaping oppression and mortality, fleeing social madness and physical contingency into a spiritual realm of your own, and I say they get away clean. As the Godfather taught and the Planets agree—on "Escape-Ism" and "Escapism (Gettin' Free)," respectively—all music is escapist one way or another, a symbolic/sensual refuge no matter how cerebral, demanding, or hard to take. The test is the alternate reality it creates, and by exploiting the solid tunes and light feel of jazz from Sonny Rollins to Lonnie Liston Smith, these hip hop bohemians come up with a credible one. The airy delicacy of their sampled groove seems hyperreal in this pop context, transforming Butterfly and Doodlebug's weakness into wit and Ladybug's samba-like skippity-skip into a come-on that's equal parts sexuality and self-respect. The specific "Pacifics," about Sunday in New York, respects the literal here-and-now more observantly than any number of gat-filled street whoppers, and "La Femme Fétal," about Butterfly's conversation with a female friend, is the most humane, didactic, and politically informed prochoice song ever recorded. They could be in for some nasty moments if they expect full acceptance in the so-called hip hop community, but what can you do? Alternate on over here. **A**

Digable Planets: *Blowout Comb* (Pendulum/EMI '94) Their edge was music not attitude, vocals not words—they had 'em both, their fellow middle-class revolutionaries in Arrested Development didn't. So while the follow-up rhymes could be more down-to-earth, it's amazing how good they sound with a live band and limited samples—less jazzy, a loss, but still thick, warm, and smoove. They rap like themselves and no one else, and as skilled as the guys are, Ladybug is the genius, even putting across rap's most (nay, only) charming piece of sun-people demonology: "I'm 62 inches above sea level/Ninety-three million miles above these devils." **A–**

Digital Underground: "The Humpty Dance," "Doowutchyalike" (*Sex Packets,* Tommy Boy '90) 🐚
Digital Underground: *This Is an EP Release* (Tommy Boy, '91) There's no "Doowutchyalike" or "Humpty Dance" here, but those aren't true album cuts anyway; there's also no "Gutfest '89," the frat-boy fantasy about girls in cages that put the rest of *Sex Packets* beyond my ken until these remixes sent me back to compare and contrast. The hectic dissonances underneath the original "Sex Packets" jar the senses nicely, but I'll take the slick byplay of this laid-back in-your-face, which sets out to prove that funky doesn't mean hard. Nor is "Same Song" a novelty, baby brutha. And in case you're worried they're going quiet storm on you, Humpty Hump gets chicken grease on a young thing's pantyhose. **A–**

Digital Underground: *Sons of the P* (Tommy Boy '91) you can wear out the hard and the brother-brother-brother, but you can't wear out the cosmic slop ("The Dflo Shuffle," "Kiss You Back") ★★★
Digital Underground: *The Body-Hat Syndrome* (Tommy Boy, '93) After three tries, here's the P-Funk album of their destiny—tasteless, compassionate, uproarious, private, cultural. Given their frat-boy tendencies, maturity suits them—if you're going to tell tales on that special friend who ate peanut butter out of your asshole, it helps to compensate with sad, shocked reports from the front. The key is "Doo Woo You," in which a smooth freaky brother talks a woman into his bed and a white guy into his head simultaneously. **A–**
Digital Underground: *Who Got the Gravy?* (Jake '98) imparts new flavor, if not flava, to the word "lubricious" ("Who Got the Gravy?" "Wind Me Up," "The Odd Couple") ★★★

Henri Dikongué: *C'Est La Vie* (Tinder '98) A Camerounian who left law school in Paris for a pan-African theater troupe in the self-same city, this thoughtful songwriter and fluent guitarist is a hit in the genteel mold of Lokua Kanza and Geoffrey Oryema. He's what happens when Afropop becomes world music—when it targets broad-minded European connoisseurs rather than rhythm-schooled African sophisticates. In short, he's a folkie. But he's more rhythm-minded than most, rival Africans included, melding piano here and clave there into arrangements whose weave launches his plaintive tunes the way genteel beauty should. And when he sings declaratively, you believe he's saying something. **A–**
Henry Dikongué: *Wa* (Shanachie '99) 🎯

Leonard Dillon the Ethiopian: *On the Road Again* (Heartbeat '91) difficult love, endless sufferation, sweet-souled music ("On the Road Again," "One Step Forward," "Feed the Fire") ★★★

Dillon Fence: *Rosemary* (Mammoth '92) Sooner or later, "alternative" recycles everything. Including Pablo Cruise. **C–** 🦃

Dim Stars: *Dim Stars* (Caroline '92) Ⓝ

Dinosaur Jr.: *Fossils* (SST '91) best-of EP masquerading as singles comp, complete with fucked-up Frampton cover ("Just Like Heaven," "Little Furry Things") ★★★

Dinosaur Jr: *Green Mind* (Sire/Warner Bros. '91) J Mascis is a one-trick guitar god whose act gets sloppier and samier as his adolescence becomes more figurative. He does have his own instrumental sound, a roiling whine that's the essence of grunge on pot. Unfortunately, he also has his own vocal sound, ditto. Grunge's pothead contingent will adore him until he succumbs to male-pattern baldness. But someday archaeologists will wonder just exactly what was the point. I wonder now. B 🐢

Dinosaur Jr: *Whatever's Cool with Me* (Sire/Warner Bros. '91) Ⓝ

Dinosaur Jr: *Where You Been* (Sire/Warner Bros. '93) somehow his axe and his voice sing the same tune, momentarily transmuting self-pity into simple sadness ("Out There," "Start Choppin") ★★

Dinosaur Jr: *Without a Sound* (Sire/Warner Bros. '94) 🎸

Dinosaur Jr: *Hand It Over* (Reprise '97) 🎸

Celine Dion: *Celine Dion* (Epic '92) Montreal chanteuse goes gold Stateside, and I'm thinking, hey, North American Eurodisco for Anglophones, could be OK. Not hardly. Though the two Ric Wake productions lilt sweetly enough, she's a creature of the power ballad, with tympani all over her drum pads and Diane Warren hand-me-downs for hooks. Worst album of the year—that I can remember. D+ 🐢

Wasis Diop: *No Sant* (Triloka '96) 🎸

Dirty Three: *Horse Stories* (Touch and Go '96) 🎸

The Dismemberment Plan: *The Dismemberment Plan Is Terrified* (DeSoto '97) They're D.C. boys who sound sort of the way Primus might if Primus enjoyed a normal sex life. Not that they aren't frustrated; "The Ice of Boston" stands tall in the overcrowded canon of not-getting-laid songs. But their affective impulses are well-integrated, and they're bright and well-meaning enough that I'm here to assure them eros will give them a ride eventually. I know from the tunes, surprisingly thoughtful for posthardcore. And from the way the guitars and such come crashing down to break up a good party and set off a better one. A–

The Dismemberment Plan: *Emergency and I* (DeSoto '99) Hardcore's gotten confusing for oldsters; in these post-Fugazi days, a lot of it sounds like jazz. But it sure beats the folk-rock that used to sound like jazz. Here's a D.C. unit that convened in 1993 and made this third album on Interscope's dime during the merger mess. The only way they're punk anymore is that there aren't very many of them and that none of them seems to be playing keyboards even though most of them can. What they are instead is a much rarer thing, no matter what Ron Sexsmith and Richard Buckner pretend—bright, thoughtful, quirky, mercurial young adults skilled at transforming doubt into music. Tracking his feelings through irregular structures and jumpy rhythms, Travis Morrison is always lyrical, even celebratory—full of regrets like many honest men, but never ever a sad sack. A–

The Disposable Heroes of Hiphoprisy: *Hypocrisy Is the Greatest Luxury* (4th & B'way '92) As critics kvell, skeptics eye their p.c. quotient: black rapper with white adoptive parents and Asian American DJ who subsumes his racial analysis in an explicitly antihomophobic, antixenophobic leftism and allies himself with the Piss Christ and the Dead Kennedys. And for sure a few of the ideas are pat or simplistic and a few of the metaphors flat or anticlimatic ("politics is merely the decoy of perception"? wha?). But if Michael Franti is no Linton Kwesi Johnson, neither was LKJ at 25. His wordslinging isn't quite

Chuck D., subject of the ballsy imitation/ tribute/parody/critique "Hypocrisy Is the Greatest Luxury," but his intellectual grasp thrusts him immediately into pop's front rank—I'd put money on his thought quicker than Michael Stipe's or Michelle Shocked's, not to mention Richard Thompson's or Black Francis's. And then there's the DJ that isn't—with crucial help from Consolidated's Mark Pistel, industrial percussionist Rono Tse is a one-man hip hop band. He creates more music than he samples, stretching Bomb Squad parameters to carry the tracks whenever Franti falters. I'd like to think the two could penetrate right to hip hop's fragmented core. But if they never achieve full cultural resonance, their art will have to suffice. And it will. **A–**

Divinyls: "I Touch Myself" (*Divinyls,* Virgin '91) 💣
Divinyls: *Essential Divinyls* (Chrysalis '91) desperately seeking Hitsville ("Hey Little Boy," "Don't You Go Walking") ★★

Dixie Chicks: *Wide Open Spaces* (Monument '98) blondes have more brains (than they get credit for) ("Wide Open Spaces," "Give It Up [Or Let Me Go]") ★★
Dixie Chicks: *Fly* (Monument '99) unlike three virgins ("Goodbye Earl," "Sin Wagon," "Ready to Run") ★★★

DJ Clue?: *The Professional* (Roc-A-Fella/Def Jam '99) 🎸

DJ DMD and the Inner Soul Clique: *Twenty-Two: P.A. World Title* (Inner Soul/EastWest '99) Ⓝ

DJ Food: "The Dusk" (*Journeys by DJ: Coldcut* [comp], JDJ import '95) 💣

DJ Kool: *Let Me Clear My Throat* (American '96) just keeps on go going ("Let Me Clear My Throat," "Let Me Clear My Throat [Old School Reunion Remix '96]") ★★★

DJ Quik: *Quik Is the Name* (Profile '91) 🎸
DJ Quik: *Safe and Sound* (Profile '95) Ⓝ

DJ Shadow: *Endtroducing . . . DJ Shadow* (FFFR/Mo Wax '96) Armed with a sampler, a sequencer, and the black plastic he gave up trying to catalogue in 1989, 24-year-old Josh Davis of Davis, California, and London, England, distills everything he loves about drumbeats, symph-schlock, and oddball Americana into a 63-minute work with a beginning, a middle, and a to-be-continued. Some under a minute, some over nine, the 13 tracks are designed for headphones— Apollonian even if beat-driven, their only vocals spoken-word and comedy samples that accrue a mysterious fascination without ever revealing their relevance to each other or anything else. Except, that is, for the 30-second intro to the six-minute "Building Steam with a Grain of Salt," in which a square, self-taught drummer explains himself as a reassuring crackle attests to his vinyl authenticity down in the mix: "I'd like to just continue to be able to express myself as best as I can. And I feel like I'm a student of the drums. And I'm also a teacher." And then he chuckles nervously. And then Davis loops that chuckle for a second or two, making of it music and chaos and satire and self-mockery and music all at once. **A+**
DJ Shadow: *Preemptive Strike* (Mo Wax/FFRR '98) his best was better the first time ("In/Flux," "Organ Donor [Extended Overhaul]") ★

DJ Spooky: "Hologrammic Dub," "Anansi Abstrakt" (*Songs of a Dead Dreamer,* Asphodel '96) 💣
DJ Spooky: "Remix Sistrum" (*Drop Acid . . . Listen to This!!* [comp], Knitting Factory Works '97) 💣

DMX: "Ruff Ryders' Anthem," "Stop Being Greedy" (*It's Dark and Hell Is Hot,* Def Jam '98) 💣
DMX: *Flesh of My Flesh Blood of My Blood* (Def Jam '98) 🎸

DNA Featuring Suzanne Vega: "Tom's Diner" (*Tom's Album* [comp], A&M '91) 💣

D.O.A.: *Murder* (Restless '90) 🎸

Dr. Dooom: *First Come, First Served* (Funky Ass '99) Having offed porn junkie Dr. Octagon and bought some incense to hide the smell, Kool Keith's serial killer gets as funky as your bedmate's breath in the morning. Old tropes remain—ass cracks, organ damage, race baiting, second-level sports stars, claims of biz savvy. But though the beats remain electro, the slasher-movie shtick moves his buddies the Diesel Truckers to find out how low his production can go, including a hook that has Peter Lorre wheedling "I'm very hungry" again just when you thought it was safe to get back in the elevator. No rapper has ever imagined such disgusting apartments—lurid locales with fluorescent cereal on the floor. More than all the "body parts in shopping carts," it's the decor that puts the "fake gangsta hardcore stories" Dooom despises to shame. **A–**

Dr. Dre: *The Chronic* (Interscope '92) The crucial innovation of this benchmark album isn't its conscienceless naturalization of casual violence. It's Dre's escape from sampling. Other rappers, as they are called, have promised to create their own musical environments, usually without revealing how much art and how much publishing fuels their creative resolve. But Dre is the first to make the fantasy pay out big-time. The world he hears in his head isn't the up-to-date P-Funk fools say they hear—that would be too hard. Instead he lays bassline readymades under simulations of Bernie Worrell's high keyb sustain, a basically irritating sound that in context always signified fantasy, not reality—stoned self-loss or, at a best Dre never approaches, grandiose jive. This is bell-bottoms-and-Afros music, its spiritual source the blaxploitation soundtrack, and what it promises above all is boom times for third-rate flautists—sociopathic easy-listening. Even if it's "just pop music," as some rationalize, it's *bad* pop music. **C+** 🦃

Dr. Dre & Ice Cube: "Natural Born Killaz" (*Murder Was the Case* [ST], Death Row/Interscope '94) 💣

Dr. Israel: *Inna City Pressure* (Mutant Sound System '98) **N**

Dr. John: "Merry Christmas Baby" (*A Creole Christmas* [comp], Epic Associated '90) 💣

Dr. John: *Trippin' Live* (Surefire '97) for James Booker and Roy Byrd ("Tipitina," "Kin Folk") ★

Dr. Octagon: *Doctor Octagon* (Bulk '96) the shock horror! the shock horror! the perhaps authentically crazy! ("Earth People," "Wild and Crazy," "Introduction") ★

John Doe: *Meet John Doe* (DGC '90) 💣

Tim Dog: "Fuck Compton" (*Penicillin on Wax,* Ruffhouse/Columbia '92) 💣

Nate Dogg: "One More Day" (*Murder Was the Case* [ST], Death Row/Interscope '94) 💣

Swamp Dogg: *Surfin' in Harlem* (Volt '91) Afrocentricity with a middle-aged spread ("I've Never Been to Africa [And It's Your Fault]," "Appelle-Moi Noir") ★★★

Swamp Dogg: *Best of 25 Years of Swamp Dogg . . . Or F*** the Bomb, Stop the Drugs* (Pointblank '95) The title cut is brand-new, and so is the vintage-1955 theme song for his wife Yolanda, "Pledging My Love." The rest aren't. But like most Jerry Williams fans, I go way back with the guy, and damned if I can find half these songs in my shelves. Just as a for instance, where the hell is "I've Never Been to Africa (And It's Your Fault)," which sums up his worldview if anything does? So I guess the point is that nothing does—he's not only sui generis but completely contradictory, like most people, few of whom would think of writing 400 songs about it. By now his daring soul-rock hybrid is a studio convention, his big piercing voice arguably monochromatic. But between his wild takes on the ins and outs of the monogamy he lives for and his classic and cockamamy mix of political radicalism and cultural conservatism, this Afrocentric integrationist has written more interesting songs cruising in his cab than most tunesmiths manage in their luxury suites. Consistent? Never. In print? For the moment. Scarf it up now. **A–**

The Dogg Pound: *Dogg Food* (Death Row/Interscope '95) Ⓝ

Bo Dollis & the Wild Magnolias: See the Wild Magnolias

Domino: *Domino* (Outburst '93) Ⓝ
Domino: "Sport That Raincoat" (*America Is Dying Slowly* [comp], Red Hot '96) 👁

Tanya Donelly: *Lovesongs for Underdogs* (Reprise '97) 💣

The Donnas: *American Teenage Rock 'n' Roll Machine* (Lookout! '98) Ⓝ
The Donnas: *Get Skintight* (Lookout! '99) Teen life as teen combat, with tunes and sexual content both revved up, which synergy is the only form maturity can (as yet) take with these Bay Area molls. If more young females had a purchase on the scornful independence the Donnas transform into fun, this act might actually pose role-model problems. Let's just hope it'll loom larger in the fantasy lives of shy girls than of dirty young men. Because fun it is. **A–**

Nahawa Doumbia: *Didadi* (Shanachie '90) Ⓝ
Nahawa Doumbia: *Mangoni* (Stern's Africa '93) synths, koras, whatever—it's slow, it's impassioned, it's pop, it's from Mali ("Galoya") ★

The Dove Shack: *This Is the Shack* (Def Jam/RAL '95) Lazing around in Warren G's groove without making a pass at his tragic sense of life, these hangers-on would be yawns if they weren't the ugliest sexists to make a three-week splash all year. Although the hatred is everywhere, it's most painful on an early "skit"-song-"skit" triptych: "The Train" (a backslapper about gang rape in the dark), "Fuck Ya Mouth" ("To all our hookers and hos"), and "Slap a Hoe" (a device invented for punks too yellow to do the job themselves). Heaven forfend the rappers actually doing any of these things, except maybe buy a Slap-a-Hoe—this isn't advocacy, it's constitutionally protected representation, harrumph. What I don't understand is why anyone who doesn't hate women is outraged when C. Delores Tucker goes just as far overboard in response. If they understand when self-serving black men express themselves in these, harrumph, metaphors, why don't they understand when self-serving black women counterattack by any means necessary? **C+**

Johnny Dowd: *Wrong Side of Memphis* (Checkered Past '97) The vita that marks this middle-aged Ithaca moving man as a genuwine everyman reduces just as readily to boho-with-a-day-job, and lest you look down on him he's careful to stick an "existential" into the one about the "Average Guy," so-called. When he finds "tender love," his tropes pick up considerable—"Like beans and rice she's a total plateful," nice and homely. But soon it's back to murder and misery in the dismal swamp quote unquote, with malnourished blues to match. Gangsta folk—not only are the stories old hat, the beats suck. **B–** 🦃

Downtown Science: *Downtown Science* (Def Jam/Columbia '91) "I could have went to Yale but I wasn't accepted/ You know why?/I didn't apply." Deep, linear, never in a hurry, Sam Sever's grooves are as simple and inexorable as War, whose time is coming. Intelligent, confident, in love with words and the world, Bosco Money's rhymes assume a humanism too natural to preach about. The raps aren't especially unmacho or correct—in fact, you might say they're beyond attitude. So it's possible they're not macho or incorrect enough to get over. That would be tragic. **A–**

Dramarama: *Live at the China Club* (Chameleon '90) This bargain EP exploitation includes: three selections from the unblemished *Cinéma Vérité* and *Box Office Bomb,* the two finest songs from the spotty *Stuck in Wonderamaland,* and a non-LP B side exhibiting an abandon appropriate to both a Dolls cover and post-punk performance philosophy. It's only a live holding action, and let's hope the writing returns to form. But now everybody who began with *Wonderamaland* knows how much form they have to return to. **B+**

Dramarama: *Vinyl* (Chameleon '91) Their existential confusion goes global, especially with the nonprotest protest of "What Are We Gonna Do?" But as they burst upon the world after a maturing process without a public history, I'm sorry, they're a touch too slow. And long—the three six-minute jobs sink them in the very ponderousness skewered by the four-minute "Classic Rot." Not a very vinyl length, six minutes—especially in songs that might be as sharp as the rest speeded up and cut down. **B+**

Dramarama: *Hi-Fi Sci-Fi* (Chameleon '93) Although "Incredible" uses the present tense to hail the perfect love of younger days—she smokes his brand of cigs and runs up a $12.37 electric bill ("our great expense") because (the historicizing clincher) she never turns off the radio—the bloody snot and lost year of "Prayer" and "I Don't Feel Like Doing Drugs" suggest yet more maturity. What's confusing, and a stroke, is that with Clem Burke pounding the skins and the band mixing and matching, it rocks louder, harder, and faster than anything they've done since going pro—or ever. Assuming the content is autobiographical, which given John Easdale's gift for covering his tracks is only a conceit, this makes it the best just-say-no advert since "Tonight's the Night." Neil's, not Rod's, and you'd best believe pop polymath Easdale knows and admires both but prefers to evoke Neil, whose sister does a backup turn. He also lifts "Prayer" from "Search and Destroy." **A–**

Dramarama: *The Best of Dramarama: 18 Big Ones* (Elektra Traditions '96) Imagine John Easdale as a cross between Richard Butler (P-Furs, fame fades) and Elliott Murphy (referenced in the notes, best on his 1973 debut *Aqua-*

show), only (a) a fan first and (b) less rich than either. A beautiful loser manqué in music for love—lucky for him he's got the tunes. If this sounds beguiling and you've never heard his finest album—the 1984 debut *Cinéma Vérité* (although his later efforts sure topped Murphy's)—this will tempt you to give it a try. **A–**

Dread Zeppelin: "All I Want for Christmas Is My Two Front Teeth" (*Just in Time for Christmas* [comp], I.R.S. '90) 🐟

Dreams Come True: *Dreams Come True* (Antone's '90) Wrapping her warm, slinky voice around lyrics borrowed and dreamed up, Marcia Ball earns top billing in this ad hoc Austin blues trio. Lou Ann Barton, a professional tramp who's done her share of rehab, and Angela Strehli, a sensible sort who runs the label, must have figured it would be neighborly to help their old pal turn in a decent follow-up to *Soulful Dress,* which is eight years old now. Sure they did—they love each other like Ike and Tina, whose "A Fool in Love" they covered to initiate this mission impossible in 1985. Congratulations to coordinator-bassist Sarah Brown for getting a record out of them, and to producer-pianist Dr. John for easing it up toward the sum of its parts. **A–**

Dream Warriors: *And Now the Legacy Begins* (4th & B'way '91) West Indian daisy age from boogie-down Toronto ("Ludi," "My Definition of a Boombastic Jazz Style") ★★★

Dream Warriors: *Anthology: A Decade of Hits 1988–1998* (Priority '99) Once these black Canadians put out a well-liked album that missed the tail end of daisy age. Then they vanished. Gang Starr and Digable Planets connections got their next CD a token U.S. release, but the one after was strictly commonwealth—as far as the south-of-the-border rap community was concerned, King Lu and Capital Q no longer existed. So maybe nobody told them that you claim street no matter how middle-class you are, that jazz samples were a doomed fad, that Digable Planets blinked out faster than the evening star. And maybe that was good. Probably it didn't feel like that to them; one of their best songs is called "I've Lost My Ignorance," and I'm sure the disillusion hurt. But though their inspiration wanes slightly, they never surrender their thoughtful intricacy or raceman lyricism. Certainly they belong in the same sentence as De La Soul and A Tribe Called Quest. And "Test of Purity" is the best song about nasty sex a nasty music has ever produced—in part because it's so explicit, in part because it's so imaginative, in part because it's so kind. **A–**

Drive-by Truckers: *Pizza Deliverance* (Soul Wax '99) Rockers playing sortacountry with rough enthusiasm and nothing like a sound, they make their mark detailing the semivoluntary poverty DIY musicians share with the highly subsuburban constituency they imagine. These are people who'd love to have more money, shit yes, but don't know the first thing about kissing ass, people who think sixpacks are necessities of life and Dixie Chicks CDs aren't. So they fuck up as a life principle and then write or listen to songs about it—songs about getting loaded and screwing your sister-in-law, about shooting that lady at the laundromat who stole your sock. About fucking up just like your daddy. About G. G. Allin changing your life, never mind exactly how. **A–**

Dru Hill: *Dru Hill* (Island '96) 💣

Lucky Dube: *Victims* (Shanachie '93) 💣

Dulce & Orchestra Marrabenta Star de Mozambique: "Tsiketa Kuni Barassara" (*Women of Africa* [comp], CSA import '90) (CC)

Francis Dunnery: *Tall Blonde Helicopter* (Atlantic '95) Bob Geldof with no pretensions, no investments, and a pickup band ("Too Much Saturn," "I Believe I Can Change My World") ★

Champion Jack Dupree: *Forever and Ever* (Bullseye Blues '92) On the label de-

but of this long-exiled songster-pianist, the Rounder folks worked session men, thematic material, and MLK rumination into a standard Crescent City hustle, sending the roots claque into paroxysms of approbation. Here the quality control board lets up some, with results that seem far more personal and overheard—a dirty old man in fine fettle entertaining the room. And for sure his age is part of the charm. When an 82-year-old can sing the blues about how his family gave him away when he was one, you know his shtick has staying power. **A–**

Champion Jack Dupree: *One Last Time* (Bullseye Blues '93) the boys in the band listen like it's their last chance ("Bad Blood," "School Days") ★

Jermaine Dupri: *Life in 1472* (So So Def '98) why hoochies give coochie ("Get Your Shit Right," "All That's Got to Go") ★

Ian Dury & the Blockheads: *Mr. Love Pants* (Ronnie Harris import '98) Mr. Smarty Pants mocks meritocracy and enjoys his body ("Jack Shit George," "Geraldine") ★★★

Dust Devils: *Geek Drip* (Matador '90) Ⓝ

Bob Dylan: *Under the Red Sky* (Columbia '90) This Was Bros. pseudothrowaway improves on the hushed emotion, weary wisdom, and New Age "maturity" of the Daniel Lanois–produced *Oh Mercy* even if the lyrics are sloppier—the anomaly is what Lanois calls *Oh Mercy*'s "focused" writing. Aiming frankly for the evocative, the fabulistic, the biblical, Dylan exploits narrative metaphor as an adaptive mechanism that allows him to inhabit a "mature" pessimism he knows isn't the meaning of life. Where his seminal folk-rock records were cut with Nashville cats on drums—Kenny Buttrey when he was lucky, nonentities when he wasn't—here Kenny Aronoff's tempos are postpunk like it oughta be, springs and shuffles grooving ever forward. The fables are strengthened by the workout, and as a realist I also treasure their literal moments. I credit his outrage without forgetting his royalty statements. I believe he's gritted his teeth through the bad patches of a long-term sexual relationship. And when he thanks his honey for that cup of tea, I melt. **A–**

Bob Dylan: *The Bootleg Series Volumes 1–3 (Rare and Unreleased) 1961–1991* (Columbia '91) Dylanology—the thinking man's philately ("Catfish," "It Takes a Lot to Laugh, It Takes a Train to Cry," "Blind Willie McTell," "Quit Your Low Down Ways," "Call Letter Blues," "Last Thoughts on Woody Guthrie") ★★

Bob Dylan *Good As I Been to You* (Columbia '92) Dylan's last cover album confused his followers mightily, not least because he called it *Self-Portrait.* And maybe he tossed this one off as per contract too—his boyish tenor and nimble acoustic guitar don't rescue "Frankie and Albert" or "Sittin' on Top of the World" from the taxidermist, and though "Tomorrow Night" could be a mean parody of Lonnie Johnson's sour-voiced original, it probably just sucks. But most of these old tunes he gooses or caresses to some kind of arousal—he clearly knows the sensitive spots of Stephen Foster's "Hard Times" and the antiredcoat jig "Arthur McBride." Not that he thinks such intimacy yields a self-portrait. Older than that now, he merely explores a world of song whose commonness and strangeness he knows he'll never comprehend. **B+**

Bob Dylan: *World Gone Wrong* (Columbia '93) Dylan's second attempt to revive the folk music revival while laying down a new record without writing any new songs is eerie and enticing. He cherishes the non sequiturs, sudden changes of heart, and received or obscure blank spots in these buried songs—all usages he's long since absorbed into his own writing because he believes they evoke a world that defies rationalization. Me, I'm not so sure it doesn't just seem that way because there's no way we can be intimate with *their* worlds anymore. And while only a crank could resist his liner notes, that doesn't mean it isn't cranky in the extreme to hold, for instance, that the two-timing aristo who gets his in "Love

Henry" is "modern corporate man off some foreign boat, unable to handle his 'psychosis' responsible for organizing the Intelligentsia," *und so weiter.* We do not live in "the New Dark Ages." And if we did, Dylan would call out for rationalization right quick. **A–**

Bob Dylan: *Greatest Hits Volume 3* (Columbia '94) He can climax with "Knockin' on Heaven's Door" if he wants—*Pat Garrett and Billy the Kid* is a piece of crap, the song a work of genius, which is the basic idea on this living testament to random forethought. But shaggy dog story or no shaggy dog story, "Tangled Up in Blue" doesn't belong, and neither does that supernal piece of crap "Forever Young," because both are classic tracks from albums that precede Rolling Thunder and *Desire,* events that marked his epochal commitment to hackdom even if no one dreamed it at the time. On 14 cuts employing 57 session musicians, four of whom appear twice and none thrice, this collection celebrates that commitment. Its sonic trademark is the soulettes who underpin "Changing of the Guards" (*Street Legal,* 1978), "The Groom's Still Waiting at the Altar" (*Shot of Love,* 1981), "Silvio" (*Down in the Groove,* 1988), and the magnificent 11-minute Sam Shepard collaboration "Brownsville Girl" (*Knocked Out Loaded,* 1986)—all obscure, all compelling, all cockeyed flights of prophecy or mythic narrative, and all featuring the backup pipes of Carol (sometimes Carolyn) Dennis, who I bet has been feeding him lines for two lost decades. **B+**

Bob Dylan: *Unplugged* (Columbia '95) excellent songs pronounced with gratifying clarity ("Knockin' on Heaven's Door," "Dignity") ★

Bob Dylan: *Time Out of Mind* (Columbia '97) A soundscape as surely as *Maxinquaye* or *The Ballad of Tom Joad,* only more tuneful and less depressive—that is, merely bereft rather than devoid of affect or will. Lyrically, it splits the difference between generalized El Lay schlock and minor Child ballad; a typical couplet goes,

"You left me standing in the doorway crying/In the dark land of the sun." So the words are good enough except on the Billy Joel–covered "Make You Feel My Love," yet seldom what you come back for. The hooks are Dylan's spectral vocals—just his latest ventriloquist's trick, a new take on ancient, yet so real, so ordained—and a band whose quietude evokes the sleepy postjunk funk of Clapton's *461 Ocean Boulevard* without the nearness of sex. Special kudos to Augie Meyers, the Al Kooper we've been waiting for. **A–**

Bob Dylan: *Live 1966* (Columbia/ Legacy '98) What no one ever mentions about this legendary Manchester concert is that the folk set stinks. It's arty, mannered, nervous, as if Dylan is sick of these songs, although three of the seven haven't even been released yet. And when they are, on *Blonde on Blonde,* they'll be band- if not Band-backed like all the others except "Mr. Tambourine Man," and as such relaxed, confident, committed, *meaningful.* Appallingly ideological though it is that anyone could have preferred this static display to what followed, the rock set is warmly received. This is not to say, however, that it lives up to its myth. You'll hear some of the most freewheeling, locked-in live music of the '60s—far more detailed and responsive than comparable Stones or Who, with Robbie Robertson so cockeyed funky he almost careens off the stage. You'll also hear some folkie fool shouting "Judas" and Dylan calling him a liar and, if you strain, somebody muttering "play fucking loud." But you will not hear the times a-changin' or Robert Zimmerman jousting with destiny. That stuff's for historians. And if we owe the historians for a terrific electric disc, they owe us for the awful acoustic one. **B+**

D/COMPILATIONS

Chuck D Presents Louder Than a Bomb (Rhino '99) exhortations and commonplaces, old school style (Common Sense, "I Used to Love H.E.R. [Radio Edit]"; Ice Cube, "A Bird in the Hand") ★★★

Dada Kidawa/Sister Kidawa (Original Music '95) more '60s dance hits from Tanzania, which improve as they Congo-Cubanize (Njohole Jazz Band, "Mpenzi Zaina"; Dares Salaam Jazz Band, "Mpenzi Sema") ★★

Dancehall Stylee: The Best of Reggae Dancehall Music Vol. 4 (Profile '93) As if to prove Jamaica isn't totally overrun by electric percussion and macho bwoys grunting about guns and punany, this comp centers on two winsome pieces of lover's rock, one male and one female. It also makes room for numerous melody instruments, most of them saxophones repeating phrases you'll want to hear again (and will). For all I know, hardcore dancehall users will find it, to employ an expression current in my country, soft. But old reggae heads who can't be bothered distinguishing between Buju Banton and Wu-Tang Clan can start here. **A–**

Dance Hits U.K. (Moonshine Music '94) Only a hardcore club kid with connections could tell you what kind of "hits" these were, if any. I don't care because strung together they pass the sole test of a hedonistic disposable, which is personal—they do it for me. I surmise that continuous mixer DJ Tall Paul Newman splits the difference between house and jungle, favoring strong, postmechanical grooves with avant breaks and Snappy pseudorap like Tin Tin's "The Feeling" and his own "Rock Da House." Toward the end mere grooves take over; toward the end I stop shouting out hooks from my living room. **A–**

Dangerhouse: Volume One (Frontier '91) L.A. circa 1977—let's get rid of *everything* (Randoms, "Let's Get Rid of NY"; Howard Werth, "Obsolete") ★★

Dazed and Confused (Medicine '93) But it's really great junk. Seventies AOR as hard-rock utopia, with all the El Lay wimp-out, boogie dumb-ass, and metal drudge-trudge surreptitiously excised, enabling the escapist to bask in history without actually encountering any Montrose or Outlaws records. A few of the selections are ringers—unjustly, neither the Sweet's "Fox on the Run" (too pop) nor the Runaways' "Cherry Bomb" (too chick) ever gained much stoner credibility. Most are by major artists (Skynyrd, War, Alice Cooper, ZZ Top) or indisputable legends (Sabbath, Kiss, Deep Purple, Ted Nugent). But only someone who suffered his first nocturnal emission between 1970 and 1975 will be motivated to collect the catalogue it implies. For the rest of humanity, this is an ideal way to enjoy what for all its high volume, guitar excess, and muddled longueurs remained a pop sensibility that harked back to the '50s. Jim Dandy to the rescue indeed. **A–**

Deadicated (Arista '91) 💣

Dead Man Walking (Columbia '95) Ⓝ

Deep Blues (Atlantic '92) Mississippi jook music today (R. L. Burnside, "Jumper on the Line"; Big Daddy Johnson, "Daddy, When Is Momma Coming Home") ★

Detroit: Beyond the Third Wave (Astralwerks '96) Ⓝ

Diggin' in the Crates: Profile Rap Classics Volume One (Profile '94): linear beatbox fantasias, no fresher or sillier now than they were then (Rammelzee Vs. K-Rob, "Beat Bop"; Word of Mouth Featuring D. J. Cheese, "King Kut") ★★

The Disco Years, Vol. 1: Turn the Beat Around (1974–1978) (Rhino '90) With its beatwise hooks, generic soul, and cheap orchestral effects, disco was the great singles music of the '70s, finally ripe for rediscovery unimpeded by the territorial imperatives of individual labels. Compiler Ken Barnes tries to stick in some bad records, for history's sake. But though only "Shame, Shame, Shame" could qualify for volume two's "Ring My Bell"-"I Will Survive"-"Ain't No Stoppin' Us Now" run, Andrea True and Peter Brown are commercial crap like it oughta be, and

once "The Hustle" makes its statement the hits just keep coming on, untouched by electro blandout. Seven songs here went number one, and all four non-top-10 choices belong. Travails that touch the heart, relieved by the phony good cheer that makes life worth living. **A**

The Disco Years, Vol. 2: On the Beat (1978–1981) (Rhino '90) I know that (a) it never really died and (b) if it did it was killed by rockist philistines and the homophobic media. So basically this is a fairly ace singles comp. But since formal exhaustion happens, and so does commercial exploitation, disco does begin to suck a little here. Case in point: Lipps, Inc.'s "Funkytown," a better-than-average novelty record so brittle that to place it up against the magnificently novel "Ring My Bell" is to tempt the wrath of the gods. So let it be noted that two of Rhino's evil "CD bonus tracks" (by GQ and the B.B.&Q. Band) are so bland that I'm tempted to recommend the cassette. Best novelty sound: the flushing toilet of Indeep's "Last Night a D.J. Saved my Life"—one more proof of the inexhaustibility of human ingenuity and human chutzpah. **A–**

The Disco Years, Vol. 4: Lost in Music (Rhino '92) The first two volumes were so brilliant that too much of a good thing was sure to follow. Keyed to the dumber-than-ever "Rock the Boat" and "Boogie Fever," volume three is obvious when it's listenable at all; volume five at least re-exposes obscurities on the order of Secret Weapon's "Must Be the Music," Hot Chocolate's "Mindless Boogie," and Cheryl Lynn's mad, shrieking "Star Love." But this sharply conceived anthology transcends hodgepodge by tracing Chic's influence on the music of disco's deformularized commercial decline. Ken Barnes is right, damn it—not only did Rodgers and Edwards inspire rips like René & Angela's "I Love You More" and imitations like Change, they also created the market that would dance to experiments like the Peech Boys' "Don't Make Me Wait" and C-Bank's "One More Shot." And as producers they were auteurs from Nile's impossible coda on

Norma Jean's "I Like Love" to Diana Ross's single-entendre "I'm Coming Out" to Sister Sledge's uncoverable title tune—which tunnels deeper into club life than anything Elvis Costello ever wrote, and which wouldn't mean a thing without Nile and 'Nard sucking us in. **A–**

Divas of Mali (Shanachie '96) voices of authority (Sali Sidibe, "Yacouba Sylla"; Dandia Kouyate, "Jakha") ★★★

DJ Red Alert's Propmaster Dancehall Show (Epic Street '93) 💣

Drive Me Crazy (Jive '99) The time was right, so here it is—a concept album about teenpop. You get shameless, obvious, brilliant remixes on Britney (new jack title track) and BSB ("I Want It That Way" as cheese house). You get two excellent songs about how prefab teenpop is (by Barenaked Ladies and Silage, which means—I looked it up—"fodder converted into succulent feed"). You get an "I Want You Back" rip that reaffirms teenpop's inimitability. You get the Donnas proving they're whores by playing wholesome teenagers. You get Matthew Sweet sounding like an old man. You get Jive's next big push, Steps, who I hope trip, and great lost tracks by Plumb (?) and Mukala (not African, I don't think). And of course you get filler. **B+**

Dublin to Dakar: A Celtic Odyssey (Putamayo World Music '99) 💣

Sheila E.: *Sex Cymbal* (Warner Bros. '91)

Eagles: *Hell Freezes Over* (Giant '94)

Steve Earle: *Train A Comin'* (Winter Harvest '95) When the vernacular flows easy or sounds that way, a rare thing, five wives and enough heroin to destroy a saner man are the kind of myth rock and roll fools are always mistaking for reality. And clean though Earle may be, he's not above or beyond embracing that myth— among his latest celebrations of romantic dysfunction is one where he all but dares the object of his obsession to call the cops. Better the laconic narratives and pipeline to the great American tune clusters of this alternative offering, a trad reimmersion with Norman Blake and Peter Rowan picking mandolins and dobros as Earle dredges up songs by his fine young self. "Tom Ames' Prayer" and "Hometown Blues," from '76 and '77, are as undeniable as any Earle this side of "The Devil's Right Hand." And so are "Angel Is the Devil" and "Ben McCulloch," from '92 and '95. **A–**

Steve Earle: *I Feel Alright* (Warner Bros. '96) demands its own Grammy category: Best Use of Outlaw Pathology in a Roots-Rock Setting ("South Nashville Blues," "CCKMP," "More Than I Can Do") ★★★

Steve Earle: *El Corazón* (Warner Bros. '97) Earle writes with the flair and searching eye of a great talker who's also a great reader, and he can sing with anyone—on *The Songs of Jimmie Rodgers,* his dissolute "In the Jailhouse Now" keeps the ball rolling after two of the canniest vocals of Bob Dylan's and Willie Nelson's not exactly thoughtless careers. But now that he's sober he sounds drunker than ever, recalling the blurry, lost-my-dentures drawl of John Prine at his cutest. And since unlike Prine he doesn't take naturally to cute, his back-porch sentimentality can seem as unearned as any folk revivalist's; when he reflects too much, as is his current spiritual wont, he proves that the only thing softer than a tough guy's heart of gold is a populist radical's *corazón sangriento.* While hoping the born-to-lose sex problems of his rock comeback are behind him, I still find his fast ones more convincing than his slow ones. **A–**

Steve Earle and the Del McCoury Band: *The Mountain* (E Squared '99) With bluegrass "more comfortable all the time," the sometime country-rocker turns in his strongest and loosest record of the decade. But bluegrass it ain't—it's too comfortable. I was so impressed with how the music moaned and shivered and flapped around in the wind I wondered how I'd ever overlooked McCoury's outfit until I played their new CD, which is just as clean and tight and anal as every other spoor of Bill Monroe I've ever swept out the door. Slurring like a moonshiner who's been on a mush diet since his bird dog died, Earle rowdies up McCoury's sharpsters till they turn all hairy and bounce off

---

★★★, ★★, ★ Honorable Mention   🐢 Choice Cut   ◐ Neither   💣 Dud   🦃 Turkey

walls like the Pogues. And though the songs are less literary, more generic—blues and breakdown, "pinko folk song" and "real-live-bad-tooth hillbilly murder ballad"—literature is Earle's critical selling point. His stories always sing. **A–**

John Easdale: *Bright Side* (Harvey '98) Ⓝ

East River Pipe: *The Gasoline Age* (Merge '99) road songs for insomniacs just driving around ("Down 42nd Street to the Light," "Cybercar") ★★

EC80R: *World Beaters* (DHR '98) 💣

Eek-a-Mouse: *U-Neek* (Peace Posse '91) Ⓝ

Eels: *Beautiful Freak* (DreamWorks '96) 💣

Eels: *Electro-Shock Blues* (Dream-Works '98) Mark Everett is a talented 31-year-old who bravely determined to deal with the dying he's seen in song. But that didn't mean he had to make a concept album. Beyond art-rock fashion, which has rendered the static song cycle stupid-fresh again, the strategy suits a detachment he'd be drawn to in any era, a detachment that's devoid of charm—which also goes for the concept it hides behind, baggage doubly distracting for consumers without a press kit. I count three excellent songs here—a plighted troth, a teen memory, and an unexpected flight in which Everett invites one of his deceased back for a last look. I sincerely hope they're all covered by singers who can show them the love they deserve. **B** 🦃

Marty Ehrlich: "The Short Circle in the Long Line" (*The Traveller's Tale*, Enja '90) 🐦

Elastica: "Spastica" (*Connection*, Deception import '94) 🐦
Elastica: "Rockundroll" (*Stutter*, DGC '94) 🐦
Elastica: *Elastica* (DGC '95) Punk-pop as self-consciously noncanonical market ploy, wound tight as a methedrine high. The Buzzcocks weren't deep, Wire wasn't

deep, but these sassy London girls are shallow on principle, accentuating the desperation of a fun they refuse to grant any emotional resonance. I love their bright, tough veneer and hectic sexuality. I'll happily get juiced on their quick charge. And I can imagine myself discarding them without a second thought. After all, they're asking for it. **A–**

Electric Angels: *Electric Angels* (Atlantic '90) 💣

Eleventh Dream Day: *Lived to Tell* (Atlantic '91) A notable guitar sound evolves into an undeniable band sound, roots/trad sonics (steel and slide under lead) and rhythms (buried hints of r&b strut and shuffle) just barely keeping their balance as Janet Bean (she drums, she writes, she sings tail ends and revs them up) punkrushes the show. Doesn't really matter that headman Rick Rizzo's vocals are strong-that's-all and Bob Dylan is too much with them—"It's All a Game" 's fed-up get-it-together and "Daedalus"'s dippy dream notwithstanding, these songs don't signify as songs but as music. The band's alternative pigeonhole proves AOR guys are scared witless of rocking out. And its anomalous clubland profile typifies an aesthetic fallacy that long preceded the naming of postmodernism. Really, folks, irony isn't the way, the truth, and the life. It's just hard to avoid a lot of the time. So don't cast aspersions on their sincerity. They're just doing what comes naturally. **A–**

Eleventh Dream Day: *El Moodio* (Atlantic '93) postpomo guitar heroes—not quite smart enough to be slow ("Makin' Like a Rug," "That's the Point") ★★★

Missy Misdemeanor Elliott: *Supa Dupa Fly* (The Gold Mind, Inc./EastWest '97) Like a lot of young black pop artists, Missy deals in aural aura rather than song, which means that even after you connect—as I did with "Izzy Izzy Ahh" well before "The Rain" hit MTV—she can take a while to absorb. Innovative though it is, the video obscures the musical originality of "The Rain," its spacing and layering simultaneously sparer and busier than anything ordinarily allowed on the radio, and without Ann Peebles hooking you in, the rest of the album poses the same kind of congenial challenge. Sooner or later its pleasantness reveals itself as erotic—explicitly sexual enough to establish an atmosphere in which pleasure is something that happens simply and spontaneously between friendly free agents. There's no sense of conquest or surrender, humiliation or ecstasy or sin. It's summertime, and the living is easy. **A–**

Missy Misdemeanor Elliott: *Da Real World* (The Gold Mind, Inc./EastWest '99) no more Missy Nice Girl ("Busa Rhyme," "Smooth Chick") ★★★

Ramblin' Jack Elliott: *Friends of Mine* (HighTone '98) hootenannies, they useta call 'em ("Walls of Red Wing," "Me and Billy the Kid") ★

Joe Ely: *Live at Liberty Lunch* (MCA '90) not country, not rock and roll—rock ("Me and Billy the Kid") ★★
Joe Ely: *Love and Danger* (MCA '92) As these things are now measured, he's finally a country artist—a good one. You can tell by the way Tony Brown stops him from oversinging. By the way he lays into the similes on "Sleepless in Love" and the rhymes on "She Collected." By the way he writes nothing but love songs, including two stinkers. By the way Robert Earl Keen furnishes mythos and memories without filling Butch Hancock's shoes. **B+**
Joe Ely: *Letter to Laredo* (MCA '95) Ⓝ
Joe Ely: *Twistin' in the Wind* (MCA '98) Ⓝ

Embrace: *The Good Will Out* (DGC '98) 💣

EMF: *Schubert Dip* (EMI '91) The variations these self-made airheads work on their catchy tune rarely deliver anything heavier than a hook beat. At least the New Kids know there's a difference between fresh and callow. **C+** 🦃

Eminem: *The Slim Shady LP* (Aftermath/Interscope '99) Pundits who believe kids are naive enough to take this record literally are right to fear them, because they're the kind of adult teenagers hate. Daring moralizers to go on the attack while explicitly—but not (fuck you, dickwad) unambiguously—declaring itself a satiric, cautionary fiction, this cause celebre runs short on ideas only toward the end, when Dre's whiteboy turns provocation into the dull sensationalism fools think is his whole story. Over an hour his cadence gets wearing too. But he flat-out loves to rhyme—"seizure"/"T-shirt," "eyeballs"/"Lysol"/"my fault," "BM"/"GM"/"be him"/"Tylenol PM"/"coliseum," "Mike D"/"might be"—and you have to love the way he slips in sotto voce asides from innocent bystanders. Sticking nine-inch nails through his eyelids, flattening a black bully with a four-inch broom, reminding his conscience/producer about Dee Barnes, watching helplessly as an abused Valley Girl OD's on his shrooms, cajoling his baby daughter Hailey into helping him get rid of her mom's body, he shows more comic genius than any pop musician since—London Wainwright III? **A–**

Enigma: *MCMXC a.D.* (Charisma '90) On the hit, mellow electrobeat and Gregorian fog provide mutual relief, and the rest of this disco for Camille P. is filler. Some Amurricans think a whispered "*Je te desire*" is por . . . er, erotic—*sexy*! I've always preferred "I wanna fuck you" myself. **C–** 🦃

Brian Eno: *Nerve Net* (Opal/Warner Bros. '92) 💣
Brian Eno: *The Drop* (Thirsty Ear '97) Ever the bullshitter, the St. Petersburg (Russia) muso cites as influences Me'Shell NdegéOcello, Fela, and the Mahavishnu Orchestra, and as an admirer of all three I only wish I could hear the way musos hear. To me it sounds like he got stuck between *Music for Airports* and *Wrong Way Up* and spun his hard drive for 74 minutes. He hears melodies whose

vagueness he extols, I hear vaguenesses whose attenuation I rue. He hears basslines, I hear tinkle. He hears "sourness," I hear more tinkle. **C** 🦃

Eno/Cale: *Wrong Way Up* (Opal/Warner Bros. '90) After years of big-money production jobs and New Age environments, we know Eno for a middle-brow dabbler—no longer can he dazzle us with unpretentious impassivity. And if his return to song form seems too easy, well, maybe it was. Nevertheless, this sea of permutation is the follow-up *Another Green World* deserved. He's been synthesizing rhythms so long he makes them sound organic—we get not only world-beat echoes but the soul shuffle his singing is now up to. As for the other guy, he hasn't sounded so sure of his ground since he played second fiddle to Lou Reed. **A–**

En Vogue: *Born to Sing* (EastWest '90) Ⓝ
En Vogue: *Funky Divas* (EastWest '92) three years after the audition, they still don't cohere enough to let the songs quit ("My Lovin' [You're Never Gonna Get It]," "Giving Him Something He Can Feel," "Free Your Mind") ★★★

En Vogue: *Runaway Love* (Atlantic '92) As a mere admirer of *Funky Divas,* I prefer this stopgap EP's techno "What Is Love," rap "Hip Hop Lover," and dancehall "Desire." Qua song, "Runaway Love" cuts any of them. And Salt-n-Pepa's "Whatta Man" is the second catchiest and first funkiest thing they've ever put their larynxes on. Backup singing may not be their vocation, but they can always pay the bills with it. **A–**

En Vogue: *EV3* (EastWest '97) Sylvia Rhone isn't gonna pull the plug on her copyright just because Dawn Robinson has decided she's the reason for her own success. So with yeomanlike help from Babyface, the label has laboriously extracted a hit and some platinum from Rhone's three remaining charges as they strain for soul and funk as stagily and dutifully as the fabricated bevy of talent-hunt beauties they've always been. Sole exception: the Robinson-led *Set It Off* smash "Don't Let Go (Love)." There's a lesson in that, right? Only what will that lesson be when Robinson's debut does the dog? **B–** 🦃

En Vogue: *Best of En Vogue* (EastWest '99) By way of the crass product advisory they deserve, let the record show that 1992's *Funky Divas* captures their cultural moment and this one beats it song for song, including mild pleasantries from their undistinguished debut and adieu. Say ciao to the queens of air-kiss soul. **B+**

EPMD: *Business as Usual* (Def Jam/RAL/Columbia '91) Once they were winning wannabes stealing pop hooks in the basement. Now they're big-time, as rappers measure such things, and for all the difference it makes in general humanity they might as well have gotten there selling crack. Ugly as the Geto Boys and a lot dumber, the cross-dressing tale "Jane 3" climaxes with the rape she deserves; elsewhere the rhymes run three bozacks and three criminal-mindeds to one Mandela/Farrakhan. Who cares whether they're truly street or just following hard fashion? How many dope beats does the world need? **C+** 🦃
EPMD: *Business Never Personal* (RAL/Chaos/Columbia '92) 💣

Erasure: *Pop! The First 20 Hits* (Sire/Reprise '92) 💣

Roky Erickson: *You're Gonna Miss Me: The Best of Roky Erickson* (Restless '91) Discophilia or no discophilia—the title track confuses live with authentic, leaving the equally apt "You Drive Me Crazy" to true collectors—this compilation establishes a '60s casualty and various aliens as the greatest '60s band of the '80s, which didn't lack for retro pretenders. The feel is early Stones, with the very Satan the Stones pimped so pretentiously filling in for Charlie Watts—who else could have guaranteed Roky a victory over Mother Nature, not to mention

Father Time? Devils, ghosts, zombies, vampires, two-headed dogs, I got no use for any of them—except when they ride riffs, grooves, and tunes this demented and user-friendly. **A–**

Nas Escobar, Foxy Brown, AZ and Nature: *The Firm—The Album* (Interscope '97) After honoring Bernard Herrmann with some keyb-simulated RZA, Dre recedes (none too soon) and the music spares out—Wasis Diop's kora sample today, mbira tomorrow. Foxy's pussycentrism gives the finger to the funniest male orgasm on record. And Black Mafia fantasies threaten white male corporate oppression. (Just kidding.) **B–** 🦃

Alejandro Escovedo: *Bourbonitis Blues* (Bloodshot '99) *No Depression*'s "Artist of the Decade" (it says here) gets help he needs from the Wacos, Ian Hunter, and the unsinkable "Pale Blue Eyes" ("I Was Drunk," "Pale Blue Eyes") ★

ESG: *"Erase You"* (*ESG*, Pow Wow '91) 👒

Esquivel!: *Space-Age Bachelor-Pad Music* (Bar/None '94) Ⓝ

Gloria Estefan: "Rhythm Is Gonna Get You," "Conga" (*Greatest Hits*, Epic '92) 🐚
Gloria Estefan: *Gloria!* (Epic '98) 🦯

Maggie Estep: *No More Mister Nice Girl* (NuYo '94) Ⓝ
Maggie Estep: *Love Is a Dog from Hell* (Mouth Almighty/Mercury '97) namechecks John S. Hall, not Patti Smith ("Emotional Idiot," "Jenny's Shirt," "Scab Maids on Speed") ★★

Estrellas de Arieto: *Los Heroes* (World Circuit/Nonesuch '99) An amazing story. In 1979 a Paris-based Ivoirian bizzer convinced Cuba's state record company to convene a cross-generational all-star band, and for a week some 30 musicians and over a dozen singers jammed in combinations dictated by a trombone-playing a&r man. The five albums that resulted hit in Venezuela and stiffed in Cuba. But don't

think the jams didn't jell. These two CDs, a mere 14 cuts lasting two-and-a-half hours, grant a second life to what was obviously a blessed event. Simple heads-plus-improvs dominated by tres and violins, the first disc is one of those rare records that nails such pieties as the joy of music making and the pleasure of the groove. The convergence of relaxation and exhilaration, teamwork and exhibitionism, skill and fun, is nothing less than utopian, which in Cuba, where utopia was a bitter memory, may have been hard to take. The second disc overemphasizes the strident trumpets adored by Cubans who want to be modern. The first one makes me want to send Ry Cooder an ironic thank-you note. **A–**

Melissa Etheridge: *Yes I Am* (Island '93) Many of the rock belter's more overwrought cris de coeur decode nicely into SOS's from the closet. But somehow I don't expect she's going to abandon her fevered word-slinging and muscle-bound dynamics now that her open secret is officially public. She'll always do her damnedest to make sure no one misses the full significance of images like "naked soul," "ache for something new," and "stand firm in the tempest." Patty Scialfa is Shonen Knife by comparison. But I blame Etheridge on Bruce anyway. **C+** 🦃
Melissa Etheridge: *Your Little Secret* (Island '95) 🦯

Etoile de Dakar: *Volume 1—Absa Gueye* (Stern's Africa '93) Supposedly, Youssou N'Dour has gone on to better things than these first recordings, cut in 1979 with the seminal band he formed two years earlier at age 18. And without doubt his music has grown more ambitious and more accomplished. But there's nothing youthfully naive or folkishly charming about mbalax at this stage of evolution. Counterbalancing clave-inflected sway with hectic tama-drum interjections, making ample room for guitar and horns, it never shrinks from its own complexities or sinks under their weight. With five band members writing, many of the 10 tracks grab you at every turn. And unlike N'Dour's always admirable and usually enjoyable internationalist fusions, they never overreach. **A**

Etoile de Dakar: *Volume 2: Thiapathioly* (Stern's Africa '94) meaning of title: public property ("Dounya," "Thiapathioly") ★★★

Etoile de Dakar: *Volume 3: Lay Suma Lay* (Stern's Africa '96) On the final installment of their collected works, Youssou N'Dour's first band embellish their self-taught Afrocentric charanga with horn lines whose intricately percussive Islamic tune families recall no Latin record I've ever noticed. Cut into still gaudier ribbons by the hectoring tenor of the soon-departed El Hadji Faye, it's wilder and weirder than any mbalax or fusion the nonpareil vocalist has put his name on since. **A–**

Etoile 2000: *Etoile 2000* (Dakar Sound import '96) Imagine a bunch of garage musicians whose main technical limitation is that they grew up too poor to own instruments. Two genius guitarists clashing, three drummers beating the hell out of each other, crazy sax man coming and going, and then, because this is a garage band only in theory, two singers who can outwail the average gospel strongman, never mind the average Iggyphile. That's this short-lived, hot-headed Senegalese crew, who undertook the literally garage-recorded "Boubou N'Gary," all unkempt echoplexed fuzzbox and excitable tama, to give their old boss Youssou N'Dour what for, and began hearing it on the radio—constantly—about two hours after they'd finished. None of the other five tracks is quite as intense or chaotic. But this will shut up anybody who believes Afropop is too slick and anybody who believes it's too primitive simultaneously. El Hadji Faye, we salute you. **A–**

E.U.: *Cold Kickin' It* (Virgin '90) 🎣

Eugenius: *Oomalama* (Atlantic '92) irony-pop gone garage-rock—hooky whether it steamrolls, trudges, or whines ("Breakfast," "Bed-In") ★★★

Eugenius: *Mary Queen of Scots* (Atlantic '94) Ⓝ

Eurythmics: *Greatest Hits* (Arista '91) The approximate chronology follows the rough arc of their career, for it was only after establishing "Sweet Dreams" and its follow-ups that Dave Stewart and Annie Lennox dared reveal what a grand hoot they thought pop was. The fabulous disco-rock overstatement of the mid-'80s ensued, climaxing with the 1987 Stones piss-take "I Need a Man." Thereafter they can conceal neither how much they hate each other nor how much they prefer hits to hoots. "I believe in you," Annie intones richly and perfectly on the finale, "like Elvis Presley singing live from Las Vegas." **A–**

Eve: *Ruff Ryders' First Lady* (Ruff Ryders/Interscope '99) dogs can't leave that woman alone ("Heaven Only Knows," "My B******," "Love Is Blind") ★★

Everclear: *World of Noise* (Capitol '94) Ⓝ

Everclear: *Sparkle and Fade* (Capitol '95) In his thirties, with a load of drugs behind him and a young daughter waiting at home, Art Alexakis has a firm enough grip on his life to articulate the anguish other guitar-wielders yowl about. Where on the aptly entitled *World of Noise* the sharpest lyrics never quite mesh, here almost every song comes with a story, a tune, and a musical pain threshold. Its cast of struggling souls is evoked by somebody past pitying himself—somebody who's been around the block so often he's finally learned that compassion is for other people. **A–**

Everclear: *So Much for the Afterglow* (Capitol '97) Art Alexakis knows he got lucky and figures the surest way to maximize his success is to maximize his music, showing the strengths and weaknesses of someone you sincerely hope has found the investment counselor of his dreams. With his big riffs and self-aggrandizing evocations of a credible life, he's best working the audience-as-beloved trope. The title tune says everything he needs to say about follow-ups in the age of the one-shot. **B+**

Everlast: *Forever Everlasting* (Warner Bros. '90) Ⓝ

Everlast: *Whitey Ford Sings the Blues* (Tommy Boy '98) not much to boast about beyond being alive, and better for it ("The Letter," "7 Years") ★★

Evil Stig: *Evil Stig* (Warner Bros./Blackheart '95) Ⓝ

The Evil Tambourines: *Library Nation* (Sub Pop '99) 💣

Cesaria Evora: *Cesaria Evora* (Nonesuch '95) the queen of morna, which is like fado only—no thanks to the Portuguese, I'm sure—more African ("Flor na Paul," "Tudo dia de dia") ★★

Cesaria Evora: *Cabo Verde* (Nonesuch '97) I was struck by the English title of "Mar é morada de sodade": "The Sea Is the Home of Nostalgia." Usually "saudade," the equivalent of "soul" in Evora's morna style, is rendered "sadness" or "longing," terms that disguise the self-pity beneath its dignity—a self-pity that's easier to take out in the open. Rather more than on her renowned U.S. debut, that self-pity is swallowed up in the somewhat swifter flow of the grooves, a speed achieved at no loss of her fundamental fluidity. And I note that the two drop-dead melodies, both taken medium-fast and one featuring an utterly easeful James Carter, counsel confidently against despair and complacency. **A–**

Cesaria Evora: *Miss Perfumado* (Nonesuch '98) Ⓝ

Cesaria Evora: *Mar Azul* (Nonesuch '99) Ⓝ

Cesaria Evora: *Café Atlantico* (Lusafrica/RCA Victor/BMG Classics '99) I'm happy to note that Shoeless Cesaria reports herself happy. She likes being a star, and is proud to have spread the fame of her native land—now officially redesignated, in the soupiest thing here, an "Atlantic Paradise." To celebrate, she sells out big-time, and does it ever suit her—her Brazilian concertmaster's swirling strings ruin only one of five tracks, and the kora, bolero, and danzón are all to the good. Meanwhile, over on the arty side, two previously unrecordeds from her twenties are bright standouts, and the lyric booklet is full of surprises. Never got her and wondered if you were worse for it? Why not start here? **A–**

Excuse 17: *Such Friends Are Dangerous* (Kill Rock Stars '95) Carrie Brownstein finds her scream ("This Is Not Your Wedding Song," "The Drop Dead Look") ★

Exposé: *Exposé* (Arista '93) 💣

Eyuphoro: *Mama Mosambiki* (RealWorld '90) Mozambican not South African—guitar lilt soukous or chimurenga or samba or Larry Carlton, soul Riourbane not Soweto-muscular ("Samukhela," "Oh Mama") ★★★

E/COMPILATIONS

'80s Underground Rap: Can I Kick It? (Rhino '98) the obscurities kick harder than the obviosities (the Real Roxanne, with Hitman Howie Tee, "Bang Zoom [Let's Go-Go]"; Jungle Brothers, with A Tribe Kalled Quest, "Promo No. 2 [Mind Review '89]") ★★

'80s Underground Rap: Can You Feel It? (Rhino '98) no matter what they didn't know in Cali, New Yorkers were feeling EPMD and the JBs back in the day (Special Ed, "I Got It Made"; Three Times Dope, "Greatest Man Alive [After Midnight Mix]") ★★★

'80s Underground Rap: Don't Believe the Hype (Rhino '98) Ⓝ

El Caimán: Sones Huastecos (Corason '96) No hablo español, so when it comes to the Mexican songform called *son* I naturally go for what the French call *son*—sound. The unvarying structures and repetitive tunes of this northeastern style only foreground the attractions of a sound I can't do without right now—two steady guitars, one wild violin, and two eerie falsettos conjoining to call up no one knows what Arab or (anti-) Aztec ghosts. Dug it before I'd ventured south of Tijuana, love it now, and don't assume you won't until you hear the Pérez Maya brothers, amateurs on a Veracruz islet who learned their weird shtick from their father—or Dinastía Hidalguense, dulcet toasts of the subgenre. **A–**

ESPN Presents Slam Jams Vol. 1 (Tommy Boy '97) Nouveau jock jams, extreme-sports anthems, or wrinkle on a muscle-headed repackaging concept? Don't know, don't care—fabulous new wave comp is what matters. From Madness's "One Step Beyond" to the Modern Lovers' "Roadrunner," with such super-obvious milestones as "Ca Plane pour Moi" and "Dancing with Myself" marking the route, the stoopidity barrels down an expressway to your ass. You *will* drive to it. Dance too. Even bungee jump. **A+**

Éthiopiques 1 (Buda Musique import '98) notes from an aborted pop scene (Muluqèn Mèllèssè, "Wètètié maré"; Sèyfu Yohannès, "Tezeta") ★★★
Éthiopiques 2 (Buda Musique import '98) barest, craziest, sexiest, least melodic, least grooveful, most Arabic (Tigist Assèfa, "Toutouyé"; Malèfya Tèka, "Indè Lyèruzalèm") ★
Éthiopiques 3 (Buda Musique import '98) The instant cachet of a five-CD series documenting the 1969–1978 run of the only record label in Addis Ababa did not reflect the irresistibility of its parts. I doubt any reviewer bonded with many individual songs/tracks even on this superior volume, not after the three or four listens preceding publication and probably not ever. Because Ethiopia was its peculiar self—an uncolonized absolute monarchy so in-sensible to indigenous music that its national anthem was composed by an Armenian—the set also does without such world-music boons as love of the past, belief in the future, and lust for conquest. As the soundscape to a locale undiscovered by squarer, older tourists, however, it obviously has its uses, especially for an alt generation that's always mistrusted organic ecstasy. I've never encountered a more neurotic-sounding Third World sensibility. Its m.o. is to mush up Middle East, Africa, and Europe for a small-time power elite you can almost see—anxious young traffickers in court intrigue sitting around smoky, well-appointed clubs where petit-bourgeois artistes strive to give them a thrill. And just often enough, the organic—imbued with melody or hook or vocal commitment or instrumental synergy, only to be tempered and twisted by an endemic uncertainty—peeps through. **B+**
Éthiopiques 4 (Buda Musique import '98) Booker T. and Ramsey Lewis trade concepts over a drummer who first laid eyes on a trap set last month—Ethiopian-style, *mais oui* (Mulatu Astatqué, "Yèkèrmo sèw," "Mètché Dershé") ★

Ethnotechno (TVT '93) relaxed beats + sound effects con, Yoruba, etc. = "Sonic Anthropology Volume 1" (Juno Reactor, "Alash [When I Graze My Beautiful Sheep]"; Sandoz, "Limbo"; Jonah, "Algiers") ★★★

Every Road I Take: The Best of Acoustic Blues (Shanachie '99) Ⓝ

Excess Baggage (Prophecy '98) John Lurie Entertainment presents . . . movie music for people who don't like movie music—not to mention television music ★

Excursions in Ambience (Caroline '93) Ⓝ

Candido Fabré: *Poquito a Poco* (Candela '99) violins loud like horns ("Bailando con Otro," "La Mano en el Arazón") ★★★

Donald Fagen: *Kamakiriad* (Reprise '93) virtuoso time warp—as gorgeous and shallow as *Aja* ("Teahouse on the Tracks," "Trans-Island Skyway") ★★★

John Fahey: *Return of the Repressed: The John Fahey Anthology* (Rhino '94) The catch phrase I like best for his deliberate acoustic style gets its '50s-collegiate pretensions and folk/not-folk ambivalence: "existentialist guitar." A record collector who bases many songs on treasured blues and string-band obscurities, he also cops from Saint-Saëns, rock and roll, Christian hymns, Hindu hymns, and what-have-you to construct a late-night music untouched by lyrics or speed: spacy and contemplative, yet with an implacable common touch. True enough, Fahey's pioneering DIY label, named after Takoma Park, the D.C. suburb he called home, was where George Winston got his start. But after two decades of asking myself why he's any better than Leo Kottke, I've decided it's a spiritual thing—he's maintained a direct line to his inner amateur. For two whole CDs, definitely not boring. Just close enough to make you question the concept. A–

John Fahey: *City of Refuge* (Tim/Kerr '97) "My category is alternative, period," avers the last intelligent person to make such a claim in this millennium. He doesn't want to be folk or New Age, and who can blame him? But if he were, some rich dunderhead might insist that he treat blues and pop rarities to his dolorously deliberate touch, like on those old Reprise albums Byron Coley sneers at. Instead he's encouraged to stagger toward an obscure destination mere mortals would noodle around, dumbfounding bystanders with the scraps of sound that flake off his beard as he goes. Once in a while tunes poke through the refuse, notably that of "Chelsey Silver, Please Call Home." These occasion proud huzzahs from young fools who can only forgive themselves such emoluments after a good cleansing scourge of spare solo indirection. Their self-disgust is our loss and Fahey's ticket to wankdom. Even the meandering Cul de Sac get more out of him. C+🦃

David and Jad Fair: *Monster Songs for Children* (Kill Rock Stars '98) 💣

Jad Fair and Kramer: *The Sound of Music* (Shimmy-Disc '99) Kramer's settings took three days, Fair's words two listens and one day, and when it jells you'd think it was even less ("Sleeping Beauty," "Elenor") ★

Jad Fair and the Shapir O'Rama: *We Are the Rage* (Avant import '96) Although these 23 soliloquies in 46 minutes are a little long on noize-will-be-noize guitar, umpteenth collaborator Kim Rancourt (of When People Were Shorter and Lived

Near the Water, since you asked) does the 42-year-old boy wonder a favor by sticking up for himself. In fact, while nothing tops the climactic love poem only Jad could have written ("Her eyes are the color of a Slurpee"? "She smells as good as pizza"?), it was Rancourt who gave him the definitive "I Comb My Hair with My Hand." And who sings several of the best soliloquies here all by himself. **B+**

Jad Fair and the Shapir O'Rama: *I Like Your Face* (Wire Monkey '99) Ⓝ

Jad Fair & Yo La Tengo: *Strange but True* (Matador '98) Jad never runs dry, but he does trickle off sometimes ("Circus Strongman Runs for PTA President," "Texas Man Abducted by Aliens for Outer Space Joy Ride") ★★

Marianne Faithfull: *Blazing Away* (Island '90) Already too damn significant for her own good, the diva-elect displays herself and her tattered repertoire to an adoring St. Ann's claque and gets little help from a band that should know better. I could go back to the disastrous video (shots of microphone bases for variety, pans of stained-glass windows for edification, slo-mo birds for filmpoetry) to make sure that's partner-in-cultdom Barry Reynolds on guitar overkill, not wizard-for-hire Marc Ribot. But since it's definitely Ribot's pal Dougie Bowne laying on the drumrolls, I'd rather not know. Either way the misbegotten strategy is to ratchet up the melodrama until only a cad would deny's she's suffering—and not just because she's worried sick about having to pull this act off forever amen. **B-**🐝

Marianne Faithfull: *Faithfull* (Island '94) There's a bald expediency to this compiled-by-Chris-Blackwell-himself overview: what kind of a legend leads an 11-track best-of with the five keepers from her career album, now 15 years behind her? Yet though even the new Patti Smith cover has nothing on "Broken English" or "Why D'Ya Do It," every more recent song (as well as the iconic twice-15-year-old Jagger-Richards ingenue move "As Tears Go By") beats *Broken English*'s filler. So

slice it this way. For the first half she's a wreck, spitting imprecations at the world. During the second she regains her dignity. And since dignity is rarely as much fun as wreckage, there's a definite thrill in hearing her make something of it. **A-**

Marianne Faithfull: *A Secret Life* (Island '95) Ⓝ

Marianne Faithfull: "Don't Forget Me" (*20th Century Blues,* RCA Victor '97) 🎧

Marianne Faithfull: *A Perfect Stranger: The Island Collection* (Island '98) admit this—Brecht-Weill put Faithfull-Reynolds to shame ("Ballad of the Soldier's Wife," "The Ballad of Lucy Jordan") ★★

Th Faith Healers: *Lido* (Elektra '92) They're rougher, dirtier, and, despite their female lead, lower. They could make excellent use of Anton Fier. But their buzz is early Feelies, and buzz it does: sheer power-drone, never fully controlled and often breaking into something quite frantic and exciting. Very abstract, very bound up in dynamics, but abstractly *visceral,* and neither incapable nor contemptuous of the gift hook in the mouth. A left hook, I hope. Ouch, that hurts—so good. **A-**

Th Faith Healers: *Imaginary Friends* (Elektra '94) writing songs more and enjoying music less ("Kevin," "Sparklingly Chime") ★★

Faith No More: *The Real Thing* (Slash/Reprise '90) With rap, funk, hardcore, and falafel-joint rai seasoning their metallic stew, a new frontman thinks hard about life and horror comics while under the influence of I hate to think what. "Epic," which old people will think is about the terrors of sex though it's really about the terrors of everything, and "Zombie Eaters," a jaundiced if not jealous view of a baby's world, delineate their generational chauvinism, and art-AOR keybs establish the depths of their cultural deprivation. Not as stupid as they sound—but do they sound stupid. **B-** 🐝

Faith No More: *Angel Dust* (Slash/Warner Bros. '92) but it's really *great* shit

("Land of Sunshine," "Midlife Crisis," "Midnight Cowboy") ★★★

The Fall: *Extricate* (Mercury '90) indefatigable-uh ("British People in Hot Weather") ★

The Fall: *458489 A Sides* (Beggars Banquet '90) Beginning, naturally, with the least catchy thing on the record (it came first, and who are they to deny history?), this singles compilation spans the entirety of Brix Smith's controversial (especially if you're an old friend of Mark's) tenure with the eternal U.K. art punks. Their drones don't resolve or climax or even pick up speed, yet though Mark's said to be a poet, they're not just there for the words, many of them undecodable—they're there for the drones. Which just hurry you along on a nagging groove whose intimations of eternity are in no way undermined by Brix's penchant for deep detail. The only Fall record any normal person need own. A–

The Fall: *458489 B Sides* (Beggars Banquet '90) the reassuringly literate clatter of avant-garde background rock—two hours of it ("No Bulbs," "Kurious Oranj [Live]") ★★★

The Fall: *Kimble* (Strange Fruit '93) great original sound ("Spoilt Victorian Child") ★

The Fall: *The Infotainment Scan* (Matador '93) great original sound, one hell of a cover band ("Lost in Music," "I'm Going to Spain") ★★★

The Fall: *Middle Class Revolt* (Matador '94) Ⓝ

The Fall: *The Marshall Suite* (Artful import '99) alt-rock won't die till they ban Pignose amps in Mark E.'s senior residence, but that doesn't mean he'll put this much into it ("F-'Oldin' Money," "Touch Sensitive") ★★★

The Family Stand: *Moon in Scorpio* (EastWest '91) 💣

Mose Fan Fan: *Se Belle Epoque* (Retro-Afric '94) 1970–1982—Somo Somo's headman gets his feet wet in Kinshasa, his shit together in Dar Es Salaam, and his rocks off in Nairobi ("Pele Odidja," "Molema") ★★

Mose Fan Fan & Somo Somo Ngobila: *Hello Hello* (Stern's Africa '95) Insofar as soukous has room to grow anymore, it rejects Paris hyperdrive for the confident understatement of the golden era, and too often the formal energy lags the second time around. Masterminded by a veteran guitarist who was once from Zaire, this exile supersession (Quatre Etoiles, Sam Mangwana) finds the balance: bold yet complex, lively yet reflective, scintillating yet groovesome, fast yet mellow—yet fast, you know? A–

Alou Fané's Foté Mocoba: *Kamalan N'Goni: Dozon N'Goni* (Dakar Sound import '94) "the young Bambara hunter plays his guitar in the Kamalan way," aka Oumou Sangare with a penis ("Miria," "Tou lomba") ★★

Fantcha: *Criolinha* (Tinder '97) ingenue saudade ("Sonho d'um criôl," "Mi é dodo na bô Cabo Verde") ★

Dionne Farris: *Wild Seed—Wild Flower* (Columbia '94) 💣

Majek Fashek and the Prisoners of Conscience: *Spirit of Love* (Interscope '91) Ⓝ

Fastbacks: *The Question Is No* (Sub Pop '92) For all its sectarianism, one thing alt-rock produces in superfluity is nice guys—nice guys in nice bands. They're friendly and articulate, they support their scenes, they make music for love. Most likely their music ain't half bad, either. But seldom is it capable of signifying beyond the one-on-one club-circuit ambit. Such bands are praised beyond all reason by the fans they've served so faithfully for so long. In New York the prototype is Tara Key and Tim Harris's Antietam; in Seattle it's this Kurt Bloch-Kim Warnick unit. As you may have read, they're down-to-earth and pop-punky, the very model of a garage band for everyday use. Warnick sounds so sensible you'd loan her your car. And yes, some of Bloch's tunes will get her around the block. But unless you've seen them a few times, or Warnick's honest voice happens to activate your body chemistry, you'll struggle to penetrate the hoopla and then forget you own it. **B–** 🦃

Fastball: *All the Pain Money Can Buy* (Hollywood '98) "We just wanted to make a personal statement with our music," aver these three Austinites with a sincere look in their eyes. And so they yoke popcraft worthy of Three Dog Night, the Doobie Brothers, perhaps even Matchbox 20 to lyrics that speak of the dark things—institutionalization, methadone, lovers left bleeding, highways going nowhere, and, quite a few times, their own inordinate careerism. Is that personal enough for you? **C+** 🦃

Fatboy Slim: *Better Living Through Chemistry* (Astralwerks '97) bang bang bang ("Going out of My Head," "Santa Cruz") ★★
Fatboy Slim: *You've Come a Long Way, Baby* (Astralwerks '98) proving what all pop pros know—that obvious is harder than subtle ("The Rockafeller Skank," "In Heaven") ★★★
Fatboy Slim: *On the Floor at the Boutique* (Skint import '98) The stupid album he's not genius enough to make himself is a live mix tape segueing many dance records unknown to me and a few I've long loved, most crucially the Jungle Brothers' groove-setting "Because I Got It Like That." All are speeded up so that the vocalists, let's call them, sound less like cartoons—except on "Michael Jackson," which samples the J5's Saturday-morning show—than like they've just huffed helium or nitrous oxide. Jumping jack laugh, it's a gas gas gas. **A–**

Fat Joe: *Don Cartagena* (Mystic/Big Beat/Atlantic '98) Promising "the best in hardcore hip hop," the former work boy and bus robber wants to show up the—what was that again, let me check my notes—"fake niggas" who are ripping off his former lifestyle. So he orders plenty murders and disrespects plenty hos (as opposed to "intelligent, civilized divas") before proceeding to the usual violin-drenched do-what-I-say-not-what-I-did—aimed, he says, at "the drug-dealin', thug-ass motherfuckin' niggas listening to Fat Joe." Though Noreaga's cameo sounds as soulful as Otis Redding by comparison, I believe Joe is more enlightened than some of these citizens. I also believe the rest of us can live without him. **C+** 🦃

Charlie Feathers: *Charlie Feathers* (Elektra Nonesuch '91) Like most of the losers who claim they taught Elvis his tricks, this 59-year-old Memphis crackpot has his claque—fools who think his stray cuts for Sun, King, and lesser, later indies put him on a par with Carl Perkins if not Jerry Lee. But though "One Hand Loose" and "Tongue-Tied Jill" are pretty great, only nuts need Kay Records' generically rockacountry *Jungle Fever* comp. So this is a shock. Although "Mean Woman Blues" rocks out like Robert Gordon and Billy Hancock wish, Feathers refuses to insult anyone's intelligence pretending he's horny as a teenager, putting his past behind him in the forlorn collection of old song titles "We Can't Seem to Remember to Forget." His resonant bullfrog undertone and hiccuping upper register evoking a less cocky George Jones, he explores rockabilly as a musical form—the white man's blues he's always saying it is. Funny, emotional, completely personal. Play at medium volume, late in the dark night. **A–**
Charlie Feathers: *Get with It: Essential Recordings* (Revenant '98) Ⓝ

The Feelies: *Time for a Witness* (A&M '91) Though it had precedents in such influences as Brian Eno, Steve Reich, and *The Velvet Underground,* we know why the rippling quietude of 1986's electro-pastoral *The Good Earth* got Peter Buck accused of taking the city out of the boys. So when Bill Million describes this de facto will and testament as "taking several giant steps backwards," say amen. The sere minimalism of *Crazy Rhythms* was always misleading. Only here, on a harder, louder, riffier, humansticker studio expansion of their original concept, do they capture the exhilaration of the legendary shows they used to mount on national holidays—the one on Flag Day came complete with star-spangled banner. Once again they imbue oddball suburban nerdiness with spare downtown cool. Once again they rock out while shedding their grace on thee. **A**

Fela Anikulapo-Kuti: *O D O O* (Shanachie '90) ragged and unbowed ★★

Fela: *Black Man's Cry* (Eurobond import '90) Maybe I know only one of these six '73–'77 titles—"Lady," who's uppity, unlike a real "African woman"—because the others shun pidgin and sometimes lyrics. As total statements I prefer "Shuffering and Shmiling" or "Zombie." But this is his fusion in its world-beating prime, back when his bitterness was still sweet to him. **A–**

Fellow Travellers: *No Easy Way* (OKra '90) notes on the abiding pleasures and disappointments of small-town life ("Promise of a Kiss," "No Vacancy") ★★

Fellow Travellers: *Just a Visitor* (OKra '92) your typical leftist country dub ("She Moved Away," "Mary, Her Husband, and Tommy Too") ★★

Fellow Travellers: *Things and Time* (OKra import '93) Jeb Loy Nichols is a singer of helpless, studied nasality whose reference points are country, dub, and '70s soul, none of which he deems incompatible with the Carpenters or George Gershwin. And although on his third album he leaves class war to Gregory Isaacs' "Poor and Clean," he's also a lefty. In short, he's about as commercial as a Swedenborgian schismatic on public access. And so, with nothing to lose except a few creations that might otherwise fail to survive any posterity whatsoever, he puts 16 songs on a mournful, unhurried, all too hypnotic 65-minute CD. It could use some pruning, but the guy writes better all the time, with domestic epiphany,

romantic resignation, and our daily fatigue his specialties. There's a sadness here beyond self-pity, and a unique groove to match. At least your mind will wander somewhere it's never been before. **A–**

Ibrahim Ferrer: *Buena Vista Social Club Presents Ibrahim Ferrer* (Nonesuch/World Circuit '99) at 72, he has the right to take it easy—and luckily, also the ability ("Marieta," "Bruta Maniquá") ★★

Ferron: *Phantom Center* (Chameleon '90) **Ⓝ**

Bryan Ferry: *Taxi* (Reprise '93) **Ⓝ**

Field Trip: "Ballad of Field Trip" (*Ripe*, Slash '91) 🎵

Filter: *Title of Record* (Reprise '99) 🎸

Fine Young Cannibals: *The Finest* (London/MCA '96) Classy of them never to overextend a thin concept, now conveniently distilled to an essence of smooth pop-soul hip and seasoned with intimations of conscience. MTV abusers please note: lean, light Roland Gift sounds as fine as he looks. **A–**

Firehose: *Live Totem Pole EP* (Columbia '92) 🎸
Firehose: *Mr. Machinery Operator* (Columbia '93) 🎸

Firehouse: *Hold Your Fire* (Columbia '92) Metal has evolved at such a drastic pace that this assiduously inoffensive prefab seems almost folkloric, a weird anachronism in which the great tradition of Jon Bon Jovi and Mark Slaughter—manly tenor, moderate tempos, technically unassailable riffs—is preserved for the dwindling faithful. They "Reach for the Sky," they "Hold That Dream," they "Rock You Tonight," and because their "Mama Didn't Raise No Fool," they describe the inevitable bone job as "Sleeping with You." Isn't that sweet? **C–** 🐝

The Fireman: *Strawberries Oceans Ships Forests* (Capitol '94) *Riff and Variations,* or, *Techno for Seniors* ("Transcrystaline," "Celtic Stomp") ★

Fishbone: "New and Improved Bonin' " (*Bonin' in the Boneyard,* Epic '90) 💣

Fishbone: *The Reality of My Surroundings* (Columbia '91) 🎸

Fishbone: *Give a Monkey a Brain . . . and He'll Swear He's the Center of the Universe* (Columbia '93) 🎸

Roberta Flack: *Roberta* (Atlantic '94) the great black pop of middle-class dreams ("Cottage for Sale," "Let's Stay Together") ★★

The Flaming Lips: *A Collection of Songs Representing an Enthusiasm for Recording . . . by Amateurs* (Restless '98) 🎸

The Flaming Lips: *The Soft Bulletin* (Warner Bros. '99) Tiptoeing along the precipice that divides the charmingly serious from the hopelessly ridiculous, this year's Prestigious Pink Floyd Tribute by a Long-Running Band of Some Repute and Less Distinction enjoys two advantages over *OK Computer* and *Deserter's Songs.* Not only does it map out a sonic identity, the chief selling point of all these records, but it's not above pretty. And lead genius Wayne Coyne mixes up the quotidian and the cosmic in the best American psychedelic tradition, with a social dimension more grounded than the usual dystopian mishmash—heroic scientists, gosh. All that granted, however, listeners with no generational stake in how old alt bands impact history are obliged not only to contend with Coyne's wispy voice and chronic confusion, but to stifle their giggles when Steven Drozd bangs his drums all over a song mixing up summer love and mosquito bites. That is, these guys are Not Joking. Ever. Which makes them hopelessly ridiculous. **B** 🐝

The Flatlanders: *More a Legend Than a Band* (Rounder '90) In 1972 Joe Ely, Butch Hancock, and leader Jimmie Dale Gilmore—drumless psychedelic cowboys returned to Lubbock from Europe and San Francisco and Austin—recorded in Nashville for Shelby Singleton, and even an eccentric like the owner of the Sun cat-

alogue and "Harper Valley P.T.A." must have considered them weird. With a musical saw for theremin effects, their wide-open spaceyness was released eight-track only, and soon a subway troubadour and an architect and a disciple of Guru Mararaji had disappeared back into the diaspora. In cowpunk/neofolk/ psychedelic-revival retrospect, they're neotraditionalists who find small comfort in the past, responding guilelessly and unnostalgically to the facts of displacement in a global village that includes among its precincts the high Texas plains. They're at home. And they're lost anyway. **A–**

Fleetwood Mac: *The Dance* (Warner Bros. '97) Ⓝ

Flipper: *American Grafishy* (Def American '92) 🎸

Rosie Flores: *After the Farm* (HighTone '92) Formal imagination quotient: zero. She's not even pure country like the last time somebody paid her to put out a record, back in '87—just L.A. countryrock with a barely perceptible edge. But the catch in her voice has gotten so husky you want to give her a squeeze, and she writes more good songs about the usual thing than any of the young hunks who've given Nashville delusions of grandeur in the interim even bother to sing. Guess her problem is that she's kind of uppity—for a girl. **A–**

Rosie Flores: *Once More with Feeling* (HighTone '93) Ⓝ

Fluffy: *5 Live* (The Enclave '96) Guitars basic not hookless, tempos fast not hyper, attitude bombed not nihilistic, these London lasses are as pure punk as the '90s get. These songs will never again sound as raw or desperate as on this 15-minute swatch of their May return to CBGB—not on record. It's one of those rare live moments that signifies in the living room. They're pumped, and you can hear it. **A–**

Fluffy: *Black Eye* (The Enclave '96) Am I forgetting somebody, or is this the most unrelenting (and, not to hedge any bets, best) punk debut since the glory days of Ramones-Pistols-Clash? OK, Wire, but really. The big loud production by Clash/Pistols veteran Bill Price tweaks classic riffs for hard rock oomph, the riffs carry the power surges, and except for the fame one, the songs live up to the underlining. Amanda Rootes's sex life is at best a draw, but she knows its garish details thoroughly enough to convince anyone willing to stand up there while she spits them out that sooner or later she'll walk away with a victory. Her rage doesn't mean she's strong—it means she's hell-bent on getting there. **A**

Foamola: *May I Take a Bath?* (Foamola '92) There's too much art project in this five-song cassette, but fanzines hype slighter, dumber, more received stuff as if it were their holy mission, so why shouldn't I express myself? A married couple blow (flute, ocarina) and beat (chopsticks, coffee spoon, plastic fork). A buddy lays down some organ. The encomium to John Quincy Adams and the comparison of Texas and Tennessee are equally fanciful and equally educational. "Waiting for the Catfood to Come" is an East Village "Afternoon Delight." The weather report gets boring. And now I hear a one-year-old has joined the act. **B+**
Foamola: *Spit on the Dishes* (Foamola '93) **Ⓝ**

John Fogerty: *Blue Moon Swamp* (Warner Bros. '97) **Ⓝ**

Ben Folds Five: "Boxing" (*Ben Folds Five,* Passenger '95) **🍡**
Ben Folds Five: *Whatever and Ever Amen* (550 Music '97) crude piano portraits of general apathy and major boredom with a few feelings poking through ("Brick," "Song for the Dumped") **★**
Ben Folds Five: *The Unauthorized Biography of Reinhold Messner* (550 Music '99) What jerks melody inflicts on us. With no connection to any human virtue of substance, the catchy tune ushers all manner of unpleasant personality traits into our lives. And if this smart aleck is

less dangerous than Fred Durst, he also does less with what he was given. For sure he's less original musically (as opposed to melodically) no matter how many piano lessons he took, banging away like a garage guitarist with the occasional flourish to prove he has a right— God, Joe Jackson was more fun. And although he also throws in the occasional well-turned sentiment to prove he has a right—"Don't Change Your Plans" and "Mess" are recommended to nice guys seeking covers—his basic program remains revenge-of-the-nerd. He always knew he was smarter than whoever and ever amen. He always knew there were people who'd admire him just because he was clever. And unfortunately, he was right. **B 🎥**

Sue Foley: *Without a Warning* (Antone's '93) After a pleasant debut, an Austin-based Canadian comes up an original. Blues in form, she's girl-group in spirit— "Cry for Me" steps as lightly as the Magic Sam covers, and the Earl Hooker tribute has the weight of a charming novelty. Just don't trifle with her—not unless you can name another blueswoman who'd lead three instrumentals on a single album, or call her a liar when she goes out on "Put Your Money Where Your Mouth Is" and "Annie's Drifting Heart." Which latter provides at least two Inspirational Warnings: "I got a woman's body but a little girl's mind," and "Good luck follows me all around." **A–**
Sue Foley: *Big City Blues* (Antone's '95) **Ⓝ**
Sue Foley: *Walk in the Sun* (Discovery/Antone's '96) **Ⓝ**

The Folk Implosion: *Dare to Be Surprised* (Communion '97) as comforting as an old pair of jeans, and as apt to fall apart ("Insinuation," "Pole Position") **★**
The Folk Implosion: *One Part Lullaby* (Interscope '99) "I didn't leave my room till I learned how to drive," Lou Barlow recalls about being 17, which is probably why he seems retarded to this day. He's not a thug or a dolt, God knows. But he has the

awkward aura of someone whose social IQ is 100 points below his math-and-verbal, and I wouldn't bet that his socks always match. This is so pretty it's almost a joke about quiet lyricism. But it's so passive you want to put crystal meth in its apple juice. **B+**

Foo Fighters: *Foo Fighters* (Roswell/Capitol '95) the spirit is strong but the identity is weak ("This Is a Call," "Big Me") ★★★

Foo Fighters: *The Colour and the Shape* (Roswell '97) Real band, real producer, real lyrics, real pain, and, very important, real talent—put them all together and a solidly satisfying formal exercise follows a vaguely vacant one. Dave Grohl will never sing, play, or care in the same existential realm as Kurt Cobain. But the marital breakup content/concept inspires him to fully inhabit the music that meant so much to him and millions of other Kurt Cobain fans. **A–**

Foo Fighters: *There Is Nothing Left to Lose* (RCA/Roswell '99) sound there, context vanished ("Stacked Actor," "Generator") ★

T-Model Ford: *Pee-Wee Get My Gun* (Fat Possum/Epitaph '97) Ⓝ

The Foremen: *Folk Heroes* (Reprise '95) "We used to wanna sing like Joan Baez/Jesus, what were we smoking?" ("Russian Limbaugh," "Peace Is Out") ★★

The Foremen: "Hidden Agenda" (*What's Left?*, Reprise '96) 🐞

Forest for the Trees: *Forest for the Trees* (DreamWorks '97) The initial temptation is to gush over how trip-hoppy Carl Stephenson was ere world or underworld heard tell of Tricky or DJ Shadow. But in fact this 1993 recording shows its age, most tellingly by assuming that tunes are a good thing. Stephenson cut his studio chops producing rappers—first with the Geto Boys, then with the College Boyz, whose hunger for hits transcended petty differences. So when he entered the rock world, he saw no reason to believe that texture and melody were mutually exclu-

sive. And if it turns out that this was naive, well, naiveté is one thing that makes this obsession disguised as an album so appealing. Finally we who prefer *Mellow Gold* to *Odelay* have a good idea why. **A–**

Juan Formell y Los Van Van: See Los Van Van

Juan Carlos Formell: *Songs from a Little Blue House* (Wicklow '99) I knew he was the son of Los Van Van's big man first time I played his blandly pretty folk-jazz and chalked up its bloodlessness to the suburban New Age crap first harbingered when Kenny Rankin discovered chromatic chords in Marin County 30 years ago. Not until later did I read that the younger Formell had "literally re-defined the concept of Cuban music," only the Commies wouldn't let him so he went into exile, only then he suffered "rejection" "in some communities here in America too." Self-pity being folk music's universal solvent, my own suspicion is that said communities, if they exist at all, didn't dig his clave. Really, JC—I don't care whether you like Castro. I'm a major El Duque fan. I just think you're a wimp. **B–** 🦃

John Forster: "Entering Marion," "Fusion," "Article Nine," "Whole" (*Entering Marion*, Philo '94) 🐞

Robert Forster: *Danger in the Past* (Beggars Banquet '91) singer-songwriter ("Baby Stones," "Is This What You Call Change") ★★★

Robert Forster: *Calling from a Country Phone* (Beggars Banquet import '93) country-rock was never this gangly—singer-songwriter either ("The Circle," "Drop") ★★

Robert Forster: *I Had a New York Girlfriend* (Beggars Banquet import '94) a cover album that runs out of material ("Echo Beach," "Locked Away") ★

Robert Forster: *Warm Nights* (Beggars Banquet '96) songs too good for the help, subcontracted to none other than Edwyn Collins ("Cryin' Love," "I Can Do") ★★

John Forté: *Poly Sci* (Ruffhouse/Columbia '98) around the way preppie ("Poly Sci," "All You Gotta Do") ★★

Fountains of Wayne: *Fountains of Wayne* (Atlantic/Tag Recordings '96) revenge of the schnooks ("Sick Day," "Joe Rey") ★★★

Fountains of Wayne: *Utopia Parkway* (Atlantic '99) retro popcraft as the pursuit of doomed happiness ("Prom Theme," "Red Dragon Tattoo") ★★★

Four Bitchin' Babes: **"L.A.F.F. (Ladies Against Fanny Floss)"** (*Gabby Road,* Shanachie '97) 👄

4 Etoiles: See Quatre Etoiles

4 Non Blondes: *Bigger, Better, Faster, More!* (Interscope '92) Except maybe for a few pie-eyed corner-cutters over in marketing, nobody born before *Never Mind the Bollocks* thinks Linda Perry is "alternative." It was to avoid music that might distract from her big vague voice—referents: people she never heard of like Lydia Pense and people you wish she never heard of like Ann Wilson—that she axed her female guitarist for a male hotshot once her male producer took her aside. Janis is dead, unfortunately. Also unfortunately, her vision of meaningful rebellion lives on. **C** 🦃

Kim Fox: *Moon Hut* (DreamWorks '97) Ⓝ

Aretha Franklin: *What You See Is What You Sweat* (Arista '91) 💣

Aretha Franklin: *Greatest Hits (1980–1994)* (Arista '94) She's not the titanic presence of 25 years ago, but never count her out. That would require explaining away Clivillés & Cole's new "A Deeper Love," an electro masterpiece as emotional as "Ain't No Way" and as propulsive as "Chain of Fools" (and by the way, it's about God). She even makes Babyface's "Honey" sound like a song. If such late classics as "Jimmy Lee" and "Who's Zoomin' Who" are frothier than true believers might hope, that only proves her evolutionary superiority. All the principle she needs is in her voice, which should only keep adapting into the next millennium. Inspirational Verse That Isn't Even from the Michael McDonald Duet "Ever Changing Times": "I say the past is the past and it no longer matters." **A**

Aretha Franklin: *A Rose Is Still a Rose* (Arista '98) Unlike James Brown, say, or Ray Charles, the Queen of Soul is at home with up-to-the-minute black pop, cherry-picking producers the way Jerry Wexler once did songwriters. Cf. the uncountable rhythm tracks of Puffy Combs's apparently simple (and apparently unsampled) "Never Leave You Again"; Dallas Austin's long-suffering yet somehow jaunty "I'll Dip," on which Aretha sings barely a scrap of the written melody, improvising the verse and embellishing a chorus hook stated by a multitracked backup diva; Daryl Simmons's "In the Morning," disintegrating over and over into a mournful "I don't wanna be the other woman"; Franklin's own "The Woman," inarticulate in its wronged pain until she moans and scats the coda into a show of the pride she brushed by in the second verse; and Lauryn Hill's equally impressive title cut, whose unaffected big-sisterhood underpins the godmother's most credible feminist outreach ever. None of these 11 songs aspires to the declarative tunes and pungent phrases of the soul era, and at 55 Aretha is losing her high end. But after a decade in artistic seclusion, she had something to prove, and she did—with an album as audacious and accomplished as the great Wexler's *Spirit in the Sky* or *Young, Gifted and Black.* **A**

Kirk Franklin's Nu Nation: *God's Property* (B-Rite Music '97) In extremis, choirmaster Franklin's platinum-certified, year-in-the-*Billboard*-200 *Whatcha Lookin' 4* relied on the reflexive gospel strategy of bowling sinners over with solo vocal glory, leaving the skeptic impressed but kind of tired. Here, however, he's generally content to throw his appealing baritone over the sociable interplay of his 18 sopranos, 19 tenors, and 15 altos, thus keeping the enjoyment human-scale. And in extremis we get the gloriously obvious "Yes We Can-Can" and "One Nation Under a Groove" samples, which Kirk's host renders so much more righteous than Suge's posse you figure somebody up there has had it with the Devil getting all the good beats. **B+**

Scott Free: *Getting Off Scott Free* (Leather/Western '97) **Ⓝ**

Free Kitten: *Nice Ass* (Kill Rock Stars '95) **Ⓝ**
Free Kitten: *Sentimental Education* (Kill Rock Stars '97) the simple punk songs I credit to Kim Gordon, the simplistic punk noisefests I blame on Julia Cafritz ("Top 40," "Teenie Weenie Boppie") ★★★

Freestyle Fellowship: *Innercity Griots* (4th & B'way '93) **Ⓝ**

Fresh Fish: "Bang Da Bush (Cadet Mix)" (*Club Mix 96—Volume 2* [comp], Cold Front '96) 💣

The Friggs: "I Thought You Said That You Were Gonna Kill Yourself" (*Rock Candy,* E-Vil '97) 💣

Bill Frisell: *This Land* (Elektra Nonesuch '94) For the groove-minded, Frisell is a frustrating case. Unlike so many jazz guitarists, he can get loud and rock out, but for him those are but two compositional options in the grand plethora. So while most of his albums are graced by great moments or nice mood, in the end I'm too rhythm bound to want any part of the new live one or the two new soundtracks or the one where he covers Madonna or (especially) the one where he falls for a synthesizer. This beautifully constructed sextet record I come back to. It rocks out primarily by association; in fact, many of the avant-garde rags and elegiac ballads feel early 20th century as they bounce off each other like motives in a symphony. But as is often claimed and seldom achieved, the sheer sound of a few bars of guitar can evoke the whole electric blues gestalt, just as the alto-trombone-clarinet combo can evoke all

horns. On his Madonna record Frisell also covered Aaron Copland, who I keep meaning to get to. In the meantime I have this. **A–**

Fuck: *Pardon My French* (Matador '97) 💣

Fugees (Tranzlator Crew): *Blunted on Reality* (Ruffhouse/Columbia '94) pan-African as opposed to Afrocentric, militant as opposed to hard ("Nappy Heads," "Blunted Interlude") ★
Fugees: The Score (Ruffhouse/Columbia '96) They got black humanism, gender equality, and somebody to eclipse Duke Bootee in the Columbia alumni magazine. They sample "I Only Have Eyes for You" from before they were born, misprise "Killing Me Softly" like it was the Rosetta stone, emerge unscathed from the both-sides-of-gangsta trap, and aren't so nervous about being followed that they won't leave landmarks on their soundscape. And astonishingly, they're not just selling to a core audience—this is one of the rare hip hop albums to debut high and rise from there. So you bet they're alternative—they'd better be in a subculture backed into defiant self-pity by rabid reactionaries, lying ex-liberals, and media moguls suddenly conscience-stricken over the nutritional content of what they always considered swill. Forget their debut, from before they discovered the gender-equality formula in which one girl learning equals two guys calling the shots. Forget the Roots, Aceyalone, Pharcyde. This isn't another terrible thing to waste. It's so beautiful and funny its courage could make you weep. **A**

The Fugs: *Songs from a Portable Forest* (Gazell '90) Ed Sanders is a Romantic who's outlived his wild days without disowning or betraying them. As a young Fug, he affected comic hippie raunch; solo, he half realized a pseudohillbilly twang. But pushing 50 in a group that reunited for an antinuke rally, he sings all prettified like the tree-hugging published poet he is. And it's his singing that turns these 12 mostly unjokey songs from the Fugs' three '80s imports into nothing you've heard before. Sanders's care, compassion, and, yes, sensitivity are credible even when he's comparing protesters to Prometheus—the seven-part, 11-minute lifework "Dreams of Sexual Perfection" has William Blake coming in his grave. You almost begin to think any spiritually advanced rockpoet could do this—until Leslie Ritter's Maria McKee-as-Joan Baez contralto turns "World Wide Green" into a pompous preachment and brings you back to earth. **A–**

Robbie Fulks: *Country Love Songs* (Bloodshot '96) honky-tonk gems without the (choose one) soul/voice/context (soul) ("[I Love] Nickels and Dimes," "The Buck Stops Here") ★

Robbie Fulks: *South Mouth* (Bloodshot '98) in the great tradition of Dwight "Little Man Whose Name Is Saul" Yoakam (and Steve "Jap Guitar" Earle), he vows to deliver Nashville from the dread "faggot in a hat" ("Dirty-Mouthed Flo," "Fuck This Town") ★

Robbie Fulks: *Let's Kill Saturday Night* (Geffen '98) "For a life of devotion the death blow He deals/We owe Him only hatred, but God isn't real" ("God Isn't Real," "Pretty Little Poison") ★

Robbie Fulks: "Roots Rock Weirdoes" (*The Very Best of Robbie Fulks,* Bloodshot '99) 🍩

Fun-Da-Mental: *Seize the Time* (Beggars Banquet/Mammoth '95) Ⓝ

Funkdoobiest: *Which Doobie U B?* (Epic/Immortal '93) potbelly beats, empty threats ("Bow Wow Wow," "Doobie to the Head") ★

Funkmaster Flex: *Funkmaster Flex Presents the Mix Tape Volume 1* (Loud/RCA '95) freestyle rap more exciting to read about than to hear, just like free jazz ("Puerto Rico," "Get Up") ★

Funky Porcini: *Love, Pussycats and Carwrecks* (Ninja Tune USA '96) 💣

Funky Porcini: *Let's See What Carmen Can Do* (ZenCDs50 '97) Ⓝ

Funkytown Pros: *Reachin a Level of Assassination* (Peace Posse '91) All clenched throat and quick internal rhymes, Boiwundah disdains "white green," and he knows how to brag: "I'm the debate master, you're just a masturbator." Even stronger "coffee with no cream" comes from his DJ cousin Devastatin', who states his business with a "Big Payback" loop and never retreats. At their most bodacious—the twisted horn intro/refrain on "Here Me Now, Believe Me Later" could have been ripped bleeding from late Miles or choice Art Ensemble—his beats are as out as JB's spaciest and jazziest. In short, this unaffiliated L.A. crew deserves better than to go down in the juice wars. **B+**

Fun Lovin' Criminals: *100% Columbian* (Virgin '99) 💣

FU-Schnickens: *F.U.—Don't Take It Personal* (Jive '92) Not "Asiatic," and not "Asian" either. "Oriental," as in the kung FU movies where these black Brooklynites learned the warrior's way. 'Cept FU also ciphers to For Unity, and they watch a *lot* of TV, and headman Chip FU's dancehall goes by so fast you'll have trouble keeping up on the lyric sheet, especially when he throws in exextra syllallables or semyhr sdrawkcab. Armchair zucchinis with dreams of multiculti deconstruction have been on the lookout for these guys— rappers whose visions of fun, agape, and aural conquest remain open-ended, playful, and, face it, silly. Hope their ideals and/or illusions don't evaporate upon contact with the outside world. **A–**

FU-Schnickens: *Nervous Breakdown* (Jive '94) You want an inkling of how grim things are for black kids right now, try and find another current rap record that manages to mean a damn thing without slipping into gangsta suicide or Afrocentric cryptoracism. Since this one sank faster than Public Enemy, maybe it doesn't mean much either, but to me the East Flatbush trio radiates the hope hip hop was full of not so long ago. There's deep pleasure in their vocal trade-offs and hard, wryly textured tracks. There's wordwise grace in rhymes that balance B-movie fantasy against everyday brutality without denial or despair. And there's joy in the nonpareil skills of reformed backward rapper Chip Fu. He coughs, he hiccups, he snorts, he stutters; he whinnies, wheezes, wows, and flutters. **A−**

FU-Schnickens: *Greatest Hits* (Jive '96) I'd say check out the real albums—there're only two—except that I already did and you didn't, gold single with Shaq notwithstanding. So maybe you'll try four from CD A and four from CD B, including the pace-setting "La Schmoove" and the impossible "Sum Dum Monkey," a speed-rapped run of sonic laugh lines so virtuosic it rockets beyond double-dare-you into a realm of ludic delight where few dare follow. The previously uncollecteds, a soundtrack track plus three new ones, pretend FU-revels are a dancehall offshoot, which bodes poorly and will convince no one. These guys obviously came from nowhere, whence they will now return—for natural comedians, a tragic end. **A−**

Future Bible Heroes: *Memories of Love* (Slowriver '97) Ⓝ

The Future Sound of London: *Lifeforms* (Astralwerks '94) Ⓝ

The Future Sound of London: "We Have Explosive" (*Dead Cities*, Astralwerks '96) 👁️

F/COMPLIATIONS

Fat Beats & Brastraps: Battle Rhymes & Posse Cuts (Rhino '98) bitch bitch bitch, brother brother brother (Shanté, "Big Mama"; Roxanne Shanté vs. Sparky Dee, "Round 1 [Uncensored]") ★
Fat Beats & Brastraps: Classics (Rhino '98) "The rules of the game are simple and plain/Turn on the microphone and recite your name," claims the great lost Sparky-D over some breakbeats and an audacious two-note Louie Shelton loop. And beyond the two stone classics, Roxanne

Shanté's "Have a Nice Day" and the Real Roxanne's "Bang Zoom (Let's Go-Go)," that innocence encapsulates the casual charm and enduring artistic value of this femme rap comp. It's innocent when Shanté lays out the perils of the street on the rare "Runaway," when young Latifah shanks the Meters, when LeShaun dba 2 Much serves up the lovingly lubricious "Wild Thang" for the ineluctably lustful L. L. Cool J, when the great lost Ice Cream Tee disses "male chauvinists" without thinking twice. Historically and musically, the Sequence and Salt-n-Pepa are missed. What a great girls school the old school could have been. **A−**
Fat Beats & Brastraps: New MCs (Rhino '98) "Unknown MCs" is often the truth, which doesn't make it justice (Nonchalant, "5 O'Clock"; Shä-Key, "Soulsville") ★★

The Flintstones: Music from Bedrock (MCA '94) triple whopper with cheese ("Weird Al" Yankovic, "Bedrock Anthem"; Green Jelly, "Anarchy in the U.K."; the BC-52's, "(Meet) The Flintstones") ★★★

Floyd Collins (Nonesuch '96) 💣

For the Love of Harry: Everybody Sings Nilsson (MusicMasters '95) He was so great he can make Jimmy Webb and Steve Forbert sound interesting, Aimee Mann and Marc Cohn sound enduring, Jennifer Trynin and Ron Sexsmith sound like you should know who they are. He was so great Fred Schneider ain't funnier and the Roches ain't spacier. He was so great you'll play one of these things from beginning to end—twice, even more, for the fun of it. **B+**

Freedom Fire—The Indestructible Beat of Soweto (Vol. 3) (Virgin '90) Producer Trevor Herman claims the lead cut, featuring Mahlathini and the gang, is "the finest track ever released on Earthworks." I say it's high-generic, and five minutes of high-generic at that, damn near swallowing the shouting spirituality of the two Amaswazi Emvelo songs right afterward. But gradually things pick up—Zulu fear of flying, nasal Shangaan weirdness, three distinct and magnificent Mahlathini vehicles, modest accordion jive, avant Venda-Pedi instrumental, modernized marabi, hectoring Sotho shout. Out of many peoples, one compilation. **A–**

The Funky Precedent (Loosegroove /No Mayo '99) underground hip hop at its warmest, most multiculti, and least hip hop (the Breakestra, "Getcho Soul Together"; Dilated Peoples, "Triple Optics [Live Funky Precedent Mix]") ★

Future House: Best of House Music Volume 4 (Profile '93) grooviest at its least techno, when it peels back house's soul to the kernels of melody underneath (Hyper Go Go, "High"; S.A.S., "Amber Groove"; Liberty City, "Some Lovin' ") ★★

Futurhythms (Medicine '93) midrange, steady-state, "tribal" (Leftfield, "Song of Life [Radio Edit]"; the Prodigy, "Wind It Up [Forward Wind Mix]") ★★

g

Warren G: *Regulate . . . G Funk Era* (Violator/RAL '94) Where his homeboy Snoop plays a well-chilled sociopath whose indifference to pain is the centerpiece of his carefully plotted menace, Dr. Dre's kid half brother is more like a mischievous seventh-grader. Giggling at Bootsy's funny glasses one minute, selling crack on the corner the next, he could go either way, or both in tandem. His cool and his tough are less practiced, less cocksure, hence more dangerous—and more tragic. Teamed with the tunefully murderous Nate Dogg, he's nasty in a new, neurotic way. Giving work to the Twinz or Dove Shack, he's one more G. **B+**

Warren G: *Take a Look over Your Shoulder (Reality)* (Def Jam '97) 💣

Peter Gabriel: *US* (Geffen '92) His voice permanently hoarse—sounds like he's been campaigning for president since he dropped *So* in 1986, which in a sense he has—Gabriel deploys a multihued battalion of respected professionals into wave upon wave of overkill. Though the sonic layering isn't devoid of interest or even originality, the problem goes way beyond a grandeur that seems inauspiciously egotistical on "his first real record of love songs"—these arrangements would obtrude into any musical event more low-key than an Olympic anthem or a massed May Day choir singing "The Internationale." "Steam"'s googolgroove overwhelms its petty sexism, but "Kiss the Frog" wrecks a funny little idea about Pete's penis by asking it to hold up the weight of the world. And "Kiss the Frog" is the other fast one, plus one makes two. What you mean US, white man? **B−** 🦃

Chris Gaffney: "My Baby's Got a Dead Man's Number," "Loser's Paradise" (*Loser's Paradise*, HighTone '95) 🔊

Jeffrey Gaines: *Jeffrey Gaines* (Chrysalis '92) 💣

Serge Gainsbourg: "Je t'aime . . . moi non plus" (*Comic Book*, Mercury '97) 🔊

Diamanda Galas: *Plague Mass* (Mute '91) Ⓝ

Galaxie 500: *This Is Our Music* (Rough Trade '90) Look, all you young white people, I know fate has dealt you a shitty hand. Rent stabilization is a joke, safe sex isn't a joke, pollutants can really get you down, and forget the economy. Not to mention the decline of civility on our city streets. So if you just want to sit around and mope about it to each other, we understand. But if you're looking for a helping hand, you're going to have to reach out a little yourselves—that's just human nature. Show some get-up-and-go, crack a few jokes, like on the first song. As my grandpa used to say: "Laugh and the world laughs with you/Weep and you weep alone." **B−** 🦃

Game Theory: *Tinker to Evers to Chance* (Enigma '90) Ⓝ

Gang of Four: *A Brief History of the Twentieth Century* (Warner Bros. '90) A gorgeous artifact, history by a band that doesn't even control its own—all their product good (*Entertainment, Solid Gold, Another Day/Another Dollar, Songs of the Free*) and bad (*Hard*) has been deleted ("is history," one might say), replaced by one otherwise uncompromising nonvinyl retrospective. Explication aplenty is provided by the Greil Marcus essay that supports the package, though he underplays their crabwise rhythmic progress and sporadic militance. Docked a notch so you scour the remainder bins first. **A–**

Gang of Four: *Mall* (Polydor '91) and in the mall, there's a disco ("Motel," "F.M.U.S.A.") ★

Gang of Four: *Shrinkwrapped* (Castle '95) Ⓝ

Gang of Four: *100 Flowers Bloom* (Rhino '98) In a year of exploitations and misconceptions—Newman box (his albums sell cheap), Bacharach box (when will Dionne get her miniset?), Mayfield overkill-then-downsize (MCA's two-CD 1992 *Anthology* nails him)—the synchronic programming, live tracks, and five songs from 1995's disappearing *Shrinkwrapped* make this double look like another rogue Rhino. Far from it. Gof4's Warner albums always worked as albums, as they will again when they're finally rereleased, and Warner's *Brief History of the 20th Century* posits a proper beginning, middle, and end. What this jumble does is establish new interconnections—the concert versions and studio remixes hold songs you know up to the light, and mixed in among the old electrofunk adventures their recent techno moves sound principled and in character. Gof4's radical critique/embrace of commodification remains a truth, not the whole truth, so help me God. But it sure hasn't lost relevance. And when their albums do come back whole, as commodification makes inevitable, this version of their vision will still get in your face. **A**

Gang Starr: "The Illest Brother" (*Daily Operation,* Chrysalis '92) 🐢

Gang Starr: *Hard to Earn* (Chrysalis/ERG '94) Ⓝ

Gang Starr: *Moment of Truth* (Noo Trybe '98) Ⓝ

Gang Starr: *Full Clip: A Decade of Gang Starr* (Virgin '99) A longtime agnostic in re Guru and Premier except as regards the former's ill-advised Roy Ayers–Donald Byrd trip, I'm grateful for this exemplary compilation. For anybody wondering what "flow" can mean, Guru's smooth, unshowy delivery, cool in its confident warmth and swift without ever burying words or betraying rush, is one ideal, and Premier's steady drums 'n' bass, just barely touched by anything that would pass for a hook, undergird his groove with discretion and power. My problem has always been the music's formalism—the way it encouraged adepts to bask in skillful sounds and rhymes that abjure commerce and tough-guyism. But reducing five albums to two CDs not only ups the pop density, as you'd expect, but achieves variety by jumbling chronology and mixing in B sides and soundtrack one-offs that weren't cut to any album's flow. It's a credit to the duo's constancy that the result plays like a single release. And despite his occasional bad-girl tales and images of sexual submission, Guru's quiet rectitude and disdain for a street rhetoric whose reality he's seen make him a chronicler everybody can learn from. **A–**

Garbage: *Garbage* (Almo Sounds '95) if Whale is Tricky without a dark side, Garbage is Whale without Tricky and depressed about it ("Queer," "Supervixen") ★★★

Garbage: *Version 2.0* (Almo Sounds '98) The chrome-plated hooks and metronome hardbeats of this irresistibly dislikable exercise are perfect for a frontwoman whose vaunted sexuality is no more welcoming than Tina Turner's. For those of us unattracted to real-life sadomasochism, how better to combine pleasure and pain than to let 12 impregnable theoretical hits march over us in their digital boots? **A–**

Greg Garing: *Alone* (Paladin/Revolution '97) **Ⓝ**

Garmarna: *Gods Musicians* (Omnium '96) **💣**

Djivan Gasparyan: *Apricots from Eden* (Traditional Crossroads '96) **Ⓝ**

Coumba Gawlo: *Coumba Gawlo* (Africando import '94) **Ⓝ**

Gay Dad: *Leisure Noise* (London '99) **💣**

The Gear Daddies: "Boys Will Be Boys" (*Let's Go Scare Al,* Polydor '90) **👒**

Genaside II: *Ad Finite* (Durban Poison '99) Filtering Gil Scott-Heron through Linton Kwesi Johnson and Bernard Herrmann through Richard Wagner, guesting an imprisoned dancehall boomer on one track and a certified operatic contralto on the next, this Prodigy/Chems/Tricky-beloved brand name has more scope and punch than most trip hop, or whatever it is. And it holds together like—well, not Wagner probably, but at least Shadow. Unaccustomed as I am to thrilling to fake strings, I thrill to these. And not just because I've been boomed into submission, I don't think. **A–**

General Degree: "Pianist" (*Love Punany Bad* [comp], Priority '95) **👒**

Genius/GZA: *Liquid Swords* (Geffen '95) gangsta as mystery, religious and literary ("Shadowboxin'," "Killah Hills 10304") **★★**

Genius/GZA: *Beneath the Surface* (MCA '99) he means the surface of a frozen lake, if I'm not mistaken ("Victim," "Crash Your Crew") **★**

Boy George and Culture Club: *At Worst . . . The Best of Boy George and Culture Club* (SBK '93) **Ⓝ**

Boy George: "Funtime" (*Cheapness and Beauty,* Virgin '95) **👒**

The Geraldine Fibbers: *Lost Somewhere Between the Earth and My Home* (Virgin '95) alienated violin, dramatic tempo changes, stentorian vocals—if this be country music, so was King Crimson ("A Song About Walls," "Marmalade") **★**

The Geraldine Fibbers: *Butch* (Virgin '97) **Ⓝ**

Gerardo: *Mo' Ritmo* (Interscope '90) mocha ice—lick it good now ("Fandango," "Rico Suave") **★**

Lisa Germano: *Happiness* (Capitol '93) **💣**

Lisa Germano: *Geek the Girl* (4AD '94) sonics lean, drama thin ("My Secret Reason," "Cancer of Everything," "Stars") **★★**

George Gershwin: *Gershwin Plays Gershwin: The Piano Rolls* (Elektra Nonesuch '93) I know, I'm surrendering all my principles—make room for *Rhapsody in Blue* and soon Schubert's *Trout* or something will weasel into the anticanon. Actually, I've liked *Trout* both times I've played it—and not only that, remember liking it, which is more than I can say of any Mozart I've ever enjoyed, if indeed I have. But unlike *Rhapsody in Blue,* it doesn't have the B-word in its title or the B-notes in its tune—or the tricky little "Sweet and Lowdown" to lead off, or "Swanee" to arouse one's blackface anxieties. And it doesn't have the composer in higher fi than any other '20s recording technique permitted. **A–**

George Gershwin: *The Piano Rolls Vol. Two* (Nonesuch '95) **Ⓝ**

The Geto Boys: *The Geto Boys* (Def American '90) I accept the slasher-movie defense in re the racism (and antirockism) of all attempts to stop these putative tough guys from bum-rushing the marketplace. But aesthetically the analogy is null, because slasher movies suck—exploiting and exacerbating rather than "revealing" or "catharsizing," they're a social pathology, period. So whether the Boys are expressing their inner natures or one-upping N.W.A and 2 Live Crew, they're sick motherfuckers. Women get offed before or during sex in three different songs, one of which runs a chorus of "Geto Boys, Geto Boys" in back lest the misguided distance it too far from its perps, and if the merely brutal "Gangster of Love" isn't about their own experiences, they don't want anybody to know it. I'm impressed by their pungent beats and vernacular. I'm glad they put Reagan in bed with Noriega. I'm sorta touched when one of them thinks to thank the first girl to lick his asshole. I admire their enunciation on "F#@* 'Em." But fuck 'em. **B–** 🦃

Geto Boys: "Mind Playing Tricks on Me" (*We Can't Be Stopped,* Rap-a-Lot '92) 💣

Geto Boys: *Till Death Do Us Part* (Rap-a-Lot '93) 💣

Geto Boys: "The World Is a Ghetto" (*The Resurrection,* Rap-a-Lot '96) 💣

Ghazal: *As Night Falls on the Silk Road* (Shanachie '98) Ⓝ

Ghorwal: *Majurugenta* (RealWorld '93) The Mozambican music is happy yet principled, soukous-smooth even if the interlocking rhythms show off their seams and the horns are equal parts intricacy and palpable deliberation. The translations add attacks on "fashion" to various unusual, banal ways to die—no medicine, no transport, your general civil war horror. In short, three-dimensional agitprop—tragedy and left puritanism in one resolutely hedonistic package. **A–**

Ghostface Killah: *Ironman* (Razor Sharp/Epic Street '96) The most street of the Clan—not comic like Ol' Dirty Bastard or mack like Method Man, not deep like Raekwon or Genius either. In a word, gangsta—East Coast–style, reflective and observant, only he doesn't vow to go straight all the time. By his own account, he's done a lot of bad things, and within five minutes he's spewing some of the vilest woman-hate in the sorry history of the subgenre. But the detail is so vivid and complex that for once we get the gripping blaxploitation flick gangsta promises rather than the dull or murky one it delivers. True crime tales like the vengeful "Motherless Child" and the unstoppable "260" are gritty and action-packed, and even the spew plays out as exactly what a

long-dicked knucklehead would want to say to the young thing who done him wrong. Then there are moments like "Camay," in which social-climbing crew members move on a legal secretary and an assistant manager at Paragon, and the social-realist family reminiscence "All I Got Is You." Most decisive of all, RZA's music is every bit as literal as Ghostface's rhymes and rap, giving up tunes, even hooks. As soulful as Tony Toni Toné—maybe more. **A**

Giant Sand: *Swerve* (Amazing Black Sand '90) Ⓝ

Giant Sand: *Ramp* (Amazing Black Sand '92) After a decade of secondhand longhairs pushing paisley and/or Manson and/or paganism and/or mulching and/or altered states as the true flowering of that storied '60s ideal, a postpunk comes up with a new improved aural simulation of hippiedom. It probably wasn't recorded on Howe Gelb's commune—sources indicate that Gelb doesn't have a commune. But what a commune it evokes—friendly, cooperative, never so spaced out it becomes dysfunctional. Guests drift in and out, and from Indiosa Patsy Jean, who sounds about five, to Pappy Dailey, who sounds about 70, there's room for anyone with a song. The first side makes something of the dissociated atmospherics that undermined the band's previous umpteen releases; the second's almost popwise. Together they're what country-rock was never really like, or wanted to be. **A–**

Giant Sand: *Center of the Universe* (Restless '93) Howe Gelb is too smart to claim said center is him—but not too smart to suspect it ("Center of the Universe," "Thing Like That") ★

Giant Sand: *Glum* (Imago '94) the wisdom of younguns and old folks rises from the half-formed void ("Bird Song," "I'm So Lonesome I Could Cry") ★

Giant Sand: *Purge and Slouch* (Restless '94) 💣

Gift: *Multum In Parvo* (Tim/Kerr '95) Sonic Youth as Poison from a Portland married-couple-plus-dynamite-drummer who heard another album in those tricks ("Sinking Ship," "OK This Is the Pops") ★★★

Gilberto Gil: *Parabolic* (Tropical Storm '91) translations or no translations, you'll wish you knew Portuguese ("Where the Baiao Comes From") ★

Gilberto Gil/Jorge Ben: *Gil E Jorge* (Verve '92) Always ready to go further out on a beat than the other samba/bossa geniuses, they walked into a studio in 1975 and spread nine songs over 78 minutes. With percussion up front and snatches of English on the order of "Blue, blue sky/Blue, blue sea" reinforcing all the repetitions and nonsense syllables, the renowned lyricists were playing a rhythm game, and they won. They don't just vamp till ready—they vamp to live, vamp for the sheer open-ended joy of it. **A–**

Gilberto Gil: "Tatá Engenho Novo" (*O Sol De Oslo,* Blue Jackel '98) 🍭

Gilberto Gil: See also Caetano Veloso e Gilberto Gil

Vance Gilbert: *Shaking Off Gravity* (Philo '98) 🍒

Johnny Gill: *Johnny Gill* (Motown '90) Ⓝ

Vince Gill: *I Still Believe in You* (MCA '92) As bland as Nicolette Fogelberg, with Tony Brown running the broad-spectrum lyrics through his good-taste machine as if he wants to be Peter Asher when he grows up, this ex-purist is the real country-hunk menace because he's so reproducible. I admit they pin a few classics—"Don't Let Our Love Start Slippin' Away" and "Say Hello" have the ring of general truth. But when they don't, it's '70s singer-songwriter all over again. Eddie Rabbitt just didn't know how to market himself. **C+** 🦃

Vince Gill: *When Love Finds You* (MCA '94) 🍒

Jimmie Dale Gilmore: "After Awhile" (Elektra Nonesuch '91) Gilmore being something of a mystic, I expect transcendence of him, and on his two previous

records Butch Hancock gave it to me: "When the Nights Are Cold" on *Jimmie Dale Gilmore,* "See the Way" on *The Flatlanders.* This basically self-composed major-label whozis is solider than either, solid like the quality country album it ain't—Gilmore may not be writing so metaphysical anymore, though "Go to Sleep Alone" is pretty deep, but he still sings like a space cadet. Still, some kind of quality album it is. The nearest it comes to a peak is a Butch Hancock song. **A–**

Jimmie Dale Gilmore: *Spinning Around the Sun* (Elektra '93) Never one for automatic poetry, Gilmore chooses to showcase precisely four of the new songs he's managed in the past two years, and even though Butch Hancock and Al Strehli provide appropriate camouflage, somebody up there must have expected a grander statement, because this major-label follow-up is gussied up like just that. The voice transmutes Major Tom into Roy Orbison, the production glistens like Garth, and fast or slow the tempos never waver. All of which may strike the pure of heart as icky, or inappropriate, but I doubt I'll hear a more gorgeous country record—maybe a more gorgeous record—anytime soon. And unlike *"After Awhile,"* this one doesn't let up—ends with a spooky Lucinda Williams duet and three of those four new songs, two of which were definitely worth the trouble. **A**

Jimmie Dale Gilmore: *Braver Newer World* (Elektra '96) trying to prove he's not trad, which we knew already ("Black Snake Moan," "Borderland") ★★★

Gin Blossoms: *New Miserable Experience* (A&M '92) Even if you hate weak guys a lot more than I do, you can't deny that "Hey Jealousy" is a classic—Peter Buck himself would kill (or at least steal) for that gold-plated guitar lick. But though the guy who came up with it is now dead, the group and its handlers jangle on through mediocre follow-ups programmers wouldn't have played twice before "Hey Jealousy" softened them up. The marketplace—what mere journalist can fathom it? C+ 🦃

Greg Ginn: *Dick* (Cruz '94) ⓝ

Ginuwine: *Ginuwine . . . The Bachelor* (550 Music/Epic '96) mack beats bumped and grounded ("Pony," "Holler") ★★★
Ginuwine: *100% Ginuwine* (550 Music '99) thump, bump, hump ("Final Warning," "No. 1 Fan") ★★

Girls Against Boys: *Venus Luxure No. 1 Baby* (Touch and Go '93) heeding their mentor, Chicago bon vivant Louis Armstrong, they pass stool midrecord, and does it improve their sex life! ("7 Seas," "Bulletproof Cupid") ★
Girls Against Boys: *Cruise Yourself* (Touch and Go '94) 💣
Girls Against Boys: *House of GvsB* (Touch and Go '94) Usually good bands choose meaningful monikers like Stereolab or Sammy or Rage Against the Machine. But how about Hüsker Dü? The Pixies? *Nirvana?* Read into those trademarks whatever you want in retrospect, you were drawn to them by the way the attendant guitars etc. did their things. So take the name for the cheap attention-getting device it is. The main difference here is an attraction altogether less instantaneous and surefire—to a sound that's impressive but cold, suggesting the Fall as produced by Al Jourgensen or *In Utero* at a more primitive level of spiritual development. Of course, once it reveals its human frailty, its pleasures seem deeper as a result. Ain't retrospect grand? A–
Girls Against Boys: *Freakonica* (DGC '98) ⓝ

Philip Glass/Allen Ginsberg: "Song #6 from Wichita Vortex Sutra" (*Hydrogen Jukebox*, Elektra Nonesuch '93) 💿

Corey Glover: *Hymns* (LaFace '98) ⓝ

The Goats: *Tricks of the Shade* (Ruffhouse/Columbia '92) The password invoked to keep the wrong element out of the hip hop club is "beats." Shazzy, Sister Souljah, the Disposable Heroes, the Beastie Boys, all are accused of lacking beats, and no doubt these three rappers and five musicians will get the same treatment. So unless you're a joiner, home in on their fusion and call it alternative rock. Right, it so happens that this pointedly integrated group is also pointedly leftist. But while I enjoy the numerous skits partly because I approve of their messages, Columbus and flag burning and Leonard Peltier don't push my buttons even if abortion and class and pleasure do. I listen to this record because I love the way the rap vocals add muscle and edge to the hard-rock guitar and classic-rock bass. As for the beats per se, they're solid. Even slammin. A
The Goats: "Butcher Countdown" (*No Goats, No Glory*, Ruffhouse/Columbia '94) 💿

The Go-Betweens: *1978–1990* (Capitol '90) Half best-of, half collectorama, this gets you coming and going: you had no idea the album highlights would mesh into perfect pop, and you had no idea the 45-rpm obscurities would coalesce into imperfect pop. What threw you off was that they always seemed too serious for pop, too grown up. But once Robert Forster and Grant McLennan stooped or leaped to melody, they were serious fun in spite of themselves. And bookishly static though they seemed, they were also a band. Forster and McLennan provided the internal tension—subtle friction at its most personal and its most cooperative. Lindy Morrison made sure they moved. A
The Go-Betweens: *The Peel Sessions* (Strange Fruit '91) The quality of the B sides etc. on *1978–1990* surprised fans who thought they were buying greatest semihits, and like any world-historical pop band, the Go-Betweens were more than a song vehicle—they had a drummer. The four fine fast ones on this 1984 broadcast session—a B from *1978–1990* and three I'd never heard—rock tougher than you'd expect from their 1984 studio LP. I propose a posthumous live. A–
The Go-Betweens: *Spring Hill Fair* (Beggars Banquet '96) In the Indian sum-

mer of a formal moment, singer-song-writer-guitarists Robert Forster and Grant McLennan joined a shifting lineup headed by steadfast drummer-inamorata Lindy Morrison and mercurial violinist-inamorata Amanda Brown to fashion as deep and intricate and prematurely mature a body of traditional relationship songs as, oh, Joni Mitchell herself, who should only have accessed half their empathy and synergy. Hiding their hooks in arrangements and lyrics as often as they brandished them in tunes, they were modest, affectionate, funny, cheerful, never too oblique or ironic—pop for the ages if anything is. But with the *1978–1990* compilation now import-only, novice songseekers are confronted instead by a remastered, reannotated six-album oeuvre. So acquire them all, I guess, thusly: *Tallulah* (1987, Amanda and "Right Here"), *Spring Hill Fair* (1984, produced yet rough), *Before Hollywood* (1983, austere yet gorgeous), *16 Lovers Lane* (1988, poppest), *Liberty Belle and the Black Diamond Express* (1986, talkiest), *Send Me a Lullaby* (1981, punkest). Accounted too damn subtle for a U.S. market whose favorite Aussies were MTV flukes and whose favorite Brits had surrealistic haircuts, these Brisbane-bred Londoners' first three albums were never accorded the decency of official U.S. release. This is my paltry attempt to extend a nation's apology. **A**

The Go-Betweens: "Karen" (*78 'til 79: The Lost Album*, Jetset '99) 🐝

The Go-Betweens: *Bellavista Terrace: Best of the Go-Betweens* (Beggars Banquet '99) Ⓝ

God: *Possession* (Virgin '92) Ⓝ
God: *The Anatomy of Addiction* (Big Car import '94) Ⓝ

Godflesh: *Pure* (Relatively/Earache '92) Ⓝ

Go-Go's: *Greatest* (I.R.S. '90) The great album they didn't have in them, so skillfully constructed that you can't tell the *Talk Show* from the *Beauty and the Beat*—can't tell Belinda Carlisle learned

how to sing before she forgot how to live. How she thrives when she's stuck with her sisters' songs! How they thrive when they stick her with their songs! How fine they all sound covering "Cool Jerk"! How much is that doggie in the window? **A**

Golden Delicious: "Hot Corn, Cold Corn" (*Old School*, Cavity Search '97) 🐝

Golden Smog: *Down by the Old Mainstream* (Rykodisc '96) Ⓝ

Goldie: *Timeless* (FFRR '95) If Goldie is to jungle what Tricky is to trip hop—the "accessible" name brand for strangers in wonderland—then Martin Denny was Dr. Livingston. Occasionally some diva takes up a tune, but mainly this pleasant, far from arhythmic soundspace posits an impressionistic respite from hardcore techno, with warm links to fusion, movie music, and the tragically neglected legacy of Rick Wakeman. **C+**

Goldie: *Saturnz Return* (London/FFRR '98) 💣

Gomez: *Bring It On* (Hut/Virgin '98) really da roots-rock—they mean it, man ("Whipping Piccadilly," "Love Is Better Than a Warm Trombone") ★★★

Gomez: *Liquid Skin* (Virgin '99) Ⓝ

Rubén González: *Introducing . . . Rubén González* (World Circuit '97) Never much for horn sections, I've always preferred my clave straight from the timbales, perhaps with some charanga violins for accent. But in part that's because not even Eddie Palmieri gives up as much montuno as this 77-year-old Cuban virtuoso, making his first album as a leader five years after he thought he'd retired, his joints aching and his home piano consumed by woodworm. Rhythm and romance flow from his old-fashioned digital memory as he and his friends jam the classics, guaracha to bolero to cha cha cha. **A–**

Goodie Mob: "Guess Who" (*Soul Food* [ST], LaFace '95) 🐝

Goodie Mob: *Still Standing* (LaFace '98) Their drawls as thick as their funk, they create a Dirty South at once more impenetrable and more inviting than Eightball's or Master P's—in feeling, one of hip hop's most neighborly spaces. Musically and verbally, they're too textural, but not even OutKast cultivates such territory with such care, and their Allmans homage/rip is almost as inspirational as this preachment: "I'm sick of lyin'/I'm sick of glorifyin' dyin'/I'm sick of not tryin'." **B+**

Goodie Mob: *World Party* (LaFace '99) Not to truck with the boogie bromide that spiritual uplift requires certified fun, but this album is anything but the pop retreat the conscious slot it as. Quiet as it's kept, message was always icing for these Dirty South pathfinders anyway, and this is the first time their music has ever achieved the infectious agape that's always been claimed for it. The mood recalls early go go—a funk so all-embracing that anyone who listens should be caught up in its vital vibe. But after 20 years of hip hop, the rhythmic reality is far trickier than Chuck Brown or Trouble Funk ever dreamed—as is Cee-Lo's high-pitched overdrive, which may yet be remembered as one of the great vocal signatures of millennial r&b. **A–**

Steve Goodman: *No Big Surprise: The Steve Goodman Anthology* (Red Pajamas '94) Cool Hand Leuk, this impish folkie liked to call himself. When cancer finally got him after 15 years in 1984, Randy Newman could think of no apter or kinder way to open a tribute concert than "Short People," but it grieves me to report that Keith Moreland did not drop a routine fly at his funeral, as Goodman suggested in 1983's "A Dying Cub Fan's Last Request." Living in the valley of the shadow of chemo, Goodman believed in enjoying himself, and he also believed it was his job—meaning among other things the precondition of all the gratifications he refused to delay—to induce us to enjoy ourselves as well. That's one reason the live half of this double-CD is especially irresistible despite the old stuff. He's adroit, very funny, very tolerant, seldom too warm, and incorrigibly middle-class. Up

until now he had his name on a lot of great songs and nothing anyone imagined was a great album. **A–**

Goo Goo Dolls: *Hold Me Up* (Metal Blade '90) Ⓝ
Goo Goo Dolls: *A Boy Named Goo* (Warner Bros./Metal Blade '95) 💣
Goo Goo Dolls: *Dizzy Up the Girl* (Warner Bros. '98) Ⓝ

John Gorka: *After Yesterday* (Red House '98) 💣

Gorky's Zygotic Mynci: *Introducing Gorky's Zygotic Mynci* (Mercury '96) 💣

Grandaddy: *Under the Western Freeway* (V2 '98) An indelibly local unit from the sun-baked I-5 nowhere of Modesto, California, they orchestrate lo-fi so cunningly that the tunes arising from the murk seem angelic in their grace and uplift. The title instrumental, a descending scale voiced by several flutes or recorders and a roomful of busted Casios, sets the standard. But that's not to say skateboard pro turned glorified garbage man Jason Lytle throws away the words, starting with a lead track that dissents from meritocracy with a quiet defeatism too subtle and eloquent for any simple slacker. No matter how wearisome Lytle finds all the Neil Young, Howe Gelb, and Pavement comparisons, they triangulate him accurately and honorably. **A–**
Grandaddy: *Signal to Snow Ratio* (V2 '99) accomplished sound with not much new to say meets 12 minutes to say it in ("MGM Grand," "Hand Crank Transmitter") ★★

Grandmaster Flash and the Furious Five: *Message from Beat Street: The Best of Grandmaster Flash and the Furious Five* (Rhino '94) They start out as street kids trying to get over, their idea of a sales gimmick "The Birthday Party"— because everybody's got one, and because in 1981 that's still considered reason for celebration. Up till "It's Nasty" they specialize in hard dance music no more serious than, oh, Tony Toni Toné's.

But unlike Kurtis Blow, their only rival on record until Run-D.M.C. changes everything, they think like consumers, striking poses that look good on the corner, not the stage. And then a Columbia student they know writes "The Message" and it dawns on big-voiced frontman Melle Mel (and hard-nosed label owner Sylvia Robinson) that with his street cred he can put its message over. Although their protest phase may sound naive to the ignorant, it looks at the inner-city same-old with a freshness and moral certainty few have matched since, and played, scratched, or synthesized, their beats seize history. "Wheels of Steel" would have made a more poetic intro than the redundant 1994 megamix. But this is how rap began. **A**

Grandmaster Flash, Melle Mel & the Furious Five: *More of the Best* (Rhino '96) Beyond the extended "Flash to the Beat" and the essential "Wheels of Steel," these 12 tracks were recorded '84–'87, when they sounded a little lost. Heard as musical form rather than cultural positioning, however, they flesh out Flash's beat-mastery, grandly intricate yet stone solid, and establish that Melle Mel beat Chuck D to the game—the fire-and-mutant-dogs "World War III" hits like "Black Steel in the Hour of Chaos," and lays down political science in the bargain. **A–**

Grand Puba: *Reel to Reel* (Elektra '92) easygoing racist-sexist motherfucker ("Lickshot") ★

Amy Grant: *Heart in Motion* (A&M '91) Xian Xover queen: "What's the difference between a PMS'ing woman and a bulldog? Lipstick! See, only a woman can tell that joke." Don't be so sure, lady. And note *Hit's* gnostic riposte: "What do you get when you cross an atheist with a dyslexic? Somebody who doesn't believe in dogs!" **C** 🦃

Grant Lee Buffalo: *Mighty Joe Moon* (Slash/Reprise '94) Grant Lee Phillips doesn't sing subtly enough to pine so lyrically or forcefully enough to suffer so unremittingly. That folkloric drawl may be the

way he talks, but it sounds like he picked it up at the movies along with the rest of his ideas. It's pointless to suggest he stick in a few laughs because there's no chance they'll be funny. I do recommend, however, that he abandon his quest for the meaning of John Wayne Gacy. **C+** 🦃

Grateful Dead: *Two from the Vault* (Grateful Dead '92) The preserve of a huge, insular cult accustomed to rendering its very real aesthetic discriminations within a context so uncritical no outsider need pay them the slightest mind, the Dead's music has disappeared into the mythology it engendered. They were a great band—probably still are on the right night. But trying to convince an unbeliever is like trying to tell a stranger about LSD. Recorded in August 1968, when Pigpen McKernan was still living in his body, these nine songs include all six on the classic *Live/Dead;* playing is comparable, audio superior. Great drummers were hard to come by in the hippie era, and the Dead were too discursive to want one anyway—Bill and Mickey rocked out by revving tempo and volume and letting Pigpen take it away. But often the Dead's ruminations have content—they listened more responsibly than any other band of the era. And on solos of over a chorus or two, Jerry Garcia stands as the era's most inventive guitarist short of Hendrix and Page. God they were a trip. **A–**

Grateful Dead: *Dick's Picks Volume Two* (Grateful Dead '95) the good old days, circa Keith Godchaux ("Jam," "Going down the Road Feeling Bad") ★★★

Grateful Dead: *Dick's Picks Volume Three* (Grateful Dead '95) **Ⓝ**

Grateful Dead: *Hundred Year Hall* (Arista '95) **Ⓝ**

Grateful Dead: *Dick's Picks Volume Four* (Grateful Dead '96) three (more) CDs from their Fillmore East heyday ("China Cat Sunflower," "That's It for the Other One") ★

Grateful Dead: *The Arista Years* (Arista '96) **Ⓝ**

Grateful Dead: *Dozin' at the Knick* (Grateful Dead '96) For years I've sought concrete proof that two decades of Dead-heads weren't the marshmallow-ears the world believed, but after several concert tapes failed to get over I decided I had more pressing business than finding the good nights that were probably still there. Now, finally, after several half stabs (*Hundred Year Hall, Fallout from the Phil Zone*), comes this four-hour three-CD document from historic Albany, New York. Solid new Bob Weir opener, coupla excellent! Bob Dylan covers, Brett Mydland more Rod McKernan than Page McConnell, creaky and transcendent "Black Peter," "Walkin' Blues" and "Jack-a-Roe," the nightly "Drums" and "Space" excursions scenic enough. And above all, that mesh of the tight and the shambolic that on their best nights rendered their music interactive in a way marshmallow-heads will never understand and therefore never hear. **A–**

Gravediggaz: *6 Feet Deep* (Gee Street '94) turning the nightmare up a notch to find out whether the world has gone completely bonkers ("Graveyard Chamber," "6 Feet Deep") ★★

Gravediggaz: *The Pick, the Sickle and the Shovel* (Gee Street '97) Ⓝ

Macy Gray: *On How Life Is* (Epic '99) if only Esther Phillips had written her own songs, she would have sung worse ones ("I've Committed Murder," "Caligula") ★★

Green: *White Soul/Bittersweet* (Widely Distributed '91) Ⓝ

Al Green: *One in a Million* (Word/Epic '91) Al is no less a self-starting weirdo when he sings gospel than in any other showbiz context. The greatest of the soul singers barely missed a beat making his conversion—he remained all personal stamp and driven style, a purely human miracle. So maybe I relate to his gospel because that isn't really what it is, although it helps that I loved his voice like a church lady long before he turned it to the service of the Lord. Combining the best of two pretty good albums with one cut from the made-whole *Higher Plane* and another from the stiff *Precious Lord,* this is

where ye of little faith will see the error of your ways. **A**

Al Green: *Love Is Reality* (Word/Epic '92) Ⓝ

Al Green: *Don't Look Back* (BMG import '95) This hard-to-find, slightly long-winded return to Mammon isn't what it should be, might be, or in theory will be, once MCA finalizes a promised revamp with its Hall of Fame inductee (hey guys, there's an angle—and there it goes, receding into the distance). Since 8 of 13 titles feature the word "love" (OK, once it's "lovin'," and in parentheses), the pruning will presumably start somewhere in there, although as with so much great minor Green not one of those performances lacks vocal frisson. Executive mastermind Arthur Baker finds a use for Curtis Stigers on the title tune and cedes Al a nice Charles & Eddie song, but the primary hands-on guys are Fine Young Cannibals David Steele and Andy Cox. On their "One Love," which strikes my impractical ear as the sure shot MCA craves, Green negotiates a thoroughly modern electrobeat so effortlessly you gotta believe he can live the rest of his life without God or Hi Rhythm. **A–**

Al Green: *Your Heart's in Good Hands* (MCA '95) MCA is docked a notch for updating *Don't Look Back* by hiring Queen of Banality Diane Warren to write a new lead track, and then having Little King of Funk Lite Narada Michael Walden produce it. Jodeci's DeVante provides the other new one, and although Al schmears his mythic high range all over both, their timid low range sounds like nothing more than a suave market ploy up against the emulated Hi Rhythm and borrowed Young Cannibals propelling everything that follows. **B+**

Al Green: "Love God (And Everybody Else)" (*Michael* [ST], Revolution '96) 🔊

Al Green: "(Live) How Can You Mend a Broken Heart" "(Live) Love and Happiness" (*Anthology,* The Right Stuff '97) 🔊

Green Day: *1,039/Smoothed Out Slappy Hours* (Lookout '90) 🧨

Green Day: *Kerplunk!* (Lookout '92) beats masturbating ("One for the Razorbacks," "2000 Light Years Away") ★★

Green Day: *Dookie* (Reprise '94) For accuracy's sake, I should note that you haven't exactly heard it all before—the drums are punchier, the structures trickier. But insofar as you have, that's the point: punk lives, and these guys have the toons and sass to prove it to those who can live without. Before they start to wear down, they've done their bit for apathy, insanity, voluntary poverty, and the un-American way. A–

Green Day: *Insomniac* (Reprise '95) Billy Joe has an instinctive hold on the rock and roll virtue of sounding like you mean—his songs conceptualize his natural whine with a musicality that undercuts his defeatism only don't be so sure. "I'm a smart-ass but I'm playing dumb": eight million sold and all he admits to knowing is the futility of Telegraph Avenue losers who dis the rich occasionally and each other all the time. How he'll feel when this one doesn't sell two million we should all want to know. A–

Green Day: *Nimrod* (Reprise '97) punks can age gracefully, but for whiners it's hard ("The Grouch," "Walking Alone") ★★

Patti Griffin: *Flaming Red* (A&M '98) ☞

Nanci Griffith: *Other Voices, Other Rooms* (Elektra '93) ☞

The Grifters: *Ain't My Lookout* (Sub Pop '96) Southern-fried hipsters uproot some pavement ("Parting Shot," "Boho/Alt") ★★

The GrooveGrass Boyz: *Groove-Grass 101* (Reprise '99) ☞

Grooverider: *Mysteries of Funk* (Higher Ground/Columbia '98) ☞

Guided by Voices: *Bee Thousand* (Scat '94) On most of these 20-tracks-in-36-minutes, the tunes emerge if you stick around, but they're undercut by multiple irritants. The lyrics are deliberately obscure, the structures deliberately foreshortened, the vocals a record collector's Anglophilia-in-the-shower; the rec-room production is so inconsistent you keep losing your bearings, as befits resident art-rock fan Robert Pollard's boast (which echoes Lou Barlow's, what a coincidence) that some recordings aren't just first takes but first plays, of songs he'd dreamed up since the last time the band came over. In short, this is pop for perverts—pomo smarty-pants too prudish and/or alienated to take their pleasure without a touch of pain to remind them that they're still alive. B– 🐛

Guided by Voices: *Alien Lanes* (Matador '95) ☞

Guitar Wolf: *Jet Generation* (Matador '99) is that a rocket in your pocket, or is this just a concept album about electric noise? ("Fujiyama Attack," "Cyborg Kids') ★

Gumball: *Special Kiss* (Primo Scree '91) ⓝ

Guns N' Roses: *Use Your Illusion I* (Geffen '91) what pros ("Don't Damn Me") ★

Guns N' Roses: *"Civil War"* (*Use Your Illusion II*, Geffen '91) 👁

Guns N' Roses: *"The Spaghetti Incident?"* (Geffen '93) Talk about anxiety of influence. As someone who never thought punk had much to do with musicianship or musicianship much to do with GN'R, I remain impressed even with the excitement worn off. I mean, *Axl Rose* damn near stealing "Human Being" from David Johansen? Because his *drummer* is so fierce? *Fear* and *UK Subs* (!) and *Nazareth* (!!) tunes that belong on the same record? What would Harold Bloom say? Something about Axl being a shitty songwriter, I hope. Which wouldn't be altogether fair. But hey—criticism is unfair. A–

The Guo Brothers & Shung Tian: *Yuan* (RealWorld '90) Produced by Pól Brennan of Clannad, the insufferable lace-curtain-Irish folkies who bequeathed Enya unto the world, and with Guo Yue's Chinese flute and Guo Yi's Chinese mouth organ carrying the melodies and Guo Liang's plucked Chinese harp plenty prominent, the instrumental affinities are self-evident. So I worry about the spiritual affinities. My working theory is that Maoist aesthetics knows the difference between dignity and gentility, enabling these exiles to formalize folk music into art music without draining its life away. Of course, this could be utter fancy—just as likely some arbitrary synthesis of acculturation and deep bodily need inclines me toward Chinese scales. But for sure their jaunty-to-haunting tunes and mood pieces eschew the comfortable sheen one associates with Pól Brennan, not to mention the comfortable pulse one associates with Kitaro. **B+**

Guru: *Jazzmatazz Volume 1* (Chrysalis '93) 💣

Arlo Guthrie and Pete Seeger: *More Together Again* (Rising Sun '94) 💣

Gutterball: *Gutterball* (Mute '93) New Zevons for a pomo world ("Trial Separation Blues," "One by One") ★★★

Orüj Güvenç & Tümata: *Ocean of Remembrance* (Interworld '95) Güvenç is a clinical psychologist, practicing musicologist, and Sufi sheik who heads his own department of music therapy at a med school in Istanbul. He's also a warm, intent, unvirtuosic, spiritually contained singer who plays ney (a flute), oud (a lute), and rebab (a three-stringed fiddle). He and his three associates recorded these six pieces during a blizzard in western Massachusetts while fasting for Ramadan. All six are zhikrs, recitations of God's names. Their distinct rhythms are mesmeric rather than exciting, and while they're not the healing music that is Güvenç's lifework, I can testify that this hour of unassuming ecstasy helped get me through a 101-degree fever—and that I love it when I'm straight as well. Sample-ready: the chanted breaths that take over "Allah, Allah, Allah" about 10 minutes in. **A**
Oruç Güvenç and Tümata: *Rivers of One* (Interworld '97) Showcasing the Sufi healing music that Güvenç rediscov-

ered—therapeutic rather than transcendent, longer on flute, with minimal vocals—this comprises three improvisations on the *rast makam,* a tonality said to promote "inner calmness." As someone who regularly endangers his immune system with electric music, I find it useful at bedtime. But although I dig how assuredly Gulten Uralli pours the water that sets the beat, I sincerely hope the follow-up moves on to the *hicaz makam,* which "protects and strengthens the urogenital system." **A–**

Guy: *The Future* (MCA '90) As is only natural, I have as much trouble relating personally to Aaron Hall's woo-pitching Wonderisms as to, I don't know, Keith Sweat's tender Teddyisms. But I do appreciate them, and if forced to a choice I'd definitely rather suck him off than Dr. Dre. At long last male soft-core—moved, appreciative, desperate for more. Elsewhere it's the present of the funk—Prince here, Imagination there, both as new as jack can be. Plus a kissoff to Gene Griffin doubling as a get-yours-from-the-man cheer. **A–**

Buddy Guy: *Damn Right I've Got the Blues* (Silvertone '91) ⓝ
Buddy Guy: *My Time After Awhile* (Vanguard '92) ⓝ
Buddy Guy: "Country Boy" (*Feels Like Rain,* Silvertone '93) 🍬
Buddy Guy: *Slippin' In* (Silvertone '94) more voice, more soul, plenty guitar, less classic (and shopworn) songs ("Love Her with a Feeling," "Little Dab-a-Doo") ★
Buddy Guy: *Heavy Love* (Silvertone '98) past 60 and feeling it, he's relaxing more and feeling that too ("Midnight Train," "Did Somebody Make a Fool out of You") ★★★

Buddy Guy & Junior Wells: *Alone and Acoustic* (Alligator '91) au contraire—together and acoustic ("High Heel Sneakers," "Give Me My Coat and Shoes") ★
Buddy Guy & Junior Wells: *Last Time Around—Live at Legends* (Silvertone

'98) They last performed together in 1993, half a decade before Wells died, and they fit like an old pair of shoes, picking up on cues that haven't even been delivered yet. The first "What'd I Say," a highlight twice, takes off on the clicks, moans, squeals, hoots, and chicken squawks Wells cuts into Guy's vocal, and again and again classic titles from their book and everyone else's are adjusted to accommodate classic lines from the universe of blues readymades. Take this as a passport to that universe, but don't expect anyone to sell you a map. **A–**

G/COMPILATIONS

Gabba Gabba Hey (Triple X '91) Somehow I dreamed Ramones songs would resist interpretation simply enough to make a tribute fun. Instead I'm wondering whether *Sniffin' Glue* went too far when it showed the world how to play those magic chords. Double-redundant because the respectful L.A. punkoids it corrals are quadruple-obscure, this scenester showcase coughs up small surprises from L7 (gurls), the Creamers (mostly gurls), and the Badtown Boys (not gurls). Yabba dabba doo. **C+** 🦃

Get Shorty (Antilles '95) Two new compositions perform the postmodern marvel of updating the Booker T. template "Green Onions," which is included for comparison. Especially in the five-minute version featuring his happy vocal interjections, soundtrack designer John Lurie's "Stink" melds jumpy funk to Casio kalimba with fine postneoprimitivist brio. And Us3's "Chilli Hot" hot-wires both action and music with the drop-dead snap and self-referential sass they cry out for. Unfortunately much of the rest merely does its job—by declining to develop snatches like the matched pair "Bo at Airport" and "Romantic Walk," Lurie aspires to atmosphere rather than the redefinition of r&b. Too bad—better him than such

well-modulated helpmates as Morphine and Medeski Martin & Wood. **B+**

Girls Town (Mercury '96) strong womanism from Yo Yo, Latifah, Salt-n-Pepa—and that's just the stuff you know (Roxanne Shanté, "Thin Line"; Suga, "And I Say"; Tyte, "Sista"; PJ Harvey, "Maniac") ★★★

Gnawa Music of Marrakesh: Night Spirit Masters (Axiom '90) Ⓝ

The Gospel According to Earthworks (Stern's/Earthworks '98) joy to the world music, South African style (Makholwa Vumani Isono, "Izikhova Ezimnqini"; Holy Spirits Choir, "Siyakubonga") ★

Great Divorce Songs for Her (Warner Bros. '94) gals only country fans have heard of show Travis and Hank up for the blowhards they are (the Forester Sisters, "Men"; DeAnna Cox, "Never Gonna Be Your Fool Again") ★★

Guitar Paradise of East Africa (Earthworks '91) Though at least three of the artists came up in Zaire, this classic compilation comprises six four- or five-minute Kenyan dance hits and five eight- or nine-minute Kenyan dance hits. So I guess it's benga, a beat/genre/label even more all-embracing than the soukous it cheerfully lifts. Though at times the guitaristics billow like Kinshasa, they're gentler, quirkier, more rural—and they're not definitive, because this is a song album. Nasally conversational or breathily musical, the voices get catchy to impossibly fetching melodies, and though only one band can afford horns, that band comes up with a great chart—a great *cheesy* chart. Intensely pleasurable up till cut seven, Orchestre Super Mazembe's atypically dark, typically gorgeous "Shauri Yako." After that, five consecutive tunes make you sit up and exclaim, "Oh boy, *that* one." Destructible, I suppose—persuasion, not power, is the idea. But if this is one world, undeniable. **A+**

Guys and Dolls (RCA Victor '92) It's a measure of musical comedy's descent into technique that every principal in this revival has more pipes and less style than those in MCA's 1951 original-cast version. And it's a measure of the boundless melody and street cred of Frank Loesser's songs that only a curmudgeon or a critic would make the comparison. The score isn't impregnable—after enduring Debbie Reynolds's New Yawkese in Reprise's Rat Pack version, I remembered why I get paid for doing this. And to give technique its due, only diva wannabe Josie de Guzman (whose insatiable urge to peal out does actually make a kind of sense in "If I Were a Bell") fails to add entertaining details. Forget *West Side Story*—Damon Runyon's criminal-minded wiseacres and untragic romance are for every rock and roller who prefers Chuck to Elvis and the Stones to the Doors. **A–**

Half Japanese: *Fire in the Sky* (Safe House '93) fast ones fast, slow ones heartbreaking ("This Could Be the Night," "Always," "Magic Kingdom," "Everyone Knows") ★★★

Half Japanese: *Greatest Hits* (Safe House '95) It might be possible to array all their best-realized inspirations in neat rows and convert the fogies who've never given the brothers Fair a first hearing or a second thought. But if they were capable of such compromises, there'd be no point. So here are two sprawling CDs somewhat more consistent than the messes that are their albums—69 not quite randomly ordered tracks (and don't think they can't add), at least 45 or 50 of which you'll be happier for knowing, with annotations that include David's guitar lesson ("I like to put six different-sized strings on because that gives the most variety, but my brother used to put six strings of the same thickness on so he wouldn't have so much to worry about") and the news that *Loud,* which was released in 1981, was recorded in 1982. Theorem: Jad, who likes girls, is more winsome (and talented) than David, who fears them. Corollaries: their romances top their sci-fi, and despite their renowned noise, their greatest moments are slow ones about crushes, usually sweetened by competent sidemen. The imperfect introduction. **A–**

Half Japanese: *Hot* (Safe House '95)

Aaron Hall: *The Truth* (Silas/MCA '93)

Michael Hall: *Adequate Desire* (DejaDisc '94) Far be it from me to attribute his edge to the journalism on his boho résumé, but he's always been a cut or two above the dozens or hundreds of marginal or semiprofessional singing songwriters who can pull your coat for a cut (or two). In fact, he's got a best-of's worth of tunes behind him: for starters, "Sharlene," "Debi Came Back," "I Work Hard," "I'm Sorry, I Can't Rock You All Night Long," "Don't Love Me Wisely," "Let's Take Some Drugs and Drive Around." But this is the first time he's opened the door to music lovers unequipped with the aesthetic discipline or psychological serendipity cut-above music usually requires. Since cut-above artists evolve just like the ones you keep your ear on, it catches him at an unrepresentative moment—he hasn't always been so reflective, although at this late date he may be stuck with it. He's not just trying to pin the moment when love reveals its mystery—he's trying to make it last as he looks death in the eye. **A–**

Michael Hall: *Frank Slade's 29th Dream* (DejaDisc '95) a folk-rock tour de force that goes "Life is all right for the time being/Life is all right for the time being"—for 38 minutes ★★

Michael Hall: *Day* (DejaDisc '96) electric-guitar songs for the apocalypse now ("Their First Murder," "Las Vegas") ★

Tom T. Hall: *Home Grown* (Mercury '97)

Geri Halliwell: *Schizosonic* (Capitol '99)

★★★, ★★, ★ Honorable Mention   🐦 Choice Cut   N Neither   💣 Dud   🦃 Turkey

Hamell on Trial: *Big As Life* (Mercury '95) gainfully employed enough to know what he and his amplified acoustic are pissed about ("Big As Life," "Z-Roxx") ★
Hamell on Trial: *The Chord Is Mightier Than the Sword* (Mercury '97) more songs about jobs and saloons ("In a Bar," "Red Marty") ★
Hamell on Trial: *Choochtown* (Such-A-Punch '99) Ed Hamell is a DIY folkie with a punky band who inhabits the sleazy corner where boonie bohemia meets pure lowlife. Drugs can make that happen, as can marginal employment slipping toward petty crime. His pals Chooch and Joe Brush certainly don't read Hammett, maybe Elmore Leonard or Carl Hiaasen for the warm weather. I bet Hamell reads them all—and that along with talk TV, they've influenced his narrative poesy. **B+**

Hammer: See MC Hammer

Beres Hammond: *In Control* (Elektra '94) Ⓝ

Herbie Hancock: *Dis Is Da Drum* (Mercury '95) Ⓝ

Handsome Boy Modeling School: So . . . How's Your Girl? (Tommy Boy '99) This Prince Paul p-jay is more trip-than hip hop. Its irresistibility is atmospheric—a sound that pits industrial textures against quiet piano samples/parts—and its lo-res limitations are established by the fact that its standout track was produced by DJ Shadow. But guest rappers (and singers) greatly augment its musicality, and the bits that aren't simply drop-deadpan funny have the same wiggy couch-potato resourcefulness I associate with the best De La Soul—the sense that these guys know how the deck is stacked and intend to beat the game without leaving their seats. A blow for realism. A blow for positivity. A blow for getting yours without taking it from your brothers. **A**

The Handsome Family: *Through the Trees* (Carrot Top '97) digging for the great elusive motherlode of American tragic deadpan ("Weightless Again," "The Woman Downstairs," "Cathedrals") ★★★
The Handsome Family: *Down in the Valley* (Independent import '99) The reason these alt-country cult heroes stir up so much humbug is that when Rennie Sparks's lyrics don't settle for "dark," or Brett Sparks's music for lo-fi dirge, they can be miraculous. Of course Brett's no Acuff or Haggard; his static baritone barely negotiates the notes. But on this putatively Ireland-only best-of, he and his wordless wife quietly claim traditional country music for the surreal, the mordant, and the psychotic. They require attentive listening. Give it to them and you'll leave a different if not necessarily happier person. **A–**

The Hangovers: *Slow Dirty Tears* (Kill Rock Stars '98) love life of an ex-Raincoat with bad habits and a new sampler ("Sorry," "We Had a Really Smashing Time") ★★★

Hanson: *Middle of Nowhere* (Mercury '97) innocent, sure—also as layered as a $100 haircut and as mannered as a Stanislavski class ("Weird," "Man from Milwaukee") ★★

Happy Mondays: *Pills 'n Thrills and Bellyaches* (Elektra '90) their Voidoids is hotter than their "dance music" ("Grandbag's Funeral," "Kinky Afro") ★★

John Wesley Harding: *John Wesley Harding's New Deal* (Forward '96) 🎖
John Wesley Harding: *Trad Arr Jones* (Zero Hour '99) 🎖

Hard Knocks: *School of Hard Knocks* (Wild Pitch '92) Ⓝ

Ben Harper: "Mama's Got a Girlfriend Now" (*Welcome to the Cruel World,* Virgin '94) 🌀

Ben Harper: *The Will to Live* (Virgin '97) Ⓝ

Clay Harper: *East of Easter* (Casino Music '97) ex-Coolie meets Wreckless Eric in totally improbable guitar-organ garage ("The Next Contestant," "Health

Food and Homicide," "Airport Holiday Inn") ★★★

Corey Harris: *Fish Ain't Bitin'* (Alligator '97) After a debut that established his mastery of the Delta idiom, this young black Denver native does something really hard—proves he's big enough to fool around with it. The intermittent New Orleans polyphony is as warm as the tuba of fellow National steel-bodied adept Taj Mahal. And as much as Harris's cross-rhythms and vocal panoply honor his readings of the classics, his virtuosity springs to life on originals where a catfish farm saps the Red River or Mumia and Rodney King leave him nowhere to take his trunk. **A–**

Corey Harris: *Greens from the Garden* (Alligator '99) the best thing he can do for his roots is grow new songs from them ("Honeysuckle," "Basehead," "Teabag Blues") ★★

Emmylou Harris: *At the Ryman* (Reprise '92) grand old newfangled one-woman hootenanny ("Hard Times," "Guitar Town") ★★

Emmylou Harris: "Jerusalem Tomorrow" (*Cowgirl's Prayer,* Asylum '93) 👁

Emmylou Harris: *Songs of the West* (Warner Western '94) selflessly serving the song for 17 years ("Queen of the Silver Dollar," "I'll Be Your San Antone Rose") ★

Emmylou Harris: *Wrecking Ball* (Elektra '95) The reason Harris's instant comeback is an irritation, not a tragedy, is that the inspired collaborator and nonpareil backup singer has no vision of her own for Daniel Lanois to ruin. Her artistic personality has always been coextensive with her miraculously lucid voice, which now that it's fraying with age is ripe for Lanois's one seductive trick: to gauze over every aural detail and call the soft focus soul. I doubt she would have nailed the songs anyway—often she doesn't. But she would have come closer than this. **B** 🦃

Emmylou Harris: *Spyboy* (Eminent '98) 💣

Emmylou Harris, Linda Ronstadt, Dolly Parton: *Trio II* (Asylum '99) Ⓝ

Deborah Harry: *Debravation* (Sire/Reprise '93) Ⓝ

Alvin Youngblood Hart: *Big Mama's Door* (OKeh/550 Music '96) like Taj Mahal up and rose from the dead—only Taj is still alive ("When I Was a Cowboy [Western Plain]," "That Kate Adams Jive") ★

Alvin Youngblood Hart: *Territory* (Rykodisc '98) An audacious turf grab in a year when Lucinda Williams is doing for the blues she loves what Billy Bragg and Wilco are doing for the Woody Guthrie they love—reconstituting them for a greater good that may also be self-discovery or self-aggrandizement only who cares? After asserting its intentions with a Western swing original perfectly suited to Hart's keen blues tenor, it mixes landmarks like "John Hardy" and "Mama Don't Allow" with a ska original, a Beefheart instrumental, Ruth Etting's (and also X's) "Dancing with Tears in My Eyes," and the harrowing tale of "two mixed-blood brothers" who got lynched in 1886 pursuing an assault case they were right about—its guitar accompaniment blues-based, all right, but only because the Grateful Dead are too. If it doesn't flow like Williams or Bragg & Wilco, well, there's nothing gracious or integrated about Hart's claim, which is that when you start with country blues all of American pop is your territory. Conceptually, it's uncompromising; musically, it can only hit home piece by piece. **A–**

PJ Harvey: *Dry* (Indigo '92) Since she doesn't fancy comparisons to Sinéad or Kate Bush—"I'm like anyone as long as they're female. If they've got dark hair it's even better"—perhaps she'd prefer Cream or the Doors. Island Records sure would, but in a sexist world she's unlikely to achieve such heights of rockist catalogue stuffing—I just mean a band that sounds great until you listen to the words when you're not stoned and decide they're self-indulgent blather. This fate she's spared by the cloudy but essential feminist distinction between egoist bullroar and honest irrational outpouring—and of course by her postrockist guitar, where she starts to reinvent her instrument the way grrrl-punks reinvent their form. **A–**

PJ Harvey: *Rid of Me* (Island '93) Never mind sexual—if snatches like "Make me gag," "Lick my injuries," and "Rub 'til it bleeds" aren't genital per se, I'm a dirty old man. And if the cold raw meat of her guitar isn't yowling for phallic equality, I'm Robert Bly, which is probably the same thing. She wants that cock—a specific one, it would seem, attached to a full-fledged, nonobjectified male human being, or maybe an array or succession of cocks, it's hard to tell. But when she gets pissed off, which given the habits of male human beings happens all the time, she thinks it would be simpler just to posit or grow or strap on or cut off a cock of her own. After which it's bend-over-Casanova and every man for him or herself. **A**

PJ Harvey: *Man-Size* (Island import '93) album-available single plus two utterly disparate signature B sides ("Wang Dang Doodle," "Daddy") ★★★

PJ Harvey: *4-Track Demos* (Island '93) All right, so this isn't a cult artist's first ripoff. The new songs assure that. "Easy," "M-Bike," "Hardly Wait," and especially the fleshpotted "Reeling"—where "Robert De Niro sit on my face" leaves no doubt about whose blow-job queen she wants to be—share the kind of eager emotionality that makes Steve Albini cringe, and the same looseness animates this "Yuri-G." But I don't know how anyone can compare *Rid of Me*'s "Rid of Me" without succumbing to its marshaled power, or concluding that with some forethought she could find even more juice in her sexual enthusiasm. She is a *performer,* after all. **B+**

PJ Harvey: *To Bring You My Love* (Island '95) Four albums in three years, each sonically distinct, each adding a thematic facet to a coherent sensibility. Pretty good for an alleged up-and-comer, eh? In fact, major, and I'll reserve the G-word if you will. Bored with raunchy details, she's going for universals: salvation, rapture, fulfillment, escape. Putting aside her rough

lead guitar as unequal to this quest, she's applied herself instead to opera lessons that in no way prettify vocals that were pretty amazing even before they assumed all this range, modulation, and command, and traded in Steve Albini for Flood to help her get at some postsexual imperatives. The fuller sound they arrive at is far from slick—her buzzy keybs are as ominous as her guitar, her register shifts weirder than ever, and the mix can get disconcertingly murky. So watch out for pigeonholes. To fixate on blues or sex is to sell short religious yearnings, avant-garde affinities, and pop potential that are all intensified on an album whose generalization level only magnifies its impact. And to figure she's hellbent on the big time is not to think at all. **A**

PJ Harvey: **"Ballad of the Soldier's Wife"** (*September Songs: The Music of Kurt Weill* [comp], Sony Classics '97) 🕭

PJ Harvey: *Is This Desire?* (Island '98) Seeing Harvey in her most original live guise to date at the Hammerstein Ballroom, I didn't think Nick Cave or, heaven knows, Aretha Franklin. Instead I recalled the renowned art-song singer Jan De-Gaetani, who I was dragged off to see 20-odd years ago. I didn't much enjoy DeGaetani—not my repertoire, let's say. But I admired her ease, her naturalness-within-formality, and more and more that's how it is with Harvey. In a charcoal suit and stacked heels with red top, this was a concert artist repaying the adoration of her fans, but not so as she'd give them the early songs they wanted. Instead she concentrated on less immediate new material, which gained power in performance just as it does with repeated exposure on record. Melding modal tradition and concrète futurism, dancing to the strong beat as the moment required, she sounded so good she made what she has to say irrelevant. Which was and remains just as well, because what she has to say is limited. Is this desire? It must be, because all she's certain of is that her characters seldom get what they want. Hence, neither do listeners who seek release in formal command. While every song here kicks in eventually, starting with the two-minute "The Sky Lit Up," at times she could be the rock Wynton Marsalis. So thank God she'd rather be Tricky. **A–**

PJ Harvey: See John Parish and Polly Jean Harvey

Harvey Danger: *Where Have All the Merrymakers Gone?* (Slash '98) 💣

Umar Bin Hassan: *Be Bop or Be Dead* (Axiom '93) ⓝ

Jon Hassell: *City: Works of Fiction* (Opal/Warner Bros. '90) ⓝ
Jon Hassell and Bluescreen: *Dressing for Pleasure* (Warner Bros. '94) Like they say, only never before with this guy, play loud—background it ain't. Hassell's untreated trumpet leads a multipedigreed avant-pop band—from Praxis, Disposable Heroes, Tom Waits—through what most often sounds like that rare thing, good fusion. Miles and Eno, acid jazz, hip hop lessons, New Age world music BS—all are here, with barely a hint of ripoff. The minimalist experimenter/dabbler's most conventional and convincing record. **A–**
Jon Hassell: *Fascinoma* (Water Lily Acoustics '99) ⓝ

Juliana Hatfield: *Hey Babe* (Mammoth '92) ⓝ
Juliana Hatfield: *I See You* (Mammoth '92) 💣
The Juliana Hatfield Three: "My Sister" (*Become What You Are,* Atlantic/Mammoth '93) 🪰

Sophie B. Hawkins: *Tongues and Tails* (Columbia '92) 💣
Sophie B. Hawkins: *Whaler* (Columbia '94) 💣

Ted Hawkins: *The Next Hundred Years* (DGC '94) last of the independents ("There Stands the Glass," "Big Things") ★
Ted Hawkins: *Suffer No More: The Ted Hawkins Story* (Rhino '98) Maybe the radical alarm and homely detail of "Sorry You're Sick" are less unguarded than they seem—this guy made his living disarming passersby. Even so, Hawkins's

two Rounder releases achieve an aesthetic of the natural—songs about combs, about doing the dishes, about vagrant desire. The U.K.-only late-'80s selections are pedestrian by comparison—beautifully sung, but incompletely imagined and indifferently arranged. Because compiler Gary Stewart thinks like a collector and adores Hawkins, a summing-up that might have established an American original is only a misleading introduction—to an American original. **B+**
Ted Hawkins: *The Final Tour* (Evidence '98) died trying ("Bring It On Home Daddy," "There Stands the Glass") ★

Hayden: *Everything I Long For* (Outpost '96) If the 24-year-old Desser gets to be Lou Barlow when he grows up, which took Barlow years, he'll look back on most of these self-consciously casual vignettes as bores or embarrassments. He's best on young love, nice-guy style, especially when he and his girlfriend stay in bed all day. But the unnatural effort of extragenerational empathy makes him howl in agony. And if he really didn't know that the Susan Smith murders "were gonna become a huge media thing," he hasn't yet learned the first thing about the impossible border between the private and the public. **B** 🦃

Isaac Hayes: *Branded* (Pointblank '95) ⓝ

Wade Hayes: *When the Wrong One Loves You Right* (Columbia/DKC '98) 💣

Graham Haynes: *Transition* (Antilles '96) In which Roy's son the cornet player melds Vernon Reid and Jean-Paul Bourelly—not to mention hip hop scratchbeats and whoopbeats, twisted Braxtonesque march structures, Mandingo-Tunisian Islamoiserie, New Age vocal mood-setters, New Age vocal mood-breakers, bird cries, and harmolodic saxophone—into a funk few jazzbos have gotten near. The effect is '70s Miles with somewhat softer tastes in expanded consciousness, or Jon Hassell less hung up on repetition. If at times the syncretism seems slightly received, this often beautiful, often kicking record proves not just that rock can fuse with jazz and "ethnic" with "Western," but that each fusion can then fuse with the other—as long as you keep your ear on the music and your eye off the demographics. **A–**

Graham Haynes: *Tones for the 21st Century* (Antilles '97) 🎵

Lee Hazlewood: *Cowboy in Sweden* (Smells Like '99) Hazlewood is an "interesting" figure, always was. A natural hipster, in the biz but not of it, pop and rock and country and just plain weird—Duane Eddy, Nancy Sinatra, and Gram Parsons is quite a trifecta. Problem is, he's never been all that good. There's a nice best-of hiding in his collected works, including the new standards collection. But his vogue transcends crass track-by-track quality controls, combining the usual convolutional one-upsmanship, a visceral distaste for roots-rock's sonic canon, and a generation of aging slackers' discovery that doing bizness needn't deaden your mind or rot your soul. If slick blues licks make you sick, Hazlewood's studio hacks and string-section dreck will be some kind of change. If you like Nancy Sinatra almost as much as Karen Carpenter, thin-piped Nina Lizell will glean away enough Janis-and-Bonnie grit. If you doubt all shows of soul, the flaccid sentimentality of "Easy and Me" will be one more trope as far as you're concerned. But without opening a book I can recall half a dozen unreissued singer-songwriter albums that do more with their varied conventions than this Europe-only 1970 rarity—by Thomas Jefferson Kaye, Nolan Porter, Marc Benno, Hirth Martinez, Alice Stuart, Mississippi Charles Bevel. And I shudder to think of the unreasonable claims to be made when their time comes around again. **B–** 🦃

The Heads: *No Talking Just Head* (MCA/Radioactive '96) Not as horrible as lead tracks fronted by the frontpersons of Concrete Blonde and INXS promise—in fact, once you forgive Johnette her pain, hers is actually OK. As is that of Live's Ed Kowalczyk, aping not R.E.M. or U2 but (what a dandy idea) *Talking Heads,* whose frontperson is otherwise much missed—for his personality, his lyrics, his inimitable guitar, his glue. Best in show: "Punk Lolita," in which Tina, Chris, and Jerry back Tina, Debbie, and Johnette with results that recall no one so much as (what a dandy idea) *Tom Tom Club.* **B–** 🦃

The Reverend Horton Heat: *Liquor in the Front* (Sub Pop/Interscope '94) Not counting the belch-enhanced Scott Joplin closer, their best joke got lost on the way to the rack jobber: the title was *Liquor in the Front, Poker in the Rear* before somebody (the major label, mayhap?) took the punch line off the cover. This leaves us with a supposedly humorous male chauvinist trio playing rock-enhanced rockabilly Very Loud. College radio dogs find their mess authentic and postmodern all at once. Me, I listen in vain for a "Dixie Fried," a "One Hand Loose," even a "Ubangi Stomp"—hell, even a "Rock This Town," by the Stray Cats, who tried something similar in the dark ages of MTV. **B–** 🦃

Heavenly: *Le Jardin de Heavenly* (K '93) shambolic sweethearts ("C Is the Heavenly Option," "Tool") ★★

Heavenly: *P.U.N.K. Girl* (K '93) A sometime Pooh Stick and four inept-plus fellow Brits (three male, if you're counting) combine the K aesthetic—five mild-sounding ditties catchier than K's more-amateur-than-it-knows norm—with the Kill Rock Stars ethos—two of them about date rape. I wish aesthetic or ethos allowed for clearer vocals—would like to hear Melanie's dreams before the deed was done, and wonder whether p.u.n.k. really stands for "painful ways" as well as "utopia"-"new jeans"-"kid in her." Too often budget is a concept that swallows aesthetic and ethos. **A–**

Heavenly: *The Decline and Fall of Heavenly* (K '94) nice quiet girl asserts herself—quietly, but you can hear her talking ("Me and My Madness," "Three Star Compartment") ★★

Heavens to Betsy: *Calculated* (Kill Rock Stars '94) Corin Tucker is too self-aware about how "fucked up" she is to take her own rage at face value. But because she's also convinced that "everything is fucked up," she's sure her rage is here to stay, something she and the world will have to deal with, thus obliging her to imbue it with intelligible form. Lyrics are crucial—her counterattacks on sexual predators are variously voiced and passionately felt, and "Waitress Hell" should raise tips all over Grrrlland. But the clincher is the noise she and her guitar make along with bassist-drummer Tracy Sawyer—controlled, fierce, a deliberate, powerful punk derivative that's built for discomfort, not for speed. **A–**

Heavy D. & the Boyz: *Peaceful Journey* (Uptown/MCA '91) groovemaster, fast talker, all-around nice guy ("I Can Make You Go Oooh") ★

Hefner: "A Hymn for the Postal Service" (*Breaking God's Heart,* Too Pure '98) 🕭

Helium: *Pirate Prude* (Matador '94) 💣
Helium: "Pat's Trick" (*The Dirt of Luck,* Matador '95) 🕭

Helmet: *Meantime* (Interscope '92) speeding, crunching, giving as bad as they get ("Unsung," "Give It") ★★

Mike Henderson & the Bluebloods: *First Blood* (Dead Reckoning '96) Ⓝ

Jimi Hendrix: *Blues* (MCA '94) Your soul will survive if you never hear a moment of Reprise's brass-balled clearance boxes, *Lifelines* (radio music, radio chat) and *Stages* (four concerts! four cities! four years!). But on this "new" single disc, the Inexhaustible One sounds pretty fresh for somebody who's been dead 24 years. Even if you've heard him do most of these titles, even if you've committed *Rainbow Bridge*'s "Hear My Train A-Comin'" to memory, the simple concept and modest

scope do right by his uniqueness, his diversity, and the mother of all subgenres. **A–**
Jimi Hendrix: *Woodstock* (MCA '94) Transitional—less definitive than Winterland early or Berkeley late. But more essential (also historic) than any other Hendrix concert record. The ad hoc Gypsy Sons and Rainbows band goes with Billy Cox on bass, picks Mitch's sticks over Buddy's bigfoot; two percussionists sit in for a snakier groove and Larry Lee adds extraneous guitar. The loosely rehearsed music sounds that way. But it's way, way out there—"The Star Spangled Banner" is a bon-bon compared to "Voodoo Chile (Slight Return)/ Stepping Stone" or "Jam Back at the House (Beginnings)" or the unaccompanied "Woodstock Improvisation." All in all, your basic rock concert as act of flawed genius. Does this kind of thing happen anymore? Not on such a scale for sure. **A–**
Jimi Hendrix: See also Subjects for Further Research

Don Henley: *Actual Miles: Henley's Greatest Hits* (Geffen '95) 💣

Don Henry: "Harley" (*Wild in the Backyard,* Epic '91) 🕭

Joe Henry: *Trampoline* (Mammoth '96) Ⓝ

Joe Henry: *Fuse* (Mammoth '99) "characters who sing like William Burroughs while thinking they sound like Bobby Womack (is there anything sadder?)" ("Want Too Much," "Great Lake") ★★

Judy Henske: "Mad Dog Killer" (*Loose in the World,* Fair Star '99) 🕭

Meg Hentges: *Tattoo Urge* (Tim Kerr '93) straight rock by gay women ("This Kind of Love Is," "Heaven Sent") ★

The Herbaliser: *Blow Your Headphones* (Ninja Tune '97) Ⓝ

Kristen Hersh: *Hips and Makers* (Sire/ Reprise '94) Ⓝ

John Hiatt: "Perfectly Good Guitar," "Buffalo River Home" (*Perfectly Good Guitar,* A&M '93) 🕭

John Hiatt: *The Best of John Hiatt* (Capitol '98) Master of a Nashville-Memphis fusion that is all of rock and roll to his own generation and totally cornball to the next, this Springsteen-writ-small has always yoked Grade A songwriting to Brand X singing, and by now it's clear the limitation is as much intellectual as physical. Almost every individual selection here connects, the wedding plea "Have a Little Faith in Me" no less than the bank-robbing saga "Tennessee Plates." But though one doesn't negate the other—life is long, and various—Hiatt's ever more skillful shows of soul can't make them cohere, because at bottom he has nothing to say. All things considered, he might have been better off with less voice, not more. Then he wouldn't have been tempted to juggle career options on that endless road. He'd have settled into the well-heeled life of a Music Row pro. Alan Jackson would record his songs. **B+**

John Hiatt: *Greatest Hits: The A&M Years '87–'94* (A&M '99) tuneful, what else, but beware: Capitol cherry-picked these already ("The Rest of the Dream," "Real Fine Love") ★

Dan Hicks: *Shootin' Straight* (On the Spot '94) the old old-timey shtick sits better on an actual old-timer ("Up! Up! Up!" "Who Are You?") ★★

Hieroglyphics: *3rd Eye Vision* (Hiero Imperium '98) East Bay Afrocentricity, hold the pikls ("At the Helm," "All Things") ★★

Joe Higgs with the Wailers: *Blackman Know Yourself* (Shanachie '90) they are family ("Blackman Know Yourself") ★

The High & Mighty: *Home Field Advantage* (Rawkus '99) plenty to boast about, less to be proud of ("The Weed," "The B-Document") ★

The High Llamas: *Hawaii* (V2 '96) ✹

The Highwaymen: *The Road Goes On Forever* (Liberty '95) Uncle John Cash is the Monotone King, and Waylon and Willie have gotten so creaky they make the long ghastly Kris Kristofferson sound like just another old guy who can't clear his throat anymore. This million-dollar quartet was 242 years old as of last July 4, and while they open and close with two of the very few outlaw songs to enter the canon as their dotage encroached, by Steve Earle and Robert Earl Keen respectively, they concentrate on what they know best: death, immortality, and its correlatives, compassion prominent among them. Their good-hearted whore, good-hearted waitress, and good-hearted wife are idealizations, but the surpassing wisdom these idealizations express and embody is recommended to cynics everywhere. Inspirational Slogan: "I am what I am 'cause I ain't what I used to be." **A–**

The Highwaymen: *Super Hits* (Columbia '99) ✹

Faith Hill: "The Secret of Life," "This Kiss" (*Faith,* Warner Bros. '98) ☻

Faith Hill: *Breathe* (Warner Bros. '99) Hill's Shania move comes down so far on the wrong side of Bryan Adams it's a wonder she doesn't pop out of her fancy black lingerie—great color choice, gal, no grass stains. Back in the boudoir, she poses for photos, then carefully removes said lingerie so as to "make love all night long." The drums wham-bam her promises home. The guitars make noise without having any fun. Exactly what Tim McGraw deserves. **C+**

Lauryn Hill: *The Miseducation of Lauryn Hill* (Ruffhouse '98) P.C. record of the year—songs soft, singing ordinary, rapping skilled, rhymes up and down, skits de trop, production subtle and terrific ("Lost Ones," "Superstar") ★★★

Hindu Love Gods: *Hindu Love Gods* (Giant '90) ⓝ

Algia Mae Hinton: *Honey Babe* (MusicMasters/Sire '99) a great-grandmother's blues, uncannily John Hurt in the picking and domesticity ("Snap Your Fingers," "Whatcha Gonna Do When Your Good Girl Turns You Down?") ★★

His Name Is Alive: *Home Is in Your Head* (4AD '92) Ⓝ

His Name Is Alive: *Mouth by Mouth* (4AD '93) Proudly eclectic, reflective, and obscure—hell, arty—Warren DeFever's concession to rock normality is mood music for more moods than you'll first believe are there, including plenty of sex for the polymorphously inclined. Think Big Star's *Third* as witting aesthetic strategy rather than failed attempt to make the world go away. DeFever adds an electric flaneur's world music collection and an extra coupla decades of pop-studio perversity to the sonic palette. Karin Oliver sings as if being pretty is a spiritual attainment. **A−**

His Name Is Alive: *Stars on E.S.P.* (4AD '96) Warren DeFever is the cook, but don't expect extra helpings from his side projects. HNIA's artistic flavor, half homespun mysticism and half hermetic cutes, is all in Karin Oliver's cunning, simplistic verbal/vocal content. And the whole exercise in fey sexuality and childlike quietude would fall slightly flat without its greatest hit—three takes on a Woody Guthrie tune about how he was even more alienated than they are. **A−**

His Name Is Alive: *Nice Day* (4AD '97) 💣

His Name Is Alive: *Ft. Lake* (4AD '98) Ⓝ

His Name Is Alive: *Always Stay Sweet* (4AD '99) 💣

Robyn Hitchcock: "Don't Talk to Me About Gene Hackman" (*Jewels for Sophia,* Warner Bros. '99) 🔊

Susanna Hoffs: *When You're a Boy* (Columbia '91) 💣

Robin Holcomb: *Robin Holcomb* (Elektra Musician '90) *New Yorker* poetry, downhome quaver, uptown chords ("Hand Me Down All Stories," "Deliver Me," "The American Rhine") ★★

Hole: *Pretty on the Inside* (Caroline '91) *Nightmare on Gurl Street,* or *Beyond the Valley of the Sonic Youth* ("Teenage Whore," "Clouds") ★★★

Hole: *Live Through This* (DGC '94) Punk aesthetic or no punk aesthetic, Courtney Love's songs wouldn't be compromised and might be deepened by steeper momentum and more articulate guitar noise. But they prevail anyway. Their focus is sexual exploitation, and not just by the media, evil straights, and male predators of every cultural orientation. She's also exploited by Courtney Love, and not only does she know it, she thinks about it. These are the confessions of a self-made feminist bimbo—of the girl who wanted the most cake. Just because she's a phony, whatever that means, doesn't mean the world isn't out to deny her her props. **A**

Hole: *Ask for It* (Caroline '95) well before *Live Through This,* her *outtakes* have it going on ("Pale Blue Eyes," "Over the Edge") ★★★

Hole: *Celebrity Skin* (Geffen '98) better punk than actress, better actress than popster ("Celebrity Skin," "Awful") ★★

Rick "L.A. Holmes" Holmstrom: *Lookout!* (Black Top '96) 💣

Peter Holsapple & Chris Stamey: "I Want to Break Your Heart," "She Was the One" (*Mavericks,* DNA '91) 🔊

Holy Modal Rounders: *Too Much Fun* (Rounder '99) Peter Stampfel is the intense seeker, Steve Weber the mellow layabout. Where Stampfel is all comic focus, whether comic ha-ha or comic-as-opposed-to-tragic, Weber is someone who can just not give a fuck while remaining both charming and musical. Their magic isn't eternal youth—they're as much old codgers as John Hurt and Clarence Ashley in 1963. It's their argument that play is the fundamental life principle. Among the exhibits: the Henry Clay work emancipation hullabaloo "Kingdom Coming" rewritten to lay more insults on the massa, the scatted dog-yip solo and verse about Simulac-boosting junkie moms that bedeck the psychedeliprop "Euphoria," a sea chantey that climaxes "Don't you rock me daddy-o," a celebration of Buddha's fondness for caffeine and twisted '50s chord progressions, and a girl-group obscurity in which a sweetly love-struck teenager goes gaga over a "Bad Boy": "He'll sell your heart on St. Mark's Place/In glassine envelopes/He'll cut it with a pig's heart/And burn the chumps and dopes." **A**

John Lee Hooker: *Mr. Lucky* (Pointblank/Charisma '91) So primal he subsumes all corruption, the old man—he turned 131 in August—accepts as his due ace solos etc. from Robert Cray, Albert Collins, Carlos Santana, Johnny Winter, etc. The rock moves don't impede the groove any more than unaccompanied stomps would, and rarely has he enjoyed a shuffle as definitive as the one Jim Keltner, Nick Lowe, Ry Cooder, and to-the-session-born Johnnie Johnson lay under "This Is Hip." He hasn't released a more thrilling or hypnotic album since he was 112. **A–**

John Lee Hooker: *The Ultimate Collection 1948–1990* (Rhino '91) An ageless modern, the first blues primitivist-not-primitive: "Ain't no heaven/No burnin' hell/When I die." I could do with less Delta solitude and more urban anger, from 1948's "War Is Over (Goodbye California)" (on Specialty's stretched-thin *Graveyard Blues*) to 1967's "The Motor City Is Burning" (on MCA's boogieful *The Best of John Lee Hooker 1965 to 1974*). But just by collecting signature songs from 11 different labels, this 31-track double-CD captures his primal-not-simple beat at an unprecedented level of specificity. **A–**

John Lee Hooker: *Boom Boom* (Pointblank/Charisma '92) **Ⓝ**

John Lee Hooker: *Chill Out* (Pointblank '95) **Ⓝ**

John Lee Hooker: *The Best of Friends* (Pointblank '98) With the millennium approaching as speedily as Hook's 140th birthday, his brain trust devises an easy yet effective celebration, mining the interchangeable output of his hundred-thirties for standout cameos and adding yet more special guests. And though he was warned not to overtax himself, you'd never know it from the Claptonized "Boogie Chillen" that sets him in his groove. Carlos Santana, Ry Cooder, Jimmie Vaughan, Los Lobos, and Bonnie Raitt also get him hard. **A–**

Hoosier Hot Shots: *Rural Rhythm 1935–1942* (Columbia/Legacy '92) They played flute, clarinet, slide whistle, and bass horn. They specialized in Tin Pan Alley novelties like "Connie's Got Connections in Connecticut," "From the Indies to the Andes in His Undies," and "Girl Friend of the Whirling Dervish." They became stars on WLS's National Barn Dance. They grossed up to five grand a night. They're not mentioned in any encyclopedia I own. And they make Spike Jones sound like a Sartrean existentialist. This is the silliest music I've ever heard. **A–**

Hootie & the Blowfish: *Cracked Rear View* (Atlantic '94) Even when they split the difference between jangle and boogie, bands given to blunt popcraft and elementary guitars generally favor singers up toward the whiny end of the dramatic spectrum. So Darius Rucker's gruff grit adds an extra layer of substance to a music already deeply comforting in its formal certainties. As a black man who takes his vocal cues from what Gregg Allman made of blues and soul, not to mention a black man embraced as eagerly as Carl McCall by white people loath to think of themselves as "prejudiced," he's significant, with "Drowning" one more hit about racism than Tupac or Dr. Dre has bothered with. But since both patterns can be traced to late minstrelsy—by which I mean not the whiteskin brainwash of pervid radical rhetoric, merely the twisted roots of American pop—he's hardly unprecedented. And whatever his significance, a cornball is a cornball is a cornball. **B** 🐄

Hootie & the Blowfish: *Fairweather Johnson* (Atlantic '96) R.E.M.-with-soul, neither instant ear candy nor the generic dross quality controllers charge ("She Crawls Away," "Sad Caper") ★

Hot Boys: *Guerrilla Warfare* (Cash Money/Universal '99) 💣

Houndog: *Houndog* (Columbia/Legacy '99) 💣

A House: *I Am the Greatest* (Radioactive '92) the rationalizations of a million pretentious losers—not including you or me, of course ("I Am Afraid," "You're Too Young") ★★

Tom House *The White Man's Burden* (Checkered Past '98) Ⓝ

House of Pain: "Jump Around" (*House of Pain,* Tommy Boy '92) 🐝
House of Pain: *Same As It Ever Was* (Tommy Boy '94) Where the first time they rode an easy hit and easier Vanilla Ice comparisons, now they're compelled to prove that they have a right to exist, and the struggle is tonic. Plug-ugly vocals and mean lean beats make this the hardest hip hop of the year. Name checks include Hendrix, Page, Steven Tyler, Divine Styler, Salt-n-Pepa, G.G. Allin, and Pearl Jam. A–
House of Pain: *Truth Crushed to Earth Shall Rise Again* (Tommy Boy '96) 💣

Joe Houston: *Cornbread and Cabbage Greens* (Specialty '92) These 26 titles were cut some 40 years ago for three related L.A. indies by a Texas honker with one major national r&b hit—"Worry Worry Worry," not included here or ever heard by me, although I bet "Troubles and Worries" is close enough. Many were recorded in identical versions with equally anonymous sidemen for yet other L.A. indies, and only six were released. Yet I feel as if I've been waiting for this collection all my life. Sax reissues by the likes of Illinois Jacquet and Arnett Cobb retain a veneer of structural respectability, just like the official singles here—they're never all-out all-out. But at its best—which despite the fine thick raunch of the slow blues usually means its fastest, from famous flag-wavers like "Flying Home" and "Lester Leaps In" to prototypical jams like "Richie's Roll" and "Coastin'"—most of this sounds as if the engineer is holding the mike stand parallel to the floor because Houston is flat on his back. Until somebody puts "Honky Tonk," "Slow Walk," and "Walking with Mr. Lee" on one record, this will be how I explain rock and roll saxophone. A–

Penelope Houston: *Tongue* (Reprise '98) Ⓝ

Whitney Houston: *I'm Your Baby Tonight* (Arista '90) Ⓝ
Whitney Houston: "I'm Every Woman" (*The Bodyguard* [ST], Arista '92) 🐝

Adina Howard: *Do You Wanna Ride?* (EastWest '95) 💣

Ray Wylie Hubbard: *Dangerous Spirits* (Philo '97) 💣

Huggybear: See Bikini Kill

Michael Hurley: "I Paint a Design" (*Wolf Ways,* Koch '95) 🐝
Michael Hurley: *Weatherhole* (Field '99) shoebox of American folk music ("Nat'l Weed Growers Assoc.," "Your Old Gearbox") ★★★

Hüsker Dü: *The Living End* (Warner Bros. '94) Culled from their final tour, their second live album—the first was their first, with the lovely protohardcore title *Land Speed Record*—is long on late songs, its only cover the perfect "Sheena Is a Punk Rocker." But the mutual disregard that had set in well before their demise never dented their reputation as the fiercest band in el nuevo wavo. Their ordinary shows were something else, and given how dimly they were recorded at SST, the live-to-the-soundboard audio is often an improvement. Not an epiphany. But definitely a manifestation you can believe in. A–

HWA: *Hoez with Attitude: Az Much Ass Azz U Want* (Ruthless '94) this just in—rappers get head, respect you in morning ("Great Tazte—Lezz Fillaz," "All That (Just a Little Action)") ★★★

Hyper Crad: "3 (Back Door Mix)" (*Suck It and See,* Palm Pictures '99) 🐝

H/COMPILATIONS

Handraizer (Moonshine Music '94) High end mostly keyb/organ (not much fake guitar), low end more disco than funk (few nods to the unlocked pelvis), midrange provided by mostly black voices shouting out challenges and exhortations (you *will* get up now). Occasional cushy synth-symph flourishes provide what respite there is, because beyond a few of the very incidental vocals nothing here is slow—nothing. However it works in situ, I guarantee you'll clean your apartment at a record pace. **A**

Hard Rock Cafe: Party Rock (Hard Rock/Rhino '98) Lead track: "Addicted to Love." Best track: "Addicted to Love." Also includes: "Hot Blooded," "What I Like About You," "Can't Get Enough." Oldest track: "Joy to the World." Second-worst track (after "Do You Feel Like We Do"): "Joy to the World." Author of notes: singer of "Joy to the World." Black artists: one. Newest track: Tone-Loc's "Wild Thing." Tracks by legitimate album artists: one ("Gimme Three Steps"). Conflicts with *Dazed and Confused:* two. Conflicts with *Jock Jams* or *Frat Rock:* zero. In short: best stupid-rock comp in many a year. **A**

Heart of the Forest (Hannibal '93) Where *Baka Beyond: Spirit of the Forest,* the acoustic guitar jam producer Martin Cradick constructed around tunes and percussion tracks he took out of the jungle, is so easy to ignore it makes you appreciate the candid hokeyness of Deep Forest, here Cradick constructs a literally awesome and enchanting glimpse of another world. His musical record of the Baka pygmies borrows the structure Steven Feld devised for New Guinea's Kaluli on 1991's *Voices of the Rainforest,* which condenses the sounds of a village day down to an hour. But unlike Feld, Cradick doesn't try to evoke a mindset in which birds, insects, frogs, running water, and crackling brush create music so that the human beings who share their ear-space "lift-up-over sound." Instead, as in Smithsonian's recently reissued *Mbuti Pygmies of the Ituri Rain Forest,* natural sounds provide the ground of an ethno-musicological array dominated here by indigenous harps—magical incantations, nursery rhymes, work songs, occasional divertissements, and drunken revelries. Before you buy any more guff about aural environments and ambient whoziwhatsis, check out what a real soundscape sounds like. Don't miss the water drums. **A–**

Heavy on the Highlife! (Original Music '90) The six selections on this 67-minute best-of are attributed to three artists, but I say they're all the Oriental Brothers, so called because they're from *eastern* Nigeria—the biggest stars of what was once Biafra, where Yoruba juju somehow never caught on. With the polite Ghanaian horn sections that lace through the accompanying *Giants of Danceband Highlife* as passé as colonialism by the time the war was over, Sir Warrior Opara, Dan Satch Opara, and Godwin Kabaka Opara went for a wild Afropop that combined indigenous guitar hooks with the putatively Zairean rhythms then sweeping the continent. Unlike the Ibo hits preserved on Vertigo's long-lost *African Music* comp, the four-minute 1973–1974 songs are gentle and charming only in comparison to the 18-minute mid-'80s tours de force that follow. Natural soul disco from the heart of Africa, they don't relent until they fade into forever. Listening rather than dancing, your attention may wander for a minute or two, but whenever you tune back in, Dan Satch is coming at the guitar beat from yet another angle, or Sir Warrior is shouting out yet another variation on an eternal theme that transcends whatever tribal truism translation might provide—a confluence of body and spirit you wish touched those who would impoverish either, which always means both. **A**

Hedwig and the Angry Inch (Atlantic '99) **Ⓝ**

Help (London '95) 💣

Hempilation (Capricorn '95) 💣

Heritage (Six Degrees/Island '97) I don't know why Darol Anger's name was left off his pet project, but the effect is to conceptualize it. As a result, these "new interpretations of American roots music" seem of a piece with the rest of 1997's folk revival revival, in which the Smithsonian's Harry Smith reissue and Rounder's Alan Lomax exhumation joined the alt-country bubble and the revitalization of Bob Dylan in a single antifuturist countercurrent. But just as there's Americana and then Americana, there's futurism and then futurism—why do you think they call it New Age? And this, by jiminy, is New Age Americana: fiddler Anger is a Windham Hill stalwart long active on the folk-jazz cusp. Guest vocalist Jane Siberry opens 'er up and brings 'er home, and in between Willie Nelson and Mary Chapin Carpenter, who outdid themselves on Dylan's Jimmie Rodgers tribute, sink into the intelligent sentimentality that is the bane of each. Ditto for long-winded virtuosi David Lindley, David Grisman, and John Hartford, all of whom can be sharper when somebody jabs them a little. The smug soundtrack to a PBS special about tribulation and survival on the lost frontier. **C–** 🦃

Hi-Jivin' (Kijima import '90) It can't be that every group on this sweet little label sampler has the same rhythm section—certainly not Malombo, or the mbira-style percussion ensemble Amampondo—but at this remove it kind of sounds that way. Equally rustic whether the name up top is Zulu or Sotho, long on squeezebox and masculine stomp, it will come as a bit of a change to fans who hope there's more to mbaqanga than Makgona Tsohle. Those who aren't quite sure who Makgona Tsohle are should find out. **A–**

Hip Hop Greats: Classic Raps (Rhino '90) No "That's the Joint," because the concept behind this found collection of lost keepers isn't the greatest rap records from back in the day, it's crossover in the dark of history. The rhymes are silly, with moments of unimaginable grace—from Wonder Mike's bad meal to Shirl the Pearl's soft swagger, from Kurtis Blow's universal pun to "The Message"'s message. The beats are old-school funk except when Flash gets hold of them—half "The Message"'s prophecy was in its rhythms. And the youthful positivity of both style and stylists don't stop—until white lines turn into tiny chunks of poison rock. **A**

History of House Music Vol. 2: New York Garage Style (Cold Front '97) Where the Chicago-based volume one honors disco and spawned techno, the Gotham-based volume two honors funk and spawned nothing. Compressing clenched male studio voices into keyb-saturated bass-and-percussion, it's just a dense, urgent, anxious moment of dance music—unutopian even when Colonel Abrams soul-shouts that "Music Is the Answer." "Don't Make Me Wait" set it off. "Set It Off" was the answer. **A–**

A History of Our World Part 1: Breakbeat & Jungle Ultramix by DJ DB (Profile '94) Ⓝ

Holding Up Half the Sky: Voices of African Women (Shanachie '97) from the Sahara to the Cape, from pop candy to folk porridge, they have one thing in common—vaginas (Netsennet Mellesse, "Yellow Wekesa"; Kiné Lam, "Souma Sagnone") ★★

Honeymoon in Vegas (Epic '92) Elvis impersonators (best Billy Joel, worst Amy Grant) meet Elvis interpreters (best Jeff Beck, worst Bono) ★★★

Hot Latin Hits/Exitos Latinos Calientes: The '90s (Rhino '98) Doing my bit to nip a world-lounge fad in the bud, I hereby deplore not just a record but an entire sensibility—the florid Spanish-language romanticism at the root of the international ballad style. Performed mostly by one-named singers like Mijares, Lucero, Cristian, and Julian, these early-'90s cris de coeurs are all the excuse any young Spanish speaker needs to believe Los

Fabulosos Cadillacs are the Beatles. Emotion so deeply in love with itself is why irony was invented. **D+** 🐛

Hot Luv: The Ultimate Dance Songs Collection (EMI '96) Tough nooky to snobs who think good dance music now consists entirely of sensitive techies extending the frontiers of recorded sound. Its essence remains stupid singles you can't get out of your head, as on this peerlessly crass contemporary collection, which will lower your IQ so fast you'll settle for a "Macarena" with no girls on it. Sure I could nitpick about every clichéd, overexposed, blessedly obvious track. But only if you gave me more time to think about it. **A**

Hound Dog Taylor: A Tribute (Alligator '98) The natural evolution of chops and technology renders this inauspicious vehicle the best houserocking record by anyone since the honored slidemaster, who died in 1975 leaving his Houserockers to bequeath their name to a boogie blues style never truly replicated. Bigger and faster than the prototype, it lets virtuosos-in-spite-of-themselves give free rein to their baser natures: flash-fingered Luther Allison, Sonny Landreth, Dave Hole, and Warren Haynes come on every bit as crude as neoprimitives George Thorogood, Elvin Bishop, and Cub Koda. Respect to Vernon Reid and Alvin Youngblood Hart for powering up acoustic. Shame on Ronnie Earl for showing off. **A–**

Hype! (Sub Pop '96) the dream is over, long live the dream (Mudhoney, "Touch Me I'm Sick"; Nirvana, "Negative Creep") ★

Janis Ian: *Breaking Silence* (Morgan Creek '93) 🔥

Ice Cube: *Amerikkka's Most Wanted* (Priority '90) Musically it's as original as Tribe Called Quest, and probably doper: with Eric Sadler thickening the mix and the vocalist bluntly banging the tracks home, it delivers the hard beats N.W.A.'s claque clamors about, not just for a few sucker punches but from beginning to end. Lyrically it's as piggy as it wants to be: despite his gift for rhyme and narrative, Ice Cube's politics revert to victim-of-a-racist-society belligerence except maybe on the perverse (and hateful) "The Nigga You Love to Hate." It was inevitable that some black misogynist would elevate his problem into an emblem of outlaw status. But I say fuck the muthafucka, stay on his dick, etc.—anybody who's thinks it's cute to dub himself "the bitch killer" is armed, extremely dangerous, and fair game for the pickle jar. **B–**

Ice Cube: *Kill at Will* (Priority '90) I don't want to claim the criticism is getting to him—still talking tough on this interim EP, he remixes "Get off My Dick and Tell Your Bitch to Come Here." But he's keeping his woman problem to himself and putting thuggism in perspective: "The Product" tells a young black con's story from his pops's nut, "Dead Homiez" cops to a sadness a lesser outlaw might consider unmanly. With Sir Jinx running the board, the beats never work up to carpet-bomb density. And if Ice Cube keeps rhyming like this, you won't care. **A–**

Ice Cube: *Death Certificate* (Priority '91) Between "Dead Homiez," which mourned murdered friends in a voice some called soft, and *Boyz N the Hood,* which required him to simulate thought, the St. Ides spokesperson was worried about his image. To use the only noun in the hard lexicon that suggests normal human sensitivies, he was acting like a "faggot." So here he reclaims his perpetually threatened manhood. Early on he mitigates the usual gangsta shit—gat as penis and pit bull, female body as pestilence and plague—with such touches as an antigang track and a nurse with attitude. But eventually he breaks new ground. In addition to many fascinated rhymes on the complex subject of who fucks who in the ass and how, he nuts out on white devils who crave "a taste of chocolate" because "white bitches have no butt and no chest." He inveighs against "Jap" and "Jew." And he proposes a "nationwide boycott" of Korean-owned inner-city businesses that escape the torch, poking gentle fun at the Korean accent along the way. Call him Ice KKKube—a straight-up bigot simple and plain. **C+** 🦃

Ice Cube: "It Was a Good Day" (*Predator,* Priority '92) 🍥

Ice Cube: *Check Yo Self* (Priority '93) remixed two-song *Predator* best-of plus nigga-devil-bitch plaint ("It Was a Good Day," "Check Yo Self") ★★

Ice Cube: *Lethal Injection* (Priority '93) 🔥

★★★, ★★, ★ Honorable Mention   🍥 Choice Cut   ⓝ Neither   🔥 Dud   🦃 Turkey

Ice Cube: "Ghetto Vet" (*I Got the Hook-Up!* [ST], No Limit '98) 👎
Ice Cube: *War and Peace* (Priority '98) 💣

Ice-T: *O.G. Original Gangster* (Sire/Warner Bros. '91) Learning and diversifying, remembering where he comes from and sticking to what he knows, Ice-T wing big as the old school shakes out. He won't desert the hards because a hard he remains; his violence is pervasive and graphic because he knows brutalization from the inside. But he's nothing if not a moralist, and so the new jack drunk dies in his Benz, the cops break down the gangbanger's door, the gays are left to live their own lives, and the prematurely ejaculated sex jam is a dis on the horny fool who slavers for it. Since most of what I know about the hard audience comes from rap records, I can't guarantee he'll get away with it. But I can guarantee that this one has something to teach everyone who can stand to listen to it and almost everyone who can't. **A**

Ice-T: *Home Invasion* (Rhyme Syndicate '93) At first it sounds like the bad guys won—from sexy stories to O.G. kiss-offs, he spends too much time proving he's still Ice Motherfucking T. But in fact he contextualizes himself as shrewdly as ever. He may write the misogynist rhymes—"I got an ill side that drips from my brain," he explains—but he leaves the worst to DJ Evil E and 2 Live Crew sicko Brother Marquis, the conceit being that some black men think women are hos just like some black men wanna off cops, and that *every one of these black men deserves to be heard.* Which I buy, sort of, while noting that in the lead track a narrator posing as Ice-T offs a cop himself, and not for the last time. "Addicted to Danger" is a shrewd gangsta fable; "99 Problems" takes bitch-talk over the top where it belongs; Grip plays his Yo-Yo; the carefully phrased "Race War" and self-aggrandizing "Message to a Soldier" and amazing "Gotta Lotta Love" (is that a *bridge*?) are as politically felt as the greatest PE. But in a rapper as musically expedient as Ice-T, pro forma claims to hard prowess are rarely of much interest in themselves. Blame them on the bad guys. **B+**

Ice-T: *Cold As Ever* (Blue Dolphin/Hit Man '96) 💣
Ice-T: *Return of the Real* (Rhyme Syndicate '96) making one wonder yet again—what *is* reality, anyway? ("I Must Stand," "Rap Game's Hijacked," "The 5th") ★
Ice-T: *The 7th Deadly Sin* (Coroner/Atomic Pop '99) On "God Forgive Me," the finale until the wittily grandiose Zionist-baiter "Exodus" was tacked on, comes a belated hint of the persona mongering that once terrified a republic: Ice begs absolution for inventing the "gangsta rap" that "changed the course of the world." Maybe that's not as ridiculous as it seems. But certainly no such claim can be made for this clipped collection of pimp-dope-biz boasts/tales, which transcend genre hackwork only when an abused 16-year-old coos the title hook of "Always Wanted to Be a Hoe" like she can't wait to get the next dick in her mouth. Watching the O.G.'s back is a jaw-dropping procession of old-timers you hoped had gone into management, including Brother Marquis, Ant Banks, King Tee, Onyx, Kam, and, always last and always least, wee little Too Short. Proving mainly, I guess, that you can never find a cop killer when you need one. **C+** 🐢

Idle: *Downers Pharmacy* (Big Deal '94) their lives were saved by Sonic Youth ("Cathy Loves Elvis," "Rt. 17") ★

Idlewild: *Hope Is Important* (Odeon '99) Unaccustomed as I am to quoting *NME,* I can resist neither "a flight of stairs falling down a flight of stairs" nor "what Fugazi would sound like if they ate meat." Punk foursome from Glasgow—sometimes lyrical, sometimes heavy, mostly headlong, less confused than the people they write to and about. Almost as catchy as Green Day, who were (are?) cuter. I sincerely suggest they conceive a video for "A Film for the Future" or "You Don't Have the Heart" that makes good-natured fun of 'N Sync—or, failing that, Oasis. There's still time. **A−**

Billy Idol: *Charmed Life* (Chrysalis '90) 🎺

Billy Idol: *Cyberpunk* (Chrysalis '93) If Idol's interest in William Gibson's uncopyrightable neologism was originally piqued by the dollar signs that appear in front of his eyes whenever he encounters the magic rune p-u-n-k, well, the fate of any good idea is that sooner or later it touches people with no deep connection to it—like punk and the former William Broad, for instance. Not that Idol would think of offending this new generation he's read about. So "Adam in Chains," which after a long spoken intro devolves into what a vulgarian might take for his latest love-gone-bad rant, is in fact "a prayer for the tomorrow people and power junkies." And the deathless "Suck on my love meat" is intended as a critique, not a celebration. Sexist, our Billy? How cyber would that be? **C−** 🦃

Iggy and the Stooges: *Open Up and Bleed!* (Bomp! '96) Distinguishable from competing relics of the Church of Iggy by the oddly qualified boast "The Great Lost Stooges Album?" (they do enjoy their punctuation over at Bomp!!), this one recycles the *Raw Power* follow-ups of the *Rubber Legs* EP, with dimmer sound than the ruinous underbassing Bowie inflicted on that piece of classic-openers-plus-filler, and also dimmer songs—"Cock in My Pocket" might make somebody a second encore, "Rubber Legs" is a worthier title cut than "Open Up and Bleed," and the rest belonged on the cutting room floor. Plus, wouldn't you know, equally dim live tapes designed to prove yet again that they did actually vamp longer than Hawkwind and Grinderswitch put together—anything rather than get down to business. Really, folks. He was seminal. He was damn good. He's not bad to this day. He wrote more anthems than Richard Berry himself. But anyone who thinks he's the spirit of the music has been taken in by the doomed theory that

rock and roll is transgressive by definition. Like any living art form only more so, it encompasses transgression for sure. But it wouldn't be alive if it didn't also encompass a lot else. **C+** 🦃

Iggy and the Stooges: *Raw Power* (Columbia/Legacy '97) Strict constructionists and lo-fi snobs charge indignantly that by remixing his own album Iggy has made a mockery of history and done irreparable damage to a priceless work of art. This is really stupid. Before it was anointed the Platonic idea of rock and roll by desperate young men who didn't have much else to choose from, first-generation Iggyphiles charged just as indignantly that David Bowie had mixed the real thing way too thin—as Iggy observes, this classic-by-comparison always sounded "weedy" (although, not to insult a valued colleague, "David's" version was also "very creative"). So the pumped bass and vocals Iggy has uncovered on the original tapes, which were supposed to coexist with the high-end screech to begin with, are a quantum improvement. Plus you can finally hear the celeste on "Penetration"—sounds great! Only the slow ones, which like all of Iggy's slow ones are not as good as his fast ones, stand between a statement of principle and a priceless work of art. **A−**

The Iguanas: *The Iguanas* (MCA '93) ⓝ

Ill Will: "Blowin' Up the Spot" (*The D&D Project* [comp], Arista '95) 👄

Natalie Imbruglia: *Left of the Middle* (RCA '98) Compared to the diluted simple syrup of Swirl 360 or the teen-idol rappabilly of Jimmy Ray, Imbruglia's modern pop is *Rumours*. Not only is she extraordinarily pretty without being too blatant in her babitude, she's got the brains and will to make up her own songs (and did I mention how pretty she is?). Thus she's earned our respect. But under all their state-of-the-studio-art, her competent songs are no more distinctive than the competent songs of hundreds of less pretty women. This was no stiff—RCA milked platinum and a follow-up single out of the sure shot she didn't write herself. But we should be proud that iconicity proved beyond Imbruglia's means. It's three cheers for democracy every time someone goes even a little broke underestimating the taste of the American public. **C+** 🦃

Imo Brothers International: *Ije Love/Journey of Love* (Original Music '96) Ⓝ

Imperial Teen: *Seasick* (Slash/London '96) Coy about their Faith No More link, which leaves no mark on their handcrafted jangle-pop. Not so coy about their gay subtext, which—well, as they say themselves, "our subtext is our plot." A painful one, too. Postgrungers who mistake their cheery surface for happiness either aren't listening or expect too little of life. Sweet and sharp and sometimes mean, they're still feeling their way toward a personal identity as they establish a musical one. And that felt quality makes their jangle-pop come alive. **A–**

Imperial Teen: *What Is Not to Love* (London '99) These understated gender offenders respond to commercial clampdown by mooning around their bedrooms until their hooks are covered with mattress lint. They're true to their alt-bred school—foggier and coyer, yet sweeter than ever if you prove you love them, and hardly averse to reminding whoever's listening that they're "fucking congressmen," say. The brutal fact is that they're not going to break pop no matter how assiduously they polish their lissome tunes or sand down their intelligent noise. So I admire their resistance, and sometimes love it. **A–**

Indigo Girls: *1200 Curfews* (Epic '95) 💣

Inevidence: "Cum Dancing" (*Suck It and See,* Palm Pictures '99) 👁

Innerzone Orchestra: *Programmed* (Astralwerks '99) Ⓝ

Insane Clown Posse: *The Amazing Jeckel Brothers* (Island '99) Refreshing for white guys, especially white guys as dumb as these two, to complain about the slave owner on the dollar bill—simpleminded, but an act of cultural nonconformity nonetheless. Cool to give away a special-offer CD where you rap over stolen gangsta tracks, too. But when a real gangsta's bitch fucks his homey he kills everybody in sight. These kiss-offs just kill the girl, every chance they get. And though they claim clown, they rarely get funnier than "I'd cut my head off but then I would be dead," and that on the cut everybody uses to prove how dumb they are. Personally, I think saying fuck 93 times in one song is a riot. Tell Fatboy Slim the news. **C+** 🦃

Inspectah Deck: *Uncontrolled Substance* (Loud '99) foot soldiers' tales ("Movas & Shakers," "Elevation") ★★

Inspiral Carpets: *Life* (Mute/Elektra '90) 💣

Inti-Illimani: *Arriesgaré la Piel/I Will Risk My Skin* (Xenophile '96) 💣

Intro: *Intro* (Atlantic '93) 💣

Irakere: *La Colección Cubana* (Music Club '98) 💣

Iron Prostate: *Loud, Fast, and Aging Rapidly* (Skreamin' Skull/Skyclad '91) 💣

Gregory Isaacs: *Best of Volumes One and Two* (Heartbeat '92) After roots reggae and before dancehall there was lovers rock, a tag devised for U.K.-based women singers and soon seized by JA crooners who'd never escaped their tight little island. Usually for good reason, too—if you don't believe me, check out Dennis Brown next time you have a week to kill. But even if few non-Jamaicans know it, the equally prolific Isaacs—I bet by now he's recorded 500 songs—is a master. Coolly crooning lyrics that declare for self-determination up against romance or oppression, caressing and suffering with equal imperturbability, he's the aural image of an unconquerable, ganja-guzzling serenity. This showcases keepers from back when sheathing his sexism and talking that dread both came naturally, though great titles like "Slave Master" and "Night Nurse" and "Extra Classic" would follow, as would a sweeter version of the chilled baritone he eventually macked to shreds. It supplants the now semiredundant *My Number One* as your chance to decide whether to agitate for a box. **A−**

Gregory Isaacs & Friends: *Dance Hall Don* (Shanachie '94) Ⓝ

Chris Isaak: *Forever Blue* (Reprise '95) Ⓝ

Chris Isaak: *Baja Sessions* (Reprise '96) 💣

Chris Isaak: *Speak of the Devil* (Reprise '98) rockaballads AC ("Speak of the Devil," "This Time") ★

Mark Isham: *Miles Remembered: The Silent Way Project* (Columbia '99) The auteur isn't Windham Hillbilly turned soundtrack impressionist Isham, whose mushy desecrations I would have slagged bigtime if only I hadn't listened to them first. Instead, this proves the ranking companion piece to *Panthalassa,* with a proficient noname band focusing the compositional skills of the auteur, who is also the greatest musical impressionist of the century. Reducing the *Jack Johnson* theme to five minutes, they even rock like they mean it. **B+**

The Isley Brothers Featuring Ronald Isley: *Tracks of Life* (Warner Bros. '92) Ⓝ

I/COMPILATIONS

Incredibly Strange Music (Caroline '94) Despite their claims to "amazing diversity" and "unique and bizarre visions of life," all of these 13 tracks, compiled by Andrea Juno to illustrate the *RE/Search* issue of the same name, are by white people. Though rhythms tend to the "Latin," all are notably deficient in bottom. The few guitars owe more to Django than Duane, sonorities are up in the whistling-vibraphone-marimba-sitar-theremin range. The two classical covers share a take-that! antirockism with the two songs about dumb teenagers. The only other vocals are Katie Lee's "Will to Fail," from her *Songs of Couch and Consultation* LP, and Kali Bahlu's spoken-word-with-sitar "Cosmic Telephone Call," a wacky flight of pseudo-Buddhist ecumenicism that's easily Juno's most charming find. Beyond their compulsion to escape pop's Afro-American mainstream, what's most striking about these willfully marginal, grotesquely pomo selections is how suburban they are. Responding directly to the hi-fi boom of the '50s and '60s, conceived by adepts of recorded sound for people who wanted to show off their stereos, they presuppose not merely disposable income but a commitment to affluence that insures the ultimate banality of the CD's concrète-naif sound effects and whoop-de-doo chord changes. It documents not forgotten or "strange" music, but a desperately silly moment in the ongoing history of bohemia, which has been hosting this kind of stunt since the time of the dandies. **C**

Incursions in Illbient (Asphodel '96) Ⓝ

I've Found My Love: 1960's Guitar Band Highlife of Ghana (Original Music '93) cultural downmarketing in postcolonial Accra (Youngsters, "Yebewu Asee Kwaa"; Akwaboa, "Onuapa Due") ★

j

J.: *We Are the Majority* (A&M '92) ⓝ

Jack Frost: "Thought That I Was Over You," "Didn't Know Where I Was" (*Jack Frost,* Arista '91) 🐚
Jack Frost: *Snow Job* (Beggars Banquet '96) It's 1993. Grant McLennan of the much-mourned Go-Betweens meets Steve Kilbey of the barely missed Church for a second one-off, written and recorded on the spot and then stuck in a box until they find time to finalize it, which takes years. The songs evoke romantic moods and vague experiences rather than nailing the literal-cum-ineffable; the music strives for effect rather than detail or even ambience. By McLennan's standards, it's hokey, mysterioso, fulla keybs. Yet its schlock disposability and glam brio generate the crass charm McLennan's class act too often avoids. Too bad only cultists will care—and worse still that they'll probably reject it on principle. **B+**

Alan Jackson: "Gone Country," "I Don't Even Know Your Name," "Someday," "Livin' on Love" (*The Greatest Hits Collection,* Arista '95) 🐚
Alan Jackson: *Under the Influence* (Arista '99) 🎸

Janet Jackson: *janet.* (Virgin '93) At least the money that went into this obscenely expensive record comes back as physical luxury: the difference between hearing it on a cheap box and a booming system is the difference between daydreaming about sex and having somebody's crack in your face. Which is only one way it's more pornographic than obscene. And which doesn't make it Jam & Lewis's. This achievement is Janet's, period—those who disagree should send me the name of that hot number in the S.O.S. Band they couldn't wait to boff. Better nose than Michael, better navel than Madonna, better sex than either. **A−**
Janet Jackson: *Design of a Decade 1986/1996* (A&M '95) Her three count-'em three A&M albums produced 12 count-'em 12 top-five singles. All are here. So are two excellent tracks from her one count-it one Virgin album, and two rather less excellent previously unreleaseds. The three estimate-'em three million who own A&M albums two and three needn't bother. Those who begrudge her the place she's earned in the pop cosmos have some catching up to do. **A−**
Janet Jackson: *The Velvet Rope* (Virgin '97) Why do I believe that this self-made object's mild kink and coyly matter-of-fact bisexuality are functions of flesh pure and simple? That for her sex really is about pleasure rather than power—or even, except as a side issue, love? Because her sex songs are flavorful where her love songs are all cliché, and because her much-berated fluting little-girl timbre whispers innocence even when she's loosening her new friend's pretty French gown. So in the absence of total personal fulfillment, here's hoping she retains her ability to feign delight—to fool herself as well as everyone else. **A−**

Michael Jackson: *Dangerous* (Epic '91) It's hard to hear through the oversell, but—especially if you ignore the faith-hope-and-charity, bringing it down under an hour—this is plainly his most consistent album since *Off the Wall,* a step up from *Bad* even if its hookcraft is invariably secondary and its vocal mannerisms are occasionally annoying. Teddy Riley acting alone has never manufactured such abrasively unpredictable beats, much less the singer to top them—if they're not as catchy as a 10-year-old might hope, that's just Michael riding the rhythmic moment, as always. And though it's futile to analyze the love life of an invisible man who's convinced he's more popular than the Beatles now, he's hawking the most credible sex-and-romance of his career. "In the Closet" implores his mystery woman to keep their—get this—"lust" behind closed doors. Soon he's going wild, or fabricating desperate nostalgia for their used-to-be. And then he's muttering "Can't Let Her Get Away" through clenched teeth—mantralike, over and over into the void. Coulda happened, doncha think? With Brooke Shields maybe? **A–**

Michael Jackson: HIStory: Past, Present and Future Book 1 (Epic '95) if stardom is your only subject, you might as well take it to the limit ("Smile," "Tabloid Junkie") ★★

Ronald Shannon Jackson: *Red Warrior* (Axiom '90) metalhead solo room, metalhead showoff space ("Gate to Heaven," "What's Not Said") ★★

Ronald Shannon Jackson: *Taboo* (Venture '90) A departure from Shannon's overworked small-group format featuring varying horn sections and, hi there, old hand Vernon Reid. First side's a suite that'll string you along but good—kind of like Mingus, so to speak. Unfortunately, the second side doesn't exactly move as one thing—a few times its things don't even move as one thing. **B+**

The Jackson 5: "You've Really Got a Hold on Me" (*Motown Sings Motown Treasures* [comp], Motown '98) 🐝

Mick Jagger: *Wandering Spirit* (Atlantic '93) singing the erotic obsession and existential futility of any spirit too long attached to the flesh, then trying for love too late ("Evening Gown," "Hang On to Me Tonight") ★★★

James: "Laid" (*The Best of,* Fontana '98) 🐝

Boney James: *Sweet Thing* (Warner Bros. '97) 🎸

Elmore James: The Sky Is Crying: The History of Elmore James (Rhino '93) Robert Palmer (the important one, I mean) raided the vaults of eight mostly deceased labels to assemble this compiler's tour de force, designed to prove that his man belongs on Mount Bluesmore with Muddy, Wolf, and Sonny Boy II. And though that can't be done in a mere 21 songs (much less 14 on cassette), especially with the more predictable Virgin Flair and Capricorn Fire collections out there proving James's mortality, he rewrites history anyway. As a devotee who considered James a creature of "Dust My Broom," I now know him for the visionary bandleader and galvanic guitarist Palmer and his many previously uncollecteds champion. His voice vying with the harsh distortions he gets out of his amplifier, James would play any kind of blues as long as he could make a lot of noise, and he made "It Hurts Me Too" famous after he was dead. What more do you want? How about his scariest sexual rival, "The 12 Year Old Boy"? **A+**

Etta James: Mystery Lady: Songs of Billie Holiday (Private Music '94) Holiday is a great American artist, a genius whose musical improvisations only deepened an unfathomable persona that was sweet, willing, knowing, suspicious, sly, cynical, and impossibly unhappy before she hit 25 and then gained texture as her body broke down. James is merely a fine r&b singer who's been stroking her cult since before she had one. Entertaining an audience of self-anointed sophisticates who had a thing for earthy music, she fell into the habit of cutting her own earthiness with a flattering wink and coasting from there, and as she herself would tell you, preferably while signing your CD booklet. It would be stupid to buy this before taking on Holiday—Columbia's young three-disc box (with Billie, crappy material just adds to the challenge), or Verve's mature two-disc set (with Billie, a ravaged voice ditto). But short of Chess's young two-disc *Essential Etta James,* it's Etta's most consistent and musical album—her melodic nuances are every bit as hip as the ace backup of Cedar Walton's tight septet. Beyond repertoire, it has little to do with Billie—at most, Etta suggests Holiday's tough soul the way Diana Ross did her pop smarts. But compared to Miki Howard's disgracefully self-aggrandizing "tribute" or Terence Blanchard's dismayingly schmaltzy "songbook," it's an act of love. It's also a hell of a torch record. **A−**

Etta James: *Time After Time* (Private Music '95) ◐

Etta James: *Life, Love and the Blues* (Private Music '98) ◐

Etta James: *Heart of a Woman* (Private Music '99) torching cocktail cool ("My Old Flame," "I Only Have Eyes for You") ★★

Skip James: *She Lyin'* (Genes '94) James is in the canon for a few wildly unprecedented guitar and piano solos captured in 1931, his only session until he was yanked from his sickbed by the folk movement 33 years later. Although the two '60s albums he cut for Vanguard were hailed by the country blues claque, they lack the charm and commitment of John Hurt's. This contemporaneous exhumation isn't brilliant either, but it has more life. A detached noninnovator by the time it was recorded, James nevertheless maintained a personal take on an enduring entertainment music; his falsetto breathed mystery and sexual magnetism. A minor moment in the tangled history of a seminal genre. **A−**

Steve James: *Art and Grit* (Discovery/Antone's '96) jug-band hokum for slide and tuba ("Ooze It to Me, Mama,"

"Downbound Train," "Viola Lee Blues," "Wet Laundry Blues") ★★★

Wendy James: "London's Brilliant," "Do You Know What I'm Saying" (*Now Ain't the Time for Your Tears,* DGC '93) ◄

Jamiroquai: *Synkronized* (Work '99) Hoping to prepare for future outbreaks of rhythm pap by discovering what put these London clotheshorses over, I found but two clues: acid jazz and Heatwave. Both of these apply only in Britannia. How the band secured its Grammy I defy Fredric Dannen to determine. **C−** 🐛

Jam Nation: *Way Down Below Buffalo Hell* (RealWorld '93) 💣

Jane's Addiction: *Ritual de lo Habitual* (Warner Bros. '90) 💣

Jane's Addiction: *Kettle Whistle* (Warner Bros. '97) As its current projects crumble from irrelevance to negative cash flow, a band that never made music or money commensurate with its myth bestows upon a shock-sated marketplace outtakes, demos, live tracks, and four proofs of physical reunion. Chutzpah has never been Perry Bernstein's problem. **C+** 🐛

Jaojoby: *Salegy!* (Rogue import '92) 6/8 dance beats from Madagascar, by guys with their own drum set ("Samy Mandeha Samy Mitady," "Mampanino Anao") ★★

Jali Musa Jawara: See Djeli Diawara

The Jayhawks: *Hollywood Town Hall* (Def American '92) ◐

The Jayhawks: *Tomorrow the Green Grass* (American '95) always sincere, never wimpy, can write some ("Miss Williams' Guitar," "Ten Little Kids") ★

The Jayhawks: *Sound of Lies* (American '97) 💣

Jay-Z: *Reasonable Doubt* (Roc-A-Fella/Priority '96) "watching every ***** watching me closely" ("Friend or Foe," "Cashmere Thoughts") ★

Jay-Z: *In My Lifetime, Vol. 1* (Roc-A-Fella/Def Jam '97) arrogant yet diffident, ruthless yet cute—a scary original ("[Always Be My] Sunshine," "Real Niggaz") ★★

Jay-Z: *Vol. 2 . . . Hard Knock Life* (Roc-A-Fella/Def Jam '98) meet keybmaster Swizz Beats, the missing link between Charles Strouse and Too Short ("Hard Knock Life," "If I Should Die") ★★★

Jay-Z: *Vol. 3 . . . Life and Times of S. Carter* (Roc-A-Fella '99) Sean Carter isn't the first crime-linked hitmaker with a penchant for kicking broads out of bed at 6:15 in the morning. Frank Sinatra beat him to it. Right, Sinatra never boasted about his own callousness—not publicly, in song—and that's a big difference. Jay-Z has too many units tied up in playing the now-a-rapper-now-a-thug "reality" game with his customers, thugs and fantasists both, and only when he lets the token Amil talk back for a verse does he make room for female reality. But he goes for a rugged, expansive vigor, nailing both come-fly-with-me cosmopolitanism and the hunger for excitement that's turned gangster hangouts into musical hotbeds from Buenos Aires to Kansas City. You don't expect a song called "Big Pimpin'" to sound as if the tracks were recorded in Cairo. This one does. **A**

Jazz Passengers: *In Love* (High Street '94) artful artsongs, arty artsongs—nu? ("Dog in Sand," "Think of Me," "Imitation of a Kiss") ★

Jazz Passengers Featuring Deborah Harry: *Individually Twisted* (32 '97) A friend of Roy Nathanson since long before this band began a decade ago, I've loved the Passengers onstage, where the saxophonist kept the interactions grooving like the comic actor he also is, and found their records arty. Here the artiest track is Elvis Costello's (and bassist Brad Jones's) long-lined "Aubergine," the runner-up "Imitation of a Kiss," originally the pick to click on *In Love,* counted the Passengers' pop move in 1994 because it had lyrics. From Nathanson and Harry's slantwise opener to Blondie's loopy closer, from David Cale's mock-'40s exot-

ica to Nathanson's jump blues homage, its pleasures are various and manifest, and if they're over the head of the average Costello completist, that's because this pop move isn't aimed at any kind of average. Starting with the girl singer, it's real musicians tweaking real sophistication into something genuinely cooler—and warmer. **A–**

The Jazz Passengers Featuring Deborah Harry: *Live in Spain* (32 '98) who says a rock chick can't sing jazz music? ("Fathouse," "Dog in Sand") ★★

Jazzy Jeff & Fresh Prince: *Greatest Hits* (Jive '98) the antigangsta, as only a master of light comedy could render him ("Summertime," "Lovely Daze") ★★

Wyclef Jean: *Wyclef Jean Presents the Carnival Featuring Refugees All-stars* (Ruffhouse/Columbia '97) From kompas to reggae, Celia Cruz to Neville Brothers, the diasporan flavors ("Jaspora," one title spells it, nicely kreyolizing the Greek/Jewish term) are half decoration, half concept, and less than integral either way. Like his soul brother Puff Daddy, master of the simplistic strategy with which the Fugees wrested dominance of hip hop songwriting from the moribund Death Row consortium last year, Wyclef doesn't feature the grandiose depth charges with which Wu-Tang torpedoed hip hop beatmastering well before that. He uses the sampler—augmented by the live quote, the honored guest, and now the genre excursion—like MC Hammer before him, for one-dimensional tunes on which to float his well-articulated morality tales and popwise carnivalesque. Cognoscenti may bitch that it's only r&b, but r&b has been the shit for half a century, and this is where it lives. **A–**

Garland Jeffreys: *Don't Call Me Buckwheat* (RCA '92) Bigotry 101, from a professor with tenure ("I Was Afraid of Malcolm," "Murder Jubilee") ★

Jelly Roll Kings: *Off Yonder Wall* (Fat Possum/Capricorn '97) **Ⓝ**

Jane Jensen: *Comic Book Whore* (Flip '96) 'twixt Courtney and Alanis on the noise and normality scales, only sexier ("Luv Song," "Highway 90") ★★★

Jeru the Damaja: *The Sun Rises in the East* (FFRR '94) rhythmic dissonance for the beat connoisseur ("D. Original," "My Mind Spray") ★

Jeru the Damaja: *Wrath of the Math* (Payday/FFRR '96) no metaphor, fantasy, or conspiracy theories—just straight postgangsta dope ("Tha Frustrated Nigga," "Tha Bullshit") ★

Joan Jett: *The Hit List* (Epic '90) 💣

Joan Jett & the Blackhearts: *Notorious* (Epic Associated/Blackheart '91) 💣

Joan Jett and the Blackhearts: *Flashback* (Blackheart '93) A career's worth of outtakes, half covers and 13 of 22 from her 1983–86 heyday, this may end up a last gasp. But her simultaneous rediscovery by Warner bigshots and angry old gurls leaves room for hope that instead it will prove a marker. And either way it's her strongest album ever, full of stuff originally judged not weak but impolitic—the censored "Starfucker," the girl-loving "Play with Me," "EMI" as "MCA"—as well as Jett standards backed by Sex Pistols and Melle Mel and L7, soundtrack finds penned by Bruce Springsteen and Janna Allen, oldies new to me like "Hide and Seek" and "She Lost You," oldies forever young like "Rebel Rebel" and "Call Me Lightning," and "Activity Grrrl," in which she advises her spirit children to forget the animal rights stuff and buy a set of leathers. She still loves rock 'n roll. And vice versa. **A–**

Joan Jett and the Blackhearts: *Pure and Simple* (Warner Bros. '94) hasn't lost a step, hasn't gained one either ("Spinster," "You Got a Problem") ★★

Joan Jett and the Blackhearts: *Fit to Be Tied: Great Hits by Joan Jett and the Blackhearts* (Blackheart/Mercury '97) Now semiretired, I guess, an honored spinster godmother throughout grrrlland, she's always been endearingly, maddeningly consistent, stubbornly unimaginative in all matters of form. Hence her albums have failed to ignite even though explosions were what her commitment to the rock and roll basics was supposed to insure. But this compilation is the cherry bomb. Combining her own songwriting peaks—from "Bad Reputation" and "I Love Rock n Roll" to "Fake Friends" and the *Light of Day* non-Oscar winner—with the like-minded strokes of such symbolic friends as Sly Stone, Jonathan Richman, and Tommy James, the material only dips as semiretirement approaches. And she goes out on the Mary Tyler Moore theme. **A**

Joan Jett: See also L7 & Joan Jett

Jewel: *Pieces of You* (Atlantic '97) Worth ignoring while she was merely precious, she demands our attention now that she's becoming overvalued as well. With the possible exception of Saint Joan, who at least had some stature, this is the bad folkie joke to end all bad folkie jokes. With her self-righteousness, her self-dramatization, her abiding love for her own voice, her breathy little-girl innocence and breathless baby-doll sexuality, her useless ideas about prejudice and injustice and let us not forget abuse, she may well prove as insufferable as any hollow-bodied guitarist ever to get away with craving the world's adoration. End of story—I hope. **C–** 🦃

Bobby Jimmy: *Erotic Psychotic* (Priority '91) roll over Ogden Nash and tell Jimmy Castor the news ("Rapper Rapper," "Minute Man Man") ★★

Antonio Carlos Jobim: *Composer* (Warner Archives '97) 💣

Jodeci: *Diary of a Mad Band* (MCA/Uptown '93) Ⓝ

Jodeci: *The Show, the After-Party, the Hotel* (Uptown/MCA '95) No way does the sex on this concept album recall Prince or Marvin Gaye—spiritually, its precursors are Kiss and Judas Priest. Rather than lust between equals, it's powerful men manipulating starstruck girls. And since the backstage adventure with the lawsuit attached somehow goes unrecounted—supposedly, DeVante pointed a gun while K-Ci felt the complainant up, with both love men pleading guilty to less specific charges—only a fool would take their word about how knowing their honeys are. So here's hoping your mama didn't raise no fools. And here's hoping this papa didn't either. **B–** 🦃

Billy Joel: *River of Dreams* (Columbia '93) 💣

The David Johansen Group: *Live* (Epic Associated/Legacy '93) A Bottom Line show from the beginnings of his solo run, before he had the arena-rock flourishes down pat, this isn't quite the song showcase it might have been later—no "Bohemian Love Pad," no "Wreckless Crazy," no "She Loves Strangers." But on the other hand, no "Melody," no "Marquesa de Sade," no "Flamingo Road," no enjoyable-to-forgivable gestures that aged even more awkwardly than the rest of his Grass Roots phase. In retrospect, this Staten Island band sounds a lot more like the Dolls than it did at the time. And if it's less inspired and more in control—cf. Johnny Thunders's veering cameo—that's not entirely a bad thing. **A–**
David Johansen: "Alabama Song" (*September Songs: The Music of Kurt Weill* [comp], Sony Classics '97) 🔊

Elton John: *The One* (MCA '92) Fun automaton, floundering has-been, or unnoticed fixture, he hung in there, so that 1992 was the *23rd consecutive year* he put a single in the top 40. Since Elvis himself only got to 22, this statistical aberration merits a tribute, and though I was disarmed by the news that he'd not only come out but was donating all singles royalties to AIDS research, I decided to take it as a long-overdue hint to ignore his albums. Unfortunately, the first single was an all-too-well-plugged Eric Clapton feature. Then came an AIDS ballad drenched in midtempo melodrama, followed by a title tune that's just as soupy with less content. So here's hoping somebody at MCA

likes "Sweat It Out," a fast dance number about vanquishing the forces of reaction. Inspirational Verse That Saves Me a Review: "No more Tears for Fears/Give me tears of rage." **C+** 🦃

Johnnie Johnson: *Johnnie B. Bad* (Elektra Nonesuch '91) 💣

Linton Kwesi Johnson: *Tings an' Times* (Shanachie '91) A concept album about political fatigue, a theme the man understands deeply and cogently and aphoristically and colloquially and polysyllabically. Johnson always talks, never sings, but his assumed patois is like Leonard Cohen with funkentelechy—the speech of his people is music to his ears, and the music of his people is manna. So the riddims skip by on Dennis Bovell's ska-speedy tempos, graced with tricky guitar hooks and colored with fiddle and accordion that sing Hungary and Algeria and Colombia and the Rio Grande as Johnson "consider how young rebels get old." "Sense outa Nonsense" is a homily about innocents and fools played out as an animal fable, its punch line not words but a regretfully disparaging click of the tongue. "Story" gets behind black masks. "Tings an' Times" starts "Beat doped demoralized/Dizzied dazed and traumatized" and goes on from there. "Di Good Life" utters the name of socialism— "Some say him is a ghost/Some say him is a sage/But nobody know him rightfully yet/Or where him come from." "Di Anfinish Revalueshan" somehow finds hope in confusion and compromise. And in "Mi Revalueshanary Fren," Linton tries to reason with an old Marxist about glasnost. Problem is, the Marxist has wigged out— all the reason is on Linton's side. Analysis, analysis, who's got the analysis? Surely not a reggae man? **A**
Linton Kwesi Johnson: *More Time* (LKJ '99) most poetic when he's most quotidian ("If I Waz a Tap Natch Poet," "Reggae Fi Bernard") ★

Pete Johnson: *King of Boogie* (Milan '92) The hero of Big Joe Turner's "Roll 'Em

Pete" was third man on a boogie-woogie totem pole topped by Albert Ammons and Meade Lux Lewis. All three formed duos; occasionally they even ganged up into a trio I'd love to hear. But on the basis of the records I know I'll just note that the hierarchy was designed for jazzbos. Especially on this mostly solo Hot Club of Paris session, but also on Delmark's small-combo *Central Avenue Boogie,* Johnson is the barrelhouse piano player of rock and roll dreams—he launches more fast ones and flexes more right-hand muscle. So I prefer him straight up—sidemen just get in his way. **A–**

Ross Johnson: "Wet Bar" (*It Came from Memphis* [comp], Upstart '95) 🕭

Syl Johnson: *Back in the Game* (Delmark '94) 💣

Vernard Johnson: *I'm Alive* (Elektra Nonesuch '91) 💣

Daniel Johnston: *Fun* (Atlantic '94) just like K. McCarty, I prefer my crazies childish and well supervised—only I also prefer their own voices ("Love Wheel," "Happy Time") ★

Daniel Johnston: "Come See Me Tonight" (*My So-Called Life,* Atlantic '95) 🕭

Daniel Johnston: "Casper," "Casper the Friendly Ghost" (*Kids* [ST], London '95) 🕭

Freedy Johnston: *The Trouble Tree* (Restless/Bar/None '90) folk-postpunk Donald Fagen ("Tucumcari," "No Violins") ★★★

Freedy Johnston: *Can You Fly* (Bar/None '92) Defying the taste for tortured chaos that the triumph of Nirvana signifies, the Kansas-born Hoboken fixture is a case study in bringing confusion under control—in loving your life as beautiful mess. Contained, mature, realistic in philosophy and aesthetic, its every song a model of open-ended lyrical detail and lithe, sly melodicism, it's a flat-out monument of singer-songwriterdom—up there with Randy Newman's *12 Songs,* Joni

Mitchell's *For the Roses,* and other such prepunk artifacts. Johnston is modest in everything but his perfectionism, his rage repressed if that and his puzzlement so permanent it comes as naturally as breathing. The epiphanies he runs through his flat Midwestern inflections evoke a heartland miniaturist like Bobbie Ann Mason more than any rock artiste. Hitting the festival circuit with the ozone layer shot to hell, losing a daughter in Manhattan's concrete dreamscape, deconstructing a house and a marriage simultaneously, his oblique, decipherable tales of not quite getting it together are summed up by the title of the first: "Trying to Tell You I Don't Know." **A+**

Freedy Johnston: *Unlucky* (Bar/None '93) new producer, so this EP can't be good outtakes from a great album—can it? ("For a Lost Key") ★★

Freedy Johnston: *This Perfect World* (Elektra '94) trying to say what he can't sing, trying to drive with the green light on ("Bad Reputation," "Evie's Tears") ★★★

Freedy Johnston: *Never Home* (Elektra '97) When *Billboard* wondered whether Freedy could fill one of those solo-male chart niches left inexplicably vacant by Rod Stewart and Bryan Adams, the object of their affections had the artistic integrity to keep a straight face about it. He's a cardplayer—so committed to the mystery of the ordinary that you have to poke a stick beneath his placid, bland catchiness to glimpse the empathy and compulsion it conceals. With '70s studio hero Danny Kortchmar replacing the mismatched Butch Vig behind the board, Johnston not only regains his grace but spells it out—most of these lyrics tell a story suitable for paraphrasing. But he'll never be accessible to consumers who can only read a heart when it's bloodying a sleeve. Our blessing, his curse. **A–**

Freedy Johnston: *Blue Days Black Nights* (Elektra '99) Sinatra he's not—maybe not Sammy Cahn and Jimmy Van Heusen either ("Depending on the Night," "Changed Your Mind") ★

Joi: *The Pendulum Vibe* (EMI/ERG '94) freedom as manumission, freedom as swinging both ways ("Freedom," "Narcissa Cutie Pie") ★

Al Jolson: *Let Me Sing and I'm Happy: Al Jolson at Warner Bros. 1926–1936* (Turner Classic Movies/Rhino '96) It's hard now to grasp that, generation gap aside, this native of Lithuania was nothing less than the Elvis of the first half of the 20th century. But fame was fleeting in that trendy, technology-driven era, and by the mid-'30s, as foolish kids embraced the big-band fad and "crooning" style, "The World's Greatest Entertainer" was slipping badly. While it's true enough that his emotionality was too cornball for an emerging generation of pseudosophisticates, the biggest problem was his resistance to new media—his radio shows were spotty, and, much worse for history, his studio recordings were stiff. As anyone who screens *The Jazz Singer* learns, however, movies were the exception. Hollywood let him roll his eyes and shake his fanny in front of onlookers who could feed him the approval he craved. Whether he's wearing burnt cork or pancake makeup, appropriating Irving Berlin or an Oedipal kiss from his mammy, his verve, spontaneity, and sexual magnetism are as startling as, well, Elvis's. A–

George Jones: *Friends in High Places* (Epic '91) friends wherever he can find them, some inspired (Randy Travis, Vern Gosdin), some otherwise (Ricky Van Shelton, Buck Owens) ("A Few Ole Country Boys," "All That We've Got Left") ★

George Jones: *And Along Came Jones* (MCA '91) and along came Tony Brown, too ("I Don't Go Back Anymore," "You Couldn't Get the Picture") ★

George Jones: *Walls Can Fall* (MCA '92) The cassette-bound are advised to fast-forward to side two, CD investors to program, oh, 6-4-7-8-9-10-1; there's no true filler here, but "Wrong's What I Do Best" is far more thematic than "I Don't Need Your Rockin' Chair," in which 10 suburban cowpeople sing the praises of

61-year-old youth, and which I conceive as a coda. George has been hitched and on the wagon since well before he cut his late-'80s dreck, but he can still sing the likes of "Drive Me to Drink" (if she can't be his wife she can be his chauffeur) and "There's the Door" (if she can walk out of the house he can walk out of the bar) as if he does a lot of listening at 12-step meetings. His problem wasn't authenticity—it was Billy Sherrill. A–

George Jones: "The Visit" (*High-Tech Redneck,* MCA '93) 🍥

George Jones: *The Bradley Barn Sessions* (MCA '94) did someone say duets with America's greatest living vocalist? ("Bartender Blues," "Where Grass Won't Grow") ★

George Jones & Tammy Wynette: "If God Met You" (*One,* MCA '95) 🍥

George Jones: *I Lived to Tell It All* (MCA '96) a drunkard's prayers ("I'll Give You Something to Drink About," "Tied to a Stone") ★

George Jones: *It Don't Get Any Better Than This* (MCA '98) old faithfuls ("Wild Irish Rose," "It Don't Get Any Better Than This") ★★★

George Jones: *Cold Hard Truth* (Asylum '99) Ⓝ

George Jones: *The George Jones Collection* (MCA '99) too obvious too often ("Wild Irish Rose," "Golden Ring") ★★

George Jones: *Live with the Possum* (Asylum '99) Ⓝ

Hank Jones Meets Cheick-Tidiane Seck and the Mandinkas: *Sarala* (Verve '96) Afro-jazz fusion with the emphasis on the Afro for once ("Touniya Kanibala," "Hadja Fadima") ★★★

Paul "Wine" Jones: *Mule* (Fat Possum/Capricorn '95) country blues in a wired world ("Diggin Mommas Tatters," "Nobody but You") ★

Rickie Lee Jones: "Rebel Rebel" (*Traffic from Paradise,* Geffen '93) 🍥

Rickie Lee Jones: *Ghostyhead* (Warner Bros. '97) 🌶

Janis Joplin: *Janis* (Columbia/Legacy '93) Having long ago wondered how she'd "hold up," I eventually concluded the answer was that I didn't feel like playing her records anymore. But it was just the opposite: one reason the music triumphs more miraculously than ever is that it's damned hard to listen to, fading into the background about as smoothly as Ornette or the Dolls or PJ Harvey. The most polished product here is the least compelling—it's in her demos, her live fracases with Kozmic Blues and Full Tilt Boogie, and especially her rough anything-goes with Big Brother that she demolishes the canards that she was a blues imitator or hippie fool. For her, blues was a language to be twisted and shredded in the service of a utopian quest, a quest I swear she had the stuff to take somewhere. My only quarrel with this superb re-creation, which unveils many terrific previously unissueds and contextualizes several older finds, is that it sacrifices live rarities like "Ego Blues" to the *Kozmic Blues* album. You want to know more, read the liner essays by Ellen Willis and Ann Powers, which I hope aren't over the Grammy guys' heads. **A**

Janis Joplin with Big Brother and the Holding Co.: *Live at Winterland '68* (Columbia/Legacy '98) the history enjoyable, the jams educational, and listen for this prophetic Inspirational Interjection: "When I say no that's exactly what I mean" ("Easy Rider," "Down on Me") ★★

Montell Jordan: *This Is How We Do It* (PMP/RAL '95) Ⓝ

Wynonna Judd: "She Is His Only Need," "All of That Love from Here," "It's Never Easy to Say Goodbye" (*Wynonna Judd,* Curb/MCA '92) 🍭
Wynonna Judd: *Tell Me Why* (Curb/MCA '93) credit to her family, credit to her sex ("Girls with Guitars," "Tell Me Why") ★★
Wynonna: "Free Bird" (*Revelations,* Curb/MCA '96) 🍭

Julie Ruin: *Julie Ruin* (Kick Rock Stars '98) "What would 'L'Ecriture Feminine' sound like as music?" the once and future Kathleen Hanna asked herself, and if this is the answer, we're in trouble. It sounds like Calvin Johnson prattle, it sounds like she needs all that sound equipment she can't afford, it sounds like she took her bat and went home. It's fine to reject confessional for narrative if you have some fictional craft, fine to let machines do the playing if you can figure out how to make them sing, but so far Hanna doesn't and hasn't. Instead she takes the obscure rants that were so compelling at Bikini Kill decibels and murmurs them into her cheap mike at two in the morning, if we're lucky to one of the simple tunes that provide meaning in a band context and relief in this. "I don't expect people to like it or anything," she told some zine, and here's hoping they don't. She's 29, and she needs to move on. **B–** 🐞

Jungle Brothers: *J. Beez Wit the Remedy* (Warner Bros. '93) Four years after, you can definitely discern an absence—of faith or community or existential confidence, youth or advance money or raw spiritual health. Where once hooks were a pop luxury their holistic groove had no time for, now the JB's sound as dissociated as some tortured hippie manqué or privileged gangsta. So catchier would be nice. Yet they remain unique—street, street-tough, no suburban patina or collegiate pretension, yet somehow free of hostility, blissed out in their blackness. Positive, I guess. And the great stuff—the beats concrète of "Blahbludify" and "For the Heads at Company Z" and "Man Made Material," maybe the headlong preclimax of "JB's Comin' Through" and "Spittin Wicked Randomness"—experiments more esoterically than Michaels D or Ivey have ever dared. **B+**
Jungle Brothers: *Raw Deluxe* (Gee Street '97) Ⓝ
Jungle Brothers: *V.I.P.* (Gee Street '99) 🎣

Junior Cottonmouth: "Physical Stuff," "Something Scratching" (*Bespoke,* Atlantic '97) 🍭

Juvenile: "HA," "Intro" (*400 Degreez*, Cash Money/Universal '98) 🔊
Juvenile: *Tha G-Code* (Cash Money/ Universal '99) celebrating an old pop reliable—new money ("A Million and One Things," "U Understand") ★

J/COMPILATIONS

The Jackal (MCA '97) the electropop moment, from spiritual jokes to fabricated enlightenment (Goldie, "Sunray 2"; Black Grape, "Get Higher") ★★★

The Jazz Age: New York in the Twenties (Bluebird '91) Crammed into Tin Pan Alley straitjackets by big bad bizzers or maybe just lacking in natural rhythm, these young white guys—Benny Goodman, Glenn Miller, Tommy Dorsey, Jimmy Dorsey, Jack Teagarden, Red Nichols, Eddie Lang, Joe Venuti—nevertheless sound intensely happy to be alive, so delighted with the freedoms come up the river from New Orleans that they can scarcely contain themselves. Disciplined but never sedulous, they're rollicking iconoclasts injecting greater musicians' mind-boggling innovations of pulse, phrasing, and intonation into the culture of Prohibition. They sing the spirit electric without uttering a word. **A**

Jazz Satellites—Volume 1: Electrification (Virgin import '96) Running the gauntlet of not just fusion but such ignominious genres as Third Stream, soundtrack, and acid jazz, kowtowing to pretenders, meddlers, mooncalves, and schlockmeisters like Jan Garbarek, Teo Macero, Alice Coltrane, Norman Connors, and a panoply of pseudonymous English cyborgs, this obscurely annotated double-CD is the great lost testament of late Miles—cacophonous, futuristic, swinging-to-spacy variations on everything he thought he was doing between *Bitches Brew* and *Agharta*. Connecting up the mind-to-the-wall charge of early Mahavishnu and Tony Williams Lifetime, it ought to demonstrate the obvious to techno-

mancers the world over—raid jazz for avant *sounds* and leave its beats for hip hop to sort out. In fact it proved so indigestible that in its native U.K. it vanished without notice. If you find one, don't let go. **A–**

Jit—The Movie (Earthworks '91) Highlighting Eddy Grant fan Oliver Mutukudzi, whose trademark cough reappears as Solomon Skuza's grunt-in-transition, six songs from the soundtrack and six from the southern African ether complement *Zimbabwe Frontline*'s earlier survey of a roughly soulful pop idiom—less mbira-rooted and more internationalist, with English lyrics that never grate. Not every musician in Harare is as vital as Thomas Mapfumo, or as light-headed as the Bhundu Boys. **A–**

Jive Nation: The Indestructible Beat of Soweto Vol. 5 (Stern's/Earthworks '95) The title is poetic license. Not only will it take a lot more than music to hold South Africa together, but the posttribal genres Trevor Herman fuses into jive aren't modern enough for the job. Nevertheless, these 18 tracks, the series's strongest since volume one, prove how robust the genres remain. Three tipico Shangaan outfits and one supertrad Sotho group hold their own and then some against the Zulus. The King Star Brothers and especially Colenso Abafana Benkokhelo render Ladysmith's absence moot. Johnny Clegg sounds like himself and fits right in. And on his sole track, Mahlathini blows everybody else away. **A–**

Jive Soweto: The Indestructible Beat of Soweto Vol. 4 (Earthworks '93) By now the availability of South African pop far exceeds the needs of the curious, and none of Trevor Herman's four follow-ups to *Indestructible Beat* is as essential as Ladysmith's *Classic Tracks* or Mzwakhe's *Resistance Is Defence* or Mahlathini's *Paris-Soweto* or Shanachie's *Heartbeat of Soweto*. But for the converted, each has its distinct rewards. Featuring the slick arrangements and syncretic harmonies of the Soul Brothers on six tracks, this one abandons basso groaners for the high-end registers of hectoring chatter-box Ihashi Elimhlophe, theatrical inter-loper Mbongeni Ngema, and pop idol Steve Kekana. It makes itself useful on sonic differentiation alone. **A–**

Journeys by DJ: Billy Nasty Mix (Moon-shine Music '93) An English DJ's one-cut, 78-minute set, comprising healthy swatches of 19 technohouse instrumen-tals. Despite occasional overdubbing and lots of switching back and forth, Nasty's basic strategy is to lay the best parts end to end and make you like it, and although I must have encountered some of these songs on ordinary dance comps, all I can tell you is that they're long on basslines, midrange coloration, and vocal sound ef-fects—and that they sound great when-ever you tune in. For years hardcore dancers have been complaining that compilations and single-artist albums don't do their experience justice—the songs remain too discrete. The few street and private tapes I've heard don't live up to the fantasy, and a second volume in this series is more like an ordinary house collection. But this—this is sort of what they're talking about. Bravo. **A–**

Judgment Night (Immortal/Epic Sound-trax '93) Here's a little something that you've never heard before: mostly black rappers rhyming over the live guitars *and drums* of mostly white bands, all alterna-tive-identified and only De La Soul help-mates Teenage Fanclub less than hard. This music knows lots of ways to say blunt; if the wordplay is minimal, that fits concept and movie, which ain't about a bobsled competition. Whoomp, there it is—beats the new Motorhead and the new Cypress Hill simultaneously. **A–**

Juice (Soul '92) **Ⓝ**

k

Cheb Kader: *From Oran to Paris* (Shanachie '91) emigré rai with hot violin ("Koumou Bih") ★★

Pépé Kallé: *Pépé Kallé* (Gefraco '90) The soft touch of Empire Babuka's head-man takes his speedy new wave soukous a crucial lift or two higher than Loketo's more masculine *Soukous Trouble.* But a Diblo Dibala record is what it is—in a style where every guitarist sounds the same and pretty damn good, the producer's ar-ticulated billows of rhythm always encour-age your faith that this time it'll be even better. And especially on the buoyant, surging "L'Argent Ne Fait Pas le Bonheur," it is. **A–**
Pépé Kallé: *Larger Than Life* (Stern's Africa '92)

Kam: *Made in America* (EastWest '95)

Ini Kamoze: *Here Comes the Hotstep-per* (Columbia '95) belated one-shot oc-casions belated mid-'80s comp as belated minor Sly & Robbie album ("Here Comes the Hotstepper," "Rough") ★★

Kanda Bongo Man: *Zing Zong* (Hanni-bal '91) Montreuil HI-NRG to the mel-low—generically, but he invented the genre ★★
Kanda Bongo Man: *Soukous in Cen-tral Park* (Hannibal '93) Prolonged com-parison to 1988's *Kwassa Kwassa* and 1991's *Zing Zong* reveals distinctions so subtle I can't swear they're there. I'm cer-tain guitarist Nene Tshakou is slightly

fleeter and more lyrical (if less dazzling) than Diblo Dibala, who went on to make greater records than the boss after help-ing him reinvent soukous, and that Tshakou was having a good day. And I'd guess that maybe the boss's music tends to take off—lifts, grooves, accelerates—in front of an audience. For sure neither live audio nor live song length are drawbacks. For sure the material is choice. Start here. **A–**

Big Daddy Kane: "All of Me," "Big Daddy vs. Dolemite" (*A Taste of Choco-late,* Cold Chillin'/Reprise '90)
Big Daddy Kane: *Daddy's Home* (MCA '94)

Ray Kane: *Punahele* (Dancing Cat '94) a commercial for paradise, if that turns you on ("Pauoa Liko Ka Lehua," "Puna-hele") ★

Mory Kante: *Touma* (Mango '90)

Lokua Kanza: *Lokua Kanza* (Salambo import '93)
Lokua Kanza: *Wapi Yo* (Catalyst '97)

Alione Kassé: *Exsina* (Tinder '98)

K-Ci & JoJo: *It's Real* (MCA '99)

Keb' Mo': *Just Like You* (OKeh/Epic '96) blues, soul, and the trouble he's seen—one big happy family ("That's Not Love," "Dangerous Mood") ★

Salif Keita: *Amen* (Mango '91)
Salif Keita: *The Mansa of Mali . . . A Retrospective* (Mango '94) I wonder

---

★★★, ★★, ★ Honorable Mention   🕭 Choice Cut    Neither   💣 Dud   🦃 Turkey

what a mansa is. Surely nothing so crass as an albino from the desert around Bamako who was ambitious enough to hit NYC back in 1980? But that's who he is and has been, as set on world conquest as Youssou D'Dour himself, even if he isn't as good at it. The baloney on this useful introduction isn't the three grand survivals from the failed Eurofusion *Soro,* which are more likable undercut by simpler stuff, or even the duly selected representative from the Republic of Zawinul, which starts out fairly pretty and gets fairly intense. And it sure isn't the legendary 1978 "Mandjou," 13 leisurely, inevitable minutes an Ambassadeurs fan might buy a whole best-of just to own. It's the three hunks of soundtrack, precisely one of which conjures up any image whatsoever. **A–**

Salif Keita: *"Folon"... The Past* (Mango '95) Malian world beat with a pan-Afropop flavor-not-flava ("Africa," "Dakan-Fe") ★★

Salif Keita: *Papa* (Metro Blue '99) This Vernon Reid coproduction is beyond fusion, crossover, world music, and the rest. The master guitarist is pure polyglot, comfortable anywhere from AOR to funk to harmolodic to aleatory, and after two decades of knocking on Euro-America's door, the master singer is at home in the white world even if he's never found the fortune he sought there. So the straightforward rhythms mesh imperceptibly with the traditional instruments Keita is forever rediscovering, and though it's not clear from the credits whether such Bamako big men as Toumani Diabate (kora) and Ousmane Kouyate (guitar) ever occupied the same room as such New York delegates as John Medeski (organ) and Henry Schroy (essential on bass), their spiritual confluence is in the grooves. Above it all Keita soars gravely in Bambara and sometimes English, his sand-blasted yearning finally kept in focus by a production that knows the difference between embellishing and bedizening. Almost as much an outsider in Mali and Senegal as in France or the U.S., he's finally arrived at

a style that's indigenous everywhere. Which is what he always wanted. **A–**
Salif Keita: See Les Ambassadeurs

Kelis: *Kaleidoscope* (Virgin '99) Kaleidoscopic not as in psychedelic—this is pop funk straight up—but as in changeable, hard to get a bead on. Beyond male-identified, that is. The many moods of Kelis only begin with the hissy fit she's gone pop with (which, I should mention, is about as riot-grrrl as Gwen Stefani on a bad hair day). She stands by her man, reasons with her man, lies for her man, watches TV alongside her man, loads his gun, fucks him in the window, hopes he misses his damn plane. She thinks about ghetto boys and girls, she thinks about outer space, and mainly she thinks about her man. Why else would she get so mad at him? **A–**

R. Kelly and Public Announcement: *Born into the 90's* (Jive '92) 🎵
R. Kelly: *12 Play* (Jive '93) In a year when the big rappers have either repeated tired outrages or outgrown them, Kelly's crude, chartwise new jack swing is black pop's most depressing development. An effective singer in the post-Stevie new-soul mode whose way with a beat is confirmed by an impressive catalogue of bestselling productions, he aims his common denominator straight at the solar plexus. He has no apparent interest in tune—the Spinners' "Sadie" sounds positively angelic after "Summer Bunnies" and "I Like the Crotch on You." And despite a few moments of class consciousness, he displays far less human decency in his quest for booty than such unaltruistic competitors as Jodeci and Boyz II Men. But lest anyone suspect he lacks moral acuity, he offers this Inspirational Liner Note: "To all those women out there when I step off in a club—don't treat me like I'm just anybody because you end up treating me like I'm nobody and that's wrong." **B–**
R. Kelly: *R. Kelly* (Jive '95) "He's grown up a little," an intelligent young member of his target audience was gratified to re-

port, and that's a reasonable explanation for his surprise abandonment of bump-and-mack banality. But as a sage old outsider, I wonder whether he hasn't also sold out a little—and whether pop music and the world aren't better off for his market-driven pursuit of the love-man demographic. Luther's ladies buy as many tapes and CDs as B-girls do, and in real stores, too. So as said B-girls evolve into job-holding consumers who won't get played, a fella with his eye on the main chance learns to improve the quality of his dubious promises: "Trade in my life for you," that's strong, and no harm in a little "goin' down on you by the fireplace." Add a dollop of Dre, a cup of Isleys, and more church than he sees the inside of in a year, and you have the smartest and sexiest new jack swing since Teddy Riley fell off the edge of the biz. **A–**

R. Kelly: *R.* (Jive '98) megaskills for megasale ("Half on a Baby," "Did You Ever Think") ★★

Kenickie: *At the Club* (Warner Bros. '97) Ⓝ

The Kennedys: *Life Is Large* (Green Linnet '96) Ⓝ

Klark Kent: "Yo Ho Ho" (*Just in Time for Christmas* [comp], I.R.S. '90) 🐟

The Kentucky Headhunters: "It's Chitlin' Time" (*Electric Barnyard,* Mercury '91) 🐟

Tara Key: *Bourbon County* (Homestead '94) 🎸

Tara Key: *Ear and Echo* (Homestead) '96 🎸

Khaled: *Khaled* (Cohiba '92) sounds more Arab with Michael Brook Frenching him than with Don Was funking him ("El Ghatli," "Wahrane") ★★★

Khaled: *N'ssi N'ssi* (Mango '94) The temptation once again is to attribute the straight-ahead passion of the big cheb's return bid to neotraditionalist Don Was, who adds funk bass, steel guitar, Was (Not Was) sax, and other unidiomatically consonant Americanisms to the already

elaborate (and funky) production strategies the artist learned from the brothers Ahmed. But once again the alternate producer's Gallicisms—this time Phillippe Eidel's musette accordion, music-hall piano, and imported rafts of Cairo violins—fill out his songs less obtrusively if less strikingly. Hey, there's a thought—songs. Most of these were hits where and when it counted even if we've never heard them before. Can't hurt, can it? **A**

Khaled: *Sahra* (Island '97) panpop move ("Lillah," "Detni Essekra") ★★

Badar Ali Khan: *Lost in Qawwali* (Worldly/Triloka '97) Cousin of Nusrat, big deal—there's probably whole villages of 'em. Only this one's released the hottest qawwali record I've ever heard. No Western instruments, just harmonium, tabla, and hand claps, but also no ghazals—at times I swear it swings, and direct comparison to the master makes startlingly clear that the higher pitches, faster tempos, and precipitate ascent into ecstasy very nearly create a new subgenre: speed-qawwali. The 13-minute lead track supposedly sold a million as a Pakistani cassingle, and I bet it created a scandal. Nonbelievers, on the other hand, will get Badar easier than they ever did the former real thing. Deep? How would I know? But as intense an hour of music as you'll hear all year. **A**

Badar Ali Khan: *Mixes* (Worldly/Triloka '97) 🎸

Badar Ali Khan: *Lost in Qawwali II* (Worldly/Triloka '98) Yankee yobs like you and me might reasonably wonder how the hell much more Sufi devotional music we need, and absent this Nusrat cousin's extraordinary, volume-one-leading, elsewhere uselessly and here curiously remixed great hit "Trance," the answer may well be none. Nevertheless, direct comparison with Caroline's honorable, vintage, budget-double *Supreme Collection Volume 1* underlines the younger Khan's distinction. To put it in yob terms that would make any radio programmer snort, he's marginally hookier. If you love the first one and *want* a little more, then you'll like this. And barring unforeseen developments, that will be that. **A–**

Chaka Khan: *Epiphany: The Best of Chaka Khan Volume One* (Reprise '96) Of her enormous gift there's no question—not just a sumptuous voice, those are commonplace, but sonic character. She sounds somehow nasal, sensuous, and "trained" all at once, like Sarah Vaughan with adenoids, and also with the rhythmic hots. On her great Rufus tracks Khan was uninhibited enough to sing funkier than any woman since. But though the solo "Ain't Nobody" and "I'm Every Woman" and "I Feel for You" top "Once You Get Started" if not "Tell Me Something Good" (wisely reprised live here), too often she's striven toward vacuity, as on the "five new songs" her label stickers so proudly—when she signs on with David Foster or asks Arif Mardin to do up a ballad for her, I remember that her voice also reminds me of Heatwave's synthesizer. But Luther Vandross, Melle Mel, Bird 'n' Diz, even Billie Holiday—these tributes and collaborations she's been equal to. Makes you wonder. **A–**

Nusrat Fateh Ali Khan: *Mustt Mustt* (RealWorld '90) sometimes—"Tracery" feh, "Sea of Vapours" pee-yoo—the master modernizer of Sufi song, well, transcends the New Age art-rock Michael Brook vouchsafes him ("The Game," "Taa Deem") ★

Nusrat Fateh Ali Khan & Party: *Devotional and Love Songs* (RealWorld '91) ◐

Nusrat Fateh Ali Khan: *The Last Prophet* (RealWorld '94) 💣

Nusrat Fateh Ali Khan & Party: *Intoxicated Spirit* (Shanachie '96) Look, it's simple. Do you want Michael Brook strumming and arranging and practicing right reason, or do you want the most awesome singer in the known universe manifesting his proximity to the divine for your voyeuristic delectation? Whatever rules apply to anyone else—Brook has done handsomely by Cheb Khaled, and

most virtuosos should damn well hone their inspirations in the studio before bestowing them on the marketplace—don't apply to Nusrat. This album grabbed me not just because it's uncut—four unfaded tracks lasting 23, 24, 12, and 14 minutes—but because its Sufi ecstasy runs so close to the surface, far wilder than on RealWorld's equally uncut *The Last Prophet.* Students of song form may want to try *Devotional and Love Songs,* its harmonium and percussion augmented by a mandolinist-guitarist less distracting than Michael Brook. Me, I'll stick with Nusrat and his boys galloping off into the stratosphere—his wails, his flights, his tongue twisters, his ululations, his naming party for God. **A–**

Nusrat Fateh Ali Khan: *Rapture* (Music Club '97) Although 100 albums in 10 years may be an exaggeration, I doubt even Urdu speakers need the entire Allah-channeling oeuvre. On the other hand, I'm so sure non-Urdu speakers don't need RealWorld's polite introductions that I do hope to try one of his Pakistani cassettes someday. Meanwhile, there's this compilation, cherry-picked from his U.K. catalogue by a supersharp Brit discount label, which means that like those cassettes it's cheap. But that's not why I don't mind the rock drums and guitar on one track. It's because this cherry-picker knew where the juicy ones were. **A–**

Nusrat Fateh Ali Khan: *Greatest Hits Vol. 1* (Shanachie '97) I can see only one upside in the dreadful rumor that Khan has blown his voice, seriously if not permanently—it will inspire entrepreneurs with a conduit to the American audience RealWorld developed and misserved to license Khan's Pakistani plethora. Whatever "hit" can mean in qawwali, the world music veterans at Shanachie tell us these four extended tracks were selected with care, not grabbed at random. Their pure power somewhat less intense and fanciful than on *Intoxicated Spirit,* they're a special boon for late converts who never got the point of his crossovers anyway. **A–**

Nusrat Fateh Ali Khan & Party: *The Supreme Collection Volume 1* (Caroline '97) two un-Westernized late-'80s CDs, eight tracks, budget-priced, so how much do you want/need? ("Tum Agar Yuhi Nazren") ★★★

Kicksquad: "Champion Sound" (*Kickin Mental Detergent Vol. 2* [comp], Instinct '93) 🐝

Kid Creole and the Coconuts: *Private Waters in the Great Divide* (Columbia '90) To the shocked rumor that label prexy (and former Dr. Buzzard manager) Tommy Mottola forced August Darnell back into the studio for a quick "Lambada" stick-on, I say the universalism of that great hit is an improvement. In general here a level of imagination that has always exceeded Loudon Wainwright's, say, has turned slightly shticky. "I Love Girls" is a sinuous sample of the album's disco-funk and a proper first panel for the roué-in-the-age-of-AIDS triptych. But it's not liberating, daring, or even surprising. For wit, all Darnell does is show off his vocabulary. The same goes for the true-crime "Taking the Rap," the sexy "When Lucy Does the Boomerang," and so forth—not even Cory Daye or Prince lift off from the pleasure zone. Biggest exception is the prophetic refrain of "Laughing with Our Backs Against the Wall": "What you gonna do when the money runs out?" Sign with Sony, of course. **B+**

Kid Creole and the Coconuts: *You Shoulda Told Me You Were . . .* (Columbia '91) Although he claims he's set "to leave his beloved Isle of York once and for all," Manhattan toned up the Kid's politics. The Cory Daye feature "Consequently," which starts with Columbus sailing the ocean blue, is as cold-eyed as the Mekons' Sally Timms feature "Brutal," and "Oh Marie" and "Madison Avenue" are more realistic about crime in the streets and crisis in the schools than most rap or any Lou Reed. As for the love songs, they're fine when love has nothing to do with it—when he's hot for a party

girl, or insisting a sex object meet his plastic surgeon. **A–**

Kid Creole and the Coconuts: *Kid Creole Redux* (Sire/Warner Bros. '92) How do you tell a Nirvana fan about Kid Creole? How do you induce a grunge teen to make common cause with a tropical dandy who proclaimed his commitment to "alternatives" back in 1987, as he completed the album cycle his label is now downsizing. How do you inspire the proud owner of Sub Pop collectibles to search for *Wise Guy,* and thus hear the deprived "No Fish Today" as well as the depraved "Annie, I'm Not Your Daddy," instead of shelling out for this expediently catchy collection? This is the "Lifeboat Party" that turned into a European toothpaste commercial—an entertaining one, I'm sure, but docked a notch for hiding the baking soda. **B+**

Kid Creole and the Coconuts: *Kiss Me Before the Light Changes* (Atoll '94) reduced to pure cult band, they're good enough for one ("To Travel Sideways," "Kiss Me Before the Light Changes") ★

Kid Creole and the Coconuts: "You Shoulda Told Me You Were Catholic" (*To Travel Sideways,* Atoll '94) 🐝

Kid Frost: *East Side Story* (Virgin '92) Ice-T as low rider ("These Stories Have to Be Told," "I Got Pulled Over") ★★

Angelique Kidjo: "Batonga" (*Logozo,* Mango '92) 🐝

Angelique Kidjo: *Ayé* (Mango '94) The queen of world music isn't merely a big voice—she's also a compact body. Plus, terrific Afro-Parisian clothes sense. And to top it all off, a crew cut. In short (five-one, maybe five-two), she's a disco queen with a gimmick—earthier than Ya Kid K, but less grounded. And the follow-up doesn't even have "Batonga"'s synth riff to jolly you past the guitar solos. (Well, actually it does—it just doesn't have another one.) **C–** 🦃

Angelique Kidjo: *Fifo* (Mango '96) 💣

Kid 'n Play: *Kid 'n Play's Funhouse* (Select '90) 💣

Kid Rock: *Grits Sandwiches for Breakfast* (Jive/Novus '90) 💣
Kid Rock: *Devil Without a Cause* (Atlantic/Lava '98) Wish this "illegitimate son of man" would stop pretending he's a pimp—he tours so much he can't possibly provide the necessary continuity. But not since great Motorhead has there been a hard rock album with so many laugh lines: "I don't like small cars or real big women/But somehow I always find myself in 'em." Belatedly fulfilling the rap-metal promise of *Licensed to Ill,* he makes the competition sound clownish, limp, and corny, respectively, and the Eminem cameo is a draw—his flow is surer even if his sound isn't. Lickin' pussy underwater blowin' bubbles up your ass, he is, and I quote, all of that and a bag of chips. **A–**

Killah Priest: *Heavy Mental* (Geffen '98) Shaolin mystagogy meets millenarian panic in music for the end time. And though the album may be paranoid, that doesn't mean nobody's out to get it—just like any other product of the projects. "Science projects," Priest calls them, amid biblical citations, images of crucifixion, *2001* fantasies, warp-speed verbal drive-bys, and this Inspirational Verse: "I roam the earth's surface snatching purses/Allergic to Catholic churches/What's the purpose?/Religious worship is worthless." Preach, Killah. **A–**

The Killer Shrews: *The Killer Shrews* (Enemy '93) This ideologically inconvenient all-male trio sounds more like the Mekons than the 3 Johns and more like great Mekons than *I Love Mekons.* Departed non–drum machine Steve Goulding rock-'n'-rolls away and Gary Lucas signifies untoward virtuosity with his guitar as Jon Langford hectors, derogates, prophesies, and propagandizes. Sure hope "It's Happening Again" is the best song about the return of fascism I ever hear. Inspirational Verse: "Just one thing you'd better understand/We know your secrets/I wrote them all down on the palm of my hand/They go naaahh nah-nah-nah-nah nah-nah." **A–**

Killing Joke: *Pandemonium* (Zoo '94) Ⓝ

Junior Kimbrough: *Most Things Haven't Worked Out* (Fat Possum/Capricorn '97) primal drone ("Lonesome Road") ★

Albert King with Stevie Ray Vaughan: *In Session* (Stax '99) About a year later, in October 1984, Vaughan would throw a birthday party at Carnegie Hall with his brother Jimmy, Dr. John, and the Roomful of Blues horns. This was just a Canadian TV taping with the stalwart bluesman, who barely remembered jamming with the skinny young kid in Austin years before. With Vaughan dead (oh right, King too), both these events are now CD-available for keepsake-hungry fans. Rockers always overrated Albert King, whose broad aesthetic was longer on power than definition, but here his presence has a quieting effect on his disciple, who in the end would do far more with a closely related aesthetic. And since King is the putative star, we get his repertoire, a big problem with the endless Vaughan reissue program, and his singing, which is stronger than Stevie's. So to my surprise, this is the one to wear around your neck. **A–**

B. B. King: *Blues Summit* (MCA '93) The artist's flair for the duet is such that the most arresting solo here comes when B. B. is driven to new heights by his favorite collaborator, the B. B. King Orchestra. And because he doesn't want to give away his come-ons yet (or else doesn't have any), he sounds more comfortable with the men than the gals. But that's not to say the likes of Robert Cray and Etta James and John Lee Hooker aren't extra added attractions. Or that they don't inspire him to focus—which is really all he needs. **B+**
B. B. King: *Deuces Wild* (MCA '97) best cameos of an albumful: Tracy Chapman, Mick Jagger, Eric Clapton ("The Thrill Is Gone," "Paying the Cost to Be the Boss," "Rock Me Baby") ★★★

Bobby King and Terry Evans: *Rhythm, Blues, Soul & Grooves* (Rounder '90) 🍴

Jimmy King: *Soldier for the Blues* (Bullseye Blues '97) Cray's best in half a decade ("Living in the Danger Zone," "Drawers") ★★★

King Missile: "Jesus Is Way Cool," "Gary & Melissa" (*Mystical Shit,* Shimmy-Disc '90) 👁️
King Missile: *The Way to Salvation* (Atlantic '91) John S. Hall wants you to believe he'll be cracking wise when the world ends, an event he once projected for 1992 or 1993, although now that he's on a major he's trying to push the date back. About time, I say—the major, I mean. Hall is completely word-dependent—when his imagination flags second half, so does the album. But it isn't just the consistency of the sarcasm that distinguishes this one. It's the way he's putting his hard-rock comedy, shaggy dog fables, and sophistical shit across. Rarely has a performance artist made a more forceful adjustment to guitar-bass-and-drums, or a college-radio band a tuffer adjustment to clean-yet-heavy. Credit indie engineer Lou Giordano for his postindie production, and Atlantic for its venture capital. **A–**
King Missile: "Detachable Penis" (*Happy Hour,* Atlantic '92) 👁️
King Missile III: *Failure* (Shimmy-Disc '98) ever the model boho, John S. Hall shrugs off the death of alt while continuing to worry the size of his dick ("Failure," "A Good Hard Look") ★

The Kinleys: *Just Between You and Me* (Epic '97) So womanly they seem almost kinky, harmonizing twin sisters explore an unusually wide range of Nashville life choices—crazy in love or desperate to get back there, lazing around or sleeping around or pondering separations that put mere breaking up in existential perspective. Sound pretty relevant to me. Young or old, married or single, straight or gay, janitor or schoolteacher or constitutional lawyer or championship computer nerd, most people I meet lead emotional lives like these. In "Contradictions" two mothers let their kids go and the first kid is older than the second mother. Then they go out on "Dance in the Boat," which rocks same. **A–**

Kix: "Girl Money" (*Hot Wire,* EastWest '91) 👁️

The Klezmatics: *Rhythm and Jews* (Flying Fish '93) Although neither band is especially pure, and a good thing too, what distinguishes their shtick from that of the Klezmer Conservatory Band, who I enjoy from a respectful distance, is that it honors the shtetl rather than the borscht belt. Their sense of drama precedes vaudeville and, more significantly, musical comedy. **B+**
The Klezmatics: *Jews with Horns* (Xenophile '95) If I was a maven, maybe the hodgepodge of influences would grate, but more likely they'd just delight more. Conceptually, the pleasure here is how subtly a free and easy universalism animates a style that's often provincial on purpose and sometimes culture-bound in spite of itself. And musically, it's how unassumingly these folks show off their endless chops. That goes even for the wonderful singer Lorin Sklamberg, who never betrays the slightest emotional or physical strain even though he's as transcendent a tenor as today's semipop can offer—and for my second favorite, violinist Alicia Svigals, and for avant-clarinetist David Krakauer, and Miles-inflected Frank London, and loose-limbed David Licht, and no doubt bassist-vocalist Paul Morrissett too. This is a wedding music for listeners of every sexual persuasion. Its object is joy. Its miracle is that they come by the joy honestly. **A–**
The Klezmatics: *Possessed* (Xenophile '97) Modern klezmer obviously celebrates Jewish roots and identity—often mixed in with Jewish eclecticism, usually with Jewish secularism, occasionally with Jewish avant-gardism, and always with Jewish celebration itself. The Klezmatics assume all that and then intensify the

Jewishness as they transcend and/or escape it. Lorin Sklamberg's ethereal yet sensual tenor epitomizes sacramental seriousness while suggesting the slippery skepticism of all traveling musicians, and the rest of the Klezmatics make congruent artistic choices—as in the "Reefer Song" Frank London composed with Yiddish lyrics by Michael Wax, or the bewitchingly traditional melody Alicia Svigals provided lyricist Tony Kushner's bereftly postmodern "An Undoing World." Anchored and turned inside out by that song, the first half of this record reaches Jewish heaven—where the undone are restored, where the Messiah gathers the gays and blacks and reefer-smokers to his bosom, where the just feast on a "fabulous and tasty wild ox" called the Shor-abor. This is a vision band with a genre, not a genre band with a vision. And both are open to all. **A–**

The Klezmatics/Chava Alberstein: *The Well* (Xenophile '98) **N**

The Klezmonauts: *Oy to the World* (Satire '99) what Manhattan holiday party couldn't use a klezmer "Jingle Bells"? ("Joy to the World," "Deck the Halls") ★

The KLF: *The White Room* (Arista '91) "They're justified/And they're ancient/And they like to roam the land," croons anonymous disco soulgirl P. P. Arnold. "They don't want to upset the apple cart/And they don't want to cause any harm/But if you don't like what they're going to do/You'd better not stop them 'cause they're coming through." Whereupon follows a famous sample from the MC5's "Kick Out the Jams" and a welter of pop-industrial body grooves. These voracious smarty-pants Brits—aka the Timelords, the Justified Ancients of Mu Mu, the Jams—are sampling less and copycatting more these days, and whatever they mean or don't mean, deconstruct or reify or exploit, they like everything I like about house and are canny enough to can the boring parts. Somebody at the label that brought us Snap has an ear for the rap-Eurodance cusp. **A–**

Klover: *Feel Lucky Punk* (Mercury '95) Ever since Green Day had the gall to go multiplatinum, purists and fools have whined themselves hoarse about safe punk. Only who's stupid enough to try and make money that way? Besides Mercury Records, I mean. Oh, I know—it's Gang Green, who enjoyed a long subsistence career as beer-swilling Beantown skateboarders before they uncovered that elusive note of sincerity in bemohawked young Mike Stone. As if by magic, singer-guitarist Chris Doherty became guitarist-gray eminence Chris Doherty, L.A. producer Roy Z. acquired five cocomposing credits, and Stone was yelling about something called "the Radiation Generation." **C+** 🦃

KMD: "Mr. Hood at Piocalle's Jewelry/Crackpot," "Mr. Hood Gets a Haircut" (*Mr. Hood,* Elektra '91) 💿

KMFDM: *Retro* (Wax Trax! '96) not fascist, just German—and also, not fascist, just industrial ("A Drug Against War," "More and Faster") ★★

Chris Knight: *Chris Knight* (Decca '98) This being Nashville, of course they claim his secret is reality, but I say it's literature. He's a writer pure and simple, schooled in the economical everyday; if he'd grown up in California instead of Kentucky, he'd have tried his hand at sitcoms. I love the way he finds a pungent trope and tops it—drives his truck to Timbuktu and then lies down on a bed of nails. The music is spare enough to signify reality, and big enough to heighten it. **A–**

Jack Knight: "Who Do You Love" (*Gypsy Blues,* Universal '99) 💿

Jordan Knight: *Jordan Knight* (Interscope '99) a much tastier Michael McDonald than Duncan Sheik (or Michael McDonald) ("Give It to You," "A Different Party," "I Could Never Take the Place of Your Man") ★★

Chris Knox: "Song to Welcome the Onset of Maturity" (*Songs of You and Me,* Caroline '95) 💿

Koerner, Ray & Glover: *One Foot in the Groove* (Tim/Kerr '96) ⓝ

Ami Koita: *Songs of Praise* (Stern's Africa '93) ⓝ

Habib Koité & Bamada: *Ma Ya* (Putumayo Artists '99) ⓝ
Habib Koité & Bamada: "Cigarette A Bana (The Cigarette Is Finished)" (*Muso Ko*, Alula '99) 🕭

Kool G Rap & D.J. Polo: *Wanted: Dead or Alive* (Cold Chillin' '90) hard again ("Streets of New York," "Erase Racism") ★★
Kool G. Rap & D.J. Polo: *Live and Let Die* (Cold Chillin' '92) 💣

Kool Keith: *Black Elvis/Lost in Space* (Ruffhouse/Columbia '99) you know: space—where he rules the world ("Fine Girls," "Intro") ★★

Kool Moe Dee: *Funke Funke Wisdom* (Jive '91) back in command ("Funke Wisdom," "Rise 'n' Shine," "Death Blow") ★★★
Kool Moe Dee: *Greatest Hits* (Jive '93) This safe, sane 15-track summation is sufficient to the old-school veritas of Mohandas Dewese's declaratory beat. It don't stop, and it don't stop. But on his first two albums, and more explicitly if less consistently later, he was also a bridge to the conscious rap that made the old school seem so elementary. How ya like him now depends on how well ya knew him back when. **B+**
Kool Moe Dee: *The Jive Collection Volume 2* (Jive '96) Volume 2 not for the artist, but for his label's new catalogue exploitation; nine of the 12 tracks also appear on Moe Dee's 1993 best-of, with which it shares its inferiority to his first two solo albums. But the three additions— "Knowledge Is King," "Funke Wisdom," "The Avenue"—show off his brainy independence. Both comps fulfill their destiny. This one goes in the changer. **B+**

Al Kooper: *Rekooperation* (MusicMasters '94) unsung neoclassical r&b ("Soul Twist-ed," "Don't Be Cruel") ★

Korn: *Korn* (Epic/Immortal '94) The cover depicts a frightened little girl peering up from a swing at a hook-handed rapist whose huge shadow slants across her space; the girl's shadow seems to hang from the gallows-shaped K of the band logo. They love this image, exploit it in every trade ad as Sony flogs their death-industrial. They sing about child abuse too—guess what, they're agin it. If their name isn't short for kiddie porn, they should insist on a video where they get eaten by giant chickens. **C-** 🕭
Korn: *Life Is Peachy* (Epic/Immortal '96) 💣
Korn: *Follow the Leader* (Epic/Immortal '98) Korn deny they're metal; that's Judas Priest, all four-four pomp and guitar solos. But they nevertheless demonstrate that the essence of metal—an expressive mode it sometimes seems will be with us for as long as ordinary whiteboys fear girls, pity themselves, and are permitted to rage against a world they'll never beat—is self-obliterating volume and self-aggrandizing display. Now calling up death-metal's signature groan only to prove he's authentic, poor not-actually-abused Jonathan Davis raps, recites, scats, and sings dull tunes landscaped with eerie licks, odd bridges, and a hyperactive rhythm section. How much his fans identify with "My Gift to You" ("I kiss your lifeless skin"), "Cameltosis" ("You trick-ass slut"), or the tragic "Seed" ("Do I need this fame?") remains unclear. But I'm parent enough to hope they can find a more fully formed designated someone than a guy whose idea of transgressive art is Net-casting soft-core s&m to any teenager with a logon. **C** 🕭
Korn: *Issues* (Epic/Immortal '99) 💣

Kotch: *Kotch* (Mango '90) They say this self-contained Jamaican sextet returns reggae to harmony-group truths, but with Rueben Espuet's falsetto teasing the cover versions till they giggle and Sly & Robbie exploding those beats, their traditionalism sounds pretty pomo to me. Material includes Sarah Vaughan's "Broken Hearted

Melody," three Smokey Robinson songs (one credited to "Unknown"), and a twisted six-minute "Tequila" bent further out of shape by samples from "Pump Up the Volume" and *The Marriage of Figaro*. **B+**

Kotoja: *The Super Sowalé Collection* (Putumayo World Music '94) Ⓝ

Kandia Kouyate: *Kita Kam* (Stern's Africa '99) female pride, Malian and Islamic style ("Doninké," "Douwawou") ★★

The Ousmane Kouyate Band: *Domba* (Mango '90) The rockish grandeur of this Guinean world music ensemble sounds like it owes Santana. Probably doesn't, of course—we know where the polyrhythms started, and in 24 years Carlos has never risked a singer who could steal his thunder like this hereditary troubadour. On the other hand, Carlos can outplay the troubadour even though the troubadour counts himself a guitarist by trade. The crux is that most of the time Carlos's corn just sounds like corn. Kouyate's sounds like the staff of life. **A-**

Sanougue Kouyate: "Tenin Sama" (*Balendala Djibe*, Mango '90) 🞋

Kraftwerk: *The Mix* (Elektra '91) best-of with the bass boosted—very funktional, meine Herren ("Pocket Calculator," "The Robots") ★★★

Kramer: "She's Everything Mr. R" (*Drop Acid . . . Listen to This!!* [comp], Knitting Factory Works '97) 🞋

Wayne Kramer: "Crack in the Universe," "Incident on Stock Island" (*The Hard Stuff*, Epitaph '95) 🞋

Wayne Kramer: *Dangerous Madness* (Epitaph '96) visionary guitar, '60s-style, plus lowlife lyrics by Mick Farren, who should know ("Dangerous Madness," "A Dead Man's Vest") ★★

Wayne Kramer/Deniz Tek/Scott Morgan: *Dodge Main* (Alive '96) so it's never too late for an MC5 tribute ("Future/Now") ★★

Wayne Kramer: *Citizen Wayne* (Epitaph '97) The punk line on the MC5 is that their revolutionary pretensions were imposed by conniving hippie John Sinclair. So how come it was Fred Smith who got "People Got the Power" out of Patti? And how come Wayne Kramer has now enlisted ex-rad David Was in the most political record of either career? Despite one small-minded sectarian dis—nobody in *my* Trotskyite cell would be so gauche as to serve chips with pesto, let me assure you—these songs talk class and counterculture simultaneously, a rare thing, especially with the emphasis on the class. And musically, the two Detroiters tear up each other's roots as Was tilts Kramer's good old guitar toward the avant-funk it has long since deserved. **A-**

Alison Krauss: *Now That I've Found You: A Collection* (Rounder '95) Even with the greatest voices, tastes are personal—where you might prefer Aretha's Diane Warren song, I'd probably go for Al Green's. Krauss isn't quite in that class, but after this compilation-plus overcame my penchants, I began to think she was only a notch below. However much fans appreciated the child prodigy for her fiddle, they love the woman for her kind, precise, intent soprano. And not only is this a singer's showcase, it's a pop singer's showcase. Sure she's still country—bluegrass, even. She's nothing if not principled. But she also ropes in not just the Beatles but the Foundations and, believe it or not, Bad Company. And by reclaiming guest tracks from specialist albums by Jerry Douglas, Tony Furtado, and the Cox Family, she oversteps the sonic boundaries of her admirable but specialized band. Best in show (after the Beatles, the Foundations, and Bad Company): a sexy little sacred number. **A-**

Lenny Kravitz: *Mama Said* (Virgin '91) don't think Hendrix-Beatles, think Prince–George Michael ("Fields of Joy," "Stand by My Woman," "Stop Draggin' Around") ★★

Lenny Kravitz: *Are You Gonna Go My Way* (Virgin '93) 🞍

Lenny Kravitz: *Circus* (Virgin '95) 🞍

Lenny Kravitz: *5* (Virgin '98) His racially convoluted formalism having long since come clean as a total absence of original ideas, he grabs the brass ring from the back of a tacked-on Guess Who cover best heard on the far more imaginative *Austin Powers* soundtrack. Lenny, your work here on earth is done. We've got Derek Jeter now. **C** 🐝

Kraze: "The Party" (*Start the Party! Volume 1* [comp], Big Beat '94) 👁️

Kris Kross: *Totally Krossed Out* (Ruffhouse/Columbia '92) One step up the evolutionary ladder from the cute boy on the steps who's rechristened Fabian or Vince Eager, these two Atlanta 13-year-olds are totally fabrikated. They contributed less to their beats, lyrics, and look than the New Kids. And not only is "Jump" one of those works of art that makes rock and roll worth living for, a trifle that sweeps all questions of import and integrity aside, but there's an album to go with it. Nineteen-year-old producer Jermaine Dupri writes for irrepressible 13-year-olds so set on enjoying the full privileges of adolescence that only a bad cop would enforce their curfew. Dupri exploits their preadolescent tempos and timbres to the max. And he shades their ebullient music with subtly disturbing samples only lil boys from the hood could be sad and savvy enough to call their own. **A–**

Kris Kross: *Da Bomb* (Ruffhouse/Columbia '93) producer's pawns, voices changing, they hang in there ("Da Bomb," "Alright") ★★

Kris Kross: *Young, Rich and Dangerous* (Ruffhouse/Columbia '95) 💣

Kronos Quartet: *Pieces of Africa* (Elektra Nonesuch '92) Ⓝ

KRS-One: *Return of the Boom Bap* (Jive '93) His best, because the music has finally subsumed the lyrics—with outside guidance from Gang Starr's DJ Premier and others, the rapmaster's bassy beats and monophonic hooks have never sounded more catchy or more his own. Horn blats, "Three Blind Mice" guitar, siren imitation, human beat-box, whatever—all

recur hypnotically and leave you hungry for more. Nor have the words fallen off. The history he teaches is mostly his own. And a couple of times he just kills the cops. **A–**

KRS One: *KRS One* (Jive '95) 💣

KRS-One: *I Got Next* (Jive '97) what he really got is beats, for once ("Heartbeat," "Step into a World [Rapture's Delight]")★

KRS-One: See also Boogie Down Productions

K-Solo: "Tales from the Crack Side" (*Tell the World My Name,* Atlantic '90) 👁️

K-Solo: *Times Up* (Atlantic '92) Ⓝ

Ali Hassan Kuban: *From Nubia to Cairo* (Shanachie '91) Candidly commercial if not cockeyed drunk, a veteran entertainer from the melanin-rich upriver highlands leads a thoroughly modern band that favors the same stop-and-go tricks polka strategists love so. His horn players live for their solo features, and that's not to mention his accordionists—or his bagpipers. And throbbing and clattering incessantly behind, what else? The drums, the drums, the drums, the electric bass. **A–**

Ali Hassan Kuban: *Walk Like a Nubian* (Piranha import '94) it's a geometrical diddybop—a tad too mechanical this time ("Om Sha'ar Asmar Medaffer") ★

Ali Hassan Kuban: *Nubian Magic* (Mercator '95) Sudanese wedding music for the Aswan diaspora—fast by rustic standards, James Brown–influenced but who isn't ("Mabrouk Wo Arisna," "Maria-Maria," "Al Samra Helwa") ★★★

Joachim Kühn: See Ornette Coleman

Kula Shaker: *K* (Columbia '96) What Happy Mondays did for substance abuse these fools vow to accomplish for spirit abuse. Drunk on Krishna, they take an anonymously commonplace chorus-guitar melange and stir in some sitar/tabla/tamboura and banalities I hope aren't translated from the Hindi. Bet it wouldn't occur to Cornershop to inform *Billboard* that Indians are "content" because they have "faith." Kaleidoscope either. **C** 🐝

Forward Kwenda: *Svikiro* (Shanachie '97) if meditate you must, better a mbira than a didgeridoo ("Chiahangechid-hange," "Kanhurura") ★

Kyuss: *Kyuss* (Chameleon '94) 💣

K/COMPILATIONS

Kalesijski Svuci: Bosnian Breakdown: The Unpronounceable Beat of Sara-jevo (GlobeStyle import '92) Muslim polkas from the good old days, when the disaster was economic ("Oho Ho Sto Je Lijepo," "Ramino Kolo") ★

Kenya Dance Mania (Earthworks '91) A more Zairean—hornier, earlier, less dis-tinctive—mix of soukous, salsa, mba-qanga, and indigenous whatever than the transcendent *Guitar Paradise of East Africa,* but with the same fundamental virtue: a melodic gift that only asserts itself after a few beloved grooves work their not-quite-exportable charm. Pretty home-spun for disco, its most impressive (trans-lated) lyric is a survey of siesta folkways entitled "Lunch Time." If music be the food of underdevelopment, play on. **A–**

Kerestina: Guitar Songs of Southern Mozambique 1955–1957 (Original Music '95) Shangaan roots of Thomas Chauke and Obed Ngobeni (Mahikwani Makhu-vele, "Ugandzibyeli Akuxonga"; Alberto Tentowani Mwamosi & Gabriel Maopana Bila, "Achifa Dukwana Chamina") ★★

Kickin Mental Detergent (Kickin USA '92) This U.K.-label comp proved so sem-inal that it spawned 1993's *Vol. 2,* which is merely less consistent, and 1994's *Kickin Hardcore Leaders,* which is scene-specific to the verge of abstraction. And after trolling among competing fast-techno collections, I see the downward spiral as an omen. Early on, with label and move-ment still worried about being liked, songs of dread and abandon bedeck them-selves with spoken-word hooks, lending their apocalyptic aura an illusion of coher-ence that squares can relate to, and aren't above other vulgar fripperies—lay-ers of texture, sound effects, tunes. How-ever impure they are counted by the small legions who have since undergone full au-ral immersion, they're as cleansing as claimed when approached from the other side—from the rest of music. **A–**

The Kings and Queens of Township Jive: Modern Roots of the Indestruc-tible Beat of Soweto (Earthworks '91) If the successors to Earthworks's epochal mbaqanga comp have been too profes-sional, the predecessors from Rounder and such haven't been professional enough. So finally, here are the '60s/'70s hits. Though it stars the usual great names—Mahlathini, the Queens, West Nkosi—its highs surprise: a beleaguered Soul Brothers boast hooked to a rumbling organ sound effect, a Lulu Masilela one-shot as self-evidently classic as "Walking with Mr. Lee," the rest of the sax jive. I used to get an r&b rush off these folks' mature work. Little did I know how much fun they'd already had. **A**

Kings of African Music (Music Club '97) Ali Farka Toure's folkloricism to Manu Dibango's dance jazz is a leap for anyone who can hear, and as a listener who has learned to distinguish instinctively among the vocal approaches of Zimbabwe, Congo, and Senegal (to overgeneralize shamefully, call them rough, sweet, and piercing), I object in principle to the pan-African conceit. But essentialism has its lessons, such as how overtly dramatic—ergo individualistic?—pop vocals have gotten continent-wide since the ebullient postcolonial communitarianism captured by John Storm Roberts's *Africa Dances.* And done as well as this, essentialism also has its uses—as a budget-priced in-troduction for theoretical Afrocentrists ready to confront musical reality, and a minor treasure trove for supposed experts like me. How can it be that I never heard Franco's "Tres Impoli" before? **A–**

The King's Record Collection (Hip-O '98) A great gift idea for that Elvis nut, this collection of records Elvis covered hits every Sun nonoriginal except "Milkcow Blues Boogie" and establishes his superiority to Arthur Crudup and Big Mama Thornton (though not the Drifters or Joe Turner) for anyone who's never located the records in question. A vivid representation of both his voracious tastes and the musical ferment from which he made what he made. D.O.A.: Leon Payne's dull "I Love You Because." Born again: the Shelton Brothers' deadpan "Just Because." **A–**

Kneelin' Down Inside the Gate: The Great Rhyming Singers of the Bahamas (Rounder '95) think field hollers, mbube, doowop (Joseph Spence and the Pinder Family, "Standing in the Need of Prayer"; Clifford Ellis with Stanley Thompson and Group, "I Met My Mother This Morning") ★

Knitting on the Roof (Knitting Factory '99) *Fiddler* fiddled with, less arrantly than you might fear (Magnetic Fields, "If I Were a Rich Man"; Come, "Do You Love Me?") ★

Kwanzaa Music (Rounder '94) Kwanzaa, Black History Month, whatever—Africa's musical diaspora is worth celebrating by formal imperative. So instead of flowing like a good multiple-artist compilation should, this one parades the startling diversity generated by a root aesthetic of body-based polyrhythm, expressive emotion, and speechlike song. You'll hardly notice the three subclassic New Orleans/Texas tracks as you're transported Bahamas to Brazil, Peru to Mali, Sudan to Haiti to Zimbabwe. An inspiring, educational tour de force. **A–**

Kwanzaa Party! (Rounder '96) On the second installment of what deserves to be a long series, Daisann McLane joins Earthworks's Trevor Herman and Original Music's John Storm Roberts among world-class "world beat" compilers. Where 1994's *Kwanzaa Music* exploded in star drive all over the African diaspora, this one gets an intensely listenable flow from an equally far-flung bunch of less renowned artists. I've never heard of some of these musicians and listened right through others; not even tunes as classic as Trinidad's/Roaring Lion's "Marianne" or Haiti's/Ensemble Nemours Jn. Baptiste's "Rhythme Commercial" seem obvious. Neophytes are in for bigger revelations and just as much fun. Merry Whatever. **A–**

Patti LaBelle & Travis Tritt: "When Something Is Wrong with My Baby" (*Rhythm Country and Blues* [comp], MCA '94) 🐚

La Bottine Souriante: *Rock & Reel* (Hemisphere '99) Winking whenever the folk do something cute or dirty, wearing an I ♥ Jazz button on their collective sleeve, this accordion-fiddle-horns nonet epitomizes the cloying multicultural sophistication that infests "world music." I'd hoped they were French, but in fact they're Québecois, which makes sense—the Breton-Celt connection. Austin's Brave Combo prove it's possible to make "fun" fun. Bilbao's Kepa Junkera proves it's possible to keep eclecticism clean. This kind of stuff gives purism a good name. **C+**

La Bouche: *Sweet Dreams* (RCA '96) are made of (Euro) disco (as if there's another kind anymore) ("Be My Lover," "Le Click: Tonight Is the Night," "Sweet Dreams") ★★

The Ladybug Transistor: *The Albemarle Sound* (Merge '99) 💣

Lady Saw: *Passion* (VP '97) Seated in red suit and executive chair on the cover, the buxom Jamaican blonde sprawls on a striped couch in halter and who-knows-what inside—her hands cover her split beaver and the CD hole covers her hands. It's the new slackness, confidently and voraciously refusing to become the last big thing. Cribbing "That's Amore" and a generic country tune and a properly credited "Love Is Strange," ranging riddimically from something we call oompah to something she calls joy ride, she sings about sex while never confusing power with pleasure or sounding beholden to anyone but herself. Do I like it raw? Well, since you were nice enough to ask . . . **B+**

Lady Saw: *Raw: The Best of Lady Saw* (VP '98) cock-rock lives inna dancehall stylee ("Find a Good Man," "Eh-Em") ★

Ladysmith Black Mambazo: *Two Worlds One Heart* (Warner Bros. '90) Joseph Shabalala is a modest fellow only on the surface—black South Africans neglect that role at their peril. From the stylistic revolution he imposed on his chosen genre to his principled pursuit of international glory, he has the lineaments of a pop visionary, and here he arrives at a crossover that does his style proud, moving gracefully from Zulu to English within and between songs and pumping the a cappella rhythms with instruments on three cuts. Twice Ray Phiri masterminds suitably simple mbaqanga tracks, but the big man is George Clinton, whose "Scatter the Fire" neither obscures nor ignores the singers with their name on the cover. I urge the Jungle Brothers to volunteer for a remix. **A–**

Ladysmith Black Mambazo: *Classic Tracks* (Shanachie '90) Having beaten *Graceland* to the gate with the first (and till now best) U.S.-available Ladysmith al-

---

★★★, ★★, ★ Honorable Mention   🐚 Choice Cut   🚫 Neither   💣 Dud   🦃 Turkey

bum, *Induku Zethu,* and then gotten sandbagged by Warner, Shanachie gives up on the easy way out: instead of licensing yet another high-generic LP whole, it shuffles a dozen of them into a great one. By selecting for "musical quality" from the wealth of product Joseph Shabalala has conceived for presold Azanian fans, Randall Grass concentrates the lively and tuneful while respecting the intricately harmonized and subtly dramatic. One man's sustained vibrato and a whole language's clicks, trills, and amens. **A–**

Ladysmith Black Mambazo: *Greatest Hits* (Shanachie '92) Three tracks from 1990's *Classic Tracks* (their strongest), three from 1988's *Umthumbo Wamanzi* (their weakest), four new to me, six culled from the rest of their Shanachie catalogue (including two in English, both from *Inala*). Flow: liquid, bubbly. Redundancy: tolerable. Verdict: excellent place to start, pretty good one to continue. **A–**

Ladysmith Black Mambazo: *Liph' Iquinso* (Shanachie '94) Any American who already owns *Classic Tracks,* or *Induku Zethu,* plus maybe *Two Worlds One Heart* or *Greatest Hits,* obviously doesn't need album 36 from the definitive Zulu chorale. But not only have they avoided the rut, they've reinvented themselves—with one brother murdered, another departed, and a cousin also gone, Joseph Shabalala enlisted three of his sons and pushed on. And if anything, he's gotten better at arranging and producing the comic details that are the unsung delight of the vocal beauty he perfected. **A–**

Ladysmith Black Mambazo: *Thuthukani Ngoxolo (Let's Develop in Peace)* (Shanachie '96) have they ever made a bad record? not that we've heard ("Sisesiqhingini [Everything Is Stupid]," "Hlanganani Siyobula [The Guests Are Arriving]") ★

Ladysmith Black Mambazo: *Heavenly* (Shanachie '97) Joseph Shabalala & Co. sing the pop-gospel songbook (best cameo: Dolly Parton) ("Knockin' on Heaven's Door," "I'll Take You There") ★★★

Ladysmith Black Mambazo: *The Best of—Vol. 2* (Shanachie '98) Absolute masters of a self-invented formula neither they nor their fans ever weary of, Ladysmith are like the Ramones at a higher level of musical if not philosophical development. And now they've outlasted these great rivals. Sixteen tracks, mostly new to U.S. consumers, showcase their a cappella trickery with daunting subtlety and never-ending smarts. **B+**

Ladysmith Black Mambazo: *Live at the Royal Albert Hall* (Shanachie '99) Their first live album in a quarter century of taking it to the stage disperses the pious aura with which their religious faith and "world music"'s self-righteousness conspire to surround them. Their sound effects ought to be funny enough in themselves (try the kisses on "Hello My Baby"), but their awkward repartee will convince the properest sobersides that it's OK to laugh. Their rhythms are more pronounced as well—too bad you can't see the steps. Their English repertoire is limited, so the half where you'll understand the words is remakes; their Zulu repertoire is vast, so the half where you won't isn't. Inspirational Chorus: "Everything's so stupid stupid stupid stupid stupid stupid"—sung with a smile. **A–**

Laika: *Silver Apples of the Moon* (Too Pure/American '95) proof the Moog has progressed since Kapp 3562 went to 193 in the summer of '68 ("44 Robbers," "Honey in Heat") ★

Lamb: "Lusty" (*Lamb,* Mercury '97) 👁

Sonny Landreth: "Shootin' for the Moon" (*South of I-10,* Zoo '95) 👁

Mark Lanegan: *I'll Take Care of You* (Sub Pop '99) by my count, seven varieties of musical "authenticity" in 11 cover takeovers ("Together Again," "I'll Take Care of You") ★★

Jonboy Langford and the Pine Valley Cosmonauts: *Misery Loves Company* (Scout import '96) they "explore the dark and lonely world of Johnny Cash" with more cojones than Rick Rubin ("Cocaine Blues," "What Is Truth?") ★★

Jon Langford: Skull Orchard (Sugar Free '98) The difference is palpable. The Mekons, Waco Brothers, Killer Shrews, and I forget who are/were groups that couldn't do without Langford, whereas this is Langford with backup musicians, aides-d'arte who happen to be Wacos as well. There's no band feel, no sense of music-in-process—the garrulous artiste is audibly up top, organizing structural support for a sheaf of good tunes, and while the best of these is courteously passed on to Gertrude Stein, who wrote the words to "Butter Song," all the rest belong to Jonboy. Motormouth that he is, he's better off when he doesn't have to get to the end in 75 words or less, which is why his country band has always thrived on covers. Here he runs on, confessing his antisocial tendencies like the singer-songwriter he temporarily is—without forgetting that capitalism is antisocial too. A–

Jon Langford: Gravestone EP (Bloodshot '98) two enduring rerecorded highlights, one fine recycled obscurity, one excellent new song, mail-order only ("Nashville Radio," "The Return of the Golden Guitarist") ★★★

Laquan: Notes of a Native Son (4th & B'Way '90) Ⓝ

The La's: The La's (London '91) Blimey, another pop group with guitars—quartet from Liverpool, no less. Once in a blue moon, though, somebody with the gift comes along, and frontman Lee Mavers is that somebody. Given his spunky-to-grotty voice (think Colin Hay or early Cat Stevens—of Men at Work and "Matthew and Son" respectively, you uncultured dolts), they don't sound *enough* like the Beatles, and I hope that in a hit or two they find themselves a drummer they can tie to his or her chair, because too often the beat is vestigial (think Quarrymen). But don't look a gift genius in the adenoids—not until he turns into Billy Joel on you. A–

The Last Poets: Scatterap/Home (Bond Age import '94) corny-fresh conga-funk like they still mean it ("Reasoning," "See") ★★

Latin Alliance: Latin Alliance (Virgin '91) politics inevitable, music meant to be ("Lowrider [On the Boulevard]," "Latinos Unidos [United Latins]") ★

Latin Playboys: Latin Playboys (Slash/Warner Bros. '94) On *Kiko,* new producer Mitchell Froom, aided materially by wizard engineer and aural archivist Tchad Blake, transmuted Los Lobos's folkier textures into a kind of amniotic sound-surf, sustaining their rock noises and rhythms in swells of offhand accordion, rippling guitar arpeggio, whiskey-breathed brass, and articulated percussion. Here David Hidalgo and Louie Pérez rework *Kiko* outtakes to undercut the band's Springsteenian quest for meaning. Whenever the lyrical impressions lapse toward the stolid or sodden, they're lifted by the spare, bent music: echoes and silences, filtered voices and ancient klaxons, Indian film sounds and scratchy samples of street bebop, jagged Beefheart rhythms and idle guitar thoughts, friendly melodies from a Victrola perched on a barrio windowsill. Magical, mystical, the kind of inner-child fantasia that usually guarantees self-indulgence, but here is a field recording from two amigos' mutual unconscious. A+

Latin Playboys: Dose (Atlantic '99) Ultimately, they're rock and rollers, and this is more a collection, less a soundscape. But because it still morphs song forms toward the overheard, atmosphere and structure remain the stuff you listen for. Making something of the musique concrète palaver that sounds reflect the life of the people more truly than elitist notes, it evokes everyday street culture with vrooms and honks and revs and rumbles, argument and byplay and revelry and casual chitchat, and, most important, the garbled layering that inflects all sounds as they are usually heard, notes included.

But out of this quiet clamor, both natural outgrowth and blessed relief, emerge little melodies that seem deeply familiar even to a non-Chicano—cultural, tipico, imprinted in memory and collective subconscious. The effect is arty for sure, maybe even genteel in its calculatedly unkempt way. Yet it demonstrates once again that at times arty is like its fraternal twin pretentious—a means to something genuinely difficult and beautiful. **A**

Kenny Lattimore: "While My Guitar Gently Weeps" (*From the Soul of Man,* Columbia '98) 👓

Latyrx (Lateef & Lyrics Born): *The Album* (SoleSides '96) Lyrics Born is deep and contemplative, Lateef speedy and confrontational, and together—on DJ Shadow's heads-up lead track, simultaneously, with only a balance knob and some small print between you and the crash of your rhyme-processing program—their playful mastery has no parallel in today's rap. Not all that many precedents either, although it's significant that several aren't ghettocentric: early De La, 3rd Bass. They take more pleasure in words themselves than in tales, messages, explicit content. That granted, note that Lateef's riff on "those that talk most got the least to say" merits all the attention it gets, and that Lyrics Born's "Balcony Beach" is rap at its most spiritual—actually seems *wise.* Except on the boast tracks toward the end, their language elevates the music even when homeboy Shadow isn't producing, as he usually isn't. **A–**

Latyrx (Lateef & Lyrics Born): *The Muzapper's Mixes EP* (SoleSides '97) endorsing Alice Walker and Rayovacs ("Lady Don't Tek No," "The Bumpin Contraption [The Recalibration]") ★★

Cyndi Lauper: *Twelve Deadly Cyns* (Epic '94) The statistics are brutal. The six best tracks on this 10-year retrospective, arrayed all in a row after a bombastic new Mann-Weil cover, are all from her decade-old debut, and if "When You Were Mine"

had been thrown in the figure would have been seven. So you decide—wanna buy this for "True Colors" and "I Think About You"? I thought not, and that was without mentioning the "Girls" remix or the Mary Chapin Carpenter song about pigeons. Maybe she was so set on fun because she guessed it would be hell from there on in. **C** 🦃

Christine Lavin: *Compass* (Philo '91) meaningful when funny, wry when serious, lugubrious when artistic ("Blind Dating Fun," "Until Now") ★★

Christine Lavin: "What Was I Thinking?" (*Live at the Cactus Cafe: "What Was I Thinking?,"* Philo '93) 👓

Tracy Lawrence: "Sticks and Stones" (*Sticks and Stones,* Atlantic '91) 👓

Leaders of the New School: *A Future Without a Past* (Elektra '91) 💣

Leatherface: *Mush* (Seed '92) 🅝

The Leaving Trains: *Loser Illusion Pt. 0* (SST '91) Not exactly original, if that's what you call that monkey on your back—the six tracks run Ramones, Pistols, Jim Carroll, Angry Samoans, Replacements, Green on Red. Classic Ramones, Pistols, etc.—Pistols song goes: "Fuck you, God! I'm already living in hell." Punk lives, eats itself, or whatever. I love it. **A–**

The Leaving Trains: *Sleeping Underwater Survivors* (SST '92) 💣

Le Commandant de Bord: *Kiambukuta* (Musicanova import '91) Franco's head baritone Josky leads the lads through two LPs worth of sweet paces ("Selengina," "Chandra") ★

Led Zeppelin: *BBC Sessions* (Atlantic '97) 🅝

Leftfield: *Leftism* (Hard Hands/Columbia '95) 🅝

Legal Weapon: *Take Out the Trash* (Triple X '91) Exene without sensitivity, folk music, a notebook—with hard rock and a voice like a fire alarm ("Under Fire," "96 Tears") ★★

Keri Leigh & the Blue Devils: *No Beginner* (Amazing '93) forget Lou Ann and think Janis cum Bonnie—a voice to make Austin's dreams come true ("Locomotive Blues," "Wild Women Don't Get the Blues") ★★

The Lemonheads: *Come On Feel* (Atlantic '93) Evan Dando is a good-looking guy with more luck than talent and more talent than brains who conceals his narcissism beneath an unassuming suburban drawl. Twenty years ago he would have affected an acoustic guitar and acted sincere; now he affects a slacker-pop band and acts vulnerable. His songs don't bite, they sidle over and nibble your ear when you're not looking, and if you throw him a withering glance, no problem—he'll just move on to someone else. Exception: the one about drugs. **C+** 🦃

Ricardo Lemvo & Makina Loca: *Mambo Yo Yo* (Putumayo Artists '98) Californian Afro-salsa, sweet and mild ("Mambo Yo Yo," "No Me Engañes Más") ★

Lemzo Diamano: *Marimbalax* (Stern's Africa '97) Ⓝ

Len: *You Can't Stop the Bum Rush* (Work '99) good clean fun, right—plus, it raps ("Beautiful Day," "Cheekybugger") ★

John Lennon: *Wonsaponatime* (Capitol '98) As someone who scoffs at the outtake collections of known improvisers, I doubt I'll be delving into the box too often, although much of the live stuff is worth hearing. But not only does this one-disc distillation spare borderline obsessives financial anxiety, it proves Lennon the great singer he's rarely remembered as. Whether the alternate rearrangements are drastic (Cheap Trick on "I'm Losing You," strings on "Grow Old with Me") or subtle (pianoless "God," single-tracked "Oh My Love"), every song is renewed by a vocal commitment that shades the canonical take, usually toward sweetness or rage. There's new material too: blues cover, Platters cover, pledge of love, and the priceless Dylan answer song "Serve

Yourself." Lennon wasn't above dabbling in religion. But he never got so down he mistook God for more than a concept by which he measured his pain. **A–**

Sean Lennon: *Into the Sun* (Grand Royal '98) Ⓝ

Annie Lennox: *Diva* (Arista '92) The honorable Timothy White avers, "Her vocals have never felt performed," which those of us who don't commune regularly with the stars can take as a sign that the guy's been in show business too long. It's our belief that Ms. Lennox's vocals have never felt anything *but* performed—and that this palpably phony quality was her chief charm even though it meant that at her most nuevo wavo she was destined to turn conventional pop singer sooner or later. So here she goes normal, if that's what you call somebody who emotes banalities to her baby daughter loud enough to wake the disco: "precious little angel . . . [percolating bass] . . . bundle full of love . . . drowned in my own tears . . . [cool trumpet solo] . . . gift from heaven . . ." Thank your maker she fades it instead of going out on a high note. And give Dave Stewart this: he kept her dishonest. **C+** 🦃

Annie Lennox: *Medusa* (Arista '95) Ⓝ

Les Ambassadeurs Internationales: *Les Ambassadeurs Internationales Featuring Salif Keita* (Rounder '92) Where Rounder's first Ambassadeurs reissue was a vocal treasure house billed to the band, this attempt to cash in on Keita's small portion of fame is a band showcase headlined by the vocalist. Keita had left before one track was recorded, and on all five the instrumental bed is more seductive than the excellent singing it supports. You wait for Kante Manfila's guitar, for the oddly tuned horn riffs, for the unidentified keyb (Farfisa? Casio?) that evokes heavy wah-wah, cheap alto sax, unalloyed synthesizer. Penciling shadows of kora and kalimba behind local beats and copycat tintinnabulations, it documents a moment before West African dance music had figured out what to do with Congolese hegemony or its own traditionalism, and a lovely moment it must have been. **A–**

Les Nubians: *Princesses Nubians* (OnTown '98) Certainly not "Nubian." Biology not being destiny, not "Cameroonian" either. "Princesses" metaphorically if at all. Not "Miriam Makeba meets Wyclef Jean" or any half of same. "Soul II Soul meets Zap Mama" a smidgen. "Sisters" if they say so, "soul" if the "5th Annual Soul Train Lady of Soul Awards" says so. "French" definitely, "hip hop" forget about it. Coverers of Sade with rhythmic spoken-word interlude indubitably. Blander than their bass lines you bet. French definitely. **C+**

Les Thugs: *As Happy as Possible* (Sub Pop '93) These anthemic Parisian punks are all form and no conviction, except for the conviction that form is everything. And despite the always uncharismatic and often choral vocals, this suffices. The proximate source is probably PiL—if "Papapapa" isn't their "Poptones," my name is Jah Wobble. But because they mean to be inspirational, even uplifting, they also evoke the Buzzcocks, not to mention Brian Eno (not to mention 999). Trust the French to do neoclassicism right. **B+**

Le Tigre: *Le Tigre* (Mr. Lady '99) In which Kathleen Hanna does the unprecedented—if not, apparently, impossible—and reinvents punk again. The first time seems a snap in retrospect, a straightforward seizure of formal strategy and emotional stance for grrrl rage and female discovery—between Hanna's instinct for the ditty and her big pipes, Bikini Kill was an instant sure shot. But she got too old for that, and maybe a little too fulfilled as well. So having passed through her woebegone Julie Ruin project, she gets together with two arty girlfriends and makes deceptively simple music about her arty life. Topics include aesthetic theory, millenarian hippies, John Cassavetes, the pleasures of the MetroCard, who put the ram in the rama-lama-ding-dong, and "Hot Topics" ("Nina Simone!" "Ann Pee-

bles!" "The Slits!" "James Baldwin!" "Mia X!" "Billy Tipton!" "Shirley Muldoon!"). Dynamic synthbeats. Spirited choruses. Even some trick guitar. **A**

Letters to Cleo: *Aurora Gory Alice* (Giant '94) 💣
Letters to Cleo: "Dreams" (*Spirit of '73: Rock for Choice* [comp], 550 Music/Epic '95) 🔊

Barrington Levy: "Here I Come (Broader than Broadway)" (*The Best of Reggae Dancehall Music Volume 2,* Profile '90) 🔊

Donna Lewis: *Now in a Minute* (Atlantic '96) 💣

Huey Lewis: *Hard at Play* (EMI America '91) 💣

Jerry Lee Lewis: *Rockin' My Life Away* (Tomato '90) Last time I saw this fugitive from Madame Tussaud's was a 1984 performance video that convinced me Mr. Scratch had collected his half of the bargain in advance. So I expected nothing from this slightly earlier live-at-the-Palomino rehash, James Burton or no James Burton. And was immediately confronted with a "You Win Again" so bitter, so reconciled, so defeated, so above-it-all, so miserable that for a few songs I suspected the monkey-gland shots had worked—except that he sounds old, old and lecherous, old and lecherous and determined to enjoy it. Things do wear down in the middle, the voice can get weird, and caveat emptor: if these versions aren't identical to the 11 duplicated songs on Tomato's companion volumes, the country *Heartbreak* and the rockin' *Rocket '88,* Jerry Lee taught his best tricks to Milli Vanilli. Nashville-haters may prefer *Rocket '88*—"Chantilly Lace" and "Headstone" are keepers. But the true-pop "Harbor Lights" and "You Belong to Me" suit his ecumenical voracity, and James Burton is hot wherever. When and if he finally dies, the Killer's gonna challenge Mr. Scratch to a piano-playing contest. Then he's gonna show Cousin Jimmy his ass. **A–**

Jerry Lee Lewis: *Young Blood* (Sire '95) If the blood were literally young, the Killer would now be the Vampire. Instead, producer-wunderaltekacker Andy Paley is the Ghoul. Jerry Lee can still rock the eighty-eights, but his natural voice is a croak or a wheeze, as he proves by hero-ically holding "Gotta Travel On"'s final "long" until it tails into the pitchless pit he's already filled with croaks and wheezes. He couldn't get away with "Thirty-Nine and Holding" at forty-five. Yet at sixty he still wishes he was eighteen again. **C+** 🐢

Linda Gail Lewis: *International Affair* (New Rose import '91) The long-ago costar of the lowbrow gem *Together* reg-isters more twang per syllable than prime Duane Eddy, belting and screeching like a flat-out hillbilly—Jeannie C. Riley, say. But though I'd love to hear her "Harper Valley P.T.A." (or "Fist City," or "9 to 5"), she's Jerry Lee's sister, wild-ass before she's anything else. She doesn't ignore country on this band-centered studio job, but ex-cept for Billy Swan's "I Can Help" ("If your child needs a mama we can discuss that too"), the standouts are from Wolf-Justman, Dave Edmunds, Bob Dylan, all of whom should be damn proud. Cover-ing "They Called It Rock," she gets up to "Someone in the newspaper said it was shit," and instead of rushing discreetly on to the next line she draws out that last word with the relish of a gal who's waited to sing it all her life. **A–**

LFO: "Summer Girls" (*LFO*, Arista '99) 👁

Ottmar Liebert & Luna Negra: *Rumba Collection 1992–1997* (Epic '98) 💣

Lifers Group: *Lifers Group* (Hollywood Basic '91) Gangsta gangsta: "The Real Deal." Some of these Rahway State in-mates rap like pros, some sing like they remember how a street corner feels. All of them want you to know that dealers are sellouts and prison is "The Belly of the Beast": a temple of slavery and rape and broken bones, of suicide and genocide and acquired immune deficiencies. Both theme songs are powered by beats that might as well be punching you in the stomach, and for nightmare relief there's Crazy Chris, photographed in all his mad-eyed, ham-armed, white-skinned glory. If you're dumb enough to get inside, he's going to fuck you up personally. **A–**

Lifers Group: *Living Proof* (Hollywood Basic '93) "Fuck N.W.A, put down your watergun" ("One Life to Live," "Prison Is the Death of a Poor Man") ★★★

Lukas Ligeti & Beta Foly: *Lukas Ligeti & Beta Foly* (Intuition Music import '97) avant German trap drummer and ea-ger Ivoirians with something to teach Mick Fleetwood, Byrne & Eno, and all too many patronizing jazzmen ("René," "African Loops") ★★

Liliput: *LiLiPUT* (Off Course import '93) Completism is for obscurantists, only not this time. You want everything ever recorded by these English-speaking English-singing, English-yelling, English-murmuring Swiss maids—46 1978–1983 tracks, precisely 11 of which were ever al-bum-available in the U.S., where they sold some 600 copies. The evolution of For-merly Kleenex from punk primitives to postpunk postprimitives proceeds as if God planned it, without dead ends or maladaptations. They burst out with some of the funniest jump-up-and-down ditties ever to jolly bohemians into danc-ing. Then they mellow, musing sinuously without losing their feminism or their sense of humor. They remain my favorite girl band of all time. And their sound ef-fects are a universal language. **A**

Lil' Kim: "Spend a Little Doe" (*Hard Core*, Undeas/Big Beat/Atlantic '96) 👁

Lil Wayne: *The Block Is Hot* (Cash Money/Universal '99) tough-guyisms so steeped in convention they disappear into the bounce ("Drop It Like It's Hot," "Tha Block Is Hot," "F*** Tha World") ★★

Lilys: *The 3 Way* (Sire '99) Ⓝ

Limp Bizkit: *Three Dollar Bill, Y'All* (Flip/Interscope '97) 💣

Limp Bizkit: *Significant Other* (Flip/Interscope '99) give their image credit for having a sound ("Just Like This," "N 2 Gether Now") ★

Abbey Lincoln: *A Turtle's Dream* (Verve '95) ⓝ

Arto Lindsay Trio: *Aggregates 1-26* (Knitting Factory Works '95) ⓝ

Arto Lindsay: *O Corpo Sutil/The Subtle Body* (Bar/None '96) For over a decade, while Lindsay promoted samba's whispery vocals and fancy-pants chords as makeout music for sensual intellectuals, many who by some mischance lacked Portuguese continued to find those very selling points precious, schlocky, or both. So now Arto flexes his connections and writes his own jazzboistic verse, and, well, there's nothing like a lyric you can understand. After leading with something about the colors of the sky that's way too sensitive for this reporter, the man sounds like the bedroom astronaut he says he is even when he's celebrating a superbright two-year-old on the most seductive song here—even when he reverts to Portuguese. Reason to regret one's unimaginative personal relationship with Caetano Veloso. **A–**

Arto Lindsay: *Mundo Civilizado* (Bar/None '97) Even when he was an enraged and alienated no wave mutant there was wit and rhythm in his tantrums, and it was only a few years after he unveiled DNA and undermined the Lounge Lizards that this shy, suave, calculating lover boy bowed as a crooner. But even so it's wonderful and normal that he's grown up this far. Laying drum 'n' bass on deep Bahia, boldly and reverentially covering the two premier African-American singers of our era, hocking Brazilian tunes from Caetano on down, he calmly and erotically bridges English and Portuguese, art tourism and manor-born tropicalia, self-conscious sweetness and unkempt literacy. This be lounge-torch jungle-samba: a fragile, lyrical, sly, beatwise, embarrassingly beautiful cross-cultural appropriation that just goes to show how people grow up and settle down even when they don't. **A+**

Arto Lindsay: *Noon Chill* (Bar/None '98) Lindsay has always promoted samba as the motherlode of contemporary art-song, and after several homages this is where he claims auteurship. Highly verbal, very textured, kinda lovely. But only on "Simply Are" does song sweep art off its fundament. I like my sex subtle sometimes, but never this subtle—which goes double for beats. **B+**

Arto Lindsay: *Pride* (Righteous Babe '99) Although he'll never make as much money as the samba masters he takes after, Lindsay's jeu d'esprit has turned modus operandi. He seems fully capable of an album like this every year or two: a dozen or so songpoems in English or Portuguese, floating by on the sinuous current and spring-fed babble of a Brazilian groove bent, folded, spindled, and mutilated by the latest avant-dance fads and electronic developments. The weak link is the poetry, which wouldn't be as much fun as the music even if it was as well realized. The selling point is the fads and developments, and the faux-modest singing that renders them so organic. **A–**

John Linnell: *State Songs* (Zoë '99) darn—not 69, 50, or even 48, only 15, none of them up for legislative ratification ("The Songs of the 50 States," "New Hampshire") ★★

Liquid Todd: *Action* (Ultra '99) Former college sportswriter Todd Wilkinson didn't get to host K-Rock's syndicated Saturday-night mix show by pumping exotica. The interlocking beats and catch phrases of his first mix CD aren't what any Z-100 fan would call pop, but they're cheap, effective, and party-hearty enough to insure fun-fun-fun from beginning to end. Having gotten our attention with the church-bell tune of Mike & Charlie's "I Get Live," he cedes the floor to Fratboy Slim for five minutes and we're off to the races. The ebullience flags as ass-shaking turns endurance contest, but never settles for the functionalist minimalism this supposedly hedonistic scene runs on. Compiling such an hour from the tens of thousands of hours of techno product out there ought to be easy. I've begun dozens of CDs that prove it isn't. **A–**

Lisa Lisa: *LL 77* (Pendulum '94) ⓝ

Lit: *A Place in the Sun* (RCA '99) Led by two Orange County lads whose dad was a pop DJ, they like Vegas and old Cadillacs, make too much of their play on "come," "complete," and "completely miserable," and serve as a dull-dull-dull reminder to anyone besotted with Blink 182 that punk in itself guaranteed nothing even in the days of the Real Kids and the Suicide Commandos. **C** 🐛

Little Axe: *The Wolf That House Built* (OKeh '94) Adrian Sherwood dubz the bluez ("Ride On," "Here My Cry") ★

Little Charlie & the Nightcats: *Captured Live* (Alligator '91) ⓝ

Little Charlie & the Nightcats: *Night Vision* (Alligator '92) They get your attention by surpassing the potential of such titles as "My Next Ex-Wife," "Can't Keep It Up," and "I'll Never Do That No More"— the finest Coasters routine since "D. W. Washburn," and Jerry Leiber doesn't know it exists. Then they sail out on a groove. For white blues, as we used to call it, positively innovative. **B+**

Little Charlie and the Nightcats: *Straight Up!* (Alligator '95) It would be nice to think Rick Estrin cares that his persona is an anachronism—that in 1995 the streetwise standard of automotive savoir faire is the Lexus, not the Cadillac. But houserockin' bands are proud to be retro, so thank whomever there's one that doesn't stop at fleet solos and beer-soaked boogies. Estrin sings in the voice of a natural sophisticate whose day is made by a few pithy lines of well-chosen vernacular. He punctures phonies, rolls with the woman problems, has trouble buttoning his lip before his foot jumps in. And his best buddy is a guitarist who can play the blues and tell Charlie Parker jokes simultaneously. **A–**

Little Charlie and the Nightcats: *Shadow of the Blues* (Alligator '98) ain't love a bitch, ain't Stratocasters bitchin ("New Old Lady," "Dirty Dealin' Mama") ★

Little Richard & Tanya Tucker: "Somethin' Else" (*Rhythm Country and Blues* [comp], MCA '94) 🍭

Little Village: *Little Village* (Reprise '92) 💣

Live: *Throwing Copper* (Radioactive '94) On stage, this intently mediocre young band is U2 without a guitar sound. On record, it's R.E.M. without songs. Fittingly, it generates the "idealistic" arena-rock U2 is no longer hungry enough to bother with and R.E.M never had the stomach to work up. Only with the old guys I wouldn't put the saving word in quotes. **C+** 🐛

Live: *Secret Samadhi* (Radioactive '97) 💣

Living Colour: *Time's Up* (Epic '90) The latest target of the black superman theory won't write history like Harold Cruse and spout Afrology like Robert Farris Thompson any more than Darryl Strawberry will act the mensch like Don Baylor and hit .330 like Rod Carew. That's not his job— leading an arena band is different, and plenty difficult. It's amazing enough for a jazz musician like Vernon Reid to make the transition to pop accessibility, proving that even art-rock can signify with the best album in that meaning-laden genre since Pink Floyd was in mourning. Though the striking choruses and fancy structures are pretty Euro, the proximate model is Bad Brains sans Jah. If MTV's millions have heard Reid's more panhuman messages before, I doubt they've heard them expressed so coherently—or by a black person. Both factors count for something. **A–**

Living Colour: "Talkin' Loud and Sayin' Nothing" (*Biscuits,* Epic '91) 🍭

Living Colour: *Stain* (Epic '93) The best thing about this excellent record is how hard it crunches. From the antiliberal "Go Away" to the propansexual "Bi," the first four songs combine simplicity and savvy like no big-guitar music since vintage Aerosmith, and these smarts ain't stoopid. After that the songwriting dips some, although God knows they describe alienation as knowledgeably as any college-rock band. The weak link is Corey Glover, who still sings too well for his own good (cf. Jack Bruce). The fresh blood is Doug Wimbish, who still plays great (also cf. Jack Bruce). **A–**

The Living End: *The Living End* (Reprise '99) 💣

L.L. Cool J: *Mama Said Knock You Out* (Def Jam '90) This isn't groundbreaking like *Nation of Millions*, but it shouldn't be pigeonholed as a terrific rap record. It's an exceptionally consistent and entertaining *record*, period, on a par with *Goo* or *Freedom* or *Rock 'n' Roll* or maybe even *Sign "O" the Times*. Hilariously unreconstructed, it takes shit from no one and gives shit only in the most high-spirited way—the targets it disses hardest are Mike Tyson, whose mama would say knock the mother out if the poor fucker had a mama, and famed rapper L.L. Cool J, aka Cheesey Rat. It's avowedly street, but star street, voicing sympathy and solidarity rather than bullshitting about where he comes from after five years somewhere else. Marley Marl and assorted live human beings jam into the mix. Great music, great vocals, great lyrics, from beginning to end, by a proud pro with something to prove. **A**

L.L. Cool J: "I Be Gettin' Busy" (*Marley Marl in Control Volume II—For Your Steering Pleasure,* Cold Chillin'/Warner Bros. '91) 🐦

L.L. Cool J: *14 Shots to the Dome* (Def Jam/Columbia '93) Proof we didn't need that his talent is as phat as an elefant's phart and his brain is the size of a pea. Only it isn't his brain—it's his ability to comprehend contradiction. Like Michael Ivey, of all people, he flunked his follow-up because he can't figure out how to put success and rap together. Where Ivey (or the Basehead "character," ha ha) takes

his dorky confusion out on women, L.L.'s sexism is love-man suave—his "It's so relaxin'" after a piece of pussy gets off in the back of his Jeep is a rare moment of grace. Instead he slings the gangsta metaphors and handgun memories in the vain hope that the guys hanging out by the check-cashing place will think he's hard. But from the look of the crotch he's grabbing in several photos, as of now he just ain't. **B** 🦃

L.L. Cool J: "Doin It" (*Mr. Smith,* Def Jam '94) 🐦

L.L. Cool J: *All World* (Def Jam '96) He can be better than his singles, but more often he's been worse, and no other rapper has maintained the hitmaking knack so long. The coups are the sex raps "Back Seat" and "Doin It." I must counsel against aspiring to his superstud fantasy. But it's a measure of his pop credibility that I suspect he could be telling some sort of truth. Oohh. **A**

L.L. Cool J: *Phenomenon* (Def Jam '97) astride the world as R-rated pop staple ("Father," "Nobody Can Freak You") ★★★

Cheikh Lô: *Né La Thiass* (World Circuit '97) neotraditionalism hits Dakar ("Ndogai," "Boul di Tagale") ★

Ismaël Lo: *Jammu Africa* (Worldly/Triloka '97) Like any aspiring pop star, this sweet-voiced world music natural from Niger and Dakar thrives on a format that isolates his trickiest tunes. Not especially danceable, too slick to power through the wall of incomprehension that separates Anglophones from his multilingual homilies, this best-of showcases an expansive adept of Eurovision style. The synthesizer isn't my favorite axe either. But it can cut through the undergrowth like anything else. **B+**

Local H: *Ham Fisted* (Island '95) brighter than *Bleach,* less fly than *Incesticide* ("Chicago Fanphair '93," "Grrrlfriend") ★★★

Local H: *As Good As Dead* (Island '96) Quintessential exponents of what the cynics at *Spin* call scrunge, these two young guys from Illinois are a study in the uses and limits of originality. After their debut proved that singer-guitarist-bassist-headman Scott Lucas and drummer-dynamo Joe Daniels were to the bash-roll-howl born, they figured out enough about riffs and hooks to transform sound into song, and now evoke a tragic Seattle trio who shall remain nameless. I wish Pearl Jam, whose leader stars in the title song, packed such isometric power—that sense of tremendous force bravely exerted against implacable reality—and I say the exercise makes all of us stronger. Even if it develops further, which is about as unlikely as it having gotten this far, it will never replace the original. But these days we need any reassurance the music machine can cough up. **A–**

Local H: *Pack Up the Cats* (Island '98) At first I was just glad to ascertain they weren't a fluke. Now I think they've gone and made themselves the straight rock album of the year. Their idea of roots Hüsker Dü, their idea of avant-garde also Hüsker Dü, they attack the 100-bpm four-four with a singleness of purpose unknown to rap-fearing new metalists, ska-loving old hardcorists, and indie adventurers adrift on the great unknown. They're not true believers, writing early and often about just how far straight rock can't take you. They address an audience they swear is still there. And they have something to prove, even if it's only that a duo from the same Illinois town that produced the Shoes can make more noise than a pumpkin-smashing factory. **A–**

Lisa Loeb & Nine Stories: *Tails* (Geffen '95) **Ⓝ**

Nils Lofgren: *Silver Lining* (Rykodisc '91) 💣

Lo-Fidelty Allstars: *How to Operate with a Blown Mind* (Slint/Columbia '99) **Ⓝ**

Jack Logan and Liquor Cabinet: "Teach Me the Rules" (*Mood Elevator,* Medium Cool '96) 💿

Lois: *Bet the Sky* (K '95) 💣

Lokassa et Soukous Stars: *Megamix Vol. 1* (Stern's Africa '93) high-grade all-star Afro-Parisian best-of medley/remake ("'Lagos Night'/'Sweet Mother'/'Christiana'/'Aki Special'/'Stella'/'Wellenga'/'Oh Death'/'Lagos Night'") ★★★

Loketo: *Soukous Trouble* (Shanachie '90) Shared personnel notwithstanding, Diblo's *Super Soukous* was a guitarist's record and this is a band's. Six titles, six composers (three singers, two guitarists, one drummer), each of which achieves the same HI-NRG with a different deployment of stripped-down resources (the aforementioned plus bass, synth, percussion, a two-man horn section, and the occasional female chorus). Sure it's all up-up-up. They'll take you there. **A–**

Loketo: *Extra Ball* (Shanachie '91) They've subdivided now—Aurlus Mabele keeps the logo, Diblo Dibala takes the John Hancock. But your last chance at a great band is also your best. Mabele's warm, rich, relaxed baritone is merely foremost among several engaging voices, and the guitar dominates, as it should. Endlessly, effortlessly fluent, Dibala pours his most gorgeous effects into a hornless format that varies and repeats like prime James Brown. I just hope he meshes with bassist Miguel Yamba in real life. They should be together. **A**

Londonbeat: "I've Been Thinking About You" (*In the Blood,* Radioactive '91) 💿

The London Suede: *Suede* (Columbia '93) Make-or-break is "Sleeping Pills," when Brett Anderson drawls/whines/croons "You're a water sign, and I'm an air sign" so tunefully, repetitively, naggingly, inescapably that you swear he said "I'm an asshole" even though he pronounces "air sign" a lot more clearly than the line about Valium that follows. It's fingernail-on-blackboard city for anyone who doesn't believe Marc Bolan is Chuck Berry, and at first I couldn't stand it. Now it's a fave moment on this appropriately overhyped, surprisingly well-crafted coming out. More popwise and also more literary than the Smiths at a comparable stage, Suede's collective genderfuck projects a joyful defiance so rock and roll it obliterates all niggles about literal truth. If you think their victories over depression have nothing to do with you, be grateful you can make do with a report from the front. **A–**

The London Suede: *Dog Man Star* (Nude/Columbia '94) 💣

Lonesome Bob: *Things Fall Apart* (Checkered Past '97) A Nashville naysayer with an excoriating vision of domestic truth, a robust rocker who's fond of words like "overidealized" and "problematic," an organic intellectual who looks on the dark side, this guy is too sly to let the music take care of itself, but music isn't where he puts his conceptual energy. On maybe half these songs, he gets the words just right—cf. the outrageous "My Mother's Husband," about not always getting what you want, and the merely clever "What Went Wrong," about the practical parameters of psychotherapy. Every time he does, the music sounds fabulous. **B+**

Long Beach Dub All-Stars: *Right Back* (DreamWorks '99) 💣

Loop Guru: *Duniya* (Waveform '96) 💣

Jennifer Lopez: "Let's Get Loud" (*On the 6,* Work '99) 🐝

Mary Lou Lord: *Got No Shadow* (Work '98) Only indie perverts would hyperventilate over Lord's breathy voice, which needs every booster jet mind can devise or money can buy. And only indie perverts would object to her long-aborning major-label debut, where she gets the help she needs. The production is Amy Rigby–style neotraditionalism, with Roger McGuinn rippling under one flowing surge just to mark the concept, and, overcoming her fondness for Nick Saloman (Bevis Frond, don't you know anything?), she makes the most of covers from Elizabeth Cotten to Freedy Johnston. Equally impressive, every once in a while she finds the gumption to eke out a song so winsomely conceived and solidly constructed it belongs

in the canon she adores. Sometimes Saloman even helps—the cowritten lead track is a hummer worthy of Stuart Murdoch (Belle and Sebastian, don't you know anything at all?). **A–**

Lord Kitchener: "Fever" (*Klassic Kitchener Volume Three,* Ice '95) 🐝
Lord Kitchener: "Nora," "When You're Brown" (*Klassic Kitchener Volume One,* Ice '95) 🐝

Lord Melody: *Precious Melodies* (Ice '95) Although he doesn't have the voice to ape Cassius Clay or picong-wrestle with Sparrow, he does have the lyrics. A good half of these songs abound in calypso's outrageously observed hyperbole, and his failures with women are a relief from the usual BS even if they're hyperbole too. As for "Crazy Love" and "My Baby Is All Right," well, they don't merely justify his sobriquet—they make you think maybe this plug-ugly cared more for women than his better-endowed rivals. I still covet his gibberish-German Hitler farewell, not to mention the original of Harry Belafonte's "Mama Look at Boo Boo." But the compilation he deserves might as well be this one. **A–**

Traci Lords: *1,000 Fires* (Radioactive '95) 💣

Lords of Acid: *Lust* (Caroline '91) Though I wish they'd re-remixed the I-wanna-sit-on-your-face one even further into the pornographic stratosphere, here at last is product brazen and unwavering enough to live up to the canard about never underestimating the power of cheap music. Sure disco denizens already know its four hooks and big-beat blare. But ignoramuses like me might as well pick up a few sex tips while broadening our cultural horizons. **B+**
Lords of Acid: *Voodoo-U* (American '94) 💣
Lords of Acid: *Expand Your Head* (Antler Subway '99) ⓝ

Lord Tariq & Peter Gunz: "My Time to Go" (*Make It Reign,* Columbia '98) 🐝

Loretta/Dolly/Tammy: *Honky Tonk Angels* (Columbia '93) Ⓝ

Los Amigos Invisibles: *The New Sound of the Venezuelan Gozadera* (Luaka Bop/Warner Bros., '98) *Inglés, español, japonés, lo que sea*—as members of the international brotherhood of bored middle-class collegians, their specialty is crappy music with a concept. And the concept is—crappy music! See Combustible Edison, Pizzicato Five, *lo que sea.* C+ 🦃

Los Companeros de Valle: *The Muse* (Corason '95) Ⓝ

Los Del Rio: "Macarena (Bayside Boys Mix)" (*Macarena Club Cutz* [comp], RCA '96) 👁

Los Fabulosos Cadillacs + Fishbone: "What's New Pussycat?" (*Silencio = Muerte: Red Hot + Latin* [comp], Red Hot '96) 👁

Los Guanches: *The Corpse Went Dancing Rumba* (Corason '96) Spawned by the steady old Cuarteto Patria, the most renowned of Santiago de Cuba's dozens of son ensembles, this young quintet hypes things up—leads keener, harmonies tenser, percussion busier, guitar more intrusive. And for a non–Spanish speaker like me, the time-tested melodies levitate with every boost, getting over on interactive intricacy and vocal high spirits alone. A–

Los Lobos: *The Neighborhood* (Slash/Warner Bros. '90) Ⓝ

Los Lobos: *Kiko* (Slash/Warner Bros. '92) sounds great, but still—one song about angels, one about rain, one about a dream, one about a train ("Kiko and the Lavender Moon," "Saint Behind the Glass") ★★

Los Lobos: *Colossal Head* (Warner Bros. '96) Set on proving how big a band from East L.A. could rock, they painted themselves into a cornball corner until Tchad Blake lured two of them out with his cache of found sounds. Result: *Latin Playboys,* impressionistic fragments coalescing into a self-sustaining counterreality. And although this return to their primary identity masquerades manfully as an arena-ready song collection, more songs about rain and trains fail to convince me they'll ever revert. From enchanted-island salsa to Santana solo, from revolutionary disillusion to feeling happy anyway, their infinitely absorptive eclecticism feels blessed rather than bombarded. They're not dealing with it, they're digging it, And if you're as big as they are you will too. A

Los Lobos: *This Time* (Hollywood '99) chewing their cud for one album too long ("Oh, Yeah," "Corazon") ★★★

Los Super Seven: *Los Super Seven* (RCA '98) 💣

Los Van Van: *Azúcar* (Xenophile '94) coro as groove instrument ("Disco Azúcar") ★

Juan Formell y Los Van Van: *Te Pone La Cabeza Mala* (Metro Blue '97) stretching out now ("Te Pone Le Cabeza mala," "Ni Bombones ni Caramelos") ★

Los Van Van: *Best of Los Van Van* (Milan Latino '97) Catchy, simplistic, ramming home the clave, not shy of syndrums or syn-anything else, Los Van Van are the class of Castro-era Cuban pop. I still prefer Mango's rerecorded *Songo,* where four of the great hits here got richer, longer, and an elegant touch slower. But the cheesy '70s originals are the golden oldies of underdevelopment. Sometimes their high spirits seem forced, and sometimes their forced quality seems a mark of distinction, like the ingrown musical resources Juan Formell and his comrades had no choice but to make something new of. A–

Los Van Van: *La Colección Cubana* (Music Club '98) These dozen tracks from the decade-plus following Milan Latino's comp reinforce my suspicion that Cuba's essential postcharangists only got better as they went along. The songs roll their hips for an extra minute or two, which never hurts when the grooves are so sexy, and the comedy comes through even if you don't understand one word in 50

("Hey, *playa,* I know that one, and they sure say *más* a lot, must be what they want"). I also appreciate the synth splats on "De La Habana a Matanzas." And the two minutes of percussion—most definitely including their secret weapon, vocal percussion—that is "Llegada." **A**

The Lounge Lizards: *Queen of All Ears* (Strange & Beautiful Music '98) the inevitable progress, as they say, from fake jazz downtown-style to progressive jazz downtown-style ("The First and Royal Queen," "Queen of All Ears") ★

G. Love & Special Sauce: *Coast to Coast Motel* (Okeh/Epic '95) ⓝ

Laura Love: "Less Is More" (*The Laura Love Collection,* Putumayo World Music '95) ◒

Monie Love: *Down to Earth* (Warner Bros. '90) Set loose on a saturated market, female rappers must overcome overproduction—like indie rockers before them, they're competing for a store of compelling musical ideas that's diminishing even though its limits will never be determined. But rhymewise—contentwise—they're just getting started. Connected to the street and her family's front steps, Monie's shtick is proud rather than hostile, as in "R U Single," where she sees through a casanova's bull to what's "cute and smart" about him. She radiates sisterhood even though she concentrates on the guys, and positivity and tradition even though her only political/cultural move is "Swiney Swiney," the most disgusting antimeat song you ever heard. And she finds way more than her statistical share of beats. Cute and smart—also tough. **A−**
Monie Love: *In a Word or 2* (Warner Bros. '93) ☛

Love Battery: *Dayglo* (Sub Pop '92) ⓝ

Love Child: *Okay?* (Homestead '91) Too bad these punk-going-nowave neotraditionalists didn't study their Ramones harder—instead of crowding 21 songs into 45 minutes, they might have grouped the 14 snappiest into a dandy 27-minute shot in the dark. Of course, that would have consigned most of conceptualist Alan Licht's to the cutting-room floor. Here's hoping Licht gets bored like the arty dilettante he is. Then liberated girl Rebecca Odes could join punk-going-pop Will Baum in a band of their own. **B+**

Love/Hate: *Black Out in the Red Room* (Columbia '90) ☛

Love Jones: *Here's to the Losers* (Zoo '93) ☛

Patty Loveless: *Up Against My Heart* (MCA '91) solid-plus plus a stone godsend ("God Will") ★
Patty Loveless: "On down the Line" (*Black Dog [ST],* Decca '98) ◒
Patty Loveless: *Classics* (Epic '99) ⓝ

Love Spit Love: *Trysome Eatone* (Maverick/Warner Bros. '97) ☛

Lyle Lovett: "Church," "She Makes Me Feel Good," "She's Leaving Me Because She Really Wants To" (*Joshua Judges Ruth,* Curb/MCA '92) ◒
Lyle Lovett: *I Love Everybody* (Curb/MCA '94) What his claque cheered as wit, wisdom, and soul I suspected of meanness, pretension, and bald (ha ha) expropriation, but now that he's gone Hollywood, I enjoy his imagination and his sound. Right, there is the character who killed his grandma for her gold tooth ladee-dah. But whether he's flattering penguins, flirting fruitlessly with waitresses and record ladies, getting Dr. King's picture out of South Carolina, or nailing the limits of somebody else's soulful sincerity, he keeps it sprightly. This is pop, where clever gets you further than wise. **B+**
Lyle Lovett: *The Road to Ensenada* (Curb/MCA '96) funny guy, but who can trust him? ("Long Tall Texan," "Don't Touch My Hat") ★★★
Lyle Lovett: *Step Inside This House* (Curb/MCA '98) ⓝ
Lyle Lovett: *Live in Texas* (Curb/MCA '99) entertaining to the converted ("Here I Am," "I've Been to Memphis") ★★

Nick Lowe: *Party of One* (Reprise '90) The latest old fart to slip into limbo and come back to play another day, Nick the Knife is a writer again, every song honed and there for a reason. With the likes of Ry Cooder and Jim Keltner spiking his wry cool, he yearns for yen, makes Boeing a modest proposal, spins off pungent epithets ("Refrigerator White"), nonsense syllables ("Shting-Shtang"), and sexual metaphors ("Honeygun"). In a shameless bid for the rockcrit vote, he also finds the perfect rhyme for "ghastly" (starts with "Rick," lest you already forgot). And just like with *Labour of Lust* in 1979, he makes it sound so easy you expect a reprise a year for the rest of his life. **A−**

Nick Lowe: *The Impossible Bird* (Upstart '94) Ⓝ

Nick Lowe: "Man That I've Become," "Failed Christian" (*Dig My Mood*, Upstart '98) 🐝

Lower East Side Stitches: *Staja 98 L.E.S.* (Ng '98) Ⓝ

The Lox: *Money, Power and Respect* (Bad Boy '98) As a statement of principle, the title track is scary-good and creatively derivative; put into practice, it's scary-stupid and oppressively ordinary. How do we get MPR? By playacting bully-boy scenarios that sound petty enough to be from life and making up others we'd never have the guts for—one production number climaxes with, eek, a hand grenade! And by showing an endless profusion of imaginary bitches who the man is—the other production number climaxes when three gold-digging skeezers, as they were called in the good old days, end up with their blood all over the tracks. **C+** 🐝

L7: *Smell the Magic* (Sub Pop '90) Generalizing the hostile "Shove" with the balls-to-the-wall "Fast and Frightening," dissecting everybody else's suicidal tendencies on "Deathwish" before joining the fun on "'Till the Wheels Fall Off," humping a "Broomstick" as a preamble to "Packin' a Rod," these clitocentric trouble girls are everything the Runaways were supposed to be. Afraid of nothing including the four-syllable F-word, they go for an obsessive, dirty, punk pop-metal so aggressive it'll scare damn near every sister in sight. But the bravest will grow stronger. Soon they'll tell others. And start their own bands. And conquer the world. Right? **A**

L7: *Bricks Are Heavy* (Slash '92) Once again Butch Vig's mission is to smelt speed-sludge into grunge-metal alloy, which with this band involves intense admixtures of ditty and power chord. Although the passion of their major-label stab may not match Nirvana's, it's just as catchy and a touch nastier. Driven onward by the quick and muscular Dee Plakas, their buzzing textures and heavy hooks are streamlined rather than softened or dulled even if they don't accelerate like on last year's thrash longform. Read-my-title outbursts like "Wargasm," "Diet Pill," and "Shitlist" fulfill the ancient prophecy of a time when gurls would reinvent punk out of sheer delight in their own power. Girls will be grrrls. **A**

L7: *Hungry for Stink* (Slash/Reprise '94) Always a song band, they reverse the usual evolution by slathering themselves with grunge, which they play for weird sounds rather than dull despair. Hence their anger seems more metal-generic than punk-programmatic—rooted in the rock and roll everyday, where it belongs. It should go without saying that it's often about gender nevertheless; how anyone can accuse them of riding a bandwagon is beyond me. Every day, women is what they are, and there are lots of ways that can be shitty—the rape-avoidance diary "Can I Run" describes only a few. But every day, rock and rollers is also what they are, and they're much better at it than Candlebox or Alice in Chains. And yes, the songs help. **A−**

L7: *The Beauty Process: Triple Platinum* (Slash/Reprise '97) Divested of Jennifer Finch's liberal conscience, bad girls Donita Sparks and Suzy Gardner are she-cats with a bitch's vocabulary, yowling and whining the basics: "Me, Myself and I," "I Need," "Must Have More." Brazenly revving even further toward metal, they work their claim to "the urban din" till it yields the slag and shiny things they won't do without. **A–**

L7: *Live Omaha to Osaka* (Man's Ruin '99) "It's a long way to stay where you are in rock and roll," and also, "L7 would rather be with you people here tonight in Omaha than with some of the finest people in the world" ("Shitlist," "Lorenza, Giada, Allessandra") ★

L7: *Slap-Happy* (Wax Tadpole/Bong Load '99) "Place my bet on my rockin' machine" ("Livin' Large," "Crackpot Baby") ★★

L7 & Joan Jett: "Cherry Bomb" (*Spirit of '73: Rock for Choice* [comp], 550 Music/Epic '95) 🔊

LSG: *Levert-Sweat-Gill* (EastWest '97) manly, masculine, male—they cover the bases ("Door #1," "My Side of the Bed") ★★

Pablo Lubadika: *Okominiokolo* (Stern's Africa '93) Lubadika's guitar is one of the almost interchangeable signatures of the Hi–NRG Paris soukous sound. Delicate, nimble, tripping the light fantastic where Diblo Dibala and Syran M'Benza peal and billow, he is nevertheless delighted to feature each on a different three of these nine tracks. Generic Franco-Zairean at its most beguiling—the kind of record that makes you get serious about loosening up your pelvic girdle. **A–**

Luciano: "Messenger" (*Messenger*, Island Jamaica '96) 🔊

Luke: *I Got S--t on My Mind* (Atlantic '92) equal-opportunity doo-doo brown from the nicest guy in the Crew ("Fakin' Like Gangsters," "Head Head and More Head") ★

Luna^2: *Lunapark* (Elektra '92) Reedy, velvet, chilly, and feelful though it may be, I doubt I'd like this so much if Galaxie 500 sad sack and smart person Dean Wareham weren't fed up with his stupid sad-sack friends: "You're always loaded/Your life has imploded." I also like his perspec-

tive on his own bad character—a record that begins "You can never give/The finger to the blind" can't get too serious, or too nice. I like how the drummer pushes the music away from the slough of despond. And of course I like the guitar, which is pretty and ugly in all the right places. **A–**

Luna: *Slide* (Elektra '93) More than a stopgap, by addition (one guitar) and subtraction (one superscript 2). Who cares if the best cut on the EP is the best cut on the LP and the three runners-up are all covers—Velvets/Dream Syndicate/Beat Happening, yet. Every song is good, and several are fast. I do believe Dean Wareham wants people to type the group's name right as a first step toward putting it in lights. **A–**

Luna: *Bewitched* (Elektra '94) Pale Blue Eyes play ambient alternative ("Friendly Advice," "Going Home") ★★

Luna: *Penthouse* (Elektra '95) "If the war is over/And the monsters have won/If the war is over/I'm gonna have me some fun," confides born noncombatant Dean Wareham, whose only recorded partisan act is rooting for Nixon to expire. Wareham creates his music from the vantage of a slacker of independent means. Once darkness falls, all Manhattan (or Tacoma, Brussels, wherever he gets to tour) is his playground. But he spends most of his life in what sure sounds like a high-rise, where he drinks in the afternoon, wheedles his good-for-nothing girlfriends, studies his record collection, and cooks up guitar parts. Being as he's discovered the Go-Betweens, that seems like redeeming social value enough for me. **A**

Luna: "Season of the Witch" (*I Shot Andy Warhol* [ST], Tag Recordings '96) 🔊
Luna: *Luna EP* (No. 6 '96) ⓝ
Luna: *Pup Tent* (Elektra '97) Within the cushy parameters of the smoothness that is Dean Wareham's spiritual discipline, this sonic construction is all stakes and clothesline, relishing the jerry-built almost as much as *Penthouse* did the luxurious. It's still hooky pop as well-savored guilty pleasure, still undercut by Wareham's

pleasantly alienated lyrics. But voice and guitars sound more, well, tentative (get it?). Having given his all to the market-place and stood there bemused as it gave him Smashing Pumpkins back, he isn't throwing in the towel yet. But damned if he's going to hire a cleaning service just to have people over for drinks. **A–**

Luna: *The Days of Our Nights* (Jericho/Sire '99) downsized no, privatized yes ("Sweet Child o' Mine," "U.S. out of My Pants!") ★★

Lunachicks: "I'll Be the One" (*Luxury Problem*, Go–Kart '99) 🐝

Lung Leg: *"Hello Sir"* (Kill Rock Stars '97) 💣

Luniz: "I Got 5 on It" (*Operation Stackola*, Noo Trybe '94) 🐝

Evan Lurie: *Selling Water by the Side of the River* (Island '90) Fake jazz was all well and good, but fake tango? With world music already functioning as dinner music and background music here in the nonworld, why art it up with an extra layer of secondhand knowingness? Inconveniently, however, I liked the Lounge Lizards' bandoneon features, and my middle-aged friends kept asking what they were. Exactly how tango it all is I couldn't tell you, although Alfredo Pedernara would appear to be the genuine article and the four others would appear to be old friends of Evan's. But compared to his choppy first efforts for Argentina's favorite accordion on 1988's import-only *Pieces for Bandoneon*, the new melodies flow with an ease that transcends the idiomatic. Must be world music. Also dinner music. And pleasantly acerbic background music too. **A–**

Luscious Jackson: *In Search of Manny* (Grand Royal '93) Ⓝ
Luscious Jackson: *Natural Ingredients* (Grand Royal '94) These four estimable women exemplify the limitations of scene loyalty and good intentions. Only a killjoy would piss on their project—friendly alternative funk that stands as a

confident reproof to the usual sexual and racial caricatures. I like them fine as people, and I wouldn't even say I don't like their music. It's just that I don't, well, *like* their music. The ear food it provides is so scant that all you want to know about "Energy Sucker"'s hook riff is where they found the sample, and I just can't believe they pack an irresistible aural buzz even for those who experience their project as a cause. **B–** 🦃

Lustre: *Lustre* (A&M '96) "What these boys do is what they call muscle pop. Turned up axes, muthafied drums and some soul-waking [get this—ed.] sweet-Jane vocals, shaken and stirred, slurred and purred . . ." Never blame a band for its press release, but having ingested the music first, I'll swear they're *even worse* than this all-purpose so-square-they're-hip. North Carolinians, drummer from Antiseen ("That's why you never pick up a drummer, dear—there's no telling where he's been"), other two coy about pedigree and (probably) too young for Bread or Journey, which are far more plausible analogies than the Teenage Fanclub and (get this) Hüsker Dü *Billboard* supposedly came up with. My guess: roadies from Collective Soul and Better Than Ezra getting greedy. The New South! **C–** 🦃

Lutefisk: "Rebel Girl," "Something in It" (*Burn in Hell Fuckers*, Bong Load Custom '97) 🐝

John Lydon: *Psycho's Path* (Virgin '97) 💣

L/COMPILATIONS

Lach's Antihoot: Live from the Fort at Sidewalk Cafe (Shanachie '96) 💣

La Iguana: Sones Jarochos (Corason '96) the most intensely strummed Mexican son style, strongest at its slickest (Conjunto Los Jarochos, "El Jarabe Loco"; Conjunto de Santiago Tuxtla, "La Bamba") ★

Christine Lavin Presents Laugh Tracks Volume 1 (Shanachie '96) "20 funny folk songs—I just hope they have security at Tower Records when this goes on sale" (Andy Breckman, "Andy Breckman Tells Us How He Really Feels"; Andy Breckman, "Don't Get Killed"; the Chenille Sisters, "Blowin' in the Wind—A Female Perspective"; Rob Carlson, "[These Eggs Were] Born to Run") ★

Lesbian Favorites (Rhino '98) big solid emotions, woman to woman, easiest to take underplayed a little (Gretchen Phillips, "Swimming"; Jill Sobule, "I Kissed a Girl") ★★

Lightning over the River (Music Club '99) Although compiler Christina Roden rightly distinguishes between speed soukous and the old bipartite kind that gives the singer some, the thunderbolts she catches in her bottle are all thrown by guitarists. Admirers of Kanda Bongo Man, Tshala Muana, and especially Syran M'Benza (*Symbiose*, two tracks) may find a few selections familiar. More likely, however, they'll just own them. Even for Afropop fans, an enjoyable tour of a terrain that tends to blur into itself without a guide. **A−**

The Lion King (Walt Disney '94) The Afropop Fund has less of a beef than do parents and plain old pop fans—better secondhand mbube jive (Mbongemi Ngema simulating pan–Africana) than thirdhand razzamatazz (Elton John and Tim Rice dusting off the big themes, dull hooks, and *Jungle Book* shtick). With half an exception for Nathan Lane's meerkat, the voices are even more negligible than the songs, which number five in all—it takes three Elton versions plus four Eurocentric instrumentals to bring a lousy EP up to 12 tracks. **C−** 🦃

Lipstick Traces (Rough Trade import '93) punk as Ur–political vanguard as per G. Marcus, a man who considers the Firesign Theatre background music (Adverts, "One Chord Wonders"; Mekons, "Never Been in a Riot") ★

Live at the Social Volume 1 (Heavenly import '96) Chem Bros. party mix, livest when it's r&best (Meat Beat Manifesto, "Cutman"; Selectah, "Wede Man [Hoody Mix]") ★★★

The Look of Love: The Burt Bacharach Collection (Rhino '98) Now it's official: Dionne Warwick and Burt Bacharach were the best things ever to happen to each other. She's a bore without him, and he brings out the best in none of the other singers here. If anything, his fancy hackwork diminishes them a little—whether it's starters like the Drifters, the Shirelles, and Dusty Springfield or second-stringers like Gene Pitney, Jackie DeShannon, and end-of-the-bencher Chuck Jackson, all sound about as good as you'd expect and all peaked elsewhere. Then there are Lou Johnson, B. J. Thomas, Bobby Vinton, and the hapless Bacharach himself, not to mention horrid one-shots by Richard Chamberlain, Bobby Goldsboro, Trini Lopez, Jill O'Hara, gad. It's enough to renew your faith in Elvis Costello. **B−** 🦃

Lyricist Lounge Volume 1 (Rawkus '98) can't beat the atmosphere (Word a' Mouth, "Famous Last Words"; Bahamadia and Rah Digga, "Be OK") ★

Baaba Maal: *Taara* (Mélodie import '90) 🧨

Baaba Maal: *Lam Toro* (Mango '93) Ⓝ
Baaba Maal: *Firin' in Fouta* (Mango '94) so intensely beautiful you can hear through all the instruments from the right angle ("Sama Duniya," "Swing Yela") ★★
Baaba Maal: *Nomad Soul* (Palm Pictures '98) Ⓝ
Baaba Maal: *Live at the Royal Festival Hall* (Palm Pictures '99) "My voice was always very loud but very thin," so this border Tukolor bulked up his God-given instrument with the same conscious discipline that enabled him to attend law school and penetrate Wolof Dakar. But as with so many ambitious young men from the provinces, there's always been an awkwardness about him, and his Chris Blackwell–backed attempts to follow Youssou N'Dour and Salif Keita into the so-called world music market have been cluttered with horns, stabs in the dark, and invited guests. The shows have varied too, but this four-cuts-in-40-minutes EP is the heart of a good one. It's got a montuno-driven salsa. It's got reggae universalist Ernest Ranglin in Tukolor drag. And everywhere it's got tamas wrangling into the night. **A–**
Baaba Maal: *Jombaajo* (Sonodisc import '99) cut circa 1990, unreleased because it seemed too loose, and better for it ("Baydikacce," "Farm") ★★★

Aurlus Mabele and Loketo: *King of Soukous* (Soundwave '91) attempted singer's record ("Embargo") ★

Macha: *See It Another Way* (Jetset '99) 🧨

Kirsty MacColl: *Electric Landlady* (Charisma '91) Ⓝ
Kirsty MacColl: *Galore* (I.R.S. '95) Be they folk, pop, or country—or hybrid, like this second-generation folkie come of age in postpunk Thatcherland—purebred song hounds have lower standards than we who demand more of music than a catchy lyric. But in a decade and a half she's written 'em and picked 'em, adapting to spare guitars and big keybs, Latin and rap, Shane MacGowan and Johnny Marr. She has a political mind and a personal life, high times and second thoughts. Music hounds will enjoy making her acquaintance. **A–**

Shane MacGowan and the Popes: *The Snake* (ZTT/Warner Bros. '95) Fuckin' right he's still alive, and without stooping to abstinence either. He abuses any substance you got, addresses love bitter love with the unexampled expertise of a snaggle-tooth who might have fucked your missis but never fucked your daughter, bawls catchy tone-deaf tunes, and entrusts his life to the Church of the Holy Spook. The only great Pogues album was *Rum Sodomy and the Lash*, 10 years ago. This is the next best thing. **A–**
Shane MacGowan & the Popes: *The Crock of Gold* (SPV import '98) "F yez all, F yez all, F yez all" ("St. John of Gods," "Paddy Public Enemy No. 1") ★★★

★★★, ★★, ★ Honorable Mention   🍽 Choice Cut   Ⓝ Neither   🧨 Dud   🦃 Turkey

Machines of Loving Grace: *Machines of Loving Grace* (Mammoth '91) humanist industrial ("Cicciolina") ★

Macka-B: *Looks Are Deceiving* (Ariwa '90) Seven songs instead of eight or nine, with room for codas that wore thinner for me than they will for the dancehall-friendly. But the songs themselves don't quit—the disses drop science, "Unemployment Blues" gets down to business, "Proud to Be Black" sticks to the proud facts of that overburdened theme. And "Drink Too Much" fulfills the promise of its brief, eloquent spoken intro: "Now you have some people feel dem idea of a good night out is to go to the pub, drink 15 pints of lager, and then *vomit*." **A–**

Macka-B: "False Preacher" (*We've Had Enough*, Ariwa '90) 🐝

Macka-B: *Buppie Culture* (Ariwa '90) Rapid rhymes, crisp enunciation, commonsense politics, and pop-weird dub give this English toaster the most auspicious U.S. debut of 1990—a best-of from all his just U.S.-released albums could be a meliorist *Fear of a Black Planet* or a socially responsible *Mama Said Knock You Out*. High points here include "Coconut"'s African Methodist accent and a climactic third-world threefer. But the title tune isn't what it could have been. And though I bet the man could write a passable "We Love the Children," he didn't. **B+**

Macka-B: *Natural Suntan* (Ariwa '90) He's too big to talk revenge, not unlike his hero Nelson Mandela—even when he's boosting melanin, he thinks it's a shame his oppressors turn the color of watermelon out in the sun. There are a lot of rhymes here because he has a lot to say, and just in case you think the truth is always neat, a lot of the rhymes are charged with dissonant synth splats. The motormouth insults of "Get Rid of Maggie" are fit company for "Stand Down Margaret" or "Madame Medusa" or "Tramp the Dirt Down." When the nearest thing to a low point is a sweet Mandela tribute that steals a chorus from Curtis Mayfield, you're up there. **A–**

Macka-B: *Peace Cup* (Ariwa '91) 💣
Macka-B: *Jamaica. No Problem?* (Ariwa '92) Ⓝ
Macka B: *Roots Ragga* (Ariwa '93) Ⓝ
Macka-B: "To Be Racist" (*Discrimination*, Ariwa '95) 🐝

Craig Mack Project: *Funk Da World* (Bad Boy '94) Biz Markie as postgangsta ("Flava in Ya Ear," "Funk Wit Da Style") ★★★

Craig Mack Operation: *Get Down* (Street Life '97) Ⓝ

Mack 10: "Backyard Boogie" (*Based on a True Story*, Priority '97) (CC)

Marlee MacLeod: *Vertigo* (TRG '97) I don't know how or why (although she was a rock critic once), but this practical independent's cadences eerily evoke those of . . . Trotsky Icepick? ("Me and Shelley Winters," "Mata Hari Dress") ★

Mac Money: "Respect Yourself" (*One Voice: Pride* [comp], Enigma/Ruffhouse '90) 🐝

Madder Rose: "Bring It Down" (*Bring It Down*, Seed '93) 🐝
Madder Rose: *Panic On* (Atlantic '94) Ⓝ

Made: "Joanne" (*Bedazzler*, MCA '97) 🐝

Madilu System: *Sans Commentaire* (Stern's Africa '94) Ⓝ

Madonna: *I'm Breathless* (Sire/Warner Bros. '90) There are no doubt hundreds of frustrated chorines who could sing the three Sondheim originals "better" than the most famous person in the world. But with its pedigree of wit and musicality, show-tune pop-schlock sure beats the direct-to-Vegas power ballads with which she's heretofore betrayed her dance-rock roots. Especially when she writes it herself—except for the "Material Girl"–inspired "More," the Sondheim tunes are fussy and genteel (with Mandy Patinkin's "well-sung" cameo the nadir), but such fake period pieces as "Cry Baby," "He's a Man," and the risqué s&m-lite "Hanky Panky" are all her. This is a woman whose great gift is for the mask. Camp isn't everything she can do, but she sure knows how to do it right. **A**

Madonna: *The Immaculate Collection* (Sire '90) Seventeen hits, more than half of them indelible classics: "Holiday" (ebullient), "Lucky Star" (blessed), "Like a Virgin" (wicked), "Papa Don't Preach" (immoral), "Express Yourself" (feminist), "Material Girl" (dialectical), "Vogue" (expressive), "Open Your Heart" (naked), "Justify My Love" (erotica), "Into the Groove" (disco). Style-swallowing opportunist though she is, every one could have been cut yesterday—they're unified by the plastic practicality of her voice and the synthetic electricity of her groove. Right, she's all image. Couldn't have done it without MTV. Tell me about it. **A+**

Madonna: *Erotica* (Maverick/Sire '92) OK, everybody, let's use our *imaginations*, shall we? It may be a little hard at first, but if we try we can have lots of fun. To start, let's pretend that we have nothing against dance music—that instead of fixating on impersonal and mechanical and all those obvious things we can just enjoy it for what it is, as innocently as babes. Come on now, really try. Got it? Good. Because now I'm going to suggest something even harder—that we pretend we've never heard of Madonna. I know that's like asking you not to think of a purple polar bear, so just pretend to pretend, if you know what I mean, which as good postmodernist children you do. Now, put the record on. Hear those bass and synth beats? Sinuous and subtle and sexy, aren't they? How 'bout the faux-Arab electro on "Words"? And aren't the techno effects all nice and cheesy-futuristic? The singer doesn't have great pipes, but because she's too hip to belt (this time), she doesn't need them. She's in control, all understated presence and impersonal personality except when she's flashing some pink. Also, not counting that "Love your sister, love your brother" thing, the lyrics are not stupid. I love the rap where the boast turns out to be a lie. And whoever thought of recording the breakup

song through the phone hookup was a sharp cookie, wasn't he or she? She, I bet. A find. **A**

Madonna: *Bedtime Stories* (Maverick/Sire '94) seductive self-regard over the best tracks fame can buy ("Secret," "Bedtime Stories") ★★

Madonna: *Something to Remember* (Maverick/Warner Bros. '95) 💣

Madonna: *Ray of Light* (Maverick/Warner Bros. '98) pretty sensual for pop enlightenment, thank God ("Skin," "Candy Perfume Girl") ★

Kasse Mady: *Fode* (Stern's Africa '90) Malian *Kutché,* with classically trained Fania All-Star Boncana Maiga as Fafy Boutella ("Laban Djoro") ★

Magnapop: *Hot Boxing* (Priority/Play It Again Sam '94) Ⓝ

Magnapop: *Rubbing Doesn't Help* (Priority '96) Ⓝ

Magnet: *Don't Be a Penguin* (PC '97) if Moe Tucker can forgive the Yule brothers, so can you ("Summer & Winter," "Don't Be a Penguin") ★

The Magnetic Fields: *Distant Plastic Trees* (Red Flame import '91) Ⓝ

The Magnetic Fields: *The Wayward Bus* (PoPuP '92) In this Amerindie version of the Eurythmics, Stephin Merritt pulls Susan Anway's strings: where Annie would belt these metronomic tunes all the way to Vegas, Anway trills them in a sweet monotone and is grateful she can manage that. She's proud to play the puppet, which is a good thing because synthere thongwriter Merritt would drop her if she wasn't. First time out the literary brilliance of his doggerel lapped over into an obscurity his crude sonic eccentricities sometimes rendered unlistenable. Here he's learned to mesh straight pop parodies with well-turned, thought-through, not-quite-representational lyrics in which Anway usually plays a guy. Many are just mildly subversive love songs. But my favorite is so flat-out campy it could have been inspired by a *Man from U.N.C.L.E.* rerun. **B+**

The Magnetic Fields: *Holiday* (Feels Good All Over '94) more songs about songs and songs ("Swinging London," "Strange Powers") ★★★

The Magnetic Fields: *The Charm of the Highway Strip* (Merge '94) Those who haven't already memorized Stephin Merritt's oeuvre will have to expend real effort acquiring a taste for him this late in the game, so they might as well experience the full glory of his eccentricity. The 6ths' album isn't just for his cult but by it, and *Holiday* may mislead the unwary into believing there's some warmth to him. This is where his dolorously impassive baritone and fugueing toy keyboards are at their most anonymous, original, tuneful, and forbidding. Since every single lyric mentions roads or trains, call it a concept album about escape, probably from himself. Even though it isn't where he rhymes "Coney Island" and "prostitutes in Thailand," it's verbal enough to inspire willing workers to decipher the lyric sheet, and its sonic identity takes the Casio demo to unheard-of extremes—like something conceived by a Martian who'd read about country music in *The New Grove* but didn't happen to own any guitars. **B+**

The Magnetic Fields: *Get Lost* (Merge '95) Reflecting a recording budget rumored to have risen by as much as $450, Stephin Merritt's craft shines brightly half the time—the song that mentions the Beach Boys actually feigns happiness. Just as important, his largely theoretical group starts to resemble a band—although cheap synth rhythms remain their thing, the banjo, flute, and ukulele are felt as unique sound, not just arch affectation. Here and there, you'd even swear Merritt is singing about his own feelings. How'd he ever come up with *that*? **A–**

The Magnetic Fields: *69 Love Songs* (Merge '99) Accusing Stephen Merritt of insincerity would be like accusing Cecil Taylor of playing too many notes—not only does it go without saying, it's what he's selling. If he'd lived all 69 songs himself he'd be dead already, and the only reality I'm sure they attest to is that he's very

much alive. I dislike cynicism so much that I'm reluctant ever to link it to creative exuberance. But this cavalcade of witty ditties—one-dimensional by design, intellectual when it feels like it, addicted to cheap rhymes, cheaper tunes, and token arrangements, sung by nonentities whose vocal disabilities keep their fondness for pop theoretical—upends my preconceptions the way high art's sposed to. The worst I can say is that its gender-fucking feels more wholehearted than its genre-fucking. Yet even the "jazz" and "punk" cuts are good for a few laughs—total losers are rare indeed. My favorite song from three teeming individually-purchasable-but-what-fun-would-that-be CDs: "The Death of Ferdinand de Saussure," who has the savoir faire to rhyme with "closure," "kosher," and "Dozier" before Merritt murders him. **A+**

Ann Magnuson: *The Luv Show* (Geffen '95) 🎸

Taj Mahal: *Taj's Blues* (Columbia/Legacy '92) I used to regard Taj as a walking Afro-musical encyclopedia, but the more I listened to this endlessly listenable anthology the less derivative he seemed. Nobody else has ever sung blues this way—cutting rural slack with urban hyperconsciousness, he's Jim Crow's bumpkin turning into Zip Coon's dandy without the negative vibe of either stereotype. Sly and cocky, but so full of fun you don't resent it, he sneaks beats from all over the diaspora under these mostly classic tunes as he shows off the effortless size and avidity of his voice and the National steel-bodied and acoustic 12-string he tiptoes out with. **A**

Taj Mahal: "Ooh Poo Pah Doo" (*Phantom Blues*, Private Music '96) 🐟

Taj Mahal: *An Evening of Acoustic Music* (Ruf '96) old dog's blues ("Satisfied 'n' Tickled Too," "Sittin' on Top of the World") ★★★

Taj Mahal and Toumani Diabate: *Kulanjan* (Hannibal '99) No longer does Mahal talk a bigger African diaspora than he walks. He deserves his top billing, but every other musician on this piece of serendipity is a West African retrofitting a simple little studio in Athens, GA. Like the guitar hotshot he'd have turned into Stateside, costar Diabate is a virtuoso and nothing more, and his Manding songs are mostly some kind of change. But when his kora echoes the happy-hollering "Ol' Georgie Buck" or the deep-Delta "Catfish Blues," those straightforward old blues take on a filigree Diabate's percussive confederates can go to work on. And when Mahal's piano strides beneath the balafon of a Diabate named Lasana, the rhythms canter so comically you wonder who said open sesame. **A–**

Mahavishnu Orchestra: *The Lost Trident Sessions* (Columbia/Legacy '99) from before John McLaughlin discovered Barney Kessel and Jan Hammer discovered Jan Hammer ("John's Song #2," "Trilogy") ★★★

Mahlathini and Amaswazi Emvolo: *You're Telling Tales* (Shanachie '90) Mbaqanga maestro West Nkosi long ago commandeered the above-named male vocal combo to inject Swazi traditions into his basically Zulu product. They're movers on Mahlathini's definitive *Paris-Soweto*, and get numerous leads and writing credits on this robust exercise as well. The track where their backing resembles barking will frighten Arsenio. **B+**

Mahlathini and the Mahotella Queens: *Rhythm and Art* (Shanachie '90) 💣

Mahlathini and the Mahotella Queens: *The Lion Roars* (Shanachie '91) for his supper ("Masole A Banana," "Amaqhawe Omgqashiyo") ★★

Mahlathini and the Mahotella Queens: *Mbaqanga* (Verve World '92) 💣

Mahlathini: *King of the Groaners* (Earthworks '93) Powered by studio stalwarts who know their own strength, the music he's aimed for since his early-'80s comeback has been a runaway train, as unwithstandable as a prime metal anthem. The late-'70s stuff on *The Lion of Soweto* often seems despondently formulaic. This early-'70s music is spare, exploratory, feeling its cornmeal—always less luxurious than the songs of his maturity, sometimes more fun. And let's hear it for Alfius Madlokovu, whose bass has strings. **A–**

Mahlathini & the Mahotella Queens: *Stoki Stoki* (Shanachie '96) after 30 years, not everything (or everywho) they used to be ("Ilamba Lidlile," "Umgqashiyo") ★★

Mahotella Queens: *Marriage Is a Problem* (Shanachie '90) 💣

Mahotella Queens: *Women of the World* (Shanachie '93) 💣

Main Source: *Breaking Atoms* (Wild Pitch '91) Ⓝ

Makavelli: *Don Killuminati: The 7 Day Theory* (Death Row/Interscope '96) 💣

Miriam Makeba: *Eyes on Tomorrow* (Polydor '91) It was made in Johannesburg, and that's a triumph. But unless you live there yourself, which means taking your uplift where you find it, save this genteel schlock for your Afrocentric grandma, who may not appreciate the gesture—she knows how much vague promises are worth. Even if you ignore the corny crossover lyrics, the all-purpose synthesizers, and the received licks from many lands, Dorothy Masuka is singing better, and without dated stabs at modernization. Dizzy Gillespie don't sound so hot either. **C** 🐢

The Make-Up: *The Mass Mind* (Dischord '98) 💣

Malka Family: "Malka on the Beach" (*Africolor 2* [comp], Celluloid import '91) 👝

Michelle Malone: *New Experience* (Sky '93) 💣

Malouma: *Desert of Eden* (Shanachie '98) Ⓝ

Nada Mamula: "Kad ja podjoh na Benbasu" (*Bosnia: Music from an Endangered World* [comp], Smithsonian Folkways '93) 👝

The Mandators: *Power of the People: Nigerian Reggae* (Heartbeat '94) militant roots and sufferation, Afrobeat-style ("Coat of Many Colors," "Injustice," "Bubbler") ★★

Kante Manfila: *Ni Kanu* (Hemisphere '95) ⓝ

Sam Mangwana: *Megamix* (Mélodie import '90) ⓝ

Sam Mangwana: *Rumba Music* (Stern's Africa '94) As he nears 50, the citizen of world soukous has never filled his large legend on any album to come my way, and although his official U.S. debut reprises several great hits, I'm peeved that I still haven't heard "Georgette Eckins" or "Maria Tebbo." On the other hand, the classic "Suzana" and the gorgeous "Fati Mata" were worth the wait. As was the Fania All-Stars approach to Kinshasa rumba, especially on the infinitely reprisable "Afrika-Mokili-Mobimba," which somebody with more right than me must already have nominated for continental anthem. **A−**

Sam Mangwana: *Maria Tebbo* (Stern's Africa '95) On two renowned late-'70s albums, seven cuts totaling about an hour, the polyrhythms are far less elaborate than in present-day soukous, the tunes far more direct. The booklet attributes their winning confidence to the vibrant culture of early independence, and though artistic and commercial logic would have led to overdevelopment anyway, the metaphor is evocative. It's that the-world-is-in-front-of-me thing. Think early hip hop—or early Beatles. **A−**

Sam Mangwana: *Galo Negro* (Putumayo Artists '98) obliging ethnic Angolan adds Lusophone accordion to Zaire-rooted pan-Afro-Latinism ("Galo Negro," "Maloba") ★★

Maniac Mob: "Get Up" (*The D&D Project* [comp], Arista '95) 👁

Barry Manilow: *Singin' with the Big Bands* (Arista '94) Tempting though it would be to tweak reformed Halo of Flies fans for going gaga over Tony Bennett, the wily codger's as prudent as ever about deploying his lovingly preserved pipes. Trevor Horn's Tom Jones joke travesties an artist who's long clocked dollars making fun of himself. But this guy's got a nerve. It's less ghoulish than some "Unforgettable"-style computer nightmare in which Barry magically replaces Martha Tilton or Tex Beneke on classic swing records, but it's also worse—swing as '50s television music, stupefying chestnuts (three each from Sinatra and the Andrews Sisters, what taste) backed by recreated or reconceived live big band arrangements (sometimes from the originals, whatever that can mean after 50 years, more often from "the Big Band Orchestra"). Fronted, of course, by Manilow's uncompromisingly inoffensive voice—a voice that never hints at sex or history or even chops. Incomprehensible Press Quote: "I've found a funkiness and intelligence in the music that will last forever. Hopefully, everyone can feel the honesty and grit on the album that will remind us of what a hip era this was." **C** 🦃

Manitoba's Wild Kingdom: *. . . And You?* (Popular Metaphysics/MCA '90) 👋

Aimee Mann: "Mr. Harris" (*Whatever*, Imago '93) 👁

Aimee Mann: *I'm with Stupid* (DGC '96) ⓝ

Barbara Manning: *One Perfect Green Blanket* (Heyday '91) her hopes as realistic as her words, which in today's bohemia makes her an optimist, she stumbles like Sonic Youth and strums like the Fall ("Sympathy Wreath," "Someone Wants You Dead") ★★★

Marilyn Manson: *Smells Like Children* (Nothing/Interscope '95) Unmitigated consumer fraud—a mess of instrumentals, covers, and remixes designed to exploit its well-publicized tour, genderfuck cover art, titillating titles, and parental warning label. The lyrics to "S****y Chicken Gang Bang" are nonexistent, those to "Everlasting C***sucker" incomprehensible. Only "F*** Frankie," a spoken-word number in which a female feigning sexual ecstasy reveals that it isn't "Fool Frankie" or "Fire Frankie" or "Fast Frankie" or "Fist Frankie," delivers what it promises. It's easily the best thing on the record. **D+** 🦃

Marilyn Manson: *Antichrist Superstar* (Nothing '95) 💣

Marilyn Manson: *Mechanical Animals* (Nothing '98) If only the absurd aura of artistic respectability surrounding this arrant self-promoter would teach us that not every icon deserves a think piece, that it's no big deal to have a higher IQ than Ozzy Osbourne, that the Road of Excess leads to the Palace Theater. Instead, his banned-in-Wal-Mart slipcase job will fade into the haze of records people found interesting at the time. Its strategy is to camouflage the feebleness of La Manson's vocal affect by pretending it's deliberate—one more depersonalizing production device with which to flatten willing cerebella whilst confronting humankind's alienation, amorality, and failure to have a good time on Saturday night. Catchiest songs: "The Dope Show" and "I Don't Like the Drugs (But the Drugs Like Me)." Duh. **C+** 🦃

Samba Mapangala & Orchestre Virunga: *Virunga Volcano* (Virgin '90) One of numerous wannabes who departed a Kinshasa controlled by Mobutu and/or Franco and Rochereau to service rumba-starved Kenyans, Mapangala named his band after a Zairean volcano. And up against the rustic underdevelopment of Nairobi pop in the '70s, any soukous variant could pass itself off as an eruption. But in the world beat disco of 1990, Virunga's snaky bass and nimble guitar come off as spaced and delicate as the falsetto leads Mapangala trades with Fataki, his only permanent sideman, and the twin saxophones are low-budget funky, their cheesy embouchure stuck between alto and soprano. So for outsiders the music's beauty is far more fragile, or spiritual, than artist or natural audience believe. Which doesn't mean we can't sway to it. **A−**

Samba Mapangala: See also Virunga

Thomas Mapfumo: *Shumba: Vital Hits of Zimbabwe* (Virgin '90) dread-roots counterpoint ("Shumba," "Pachinyakare") ★★★

Thomas Mapfumo and the Blacks Unlimited: *Chamunorwa* (Mango '91) Ⓝ

Thomas Mapfumo & the Blacks Unlimited: *Hondo* (Zimbob '93) Ⓝ

Thomas Mapfumo & the Blacks Unlimited: *Vanhu Vatema* (Zimbob '94) Ⓝ

Thomas Mapfumo: *Chimurenga Forever: The Best of Thomas Mapfumo* (Hemisphere '95) Having first invented a genre and then deployed it against colonialism, Mapfumo would rank with Franco or Youssou N'Dour if only his usages were pan-African instead of southern African or Zimbabwean or Shonan. While he's remarkably reliable—now past 50, he's less rote than Rochereau or Mahlathini, neither of whom phones his music in—his adaptation of thumb piano effects to guitar-band dynamics will remain marginal except among Afropop acolytes. So the more accessible of two compilations is a good place to pick up on him. Sharply danceable as often as not, it cherry-picks 12 especially catchy 1978–1993 tracks. You can tell the newer ones because his voice is deeper. **A−**

Thomas Mapfumo: *The Singles Collection 1977–1986* (Zimbob '96) The 16 cuts on this remastering of a cassette compiled by Mapfumo circa 1993, all of which originally surfaced as Zimbabwean seven-inches, consume pretty much the same 70-plus-minutes as the 12 on the Hemisphere collection. Which means that, relatively speaking, they're more about song than groove, and that their groove has a little more reggae/herb skank and a little less benga/whatever propulsion—they're gentler, more ruminative. The earlier dates are also a plus in theory, although I can't claim to distinguish the fresh from the formulaic even so. In fact, I doubt the artist knows the difference himself. **A−**

Marcy Playground: *Marcy Playground* (Capitol '97) 💣

Teena Marie: *Lovergirl: The Teena Marie Story* (Epic/Legacy '97) an original even on her endless ballads, conflating florid and soulful without ever sounding like the wannabe she is ("Ooo La La La," "Lovergirl") ★★

Marky Mark and the Funky Bunch: *Music for the People* (Interscope '91) one of the good guys ("So What Chu Sayin," "Wildside") ★

Bob Marley & the Wailers: *Talkin' Blues* (Tuff Gong '91) With Joe Higgs standing in for Babylon-shy Bunny Livingston, the seven songs they recorded before an audience of half a dozen at the KSAN studios one morning in 1973—maddeningly interspersed with separately tracked bits of a 1975 interview that make a CD you can program a must—isn't just the best live Wailers I've ever heard, but the best Wailers I've ever heard. The ensemble—which by the time of 1976's *Live!* will substitute the dutifully beautiful I-Threes for his male mates and adjust the instrumentals to arena scale—is at a supple, subliminal peak of interactive intimacy and intensity. The previously unreleased "Am-A-Do" plus three later outtakes are a letdown only by comparison. **A–**

Bob Marley and the Wailers: *One Love* (Heartbeat '91) 1963–66 Studio One ska/rocksteady—gems you'll play again amid curiosities you'll be glad you heard once ("Who Feels It Knows It," "Bend Down Low," "Hooligan," "Let Him Go") ★★★

Bob Marley: *Chant Down Babylon* (Tuff Gong/Island '99) **◑**

Ziggy Marley and the Melody Makers: *Jahmekya* (Virgin '91) Slowly—too slowly, but faster than we had any right to hope—he's getting it: if "This generation will make the change" doesn't convince, "When will the innocent stop being punished for their innocence" will certainly do. And the complex drive of the music, cut this time in full Tuff Gong regalia, could pass for innovative: a genuine reggae groove at pop speeds with pop horns.

More likely to endure as a turning point than to pass into half-assed oblivion. **B+**

Chris Mars: *75% Less Fat* (Smash '93) 💣

Ricky Martin: *Ricky Martin* (C2/Columbia '99) The boy-group boom is harmless-if-bad. Martin is more like bad-if-not-worse. Since he was already marked for death with Menudo, don't be so sure his rebirth is a one-shot. But don't make him a Latin-pride poster boy either. Slicked-up rhythm workouts and romantic pap were tokens of progress circa Xavier Cugat and Desi Arnaz. In an America where Spanish is a second language, they're the reactionary stratagems of one more crappy pop star. **C** 🦃

Mary's Danish: *Circa* (Morgan Creek '91) Led by matched admirers of Jimi Hendrix and Charlotte Perkins Gilman, anchored by a former Anita Baker road drummer, and spiced by a former Three O'Clock gittar man, their sorta-major sorta-debut is way too all-embracing at 17 songs and umpteen cross-genres, following their sorta-indie demo album and live EP into college-radio nowhere. I don't care whether they're progressive and postmodern and goofy and smarter than the person next to you (but not you). And I also don't care whether they can play their instruments. Because they can't play their influences. **C+** 🦃

Mase: *Harlem World* (Bad Boy '97) This hugely appealing, moderately disturbing piece of pop has no more credibility with the keepers of hip hop's gated community than Calvin Butts, Al Roker, or the great neglected legacy of the Fat Boys. Mase's phlegmatic, just-woke-up drawl earns the overused term "flow" more than any delivery since Snoop's—unflappably indolent, fonder of vowels than consonants, he has no trouble rhyming "my limo" and "sex symbol" and is at ease with both tropes. His congested timbre warm rather than cool, he sounds goofy and utterly confident at the same time, the cuddliest rapper ever. But for his audience, cuddly and raunchy are anything but mutually exclusive, and like most ass men only more so, Mase isn't always so cute. He has his "four pimp rules," his "please no hickeys 'cause wifey's with me," his detailed list of freak-me requirements that climaxes with the sudden "If she make my nuts itch I kill that slut bitch." Black Barney, if you're talking this shit just to impress your boys, forget it, because it won't. You know the score: "Niggaz say they love me, they dont love me/I know deep down they wanna slug me/I feel the vibe when they hug me." A–

Mase Presents Harlem World: *The Movement* (All Out/So So Def '99) can't stand the way he fronts but I love to hear him talk ("Crew of the Year," "We Both Frontin'") ★

Mase: *Double Up* (Bad Boy '99) 💣

Massive Attack: *Blue Lines* (Virgin '91) from soul ii skank, those postindustrial blues got them down ("One Love," "Be Thankful for What You've Got") ★★★

Massive Attack: *Protection* (Virgin '95) Trip hop without pain or mess, thick-textured and clean-etched, doing a solid for vocalists in need (they return Tracy Thorn's favor with interest, including an introduction to unknown-but-equal Nicolette) and stretching instrumentals into a weird comfort zone (e.g., the almost literally atmospheric "Weather Storm," which I assume was a little too unusual for the funk-lite hedonists in producer Nellee Hooper's own band). Definitive: "Karma-coma," a title that would say everything you need know about the killing pleasures of killer weed if Tricky's stoned vocal didn't say so much more. A–

Massive Attack V Mad Professor: *No Protection* (Gyroscope '96) The most ballyhooed dub album of the current resurgence does reveal a few secrets to nonbelievers. Juicier, funnier, and more eventful than the desiccated run of *Macro Dub Infection,* it also sustains a convincing gravity—a sense that all these whooshings and clangings and suckings and scrapings and boomings and snatches of tune relate to each other and the rest of the physical universe. Not that they do, necessarily. But aren't you glad they care enough to fib about it? A–

Massive Attack: *Mezzanine* (Virgin '98) pre-millennium unction ("Risingson," "Man Next Door") ★★

The Master Musicians of Jajouka Featuring Bachir Attar: *Apocalypse Across the Sky* (Axiom '92) Apocalypse my ellipsis, pipes of Pan my patootie. Forget the delusions of grandeur this Tunisian mountain music has given rock and rollers since Brian Jones expected to fly and settle for a few facts, because the facts are grand enough. We have here an incontrovertibly sacred music with no regard for what any theocrat would validate as decorum or beauty. Dominated by screechy horns, it's loud, fast, percussive, and, whatever its scalar conventions, dissonant. Not only is it exciting because it's ugly, it's supposed to be exciting because it's ugly. That's why Bill Laswell went and recorded it again. And a good thing too, because a quarter century after Jones died, we rock and rollers know its scales well enough to find it beautiful too. Excitingly ugly we already knew about it. A–

Master Musicians of Jajouka: *Master Musicians of Jajouka* (Genes '95) recorded 1972, in an earlier stage of professionalism, which juices the reality effect, and technology, which saps it ("Sidi Hamed Sherk," "Teasing Boujeloud") ★

Master P: "Time to Check My Crackhouse" (*The Ice Cream Man,* No Limit/Priority '96) 👄

Master P: *Ghetto D* (No Limit/Priority '97) The title track is noxious and miraculous, hooked to a hectoring male singsong unlike anything I've ever heard. Subject: how to manufacture and distribute rock cocaine. The hit vies in rank sentimentality with "Candle in the Wind," hooked to a male groan also unlike anything I've ever heard. Subject: dead homies, a hard reality turned soft metaphor. The rest is underproduced propaganda for, reflections of, or fantasies about thug life that hold intrinsic interest only for live homies and their wannabes. Question: why aren't crack buyers also victims of this "black-on-black crime" that must stop? And another: why aren't there better things to do with talent and initiative? **C+** 🦃

Master P: *MP Da Last Don* (No Limit '98) The beats speed up without losing their deep post-Cali bump, especially on the nonstop "Make Em Say Uhh #2." The artiste camouflages his rapping by passing work to his brothers and collecting chits from Bone-Thugs and Snoop. Political analyses are essayed. So the brutally predictable solo smashes by said brothers, the cold Silkk the Shocker and the crude C-Murder, are less fun. But they're also less aggravating. In addition to givens about social services and law enforcement, we get "Niggas don't kill niggas—media kill niggas," "why the government don't protect superstars," "no Grammy nominations," and complaints that his taxes are too high. We get all the usual misogynist ugliness and black-on-black crime. We get Snoop calling Puffy out without going so far as to utter his name. "The ghetto's got me crazy" I know—that's the cliché P patented with his groan. But "too legit to quit"? Where have I heard that before? **C+** 🦃

Masters of Reality: *Sunrise on the Sufferbus* (Chrysalis '93) Chris Goss still ain't Eric Page, but his songs beat Peter Bruce's, and Ginger Baker makes a difference ("Ants in the Kitchen," "T.U.S.A.") ★★★

Dorothy Masuka: *Pata Pata* (Mango '91) Masuka's an old-timer, a Zimbabwean with South African tribal ties who came up in the upwardly mobile artistic ferment of the Jo'burg '50s. Because there's not much country in her, her "marabi" derives from Sophiatown musical theater rather than, say, Zulu wedding music. Sprucing up tried-and-true melodies with mbira-based chimurenga effects, she constructs a swingingly syncretic popular style that partakes of more than its allotted portion of pop—and that sounds *southern* African, not South African, with none of mbaqanga's guttural thrust or mbube's intricate spirituality. Nobody this side of Abdullah Ibrahim has made the musical aspirations of genteel black South Africans so credible. **A–**

Matchbox 20: *Yourself or Someone Like You* (Lava/Atlantic '96) clods have feelings too ("Real World," "Long Day") ★

Material: *Seven Souls* (Virgin '90) The male version of Laurie Anderson's *Strange Angels* is a marriage made in purgatory between two cold motherfuckers: Bill Laswell and Bill Burroughs. Seamlessly synthesizing New Age atmospherics, authentic African passion, and arena-rock dramaturgy, Laswell devises settings for the sci-fi ecopessimism of the greatest reader of our time. Not that it's all dead souls and dire consequences—for balance and to prove he can do it, Laswell also constructs an inspiriting third-world anthem from the remains of John Lydon's "Pop Tones." **B+**
Material: *The Third Power* (Axiom '92) 💣

Kathy Mattea: *A Collection of Hits* (Mercury '90) here's hoping her real marriage is this real ("Where've You Been," "Life as We Knew It") ★

The Dave Matthews Band: *Under the Table and Dreaming* (RCA '94) Popular groundswells do vary in discernment, as students of jogging, nail care salons, and tax limits know. Like his homeboy and forebear Bruce Hornsby, Matthews jams politely. His instrumentation invokes classical, jazz, and bluegrass niceties. And although one can understand the deep-seated impatience with agony-as-entertainment his renown reflects, he's as bland as a tofu sandwich. **C+** 🦃
Dave Matthews Band: *Crash* (RCA '96) 💣

Eric Matthews: *It's Heavy in Here* (Sub Pop '95) Beatles, Bee Gees, who's he trying to kid? The template for these sensitive scores, useless songs, and breathy vocals was forged by failed Zombie and insurance man Colin Blunstone, whose solo LPs are now going for as much as five bucks at garage sales up and down the Portland-Seattle corridor. I know Matthews isn't old enough to know better. I just hope the world is. **C+** 🦃

The Mavericks: *What a Crying Shame* (MCA '94) the best Cuban-American Texas music Nashville can capitalize ("All That Heaven Will Allow," "There Goes My Heart," "I Should Have Been True") ★★★
The Mavericks: *Music for All Occasions* (MCA '95) 💣
The Mavericks: *Trampoline* (MCA Nashville '98) 💣

Maxwell: *Maxwell's Urban Hang Suite* (Columbia '96) 💣
Maxwell: "Luxure: Cococure" (*Embrya,* Columbia '98) 👁

Curtis Mayfield: *New World Order* (Warner Bros. '96) floating free of the merely corporeal, just like always ("Here but I'm Gone," "The Got Dang Song") ★

Mazzy Starr: *She Hangs Brightly* (Rough Trade '90) hippie imitation of the year, sad division ("I'm Sailin," "Holah") ★★
Mazzy Star: *So Tonight That I May See* (Capitol '93) 💣

Jimmy Mbaye: *Dakar Heart* (Shanachie '97) Ⓝ

Syran M'Benza: *Symbiose* (Hysa import '93) M'Benza promises "the best of Paris" for his state-of-the-tech Les Quatre Etoiles moonlight. Organ-synth, string-synth, drum-synth, supervoices, balafon, accordion—we get 'em all. And when the sweet male chorus inserts gruff commands, or M'Benza makes his soukous guitar hop mbira-style or sway like pedal steel, I'm willing to ignore the horns, which I swear come off some old Kassav' album. **B+**

Mzwakhe Mbuli: *Resistance Is Defence* (Earthworks '92) South African pop moves cozy up to African-American no-

tions of sophistication, and South African pan-Africanist moves graft a fabricated tradition onto a musical history with no parallel in Africa or anywhere else. Mbuli's fusions are more visionary and more local. Singing or chanting mostly in English or Zulu but occasionally in Xhosa or Venda, his relaxed, pantribal township jive owes all the urban South African styles—mbaqanga, kwela, marabi, even a little mbube. It's pop on South Africa's own terms, too swinging for retro and too jumpy for slick. What's more, this man didn't start out as a musician—like Linton Kwesi Johnson, he's just a poet who loves music enough to do it right. Although he's not as learned as LKJ, his songs are as complete a tour of the apartheid struggle as you're likely to get without reading—and his lyric sheet is a good place to begin. **A**
Mzwakhe Mbuli: "I Am a Cloud," "I Am No Longer the Same," "Richman" (*Izigi [Footsteps],* CCP/EMI import '94) 👁
Mzwakhe Mbuli: *KwaZulu Natal* (CCP import '96) even protesting Zulu-on-Zulu violence, he's ill at ease rounding mbaqanga into a vehicle of pop reconciliation ("Freedom Puzzle," "Our Music") ★

M. C. Brains: *Lovers Lane* (Motown '92) In his dick, of course. Where else should they be, he wants to know. **B−** 🦃

Martina McBride: "Independence Day" (*The Way That I Am,* RCA '93) 👁
Martina McBride: *Wild Angels* (RCA '95) a marriage manual like only Nashville can make them ("Crying on the Shoulder of the Road," "All the Things We've Never Done") ★★

Paul McCartney: *Run Devil Run* (Capitol '99) I don't want to call McCartney the most complacent rock and roller in history. The competition's way too stiff, especially up around his age, and anyway, I'm not judging his inner life, only his musical surface. From womp-bom-a-loo-mom to monkberry moon delight, his rockin' soul and pop lyricism always evinced facility, not feeling, and his love songs were, as he so eloquently put it, silly. This piece of starting-over escapism isn't like that at all, as, robbed of the wife he loved with all his heart, McCartney returns to the great joy of his adolescence in a literally death-defying formal inversion. So light it's almost airborne, Gene Vincent's "Blue Jean Baby" opens; so wild it's almost feral, Elvis Presley's "Party" closes. Some familiar titles are merely redone or recast, which beyond some Chuck Berry zydeco gets him nowhere. But arcana like Fats Domino's "Coquette" and Carl Perkins's "Movie Magg" could have been born yesterday, three originals dole out tastes of strange, and on two successive slow sad ones, the Vipers' hung-up obscurity "No Other Baby' and Ricky Nelson's lachrymose hit "Lonesome Town," the impossibility of the project becomes the point. Teenagers know in some recess of their self-involvement that their angst will have a next chapter, but McCartney's loneliness is permanent. Not incurable—the music is a kind of new life. But its fun is a spiritual achievement the man has never before approached. **A–**

K. McCarty: *Dead Dog's Eyeball* (Bar/None '94) 🄝

Mary McCaslin: *Things We Said Today: The Best of Mary McCaslin* (Philo '92) progressive schoolmarm as spirit of the West ("The Bramble and the Rose," "Last Cannonball") ★★

Audra McDonald: *Way Back to Paradise* (Nonesuch '98) Compared to Streisand, Garland, and Callas, said to augur a New Era of Popular Song, this two-time Tony winner proudly situates her big range and Juilliard technique on the far side of the chasm now separating Broadway theater from American music. Aficionados may follow the (satiric?) logic of, for instance, the sudden high note that punctuates the Adam Guettel–William Makepeace Thackeray trifle "A Tragic Story." But we who prefer our singing speechlike will figure she's just showing off again, which given the songs is per-fectly appropriate. Ignorant of groove, eschewing verse-chorus-bridge, orchestrated to suggest the demon jazz only insofar as 20th-century European composition mooched off it, these are not tunes playgoers will hum as they flag cabs on West 45th Street. They are the sterile spawn of Stephen Sondheim and Ned Rorem, and although they signify little when sundered from their paltry dramatic contexts, serious they remain—what few comic moments they countenance duck their heads as McDonald prepares for her next octave leap. **C+** 🦃

Reba McEntire: *It's Your Call* (MCA '93) There's no point expecting scintillation—even her new best-of doesn't have more than two-three zingers on it. So what's most irksome about this dull, bland megahit is what it says about the new Nashville. Reba has her pride, and "For Herself," written with two other women, remains an honorable female-autonomy vignette even after you forget the tune (a good thing, because the song hasn't ended yet). But genderwise she's about as adventurous as Clint Black or Alan Jackson—just right for a world where Wynonna Judd is a protofeminist heroine. **C+** 🦃

Reba McEntire: "Please Come to Boston" (*Starting* Over, MCA '95) 🕳

Kate & Anna McGarrigle: *Heartbeats Accelerating* (Private Music '90) your living room has a computer, theirs has a synthesizer ("I Eat Dinner," "Love Is") ★★★

Kate & Anna McGarrigle: *Matapedia* (Hannibal '96) With their mom in the ground and their kids grown up, these tart schoolmarms manqué are left with the sun in the morning and the moon at night, both of which have their drawbacks. So they ponder the tangled history of folk music and their own irretrievable pasts, indulge their fatalism about serial monogamy and the poor getting poorer, and sum up their message in two terse titles with songs attached: "I Don't Know" and "Why Must We Die?" And now, if you'd care to come upstairs, they'd just as soon make love. Save the postmortems for morning. Which always comes, for better or worse. **A–**

Kate & Anna McGarrigle: *The McGarrigle Hour* (Hannibal '98) The secret message of this family get-together, which literalizes the well-tended domesticity underlying every record they've made, is that self-expression is for kids. Let Rufus and Martha confess and emote, and sure, jolly Uncle Chaim into going public with that lonely tune of his, it's so modest it'll fit right in. Because what the grownups in charge are after is songs per se, songs of every provenance and orientation. Berlin and Porter and Foster at their most quiet and obscure, folk songs from hither and yon, that hootenanny refrain they were once so sick of, good old "Young Love." Loudon has no choice but to sing his heart out for once, and Linda is so peripheral she wonders why she dropped in. By the time Martha hits that impossible high note on a slow-dance finale originally cribbed from Schubert and Liszt for *Earl Carroll's Vanities of 1931,* we know she's not putting Mom and Dad on notice. She's just loving the song, loving the song. **A–**

Tim McGraw: *Not a Moment Too Soon* (Curb '94) McGraw draws his phony drawl so tight he sounds like a singing penis, or at least one of those guys who can make his prepuce mime the Pledge of Allegiance when his boner is right. He got interested in country when he heard about farmer's daughters, and learned everything he knows about Choctaws and Chippewas from Chief Nokahoma. Still hasn't outearned his daddy, though. **C+** 🦃

Tim McGraw: "She'll Have You Back" (*A Place in the Sun,* Curb '99) 🌑

Roger McGuinn: *Live from Mars* (Hollywood '97) 🎸

MC Hammer: "U Can't Touch This" (*Please Hammer Don't Hurt 'Em,* Capitol '90) 🌑

Hammer: "Brothers Hang On," "Street Soldiers," "Good to Go" (*Too Legit to Quit,* Capitol '92) 🌑

Joey McIntyre: *Stay the Same* (C2 '99) After taking in Girls Against Boys' incisive analysis of the culture-killing boypop scam in *The Nation,* which certainly needed the heads-up, I sought a class enemy to hit on, but the best I could do was this mildly annoying Old Kid. Featureless funk holds up an album that rode to gold on the back of the overstated title ballad. It's not even tripe—more in the line of twaddle, only less pretentious. Right, he should act his age like his ex-bandmate Jordan, and deserves the obscurity to which he will soon return. But in a world that contains George W. Bush, we're well advised to figure out at just what point bland feel-goodism becomes murder. **B–** 🦃

Freddy McKay: "Keep Your Mouth Shut" (*Holy Ground: Alvin Ranglin's GG Records* [comp], Heartbeat '90) 🌑

Loreena McKennitt: *The Mast and the Mirror* (Warner Bros. '94) 🎸

Brian McKnight: "You Should Be Mine" (*Anytime,* Mercury '97) 🌑

Sarah McLachlan: *Surfacing* (Arista '97) Fearing serial tsunamis of subcosmic truism and womanist gush, I'd always kept away from the edge of this Canadian, such as it was. But between her Lilith Fair counterpalooza and "Building a Mystery" bonanza, I had to dive in, and got less than I'd bargained for. McLachlan isn't a mystic, a sister, even a New Ager—merely a singer-songwriter of monumental banality. Now ensconced in the mature satisfactions that come eventually to many unhappy young women, most of whom don't possess a clear multioctave voice or modest tune sense, she's proud to encase her homilies of succor and self-acceptance in settings that don't call undue attention to her compositional ambitions. Renormalized pop at its most unnecessary. **C–** 🦃

Malcolm McLaren: *Paris* (No!/Gee Street '95) Situationism? Get real. This is the Paris of feelthy pictures, of Chirac jingles, of jazzbolism as jungle fever, of a climacteric dickhead tunelessly mimicking latter-day yé-yé girls. It didn't sell—why in the world should it? Problem is—the old hustler is beyond sales. All he wants is loads of publicity and enough of somebody else's money to get Catherine Deneuve within range of a copped feel. Presumably, Deneuve can fend for herself. What kills me is that my punk-besotted colleagues can't. Suggested parental advisory: "Features nine-track bonus CD containing ambient remixes." C 🦃

G. W. McLennan: *Watershed* (Beggars Banquet '91) The Go-Between with the weakness for wilderness was Robert Forster, a thoughtful guy given to rambling through the melodic underbrush. McLennan was the hooky one, and though at first I found his solo music irritatingly prefab, his techno tendencies have grown on me like a good Go-Betweens tune—the synthy guitar and hot drum programming put welcome glitz and steel into his romantic verse. In "Haven't I Been a Fool?" he's scrambling to cement the relationship he undermined. In "Just Get That Straight" he's trying to make the break final. In between he gets out of himself a lot. **A–**

G. W. McLennan: *Fireboy* (Beggars Banquet import '93) living tunes in studio-rock amber ("The Dark Side of Town," "Riddle in the Rain," "Whose Side Are You On?") ★★

Grant McLennan: *Horsebreaker Star* (Beggars Banquet/Atlantic '95) The pop Go-Between cut his most consistently catchy solo album by getting off the plane in Georgia and recording 30 snapshots of a resigned romantic, every damn one he had, with a producer and musicians he'd never met. The U.S. version borrows one track off the import-only *Fireboy* while dropping six from the worldwide double-CD, unrolling tune after sweet, simple-seeming tune for 77 minutes. My favorite lines involve, of all things, songs: "Really loved the one about those L.A. freaks/Did it take a day to write or was it weeks?"; runner-up is one of 24 examples of "Lovers living on what went wrong": "You can't find a kidney in Hong Kong." With too many backing vocals, not enough licks, and a rather mild lead singer, the pleasures emerge gradually, mmm by mmm and aha by aha. But play these songs five years from now and every one will be yours. **A–**

Grant McLennan: *In Your Bright Ray* (Beggars Banquet '97) 🅝

MC Lyte: *Act Like You Know* (Atlantic '91) knows what she knows ("When in Love," "All That") ★★

MC Lyte: *Ain't No Other* (First Priority '93) An around-the-way girl who's always dissed the gangsta life from a street perspective, her greatest charm is the ordinariness that's also her biggest liability. In 1991, with Latifah and Monie Love passing her by, she failed to go pop with *Act Like You Know;* in 1993, with Latifah and Monie Love falling off, she's acting like she knew: "Never ever have I ever said I was good-lookin'/Just one bad-ass bitch from Brooklyn." But finally she's hitting her self-conceived rhymes and beats with some regularity—on the turf-proud "Brooklyn," the jilted-and-glad "Lil Paul," the bloodied-and-unbowed "I Go On," the jovial "F—k That M—— F—kin' Bulls—t." And on the boy-loving "Ruffneck," over a male chorus cheering like the studio was a football terrace, Lyte raps the praises of her hardcore boyfriend. "Fiddling with his dickhead" or sneaking away from the cops, he's always rude and not always what he pretends to be, but when she's got a problem: "He'll be there/Right by my side with his ruffneck tactics." I hope so. Because they're going to need each other. **A–**

MC Lyte: *Bad As I Wanna B* (EastWest '96) as sane as Chuck D, plus she likes to have her toes sucked ("TRG [The Rap Game]," "Everyday") ★★

MC Lyte: *Seven & Seven* (EastWest '98) Missy-of-the-Year jump start, '70s-funk cruise control ("In My Business," "Top Billin' ") ★★★

MC Ren: *Shock of the Hour* (Ruthless '93) Ren isn't as half-assed or bald-faced as Eazy-E. But at least Eazy serves the social function of attacking Dr. Dre—while his delightful inner-sleeve photo of his homie in sequins and eye makeup doesn't make Dre a "bitch," and wouldn't make him less a man if it did (though it may help explain Dre's, what shall we call it, insecurity around women), I figure the more energy these characters devote to tearing each other down the less we do. Ren, on the other hand, raps as dully as Dre himself—his blunt instrument doesn't approach the loud arrogance or thick timbre of, to choose an example strictly at random, Tim Dog's "F—k Compton." His rhymes are dumbass. To save on publishing he leaves most of the beats to his boys. And oy, what concepts. On side one he brutalizes black people, especially but by no means exclusively black women (sample witticism: "Your pussy really stinks/Who the fuck bought you drinks?"). Then, to cover his tracks, he turns around and spouts the most ignorant, racist Afrocentric bullshit yet to hit the charts. Not only does he daydream about the random slaughter of "Caucasians," he also advocates the murder of any black person disloyal enough to befriend them. Hey—I know those people. **D** 🦃

Meat Beat Manifesto: *99%* (Mute '90) Its relentlessness ineluctable rather than sadistic, its pessimism cut with sardonic whimsy, its multistructures pop enough, its electrobeats funky enough, this is dance-industrial that doesn't just seem like a good idea at the time. Whenever things get too skeletal here comes—well, if not one of the preclimaxes dance rats live for, maybe a laugh line, a tune, a Horace Silver sample. Never before have synthesizers sounded like a well-tempered sheet-metal shop for a whole album at a time. Play loud. **A–**

Meat Beat Manifesto: *Satyricon* (Mute '92) 💣

Meat Loaf: *Bat out of Hell II: Back to Hell* (MCA '93) this time he plays it for laffs ("Life Is a Lemon and I Want My Money Back," "Everything Louder than Everything Else") ★

Meat Puppets: *No Strings Attached* (SST '90) "I got a shirt that cost a dollar twenty-five/I know that I'm the best-dressed man alive," sings the same goof—well, sounds more like his brother, but only their mom cares—who gets lost on the freeway/in the breezeway and escapes Satan's lake of fire in a swimming hole that sounds like heaven itself. How did music so resilient bubble out of the desert wastes? How did music so sweet top hardcore mess? No one ever accused them of reliability, but in this astutely compiled account, having established their noisy principles and done "Tumblin' Tumbleweeds" as Sid's "My Way," they never touch the ground. Amerindie at its most blessed. **A**

Meat Puppets: "Six Gallon Pie" (*Forbidden Places,* London '91) 🍬

Meat Puppets: *Too High to Die* (London '94) if tunes were everything, they'd be famous ("Comin' Down," "Shine") ★

Meat Puppets: *No Joke!* (London '95) Ⓝ

Meat Puppets: *Live in Montana* (Rykodisc '99) Ⓝ

The Meat Purveyors: *Sweet in the Pants* (Bloodshot '97) alt because Nashville can't convey their desperation and rage, high mountain "Burnin' Love" notwithstanding ("Dempsey Nash," "Go Out Smokin' ") ★★

The Meat Purveyors: *More Songs About Buildings and Cows* (Bloodshot '99) bluegrass with attitude—radical, maybe even lesbian attitude ("More Man," "Travel and Toil") ★★★

Mecca Normal: *Sitting on Snaps* (Matador '95) 💣

Mecca Normal: *The Eagle and the Poodle* (Matador '96) Humorless, devoid of rebop, admired by a pretentious minority of an alt-rock subculture already way too full of itself, Jean Smith is a typical avant-garde hustler, her self-promotion harmless as long as innocent bystanders don't get guilt-tripped into deciding she gives them a thrill. I prefer her poetry to her songs because it's over faster, and because I can absorb it without hearing David Lester's freeee guitar. Naive interviewer (and jerk): "Do you listen to any music that you would consider obscure or different?" Smith: "I'm not really into all that record crap to tell you the truth." **C** 🦃

Medeski Martin & Wood: *Friday Afternoon in the Universe* (Gramavision '95) Supporters apologize for calling this stuff "eclectic" not because the cliché embarrasses them, but because they know the band's much-bruited groove will sound suspiciously like a hodgepodge to heathens like me. Bad Brubeck, Jimmy Smith as fusion, musique concrète ordinaire, soundtracks for arty shorts about urban hyperactivity—it's all these things and more, one after the other in apparent perpetuity. Please let me out of the basement before they think of something new. **B–** 🦃

Joe Meek: *It's Hard to Believe: The Amazing World of Joe Meek* (Razor & Tie '95) damn right he's like Phil Spector—Spector wasn't all he's cracked up to be either (the Tornados, "Telstar"; the Honeycombs, "Have I the Right") ★

The Mekons: *F.U.N. '90* (A&M '90) Such traditionalists yet such parodists, such idealists yet such cynics—such pomo conflaters. Their latest interim EP is another all-cover job: Robbie Robertson as Gram Parsons, Kevin Coyne as Sally Timms, the supposedly trad. arr. "Sheffield Park," and a hotel-room vocal by Lester Bangs turned muffled centerpiece of . . . what have we here? A dance record, maybe they think—except for the "country" song, every track motorvates off an atypically insistent and/or electronic riff or obbligato. So maybe it isn't interim

after all—maybe it marks one of their big transitions. And maybe it's a goof. **A–**

Mekons: *The Curse of the Mekons* (Blast First import '91) Repulsed after storming capitalism's citadels with the well-named *Rock 'n' Roll,* they fall back exhausted, dissociated, spewing analysis and country songs and putting more oomph into the latter. The same Sally Timms who sounds suspiciously like Susie Honeyman outlining the history of the heroin trade delivers John Anderson's putatively apolitical "Wild and Blue" like a sybil at a battered women's shelter; the same Tom Greenhalgh who calls out a "bourgeois sorcerer" in a bemused falsetto praises "magic, fear, and superstition" as lustily as George Jones. Yet they continue to face down bourgeois sorcerers, earning the right to thank Jesus that "beer" rhymes with "career." **A–**

Mekons: *I Love Mekons* (Quarterstick '92) Right, love songs, laid out casually across disc and lyric sheet—a country album without a happy ending. Jon and Tom are too cynical, but they're not too callow, so their scenarios generate recognizable permutations of lust if not ecstasy, emotion if not devotion, and when Sally Timms sings about that "Millionaire," they sound like the great old pros they are. Too often, though, love just doesn't seem like their subject—the only time the music achieves carnal knowledge of the message is on the sarcastic "Special" and the confused "I Don't Know." **B+**

Mekons: *Retreat from Memphis* (Quarterstick '94) Ⓝ

Mekons: "Men United," "Have a Go If You Think You're Hard Enough" (*Me,* Quarterstick '98) 🐢

Mekons: *I Have Been to Heaven and Back: Hen's Teeth and Other Fragments of Unpopular Culture Vol. 1* (Quarterstick '99) Once table scraps, now a damn fine buffet, ranging from superb songs done dirt by label politics to intelligent songs that never erupt to an outtake from *The Mekons Story,* which is kind of like saying a reject from the Bad News Bears ("Roger Troutman," not a Zapp ref-

erence, worth preserving). Tastier orts include the ghostwritten autobiography of Sally Timms, a Rod Stewart cover, well-conceived donations to Rock for Choice and a "Lounge Ax" benefit, and a techno-rock football cheer. **A–**
Mekons: "Fancy," "1967 Revisited," "Where Were You?" (*Where Were You? Hen's Teeth and Other Lost Fragments of Popular Culture Vol. 2,* Quarterstick '99) 🐝

Melky Sedeck: *Sister and Brother* (MCA '99) conscious siblings though they may be, they do sex best ("Shake It," "Attraction") ★

John Mellencamp: "Love and Happiness," "Get a Leg Up" (*Whenever We Wanted,* Mercury '91) 🐝
John Cougar Mellencamp: *Human Wheels* (Mercury '93) 💣
John Cougar Mellencamp with Me'Shell NdegéOcello: "Wild Nights" (*Dance Naked,* Mercury '94) 🐝
John Mellencamp: *The Best That I Could Do 1978–1988* (Mercury '97) the best that he could do was all he ever was—a well-meaning cornball with Kenny Aronoff in his band ("Jack and Diane," "Small Town") ★

Little Jack Melody with His Young Turks: *On the Blank Generation* (Four Dots '92) ⓝ

Melvins: *Stoner Witch* (Atlantic '94) I know why they retain their aura of hip. It's because the drummer comes from Aberdeen and used to play in Nir . . . no no, that can't be it—oh, I remember, it's that they're pure. They're always slow, always ugly, always protodeath, always proto-industrial. And always slow. Faster here, actually, up to Sabbath speed at times, with nine minutes of din at the end to shore up their cred. If you're young and depressed and too bright or not too bright, this sound may speak to your condition, and far be it from me to suggest volunteering for Rock the Vote instead. The rest of us can read about them. **C** 🦟

E. T. Mensah: *Day by Day* (Retroafric '92) This isn't the music that revolutionized Ghanaian highlife circa 1948—it's the music that rationalized it a decade or so later. On the sweeter, simpler, early-'50s *All for You,* you can hear how Mensah must have jolted local swing worshipers when he pared down the horn sections and added beaters and shakers from Cuba and Trinidad. But like so many musicianly concepts, his synthesis flowers as his players gain assurance and chops, and for that matter so do his songs, rendered in six different languages and (at least) five different rhythms. Though the segue from the Twi "Traditional" "Kaa No Wa" to the Spanish "Congo" "Senorita" is genuinely surprising, it also makes perfect sense. It sounds like an artist at ease in a world of music that exfoliates out from the place he calls home. **A–**

Natalie Merchant: *Tigerlily* (Elektra '95) ⓝ

Freddie Mercury & Montserrat Caballe: *Barcelona* (Hollywood '92) I can't deny it because I catch myself grinning—distanced in years, and with the campy kicks magnified by a heightened awareness of Freddie Mercury's sexuality, the music of Queen has accrued the high gloss of committed kitsch, where that of Journey, say, has assumed the dull shapelessness of utter crap. Although I don't enjoy all of *Classic Queen* or *Queen's Greatest Hits*—the material's not quite that deep—they're often funny and they're also pop, oddly reminiscent of top-grade Cheap Trick. So lest anyone suspect me of sentimentalizing the dead, let me isolate this resurrected cult item, proof that you don't have to be homophobic to hate opera fantasies. Mercury's voice, unnecessarily strong and pure by rock standards, sounds like a ragged old thing up against that of a true diva well past her prime, while the diva trips over the elementary rhythmic demands of the Brian May–less material, which imparts new meaning to the concept of not quite that deep. **C–** 🦟

Mercury Rev: *Deserter's Songs* (V2 '98) Reluctant to elevate Radiohead into a first cause, I blamed their pompous whisper first on arena-rock, then classical music. But in fact it's something newer: the album that became inevitable as soon as rock and rollers began allowing as how, damn it, they really *liked* Ennio Morricone. Say hello to—and not for the last time, God help us—soundtrack-rock. Just don't ask what it's the soundtrack *to*. **C+** 🦃

Metallica: *Metallica* (Elektra '91) 💣
Metallica: *Load* (Elektra '96) One of the nice things about being old is that I'm neither wired to like metal nor tempted to fake it. Just as I figured, these here-come-the-new-heroes-same-as-the-old-heroes could no more make a "grunge" album than they could do double-entry bookkeeping. Grunge simply isn't their metier. So no matter what riff neatniks think, for outsiders this is just a metal record with less solo room, which is good because it concentrates their chops, and more singing, which isn't because they can't. **C+** 🦃

Pat Metheny: *Zero Tolerance for Silence* (DGC '94) 💣

Method Man: *Tical* (Def Jam '94) I dunno—maybe he's a great rapper because he doesn't distract from the beats ("Bring the Pain," "All I Need") ★
Method Man: "Suspect Chin Music," "Sweet Love," "You Play Too Much" (*Tical 2000: Judgement Day*, Def Jam '98) 🔊

Method Man/Redman: *Blackout!* (Def Jam '99) "Turn the rap game into WCW" ("Blackout," "Run 4 Cover") ★★★

Busi Mhlongo & Twasa: *Babhemu* (Stern's Africa '94) amandla ("Izinziswa," "Mfaz Onga Phesheya") ★★★

George Michael: *Listen Without Prejudice: Vol. 1* (Columbia '90) Who has this boy been listening to? Morrissey? Anita Baker? June Christie? Harry Connick Jr.?

Whatever the sleazy details, his announced decision to hold off on the dance music till next time half proves he doesn't know as much about stardom as he thinks, and the ruminations with which he proclaims his seriousness finish the job. As a public figure he's no Bono or Boy George—he's a good-looking, replaceable teenybop idol. So only teenyboppers, and not too damn many of those, are likely to care that he feels demeaned by false fame. It's as a musician that he's won respect, and not even a pop musician—a dance musician. Ironic, isn't it, that the danciest thing here is yoked to (and undercut by) his highly unoriginal thoughts on this matter? And though the McCartneyesque "Heal the Pain" sounds like a hit ballad, most of this cocktail music is no more interesting than the cipher who sings it so "well." I'm betting it doesn't move a quarter of *Faith*'s units, which ought to enhance his appreciation of dance music pronto. **C+** 🦃

Midi, Maxi & Efti: *Midi, Maxi & Efti* (Columbia '92) ragamuffin world-pop, Anglophone Ethiopian-Swedish division— light as a feather, sank like a stone ("Ragga Steady," "Poppadink Tribe") ★★

Bette Midler: "From a Distance" (*Some People's Lives*, Atlantic '90) 🔊
Bette Midler: "From a Distance," "In My Life," "One for My Baby (And One More for the Road)" (*Experience the Divine: Greatest Hits*, Atlantic '93) 🔊
Bette Midler: *Bathhouse Betty* (Warner Bros. '98) reclaiming her integrity if not—waddaya want?—her edge ("I'm Beautiful," "Lullaby in Blue") ★

The Mighty Sparrow: *We Could Make It Easy If We Try* (BLS '92) Ⓝ
Mighty Sparrow: *Dancing Shoes* (Ice '93) 💣
Mighty Sparrow: *Volume One* (Ice '93) Thirteen varied songs from Slinger Francisco, this hemisphere's most underutilized musical resource. They slip only slightly with "Calypso Twist," the first of his

many unflappable attempts to keep up with the rhythmic times, and the best of these lyrics stand with anyone's: "Congo Man," a wildly perverse piss-take on African roots, interracial revenge, interracial sex, male-female relations, and cannibalism, or the education satire "Dan Is the Man (In the Van)." Sparrow's career as a sympathetic critic of democratic socialism begins with "Our Model Nation" and "Federation." And while Yank-lover putdowns like "Jean and Dinah," "Jack Palance," and "Don't Go Joe" incur feminist dismay, they're about the pain of imperialism, not the treachery of woman. **A+**

Mighty Sparrow: *Volume Two* (Ice '93) Daisann McLane, aka Lady Complainer, believes the most impressive thing about Sparrow is that back-stabbing Trinidadians still consider him theirs. With his suave delivery, he's a superstar synthesizer like Frank Sinatra, moving confidently from the tourist-board "Pan Man" to the Brooklyn-minded "Calypso Boogaloo," the come-fly-with-me exotic "Oriental Touch" to the she'll-fly-to-mas sexy "Same Time, Same Place." But it's hard to imagine the Chairman daring the equivalent of "Sparrow Dead"—much less observing "These good citizens are the architects of economic slavery." **A–**

Mighty Sparrow: *Volume Three* (Ice '93) too long on "Soca Man" and "Boogie Beat" ("Idi Amin," "King Kong") ★★

Mighty Sparrow: *Volume Four* (Ice '95) He's always urbane, good-humored, devilishly at ease, and like most professional hitmakers, he isn't averse to coasting—"Sailor Man," "Dear Sparrow," "Trinidad Carnival." But as a born word man he usually gets something going even when he doesn't come up with a horn part or choral hook, and even when his lyrics are predictable, his music is usually a pleasure. If there are no works of world-historic genius hidden away on his fourth semirandom best-of, the logocentric really ought to hear "Well Spoken Moppers" anyway. **A–**

Mighty Sparrow & Lord Kitchener: *16 Carnival Hits* (Ice '93) road marches, mostly—kind of like disco songs about going to the disco (Mighty Sparrow, "May May"; Lord Kitchener, "Rain-O-Rama") ★

Buddy Miller: *Cruel Moon* (HighTone '99) Ⓝ

Paul D. Miller: *Death in Light of the Phonograph* (Asphodel '96) 💣

Steve Miller Band: *Wide River* (Polydor '93) Anyone naive enough to believe there's nothing more distasteful than a middle-aged man pretending his hormones are too much for him has never encountered a middle-aged man trying to act cute. Especially if he's also a middle-aged white "bluesman" who compares himself to Picasso whilst suing black people who sample his hooks. **C** 🎺

Ministry: *In Case You Didn't Feel Like Showing Up (Live)* (Sire '90) For fanatics and curiosity seekers, a 40-minute "mini" showcasing these professional anarchists' six most gripping, ripping songs. If you can't vote yet you're still too old for their brains-to-the-wall barrage—it vents aggressions so immature they're barely articulate, triggered by the political frustration that makes voting so meaningless these days. But once you regain consciousness it'll leave you humming, in a fragmented kind of way. You like your rock hard, right? So why the hell aren't you curious? **A–**

Ministry: *Psalm 69: The Way to Succeed and the Way to Suck Eggs* (Sire/Reprise '92) Like the good orthodox category-haters you'd figure, these perverts claim they're not industrial, which is true only in the sense that Led Zeppelin wasn't metal: they may be too good for the category, but that doesn't mean they're not of it. And like Led Zep, they're cold bastards who are worth your time even if you think you don't like what they do, which is toning up your cardiovascular system by running you over with a tank. Their rockism is checked somewhat this time by a meticulousness that may put off casual sympathizers, but from synth-ooze to caterwaul, the care they put into their din connects as an aural wit that complements and undercuts their over-the-top doom-mongering. You don't laugh with them and you don't laugh at them—you just throw back your head in glee at the unlikely fact that they exist. **A–**

Ministry: *Filth Pig* (Warner Bros. '96) As a joke about disco and a joke about heavy, Al Jourgenson's dance-industrial had some wit to it. Here the motherfucker realizes that metalheads will throw money at you long after your hip cachet has gone the way of your hard-on. Result, not counting the funnier-than-shit "Lay Lady Lay": a grindcore album worth hating. **C** 🦃

Missing Foundation: *Ignore the White Culture* (Restless '90) OK, if you say so—but only if you promise your feelings won't get hurt. **D** 🦃

Joni Mitchell: *Night Ride Home* (Geffen '91) 🎯
Joni Mitchell: "Last Chance Lost" (*Turbulent Indigo,* Reprise '94) 🐢
Joni Mitchell: *Hits* (Reprise '96) Would it were modesty that inspired her to release the hour-long *Hits* and *Misses* rather than the usual multi-CD doorstop. But given that she's fed her enormous ego hunks of what was once an equally enormous talent for 20 years now, figure the opposite. Unable to abide the thought of superseding any portion of her catalogue, much less adjudging some of it less worthy than the rest, the Grammy-winning *Billboard* and BMI awardee elected to concentrate beloved older songs in one compilation and leaden newer ones in another. The result is an uncommonly fabulous educational tool for the Ani DiFranco fan on your list that does more for the two post-1980 items it tacks on than *Misses* does for the seven that weigh it down. But since the cream of the 15 selections can also be found on her four prime early-'70s albums—*For the Roses, Court and Spark, Blue,* and *Ladies of the Canyon*—it's docked a notch for in-utility. **A–**

Joni Mitchell: "Lead Balloon" (*Taming the Tiger,* Reprise '98) 🐢

Mlimani Park Orchestra: *Sikinde* (Africassette '94) two dozen or so Tanzanians groove and articulate as one highly evolved creature ("Ubaya," "Neema") ★★

Mobb Deep: *Murda Muzik* (Loud '99) "Guns, money, pussy, cars, drugs, jewels, clothes, brawls, killings, buroughs, buildings, diseases, stress, the D's." And then: "Straight reality." Yeah, right. **B–** 🦃

Moby: *Moby* (Instinct '92) trancelike or ecstatic, techno with a spirit-feel—modest and luxuriant, compelling and humane ("Go," "Electricity") ★★
Moby: *Ambient* (Instinct '93) his best since *Before and After Science* ("Heaven," "J Breas") ★★★
Moby: *Move* (Elektra '93) Ignore techno all you want, you'll still be stuck with Moby. Surrounded by meaningless glitz, he's subtle not so he won't offend but because he thinks musical sensationalism is a means to spiritual exaltation. And because he's subtle he'll be large—sooner or later he'll devise something else as universal as "Go," and when he does his label will be prepared to cross it over. Meanwhile there's this half-hour foray into the big time, keyed to the divaesque title anthem and including electronic tribal drums, drumless atmospherics, and a six-minute symphony you can dance to. **A–**
Moby: *Everything Is Wrong* (Elektra '95) Is it strange that a studio wizard of Moby's evident genius makes such flawed records? Not if he's really a dancefloor wizard—not if the communal-ecstatic is his artistic ground. Where in concert he subsumes rockist guitar and classical pretensions in grand, joyous rhythmic release, on album his distant dreams remain tangents. "What Love" challenges Metallica as incidentally as "God Moving Over the Face of the Waters" does Philip Glass, and all I can say for sometime cocomposer Mimi Goese is that she sounded even prissier in Hugo Largo. Martha

Wash, call your agent. I mean, he's a *Christian*, girl. **A−**

Moby: *Animal Rights* (Elektra '97) To his credit, the hustling little visionary didn't go for an ingratiating follow-up. With the vocals proffering all the human comfort of a loony bin, the hortatory punk with which he betrays his appointed calling assails the central nervous system even more abrasively than his electroraves did. I mean, why do you think they call both styles hardcore? But on the one-CD U.S. version the calmer techno his U.K. label relegated to a bonus disc cuts the speed-rock sex and desperation, so that the two musics enrich and play off each other with the flow and coherence *Everything Is Wrong* lacks (meaningfully, perhaps by design, but lacks nevertheless). "Alone" wouldn't assuage the way it does if just minutes earlier he hadn't been swearing "When you're fucking me it powers up my soul" in his best messiah-cum-üebermensch monotone. **A−**

Moby: *I Like to Score* (Elektra '97) 🎣

Moby: *Play* (V2 '99) I doubt the hyperactive little imp sat down and "composed" here. There are no reports he even strove to unify à la DJ Shadow. And *Endtroducing . . .* is the reference point nevertheless. It's because Moby still loves song form that he elects to sample Alan Lomax field recordings rather than garage-sale instrumental and spoken-word LPs. But though the blues and gospel and more gospel testify not just for song but for body and spirit, they wouldn't shout anywhere near as loud and clear without the mastermind's ministrations—his grooves, his pacing, his textures, his harmonies, sometimes his tunes, and mostly his grooves, which honor not just dance music but the rock tradition it's part of. Although the futurist's dream of Blind Willie Johnson that opens this complete work was some kind of hit in England, here it'll be strictly for aesthetes. We've earned it. **A+**

The Modern Lovers: *Precise Modern Lovers Order* (Rounder '94) live Harvard '71 and Berkeley '73, back when Jonathan thought cute was pretending he couldn't spell "girlfriend" ("A Plea for Tenderness," "The Mixer [Men and Women Together]," "I'm Straight") ★★★

Modest Mouse: *This Is a Long Drive for Someone with Nothing to Think About* (Up '96) Long-winded young wankers so insularly indie they're incomprehensible to anyone who hasn't been softened up by *Wowee Zowee* and the Meat Puppets, these young Northwesterners have nevertheless stumbled into their own sound. It's tuneful, so what; it's halting, even worse; it's funny, now we're getting somewhere; it's direct albeit arch, ahh youth; it's harmonically quirky, there's the nub. The nicest thing I can say about it is that in a just educational system it would earn them all music scholarships. The worst thing I can say about it is the same thing. **A−**

Modest Mouse: *The Lonesome Crowded West* (Up '97) With unadorned melody suddenly fashionable among superannuated indie-rockers who have seen the limits of both irony and techno, I still prefer my tunelets noised up. And until these become the exclusive province of undistinguisheds and indistinguishables like, oh, Versus or Polvo, I'll crow about every exception. Skirting the professional class they were born to for a poverty that's real if voluntary, these three youngsters are probably wise-asses, probably thieves. But their songs never quit even when they're divided into the kind of stylistic segments that usually irritate the hell out of me. Although their glimpses of a cockroach world living on its own discards may seem jejune to some and homely to others, the lyrics are observed, informed, and explicit enough—in fact, as brave and beautiful as the blues, albeit at a more rarefied level of cultural specificity. **A−**

Mogwai: *Come On Die Young* (Matador '99) Young Glaswegians extolled by those weary of verse-chorus-verse as "radical," "beautiful," and other things that would never occur to the rest of us, they mutate the forgettable mess of their debut into something altogether more deliberate and kempt—occasionally tuneful, invariably slow. Only on the ocean-bound land mass where acid house was Beatlemania would anyone sit still for such earnest postrock tripe. **C** 🦃

Mold: *Sonic Youth at Disney World* (Funky Mushroom '94) contra Our Anti-heroes—also Hüsker Dü, King Missile, and (duh) the Spin Doctors ("Sonic Youth in Disney World," "Bob Mould Hates Me") ★
Mold: *Reject* (Funky Mushroom '95) Henry Street settlers ("We're an Alternative Band," "Me") ★

Momus: *Ping Pong* (Le Grand Magistery '98) In one of his many clever songs, Nick Currie compares his quest for fame to God's and wonders why the big fella gets all the coverage. The answer is that God is a nicer guy. Performers like Currie believe "all interesting behaviors, whether moral or not, are salable in our culture" because they don't have much choice—it's that or a day job. But no matter how well turned the lyric, very few listeners actually enjoy songs in which snobbish dandies trot out their sexual egomania and baby envy. Deep down, most people have some cornball in them. And this is a good thing. **B–** 🦃

Money Mark: *Push the Button* (Mo Wax/London '98) 💣

Monica: *The Boy Is Mine* (Arista '98) B diva with actual vocal technique, and why not? ("The Boy Is Mine," "Misty Blue") ★

Monifah: *Moods . . . Moments* (Uptown/Universal '96) 💣
Monifah: "Touch It" (*Mo'Hogany,* Universal '98) 🦃

Monster Magnet: *Powertrip* (A&M '98) more jokes about dominance and Mr. D. ("See You in Hell," "Bummer") ★

John Michael Montgomery: *Kickin' It Up* (Atlantic '94) 💣
John Michael Montgomery: *John Michael Montgomery* (Atlantic '95)

Nashville belched up the usual candidates for ritual slaughter this year, but most of them just weren't worthy. From ten-gallon wimps like Clay Walker to Village People rejects like Tim McGraw, the hunk boom of the early '90s is already playing out, and though Clint Black could have been so much more, he still shows flashes even if he did check in with a Christmas album. This guy is slipping from lower on the evolutionary ladder and higher up on the heap. He took album three double-platinum on a bare-faced, two-fisted imitation of Garth Brooks, whom he has the gall to cut with Hank Williams Jr. Garth is great in part because he'd never give a woman a 10 or cap a well-reported verse-and-chorus about the hard labor of divorced motherhood with a covertly resentful verse about how the little lady needs a man. **C+** 🦃

Monty Python: *Monty Python Sings* (Virgin '92) Greil Marcus wrote *Lipstick Traces* over the background buzz of the comedy albums where most of this music first appeared, but I feed my absurdism jones more cautiously. So I'll save these 14 songs plus 11 jokes/fragments for whenever the specter of cosmic frailty starts getting me down—at least 20 of them tickled me first time through, and half still make me smirk four or five plays later. Rarely has any professional wag, singing group, or existentialist philosopher showed off his, her, or their reading like these too, too mortal polymaths. Their idea of a good joke is a pimple on the Milky Way or a king with his head cut off. Sex, race, and class also interest them. Inspirational Chorus: "Gonococcal urethritis, streptococcal ballinitis/Meningo myelitis, diplococcal cephalitis/Epididimitis, interstitial keratitis/Syphilitic choroiditis, and anterior u-ve-i-tis." **A–**

Thurston Moore: *Psychic Hearts* (DGC '95) bosser tunes than Free Kitten—bosser guitar too ("Queen Bee and Her Pals," "Ono Soul") ★

Morcheeba: *Who Can You Trust?* (Discovery '96) A brother who's into blues, a brother who's into technology, and a sister (no relation) who sings so kind and calm there's a temptation to brand her bland. Believe me, that's just her soul talking. She and her place-setters are always thoughtful, often sad, rarely neurotic, never scary. Their record listens so easy you don't want me to classify it as trip hop, and neither do I. But that's what it is. **A–**

Morcheeba: *Big Calm* (Sire/China '98) **Ⓝ**

Lorrie Morgan: *Something in Red* (RCA '91) 🗡

Lorrie Morgan: "The Things We Do" (*My Heart,* BNA '99) 🖤

Alanis Morissette: *Jagged Little Pill* (Maverick/Reprise '95) I was down with the Riot Grrrl Appreciation Society on this reluctant refugee from Canadian children's television, who some say was invented by Madonna herself so she could distract the publicity machine while raising her own biological girl. That is, I approved when she played the pissed-off spikehead and recoiled from such candid self-dramatizations as "Perfect" and "Mary Jane." But with help from six or seven arrantly effective songs, she's happy to help 15 million girls of many ages stick a basic feminist truth in our faces: privileged phonies have identity problems too. Not to mention man problems. **B+**

Alanis Morissette: *Supposed Former Infatuation Junkie* (Maverick/Reprise '98) If "pop" means anything anymore, it ain't this. As a SoundScan-certified megadeal, she's outgrown the bright appeal of pop the way she's outgrown the punky abrasions that gave the debut its traction off the blocks. The mammoth riffs, diaristic self-analysis, and pretentious Middle Eastern sonorities of this music mark it as "rock," albeit rock with tunes. And in this context I suck it up, feeling privileged to listen along with all the young women whose struggles Morissette blows up to such a scale. Here's hoping lots of young men feel the same. **A–**

Alanis Morissette: *MTV Unplugged* (Maverick '99) why do you think they love her? because she's lovable, stupid ("Princes Familiar," "You Learn") ★

Morphine: "Thursday" (*Cure for Pain,* Rykodisc '93) 🖤

Joe Morris: *Sweatshop* (Riti '90) through-improvised instrumental rock as per postharmolodic jazz guitarist ("Teeming Millions," "Well Put") ★★

Joe Morris/Ken Vandermark/Hans Poppel: *Like Rays* (Knitting Factory Works '98) 🗡

Van Morrison: *Enlightenment* (Mercury '90) Only a perverse motherfucker would choose such a title for an album whose title refrain goes "Don't know what it is." What's he trying to do, fake out the satori market? Also: orchestras, the names of r&b singers, a weird recitative about the radio, and other tried-and-trues, all executed with faith, hope, and charity. Inspirational Verse: "In my soul, in my soul, in my soul." **B+**

Van Morrison: *Bang Masters* (Epic/Legacy '91) New York 1967—hungry young Irishman spouts blues poetry in a roomful of session pros ("T. B. Sheets," "Brown Eyed Girl," "The Back Room") ★★★

Van Morrison: *Hymns to the Silence* (Mercury '91) The usual wealth of fertilizer spread over two shortish CDs, long on love songs and the aforementioned hymns—wish the rejected title *Ordinary Life* was more accurate. Maybe they renamed the thing so churls like me wouldn't ask why nobody 86'd a few hymns. Like all of his recent and no doubt future work, it's slower than necessary, even in an artist of Van's advanced years. And like so much of his recent and I expect future work, it's more affecting than you'd figure. True love, eh? The simple life, huh? The days before rock and roll, did you say? Sounds kind of good. **B+**

Van Morrison: *Too Long in Exile* (Polydor '93) You know, exile—like Joyce and Shaw and Wilde and, oh yeah, Alex Haley. All on account of those "Bigtime Operators" who bugged his phone back when he was green. Now getting on to grizzled, he seeks guidance from the kas of Doc Pomus and King Pleasure and "The Lonesome Road," an unutterably sad spiritual recast as an upbeat vibraphone feature. And especially, on three cuts, his old soul mate John Lee Hooker, who doesn't come close to sounding overexposed on Them's "Gloria" and Sonny Boy's "Good Morning Little Schoolgirl" and something new by Van called "Wasted Years," about how the dumb stuff is behind them now. I don't know about Hook, but Van's just jiving—when he wanders "In the Forest," it's never a safe bet that he'll get out. **A–**

Van Morrison: *The Best of Van Morrison Volume Two* (Polydor '93) post-'84—the Great Ruminator ("Real Real Gone") ★

Van Morrison: *A Night in San Francisco* (Polydor '94) having fun with Van, John Lee, Junior, 'Spoon, Shana (Morrison), and Georgie Fame on stage ("Jumping with Symphony Sid," "Good Morning Little School Girl") ★★

Van Morrison: *Days Like This* (Polydor '95) "I'm a songwriter, and my check's in the mail" ("Songwriter," "You Don't Know Me") ★

Van Morrison with Georgie Fame & Friends: *How Long Has This Been Going On* (Verve '96) ⓝ

Van Morrison: *The Healing Game* (Polydor '97) ⓝ

Van Morrison: "Drumshanbo Hustle" (*The Philosopher's Stone,* Polydor '98) 🗑

Van Morrison: *Back on Top* (Virgin '99) ⓝ

Morrissey: *Bona Drag* (Sire/Reprise '90) To Anglophiles, Anglos, and young alternative rockers who've never known another world, Morrissey's solo singles are fraught with paradigm, but to the rest of us they're a chapter in the life of a great twit. Less secure in his delusions of grandeur and worthlessness than when he was top of the pops, he hides behind the bitchy jokes his followers consider beneath him. At least half of these fizzle-prone chart charges will amuse and excite the curiosity seeker. That any of them could be conceived as pop hits is why there are still Anglophiles. Inspirational Verse: "This is the last song I will ever sing (*yay!*)/No I've changed my mind again (*boo!*)." **B+**

Morrissey: *Kill Uncle* (Sire/Reprise '91) What kills the faithful is the anonymously supportive production, never distinctive enough to threaten (or challenge) a fading superstar in the throes of permanent identity crisis. But though they do meander into the insufferably ruminative self-pity that never used to bother Smiths fans, the songs start out plenty striking, guitar signature or no guitar signature. Tart as a grand aunt, louder on the gay subtext now that he's no longer an antipinup, Morrissey isn't just another English eccentric. He exemplifies what's made eccentricity a staple export of that once-proud nation for generations. Good show. **B+**

Morrissey: *Your Arsenal* (Sire '92) Most consistent solo set to date from talented singer-songwriter who made his name fronting popular British cult band the Smiths. Highlights include the plaintive "Seasick, Yet Still Docked," the kindly "You're the One for Me, Fatty," the cynical "Glamorous Glue," the cynical "Certain People I Know," the cynical "We Hate It When Our Friends Become Successful," and the satiric (we hope) "National Front Disco." **A–**

Morrissey: *Vauxhall and I* (Sire/Reprise '94) 💣

Morrissey: *Maladjusted* (Mercury '97) 💣

Bill Morrissey: "Inside" (*Inside,* Philo '92) 🗑

Mos Def: *Black on Both Sides* (Rawkus '99) "Building it now for the promise of the infinite," Black Star's star overreaches; delete the right tracks, which is always the catch, and his solo CD would pack more power at 55 minutes than it does at 71. I hope someday he learns that what made Chuck Berry better than Elvis Presley wasn't soul, even if that rhymes with rock and roll the way Rolling Stones rhymes with (guess who he prefers) Nina Simone. But the wealth of good-hearted reflection and well-calibrated production overwhelms petty objections. "New World Water" isn't just the political song of the year, it's catchy like a motherfucker. "Brooklyn" and "Habitat" are no less geohistorical because they act locally. **A−**

Pablo Moses: *Mission* (RAS '95) 💣

M.O.T.: *19.99* (Sire/Warner Bros. '98) Borscht Belt hip hop from Ice Berg and Dr. Dreidle, who sold their Chevy to the Levys but the Levys can't drive ("Town Car," "Double Dutch Lunch") ★★★

Mötley Crüe: *Decade of Decadence '81–'91* (Elektra '91) Ⓝ

Motorhead: *1916* (WTG '91) Sonically retrograde and philosophically advanced, this is the testimony of a mad raver at peace with his lot in the world—but not with the world, not by a long shot. As Pete Solley muddies the mix back toward classic grunge, Lemmy rages against war—sometimes in so many words, sometimes by metaphorical imprecation, sometimes by standing tall amid the barrage. But an embittered artiste he's not—riding their iron horses into the sunset, tributes to L.A., Rio, and the Ramones prove he knows how good he's got it, and prove it full-throttle. **A−**

Motorhead: *March or Die* (Epic/WTG '92) eternal rage ("Bad Religion") ★

Motorhead: *Bastards* (ZYX '93) but it's really great shtick ("On Your Feet or on Your Knees," "Born to Raise Hell") ★

Motorhead: *Snake Bite Love* (CMC International '98) 💣

Bob Mould: *Black Sheets of Rain* (Virgin '90) 💣

Bob Mould: *Bob Mould* (Rykodisc '96) Ⓝ

Bob Mould: *Egoverride* (Rykodisc '96) sole great song-sound off latest go-it-alone plus three crisply creditable outtakes equals one decent EP ("Egoverride") ★

Mouse on Mars: *Vulvaland* (Too Pure/American '94) 💣

Mouse on Mars: *Iaora Tahiti* (Too Pure/American '95) It's a shuck to apply the postfelicitous prefix "post" to instrumental rock, which has been a nothing tradition for a long time. In 1995 as so often before, chops were laughable, compositional notions paltry, big concepts quickly exhausted, and from Pell Mell to Eno/Wobble to FSOL to four out of five ambient comps to two out of three dance comps, the records weren't just forgettable, they were inconsequential. That's not true of this German duo, who care far more about details than their obvious godfathers Kraftwerk and at least as much as their vocal labelmates Pram. They may be quiet, but they ain't ambient—as background music, they're pretty irritating. Unfortunately, they're irritating up front as well. There's plenty of variety, and a well-constructed multibeat fantasia called "Saturday Night Worldcup Fieber" tickles me every time. But all this occurs within an aural universe that has little use for the left-hand three-quarters of the piano. Its philosophical roots are in the so-called space-age pop that will remain lounge-rock's legacy long after joke bands from Black Velvet Flag to Friends of Dean Martinez have moved on to prostitution or website design—the vague sound/approach now reified in a three-disc RCA exhumation, a reminder that nothing released under the auspices of a major label stays incredibly strange for long. **C+** 🦃

The Movement: *The Movement* (Arista '92) jump, jump, jump, jump, don't OD, bingo, yo mama ("Jump!," "B.I.N.G.O.") ★

M People: *Elegant Slumming* (Epic '94) Perfect records are so rare that it's foolish to cavil about the scope of the great disco album Soul II Soul and Yaz never got near (although Donna Summer did once). Each five-minute song clicks into its slot on the Michael Pickering–Paul Heard beats and hooks and special effects, with low tenor Heather Small gender-bending her diva devotion and deep, robust, confident shout over the top. What's a rock and roller to do with such music? Proud Heather puts it perfectly in her angriest moment: "Take it like a man baby if that's what you are." **A**

M People: *Bizarre Fruit* (Epic '95) Second time out they're obliged to prove their staying power—not just produce a new batch of sure shots, but add the weight of a few slow grooves and tokens of conscience, with no beginner's backlog or U.K. singles-only to fill in the blanks. So, as is only human, they don't go all the way. Michael Pickering and Steve Heard like to say that their songs are getting more soulful and meaningful, but the deepest meaning they have to offer is bound up in their formal commitment to what's most frivolous in classic disco—the fun positivity of Saturday night fever. Only the one about heroes is altogether leaden, and "Drive Time" is the radio move of every club band's prospectus. But where *Elegant Slumming* was pure pleasure machine, this stops at intensely likable—a band record rather than a producer's record, with trickier percussion and subtler hooks. **A–**

M People: *Testify* (Epic '99) four years later, 13 new tracks including five remixes—who do they think they are, Sade? ("What a Fool Believes," "Testify") ★★

The Mthembu Queens: *Emjindini* (Rounder '90) girl-group mbaqanga ("Phansi Komthunzi," "Asambeni") ★★

Oliver Mtukudzi: *Shoko* (Piranha import '92) **N**
Oliver Mtukudzi: *Tuku Music* (Putumayo Artists '99) **N**

Tshala Muana: *Soukous Siren* (Shanachie '91) A showbiz kid who broke in as a dancer, she followed a few late-'70s hits from Kinshasa to Abidjan and then Paris, where she cut her debut album in 1984. Truth to tell, her voice isn't a lot stronger than Paula Abdul's. But her music sure is, and though she does consult her arranger, hers he is—if the songwriting on this best-of doesn't prove her the most conceptually accomplished female musician in Africa, it certainly shows a hell of an ear. Varied and consistent. Catchy and uplifting. Pretty great. **A–**

Tshala Muana: *Mutuashi* (Stern's Africa '96) Out of shrewdness or raw adaptability, this spectacular dancer and savvy singer knows how to find music that does her songs proud. Here she entrusts her Luba soukous to Sahel-salsa masterminds Ibrahim Sylla and Boncana Maiga for a modernization that altogether avoids Euroschlock. Coros and montunos dominate a groove that's cut with West African instrumentation and interrupted by soft ballads, with the standard Zairean guitar peals deployed so economically that when she breaks out a Pépé Kallé cover on the next-to-last cut, it's ecstasy, and pan-Africanism in action. **A–**

Mud Boy & the Neutrons: *They Walk Among Us* (Koch '95) r&b as self-induced dementia ("Power to the People," "Money Talks") ★
Mud Boy and the Neutrons: "Money Talks" (*It Came from Memphis* [comp], Upstart '95) 🔊

Mudhoney: *Five Dollar Bob's Mock Cooter Stew* (Reprise '93) **N**

The Muffs: *The Muffs* (Warner Bros. '93) Blackhearts as Descendents or vice versa—10 years late it's hard to tell ("Lucky Guy," "Everywhere I Go") ★★
The Muffs: *Blonder and Blonder* (Reprise '95) and a damn fine formula it is ("Agony," "Oh Nina") ★★★
The Muffs: *Happy Birthday to Me* (Reprise '97) 💣

Maria Muldaur: *On the Sunny Side* (Music for Little People '90) could be (even) cuter ("Would You Like to Swing on a Star," "The Circus Song," "Never Swat a Fly") ★
Maria Muldaur: *Meet Me Where They Play the Blues* (Telarc '99) last of the red-hot mamas ("Soothe Me," "It Ain't the Meat, It's the Motion") ★

Shawn Mullins: *Soul's Core* (Columbia '98) Sincerity was smug long before irony was, and while Mullins devoted a long, honorable folk-circuit career to reinventing the feeling before he stumbled on his very own "Taxi"—six indie albums in the trunk of his car and he could still muse, "I don't know what I've been lookin' for, maybe me"—I figure he'd rather be called smug than dumb or, heaven knows, *insincere.* Pretty good at observing/concocting the kind of composite characters journalists get fired for, he's so wrought up about their humanity that he rarely captures their humor or grace. That would require establishing a distance from them, and while they may live with distance, poor souls, he can't countenance it in himself. He's like a one-night stand who feels constrained to tell you he loves you instead of making clear why he finds you attractive. Feels icky, right? **C+** 🐝

The Murmurs: *Pristine Smut* (MCA '97) Outgrowing the bland preciosity of their debut (as in "You Suck," where cute was supposed to sharpen mean and muddled it instead), showbiz kids reemerge as pro-sex lesbians with a weakness for romance and the lissome, breathy country-rock to match. Not since Liz Phair's "Flower," Janet's "Throb," and Madonna's *Erotica* has pop softcore attended so sweetly to the erogenous zones. **A−**

The Murmurs: *Blender* (MCA '98) Replaces the two filthy cuts that gave *Pristine Smut* its name with one called "La-Di-Da" that says it all and an I-had-a-hit-and-you-didn't Go-Go's collaboration. They were cuter with slime on their pudenda. Docked one notch apiece for pusillanimity. **B−** 🐝

Eddie Murphy: *Love's Alright* (Motown '93) 💣

Trish Murphy: *Crooked Mile* (Raven '97) you say you're really sick and tired of waiting for that Lucinda Williams record? ("Scorpio Tequila," "She Belongs to Me") ★

David Murray: *Shakill's Warrior* (DIW/Columbia '92) Murray is the most fluent saxophonist this side of Sonny Rollins, a far more expansive leader than King Wynton. His new big-band album serves up plenty of thrills and chills; hell, when he composes a string quartet I'll give it a shot. But I reserve the right to believe that his least pretentious record is his best. Backed by swinging beatmaster Andrew Cyrille on drums and tasty high school bandmate Stanley Franks on guitar, Murray enlists Don Pullen on organ in a knowing encomium to lounge r&b. Though too often the Hammond B-3 is a one-way ticket to Cornytown, Pullen the pianist is capable of clusters as abstract (not to say unlistenable) as Cecil Taylor's, and the tension works perfectly: his harmonic cool keeps the music honest and a little strange without ever stinting on emotion. As for Murray, you know he can blow—hot and hard, warm and soulful, sly and sleazy. He even rollicks through a Rollins-style calypso. The title tune owes Sammy Davis Jr.'s "The Candy Man." And the moody avant-garde move "Black February" swings anyway. **A+**

David Murray: *Jug-a-Lug* (DIW import '95) Recommended recent jazz titles by this endlessly resourceful if suspiciously prolific recording artist include the Malcolm tribute-quickie *MX* (Flying Dutchman), stirred and soured by Bobby Bradford's cornet; *Saxmen* (Flying Dutchman), which knocks back Young-Rollins-Parker-Rouse-Stitt-Coltrane standards guaranteed to knock new jazz fans out, and *Special Quartet* (DIW/Columbia), featuring McCoy Tyner and Elvin Jones to guess what conceptual end (start with Rhino's Coltrane box and proceed). I can also dig *Shakill's II* (DIW import), a less audaciously greasy follow-up to his first Don Pullen–drenched avant-lounge organ outing. But more to the pop point is the leap he takes here and on *The Tip,* cut during the same four-day burst: a funk band, period, or do I mean question mark-explanation point?! Imperfect for sure, but although I'd prefer it didn't swing so much, in fact the full-bodied confidence of the only-jazz that begins this set gives it the edge over *The Tip,* which never equals the Sly Stone and David Murray classics it takes off from. The drag throughout is keybman Robert Irving III, whose adoration of Joe Zawinul almost transforms *The Tip* into the darn good Weather Report album Murray's damn lucky this one ain't. The motorvator is bass-whomping Darryl Jones, who is all over this record once it gets going—most spectacularly on the loosey-goosey bass-clarinet workout "Acoustic Octo Funk," where Irving has the common sense to imitate Pullen for a while. They should have made a single album out of all this—real pop pros know an outtake when they hear one. But it frees both Branford Marsalis and Maceo Parker to go back where they came from. **A–**

David Murray Octet: *Dark Star (The Music of the Grateful Dead)* (Astor Place '96) Ⓝ

David Murray: *Fo deuk Revue* (Justin Time import '97) What generally costs African-jazz fusion its spark is that for the principals, jazz is hegemonic. However admiring the American instigator, he feels he has something to teach, and however proud his African collaborators, they adjust. In this Dakar-recorded big-band project, Murray and his New York cohort do the adjusting. After leading off with a typically attention-getting sax showcase, he hands the rhythms over to the mbalax-tinged Dieuf Dieul band and surrenders center stage to matched clarions Tidiane Gaye, Doudoud N'Daiye Rose, and Baaba Maal's brother Hamet; Dakar rappers Positive Black Soul; and the very New York–sounding Amiri Baraka. This music swings only as part of the total package, which has more forthright and complex beats to make its own. **A–**

David Murray: *Creole* (Justin Time import '98) carnivalesque as sonny idea, or, one nice thing about rock and roll is you don't have to like flutes ("Mona," "Flor Na Paul") ★★★

Maryam Mursal: *The Journey* (Real-World '98) a Somalian with a parlor trick—making Danes sound Ethiopian ("Qax," "Fejigno") ★

Music Revelation Ensemble: *In the Name of . . .* (DIW import '95) Blood Ulmer's 1977 debut *Revealing* reveals how articulately George Adams's saxophone answers his guitar and how drastically that guitar was to change—he's quickly evolved away from Montgomeryesque sonics toward blatant distortions and dense note clusters that take Hendrix down the road a piece. The rockish cult this sound attracted encouraged him to sing in a mumble of real but limited charm, and soon he was collaborating with David Murray on the most galvanizing live music I've ever heard him make. On this briefly domestic release as well as 1996's somewhat milder import-always *Knights of Power,* a horn man—Arthur Blythe on alto, Hamiet Bluiett on baritone, or (here only) Sam Rivers on soprano/tenor/flute—leaps to the fore the way Ulmer's voice ordinarily would, with the guitar chording and commenting and laying down a bed of noise more than it solos. His peak is still *Odyssey,* featuring one violin, no bass, and his finest all-around performance on record. But for a taste of how exciting he and Murray could be, listen to Bluiett blow out "The Dawn." **A–**

Charlie Musselwhite: *Continental Drifter* (Pointblank '99) Ⓝ

Mutabaruka: *Blakk Wi Blak . . . k . . . k . . .* (Shanachie '91) all-over-the-place pop genius, scattershot Rasta crank ("The People's Court," "Letter to Congress [Is It Because Wi Blakk]" ★★★

Mutabaruka: *The Ultimate Collection* (Shanachie '96) In which a health-food nut whose definitive album is a decade behind him reconstitutes himself as a people's prophet who has problems with ice cream. Only four of the 16 tracks, including the unanswerable spoken "Dis Poem," are from *The Mystery Unfolds*; there are just as many nonalbum singles, plus several worthy remixes and a live "Witeman Country." Muta's wisdom and humor greatly exceed the Rasta norm, and since he's always been dub poetry's most musical performer, the working peace he's negotiated with dancehall is no surprise. The surprise is how coherent and compelling his best music seems when it's gathered in one place awaiting humanity's attention and respect. **A**

Mu-Ziq: *In Pine Effect* (Astralwerks '95) Oh goodie—after two years of Les Baxter and Ennio Morricone assailing my precious hegemony, I finally get to apply for membership in the too-hep-to-be-square club. Sired by Esquivel out of rockist techno, it's *Another Fluorescent World,* in which moderately intricate synthbeats drain a kitschy kitchen sink of electronic harpsichords, foghorns, string quartets, bubble machines, tintinnabulations, screams, and what can only be called natural synth noises. Anything but ambient (although hum a few bars and they'll fake it for you) and not about cool, it maintains its spritz at all times, so that even the atmospheric low points sound something like fun. I miss the illusion of a centered subject that only a singer or soloist can provide, and am not overrating schlock's use value. But it's my highly complimentary guess that this schlock is way too fine to get me into the aforementioned club—or any other. **A–**

Mu-Ziq: *Urmur Bile Trax Volume 1 Volume 2* (Astralwerks '97) 🎸

Mu-Ziq: *Lunatic Harness* (Astralwerks '97) Ⓝ

Mu-Ziq: *Royal Astronomy* (Astralwerks '99) 🎸

My Bloody Valentine: *Glider* (Sire/ Warner Bros. '90) The first two cuts all but worthless, the final two murmured in a studio-stoned trance, this is the industrial New Age their organlike guitars have always promised—the reliable rhythm of a giant linoleum buffer systematically rubbing the skin off your soul. **A–**

My Bloody Valentine: *Tremolo* (Sire/ Warner Bros. '91) A four-song sampler builds off an anthem from the forthcoming *Loveless* to the spectacular guitaristics of "Honey Power," a pomo "Telstar" that shifts midway into doo-doo-doo—from which it segues into something depressive but not therefore unreminiscent of "Telstar." So take the test. Can you stand it? If so, you're ready for the longer stuff. **A–**

My Bloody Valentine: *Loveless* (Sire/ Warner Bros. '91) If you believe the true sound of life on planet earth has gotten worse than bombs bursting midair or runaway trains—more in the direction of scalpel against bone, or the proverbial giant piece of chalk and accoutrements—this CD transfigures the music of our sphere. Some may cringe at the grotesque distortions they extract from their guitars, others at the soprano murmurs that provide theoretical relief. I didn't much go for either myself. But after suitable suffering and peer support, I learned. In the destructive elements immerse. **A–**

Heather Myles: *Untamed* (HighTone '95) Ⓝ

My Life with the Thrill Kill Kult: *Sexplosion!* (Wax Trax '91) Disco-porn lite for kids who have so much trouble figuring out kink isn't sinful that they flip to the jive about how it captures the truth of male-female dynamics, patriarchal oppression, human nature, or feels-good-do-it. It beats S'Express's *Intercourse,* which must have been named after the town in Pennsylvania, but if you crave the real thing, sample the Lords of Acid's *Lust.* These Chicagoans are betting you'll feel more comfortable with a fake. In the '90s, when artists start talking both-a-parody-and-a-celebration, it's 50-50 the concept they can't put their finger on is exploitation. **C+** 🦃

Mystikal: *Mind of Mystikal* (Jive '95) Howlin' Wolf as gangsta psychopath/ boogeyman ("Y'All Ain't Ready Yet," "Here I Go") ★

Mystikal: *Unpredictable* (Jive/No Limit '97) The only No Limit rapper with a style worth talking about fires the words rough and fast, like a dancehall toaster without Jamaica, or Busta Rhymes without a sense of humor. Its boasts, doubts, and recriminations clearly audible through the gravelly buckshot of the rap, its only humanizing inflections Bernie Worrell–style hooks that hover eerily above the subwoofer boom, the CD remains unbearably intense well past the usual N.O. breaking point, leaving Mystikal one of the rare gangstas whose regrets seem powered by anything deeper than self-pity—a brush with the demonic, say. It adds a killer emotional twist by going out on what sounds like a home-recorded vocal chorus by the dead sister whose murder he'd promised to revenge an hour before. **A–** **Mystikal: "I'm on Fire"** (*Ghetto Fabulous,* Jive/No Limit '98) 🔊

M/COMPILATIONS

Magnolia (Reprise '99) Aimee Mann's most flattering setting to date, not to mention Supertramp's (Aimee Mann, "One," "You Do") ★

Make 'Em Mokum Crazy (Mokum '96) Records this idiotic don't come along every day. They don't even come along every year. Anybody remember Hot Legs' "Neanderthal Man"? I mean that idiotic. Apply the broad brush it deserves and call it *The Chipmunks Go Techno*—"Happy Tunes" in high registers that range from unnatural to very unnatural. The so-called Party Animals do *Hair* and Olivia Newton-John and "Hava Naquila" (*sic*); alias Technohead make up songs called "Happy Birthday" and "I Wanna Be a Hippy," which quotes David Peel, which has nothing on the MLK sample. Intensely irritating, perversely delightful, and (trust me on this) just the thing for a 12-year-old's coming-out party. "From The Underground Raves of Holland To The Top of The Euro Pop Charts," eh? No wonder the Euro is in trouble. **A–**

Mama Don't Allow No Easy Riders Here (Yazoo '98) Most Yazoo compilations take egalitarianism too literally, mixing the classic and the generic so that every 78 in the vault stands a fair chance of digitalization. That may happen on this collection of "Piano Rags, Blues & Stomps 1928–35" as well—note that Cow Cow Davenport's hit "Cow Cow Blues," which is definitive by definition, "will be included on a later album"—but boogie-woogie is so much more fun than country blues it doesn't matter. Beyond the distinct voices—Davenport's barrelhouse solidity, Arnold Wiley's quicksilver chromatics, Will Ezell's playful chopsmanship, Speckled Red's errant enthusiasm—a single rhythmic idea animates the flow, and just when you're tired of piano Red opens his mouth and teaches America the dozens. Plus on the ride out we have the lost Oliver Brown classic "Oh You Devil You," about which we know nothing, including how Harry Smith missed it. **A–**

Mandela (Mango '97) The heart of this soundtrack is eight pieces of ebulliently sophisticated '50s pop from South Africa's swing era, before the cultural genocide that was the razing of Sophiatown. Their lilt is like no other pop groove, a diasporan dream apartheid would soon destroy, and I pray Jumbo Vanrenen won't resist putting out a whole album of it now that he's gotten started. But while the rest is typical soundtrack hodgepodge, it's a hodgepodge of quality—from the African National Congress Choir to Johnny Clegg, from predub poet Lesoko Rempolokeng to pop queen Brenda Fassie. Perhaps most important, the "original score" interludes recognize that South Africa's classic tradition is choral, not symphonic. The Choir Gauteng A Team has the chops to tell Mambazo the news. **A–**

M-Boogie: Laid in Full (Blackberry '99) here comes the West Coast underground, sunnier than the East Coast underground (Kut Master Kurt Presents Masters of Illusion Featuring Motion Man, "Magnum Be I"; Rasco Featuring Defaro & Evidence, "Major League") ★

Mbuki Mvuki (Original Music '93) Formally, this is more sampler than compilation—23 tastes of an Afrocentric catalogue that's long on cultural idiosyncrasy, highlighting many Islamic and Caribbean genres and several so local they're barely commodified. You figure that even if it induces some inquisitive soul to try *Tumba, Cuarta and Kai* and *Songs the Swahili Sing*—or, more fruitfully, *Azagas and Archibogs* and *The Kampala Sound*—there's no way so much weirdness can hang together. But back in the '70s, when *Africa Dances* made the entire sub-Sahara its oyster, it wasn't just because we didn't know any better that we didn't notice the clash of styles. The unifying force was John Storm Roberts's passion for the simple melody and the folk-pop cusp—the best term I can think of for the fusion of village ways and urban overload, naive curiosity and pancultural daring, that permeates the musics he tells the world about. On this labor of love from Roberts's associate Richard Henderson, the same spirit connects Professional Uhuru's "Medzi Me Digya" to, say, Unknown Street Group's "Asoi." You could carp about folkloricism on a couple of early selections, but starting no later than cut six, an eternal New Year's call-and-response from the Dutch Antilles, the tunes just keep on coming. **A**

Millennium Hip Hop Party (Rhino '99) Following rap crossover from Flash to Dre, this deflates big-time. Hard to believe some find "Baby Got Back" and "Now That We've Found Love" as much fun as not "It Takes Two" (what is?) but "Bust a Move" or "U Can't Touch This." Circa 1991, as aspiration gives way to calculation and entertainment becomes subculturally suspect, shame enters game—though if the compilers had stuck in "Jump" and "Shoop," who'd notice? **A−**

Money No Be Sand (Original Music '95) Ⓝ

Monsters, Robots and Bug Men (Virgin import '96) 💣

The Most Beautiful Christmas Carols (Milan '91) Though this European tour by the Psalette de Lorraine, a multilingual French choir so famous its name appears nowhere on the package, could be less Catholic—I miss "Adeste Fidelis" and "It Came upon a Midnight Clear," especially with 3:28 expended on "White Christmas," where der Bingle and les Drifters still rool—it's ideal seasonal background kitsch nevertheless. Beautiful. Really. **A−**

Move to Groove: The Best of 1970s Jazz-Funk (Verve '95) The jazzmen who named funk thought it should swing; the black rockers who stretched its foregrounded bottom every which way thought swing was only the beginning. Hence, "the best of 1970s jazz-funk" is an oxymoron. Funk is muscle on the one, yet most of the drummers here are lightweights, most of the bassists nonentities, and that's to leave hacks out of it. As for the slumming improvisers and pop wannabes up top, not only does this half-measure elicit their worst, but from Chick Corea and Roy Ayers to Sea Level and (jeez, who remembered him?) Jess Roden, their best is none too good. We get Jimmy Smith trading B-3 for synth, Famous Flames going Vegas, Corea going nowhere, and a few good players whose rent is due. Jazz lifers—Monty Alexander, Houston Person, and especially Randy Weston—contribute the only enjoyable minutes on a 29-track double-CD. Remember, this is the breeding ground of acid jazz and rap jazzmatazz. Now you can't say you didn't know. **C** 🐢

MTV Party to Go Volume 2 (Tommy Boy '92) great singles from good albums for the harried host, casual fan, and amateur cultural historian (the KLF, "3 AM Eternal [Live at the SSL Extended Mix]"; Heavy D. & the Boyz, "Now That We've Found Love [Club Version]") ★★★

MTV Party to Go Vol. 4 (Tommy Boy '93) At the same moment *Vol. 3* convinces me I can live forever without "Baby Got Back," Mary J. Blige, and "I'm Too Sexy," the simultaneous *Vol. 4* fires up my affection for "They Want Efx," En Vogue, and "Give It Away" (I kind of dig "Baby-Baby-Baby" too) (and hey, "Hip Hop Hooray" and "Back to the Hotel" are cool, and "Jump" and RuPaul you know about). It's enough to renew my faith in confluences of taste—sometimes even dance disposables sort out. So what if the higher-grade collection mines higher-grade albums—these are remixes, right? Kris Kross's has Super Cat on it. Fun. **A–**

MTV Party to Go Volume 6 (Tommy Boy '94) remedial dance-pop for a retrograde age (A Tribe Called Quest, "Award Tour"; Aaliyah, "Back and Forth") ★★

MTV's Amp 2 (MTV/Astralwerks '98) Defined by Fatboy Slim's irresistible new "Rockafeller Skank," this is rap-techno fusion in the great tradition of Snap's "The Power," which is best at its cheapest—Chuck D sounds disoriented while KRS-One is saved by, of all people, Goldie. And if you think Fatboy Slim gets boring pretty fast, that's the beauty part. After all, Roni Size gets boring pretty fast too. But with the concept providing unity as the multiple choice provides variety, you can enjoy these obvious macho beatfests for as long as they're worth. Here we go, let's rock and roll. **A–**

MTV: The First Thousand Years: R&B (Rhino '99) Love the title, which mocks both millennium hype and music television while implicitly acknowledging that this is but the latest slice of what the cognizant would call r&b—the part hip hop thinks is for bitchez, the sexy part that finally cracked MTV halfway into the network's going-on-two-decades life. Two of 16 tracks predate 1990, including Tina Turner's semiringer. Two fall flat—wrong Brian McKnight, any Deborah Cox. R&b being a singles music in every phase of its evolution, the few from albums worth owning all sound better here with the sole exception of P. M. Dawn's semiringer. Soft-core come-ons from Johnny Gill, Montell Jordan, Jodeci, and R. Kelly sound a *lot* better—they sound like a subculture seeking xscape rather than four

damn liars. Even when the words dissemble, the music does not. This *is* how we do it—or try to do it, anyway. **A**

Muggs Presents ... The Soul Assassins Chapter 1 (Columbia '97) Freed from the big-buddah boom of H.O.R.D.E. hip hop, the Cypress Hill DJ concocts an album's worth of phantasmagoric Wu-scape and farms out the lyrical terrorism to two coasts worth of tough talkers, most of whom give the job some thought and all of whom provide welcome relief, if only from each other. Atlanta's Goodie Mob sound plenty goodie between Dre and RZA, LA the Darkman's yknowwhat-imsayin adds street, a Fugee rewrites John 3:16, and that ain't all. Not too many crime how-tos and lots of embattled postgangsta militance define a music prepared to survive its own self-abetted demise. **A–**

The Music in My Head (Stern's Africa '98) Although piercing vocals, contentious percussion, and kora guitar are constant, all that really unifies this feverish, coruscating soundtrack to the Mark Hudson novel is Senegal, with one atypically Islamic-sounding Franco track standing in for soukous's pan-African inescapability. Yet with half its tracks recorded 1970–1980 and the other half 1992–1995, so that they segue from 1977 to 1994, 1993 to 1980, it cleaves faithfully only to itself—crossover dreams notwithstanding, only a reggaeish Omar Pene unemployment anthem hints anything round, comfy, Euro. Franco elegy and Wassoulou hunting poem and not-for-export mbalax all project congruent rhythmic angles, and watch out you don't trip yourself as musicians jockey for position, vying with their bandmates while continuing to serve the band as they jam rock sonorities into salsa-inflected Senegalese grooves. Desert mystics conquer the fleshpots. Overloaded camions careen down a potholed road. Frantic macho coheres and clashes, stops and goes, crashes and coheres again. **A+**

Music of Indonesia 2: Indonesian Pop-ular Music: Kroncong, Dangdut, and Langgam Jawa (Smithsonian/Folkways '91) schlock-rock fun, kitsch-pop educational (Soneta Group, "Qur'an dan Koran") ★

Music of Indonesia 3: Music from the Outskirts of Jakarta: Gambang Kromong (Smithsonian/Folkways '91) don't miss the modern stuff—a Dixieland-gamelan head trip you have to hear with lyrics you'll want to read (Gambang Kromong Slendang Betawi, "Stambul Biya") ★★★

Muziki Wa Dansi (Afrocasette '95) Showcasing four cynosures of the Dar es Salaam dance circuit, where they rotate nightly from neighborhood to neighborhood, and ever since I read the notes I've wanted to go there. It would be boorish to single out the tune sense of Orchestra Maquis Original, so I'll merely grant that it may take a while for individual tracks to sink in, and promise that they will. Post-soukous Tanzanian style, rough and sweet in all the right places. **A–**

The Mystic Fiddle of the Proto-Gypsies (Shanachie '97) from Baluchistan, wherever that is, sorud melodies over lute drone—very intense, rather narrow ("Suite of *damali* pieces, performed by Ramazan") ★★★

Paul Nabor: "Naguyane" (*Paranda: Africa in Central America,* Detour '99)

Nada Surf: *High/Low* (Elektra '96) ✴

Najma: *Atish* (Shanachie '90) ✴

Naka: *Salvador* (Mango '92) Ⓝ

Nas: *Illmatic* (Columbia '94) street poet as realist-not-fabulist—staving off alienation and defeat with whatever you got, sex-and-violence not excluded ("It Ain't Hard to Tell," "Represent") ★★★

Nas: *It Was Written* (Columbia '96) Ⓝ

Nas: *I Am . . .* (Columbia '99) Nas covers his ahzz. If in one song he's "wetting" (lovely word) "any nigga" (another) his fellow playa Scarface doesn't like, in another he's fomenting revolution: "Combine all the cliques and make one gang." Yeah sure. The question is how convincing he is, and only two themes ring true—the bad ones, revenge and money. His idea of narrative detail is to drop brand names like Bret Easton Ellis; his idea of morality is everybody dies. Ghostface Killa's "Wildflower" is far more brutal than the she-cheated-while-I-was-playing "Undying Love," and far less bloody; Biggie's "Playa Hater" is far more brutal than the Wu-Puff cameo "Hate Me Now," and far more humorous. Blame his confusion and bad faith on a conscience that's bothered him ever since he bought into the Suge Knight ethos. I've never met a ho in my life. This kind of sellout starts with a "W." **B–** 🦃

Nas: *Nastrademus* (Columbia '99) Ⓝ

Nas: See also Nas Escobar

Nashville Pussy: *Let Them Eat Pussy* (The Enclave/Mercury '98) ✴

Nasida Ria: "Keadilan" (*Keadilan,* Piranha import '94) 🍲

Roy Nathanson & Anthony Coleman: *The Coming Great Millenium* (Knitting Factory Works '92) the avant-garde klezmerized ("You Took Advantage of Me," "Birds/Jews") ★★

Naughty by Nature: "Ghetto Bastard," "O.P.P." (*Naughty by Nature,* Tommy Boy '91) 🍲

Naughty by Nature: "Hip Hop Hooray" (*Nineteen Naughty III,* Tommy Boy '93) 🍲

Naughty by Nature: *Poverty's Paradise* (Tommy Boy '95) I wouldn't swear "Feel Me Flow" or "Clap Yo Hands" is the kind of singalong they can live by (and off). But they're no longer working an anthem thing—it's an album thing. Uncompromisingly street without indulging their anger, unmistakably good-hearted without repressing their aggressions, "Hang Out and Hustle" is their calling card and call to arms. Much respect for the will and skill that can expand their standard five minutes of jubilant escape into an hour of tough, beatwise congeniality. **A–**

Naughty by Nature: *Nineteen Naughty Nine* (Tommy Boy '99) Ⓝ

Me'Shell Ndegé'Ocello: *Plantation Lullabies* (Maverick/Sire/Reprise '93): deprived of womanist rap, we settle for strong-woman singsong ("I'm Diggin' You

[Like an Old Soul Record]," "Picture Show") ★★

Me'shell Ndegéocello: *Peace Beyond Passion* (Maverick/Reprise '96) Anything but a sucker for texts from the Old Testament, Jesus, Shiva, and Kahlil Gibran, I kept wondering who the bass player was. As I should have known and kind of guessed, it was the text borrower in question. So never mind about Leviticus—this is the humanistic groove never quite made flesh by the jazz-tinged ambient foreground of Sade, Anita Baker, and D'Angelo. Then go back and admire the text from Bill Withers. **B+**

Meshell Ndegéocello: *Bitter* (Maverick '99) slow is beautiful ("Loyalty," "Sincerity," "Satisfy") ★★★

Youssou N'Dour: *Set* (Virgin '90) After five years of struggle he creates . . . a pop record, damn it, a pop record from Senegal and no place but: 13 shortish songs replete with catchy intros, skillful bridges, concise solos, hooks. Americans should find them emotionally accessible with the help of a trot and musically accessible with no help at all: try "Toxiques," ecology the third-world way, or "Alboury," a list of progenitors you never heard of. As for aura, say he sounds like a citizen who knows exactly what he wants and exactly how to get it. Say occasionally the tama is too hectic and the horns are too hackneyed. Say everything is beautiful anyway. That exotic enough for you? **A–**

Youssou N'Dour: *Eyes Open* (Columbia '92) The arranged rock song may be slipping beyond the reach of white men. In a context defined by Paul Simon and Robbie Robertson, even a talent like Freedy Johnston risks sounding smug by association, while many women—Sinéad O'Connor, Bonnie Raitt, Rosanne Cash, Laurie Anderson—escape the taint. So does Living Colour. And so does N'Dour, whose mbalax commitments mitigate any conceptual link to studio-rock. On 14 songs that once would have required double vinyl, he strikes an African tone far from pop's confessionals and attempted

empathy. Directing matter-of-fact moral warnings at the powerful and the disenfranchised like the griot he might have been, he's confident of his social function as he tours the world. And for all that, the set-piece stiffness seems as outmoded in America as it must seem modern in Senegal. Since N'Dour usually sings in Wolof, the lyric sheet is a necessity. But I wish once in a while I could do without it. **B+**

Youssou N'Dour: *The Guide (Wommat)* (Chaos/Columbia '94) **Ⓝ**

Youssou N'Dour: *Lii!* (Jololi import '96) Global conquest hasn't come easy, so it's a good thing N'Dour was smart enough and a smart thing he was good enough to stay in Dakar. This isn't the rough rhythming of his youth—he's popwise now and always will be. You can hear Jean Philip Rykiel's gelatinous Clavier, Cheikh Lô's rival voice. But as N'Dour and Lô both know, there are no rival voices—not really, not with this much clarity, power, ductility, serration. And as N'Dour understands far better than any other Senegalese, tunes are a boon. Here they connect more unfailingly than on any of his U.S. releases, with rhythming to spare. Move over, Tony Tone Toné. He is the world. **A–**

Youssou N'dour: *Best of 80's* (Celluloid import '98) Not a reissue, or anyway not an '80s reissue, this comprises 1995's Senegal-only *Dikkaat* and 1997's Senegal-only *St. Louis,* which in turn comprise a dozen songs supposedly composed (and recorded?) in the '80s, although none of my sources has unearthed them all. I own two: the strictly indigenous title song of Etoile de Dakar's *Thiapotholy,* and a David Sancious stinker buried at the tail end of *The Lion.* The former reemerges cleaner, faster, and more professional, none of which are necessarily positives; I'll take the rock sonics of renegade guitarist Badou N'Daiye over Jimmy Mbaye's lithe new jack lines any day. But the latter is improved so much it's almost unrecognizable, rougher and shapelier simultaneously. Everywhere guitars, horns, and tama drums interact with sharper punch and tighter pizzazz than in his wild dance music or his crossover set pieces. And sometimes—I'd single out "Xarit," "Diambar," and the unabashedly beautiful "Njaajaan Njaay"—the songwriting is even more inspired than the playing. **A–**

Youssou N'dour & le super etoile: *Spécial fin d'année plus* (Pape Thiam import '99) could use more guitar—and songs, though the CD-only add-ons help ("Birima," "No méle") ★★

Youssou N'Dour: See also Etoile de Dakar

Nearly God: *Nearly God* (Island Independent/Durban Poison '96) Tricky in Unwonderland, achieving the stasis true Tricky albums only play with ("Together Now," "Children's Story") ★

The Neckbones: *Souls on Fire* (Fat Possum/Epitaph '97) Essence-of-garage is hard to hit on the nose because so-near-and-yet-so-far is simple—with three months' practice, anyone can almost do it. Hell, with a little talent you can be New Bomb Turks, Humpers, even Rocket from the Crypt, all now adduced to explain an Oxford, Mississippi, quartet who deserve better. Thomas Jefferson Slave Apartments, I say, and though I miss Ron House's postdoctoral work, they actually put out more noise, riff, and especially groove, I mean beat. Lyres? Mere myths. Lynnfield Pioneers? Arty-farties. **A–**

The Neckbones: *The Lights Are Getting Dim* (Fat Possum/Epitaph '99) the dissolute tradition, with nuggets as roots ("Cardiac Suture," "Reckless Night") ★★

Ned's Atomic Dustbin: *God Fodder* (Columbia '91) 💣

The Need: *The Need* (Chainsaw '97) 💣

The Negro Problem: *Post Minstrel Syndrome* (Aerial Flipout '97) **Ⓝ**

The Negro Problem: *Joys & Concerns* (Aerial Flipout '99) prefer XTC to Love and love to ecstasy ("Come Down Now," "Mahnsanto") ★

Nelson: *After the Fall* (DGC '90) Poignant in a way that sons of a drug-abusing father who was out of the house plenty even before the divorce should come up with such, er, positive messages. Disgusting in a way that children of pop privilege should also luck into the sales gimmick of twinhood. And utterly apropos that Rick's boys are *fifth*-generation entertainers—circus, vaudeville, situation comedy, Hollywood rockabilly, and now . . . "dynamic melodic vocal guitar rock." "Stylistically no one's doing what we're doing," Gunnar boasts, and he's right in a way. But what makes them truly unique is that he could just as well claim *everyone's* doing what they're doing. **D+** 🦃

Shara Nelson: *What Silence Knows* (Chrysalis '94) **Ⓝ**

Willie Nelson: *Across the Borderline* (Columbia '93) his best in a coon's age, and a touch too artful all around ("She's Not for You," "Don't Give Up," "American Tune") ★★★

Willie Nelson: *Moonlight Becomes You* (Justice '94) *Stardust* for swinging lovers ("Moonlight Becomes You," "Please Don't Talk About Me When I'm Gone") ★★★

Willie Nelson: *Healing Hands of Time* (Liberty '94) 10 standards—six Nelson, four ASCAP—meet more orchestral instruments than you could shake a stick at ("Night Life," "There Are Worse Things than Being Alone") ★

Willie Nelson: *Spirit* (Island '96) So bare-boned in language, instrumentation, and melodic contour you barely notice it at first, this turns out to be Nelson's strongest new album in over a decade, his most indelible songwriting in at least two. His latest case of love lost leaves him meeting his maker but not his mortality—if his "life will never be the same again," it's not because he's gonna keel over like some 63-year-old. In fact, the pain has fired him up, so that he not only surrounds the winning "We Don't Run" with new standards but plays the hell out of that acoustic guitar with the big hole in it. **A–**

Willie Nelson: *I Let My Mind Wander* (Kingfisher '97) Hardly new music. Nelson's stark, efficient Pamper demos, cut without fuss in 1961, briefly surfaced on *Face of a Fighter* at *Stardust* time and are the best things on Rhino's messy three-CD collectorama. Selections vary—this version omits "Face of a Fighter" itself, a loss. But as a songwriter he was on a roll back then, and nobody understood his singing, which means Rhino's *Nite Life* and RCA's *Essential Willie Nelson* are cluttered with off-the-rack Nashville arrangements that become a classic catalogue only in spite of their tailoring. These songs are less famous; no "Funny How Time Slips Away" lies in wait. But "Healing Hands of Time," "You Wouldn't Cross the Street to Say Goodbye," and "I Let My Mind Wander" will surprise the hell out of you, especially after you realize you haven't heard them a thousand times before. **A–**

Willie Nelson: *Teatro* (Island '98) for all Daniel Lanois's pet drummers, an honorable attempt to recreate his live unflash ("Everywhere I Go," "I've Loved You all over the World") ★★

Willie Nelson: *Night and Day* (Pedernales/FreeFalls '99) In the Nashville era, country instrumental albums have been models of dexterous precision and dispatch dominated by the sterile expanses of the Chet Atkins catalogue, a tradition that shares as much with this gift from God as Nelson's singing does with Brooks & Dunn's. Even simpatico analogies—early string bands, the looser Western swing units, the relaxation Merle Haggard's guys go for, or for that matter, Django Reinhardt—don't suggest the casual musicality this long-running off-and-on octet achieves without apparent effort every time it sits down, which happens 150 nights a year. Musicians for life who've achieved a satori that barely skirts virtuosity, they adore the melody. But they adore it after their own fashion, which is Willie's fashion whether he's singing or, as here, only playing lead guitar—pretty much on the note when you listen up, only you don't because the timbre and phrasing are so talky. Is this a species of jazz? Given the awkwardness of the session

Nelson once cut with jazz-identified Nashvillian Jackie King, I wouldn't bother calling it that. It's just Willie, who wants folks to think everything he does is simpler than it is and in some mystical sense may be right. **A**

Nerdy Girl: *Twist Her* (No Life '96) nonpareil miniatures ("Single Bed," "Casa Nova") ★

Nerf Herder: *Nerf Herder* (Arista '97) 💣

Mike Ness: *Cheating at Solitaire* (Time Bomb '99) Ⓝ

Neurotic Outsiders: *Neurotic Outsiders* (Maverick/Reprise '96) 💣

Neutral Milk Hotel: *On Avery Island* (Merge '96) Ⓝ

Neutral Milk Hotel: *In the Aeroplane over the Sea* (Merge '98) Ⓝ

The Neville Brothers: *Family Groove* (A&M '92) On a braver album, "Fly Like an Eagle" might be a coup, freedom fighters seizing the '60s-are-over sentimentality of a pop tune about a revolution Steve Miller wasn't so sorry we lost. On this record it's a reproach—the hook no song doctor can sell. Socially conscious, romantically ardent, or trading on their good name, their material just sits there waiting for you to like it. Where on the notorious *Uptown* they were a confused CHR band who deserved more airplay than they got, here they're a second-rate commercial funk band who get more than they deserve. At least Aaron's Ronstadt outing had the courage of *her* aesthetic convictions. **B–** 🌹

New Edition: *New Edition's Greatest Hits* (MCA '91) sometimes bubblegum grows up into redpop mousse, sometimes into gunk you stick under your seat ("Candy Girl," "Mr. Telephone Man") ★★

New Kids on the Block: "You Got It (The Right Stuff)" (*Greatest Hits,* Columbia/Legacy '99) 👁

New Kingdom: *Paradise Don't Come Cheap* (Gee Street '96) like taking a bath in the Gowanus Canal ("Paradise Don't Come Cheap," "Kickin' Like Bruce Lee") ★

Randy Newman: *Randy Newman's Faust* (Reprise '95) "What did you discover about musical theater?" wondered a Hollywood reporter more impressed by Newman's Broadway aspirations than by his Faustian ambition. "There's no money in it," replied the artiste, who holds down a day job in the family business, which is scoring movies. And though Newman's pact with musical theater requires him to sacrifice music, where his gifts are huge, for theater, where he's a novice, the songs themselves are rich, mocking rock, religion, musical comedy, the classix, and American culture all at once. Newman's Devil is a midlife whiner, James Taylor's God a palavering politician, Don Henley's Faust a bigger creep than both of them put together, Bonnie Raitt and Linda Ronstadt's good-girl-bad-girl a set piece. Yet these brontosauri dance through their dress rehearsal with the found grace of busmen on holiday, and the pleasure Newman takes in his hubris is so ebullient that the satire never turns cheap. If the project reeks of concept album, well, pardon me for reading—the songs do get even better once you take in the plot summary. And if it reeks of burlesque, well, how better to bum-rush Western civ and "America's greatest art form" simultaneously? **A**

Randy Newman: "Heaven Is My Home" (*Michael* [ST], Revolution '96) 🕿
Randy Newman: *Bad Love* (DreamWorks '99) After an annuity's worth of soundtracks, a box stuffed with marginalia, and *Faust,* his first true album since 1988 finds him more cynical than ever, about himself above all. Having called one cheap joke "I'm Dead (But I Don't Know It)," he explains the belated tribute to the wife and family he kissed off in the '70s with a simple "I'd sell my soul and your souls for a song," then announces: "But I wanted to write you one/Before I quit/And this one's it." Thing is, cheap jokes and cynicism have always been his gift to the world, and when he's on he can twist the knife. In joke mode, check out not only "I'm Dead," so anti-Randy it'll have young yahoos saying amen like they just discovered Mahalia Jackson, but two of his cruelest political songs ever: one a history of early imperialism where the punch line is HIV, another addressed with dulcet malice to Mr. Karl Marx. For cynicism, try "My Country," which might just be about his family too, and "Shame," where Newman plays a hateful old hard-on indistinguishable from himself. Twisting his croak a turn further are the most articulate arrangements of his singer-songwriting life: jazzlike, but in a piano-based rock context that shifts at a moment's notice to any voicing (Hollywood-symphonic, country march, pop-schlock) that might reshade a meaning or make the ear believe what the mind can't stand. There are a few ringers. But the last time he was so strong in this mode he was married to a wife he misses. **A**

New Order: *Republic* (Qwest/Warner Bros. '93) not techno and proud ("Regret," "Young Offender") ★★★
New Order: *The Best of New Order* (Qwest/Warner Bros. '95) Marvel all you want over Ian Curtis's desperation—I dig the band on the matched Joy Division comp *Permanent* and prefer detached techie Bernard Albrecht here. Where 1987's *Substance* showcased the music's remixed, interwoven glory, this pushes Albrecht's mild-mannered vocals as far front as they'll go. Turns out he has normal feelings about love and rejection and such, dislikes war and guns without getting preachy—just super-unassumingly super-catchy, as befits Britannia's ranking pop group. I mean, could Blur or Oasis write a World Cup anthem so rousing, danceable, and informative? **A**

New Radicals: *Maybe You've Been Brainwashed Too* (MCA '98) Bizwise wiseass Gregg Alexander is a postall type we'll be seeing more of—schooled in pop values he knows as a careerist rather than an aesthete, his tough times the ones that come naturally to young entertainers on the make in a world where rebelliousness isn't necessarily faked just because it's salable. As the tunes wind down in that CD-era way, even the lesser ones grow on you in all their plethora of words and paucity of meaning, evoking the pathos of the fame game for anyone with a sense of biz mechanics. Clearest musical referents: Todd Rundgren and Hall & Oates. How many boho bands have the uncool to inspire such comparisons? How many have the knowledge? How many have the chops? **A–**

New York's Ensemble for Early Music: *Istanpitta Vol. 1* (Lyrichord '95) Except perhaps in matters of tempo, where the most leisurely citizens of the machine age feel speed's tug in their bones, there's no way this music could sound as raw as it did back in the day. There's a class bias inherent in the survival as written texts of three saltarellos, which probably involved leaping, and 11 other even more obscure dances—whether or not they started with peasants (or Arabs), presumptive gentlefolk put their estampie on them. What's more, moderns who can play archaic bowed, plucked, strummed, blown, and beaten instruments inevitably come out of the classical world, where they are trained in the sweet, precise intonation that was standardized by the 19th-century orchestra, and director-arranger Frederick Renz is not known for rocking the boat. But frame drummer Glen Velez, who guests on three tracks, can make some noise, and courtly or not, you have to grant these tunes a decisive victory over ye olde test of time. So take this careful, lovely, not altogether unlively collection as a romance about aristocrats who ate with their hands. Anyone with a thing for Shakespearean interludes will love the shit out of it. **A–**

Next: *Rated Next* (Arista '97) cute pop songs about—among other less significant matters—their erections and her clitoris ("Too Close," "Butta Love") ★★

Samba Ngo: *Metamorphosis* (Compass '99) late soukous for Americans, somehow whole despite mbira, jujubeats, and circular breathing ("Midi Passé," "Mwana Congo") ★★★

Wally Ngonda: *Modo* (Stern's Africa '95) soukous after the storm ("Roger Lino," "Mody") ★

Prime Minister Pete Nice & Daddy Rich: *Dust to Dust* (Def Jam/Columbia '93) Ⓝ

Nice and Smooth: *Jewel of the Nile* (RAL '94) hip hop's pop dream—living large, acting nice, staying smooth ("Let's All Get Down," "Save the Children") ★

Jeb Loy Nichols: *Lovers Knot* (Capitol '97) The former Fellow Traveler is so subtle it's hard to see how he'll ever crash out of the Americana ghetto—or into it, since his Wyoming-Missouri pedigree quickly gave way to postpunk New York and then London, where he once roomed with Ari Up. Maybe a Don Williams cover, if anybody this side of the Eric Clapton Fan Club remembers that hummable hubby anymore. Until then you'll have to make do with Nichols's less pushy tunes, rendered in a country-soul drawl that rarely ventures above a sleepy murmur and undergirded by a sinuous funk-reggae groove that reads incongruous and sounds ordained. He sings mostly about married love, as strung out as a week of insomnia and as pleasant as an after-dinner stroll. **A–**

Stevie Nicks: *Timespace: The Best of Stevie Nicks* (Modern '91) not a diva—a transgendered arena-rock god in all his/her grand self-regard ("I Can't Wait," "Has Anyone Ever Written Anything for You") ★

Nicole: *Make It Hot* (The Gold Mind, Inc./EastWest '98) Ⓝ

The Nields: *Gotta Get over Greta* (Razor & Tie '96) 💣

Nine Inch Nails: *Broken* (Halo Five '92) Ⓝ

Nine Inch Nails: *The Downward Spiral* (Nothing/TVT/Interscope '94) musically, Hieronymus Bosch as postindustrial atheist; lyrically, *Transformers* as kiddie porn ("Heresy," "Reptile") ★★

Nine Inch Nails: *The Fragile* (Nothing '99) After six fucking years, genius-by-acclamation Trent Reznor delivers double-hoohah, every second remixed till it glistens like broken glass on a prison wall. Is the way he takes his petty pain out on the world a little, er, immature for a guy who's pushing 35? Never mind, I'm told—just immerse in the music. So I do. "Dream job: emperor," it says. "More fun than death by injection." **B** 🐝

98°: *98°* (Motown '97) With Cincinnati a hotbed of racial meshugas from *Uncle Tom's Cabin* and Stephen Foster to Marge Schott and the Afghan Whigs, why shouldn't these four white boys be the younger generation's answer to Boyz II Men? They're certainly realer than the Backstreet Boys. But no way does that guarantee they're as good. Their mild singing is soulful only because there's no competent pop that isn't anymore. Their goopy hit ballad has nothing on a little something called "Heaven's Missing an Angel." And next time—they promise, assuming like so many young fools before them that there'll be one—they're going to write the material themselves. **C–** 🐝

Nirvana: *Nevermind* (DGC '91) After years of hair-flailing sludge that achieved occasional songform on singles no normal person ever heard, Seattle finally produces some proper postpunk, aptly described by resident genius Kurt Cobain: "Verse, chorus, verse, chorus, solo, bad solo." This is hard rock as the term was understood before metal moved in—the kind of loud, slovenly, tuneful music you think no one will ever work a change on again until the next time it happens, whereupon you wonder why there isn't loads more. It seems so simple. **A**

Nirvana: *Hormoaning* (DGC import '92) Four 1990 Peel-session covers plus two sides of a theoretical single, none duplicated on *Bleach,* which it smokes (without David Grohl they're sludge monkeys), or *Nevermind,* which it can hang with (Kurt Cobain yowls like John Hancock crosses his K's). They're obviously a band to hear live (with a multiplatinum sound system, please). Especially since the ticket won't cost much more than this yen-pegged EP. Aren't you glad Mitsubishi owns MCA, so you can home-tape it legally? **A–**

Nirvana: *Incesticide* (DGC '92) A lot of these rags and bones and demos and B sides (including four *Hormoaning* collectibles) are so on that I figured maybe I'd underrated *Bleach* until I played it again. But though memorable albums have been recorded for $600, they haven't usually been memorable rock albums—electric music doesn't travel without quality controls. In any case, the trademark interactions are more emphatic on the tracks *Bleach's* Jack Endino didn't record, which generally means the recent ones. Not a great song band yet. Just a great, um, alternative band, which is rare enough. **A–**

Nirvana: *In Utero* (DGC '93) "How 'bout some Nirvana?" you'll say. "Oh yeah, great band," the reply will go. "Really had their own sound. What do you wanna play?" "It don't matter that much, any of the first three." "You mean *Bleach?*" "Nah, the Geffen albums—not that outtakes thing, but *Nevermind* or *Bluebaby* or . . . what did they call the Steve Albini one?" "You mean the really hard one. *In Utero.* The guitar one." "What do you mean guitar? It had songs on it." "Well, so did the outtakes thing." "The Albini one had better songs, actually. And it was real cadmium besides. Toxic." "You have to play it loud, though. And aren't you supposed to crank the treble too? I liked *Nevermind* better." "I liked *Bluebaby* a little better too. But that was a good album. Go ahead. Once Madonna conks out, she sleeps through the night. She's a good baby that way—nothing wakes her up. Come on, let me relive my youth." "I hope you don't regret it in the morning." "These days, I never regret anything in the morning. I'm too fucking tired to bother. Let her rip." **A**

Nirvana: *MTV Unplugged in New York* (DGC '94) Not only did Kurt Cobain transcend alt-rock by rocking so hard, he transcended alt-rock by feeling so deep. On this accidental testament, intended merely to altify the MTV mind-set by showcasing the Meat Puppets and covering the Vaselines, Cobain outsensitives Lou Barlow and Eddie Vedder in passing. His secret is sincerity, boring though that may be—he cares less than Barlow without boasting a bit about it, tries harder than Vedder without busting a gut about it. The vocal performance he evokes is John Lennon's on *Plastic Ono Band.* And he did it in one take. **A**

Nirvana: *From the Muddy Banks of the Wishkah* (DGC '96) One new song and 15 old ones—intense renderings of familiar arrangements recycled for the buying season. Maybe it wouldn't carry the same weight if Kurt Cobain were alive. But it wouldn't carry the same weight if everybody had a good job or plague wiped out half the planet either. Cobain is dead, alienated labor is everywhere, plague is something we worry about, and this is a great record for a world where those three truths are on the table. Less precise and contained than *Nevermind* or *In Utero,* it serves an unduplicated function for a band that changed the pop world with four dozen songs. I play *Unplugged* to refresh my memory of a sojourner's spirituality. I'll play this one when I want to remember a band's guts, fury, and rock and roll music. **A**

Mojo Nixon: "Don Henley Must Die," "Destroy All Lawyers" (*Otis,* Enigma '91) 🕭

Mojo Nixon & the Toadliquors: *Horny Holidays* (Triple X '92) Ⓝ

West Nkosi: *Rhythm of Healing (Supreme Sax and Penny Whistle Township Jive)* (Earthworks/Caroline '92) think late M.G.'s, trying to consolidate what they'd accomplished—with the Bar-

Kays in the house ("Mazuzu," "Marabi Kwela") ★★★

Nkuku and Jopie Sisters: "Tana Kamina" (*Homeland 2* [comp], Rounder '90) 🕭

No Doubt: *Tragic Kingdom* (Trauma/Interscope '95) Like any pop skyrocket, Gwen Stefani is video-driven, and so hebephrenic you know she unprotests too much. The production's as bizzy as the Ivy at lunchtime too. But this act's real problem is ska. Since the dawn of two-tone there hasn't been a single band in the style—excluding the punk Rancid but including Madness and the Specials—that was as songful as its fun-besotted partisans claimed. When that hippity-hop beat is hyped up for postpunk consumption, its energy somehow precludes tune. Not that she could sing in the same shower as classic Cyndi Lauper anyway. But classic Belinda Carlisle is another story. **C+** 🦃

No Face: "We Wants to Fuck," "Spanish Fly" (*Wake Your Daughter Up,* No Face/RAL/Columbia '90) 🕭

NOFX: *Ribbed* (Epitaph '91) as in condoms—also kidded ("Just the Flu," "Where's My Slice?") ★★

NOFX: *White Trash, Two Heebs and a Bean* (Epitaph '92) growing in wit, growing in wisdom ("Liza and Louise," "Please Play This Song on the Radio") ★★★

NOFX: *Punk in Drublic* (Epitaph '94) In which these pranksters proceed to prove absolutely that a sense of humor provides useful training in broader human feelings. Among those they don't put down are a porn actress, a happy born-againer, a guy in Birkenstocks and a tie-dyed Rancid T-shirt, Hasidic O.G.'s, and—implicitly—people who like tunes with their rant and rave. They're a six-figure advance away from that exalted state where assholes everywhere can call them shallow and suburban. **A–**

NOFX: *Heavy Petting Zoo* (Epitaph '96) Ⓝ

NOFX: *So Long and Thanks for All the Shoes* (Epitaph '98) "All Outta Angst," so "The Desperation's Gone" ("Monosyllabic Girl," "All His Suits Are Torn") ★★★

No Safety: *Spill* (Knitting Factory Works '92) Henry Cow meets da funk on da Lower East Side ("Sad," "Saturday Morning") ★★★

No Safety: "Balm" (*Live at the Knitting Factory,* Knitting Factory Works '94) 👄

The Notorious B.I.G.: *Ready to Die* (Bad Boy '94) As a white person in an integrated, how do we say it, nabe, I should breathe a sigh of relief that pithy Christopher Wallace seems content to exploit his own people—"I been robbin' motherfuckers since the slave ship," or, if you prefer, "I be beatin' motherfuckers like Ike beat Tina." As a male person, I should be grateful he doesn't want to pimp my kind either. But because I live a lot farther from the edge, these things don't make me feel better at all—I'm outraged when anyone gets robbed, beaten, or pimped, descendants of slaves especially. Hence I'm not inclined to like this motherfucker. But the more I listen the more I do. Wiping the cold out of his eyes at 5:47 a.m. or pulling his gat as the wrong guy comes down the street, he commands more details than any West Coast gangsta except carpetbagging Ice-T. His sex raps are erotic, his jokes are funny, and his music makes the thug life sound scary rather than luxuriously laid-back. When he considers suicide, I not only take him at his word, I actively hope he finds another way. **A–**

The Notorious B.I.G.: *Life After Death* (Bad Boy '97) Biggie's murder made it too easy to romanticize intimations of mortality that don't truck with any Tupac-style martyr complex. Equally devoid of morbidity and joie de vivre, Biggie is far more sardonic, self-deprecating, and tough-minded, "ready to die" in the cast-a-cold-eye sense. Although his moments of warmth for family and comrades seem real enough, he proves one funny son of a bitch on the love-man parody "#!*@ You Tonight," the achingly lyrical slow-falsetto showcase "Playa Hater" ("Open the Door/Lay on the floor/You've been robbed"), and the tall tale about being caught in some bitch's crib by her Knick boyfriend ("one of those six-five niggas, I don't know"), done first as a rap and then as a story for his boys. Where Cali hides behind funkamysterioso, Puffy Combs's chart-friendly r&b hooks rub comically against Biggie's unoratorical street style, with its trademark Schoolly D cum Butt-head "huh huh," as the likes of RZA, Bone-Thugs, and Lil' Kim add flavor. In short, way more fun and somewhat more moral than the look-Ma-no-hands unaccountability promoted by showbiz outlaws from Mobb Deep to Westside Connection. **A**

The Notorious B.I.G.: *Born Again* (Bad Boy '99) 💣

Nova Mob: *The Last Days of Pompeii* (Rough Trade '91) 💣

NRBQ: *Peek-a-Boo: The Best of NRBQ 1969–1989 Disc One* (Rhino '90) Ⓝ
NRBQ: *Peek-a-Boo: The Best of NRBQ 1969–1989 Disc Two* (Rhino '90) Ⓝ

'N Sync: *'N Sync* (RCA '98) Ⓝ

N.W.A: *100 Miles and Runnin'* (Ruthless EP '90) Too used and abused to pursue their business interests, the self-appointed "real niggaz" watched other fake gangstas climb the charts till they could bear it no more. So they threw together this $6.98-list shortie and hoped Amerikkka would want it. Their best riff of 1988 is their best riff of 1990, attached to a blaxploitation docudrama pitting fake gangstas against fake cops (probably played by members of their management team). And for that 2 Live touch they hire a woman (as we'll call her) to mouth their instructions on cocksucking technique, one of many things they don't know dick about. To wit: first "grab" (ouch); then "lick" (just twice, before you get down to bidness); then "insert" (now "take it slow"); and "before you know it" (damn soon), "splash." When she swallows, she inspires such a conflation of awe and disgust she's forced to service the rest of the crew forthwith. **C–** 🦃

N.W.A: *Niggaz4life* (Ruthless '91) This is supposed to be where they finally slam nonstop. In fact, however, the music's just like the lyrics—market-ready. Catchy, yes, and funky in its laid-back electro way, but never hard enough to scare off the novelty audience. Which might be fun if they didn't outpig the LAPD in the bargain. Can Chuck D really believe they mean what they say? Sure they really hate women, and anybody else who looks at them funny. But unless they're even sicker than they seem, they're too greedy to murder anybody as long as they can make so much money fronting about it. And so they've calculated every rhyme to push somebody's button—to serve up the thrill of transgression to ghetto-bound and merely ghettocentric young-black-males, and also to the big score, culturally deprived white boys seeking exotic role models. That kids will take them at their word obviously doesn't concern niggaz who'll be hard pressed to contain their pent-up hostility after the bubble bursts. So in the interests of public safety, pray they don't get taken by their investment advisers. **C–** 🦃

Nyboma: *Anicet* (Stern's Africa '94) not soukous paradise—just a sweet stopover ("Anicet") ★

Sally Nyolo: *Multiculti* (Tinder '98) Ⓝ

N/COMPILATIONS

Naked Lunch (Milan '92) Ⓝ

New Groove 3: Déconstruire le groove esoterique (REV '99) at long last acid jazz (Swoon, "Pomegranate garrote"; Henri Lim, "Aria [Ether Edit]") ★★

New Jack City (Giant '91) So what if the ballads are soul on dry ice, not even prime Sweat/Gill? The fast stuff dances the synth-beat interface between rap and disco in a state-of-the-craft showcase. This is black contempopop without filler or stupidity—from Color Me Badd's explicit sex to 2 Live Crew's Afrogangsta pride, the songs are exhibits in a morality play that, like the movie, would lose bite if it didn't flirt with exploitation. **A–**

The Night Shift (C&S '96) "laid-back trip hop and ambient grooves" that recline so indolently their souls sometimes fall out (Purple Penguin, "Tribhuwan"; Kitachi, "Spirit [Hip Hop Mix]") ★★★

No Easy Walk to Freedom (Music Club '98) South African roots-pop K-Tel style (Sister Phumi, "Ithemba"; Sipho Mabuse, "Jive Soweto") ★

No More Prisons (Raptivism '99) convicts not gangstas, agitrap not CNN (Hurricane G, "No More Prisons"; dead prez & Hedrush, "Murda Box"; Daddy-O, "Voices") ★★★

No Prima Donna: The Songs of Van Morrison (Polydor '94) 💣

Nova Bossa: Red Hot on Verve (Verve '96) proving once more that good real schlock is better than fake and bad real schlock is worse (Black Orpheus Soundtrack, "A Felicidade"; Elís Regina & Antonio Carlos Jobim, "Aguas de Março"; Walter Wanderley, "Bicho Do Mato") ★

Nuyorican Soul (Giant Step/Blue Thumb '97) 💣

Oasis: *Definitely Maybe* (Epic '94) Sixties Schmixties—back when they were a tribute band they were the Diamond Dogs ("Rock 'n' Roll Star," "Slide Away") ★

Oasis: *(What's the Story) Morning Glory?* (Epic '95) give them credit for wanting it all—and (yet another Beatles connection!) playing guitars ("She's Electric," "Roll with It") ★★

Oasis: *Be Here Now* (Epic '97) "Uncle! Uncle! Let go of my ear! Uncle, for chrissake!" ("Be Here Now," "My Big Mouth") ★★

O.C.: *Word . . . Life* (Wild Pitch '94) Ⓝ

The Ocean Blue: *See the Ocean Blue* (Mercury '96) Ⓝ

Eliades Ochoa: *Sublime Illusion* (Higher Octave World '99) Ⓝ

Phil Ochs: *There and Now: Live in Vancouver 1968* (Rhino '90) 🍒

Sinéad O'Connor: *I Do Not Want What I Haven't Got* (Chrysalis '90) Without a doubt this is subtler and more durable than most slow, long-winded records, and half of it is terrific. She has her own sound, her simulated plain-speech strikes a blow for directness and honesty without committing her to any one thing, and if you think "Nothing Compares 2 U" cuts Taylor Dayne on the radio, wait till you hear "The Emperor's New Clothes" cut Aerosmith. Not since Patti Smith has anybody had a better chance of defining rock-not-pop in a specifically female way—she's just the right mess of emotion and savvy, crudity and sophistication, fury and independence and love. If there's anything that's older news than a 20-year-old who's angry at the world, it's a 23-year-old who's discovered life is worth living. But all that means is that if she can withstand the media flood, this won't be all that hard to top. How can she possibly know what she wants when she's only 23? **B+**

Sinéad O'Connor: *Am I Not Your Girl?* (Chrysalis/Ensign '92) Over and above Irish-American backlash and papal maledictions from the depths of the catacombs, this muddled project stiffed because no one understood it, possibly including O'Connor. At least half the titles aren't "standards." I mean, Rice & Lloyd Webber? Early Loretta Lynn? "Scarlet Ribbons"? An anticlericalist sermon? A putative Marilyn Monroe song that made a bigger splash when Helen Kane did it in 1928? A samba? Doris Day's "Secret Love" (which as it happens was the first record I ever bought, though I came to prefer the B side, "The Deadwood Stage")? All they share (except for the sermon) is that they are *not rock* (and also, conceivably, that O'Connor grew up with them, as she claims). But unlike La Ronstadt, O'Connor has no not-rock audience, and little not-rock savvy. Instead of hiring some reasonable substitute for Nelson Riddle—Billy May, or her *Red Hot + Blue* crew—she relies on high-grade hacks like Torrie Zito and Rob Mounsey.

★★★, ★★, ★ Honorable Mention   🐚 Choice Cut   Ⓝ Neither   🍒 Dud   🦃 Turkey

Even through their blare she sounds so defiant, so vulnerable, so sexual that at times she could be the greatest natural singer since Aretha. So up till the last three cuts, she almost gets away with it. But she doesn't. **B** 🐦

Sinéad O'Connor: *Universal Mother* (Chrysalis/EMI '94) I confess this has grown on me. The quiet, stunning "All Apologies" is only the latest proof of the vocal gift—part physical (clarity, texture, amplitude), part spiritual (openness, commitment)—that can make her a great cover artist. Her lullaby is a stroke, and her sign-off love song arrives at a nicely unreadable tone. But from Germaine Greer's great mother of a prologue (performancewise, Farrakhan's got the sister beat) to the weeper that could tempt Bruno Bettelheim to tell moron jokes (just precisely who does "scorn" the little retard, anyway?) to the instructional rap that'll catch your ear so fast you'll waste scarcely a second pushing the next-track button (no famine OK, "post traumatic stress disorder" blarney), the framing could be a parody conceived by son of Eire P. J. O'Rourke, and it renders the album essentially inaccessible. This isn't risking foolishness—it's flaunting it. **B–** 🐦

Sinéad O'Connor: *Gospel Oak EP* (Chrysalis/EMI '97) Ⓝ

Sinéad O'Connor: *So Far . . . The Best of Sinéad O'Connor* (Chrysalis/EMI-Capitol '97) Nobody compiles better than a genius who's also a fool, and with her Gaelic/spiritual phase due to last a while, this collection is perfectly timed. I'd substitute "You Do Something to Me" and "All Apologies" for "Don't Cry for Me Argentina," which conjures Madonna with an unnecessarily competitive edge, but "Jump in the River" is the only track I miss off the tape I long ago constructed from the first two albums. A fool who knows her own strengths is a fool we want to hear from when she's feeling better. Or do I mean worse? **A**

The Odyssey Band: *Reunion* (Knitting Factory Works '98) In which James Blood Ulmer's greatest album is mined for the originality of its band concept, with Charlie Burnham the strong alternate lead the leader needs. Intimations of hoedown notwithstanding, "fiddler" doesn't capture Burnham any better than "violinist"—gypsy riffs bent by blues intonation, blues drones textured with saxophone growl. As for that lowdown meld of güiro scrape, jew's-harp thwong, and two balloons rubbing together, I assume it's Blood, who is also the straightforward vocalist and melodist on a record that starts atmospheric, turns songful, and ropes you in with a sound either way. **A–**

The Offspring: *Ignition* (Epitaph '92) Ⓝ
The Offspring: *Smash* (Epitaph '94) Ⓝ
The Offspring: *Ixnay on the Hombre* (Columbia '97) 💣
The Offspring: *Americana* (Columbia '98) Four or five years late, they make selling out seem both easy! (unlike the major-label labor *Ixnay on the Hombre*) and fun! (unlike the fluke smash *Smash*). A dozen or two bpm faster than when they caught Green Day's punk wave, they sound like a Bad Religion whose catchy drone is at long last unencumbered by any message deeper than "the truth about the world is that crime does pay"—which, to their credit, makes them indignant—or, more generally, that "The Kids Aren't Alright." This truth they explore as fully as—but, as suits their relatively privileged upbringing, less solemnly than—any gangsta. Only on the title track do they get grandiose. And while keeping it light keeps them on the right side of their frat-boy base, it also makes the fuckups they mock and mourn seem all the more hurtful. **A–**

O.G. Funk: *Out of the Dark* (Rykodisc '94) Ⓝ

Sonny Okosuns: *African Soldiers* (Profile '91) Those who wish Afropop were more political should reflect on this avowed revolutionary's *Fire in Soweto*—first banned in South Africa, which is no feat, it then became the theme music for Liberia's Samuel K. Doe, who soon proved one of the continent's worst despots. And as with most protest pros, neither Okosuns's "progressive" music, rock-colored reggae plus ye olde indigenous rhythms, nor his "progressive" lyrics, which praise Jah and Jesus and ye olde African woman, have gained passion or precision with the years. **C+** 🦃

The Okra All-Stars: *The Okra All-Stars* (Innerstate '98) any friend of Jeb Loy Nichols is a friend of country music—especially Ricky Barnes ("Big Mistake," "Shade Tree Fix-It Man") ★★

Old: *Lo Flux Tube* (Relativity/Earache '92) soundtrack to the horror movie in your dumb young mind—with band name to match ("Outlive") ★

Will Oldham: *Joya* (Drag City '97) "Why are you sad?" inquired the alt-rock mag. "I dunno," replied the former child actor dba Palace and such. "I guess I was born." Admired for his reticence, sexual ambivalence, and general refusal of formal commitment, I mean closure, Oldham lacks neither talent nor originality, and up against some truly lousy competition this is his most melodic record. But to declare him a new avatar of Appalachian purity is absurd, not just because he's a rich city kid who can't sing, but because his purity is a candid affectation—a standard variation on late alt's agoraphobic cultivation of ineptitude as a token of spiritual superiority. Why is he sad? Because sad is easier than happy—almost comforting, in a chickenshit way. **C+** 🦃

Ol' Dirty Bastard: *Return to the 36 Chambers: The Dirty Version* (Elektra '95) Yacub's worst nightmare as comedian, moral threat, and nutcase, the former Russell Jones walks that three-dimensional tightrope not with grace, and not with hope either. With faith, maybe—even charity. Certainly with an irrepressible commitment to his own history and culture, however sublumpen the sociology of class and race judges those to be. His compulsion is to turn an absence into a presence. His clownish explosions dis-

tance him from how fucked up the violence and pleasures of his culture are and appear, respectively, and his clansmen show us how complex and full of fun their treasure is. "I'm the baddest hip hop man across the world," he sputters, the prized fool in the court of King RZA. **A–**

Ol' Dirty Bastard: *N***a Please* (Elektra '99) that n***a'z *really* crazy—which doesn't make him Richard Pryor ("I Can't Wait," "Recognize") ★★

Old 97's: "St. Ignatius" (*Hitchhike to Rhome,* Big Iron '94) 👁

Old 97's: *Wreck Your Life* (Bloodshot '95) Dallas boys don't come to country naturally, not Dallas boys honest enough to open: "This is the story of Victoria Lee/She started off on Percodan and ended up with me/She lived in Berkeley till the earthquake shook her loose/She lives in Texas now where nothing ever moves." So "You Belong to My Heart" and "My Sweet Blue-Eyed Darlin'" fall as flat as their titles, and "W-I-F-E" says more about their own wimmin problems than about those of the ethos they poach so pseudosatirically. But in the back of a Bel Air with a mouthful of some girl's hair, staring at the dressing room walls blaming King Reagan for their wimmin problems, they're an uncommonly pungent bunch of alt-rockers with a sound they'll beef up yet. **B+**

Old 97's: *Too Far to Care* (Elektra '97) They get depressed a lot, actually, so what say we lump them in with the new literalism, more Ass Ponys than Uncle Tupelo? Even if Rhett Miller really thinks love always turns out as bad as it does here—hell, even if he thinks third-rate romance is just a metaphor for the musician's lot—I still give him credit for keeping his eyes open. Convincer: "Barrier Reef," which renders the high hopes and depressing mechanics of a one-night stand in equally quick and devastating strokes. **B+**

Old 97's: *Fight Songs* (Elektra '99) Now alt-country only by historical association, Rhett Miller Associates deliver what the No Depression crowd always wanted: a jangle-rock album worthy of the Byrds themselves. Miller's no McGuinn. But his conversational ache sure beats McGuire, the perfect medium for unfaltering songcraft that ambles from Crazy Horse to Poco without ever turning fussy or eclectic, and in addition his guitarist likes Lynyrd Skynyrd. The whole doesn't present itself as a concept album only because losing at love is a pop metatheme. Note, however, that for both touring postalt-rockers and the postcollegians who love them, the geographical distance these lyrics can't stay away from is now a basic coordinate of romance—a love wrecker, a pain in the heart, a way out. If you wanted to get fancy about it, and I do, you could then blame this emotional trap on the same untrammeled capitalism that turns every young job seeker into a freelance contractor and every aspiring artist into a media pro. So keep up the good fight songs, Old 97's. We'll lick this social problem yet. **A**

The Olivia Tremor Control: *Dusk at Cubist Castle* (Flydaddy '96) ◐
The Olivia Tremor Control: *Black Foliage: Animation Music by the Olivia Tremor Control* (Flydaddy '99) This division of the Elephant 6 consortium loves tunes, and its soundscraping has few equals in indiedom. When it mixes the two, the result is often kinda beautiful even though the lyrics are avowedly "not going to shed any new light on humanity," and even though the sonics tend toward the perverse—disembodied outtake snippets, mechanical malfunctions, and tape fuckups that their hip hop counterparts would bury in beats or declare inimical to organic life. But as the album goes on (and on), the strategy becomes not noize-toon synthesis, but weird song as reward for unpleasant sound. At its most generous, this may be the music of the young Brian Wilson's dysfunctional dreams. But at its most pretentious it's his bad trip. And bad trips weren't the main reason the psychedelic worldview fell into disrepute.

The main reason was that it was full of shit. **B–** 🦃

Koffi Olomide: *Tcha Tcho* (Stern's Africa '90) Floating airy synthesizers on the quietest of Paris-Kinshasa grooves, this Papa Wemba grad is class pop down to his haircut. A balladeer by soukous standards, he's a rhythm king nevertheless, a café au lait Bing Crosby with the stuff to shoot from the hips. But for all its gentle carnality, his seductive one-on-one lacks emotional detail if you don't understand the words. Fluent Francophones will swoon—especially fluent female Francophones. **B+**

OMC: "How Bizarre," "On the Run" (*How Bizarre,* Huh!/Mercury '97) 🐚

Alexander O'Neal: *All True Man* (Tabu/Epic Associated '91) ◐

Shaquille O'Neal: *Shaq Fu—Da Return* (Jive '94) he's got skillz, connectionz, a wicked laugh—and he can rhyme some ("Biological Didn't Bother," "No Hook") ★★

Shaquille O'Neal: *Respect* (T.W.IsM. '99) 💣

One Dove: "White Love (Guitar Paradise Mix)" (*Morning Dove White,* FFRR '93) 🐚

1,000 Mona Lisas: *New Disease* (RCA '96) ◐

Remmy Ongala & Orchestre Super Matimila: *Mambo* (RealWorld '92) ◐

The Only Ones: *The Peel Sessions* (Strange Fruit '91) Like the rest of the series, their compendium preserves every song they chose to try out for Uncle John, the BBC, and the great unwashed, including second-raters like the indecisive "In Betweens." But except for "The Whole of the Law," this hits the high spots. Because they always played better than the classic pop band they never really were, Peel's demand that they lay down four songs in a day of recording—half-live, as it were—gets the rough part of their groove that studio polish glossed over. And such new-ones-on-me as "Oh No," "Language Problem," and "Telescopic Love" are why people think they were a pop band. **A–**

Yoko Ono: *Walking on Thin Ice* (Rykodisc '92) Four CDs of Patsy nod me out, four of Aretha make me wonder, but six of *Onobox* get me going. Often not great and sometimes awful, they brim with previously unheard or unnoticed highs. This 19-cut condensation skips the educational stuff and ought to convert anybody with better taste than Albert Goldman—namely, you. As a student of Western composition, an adept of Japanese vocal technique, and an avant-gardist sworn to throw convention to the wind, Yoko was unready to rock three different ways. Yet on the four early songs the transparent simplicity she strives for sounds truer than the dumb authenticity of Elephant's Memory, and by the '80s she's mastered a studio-rock art-pop whose unremarkable timbres and textures are subtly transformed by her inappropriate training. A transparently simple, transcendently self-conscious triumph of the will—and of the "Woman Power" she was corny and prophetic enough to crow about back when she was the weirdo who broke up the Beatles. **A**

Yoko Ono: *New York Rock* (Capitol '95) It's reassuring that she came back to cut the album of her life, because this doomed musical's utter absence of pop instinct had me assuming the worst—that she was past learning what it means to communicate with an audience, that she'd twisted her angel's arm, that she didn't respect her own songs. Not only did she lack the discretion to stick with the best, she betrayed the good ones. The arrangements are dreck, and the performances—oy. Eminences from Rosanne Cash to the B'52's have covered her with the love she deserves, but the canniest Broadway belter would wreck material so sensibility-specific, and these unknowns are the kind they call hopefuls because deludeds wouldn't have the right ring. **D+** 🐸

Yoko Ono/IMA: *Rising* (Capitol '95) Finally history leaves Yoko free to find the music her life has taught her to make. Neither primitivist/minimalist retro nor a final awkward attempt to improve on *Season of Glass,* this brims with the calm confidence of a semidetached bystander now hailed as a direct influence by all manner of rock bohemians, including some too snobbish to understand that, actually, her late husband was the stone genius in the partnership. Its precondition is the avant-garde's new pop panache. In the world before Nirvana, I doubt any major would have bankrolled the 14-minute title track's virtuoso vocalese, or the shrieks that fill a six-minute number of identical title and lyric: "I'm Dying." What '80s bizzer would have been down with her arch, lovely animal imitations, or the starkly literal "Turned the Corner," or the plainly simple "New York Woman," or the platitudinous "Revelations"? But these days Courtney could cover "Talking to the Universe" and no one would blink. **A–**

Onyx: *Bacdafucup* (JMJ/RAL/Chaos/Columbia '93) What the Geto Boys were to the insanity defense, Onyx are to the irony defense. Not that they'd cop to it themselves. They're not honest enough, for one thing. And they're also not smart enough, which doesn't mean they're as dumb as they pretend to be—or dumb in the way they pretend to be either. The official line is that nobody takes them seriously, or literally, or something—that not only are they obviously not nigga-killing, whitey-robbing, pussy-stretching bad guys, they obviously aren't pretending to be. Instead, if you're still with me, they pretend to pretend, greatly amusing those in the know with the old nigga-in-your-nightmare routine. So for me I guess they're something like Frederick Barthelme. Vulgar fellow that I am, I still prefer my jokes boffo. **C+** 🐸

Godwin Kabaka Opara's Oriental Brothers International: *Do Better If You Can/Onye Ikekwere Mekeya* (Original Music '95) Vocal strongman Warrior Opara and guitar heavy Dan Satch Opara carried the burden of *Heavy on the Highlife!*, John Storm Roberts's 1991 introduction to the Oriental Brothers, who are more a brand name than a verifiable cohort of musicians. Although third brother Kabaka was the first to break away from the original group, his gift would appear to be mediation—between the band's Ibo loyalties and its continental ambitions, its quiet youth and its jamming maturity. These five lively 6-to-17-minute tracks are so sweetly indefatigable that their duration defines them—not polite enough for highlife, they seem almost like juju with a steadier pulse, or soukous with a less flamboyant bottom. Kabaka's guitar invokes both alien styles. **A–**

Oranj Symphonette: *Plays Mancini* (Gramavision '97) reconstructing kitsch for the music of it ("Moon River," "A Shot in the Dark") ★★★
Oranj Symphonette: *The Oranj Album* (Rykodisc '98) ❶

The Orb: *U.F. Orb* (Big Life '92) Travelogue techno. Hassell & Eno, Budd & Eno, Steve Reich, Steve Speilberg, Augustus Pablo, Davy Jones, all watered down for your trippy delectation. Not terrible, exactly, but rather silly. Free your mind and you can dance to anything. **B–** 🐛

Orbital: *Orbital 2* (FFRR '93) Mood techno. It ripples, it swells, it buzzes, it whistles, it bleeps, it annoys, all on a bed of reliable rhythm. Problem is, you have to be in the mood already. Putting you there would be too egotistical, I guess. **C+** 🐛

Orchestra Baobab: *On Verra Ça* (World Circuit '92) Rarely does Afropop's Cuban connection come out and kiss you on the cheek the way it does on "El Son de Llama," the trad. arr. charanga that sets the mood. Consciously polyglot, the band bends Mandinka and Wolof toward Togo, Guinea-Bissau, and Senegal's Cas-

samance as well as Cuba. But these 1978 Paris recordings are suffused with presalsa's elegant charm—the unostentatiously gorgeous arrangements make the less derivative Dakar-'82 *Pirates Choice* sound too off-the-cuff. Special thanks to guitarist Barthelemy Attiso for the extra melodies and saxophonist Issa Cissako for the messages from Earth. **A–**
Orchestra Baobab: *Bamba* (Stern's Africa '93) Especially on the title song, which hails a hero of Islam, this will remind *On Verra Ça* fans of how luxuriously and site-specifically this band hears classic salsa. But in addition Barthelemy Attiso has been listening to Osibisa or maybe Santana and taking the bullshit out. Two five-cut '80–'81 LPs fit on one CD, each of which breaks up the way prime African albums usually do—three-four really good ones plus pleasant filler. A bargain. **A–**
Baobab: *N'Wolof* (Dakar Sound import '98) A mere 3800 miles west of the contemporaneous *Éthiopiques* sessions, the original Senegalese salsa band surveys its turf after hiring leather-lunged Laye M'Boup to up their trad cred with his Wolof blues. Sometimes the grooves bounce and sway on their poky three-and-two, sometimes they pace soulfully forward. Either way the voice holds—first time the soon-renowned Thione Seck takes a lead, the record briefly disappears. So praise to M'Boup, dead in a car crash in 1974. **A–**

Orchestra Marrabenta Star de Moçambique: *Independance* (Piranha import '92) Said to double-time the traditional Mozambican majika, the marrabenta rhythm no doubt adds crucial subliminal novelty to Afrodance stomps like "Tsiketa Kuni Barassara," but won't signify beyond its cultural boundaries. Neither will the indigenous sources of what sounds from here like a fairly bizarre but not unexpected Afro-European-Asian-Caribbean melange. The hook is the slack horn arrangements announced on "Elisa Gomara Saia," which evoke the nutty jazz of Indonesian gambang kromong though

I doubt that's where they come from. The jewel is the preacherly melody of the supposedly unfinished "Nwahulwana." **A–**

Organized Konfusion: *Stress (The Extinction Agenda)* (Hollywood Basic '94) Ⓝ

Orgy: *Candyass* (Elementree/Reprise '98) 💣

Orquesta Aragon: *La Charanga Eterna* (Lusafrica import '99) Ⓝ

Orquestra Was: *Forever's a Long, Long Time* (Verve Forecast '97) 💣

Beth Orton: *Trailer Park* (Heavenly '97) sincere SWF, enjoys tunes on acoustic guitar, likes technology and musos with glasses ("She Cries Your Name," "How Far") ★
Beth Orton: *Central Reservation* (Arista '99) so she wasn't techno after all—glad we got that straight ("Stolen Car," "Central Reservation [Original Version]") ★

Chief Stephen Osita Osadebe: *Kedu America* (Xenophile '96) I heard this patriarch's huge 1984 "Osondi Owendi" on the Nigerian highlife compilation I found back then and never thought about him again until this delight came in the mail. Nine cuts lasting 70 minutes recorded on one day of a 1994 U.S. tour, it shambles more than Original Music's Oriental Brothers CDs; the band is so well rehearsed it makes relaxation a creative principle, interacting casually over the clattering percussion and never-ending vamps of a genre that intimates juju drums and soukous guitar within the Ghanaian dance style that defined Afropop when Osadebe was a teenager. Known for his store of traditional guitar tunes, he likes the horns to poke their noses in as well. I hope some fan constructs a compilation from his 200 albums. But though his once sonorous voice is well weathered at 60, this one-off is an honorable testament. **A–**

Joan Osborne: "One of Us" (*Relish,* Blue Gorilla/Mercury '95) 👒

K.T. Oslin: *Love in a Small Town* (RCA Victor '90) She's rooting around in her catalogue for material, and except for the incorrigibly infatuated "Cornell Crawford" ("the first song I ever wrote," and it could keep you going), the old stuff lacks the CMA-sweeping experience of "80's Ladies" or "Didn't Expect It to Go Down This Way." But the 1990 copyrights come close, the old stuff beats most folks', the covers are perfect, and she sings like Dusty Springfield. With a drawl. Her own. **A–**
K.T. Oslin: *Greatest Hits: Songs from an Aging Sex Bomb* (RCA '93) A greatest-hits it may be, a best-of it's not. Only "80's Ladies" hints at the desperate edge of "Younger Men" and "Didn't Expect It to Go Down That Way," the sexually aggressive young "Cornell Crawford" would make a dandy companion to the sexually aggressive young "Hey Bobby," and the sexually aggressive old "Oo-Wee" would make a dandy companion to the sexually aggressive old "This Woman." Oslin deserves to be famous, but if she really wants to break pop, she should convince her handlers that taking risks means more than putting 11 cuts on your retrospective where Nashville would hold the line at 10. **A–**
K.T. Oslin: *"My Roots Are Showing . . ."* (BNA '96) Ⓝ

Os Mutantes: *Everything Is Possible!* (Luaka Bop/Warner Bros. '99) Ⓝ

Outkast: *Southernplayalisticadillacmuzik* (LaFace '94) 💣
OutKast: *Aquemini* (LaFace '98) If Dre and Big Boi were addressing real "real life situations" on *Southernplayalisticadillacmuzik* or *ATLiens,* they were drawling too unreconstructedly for any Yankee to tell. This time they're clearly about babies making babies in a place with enough nature around for that kind of biology to seem like destiny. The blackstrap flow of their live slow jams ends up an evolved G-funk with denser instrumental crosstalk, no less street for putting organ rumble or soundtrack keyb where the eerie

tweedle used to be. But even so the music's Southernness signifies as rural, evoking Booker T., endless Gregg Allman ballads, humid afternoons with horseflies droning over the hog wallow. Uncosmopolitan enough to call choruses "hooks" no matter what RZA thinks, OutKast probably would have quit dealing even if said hooks didn't get bought. And if not, they would have told some unheroic, untragic stories about it. **A–**

Overweight Pooch: *Female Preacher* (A&M '91) fatback JB hip house plus handle of the year ("I Like It") ★

Isaac Oviedo: *Routes of Rhythm Vol. 3* (Rounder '92) ⓝ

Buck Owens: *Kickin' In* (Curb/Capitol Nashville '91) 💣

Orlando Owoh: *Dr. Ganja's Polytonality Blues* (Original Music '95) "toye": jujuhighlife as four psychedelic suite-jams ("Logba Logba"/"Edumare Da Mi Lihun"/"E Se Rere"/"Prof Oyewole") ★★★

O'Yaba: *Greatest Hits* (Gallo import '97) 💣

Abiodun Oyewole: *25 Years* (Rykodisc '96) 💣

Sagreddin Ozcimi/Neceti Celik/Arif Erdebil/Kemal Karaoz: "Perde Kaldirima" (*Trance 1* [comp], Ellipsis Arts . . . '95) 🎧

Ozomatli: *Ozomatli* (Almo Sounds '98) ⓝ

O/COMPILATIONS

Ocean of Sound (Virgin import '96) This gorgeously segued 32-track tour of trad ambient radiates out from Eno's 1984 *On Land* to such pop-avant types as Terry Riley, Harold Budd, Pauline Oliveros, John Zorn, and "post-orgasmic" ethnofusioneer Jon Hassell. It includes Debussy and Satie and Cage, Asians of widely disparate cultural orientation, rain-forest Yanomamis, Sun Ra and Miles and Or-nette and Herbie sounding not especially jazzlike, two dubmasters and a bunch of white "improvisers," howler monkeys and bearded seals, Aphex Twin and My Bloody Valentine, Les Baxter and Holger Czukay and the Beach Boys and the Velvet Underground. For Toop, it answers a need that's both postmodern and millennial, synthesizing insecurity and hope, "bliss" and "non-specific dread." His selections are microcosms to dive into, not magic carpets to escape on, and gently or subtly or harshly or esoterically or whimsically or just plain oddly they accommodate the disturbing and the chaotic. Those who've settled for the diverting sounds, swelling textures, and lulling grooves of the chill-out room may never buy another Quango collection again. **A**

1-800-NEW-FUNK (NPG '94) the princely funk-lite Warner wasn't actually too good for (MPLS, "Minneapolis"; Mavis Staples, "You Will Be Moved") ★

Only for the Headstrong: The Ultimate Rave Compilation (FFRR '92) Live and on the compilations that have become a soundtrack-strength commodity in the U.K., most techno is too squiggly for nondancers if not noncyborgs—the generation that's evolved to where switched-on Bach qualifies as a golden oldie has yet to reveal itself to SoundScan. But with its lower registers, human voices, and sound-effect hooks, you could almost say this one rocks. When undulating femme chorus meets percussive computer hook on the Utah Saints' "What Can You Do for Me" and DSK's "What Would We Do," it's sci-fi pop you can believe in. No way are nondancers tired of the house riff yet. **A–**

Only the Poorman Feel It: South Africa (Hemisphere '95) Relying on EMI-affiliated artists with long-term pop ambitions, this modern mbaqanga compilation seems decisively postapartheid even though not all of it is that recent. What once might have sounded like a forced identification with a contemptuous oppressor now seems more like a forced expropriation of the oppressor's cultural capital. The great moments come from 25-year expatriate Busi Mhlongo, whose only solo album begins with the same seven-minute flight of exultant woman power that kicks off this record, and urbane revolutionary Mzwakhe Mbuli, who praises a 19th-century African king to a 21st-century African arrangement. But the glitzy production extras sound as township as the kwela fiddles throughout. **A–**

Oujda-Casablanca Introspections Vol. 1 (Barbarity import '94) With Oran's chebs and chabas repressed, depressed, or scared away by the fundamentalists, superproducer Ben Omar Rachid took to prospecting just over the Moroccan border in Oujda and finally far west in Casablanca. His first export is these eight 1988-to-1993 singles, which sound from here like the rawest, most arresting rai compilation ever. Mixing old and new with a fine disregard for anybody's verities, the Berber-Gnawa-Shabi admixtures are lighter sonically and quirkier culturally, with male-female interplay a convention and battle-of-Algiers ululations a surefire attention getter. **A–**

P: "I Save Cigarette Butts" (*P,* Capitol '95)

Jimmy Page & Robert Plant Unledded: *No Quarter* (Atlantic '94) **Ⓝ**

Jimmy Page and Robert Plant: *Walking into Clarksdale* (Atlantic '98) 🍒

Brad Paisley: *Who Needs Pictures* (Arista Nashville '99) there's words in that there cowboy hat ("He Didn't Have to Be," "Me Neither") ★★

Palace Inc.: See Will Oldham

Paleface: "Burn and Rob" (*Paleface,* Polydor '91) 📀

Pan Head, "Punny Printer" (*Love Punany Bad* [comp], Priority '95) 📀

Pansy Division: *Undressed* (Lookout '93) "We're the buttfuckers of rock and roll/We want to sock it to your hole" ("Bunnies," "The Cocksucker Club") ★

Papa San: "Maddy Maddy Cry" (*Dancehall Stylee [The Best of Reggae Dancehall Music Volume 3]* [comp], Profile '92) 📀

Papas Fritas: *Papas Fritas* (Minty Fresh '95) **Ⓝ**

Vanessa Paradis: *Vanessa Paradis* (Polydor '92) **Ⓝ**

Paris: *Sleeping with the Enemy* (Scarface '92) he tries hard, but he could use a producer ("Bush Killa," "Make Way for a Panther") ★★

Paris: *Guerrilla Funk* (Priority '94) **Ⓝ**

Paris Combo: *Paris Combo* (Tinder '99) 🍒

John Paris and Polly Jean Harvey: *Dance Hall at Louse Point* (Island '96) art project, theater tryout, like that—striking proof that *her* words mesh best with *her* music ("Dance Hall at Louse Point," "Taut") ★★

Leon Parker: *Belief* (Columbia '96) A jazz record, indisputably—an acoustic jazz record. But Parker's commitment to minimal means, tiny tunes, up-front beats, and internationalist percussion suits the soundscape mind-set—if anything, ambient wonks may find his structures too clear, his melodies too direct. Moreover, his second album accomplishes these elusive goals so fully that seekers will be compelled to interface with the music as well as the ideas. Which is one idea that's almost always a keeper. **A–**

Ray Parker Jr.: *I Love You Like You Are* (MCA '91) **Ⓝ**

William Parker & the Little Huey Creative Music Orchestra: "Sunrise in the Tone World" (*Sunrise in the Tone World,* Aum Fidelity '97) 📀

Lee Roy Parnell: "On the Road" (*Hits and Highways Ahead,* Arista '99) 📀

Dolly Parton: *Eagle When She Flies* (Columbia '91) **Ⓝ**

Dolly Parton: *Slow Dancing with the Moon* (Columbia '93) 🍒

★★★, ★★, ★ Honorable Mention　📀 Choice Cut　Ⓝ Neither　🍒 Dud　🦃 Turkey

Dolly Parton: *Hungry Again* (Decca '98) 🎸

Dolly Parton: *The Grass Is Blue* (Sugar Hill '99) bluegrass isn't magic—she could put her back into these songs because she didn't get a hernia writing them ("Cash on the Barrelhead," "I'm Gonna Sleep with One Eye Open") ★★

Dolly Parton: See also Loretta/Dolly/ Tammy, Emmylou Harris, Linda Ronstadt, Dolly Parton

Pascal's Bongo Massive Vol. 2: "Gettin' Started" (*Cream of Tomato* [comp], Moonshine Music '93) 😎

Patra: *Scent of Attraction* (550 Music/Epic '95) Ⓝ

Pavement: *Demolition Plot J-7* (Drag City '90) buzzsaw industrial on a seven-inch EP ("Fork Lift") ★★

Pavement: *Perfect Sound Forever* (Drag City '91) Hüsker Dü for the age of indie irony—hooky grunge as guitar power, turnoff splatter as loyalty test, mad drummer as mad drummer. All on 10 inches of 45-rpm vinyl-only sporting seven titles and four songs. A–

Pavement: *Slanted and Enchanted* (Matador '92) Though no outsider wants to believe it, they're not just the latest scruffy rumor. And though no insider wants to believe it, they're more well schooled than inspired—skilled, gifted, of enduring artistic value, condensing a decade of indie thrashing about into a two-year recording career that takes off with their debut album. Always good at both tune and noise, they sacrifice you-know-what for you-know-what now that they're thinking about quitting their day jobs, and as you'd expect, the content is formal: noise doesn't give up without a fight, often it fights hard, sometimes it fights dirty, and tune digs where it's coming from. Yielding a message complex enough to offer hope that the lyrics— more bemused than enraged, more depressive than despairing—will catch up. A

Pavement: *Watery, Domestic* (Matador '92) The rumor that the title means "watered-down, not wild" would bewilder music lovers outside Indieland. Though it does comprise four distinguishable, hummable songs, it isn't anything the big guys would call pop music, just a dandy outro for Drag City's EP compilation. And since nobody this good lives in Indieland forever, it raises the question of what they'll do for an encore. As they brag, admit, or observe, they've got "so much style that it's wasted." Which means the content problem is staring down their throats. A–

Pavement: *Westing (By Musket and Sextant)* (Drag City '93) This concept CD about the limits of vinyl fetishism—23 cuts off EPs, flexidiscs, and other ephemera you may have read about or even purchased—is the ideal way to hear rather than collect their song-noise, which starts out as pissed-off speedtoons crackling through the pickup of an old GE portable and gradually gets (somewhat) bigger. Even irritating instrumental doodads like "Krell Vid-User" gain presence (aka "warmth") in digital form, and besides, if you get too irritated you can zap 'em. Pretend this is all that remains of a great art-punk band that never wert and chances are you won't want to. A–

Pavement: "Unseen Power of the Picket Fence" (*No Alternative* [comp], Arista '93) 😎

Pavement: *Crooked Rain, Crooked Rain* (Matador '94) Whether the tunes come out and smack you in the kisser or rise from the clatter like a forgotten promise, this is a tour de force melodywise, which is not to get dewy-eyed about its market potential. They'll never truly sell out until they take voice lessons—as alternarockers from Stipe to Cobain know full well, soulful strength is the pop audience's bottom line. Me, I find Stephen Malkmus's eternally pubescent croaks and whinnies exceedingly apt, and though in theory I always prefer songs that aren't about music, any bunch of obscurantist jokers who can inject the words "Stone Temple Pilots they're elegant bachelors" into my hum matrix have got a right to sing the rocks. A

Pavement: *Gold Soundz* (Matador '94) 💣

Pavement: *Wowee Zowee* (Matador '95) Despite their disavowals of "progress," this proceeds as you'd figure—toward lyricism rather than commerciality or some such chimera. It's seldom hard or fast or chaotic, and if it was their sacred mission to humanize guitar noise, they've betrayed it like the reprobates they no doubt are. But if their vocation is beguiling song-music that doesn't sound like anything else or create its own rut, this reinforces one's gut feeling that they can do it forever. They can't, of course—nobody can. But the illusion of eternity has been music's sacred mission for a good long time. **A**

Pavement: "False Skorpion" (*Rattled by La Rush,* Matador '95) 👁

Pavement: *Pacific Trim* (Matador '96) Not a maxisingle—an EP consisting entirely of recommended arcana, with the bonus of lyrics that actually (seem to) make sense. But note these stats: three songs totaling 7:44 for $6.98, with the prize-winning "Gangsters & Pranksters" finishing at precisely 1:30. Why do you think they call it discretionary income? **B+**

Pavement: *Brighten the Corners* (Matador '97) Mature or die is the whole of the law. So of course there's no longer much insurgency in their ill-mannered sounds, now deployed to serenade a self-sustaining subculture and celebrate a band's collective success. Moderate tempos that once breathed psychedelic wooze turn reflective if not thoughtful as lyrics reference the material emoluments of middle-class life. Yet it's still exciting, because it isn't dragged under by the nagging disappointments that generally dull such music (and security). As convinced ironists, Pavement never expected anything else. Closure is a chimera—they'll drink to that. Onetime insurgent Thelonious Monk—they'll drink to him too. A man known for his brilliant corners. **A**

Pavement: *Stereo* (Domino import '97) completists' advisory—two good otherwise unavailables, eight bucks ("Westie Can Drum," "Winner of the") ★

Pavement: *Shady Lane* (Matador '97) The named album highlight plus three-and-a-half new ones, the half being "Type Slowly" rendered as the Stones shuffle "Slowly Typed." Two of the others are also linear in groove and structure, sparely dissonant tunelets you'll love when they get broken out live. And then there's "Wanna Mess You Around," nearly 90 seconds of crammed-with-rock, a secret classic inviting infinite revision. What EPs are for. **A–**

Pavement: *Terror Twilight* (Matador '99) Since I was fooled myself until I saw them live and knew every riff, I'm wondering why some believe there are no songs here. Probably the explanation is tempo. There's never that frantic hang-on-for-your-life moment when you either pay attention or embrace brain death—when you engage at gunpoint. And though the music seems stitched together rather than wound tight, it's never in any apparent danger of falling apart; it isn't riven or driven by internal contradictions. Thus, too much meaning is left up to the words. But that's not the same as the songs not being there—or as the meanings not being there either. **A–**

Peanut Butter Wolf: *My Vinyl Weighs a Ton* (Copasetik '99) Ⓝ

Pearl Jam: *Ten* (Epic Associated '91) in life, abuse justifies melodrama; in music, riffs work better ("Once," "Even Flow") ★★

Pearl Jam: *Vs.* (Epic Associated '93) 💣

Pearl Jam: *Vitalogy* (Epic '94) Eddie Vedder's struggles with stardom have a concreteness missing from more mythic epics of resistance. But it isn't his MTV boycott or TicketMaster stand that make his third album his best—it's his need to live up to Kurt's musical example and expiate Kurt's mythic pain. Three or four of these songs are faster and riffier than anything else in P. Jam's book, token experiments like "Bugs" are genuinely weird, and in an era of compulsory irony his sincerity is something like a relief—a Kurtlike relief at that. **A–**

Pearl Jam: *No Code* (Epic '96) slowly winning a heartwarming battle against constitutional melancholia ("Mankind," "Around the Bend") ★

Pearl Jam: *Yield* (Epic '98) The reality they come to terms with here is musical, and I'm impressed they had it in them. From the electronically foreshortened riff that announces their need for attention to "Push Me, Pull Me" studio manipulations that signal their refusal to be pigeonholed, the nice techy edge of Brendan O'Brien's production can't conceal their aesthetic conservatism or materially enhance song-writing and performance skills they've never pitched higher. Like nobody less than Nirvana (right, they're dumber, thank you for sharing), they voice the arena-rock agon more vulnerably and articulately than any Englishman standing. Rarely if ever has a Jesus complex seemed so modest. **A–**

Pearl Jam: *Live on Two Legs* (Epic '98) know more Mr. Nice Guy ("Given to Fly," "F*ckin' Up") ★★

Pearl Jam: "Soldier of Love," "Last Kiss" (*No Boundaries: A Benefit for the Kosovar Refugees,* Epic '99) 👁

Ann Peebles: *Full Time Love* (Bullseye Blues '92) beats the part-time variety in life, but not necessarily in art ("Bouncin' Back," "Fear No Evil," "Miss You") ★★

Pee Shy: "Mr. Whisper," "Much Obliged" (*Don't Get Too Comfortable,* Blue Gorilla/Mercury '98) 👁

Dawn Penn "You Don't Love Me (No No No No)" (*No No No,* Atlantic '94) 👁

Pennywise: *About Time* (Epitaph '95) Ⓝ

Pere Ubu: *Worlds in Collision* (Fontana '91) pure art-rock for art-pop people ("I Hear They Smoke the Barbecue," "Worlds in Collision") ★★★

Pere Ubu: *Story of My Life* (Imago '93) postpunk as likable litterateur, band as predictable support ("Story of My Life," "Kathleen") ★

Pere Ubu: *Ray Gun Suitcase* (Tim/Kerr '95) still rockin' (again) after all these years ("Down by the River II," "My Friend Is a Stooge for the Media Priests") ★★★

Pere Ubu: *Folly of Youth See Dee Plus* (Tim/Kerr '96) 💣

Pere Ubu: *Pennsylvania* (Tim/Kerr '98) 💣

Pere Ubu: *Apocalypse Now* (Thirsty Ear '99) Something has happened to David Thomas since this "special acoustic evening" in 1991, and though I'm tempted to call it art, it's probably just the art world. Thomas has always fiddled with art-rock, but only when he hit the museum circuit in the '90s did his respectable side get the better of him. It's impossible to imagine him endangering an ICA performance piece with "mind-dead rock" like "Non-Alignment Pact" and "I Wanna Be Your Dog"—for one thing, no attendee would think of requesting such a thing. And it's all too difficult to imagine him rocking a 1999 "acoustic evening" with such benign aggression and hang-loose cheer. "Enough fun," he announces grumpily as he cuts Iggy off at 40 seconds—leaving us to discover that "We Have the Technology" is yet to come. **A–**

The Perfect Disaster: *Asylum Road* (Genius '90) unperfected ("The Crack Up," "In Conference Again") ★★

The Perfect Disaster: *Up* (Fire '90) Speaking as an anthropologist, I note the existence of a younger generation that sees no essential difference between the Stones, the Byrds, the Velvets, and Bo Diddley—all rocked, all used guitars, all preceded the Sex Pistols or Fleetwood Mac or whoever. Speaking as a critic, I note the fine taste and good sense of these know-nothings. And speaking as a fan, I thank the Lord the Velvets dominate the equation. Think Feelies (pomo momentum), Only Ones (Perrettistic Kink-ology), Chills/Clean (parallel invention), Woodentops (plus musclebottom), maybe even Galaxie 500 (minus wimpophilia). Think "We're Gonna Have a Real Good Time Together" meets "Pale Blue Eyes." **A–**

The Perfect Disaster: *Heaven Scent* (Fire '91) 💣

The Pernice Brothers: *Overcome by Happiness* (Sub Pop '98) if the Hollies had created pop so pretty and morbid it would have been great art, but these alt sad sacks are just doing what comes naturally ("Monkey Suit," "Chicken Wire") ★★

Lee "Scratch" Perry: *From the Secret Laboratory* (Mango '90) sane weirdo exploits mad genius ("Secret Laboratory [Scientific Dancehall]," "Inspector Gadget," "African Hitchhiker") ★★★

Lee "Scratch" Perry: *Lord God Muzick* (Heartbeat '91) Prophesying, imprecating, free-associating, name-dropping, rhyming, gibbering, making animal noises, the big chief of the space police inquires into the demise of King Tubby, shoots the IMF, and conquers Chris Blackwell—among other things, all of which occur in his capacious head over Niney the Observer's equally capacious dub. Never as striking as the record he did for Blackwell, it's considerably more grooveful and sustaining. Open your ears and close your eyes, and he will give you a big surprise. A–

Lee Perry & Mad Professor: *Black Art Experrryments* (Ariwa '95) "yeah, is a good joke" ("Open Door," Jungle Safari") ★

Lee "Scratch" Perry: *Who Put the Voodoo 'Pon Reggae* (RAS '96) dub for laughs—Newcleus's munchkins, Selassie's brother, Scratch's cock ("Small Morsel," "Messy Appartment") ★★★

Pet Shop Boys: *Behavior* (EMI '91) see the movie ("Being Boring," "October Symphony") ★★

Pet Shop Boys: *Discography* (EMI '91) More even than "hit" or "product," these boys know "concept," so there's no point complaining that "the complete singles collection" includes more than half the titles on their disco album (*Introspective*—*Disco* was another concept). Truth in promotion is their byword—the complete singles is what you're gonna get even if they're also the greatest album tracks. And after an early stiff, they establish a canon right down to the previously unre-

leaseds. Cerebral, sensitive, sensationalistic, shallow, this is the sound of pleasure at a distance. And also, oh yeah, pain. **A**

Pet Shop Boys: *Very* (EMI '93) Fey and ironic *naturellement,* but I wasn't ready for baroque—techno synths, massed brass, Village People chorus boys. And I also wasn't ready for sincere. For all his "I've been a teenager since before you were born," Neil Tennant finally seems, well, ready to love—finally seems to comprehend that needing another human being is more than an experiment you perform on your feelings, a way to insure that you'll not only be ravished but ravished exquisitely. Convinced cornballs may still find his emotions attenuated, but I say the production values suit the tumult in his heart and the melodies the sweetness in his soul. And I dare anybody who still thinks he's just talking to notate his high notes. **A**

Pet Shop Boys: *Disco 2* (EMI '94) 💣

Pet Shop Boys: *Alternative* (EMI '95) two discs of marginalia proving what?—that *Very* could have been more amazing yet? ("What Keeps Mankind Alive?" "Shameless," "Too Many People") ★★

Pet Shop Boys: *Bilingual* (Atlantic '96) Neil Tennant shores up his positivity with a shrug and a question mark. Does love seem arbitrary, ineffable? Well, "That's the Way Life Is"—"It Always Comes as a Surprise." Fortunately, he hasn't given up disco, or satire either. Thus he leaves us wondering whether the hustling lip-syncher of "Electricity" has the same name as the computer-toting EEC hotshot of "Bilingual"—Neil. **A–**

Pet Shop Boys: *Nightlife* (Parlophone/Sire '99) Having spent the decade risking l-o-v-e, Neil Tennant settles down with "A borderline fool/Naive and cruel," cushions the pain with melody, adds up the damages, and accounts himself ready for more. "I only worry for your sake," the altruist-as-ironist insists as he wonders where "Boy Strange" is with who. Not to worry, he will survive—for as long as he at least hears B.S.'s "footsteps in the dark." "Only love can break your heart," he observes, and that we've heard that one before doesn't make it any less poignant—maybe more. **A–**

Tom Petty and the Heartbreakers: *Into the Great Wide Open* (MCA '91) grant him this—he's a hooky sumbitch ("Into the Great Wide Open," "Two Gunslingers") ★

Tom Petty & the Heartbreakers: *Greatest Hits* (MCA '93) Sometimes it's hard to remember what a breath of fresh air the gap-spanning MTV figurehead was in 1976. So revisit this automatic multiplatinum, a treasury of power pop that doesn't know its name—snappy songs! Southern beats! gee! Like Billy Joel, say, or the Police, his secret isn't that he's a natural singles artist—it's that he's too shallow to merit full concentration except when he gets it all right, and maybe not then. Petty is the formalist of the ordinary guy, taking his musical pleasure in roots, branches, commerce, art, whatever gets him going without demanding anything too fancy of his brain or his rear end. Footloose by habit and not what you'd call a ladies' man, he often feels confused or put upon, and though he wishes the world were a better place, try to take what he thinks is his and he won't back down. He has one great virtue—his total immersion in rock and roll. **A–**

Tom Petty: *Wildflowers* (Warner Bros. '94) If he were a flower, he'd be wilted, but since he's really more a dick, call him torpid. That Rick Rubin, what a laid-back guy. **B–** 🦃

Tom Petty and the Heartbreakers: *She's the One* (Warner Bros. '96) Ⓝ

Tom Petty and the Heartbreakers: *Echo* (Warner Bros. '99) Ⓝ

Madeleine Peyroux: *Dreamland* (Atlantic '96) channeling Patsy Cline, Edith Piaf, Memphis Minnie, and Jill Corey through Queen Billie herself ("Walkin' After Midnight," "Was I?," "Always a Use") ★

Liz Phair: *Exile in Guyville* (Matador '93) She's a rebel, and if all goes well, also a pathfinder, which isn't certain mainly because the acts and attitudes that make her a rebel are so normal. Her number of partners may be over toward the right side of the bell curve. She may have commitment problems. But for at least two decades, bohemian women of a certain age have displayed this much desire, independence, bitchiness, self-doubt, and general weirdness—while continuing to pin down the unmanly emotional aperçus that make "Dance of the Seven Veils" and "Divorce Song" so gender-specific. They can behave this way if they want—they're just not supposed to come out of the closet about it. And while Phair knows more than enough about tunes and guitars to challenge the taboo, the weirdness level of her spare, intuitive, insinuating demos-plus is bohemia-specific. Which is apt for sure. But not necessarily pathfinding. **A**

Liz Phair: *Whip-Smart* (Matador '94) "I made sure it wasn't shitty, but didn't worry about whether it was, like, A+"—L. Phair, *Billboard,* 8/6/94 ("Whip-Smart," "Shane") ★★

Liz Phair: *Juvenilia* (Matador '95) One *Whip-Smart* remix, one new wave cover, and one undeveloped new song no more fascinating than the five old Girly Sound demos that are why any noncollector should hear this CD. The hands-down keepers are the dirty joke once removed "California" and the cowboy-Iggy "South Dakota," but all are a respite from her persona, her career, her sacred mission—none of which she chose, exactly, but none of which she's shown any knack for averting. Here she's the least she deserves to be—a fecund oddball so full of ideas that creaky execution is part of the excitement. In other words, an important minor artist. **A–**

Liz Phair: *Whitechocolatespaceegg* (Matador/Capitol '98) In which a girl-rock shooting star seeks recognition as nothing more but nothing less than the imaginative, eccentric singer-songwriter she always was. Her perspective remains distinctly female even when she's impersonating men. But her prim, outspoken raunch is down to a few hints, none as memorable as "Go on Ahead"'s resigned analysis of a marriage strained by the birth of a child, or "Girls' Room"'s dream of high school, or "Uncle Alvarez"'s con man hanging from the family tree. This isn't an indie babe's album, or a blowjob queen's either. It's the work of an artist testing her capacity for fictional scenarios, of an upper-middle-class woman well past worrying why she fucks and runs. Its spare, halting, impractical, distinct, blatantly hooked sound honors the home demo over the bar raveup because it was invented by someone who shares an indigenous habitat with record geeks—the kind of bedroom that's longer on stereo equipment than ceiling mirrors. **A**

The Pharcyde: *Bizarre Ride II the Pharcyde* (Delicious Vinyl '92) surrealism in African-American life, middle-class cutup division ("Ya Mama," "If I Were President," "It's Jiggaboo Time") ★★★

The Pharcyde: *Labcabincalifornia* (Delicious Vinyl/Capitol '95) **Ⓝ**

Pharoahe Monch: *Internal Affairs* (Rawkus '99) **Ⓝ**

Martin Phillipps & the Chills: See the Chills

Sam Phillips: "Lying" (*Cruel Inventions*, Virgin '91) **☁**

Sam Phillips: *Martinis and Bikinis* (Virgin '94) give her some chiliasm, all she wants is some chiliasm ("Baby I Can't Please You," "I Need Love") ★

Sam Phillips: *Omnipop (It's Only a Flesh Wound Lambchop)* (Virgin '96) **💣**

Utah Phillips and Ani DiFranco: *The Past Didn't Go Anywhere* (Righteous Babe '96) over folk-punk thrash 'n' sample, the lefty lifer just wants to say: "No matter how New Age you get, old age gonna kick your ass" ("Nevada City, California," "Bum on the Rod") ★

Ani DiFranco & Utah Phillips: *Fellow Workers* (Righteous Babe '99) old Wobbly tells war stories, young CEO watches his back ("Direct Action," "Pie in the Sky") ★

Phish: *Hoist* (Elektra '94) **💣**

Phish: *A Live One* (Elektra '95) With their damn newsletter at 80,000 and counting, the growth of their economic base is impervious not just to criticism but to any eventuality that doesn't involve the breakdown of the American transportation system. So give 'em 10 years, and don't worry you'll miss something in the meantime. Phish isn't a classic two-guitar jamming band like the Allmans or those guys from Marin. It's a keyb-guitar-bass-drums quartet, its music dominated conceptually by the high-cholestorol chords and florid arpeggios of Page McConnell's piano. Occasionally there's a good song—naif that I am, I like the one called "Simple." But they've never put more than a couple on one studio album, and this two-hour live double is where they show off their base-building specialties, e.g., "a mind-blowing 35-minute version of 'Tweezer'"—which is actually only 31, praise God, and guess what else they got wrong? **C+ 🐢**

Phish: *Billy Breathes* (Elektra '96) **💣**

Phish: *Slip Stitch and Pass* (Elektra '97) Kinda restores your faith in humanity for these guys to make like they know the difference between intelligent and pretentious. Page McConnell plays blues, Trey Anastasio plays Jerry, and David Byrne, ZZ Top, and the 19th-century team of Joe Howard and Ida Emerson beef up the fey songwriting. Plus you have to love their long overdue Doors interpolation: "Mother . . . I want to cook you breakfast." **B+**

Photek: *The Hidden Camera* (Astralwerks '96) **Ⓝ**

Phranc: "'64 Ford" (*Positively Phranc*, Island '91) **☁**

Wilson Pickett: *It's Harder Now* (Bullseye Blues & Jazz '99) so wicked it's hard to believe he consented to, ugh, "Soul Survivor"—which opens his show ("What's Under That Dress," "Taxi Love") ★★

Jo Carol Pierce: *Bad Girls Upset by the Truth* (Monkey Hill '95) A song cycle about a Lubbock girl who seeks Jesus on the two-lane blacktop of carnal knowledge and ultimately enjoys the just desert of giving birth to Her, this is clearly the product of an abusive childhood. Like, she asks her mama what women do with all those extra ova they lay and what is she told? "Color 'em, decorate 'em, and hide 'em in the yard." And what's her dad's idea of living room conversation? "I am so horny I'd fuck a rockpile if I thought there was a snake in it." Fortunately, Jo Carol overcompensates via a verbal hypertrophy she feels compelled to display over a 78-minute album featuring some dozen songs, with equal time for explanations. And she's aided handsomely by a bunch of musicians who are there for her every time she commits suicide. **A–**

The Pine Valley Cosmonauts: "Across the Alley from the Alamo" (*Salute the Majesty of Bob Wills,* Bloodshot '98) 🍢

Pixies: *Bossanova* (4AD/Elektra '90) Though the words are less willful, they're still mostly indecipherable without the crib sheet and still mostly incomprehensible with it—leisure-class kiddies grasping at straws (or women: Black Francis has gone through three girlfriends by cut five) as the solar system bangs and whimpers to a halt. But these collegians are obscurantists no longer. Announcing their newfound religious faith with a surf-metal instrumental ("Cecilia Ann," who's not a girlfriend though Francis loves her best of all), they march out tunes so simple and confident and power riffs so grandly declamatory that you learn to understand the choruses by singing them. The beats are lively. The three-minute songs don't bash you over the head with their punk/pop brevity. Neither do the two-minute songs. If they weren't still a little gothic-surrealist they might even be too easy—but they ain't. **A**

Pixies: *Trompe le Monde* (Elektra/4AD '91) Not as catchy from the git as *Bossanova,* which with eyeballs all over the cover and escape from terra firma all over the lyric sheet is risky if you want to get a rack jobber's attention or respect.

But postpunk formalists-in-spite-of-themselves, a category that includes any consumer or tastemaker who's zoned in on 50 or a hundred relevant albums, would be fools to deny themselves the feast that awaits. These devilkins have the music down, and they never overstay their welcome. **A–**

Pixies: *Death to the Pixies* (Elektra '97) Ⓝ

Pixies: *Pixies at the BBC* (Elektra '98) exactly the live testament you think they deserve ("Manta Ray," "Wild Honey Band") ★★★

Pizzicato Five: *Made in USA* (Matador '94) Avant-pop fixtures in Japan, they're considerably more skillful than our homegrown lounge-wave bands. And despite sonics brittler than anything fashioned by Juan Garcia Esquivel, their fondness for post-1963 black dance music insures a better beat. But they have an attitude problem: an affectlessness that renders them more unreadable than Madonna or John Waters or the Pet Shop Boys or any other pop ironyworker except Saint Andy, who both invented the stance and did more with it. It's my policy never to give an inch to recording artists who say things like "Without the visuals, people wouldn't understand us." And although I might get it if I were Japanese, I'm not. In fact, I could even surmise that their failure to reveal the emotional core that glints out from Madonna and Waters and especially the Pet Shop Boys bespeaks a repressed culture that has zero claim on an alien's empathy. But I won't. **B** 🦃

Placebo: *Without You I'm Nothing* (Virgin '98) Ⓝ

Robert Plant: *Manic Nirvana* (Swan Song '90) 💣

The Plastic People of the Universe: *1997* (Globus International import '98) A great band at half the age and three-quarters the speed, they fended off the dreary horror of Prague '68 with a sardonic despond that the routine oppressions of Prague '78 ground toward somber mysticism. Eventually, as happens with sects right and wrong, their fellowship soured, and only by decree of their artist president did they regroup for democracy at this gig. But though they could still play the sax-viola-guitar-keybs-gripe top and bass-forward bottom of their old music, they weren't miserable enough to re-create its mood. At a clip that suited their existential confidence and funkier, younger drummer, their spiritual alienation fell away to reveal the sonic singularity that gave it form—a Reed-Zappa amalgam so Euro it makes a nominal blues seem like sleaze for an old Elmore Leonard flick, and so intent on forward motion that the part writing only spurs it on its way. **A**

Plastikman: *Artifakts (BC)* (Novamute '98) One needn't feel deep sympathy for the minimalist project to find use and pleasure in the right Brian Eno or David Behrman, or to conclude that, all subjective affinities aside, Tangerine Dream were full of it. Richie Hawtin is at once sparer and beatier, but not by much, and anyone who would sit there for an hour finding out where he's going has too much time to kill. The belated third volume of a trilogy whose earlier installments I dutifully checked out and guiltlessly discarded, this climaxes midway through with an uncanny evocation of static going down the drain before breaking into a cute little piece of electrofunk that might be sampled by someone with more to say. Then it moves on to Tangerine Dream. **B–** 🦃

The Pleasure Barons: *Live in Las Vegas* (HighTone '93) 💣

Plush: *More You Becomes You* (Drag City '98) Feature: "The lonely, ever uncool, always corny piano man." Bio: "Liam Hayes' new record is not just about pop, it IS pop in the classic (circa 1973) sense of the term." Wha? Has Chicago moved to another planet? (Again?) Hayes's closest relative by far is Palace Inc. CEO Will Oldham whittling mountain music down to a doleful whisper. If he's anything, and his aesthetic is so attenuated you have to

wonder, he's cool, and if his aesthetic is about anything it's about being about. Hayes's snaillike, lachrymose presongs resemble no pop in history, much less 1973. (1973?) And while it's possible to imagine a piano man this anonymously self-absorbed, no cocktail lounge would permit him to sing—unless he owned it, I guess. **C+** 🦃

P.M. Dawn: *Of the Heart, of the Soul and of the Cross: The Utopian Experience* (Gee Street '91) Not only is their mind excursion less threatening than Hammer, it embraces the Beatles and Spandau Ballet with a nerdy passion that might have been designed to assuage white consciences and fears. I doubt it, though—listen true and its escapism seems not willful but willed, Prince Be's deft, thought-out response to a world that bugs him politically, spiritually, existentially, and because he's fat. This is rap that's totally idiosyncratic, yet so lost in music it's got total outreach—moving effortlessly from speech to song, the quiet storm of sweet hooks and soft beats surprises like prime Big Star or XTC, only it's never brittle or arch. The sharpest synthesis since Prince, who we should probably start calling Prince Fuck just to keep our teen spirits straight. **A**

P.M. Dawn: *The Bliss Album . . . ?* (Gee Street '93) Success has transformed Prince Be from stereo potato into overweight lover, a phrase he lifts without attribution, and like all his multifarious appropriations, this one fits him like a caftan—flatteringly, commodiously, with room to move around. Truth, sincerity, and so forth are probably present and definitely beside the point. Whether he's rapping or crooning, boasting or begging, dishing out a verbal beatdown or plumbing the sacred essence of "Norwegian Wood," his aesthetic constructs are their own socially significant reason for being. As long as he's circumspect enough to allude to his mysterious religious beliefs rather than promulgate them, he'll be a force for good in a world that generates too many misfits and not enough b-e-a-u-t-y. **A**

P.M. Dawn: *Jesus Wept* (Gee Street '95) more sampling, less singing—please ("Fantasia's Confidential Ghetto: 1999/Once in a Lifetime/Coconut," "The 9:45 Wake-Up Dream") ★★★

P.M. Dawn: *Dearest Christian, I'm So Very Sorry for Bringing You Here. Love, Dad* (Gee Street/V2 '98) *Jesus Wept* boded mediocrity—although composing is no harder than sampling, it is different, and once he'd redefined himself as one more r&b songwriter, Prince Be's all-embracing aesthetic and fluky chart run seemed over. But working with a steady band, a sometime collaborator, and the occasional borrowed riff, he revives his spaced-out spirituality as music if not commodity, transfiguring his grumpy disillusion with melodies, vocal harmonies, and now also guitar parts, all lovingly designed to convince his son Christian to be here now. **A–**

Pogues: *Pogue Mahone* (Mesa '96) 💣

Buster Poindexter: **"The Worst Beer I Ever Had"** (*Buster's Happy Hour,* Forward '94) 🐚
Buster Poindexter: *Buster's Spanish Rocket Ship* (Island '97) the concept's an excuse to do originals, the best of which stay on concept ("Iris Chacon," "Let's Take It Easy") ★★★

Polvo: *Celebrate the New Dark Age* (Merge '94) how dark can it be if it's so full of guitars? ("Fractured [Like Chandeliers]," "Every Holy Shroud") ★

Pond: *The Practice of Joy Before Death* (Sub Pop '95) not drowning in guitars, waving ("Sideroad," "Van") ★★

The Pooh Sticks: *Formula One Generation* (Sympathy for the Record Industry '90) A shambling prank-turned-tribute reminiscent in conceptual/critical complexity of *Actually* or *Kangaroo?,* and if you have no idea what I'm talking about you won't get it. The lead cut, about

falling in love with a New Kid, begins with a dim sample from the Raspberries' "Overnight Sensation" and steals the melody of Duran Duran's "Rio." The tune after that was supposedly lifted from GG Allin. Very catchy, guys and gal. As a rock critic, I love it. **A–**

The Pooh Sticks: *The Great White Wonder* (Sweet Virginia '91) I don't approve of retro, never have. But when smart young things discover crappy old records like *Frampton Comes Alive!* and great old records like *Rust Never Sleeps,* it can be infectious. The grain of eager pop greed in Hue's Brit-wimp voice, augmented by the earnest craft that enables Paul to stick whole Neil Young solos (copied, not sampled) into borrowed Strangeloves songs, reestablishes the fading distinction between parody and celebration in order to transcend it at a higher level of consciousness—an unselfconscious one. It's even possible they want to be rich and famous. **A–**

The Pooh Sticks: *Million Seller* (Zoo '93) irony-pop gone hermeneutic—with nothing to say ("That Was the Greatest Song," "Sugar Baby") ★

The Pooh Sticks: *Optimistic Fool* (Seed '95) 🄽

Poor Righteous Teachers: **"Can I Start This"** (*Holy Intellect,* Profile '90) 🐚

Iggy Pop: *Brick by Brick* (Virgin '90) 💣
Iggy Pop: **"Louie Louie"** (*American Caesar,* Virgin '93) 🐚
Iggy Pop: **"I Wanna Live," "Pussy Walk"** (*Naughty Little Doggie,* Virgin '96) 🐚

Iggy Pop: *Avenue B* (Virgin '99) Unless "A masterpiece without a frame" and "I want to fuck her on the floor/Among my books of ancient lore" are jokes no one gets, the sole compliment one can pay this confessional poetry by a fiftysomething cocksman who Cannot Love is that at least he's willing to look like a fool. But that's been his shtick since he was bleeding himself with broken Skippy jars. Right, Ig, you're "corrupt"—no news there. Unfortunately, blaming "the paranoia of the age" and bitching "I gave em every part of me" is also corrupt. Plus one more thing: until you learn to sing a little better, maybe you'd better say goodbye to Medeski Martin & Wood and put in a call to the Sales brothers. **C** 🐛

Iggy Pop: See also Iggy and the Stooges

Popinjays: *Flying Down to Mono Valley* (Epic/One Little Indian '92) Not grrrls, not gurls—girls, as in, "There were three girls in the band, and we kind of got labeled as this fluffy, pink, girly-pop, lightweight throwaway stuff." They're "not airheads" either, right, but they do want to fit in; although "Mono" is literally a lake in California and does evoke "monophonic," it could also be short for "monogamy," the root subject of every one of these sometimes rockin', sometimes dreamy tunes. Funny thing is, the only time things work out is on the obscure Mama Cass/Mann & Weil cover "It's Getting Better." Otherwise these are tales of everyday betrayal—of being manipulated, saying the wrong thing, falling short of his expectations. All so sweet and final you wonder why they bother, and won't be surprised when they give up. Inspirational Verse: "Too transparent foolish me/I showed you more than you could see." **A−**
The Popinjays: *Tales from the Urban Prairie* (One Little Indian '94) 💣

Porno for Pyros: *Porno for Pyros* (Warner Bros. '93) 💣

Portishead: *Dummy* (Go Discs/London '94) Sade for androids ("Sour Times," "Wandering Star") ★
Portishead: *Portishead* (Go! Beat/London '97) When you're this subtle, marginal differentiation is everything. Louder tracks, sparser samples, less insinuating tunes—all these changes are slight, but they impel antistar-to-die-for Beth Gibbons six inches toward stridency, and she's hard enough to take seriously when she's toning it down. The real and theoretical depressives who adore them will experience this as growth. Workaday music lovers will glance off Gibbons's shows of misery and never figure out why. **B−** 🐛

The Posies: *Amazing Disgrace* (DGC '96) Pumped by a frenetic new rhythm section and some half-earned rage, the static tunes of Alex Chilton's hottest backup band approach peak Matthew Sweet or Chris Butler–kicked dB's. Of course it's not the Beatles or Big Star—merely emulated, the formal ideas don't sustain their excitement. But it beats Bluroroasisoraimeemann. Inspirational Verse: "When I asked you, 'Why Ontario?'/You said, 'It sounds good on the radio.'" **B+**

Powerman 5000: *Tonight the Stars Revolt!* (DreamWorks '99) 💣

Pram: *Sargasso Sea* (Too Pure/American '95) 💣

Pras: *Ghetto Supastar* (Ruffhouse '98) 💣

The Presidents of the United States of America: *The Presidents of the United States of America* (Columbia '95) younger fresher fellow ("Lump," "We Are Not Going to Make It," "Kitty") ★

Elvis Presley: "Down by the Riverside" (*The Million Dollar Quartet,* Sun/RCA '90) 📀

Pretenders: *Packed!* (Sire/Warner Bros. '90) You can catch more pop with misery than you can with connubial bliss, and whether she's feeling her losses or picking up the get-down, Chrissie Hynde is on her game. Unlikely highlights include a medium-tempo take-me-back plea, a send-up of class war, an obscurely nasty animal-rights song, and yet another medium-tempo take-me-back plea. That's right, she's groveling—yet she sounds like her own woman doing it. Must have something to do with the melody lines. **A−**
Pretenders: *Last of the Independents* (Sire '94) style over substance ("Night in My Veins," "I'm a Mother") ★★
Pretenders: *Isle of View* (Warner Bros. '95) **Ⓝ**
Pretenders: *Viva El Amor!* (Warner Bros. '99) Pretenders songs post–*Learning to Crawl* emulated the concision and riff-riding lyricism of "Brass in Pocket" while doing without the passion and focus

that made it so fiercely erotic, so vivacious and fuck-you, so independent, so special. They *felt* pop, felt tuneful and shaped and legibly emotional, but in the end they were atmospheric. Here Chrissie Hynde's writing is sharp again—the riffs have an edge, the lyrics bite. There's some strong Janis Joplin soul, a pretty ballad in Spanish I bet her young Colombian husband understands, a closer with the ridiculously in-character refrain "You bring the biker out in me," a line that goes "It's only baby's breath" in your head long after it's over. And the grudge she bears against the opener's "Popstar" is such a joy to her that she rides the "Hang On Sloopy" motive as if she thought of it yesterday, driving three consecutive song-doctored classics before her: one that references her circulatory system, one that advises love "From the Heart Down," and one that begins with the latest sally in the class war she'll never surrender: "If this is public transportation/What are you doing here?" **A−**

Kelly Price: *Soul of a Woman* (Island Black Music '98) 🎸

Toni Price: *Swim Away* (Antone's '93) Ⓝ

Toni Price: *Hey* (Discovery/Antone's '95) Austin interpreter triangulated by Memphis, Nashville, and El Lay ("Bluebird," "Too Much Coffee") ★★

Toni Price: *Low Down and Up* (Sire/Antone's '99) Ⓝ

Andy Prieboy: "Whole Lotta Love" (*Montezuma Was a Man of Faith,* Doctor Dream '91) 👒

Maxi Priest: *Bonafide* (Charisma '90) The Fat Boys have had a reggae hit. So have the Bellamy Brothers. So why not a pop-funk hit for a black Brit liteweight? Catchy on jezebels and dull on world peace, he tries to shore up the formula with subtle touches rather than simple conviction, and back in Kingston, old-time bizzers from Byron Lee to Edwin Seaga are smiling. They knew it all along—though Jah did give them a scare. **C+** 🦃

Primal Scream: *Screamadelica* (Sire/Warner Bros. '91) Ⓝ

Primal Scream: *Vanishing Point* (Reprise '97) As someone who saw the title film stoned in 1971, and loved it, I agree that this is one of the few putatively psychedelic albums ever to evoke the distractible ecstasy of actual psychedelic experience, flitting from detail to fascinating, ultimately meaningless detail. Crucially, the moods and referents that flash past are anchored by tunes and sounds so simple a zonked zombie can relate to them. But as someone not altogether dismissive of the cofeature, *Panic in Needle Park* (Charles Theater on Avenue B, you could look it up), I must also note that, pace the highly apposite Stones rip that takes the trip back to earth, "medication" has never killed a hole that didn't come back gaping the next morning—a corny truth that renders this an achievement best admired from a sane distance. **B+**

Primus: *Frizzle Fry* (Caroline '90) Don Knotts Jr. joins the Minutemen ("Mr. Knowitall," "Spegetti Western") ★

Primus: *Pork Soda* (Interscope '93) quite possibly the strangest top-10 band ever, and good for them ("Bob," "DMV") ★★

Primus: *Tales from the Punchbowl* (Interscope '95) modern teen horrors simplified—and funkified ("Wynonna's Big Brown Beaver," "On the Tweek Again") ★★

Prince: *Graffiti Bridge* (Paisley Park '90) On his third studio double in a decade, he's definitely cheating. Half the music isn't really his, and the other half is overly subtle if not rehashed or just weak: title track, generational anthem, and lead single all reprise familiar themes, and the ballads fall short of the exquisite vocalese that can make his slow ones sing. But some of the subtle stuff—"Tick, Tick Bang"'s PE-style electrobeats, say—is pretty out, most of the received stuff is pretty surefire, and from unknowns to old pros, his cameos earn their billings. Also, there's half a great Time album here—did he steal it or just conceive it? **B+**

Prince and the New Power Generation: *Diamonds and Pearls* (Paisley Park/Warner Bros. '91) doesn't know his own new power ("Willing and Able," "Jughead," "Cream") ★★

Prince and the New Power Generation: *[File Under Prince]* (Paisley Park '92) Designed to prove his utter inexhaustibility in the wake of *Diamonds and Pearls,* by some stroke of commerce his best-selling album since *Purple Rain,* this absurdly designated "rock soap opera" (is he serious? is he ever? is he ever not?) proves mainly that he's got the funk. I confess I'm too square to regale the guests at my all-ages dance party with "Sexy M.F.," a title extended to six syllables in its recorded version. But "My Name Is Prince" clears up a question posed by the title, a rune available on floppy disc to any publication willing to take his guff. And "Blue Light," a ballad that's got the reggae, is a sexy motherfucker. A–

Prince: *The Hits/The B-Sides* (Paisley Park/Warner Bros. '93) Take as a given that this is an overpriced exploitation or indulgence, depending on your point of view—that is, whether you're Prince or not. The two discs of A sides are indeed choice, but most come from albums that yield more choice (not to say choicer) stuff, and their recontextualization isn't as jaw-dropping as an admirer of our greatest popular musician might hope. Whether the duplications merit the tariff you can decide for yourself. So would the B sides justify purchase on their own were the little man so generous as to make them available as such (or were the world to end, whichever comes first)? And the answer is: maybe. The porny stuff—especially "Irresistible Bitch," "Scarlet Pussy," the wicked "Feel U Up," and the absolutely classic "Erotic City"—is must-hear for any sex fan. The funky stuff is fonky. The dog bit is like bow-wow. And the ballads are of every description, including godawful. B+

Prince: *Come* (Warner Bros. '94) porn now an annoyance, funk still a surprise ("Loose!" "Pheromone") ★★★

[File Under Prince]: *The Gold Experience* (Warner Bros./NPG '95) After two or three plays, convinced that "P Control" and "Endorphinmachine" slam harder than any hip hop I've heard in years, I shrugged and recalled that, after all, I already knew he was the most gifted recording artist of the era. But this album documents more than professional genius rampant—all of them do that. This album is a renewal. It's as sex-obsessed as ever, only with more juice—"Shhh" and "319" especially pack the kind of jolt sexy music seldom gets near and hard music never does. And you'd best believe "Shhh" and "319" are hard—not for years has the auteur (as opposed to some hired gat) sounded so black, and not for years has the guitarist sounded so rock. As for the ballads, they suffer only by their failure to dominate. One of them has already stormed the radio—and another, good for him, takes too many risks to follow. A

Prince: "Don't Talk 2 Strangers," "Girl 6" (*Girl 6* [ST], Warner Bros. '96) 🐝

[File Under Prince]: *Chaos and Disorder* (Warner Bros. '96) Always a slippery devil, he's damn near vaporized commercially over the past few years, as has his promotional budget, basically because he's reached that certain age—way too familiar for ye olde shock of the new, way too boyish for intimations of immortality. So it's understandable that what's sworn to be "the last original material recorded by [File Under Prince] 4 warner brothers records" has been ignored all around. But anybody expecting a kissoff or a throwaway radically underestimates his irrepressible musicality. Apropos of nothing, here's a guitar album for your earhole, enhanced by a fresh if not shocking array of voices and trick sounds and cluttered now and then by horns. Theme song: "I Rock, Therefore I Am." And right, WEA, it wouldn't have been a hit even with some muscle behind it. A–

[File Under Prince]: *Emancipation* (NPG '96) Writing the book for the young turks of a reborn, historically hip r&b—three disks and hours of liberation, hubris, divine superfluity, and proof that he can come all night even if by six in the morning it takes too long and he never actually gets hard. Yet although there's not a bad track in the 36, I bet he himself would have trouble remembering them all, and hear nothing that tops the Delfonics and Stylistics covers, which latter wasn't the debut single for nothing and flopped anyway. Great grooves abound, however. As does great singing. Harmonies too. Did I mention that the horns are surprisingly cool? And hey, the little guy has a sense of humor. **A–**

[File Under Prince]: *Rave Un2 the Joy Fantastic* (Arista '99) put it this way—two decades after "What'd I Say," Ray Charles's shtick was a lot tireder ("Hot Wit U," "Undisputed") ★★

Prince: See also 1-800-NEW-FUNK

Prince Paul: *Psychoanalysis (What Is It?)* (WordSound '96) Melding classic reggae and Miami booty-bass, Muddy Waters harp and Schoolly D scratch, cocktail vibes and sacred quartet, the Native Tongue beatmaster turned gravedigging heretic assembles "senseless skitstyle material" by "a motley crew of ill characters and cronies from around the way who resemble a P-Funk on crack (wait, P-Funk was on crack)" into a disturbing laff riot whose dramaturgy is more musical than De La Soul's songs. There's even a sweet-chorused romantic ballad about rape and homicide, two of each, but don't worry—they're only a dream, with a fake Viennese muttering eager encouragement in the background. **A–**

Prince Paul: *Prince Paul Presents A Prince Among Thieves* (Tommy Boy '99) The main thing wrong with this record is that it's too short at 77 minutes: character sketches like Kool Keith's ordnance man, Big Daddy Kane's pimp, and Chubb Rock's crime lord could easily be fleshed out. Deploying hip hop stereotypes of mythic proportions in a coherent fable, it isn't just one of the few hip hop albums ever to make you look forward to the next skit—it's the closest thing to a true rock opera you've ever heard. So root for Chris Rock to turn it into the movie few optioned properties become. And note that while the full meaning of the title track, for instance, depends on the story, the songs hold up when you program around the skits. I'm not claiming Tommy Boy can break the steady-funking Albert King jam "What U Got," where gangsta Sha and good kid Breeze have much love for each other. But I'm not claiming Sleater-Kinney's about to go gold, either. **A**

John Prine: *The Missing Years* (Oh Boy '91) Occasionally too fantastic but never too bitter, the sagest and funniest of the new Dylans writes like he's resigned to an unconsummated life and sounds like he's enjoying one. Augmenting his droll drawl and a band comprising his producer and his engineer, the studio allstars might be visiting his living room, which is always the idea. He says he put a lot into his first album in five years because he figured it might be his last ever, which it won't be; I attribute its undeviating quality, gratifying variety, and amazing grace to talent, leisure time, and just enough all-star input. I wouldn't swear there's a stone classic here—just nothing I wouldn't be happy to hear again. **A–**

John Prine: *The John Prine Anthology: Great Days* (Rhino '93) There aren't 41 best Prine songs. There are 50, 60, maybe more; the only way to resolve quibbles would be a bigger box than commerce or decorum permits. And his catalogue's out there, with *John Prine, Sweet Revenge,* and *Storm Windows* durable favorites. But this is just the place to access his kind, comic, unassumingly surreal humanism. Prine's a lot friendlier than your average thriving old singer-songwriter (Young, Thompson, Cohen), and his disinclination to downplay his natural warmth or his folk-rock retro may make him impenetrable to victims of irony proficiency amnesia. But no one writing has a better feel for the American colloquial—its language, its culture, its life. **A**

John Prine: *A John Prine Christmas* (Oh Boy '93) you know he's a cornball at heart, and you know some of these songs, but if you're as Yule-friendly as he is you won't care ("Silent Night All Day Long") ★

John Prine: *Lost Dogs and Mixed Blessings* (Oh Boy '95) Although ex-Heartbreaker Howie Epstein gets more hooks out of his acoustic warrior than his old boss is tossing off, his idea of radio-ready does leave one waiting for the guitarist to shut up already. But usually that's because you're impatient for the next line, and usually it's a winner—if anything, Prine's waggish pathos and lip-smacking Americanese have been whetted by the divorce that keeps nosing in where it's not wanted. Homely thematic/metaphorical leaps are a common structural device—first the TV is hollering at him, then his wife ("They already think my name is where in the hell you been"), then the voice in his head that won't leave him alone. **A**

John Prine: *Live on Tour* (Oh Boy '97) four previously unreleaseds, three previously rereleaseds, who cares—he's got a million of 'em ("Lake Marie," "Stick a Needle in Your Eye") ★★

John Prine: "Let's Talk Dirty in Hawaiian" (*Lucky 13* [comp], Oh Boy '98) 🍥

John Prine: *In Spite of Ourselves* (Oh Boy '99) After two years of cancer treatments underwritten by George Strait's version of a throwaway written with Roger "I'd Like to Teach the World to Sing" Cook, the cheating songs and Nashville novelties on this duet album are a perfect way for Prine to keep his hand in until his muse feels as glad to be alive as he does. Every one of his helpmates—not just Trisha Yearwood and Emmylou Harris and Dolores Keane and Lucinda Williams, but creaky old Connie Smith and Melba Montgomery, and also feisty young Fiona Prine—pretties up his soundscape. But the costar is Iris DeMent, who kills on both the Bobby Braddock cornpone of "(We're Not) the Jet Set" (rhymes with "Chevro-let set") and the conflicted spouse-swapping of the impossible old George & Melba hit "Let's Invite Them Over"—as well as Prine's only new copyright, the title track,

in which a husband and wife who love each other to death paint totally different pictures of their marriage. **A**

Prisonshake: *Della Street* (Scat '91) 💣

The Prodigy: *Experience* (Elektra '93) assaults get irritating sometimes, sense of humor or no sense of humor ("Jericho") ★★

The Prodigy: *Music for the Jilted Generation* (Muse '95) They acted so stupid when I caught them opening for Moby that I passed off their Mercury Prize as techno tokenism. Nor was I impressed by the failed ad campaign of a title, or the picture of a longhair defending the chasm between big bad city and vernal rave with a stiff finger and a big knife. But this is stupid in the very best way. The style of sensationalism is fireworks display—pinwheels and Roman candles and star-bursts popping out of rockets midair. Sound effects too, of course—breaking glass is a favorite—and even ideas involving melody if not harmony, including a flute solo. One of the rare records that's damn near everything you want cheap music to be, and without a singer on the premises. **A**

Prodigy: *The Fat of the Land* (Maverick/Warner Bros. '97) smack them up, they deserve it, but they still got the beats ("Mindfields," "Funky Shit") ★

Professor Griff and the Last Asiatic Disciples: *Pawns in the Game* (Skyywalker '90) Of course he's serious; who could doubt it? Griff's problem (one of them, I mean) is that he's too serious—Chuck D is too serious, and Chuck is Kid if not Play by comparison. What little pleasure contaminates this music is like a Stryper solo, or a folksinger who's decided a drummer might bring his or her message to the masses—biting Chuck or the Last Poets, Griff's a lame, and the Lads are followers. Even the list of U.S. war crimes, the strongest dumbass leftist moment in a scattershot analysis, is compromised by praise for Khomeini and Lieutenant Jerry Rawlings. And though he adjudges the universal price code a tool of the Great Satan, he didn't have the clout or the principle to keep it off his package. **C** 💣

Professor Griff: *Blood of the Profit* (Lethal '99) Begins with *indisputable documentary evidence* that race mixing is a Communist Party plot. Gets worse. **D** 💣

Propellerheads: *Decksandrumsandrockandroll* (DreamWorks '98) **◐**

The Psychedelic Furs: *World Outside* (Columbia '91) 💣

Public Enemy: *Fear of a Black Planet* (Def Jam '90) All preemptive strikes to the contrary, this is a far better record than there was any reason to expect under the circumstances. It's not unusually inflated or self-involved, and though its brutal pace does wear down eventually, it's got a sense of humor, not just from a Flav who keeps figuring stuff out but from Chuck, whose "Pollywanacraka" message and voice—people keep bringing in Barry White or Isaac Hayes, but he's playing the pedagogue, not the love man, maybe some Reverend Ike figure—is the album's most surprising moment. And it's no more suspect ideologically than they've ever been, with the anti-Semitic provocation of "Terrordome" and the homophobic etiology of "Meet the G That Killed Me," both objectionable and neither one as heinous or as explicit as it's made out to be, countered somewhat by a clumsy attempt at a pro-woman slant and the spectacularly sure-footed rush of "Terrordome" itself. Shtick their rebel music may be, but this is show business, and they still think harder than anybody else working their beat. **A**

Public Enemy: *Apocalypse 91 . . . The Enemy Strikes Black* (Def Jam/Columbia '91) Hard, hard, hard—hard beats, hard news, hard 'tude. Hard on the brother man (African slave traders, black rookies, dead gangstas, malt liquor addicts, Quiet Storm, *Jet,* and anybody who calls Flav "nigga"). Trademark dissonances and quick-witted interactions are sui generis, yet it's so in-your-face spare and sneaky

deliberate that it's further from *Fear of a Black Planet* than *Black Planet* was from *Nation of Millions,* which was a lot further than a nation of others noticed. Strong top to bottom, it could peak higher: the closest thing to a "Bring the Noise" or "Terrordome" or even "911" is that nigga song. Motto: "Justice evolves only after injustice is defeated." **A**

Public Enemy: *Greatest Misses* (Def Jam '92) seven worthy remixes, two cultural criticisms, four us-against-thems cum me-against-thems ("Air Hoodlum," "Gett off My Back") ★★★

Public Enemy: *Muse Sick-N-Hour Mess Age* (Def Jam '94) For a time PE's confrontational music/ideology compelled young blacks to hope that consciousness would get them somewhere, and don't think it was the limitations of Chuck's worldview that left them hanging. He never said it would be as easy as pop fans always expect, but he must have figured racism was a little more tractable than this. And when it wasn't, well, here came da gangstas—copping instant gratification for the padded jeepbeats they dealt, they talked tough and stayed out of the man's way. Taken for granted as an elder statesman by the young turks who are always coming up, resented for leading on middle-class followers who've since discovered War and Rose Royce, what can poor Chuck D do 'cept rap in a rock and roll band? So he harangues and excoriates same as always, his dense rhetoric deep with puns, his hard beats charging you up just when you think the enamel on your bicuspids will never be the same. Over and above the gangsta-dissing "So Whatcha Gone Do Now?" and the ecology-dropping "Bedlam 13:13," half these tracks dynamite the harshly layered formula one way or another and the other half reprise a great sound. Some kind of funk, I swear, and if I understand the complaints that they sound like a damn alternative rock group, well, I always did—that's one reason I love them. **A−**

Public Enemy: *He Got Game* (Def Jam '98) Who better than the sports addict who wrote "Air Hoodlum" with no prompting from Spike Lee to comprehend and then control the soundtrack concept? Note, however, that for all the we're-back bluster and covertly sexist anti-r&b rhetoric, the closest it gets to the stressful speed of classic PE is on one of the 7 (of 12) songs Shocklee-Shocklee-Sadler didn't produce, the Danny Saber–Jack Dangers closer "Go Cat Go." Instead you'll hear backup femmes, churchy chorales, skeleton beats, Wu strings, more guest rappers than advertised, and funk samples, although these are outnumbered by hooks appropriated subtly (in fact, brilliantly) from "James Bond Theme" and the Who's "Won't Get Fooled Again" and blatantly (also brilliantly) from Buffalo Springfield's "For What It's Worth." On the latter, Steve Stills himself blubbers a climactic coda. Over-the-hill blowhards gotta stick together. **A**

Public Enemy: *There's a Poison Goin On . . .* (Atomic Pop '99) hating playas is fine, hating play amn't ("41:19," "What What") ★

Puff Daddy & the Family: *No Way Out* (Bad Boy '97) death—the greatest hook of all ("I'll Be Missing You," "What You Gonna Do?") ★★
Puff Daddy Featuring Jimmy Page: "Come With Me" (*Godzilla: The Album* [ST], Epic/Sony Music Soundtrax '98) ☻
Puff Daddy: *Forever* (Bad Boy '99) Nobody who didn't want money from him ever said he could rap, but he did have a spirit and a community, both now gone—one because it's harder to stay human on top than to act human getting there, the other because anointing Biggie your co-producer doesn't make him any less gone. Wallowing in otiose thug fantasies and bathetic hater-hating, hiring big names who collect their checks and go, he is indeed hateful if not altogether devoid of musical ideas. And for inducing a cute-sounding little-sounding girl to pronounce the words "hit-makin', money-havin', motherfuckin' pimp" he should be taken to family court. **C+** 🐝

Pulnoc: *Pulnoc* (Globus International import '91) If their Arista power-glitz leaves you craving something more mythic, murky, and underdeveloped, happy hunting. Maybe you could prevail upon a world traveler to find a copy on the far side of the EEC. Sometimes calm, often passionate, usually gloomy, always earned, and a potential boon to post-Stalinist foreign exchange. **A–**
Pulnoc: *City of Hysteria* (Arista '91) I balked because I loved the dark inevitability of my live tape, but for you, the problem will more likely be their provincial notion of good rock and roll—of "rock." And to make our unease mutual, new guitarist Tadeus Vercak's articulated strut and ex-guitarist Josef Janicek's high keybs skirt schlock-metal flash and art-rock ostinato respectively. But this is just the American studio version, complete with digital definition and dollops of English, of a music whose strength has always been a stylistic commitment, misprised though it may be, that has nothing to do with rock and rollers' provincial notions of the latest in consciousness. Existential anxieties that might merit a postcollegiate sneer in America spoke for the people in Stalinist Prague and continue to signify in the Ur-Bush version. Ditto for lovingly nurtured musical melodrama that seems more inevitable every time through. **A–**
Pulnoc: *Live in New York* (Globus International import '98) Cut the night after the U.S. debut of the Plastic People Mach II, which produced the never-released board tape I called *Live at P.S. 122* when I named it my favorite recording of 1989, this subtracts a two-song encore and adds local avant-Slavophiles Elliott Sharp on saxophone and Gary Lucas on guitar. Unbeknownst to me till I examined the booklet, it also translates half my concert review into Czech. I'm flattered, but I still prefer my blunter, wilder version. The power of this music for Americans is its reclamation of arena-rock as motor of liberation, and this illusion is not enhanced by embellishment or distraction. On the

other hand, it isn't demolished by them either. Covering William Blake and Lou Reed, deploying cello as low-tech synthesizer, betting all their marbles on a lead singer who's six months pregnant, they rock out as if they can make walls fall. **A–**

Pulp: *His 'n' Hers* (Island '94) **◑**
Pulp: *Different Class* (Island '96) The year won't produce a more indispensable song than "Common People," but that doesn't mean young Americans know enough about the bourgeoisie to get it. And when sex gods are added up, Bryan Ferry plus Blurandoasis won't equal George Michael. But beyond his devotion to songcraft, Jarvis Cocker isn't Bluroroasis—Culture Club with lyrics is more like it. Smart and glam, swish and het, its jangle subsumed beneath swelling crescendos or nagging keybs and its rhythms steeped in rave, this isn't pat enough for the disco-still-sucks crowd. And although Cocker's stick-to-itiveness over four expendable albums suggests that he's attained a measure of maturity, his breakthrough is a mutation, not a fruition. If "Common People" should fall short, I recommend Island proceed directly to "Something Changed," a happy love song every bit as clever and realistic as his class war song. **A–**
Pulp: "Help the Aged" (*This Is Hardcore,* Island '98) **☜**

Pulsars: *Pulsars* (Almo Sounds '97) record collectors and their robot trying very hard to feel ("Silicon Teens," "Tunnel Song") ★★

The Puppies: "Do Our Own Thang," "Funky Y-T-C," "Summer Delight" (*The Puppies,* Chaos/Columbia '94) **☜**

Pure Gold: *By the Rivers of Babylon* (Shanachie '90) mbube harmonies sweeten mbaqanga beats—jaunty always, inspiring sometimes, intense never ("Ubani Oku Holayo," "Nginethuba Lami") ★★★

Pylon: *Chain* (Sky '90) Their low registers, deliberate silences, and inexorably unmechanical beat all feed a muscular musical solidity with no real parallels—10 years after, the only band that sounds remotely similar is Gang of Four, who are frantically neurasthenic by comparison. Of course, Gof4 hoped to change the world, where Pylon mean merely to transcend it, which is only possible till the music's over. So 10 years after, maybe Vanessa's relatively down-to-earth lyrics mean she's headed in the right direction. And while the music's on you can still get lost in it. **A–**

Quad City DJ's: *Get On Up and Dance* (Atlantic/Big Beat '96) they think they can they know they can ("C'mon n' Ride It [The Train]," "Get On Up and Dance") ★★★

Quasi: *Featuring "Birds"* (Up '98) Unlike most young quasi-intellectuals with a keyb and a tune sense, Sam Coomes isn't too cool to sing from his own experience. Bitter but not self-indulgent about it, he's better on wage slavery, which he hates, than on love, which he merely finds wanting, and peaks when he explains how they intersect on the profoundly weary "It's Hard to Turn Me On." Nor would he give off so much life without the furious drumming of Sleater-Kinney's own Janet Weiss, who no doubt found it harder to turn him on when she was his wife. **A–**

Quasi: *Field Studies* (Up '99) if someone were to call Sam Coomes an archetypal indie whiner, how would you respond? what about if I did? ("A Fable with No Moral," "Empty Words") ★★

4 Etoiles: *Sangonini* (Stern's Africa '93) **◑**

Finley Quaye: *Maverick a Strike* (Epic '97) either too dubwise or not dubwise enough ("Sunday Shining," "It's Great When We're Together") ★★

Queen Latifah: "Fly Girl" (*Nature of a Sista',* Tommy Boy '91)
Queen Latifah: *Black Reign* (Motown '93) real Intelligent Black Woman, expedi-

ent Gangsta Bitch ("Coochie Bang . . . ," "U.N.I.T.Y.," "Black Hand Side") ★★★

Queen Latifah: *Order in the Court* (Motown '98) A success story whose taste in beats has always run pop, she vowed to "burn MC's like calories" and was off the charts in a month for her trouble. Oh well—if Chuck D can't get respect with Spike Lee behind him, what can a fat-flaunting, sitcom-fronting, dyke-playing woman expect? Here's hoping she swings every way she wants and recommending her sexual ambivalence to females everywhere. Things get bland and icky, especially when designated ingenue Inaya Jafan makes nice to the fellas, but the thematic "Yes/No" is educational right down to its tender skit. And for what it's worth, by the end of the record she seems to be proposing to the guy it's aimed at. Really, 28 isn't too old—and Latifah knows it. **B+**

Queen Pen: *My Melody* (Li'l Man/Interscope '98) 💣

Queens of the Stone Age: *Queens of the Stone Age* (Loosegroove '98) 💣

The Queers: *Love Songs for the Retarded* (Lookout! '93) for 16 songs in 36 minutes, they ♥ Ramones and rhyme with "beers" ("Ursula Finally Has Tits," "Fuck the World") ★

The Queers: *Move Back Home* (Lookout '95) ⓝ

Q-Tip: *Amplified* (Arista '99) Q-Tip's agenda is the hundred or so electrobeats that pulse identically for the first 20 seconds of the lead "Wait Up," before he opens his mouth to announce a "brand new page." Thus does the man who made Ron Carter the embodiment of hip hop humanism assert his solo personality, and let the Quest fans who'll never forgive him catch arthritis and die. He gets stronger music out of hard beats than he ever did out of soft jazz, and those surprised by how much he likes sex are in denial. He's his own man, and vivrant for it. **A**

PQ/COMPILATIONS

Passengers: *Original Soundtracks I* (Island '95) 💣

Pass the Mic: The Posse Album (Priority '96) Thirteen multirapper competitions/collaborations, most circa 1988–1992, juiced not just by shifting styles but by the pleasure-driven, word-mad forays the freestyle cutting session was invented for. Hip hop specialists will be down with Marley Marl's "Symphony Vol. 1," Main Source's "Live at the Barbeque," and Showbiz & AG's "Bounce Ta This." For most of us such happy flukes spice the far-from-overexposed likes of "Ladies First" and "Knick Knack Paddy Whack" just right. **A−**

Phat Rap Flava '95 (Cold Front '95) jeepbeats nationwide (69 Boyz, "Tootsee Roll [Set It Off Dance Version]"; Way 2 Real, "The Butterfly [Chux Party Mix]") ★★

Pimps, Players and Private Eyes (Sire/Warner Bros. '92) ⓝ

Pop Fiction (Quango '96) Thank Jason Bentley and Warren Kalodny for listening to more ambient techno and acid jazz than most humans can stand. Gleaning tracks from albums I'd already dismissed as trifles (Alex Reece, Barry Adamson, *Kids*) and albums that would have joined the pile if I'd heard them (Patrick Pulsinger, Manna, Strange Cargo), they lay a nice assortment of sonic profiles atop a nice assortment of dark grooves in a pomo-noir synthesis of Martin Denny, Henry Mancini, Brian Eno, and house music all night long. It's got a good beat and you can fall asleep to it. Only you might wake up feeling weird. **A−**

Pop-Rai and Rachid Style (Earthworks '90) Algeria's kitchen sink (Cheb Sahraoui, "Lila Sekri Andi"; Cheb Zahouani, "MaNsal") ★★★

The Preacher's Wife (Arista '96) 💣

Prodigy Present the Dirtside Recordings Volume One (Beggars Banquet '99) ⓝ

Profilin': The Hits (Arista '99) beyond "It Takes Two" and "It's Like That," which nobody considering this purchase doesn't own, long on novelty (Poor Righteous Teachers, "Rock Dis Funky Joint"; N2Deep, "Back to the Hotel") ★

Putumayo Presents the Best of World Music: Volume 1: World Vocal (Rhino '93) UNESCO greeting card for the ear (Juan Luis Guerra y 440, "Ojalá Que Leva Café"; the Bhundu Boys "Magumede") ★
Putumayo Presents the Best of World Music: Volume 2: Instrumental (Rhino '93) Essentially, this music to shop by showcases folkies from industrialized nations who correct for their deficient rhythmic élan with percussion devices more ethnic and less loud than one of those nasty trap sets. It turns the likes of Rossy and Ali Akbar Khan into easy-listening whores by association. It's why moralists think "world music" is an exploitation—and why hedonists think it's a drag. **C–** 🦃

Quannum Spectrum (Quannum Projects '99) deepest grooves in the underground (Lyrics Born, "Hott People"; Divine Styler & DJ Shadow, "Divine Intervention") ★★

Queens of African Music (Music Club '97) like most continents, Africa has more kings (Amy Koïta, "Soman"; Oumou Dioubate, "Christiana") ★

Sun Ra: *The Singles* (Evidence '96) seminal DIY, bullshit included ("Rocket #9," "The Sun One," "Big City Blues") ★★★

Radiohead: "Creep" (*Pablo Honey,* Capitol '93) 🐚

Radiohead: *The Bends* (Capitol '95) Admired by Britcrits, who can't tell whether they're "pop" or "rock," and their record company, which pushed (and shoved) this follow-up until it went gold Stateside, they try to prove "Creep" wasn't a one-shot by pretending it wasn't a joke. Not that there's anything deeply phony about Thom Yorke's angst—it's just a social given, a mind-set that comes as naturally to a '90s guy as the skilled guitar noises that frame it. Thus the words achieve precisely the same pitch of aesthetic necessity as the music, which is none at all. **C** 🦃

Radiohead: *OK Computer* (Capitol '97) My favorite Pink Floyd album has always been *Wish You Were Here,* and you know why? It has soul, that's why—it's Roger Waters's lament for Syd, not my idea of a tragic hero but as long as he's Roger's that doesn't matter. Radiohead wouldn't know a tragic hero if they were cramming for their A levels, and their idea of soul is Bono, who they imitate further at the risk of looking even more ridiculous than they already do. So instead they pickle Thom Yorke's vocals in enough electronic marginal distinction to feed a coal town for a month. Their art-rock has much better sound effects than the Floyd snoozefest

Dark Side of the Moon. But it's less sweeping and just as arid. **B–** 🦃

Radish: *Restraining Bolt* (Mercury '97) the right music at the wrong time ("Failing and Leaving," "Sugar Free") ★★

Raekwon: *Only Built 4 Cuban Linx . . .* (Loud/RCA '95) A lushly impenetrable jungle of sonic allusions transforms the nightmare of the crack era into a dream of cream skimmed and warmed for the bathtub—a dream with its own internal logic, moral weight, and commitment to beauty. It's an illusion, as any project denizen caught in the crossfire knows. But materially and metaphorically, Wu-Tang's power to create this illusion provides a way out of the hell underneath—especially, but not exclusively, for them. **A–**

Raekwon: "Skit No. 1," "All I Got Is You Pt. II" (*Immobilarity,* Loud '99) 🐚

Rage Against the Machine: *Rage Against the Machine* (Epic Associated '92) metal for rap lovers—and opera haters ("Wake Up," "Know Your Enemy") ★

Rage Against the Machine: *Evil Empire* (Epic '96) Three years late, it's the militant rap-metal everybody knew was the next big thing. Zack de la Rocha will never be Linton Kwesi Johnson. But collegiate leftism beats collegiate lots of other things, not to mention high school misogyny, and it takes natural aesthetes like these to pound home such a sledgehammer analysis. **A–**

★★★, ★★, ★ Honorable Mention   🐚 Choice Cut   Ⓝ Neither   🌶 Dud   🦃 Turkey

Rage Against the Machine: "The Ghost of Tom Joad" (*No Boundaries: A Benefit for the Kosovar Refugees,* Epic '99) 🐟
Rage Against the Machine: *The Battle of Los Angeles* (Epic '99) if only it promised as much for the future of rock leftism as for the future of rock guitar ("Calm Like a Bomb," "War Within a Breath") ★

Rahzel: *Make the Music 2000* (MCA '99) having fun with the human beatbox (and friends) in the studio (and onstage) ("Southern Girl," "Night Riders") ★

Railroad Jerk: *Railroad Jerk* (Matador '90) steam-powered industrial ("In My Face") ★
Railroad Jerk: *One Track Mind* (Matador '95) ⓝ
Railroad Jerk: *The Third Rail* (Matador '96) Marcellus Hall represents Manhattan art-slackerdom like the proud denizen he is. Whether courting a librarian or donning the left-wing blackface of "Objectify Me," he's got his vernacular literacy down, and he can also write a chorus. Talk about local color—there's even a song with "shareholders" in it. **B+**

The Raincoats: *Extended Play* (Smells Like '94) sui generis after all these years ("Don't Be Mean," "No One's Little Girl") ★
The Raincoats: *Looking in the Shadows* (DGC '96) I hate to be schematic, but they ask for it: for the first 10 tracks, the songs alternate in lockstep, Ana Da Silva–Gina Birch and forgettable-remarkable. What puts this comeback over the top is that the last two go Birch–Da Silva remarkable-remarkable—the literal "Love a Loser," which should be a single if only because the infertility fantasy and the old-age fantasy and even the pretty fantasy are a little too remarkable for MTV, and Da Silva's title tune, which summons empathy for a jilted stalker who ends up getting hold of his fantasies. And as always, only at a higher level of instrumental expertise, the band's musical charms are coextensive with its limitations. **B+**

Bonnie Raitt: *Luck of the Draw* (Capitol '91) One reason it took Raitt two decades to achieve the El Lay iconicity she deserves is her resistance to both folk gentility and studio antisepsis. So praise Don Was for humanizing the control-freak production values she could never get on top of in the '70s. Another is her moral seriousness. So praise songwriters like John Hiatt, Bonnie Hayes, and maybe even Paul Brady for combining heft with hookcraft, and Shirley Eikhard, whoever she is, for "Something to Talk About," the slyest distillation of this rowdy Quaker's sexy ways since "Love Me Like a Man." But after that tell Raitt that no commercial reservation should ever torpedo a "Tangled and Dark," about a deep, long wrangle with love itself, or an "All at Once," about losing the teenage daughter she's never literally had. It's like the guitar she's afraid she hasn't properly mastered—she stops writing at the risk of her own intelligence, idiosyncrasy, and reality. **A**
Bonnie Raitt: *Longing in Their Hearts* (Capitol '94) ⓝ
Bonnie Raitt: *Road Tested* (Capitol '95) Her supposed comeback in fact a breakthrough, she never approached gold back in the day, and hence was never big enough for a live album until now. This is lucky timing, because Grammy-era bland-out seldom dulls her concerts, where her roots-respectin' rockers come out raunchy, her tender ballads casually intimate. Even if you love *Nick of Time,* this two-CD mix of old songs and new illustrates why Raitt became an icon while Ronstadt turned into a gargoyle. She creates a world in which Bruce Hornsby and Bryan Adams project as much soul as Ruth Brown and Charles Brown. She's so free of ironic impurities she sings "Burning Down the House" as if it means one thing. And her parting words aren't "Take care of yourselves"—they're "Take care of each other." **A–**
Bonnie Raitt: *Fundamental* (Capitol '98) I'd rest easier claiming this album sounds like middle-aged sex—creaky, caring, not shy about adjusting its groove—if

it weren't for the other thing it sounds like, which is the debut album she cut with a bunch of folkie eccentrics when she was 21. So just say it sounds like Bonnie Raitt, old before her time as always. Songwise it's a little less consistent than *Luck of the Draw,* but now that Don Was has withdrawn there's finally some mess to go with her slide—Tchad Blake's kind of mess, in which junk is recycled into decor and everybody leaves coffee cups on the speaker cases. Some of them come from Starbucks. Some are straight out the vending machine. Some are Fiestaware originals. **A–**

Rakim: *The 18th Letter: The Book of Life* (Universal '97) his canon has a clarity his comeback can't match ("When I'm Flowin'," "It's Been a Long Time") ★★
Rakim: *The Master* (Universal '99) the classicism that had better be its own reward ("Strong Island," "When I B on tha Mic") ★

Rammstein: *Sehnsucht* (Slash '98) ⓝ

Ramones: *Mondo Bizarro* (Radioactive '92) More like an old country singer (George Jones leaving Epic, say) than the world's greatest rock and roll band (greater than Mick's side project, anyway), Joey and whoever (Johnny credited on guitar, Dee Dee cowriting two good songs, Marky ditto, C.J. singing Dee Dee) do right by their formula. Reasons to believe: the Dee Dee ballad Joey sings, and the Beach Boys tribute that goes, "Touring, touring, it's never boring." **A–**
Ramones: *Acid Eaters* (Radioactive '94) hippiedom as punk ("My Back Pages," "Have You Ever Seen the Rain") ★
Ramones: *Adios Amigos!* (Radioactive '95) ⓝ
Ramones: *It's Alive* (Sire/Warner Archives '95) Redundant when it was dropped on the punk-besotted U.K. in 1979, this concert is precious history now—seems so impossibly light and quick it makes you suspect they didn't sustain their live pace into their forties after all. Partly it's repertoire—the 28 songs

reprise their three best albums, and all but a couple are still classics. Mostly, though, it's Tommy, who hung in for five years without ever turning show drummer. They needed Marky (and Richie) to drive them on. But it was Tommy who designed the vehicle. **A–**

Lesego Rampolokeng with the Kalahari Surfers: "The Desk" (*End Beginnings,* Shifty import '92) 😖

Rancid: *Rancid* (Epitaph '93): punk rant at its streetest ("Rejected," "Adina") ★★
Rancid: *Let's Go* (Epitaph '94) scattershot rads in the U.S.A. ("Harry Bridges," "Burn") ★★★
Rancid: *. . . And Out Come the Wolves* (Epitaph '95) Third time out they're as far ahead of the Offspring as they are behind the Clash. Musically, their oi-ska 'core has got it going on—the 19 anthems start catchy, rev up the guitar in the middle, tail off to catch their breath, and climax with two war chants and a piece of personal invective that I hope isn't about Green Day because that would be petty. But their words only go halfway, which matters when you honor the literal and print your lyrics—their stories vague out, their slogans implode, and their politics have no future. Even in punk terms, they're not great singers either. Not only won't they change the world, they won't change rock and roll. Which is no reason not to wish them well. **A–**
Rancid: *Life Won't Wait* (Epitaph '98) With punk revivalism deemed almost as uncouth as frat-boy ska in these postalt times, the three-year hiatus since *. . . And Out Come the Wolves* may have flattened the rep of one of the few bands to get either style right. That's how pop works—you work your claim, times change, you lose. But art is more forgiving, and aesthetically, this beaty disc is an improvement—snakier in the bass and loopier in the vocals, careening forward in a lovely confusion that never approaches thrash or march (well, maybe march). Whatever their ideas about black lung, glass-pipe murder, baseball bats in Poland, liberty

failed liberty, and love redeeming love, they make you glad they have feelings about them—and convinced that for once you know the difference between feeling and pose. A–

Ranking Ann: *A Slice of English Toast* (RAS '91) "Liberated Woman" plus Mad Professor ("Kill the Police Bill") ★

Shabba Ranks: *As Raw As Ever* (Columbia '91) 💣
Shabba Ranks: *X-Tra Naked* (Epic '92) Like any dance music, dancehall is for acolytes. Trick cuts can divert the uninitiated, but there's rarely reason to buy a whole album by one artist, this one included. I'm ready to believe his crossover is about rhythmic authority, but I can't help believing that his heinous sexual politics contribute—finding-fooling-feeling-fucking-and-forgetting or declaring oral-genital contact an abomination, he must seem quite the noble savage to young pan-Africanists seeking new horizons in male supremacism. C+ 👾
Shabba Ranks: *A Mi Shabba.* (Epic '95) crossover beats, crossover 'tude—hey, "You do me and I do you" ("Ram Dancehall," "Let's Get It On") ★

Rara Machine: *Break the Chain* (Shanachie '91) ⓝ

Rare Essence: *Work the Walls* (Sounds of the Capital '92) dance single of the year plus the usual ("Work the Walls") ★

Eddy Raven: "Who Do You Know in California" (*Greatest Country Hits*, Warner Bros. '90) 🐚

Raven-Symone: "That's What Little Girls Are Made Of" (*Here's to New Dreams*, MCA '93) 🐚

Raw Fusion: *Live from the Styleetron* (Hollywood Basic '91) ⓝ

Dave Ray and Tony Glover: *Ashes in My Whiskey* (Rough Trade '90) rueful moans in the quiet night ("Uncertain Blues," "HIV Blues") ★★

Jimmy Ray: *Jimmy Ray* (Epic '98) 💣

Collin Raye: "What They Don't Know" (*In This Life*, Columbia '92) 🐚

Real McCoy: *Another Night* (Arista '95) One expediently omnivorous German hookmeister plus two soft-sung African-American army brats equals Eurodisco without overkill—every song catchy, every beat perky except on the sad one, every lyric recapitulating the pleasures and perils of l-o-v-e along the mind-body continuum. Shallow? Received? Er, *pop*? *Mais oui*—I mean *aber ja*. A–

The Real Roxanne: "Ya Brother Does," "Go Down (But Don't Bite It)" (*Go Down (But Don't Bite It)*, Select '92) 🐚

Rebekah: *Remember to Breathe* (Elektra '98) 💣

Rebel MC: "Music Is the Key" (*Rebel Music*, Desire '90) 🐚

Red Aunts: *#1 Chicken* (Epitaph '95) 💣
Red Aunts: *Ghetto Blaster* (Epitaph '97) the varied punk noisefests I credit to their learning curve, the screechy punk vocals I blame on their voices ("Alright!" "Wrecked") ★★

Otis Redding: "Trick or Treat," "Send Me Some Lovin'," "Cupid" (*Remember Me*, Stax '92) 🐚

Red Hot Chili Peppers: *Blood Sugar Sex Magik* (Warner Bros. '91) they've grown up, they've learned to write, they've got a right to be sex mystiks ("Give It Away," "Breakin' the Girl") ★★
Red Hot Chili Peppers: *One Hot Minute* (Warner Bros. '95) 💣
Red Hot Chili Peppers: *Californication* (Warner Bros. '99) New Age fuck fiends ("Scar Tissue," "Purple Stain") ★

Redman: *Whut? Thee Album* (RAL/Chaos/Columbia '92) ⓝ
Redman: *Doc's Da Name 2000* (Def Jam '98) Redman's brand of weed-fueled raunch-ruckus has never been as wild or ecstatic as Busta Rhymes's or Ol' Dirty Bastard's, but here he fuses their comic high spirits with his trademark grit into

ground-level, politically incorrect satire full of loud farts, stinkin' asses, and no-account thugs making monkey noises. In a genre where nobody wants to be a role model and everybody is, Redman cuts fresh cheese: "I'm a everyday nigga like a Toyota/The a&r hope we don't drop the same coda." People have jobs on this record—"whether it's fast food, or transportation, sneaker store, doin' hair, or straight-up strippin', we gotta get the cash"—and that includes a "round-the-clock lyricist" who claims to sleep in his workboots. Not everybody can go to work, though. So give the last word to babymama militant Liquidacia, whose demands include 40 cans of Enfamil a month and no reporting babydaddies to welfare: "We must stick together in order to survive in a world of bourgie hos." **A−**

The Reducers: *Shinola* (Rave On '95) **Ⓝ**

Alex Reece: *So Far* (Quango '96) **Ⓝ**

Lou Reed/John Cale: *Songs for Drella* (Sire/Warner Bros. '90) Lousy background music—absorb it over three or four plays, then read along once and file it away like a good novel. But like the novel it will repay your attention in six months, or 10 years. The music's dry because it serves words that make an argument worth hearing: Andy Warhol was a hardworking genius—a great artist, if you will—betrayed by hangers-on who no matter what carping philistines say gave a lot less to him than he did to them. Villain: Valerie Solanas, whose attempted assassination broke his generous spirit and turned him into "Society Andy." **A−**

Lou Reed: *Magic and Loss* (Sire/Reprise '92) **Ⓝ**

Lou Reed: *Set the Twilight Reeling* (Warner Bros. '96) Ever since *Sally Can't Dance,* if not "The Ostrich," Reed has been writing stupid-sounding songs that outrage his intellectual fans and probably his stoner fans too. On his best album in over a decade, including three consecutive "serious" ones, these include the backward-looking "Egg Cream" (only a self-hater could resist that hook) and the silly-sexy "HookyWooky" ("Reed Reveals: Fucking Is Fun!") and even the defensively macho-cynical "NYC Man" (asshole's confession as asshole's boast). Hooray for Laurie Anderson, either for distracting him from his various higher callings or for urging him to be himself. In a related development, he rocks out on guitar. **A−**

Lou Reed: *Perfect Night Live in London* (Reprise '98) honoring his own history with Dylanesque craft and disregard, only you can understand every word ("The Kids," "New Sensations") ★★

Dianne Reeves: *Art and Survival* (EMI/ERG '94) 💣

The Refused: *Shape of Punk to Come* (Burning Heart '99) 💣

Steve Reich: *Music for 18 Musicians* (Nonesuch '98) Grown even more universal (and likable) in posttechno retrospect, Reich's mathematically ebbing-and-surging facsimile of eternal return is the great classic of minimalist trance, at once prettier and more austere than any Terry Riley or Philip Glass. Eleven minutes longer than in the ECM original "owing to a tempo change governed by the breathing pattern of the clarinetist," this relaxed rerecording will appeal to graduates of the chillout room. But though rock and rollers can go with its flow, it's not a true reinterpretation like Bang on a Can's Eno, and I prefer the intensities I learned to love. Maybe Beethoven can be rehashed forever (and maybe not). With Reich, one is all any nonprofessional needs. **B+**

Hans Reichel: "Le Ball" (*Gravikords Whirlies and Pyrophones* [comp], Ellipsis Arts . . . '96) 🐚

Junior Reid & the Bloods: *Junior Reid & the Bloods* (RAS '95) that old-time riddim meets dem newfangled beats ("World Gone Reggae," "Not a One Man Thing") ★★

Vernon Reid: *Mistaken Identity* (550 Music '96) profuse guitar, 'nuff rap ("CP Time," "What's My Name") ★★

R.E.M.: *Out of Time* (Warner Bros. '91) Hiding political tics behind faux-formalist boilerplate, pop aesthetes accused them of imposing Solidarity and Agent Orange on their musical material, but in fact such subjects signaled an other-directedness as healthy as Michael Stipe's newfound elocution. Admittedly, with this one beginning "The world is collapsing around our ears," I wondered briefly whether "Losing My Religion" was about music itself, but when Stipe says they thought about calling it *Love Songs,* he's not just mumbling "Dixie." Being R.E.M., they mean to capture moods or limn relationships rather than describe feelings or, God knows, incidents, and while some will find the music too pleasing, it matches the words hurt for hurt and surge for surge. The Kate Pierson cameos, the cellos, and Mark Bingham's organic string arrangements are *Murmur* without walls—beauty worthy of DeBarge, of the sweetest soukous, of a massed choir singing "I Want to Know What Love Is." **A**

R.E.M.: *Automatic for the People* (Warner Bros. '92) eternal sleep ("Man on the Moon," "Nightswimming") ★★★

R.E.M.: *Monster* (Warner Bros. '94) Sick of dummies claiming they can't rock, the old Zepheads deliver the first power-riff album of their highly lyrical career. Peter Buck's sonic palette is rainbow grunge—variegated dirt and distortion as casual rhetoric—and he's so cranked even the slow ones seem born to be loud. As for Mr. Stipe, he's in the band, where he belongs. Message: guitars. Which after years of politics and sensitivity is well timed. **A–**

R.E.M.: *New Adventures in Hi-Fi* (Warner Bros. '96) Two years of road adventures, such as they were, that fuse spontaneity and arena scale. At sound checks and ad hoc local studios, Michael Stipe preaches and exhorts more than he rambles or muses, Mike Mills spelunks with keybs, and Peter Buck pumps the folk-rock jangle that broadened Amerindie's first wave. Nothing epochal, and there's poetry in that—the poetry of a nominal community that has learned how to keep its dreams modest and enjoy them that way. But for all the reliable melodies, momenta, and FX—*love* the siren on "Leave," guys—there's also routine in it. **A–**

R.E.M.: *Up* (Warner Bros. '98) Ⓝ

Nicole Renée: "Telephone" (*Nicole Renée,* Atlantic '98) 👁‍🗨

The Replacements: *All Shook Down* (Sire/Reprise '90) slow thoughtful rools ("Sadly Beautiful," "The Last") ★★

The Replacements: *Don't Sell or Buy, It's Crap* (Sire/Reprise promo '90) loud sloppy rools ("Satellite") ★★

The Replacements: *All for Nothing/ Nothing for All* (Reprise '97) I never bought the theory that Warner Bros. tamed them—life has that effect anyway. But the all-for-nothing disc's selection from the slide made inevitable by *Let It Be,* which stands beside *Wild Gift* as Amerindie's very peak, shortchanges the wild ("I Won't") and the tasteless ("Waitress in the Sky"); you'd be better off with *Tim.* The miscellaneous arcana on the nothing-for-all disc, however, are pretty unkempt for a pop band in the process of mastering its craft as it loses its purpose—a blues, a lo-fi proposition, a Disney cover, B sides, what-all. In fact, although or because it's a mess, it's got more pizzazz than either of their two final albums. No "Aching to Be," that's for sure. **A–**

Revolting Cocks: *Beers, Steers and Queers* (Wax Trax '90) sexist subtext (or text), no redeeming antisocial value, rock like a funk-damaged Ministry nonetheless ("Stainless Steel Providers," "Beers, Steers and Queers") ★★

Busta Rhymes: "Whoo Hah!! Got You All in Check" (*The Coming,* Elektra '96) 👁‍🗨

Busta Rhymes: "Put Your Hands Where My Eyes Could See" (*When Disaster Strikes,* Elektra '97) 👁‍🗨

Busta Rhymes: *Extinction Level Event: The Final World Front* (Elektra '98) Ⓝ

Marc Ribot: "While My Guitar Gently Weeps" (*Rootless Cosmopolitans,* Island '90) 🍥

Marc Ribot Y Los Cubanos Postizos (The Prosthetic Cubans): *Marc Ribot Y Los Cubanos Postizos (The Prosthetic Cubans)* (Atlantic '98) This witty, beautiful, slightly bent tribute to the old-time tres-playing bandleader Arsenio Rodríguez—inventor of the son montuno, the Cuban conjunto, and practically speaking the mambo—reduces all that action to a guitar-bass-drums-percussion jazz quartet, sometimes with organ and once with a few horns. Deconstructing as it adores, enjoying the rhythms and melodies of arrangements that function simultaneously as dance music, dinner music, and art music, it epitomizes what it is to love something from a distance there's no denying, yet love it well. **A–**

The Tony Rich Project: *Words* (LaFace '96) better his enlightened-bourgie Smokey than D'Angelo's pomo-new jack Marvin ("Like a Woman," "Billy Goat," "The Grass Is Green") ★★★

The Tony Rich Project: *Birdseye* (LaFace '98) 💣

Keith Richards and the X-Pensive Winos: *Live at the Hollywood Palladium, December 15, 1988* (Virgin '91) Ⓝ

Keith Richards: *Main Offender* (Virgin '92) Ⓝ

Kim Richey: *Kim Richey* (Mercury '95) 💣

Kim Richey: *Glimmer* (Mercury '99) 💣

Jonathan Richman: *Having a Party with Jonathan Richman* (Rounder '91) confessions of a reluctant grownup ("Monologue About Bermuda," "The Girl Stands Up to Me Now") ★

Ride: *Going Blank Again* (Sire/Reprise '92) high-texture also-rans process rock and roll readymades through art-school sensibilities and infernal machines ("Time After Time," "Not Fazed") ★★★

Amy Rigby: *Diary of a Mod Housewife* (Koch '96) Personalizing the political for a bohemia that coexists oh so neatly with structural underemployment, thinking harder about marriage than a dozen Nashville homilizers, the ex-Sham leaves the comforts of amateurism for an ex-Car and some El Lay roots-rockers, throwing her voice around in the process. All the ones you notice at first—the Berryesque "20 Questions," the chart-worthy "Beer and Kisses," the lovelorn "Knapsack," and the thematic "The Good Girls"—were laid down in California. But the ones you don't notice you remember, including the five where she returns to reliable locals like Tony Maimone, Doug Wygal, and her hub, who in his real-life version even gets to bang things on a couple of songs. Concept album of the year. **A**

Amy Rigby: *Middlescence* (Koch '98) What's most original about Rigby isn't her analysis of the men who fail to provide the kind of love she demands so sanely and evokes so hotly. Nor is it her designated theme, age, although I wonder how many 23-year-olds will learn as much about fun from "The Summer of My Wasted Youth" as she wants them to. It's class, which she's old enough to understand for the simple reason that she doesn't have enough money—not the way the executive mom who covets a bigger co-op doesn't have enough money, the way the temp mom who buys back-to-school outfits at Goodwill doesn't have enough money. Her voice as real as Roxanne Shanté's, Rigby sings in a material world. So Trisha Yearwood, I'm begging: cover "All I Want" if not "What I Need." **A–**

LeAnn Rimes: *Blue* (Curb '96) Ⓝ

LeAnn Rimes: *You Light Up My Life* (Curb '97) 💣

LeAnn Rimes: *Sittin' on Top of the World* (Curb '98) Not content to split the difference between Patsy Cline and Debby Boone, this young teen and her in-it-to-win-it voice turn as grotesque as a mascaraed five-year-old in a beauty pageant. She begins by imagining a guy who "worships my body." Her Dad Rimes production and Carole Bayer Warren crossovers reveal Mutt Lange as the easygoing popster he is. She never cracks a smile, rarely revs a tempo. And in the only climax she understands, she colors in the "Purple Rain" so dark I'd say its purple was black if that metaphor weren't patently ridiculous. **C+** 🐛

Riverdales: *Riverdales* (Lookout '95) **Ⓝ**

Roaring Lion: *Sacred 78's* (Ice '94) Lion (aka Hubert Raphael Charles, Raphael De Leon) was the most recorded Trinidadian of the pre–World War II era, and title notwithstanding, this selection of classics (plus a few '50s pleasantries) has nothing to do with praising the Lord—or no matter how happily he tapped into Shango ritual, the orishas either. Even more than most calypsonians, Lion played the secular sophisticate, cultivating foreigners, intellectuals, Atilla the Hun, Rudy Vallee. Because he took pride in not repeating himself, he deployed more tunes than the competition, and if some of his arrangements are almost pop, "Rhumba Dance" and "Bamsee Lambay" are almost Latin-tinge. Subjects include flies, Queen Elizabeth's royal tour, girls who dance with girls, a pyromaniac, agape, and sex, which the man who made "Ugly Woman" famous rarely if ever associates with love. **A–**

Dennis Robbins: *Man with a Plan* (Giant '92) With neotraditionalism going and outlawism gone, it's an up to run into a Nashville cat with a beard, and a boon that it could stand a trim. A Detroit native gone hillbilly and proud, he savors the details pop leaches out of country—the 300-hp galmobile, the words of the hymn he gets married to, the TV set that freaks with the sewing machine on. And like the young John Anderson, he knows enough to keep things fast and/or funny whenever possible. **A–**

Dennis Robbins: *Born Ready* (Giant '94) **Ⓝ**

Robbie Robertson: *Storyville* (Geffen '91) Robertson's unctuous undertone is the voice of a two-bit hustler who's dis-covered the big lie—the good and the beautiful, rapture and immortality, my BMW's in the shop, of course I'm not married, I can't wait to go down on you. It's disheartening that people whose age and wisdom approach my own are fussing over his New Orleans "concept"—a posse of L.A. studio hacks augmented by a few ringers and the kind of second-line once-removed horn charts the Band was hiring 20 years ago. The '70s are over, gang. Now let's dispense with the '80s. **C** 🐛

Fenton Robinson: *Special Road* (Evidence '93) his pain flows like whiskey, and he just wants to moan the blues about it ("Love Is Just a Gamble," "Crying the Blues") ★

Tom Robinson: "Green," "Fifty" (*Love over Rage,* Rhythm Safari '94) 🐚

Charlie Robison: "Poor Man's Son" (*Life of the Party,* Sony/Lucky Dog '98) 🐚

Suzzy Roche: *Holy Smokes* (Red House '97) **Ⓝ**

Tabu Ley Rochereau: *Man from Kinshasa* (Shanachie '91) The king placates soukous fashion instead of following it, and having kicked off with an electrokick-drum that's never so forward again, his third U.S.-release variety show eschews total speed trip. Catchy tunes, plangent pace changes, Cuban/Ethiopian horns, musette accordion—and enough rippling guitar to keep them coming back for more. **A–**

Rochereau et l'Orchestre Afrisa: *Exil-Ley* (Bibiche '93) **Ⓝ**

Seigneur Tabu Ley Rochereau: *Muzina* (Rounder '94) **Ⓝ**

Tabu Ley Rochereau: *Africa Worldwide* (Rounder '96) Tabu Ley never conquered his schlock habit Stateside. Even the 1989 best-of he recut for RealWorld sounded like cummerbunds and leisure suits. But as Kinshasa transformed itself from hellhole to charnel house, Afropop's smarmiest godfather withdrew not just to Paris but L.A. Then, with a quick new guitarist and dulcet vocal acolytes helping him exploit a nostalgia it would be cruel to deny, he rerecorded a magnificent dozen of the thousand or so songs he churned out when Zaire was young, and in the great tradition of classic Afropop, their airy grace still projects an illusion of possibility. This old hero no longer plans to conquer the world. He's just grateful he can remember how it felt to be looking ahead. **A–**

The Roches: *We Three Kings* (Paradox '90) **Ⓝ**

The Roches: *A Dove* (MCA '92) For a long time they seemed strangers in their own music, distracted by some purist superego whispering in their ears about acoustic guitars. Here their pop style hasn't changed that much—it's a little more eclectic, if anything. But it could almost be growing out of their three consanguineous voices; they sound as natural and gorgeous as the Comedian Harmonists, Lambert, Hendricks & Ross, maybe even the Judds. So when the words don't kick in right off, immerse in the sound until they do, because they will. Pained smiles replace nervous giggles not because they've lost their sense of humor, but because Suzzy has finally gotten sick of her own whimsy, because the '90s are even less fun than the '80s, because you can't live with them and you can't live without them, and because they thought following "You're the One" with "You're the Two" was feminist comedy enow. **A**

The Roches: *Can We Go Home Now* (Rykodisc '95) domestic nonviolence, subtly sublimated for your tranquil contemplation ("My Winter Coat," "I'm Someone Who Loves You") ★★

Pete Rock and C.L. Smooth: *All Souled Out* (Elektra '91) **Ⓝ**

Pete Rock & CL Smooth: *Mecca and the Soul Brother* (Elektra '92) **Ⓞ**

Rockin' Dopsie & the Zydeco Twisters: "Jingle Bells" (*A Creole Christmas* [comp], Epic Associated '90) 🔊

Virginia Rodrigues: *Sol Negro* (Hannibal '98) Notes by Caetano Veloso, who's clearly stunned at the ability of the daughter of a street vendor to evoke "operas, masses, lieder, and spirituals," a response shared by many Lusophiles and every fan of the Bulgarian State Radio and Television Female Vocal Choir who's in on the story. The rest of us will be stupefied that such a "celestial" voice can exist at all. She never stretches her rich, Ella-like highs into a scat—though the few midtempo numbers have a nice jazzy lilt (dig that berimbau), her instincts are exceedingly solemn. Veloso is Veloso, which means he "transcends the distinction between erudite and popular" far more vividly than he thinks Rodrigues does. High middlebrows Djavan and Milton Nascimento don't, and their cameos give the game away. **B–** 🦃

Roy Rogers: *Rhythm and Groove* (Pointblank '96) plays great slide, rides catchy rhythms, writes decent songs ("Built for Comfort," "For the Love of a Woman") ★

Rolling Stones: *Flashpoint* (Rolling Stones '91) **Ⓝ**

Rolling Stones: *Voodoo Lounge* (Virgin '94) world's greatest roots-rock band ("Brand New Car," "New Faces") ★★

Rolling Stones: *Stripped* (Virgin '95) Accepting—nay, embracing—the necessity of performing as a unit, they rehearsed. Ditto his responsibilities as a member of Great Britain's ruling class, Mick enunciated—except on the sole words not reproduced in the lyric booklet (that's right, lyric booklet), which go, approximately, "She was [n?]ifty, [sh?]ifty, she looked about 50." And macabre though it may seem, they all went out and cut not merely another unplugged recap, but a live album that reprises their classic material and groove in an honorably autumnal spirit—an album that might tell you something a decade from now. Muddy Waters would be proud. **A–**

Rolling Stones: *Bridges to Babylon* (Virgin '97) still know how to construct, play, and—sometimes—sing a song ("You Don't Have to Mean It," "Flip the Switch") ★

Rolling Stones: *No Security* (Virgin '98) 💣

Henry Rollins: *The Boxed Life* (Imago '93) *Gen X Comedy Hour* X 2 ("Strength—Pt. 2," "Airplanes") ★★

Rollins Band: *The End of Silence* (Imago '92) 💣
Rollins Band: *Weight* (Imago '94) 💣
Rollins Band: *Come In and Burn* (DreamWorks '97) Success doesn't suit this drug addict, who will kick caffeine only when they synthesize rage itself. Since I got big yuks out of 1992's spoken-word twofer *The Boxed Life,* which recalled a lab-assistant job and other homely pursuits, I am entitled to grouse about the grim star diary that is 1997's spoken-word twofer *Black Coffee Blues.* And while it's no surprise that this thrash-and-churn is his metalest metal ever, it's amazing that Spielberg-Katzenberg-Geffen made Rollins their flagship rocker—for all his corp clout and cult cred, he was off the charts a month after he muscled on. As pathetic as it is for aging Spinal Taps to fabricate melodrama out of an adolescent despair they remember via groupies and fan mail, it's even more pathetic never to feel anything else. **C–** 🦃

Linda Ronstadt & Emmylou Harris: *Western Wall: The Tucson Sessions* (Asylum '99) tribute to the modern art-song, country-folk division ("Western Wall," "1917") ★

The Roots: *Do You Want More?!!!??!* (DGC '95) Ⓝ
The Roots: *Illadelph Halflife* (DGC '96) Ⓝ
The Roots: "The Show" (*In tha Beginning . . . There Was Rap* [comp], Priority '97) 🔊
The Roots: *Things Fall Apart* (MCA '99) Stop the violence in hip hop, but make an exception if these guys will shoot the piano player. Kamal gets away with his omnipresent ostinato beds here mostly because the band is looking back to the old-school rap they loved before they discovered jazz lite. They even sample now

and then—I've never been so happy to run into Schoolly D in my life. What's so consistently annoying on their earlier intelligent records is almost hooky on this one, integral to a flow that certainly does just that, which isn't to say you won't be relieved when it rocks the house instead. Gee—maybe they've gotten *more* intelligent. **B+**

The Roots: *Come Alive* (MCA '99) world-class DJ and beatbox, excellent drummer and bassist, pretty darn good rapper(s), bourgie jazzmatazz ("Proceed," "Love of My Life") ★★

The Roots All Stars: *Gathering of the Spirits* (Shanachie '98) Mutabaruka, Sly, Robbie, and friends meet the predancehall elite (Culture, "Blackman King"; the Mighty Diamonds, "Blackman Pride") ★★

Cesar Rosas: *Soul Disguise* (Rykodisc '99) after seven long years of Mitchell Froom, Los Lobos's rocker has it his way ("You've Got to Lose," "Better Way") ★★

Michael Rose: *Michael Rose* (Heartbeat '95) badder than you know, but not than you wish ("Badder than You," "Casabank Queen") ★

Rossy: *Island of Ghosts* (RealWorld '91) Ⓝ
Rossy: *One Eye on the Future One Eye on the Past* (Shanachie '94) Ⓝ

Royal Crescent Mob: *Midnight Rose's* (Sire/Warner Bros. '91) Ⓝ

Royal Crown Revue: *The Contender* (Warner Bros. '98) 💣

The Royal Macadamians: *Experiments in Terror* (Island '90) Ⓝ

Royal Trux: *Accelerator* (Drag City '98) the snot-rock of their dreams ("Accelerator: I'm Ready," "The Banana Question") ★★★

Ruff Ryders: "What Ya Need" (*Ryde or Die Volume 1,* Ruff Ryders/Interscope '99) 🔊

Run-D.M.C.: *Back from Hell* (Profile '90) 💣

Run-D.M.C.: *Together Forever: Greatest Hits 1983–1991* (Profile '91) Use your programming buttons—the jumbled order, intended like the title to conceal how over they are, cheats them instead. Played chronologically, the music coheres—their style evolves naturally, switching gears only when they begin sweating street cred—and the rhymes lay out a tragedy. A pair of streetwise college kids inveigh against a scourge before anybody has an inkling it's going to happen. Preaching and demonstrating self-reliance, they start with a beatbox and two stentorian voices—"Unemployment at a record high"—and then incorporate just enough guitar to turn the market around. As they get famous, their boasts begin to sound out of touch—live '83 they're all camaraderie, live '84 it's already like the audience is down there somewhere—and by '87 or so their message seems formulaic. But given their bona fides, it retains a certain credibility—even the useless 1989 spiel "Pause" (rhymes with "Don't break laws") sounds like them. By the time they check out with the scary tale of a crack shooting on "The Ave.," they're packing nines—and unemployment 1983-style seems like heaven, or at least not-hell. **A**

Run-D.M.C.: *Down with the King* (Profile '93) A triumphant comeback, but the comeback is spiritual and the triumph formal, which adds up to art rather than culture. Where multiple producers usually signal identity crisis, this is debt collection—since rap as we know it proceeded from their innovations and accommodations, there's no one in the music who doesn't owe them. And though the two Bomb Squad cuts owe Cypress Hill in turn, all the other guest overseers—Q-Tip, Jermaine Dupri, Pete Rock, EPMD—drop plenty flavor without impinging on the group's aural identity. Sure of their hard-not-gangsta ethos, equally deliberate in the vocals and the bass and drums, they always sound like Jay, Run, and Darryl Mac. Yet with their own spare production style signifying only as a trademark, they live off those outside shots, and the boasts about the stages they useta rip up ring truer than the ones about the trends they're gonna start. I hope their godfather status is good for sales as well as respect, influence as well as sales. But I wonder how much their return will mean, even to rap aesthetes, if it isn't. **B+**

Run On: "Xmas Trip" (*Start Packing,* Matador '96) 🕭

RuPaul: *Supermodel of the World* (Tommy Boy '93) I know it wouldn't be an authentic disco album without filler, but he's too blandly male a singer to put over pro forma romance. The exception is "Supernatural," as you'll figure out if you match title to persona and consider the possibilities. And when he cops an attitude—on five cuts by my count, culminating in the deep-dish "A Shade Shady"—he brings off a time-warped genderfuck all his own. **B+**

Bobby Rush: "I Ain't Studdin' You" (*I Ain't Studdin' You,* Urgent '91) 🕭

Brenda Russell: *Greatest Hits* (A&M '92) ⓝ

Carl Hancock Rux: "Blue Candy" (*Rux Revue,* 550 Music '99) 🕭

RZA: *RZA as Bobby Digital in Stereo* (Gee Street/V2 '98) 💣

R/COMPILATIONS

Rawkus Presents Soundbombing II (Rawkus '99) Whoever's representing—Medina Green eating crosstown beef or Eminem tripping on a minivan or Company Flow dissing AmeriKKKa or Pharoahe Monch toasting the mayor or "hairy fat slob unshaven" R.A. the Rugged Man conjoining his "white trash nation" with "all the starvin' artists"—the Rawkus subculture is always peering over its own edge. The beats aren't invariably propulsive, but they never relent, with timeouts for DJs to scratch themselves minimized. Although the us-against-society mood is

far from asexual, nobody macks and nobody flosses. Nobody deals either. Racism is an issue, race isn't. In our present-day dystopia, no wonder so many make this imaginary world their home. **A–**
Rawkus Presents Soundboming: See also *Soundbombing*

The Real Hip-Hop: Best of D&D Studios Vol. 1 (Cold Front '99) The main thing undergrounders mean by "real" is Hold That Tune, aka Hook Junkies Keep Out. Though this ethos dates officially to the South Bronx's primordial ooze, its immediate forebear is these mid-'90s productions of Premier and his lessers. On choice singles from a singles music, the warm feelings hip hop heads cherish for M.O.P., the Lost Boys, Smif-N-Wessum, and Showbiz & AG can be shared by us hook users. An excess of celebrity similes is counterbalanced by gangsta talk as unmitigated metaphor. Competitive world, hip hop. It could kill ya. **A–**

Real: The Tom T. Hall Project (Sire/Delmore/Kickstand '98) many titles skipped by the gemlike *Essential Tom T. Hall* and the softer two-CD box, but that doesn't mean Johnny Polonsky and Ron Sexsmith are up to them (Iris DeMent, "I Miss a Lot of Trains"; Kelly Willis, "That's How I Got to Memphis") ★★

Red Hot + Blue (Chrysalis '90) Although only Shane MacGowan, David Byrne, and Debbie & Iggy have ever been identified professionally with punk, only the Jungle Brothers—whose suave rap, unlike Neneh Cherry's gauche one, ignores Cole Porter altogether—would exist as we know them without it. From U2 to K.D. Lang to Sinéad O'Connor, from Tom Waits to Salif Keita to the Neville Brothers, they've all built their market shares in fissures of taste and heightened expectation that punk opened up. And this is where punk's fierce certainty that "rock" is never enough ends up—in the suspicion that the "rock" punk changed utterly and not at all is actually a historical phase of "pop." Rarely has the pomo practice of trashing history while you honor it reached such a pitch of accomplishment. The songs are so strong that they remain Porter's whether Waits is bellowing one to death or the Fine Young Cannibals are rearranging one to a draw or Lisa Stansfield is literalizing one to within an inch of its printed lyric. Inevitably, there are duds, but listen enough and they shift on you. The recontextualizations—O'Connor's gravid "You Do Something to Me," Keita's Mandinka "Begin the Beguine," Erasure's electrodance "Too Darn Hot"—are for the ages. **A**

Red Hot + Rhapsody (Antilles '98) Bacharachians please note: this AIDS-fighting Gershwin tribute is how great songwriters make themselves felt. Beyond near has-beens Bowie and Sinéad and the all too inoffensive Natalie Merchant, the contributors are marginal. In real life, Spearhead, Sarah Cracknell, Morcheeba, Finlay Quaye, to stick to standouts, flounder as often as they fly. But entrusted with this material they soar or at least flutter about, as do Smoke City and Majestic 12, both previously unknown to me. Defined by keyboard textures from sampledelica to Hammond B-3, this is a seductive showcase of the moody sensibility shared by acid jazz and trip hop. Now if only the sensibility had Gershwins of its own—well, soon they'd no doubt find themselves something better to do. **A–**

Red Hot + Rio (Antilles '96) art-rocking up grooveful kitsch in a soulful cause (Money Mark, "Use Your Head"; David Byrne + Marisa Monte, "Waters of March") ★★

Reggae for Kids (RAS '92) dad says, "The real thing"; kid says, "I like all the songs but this one [Black Sheep's 'Time to Think']" (Eek-a-Mouse, "Safari"; Gregory Isaacs, "Puff the Magic Dragon") ★

Rent (DreamWorks '96) pretty funny for art-rock ("La Vie Boheme," "Tango: Maureen," "Happy New Year B") ★

Return of the Grievous Angel: A Tribute to Gram Parsons (Almo Sounds '99) First cut's the worst, which I blame not on

Chrissie Hynde but on "She," the softest song Parsons ever wrote (and probably the only one about black people). Last cut's the best, and although "In My Hour of Darkness" is anything but soft, I credit it primarily to Victoria Williams and a gang that owes Parsons everything, from alt-country lifer Mark Olson to Nashville darling Jim Lauderdale to in-betweeners Buddy and Julie Miller. There are plenty of great songbooks with plenty of great admirers, but damn few that define a sensibility, and even Elvis Costello and Evan Dando seem to have pondered Parsons all their musical lives—though not as much as Aunt Emmylou, who shares recipes with Beck H. and Sheryl C. As for Gram's own kids, even the slow ones—parched Gillian Welch, sodden Whiskeytown, spaced Cowboy Junkies—designed their sounds for this material, which nails their identification-alienation harder than their own ever will. **A–**

Risqué Rhythm: Nasty '50s R&B (Rhino '91) The blue blues compiled on Columbia's *Raunchy Business* and reprised on Bluesville's *Bawdy Blues* are novelty material. Voicing r&b's revolt of the body against the cerebral demands of bebop, this stuff is sexy. Even the novelties—the original "My Ding-a-Ling," say—are carnal, and though the oft-collected "Work with Me Annie" and "Sixty-Minute Man" may be mild as poetry, they're plenty physical as music. The Sultans' "It Ain't the Meat" and Connie Allen's "Rocket 69" are plenty physical as poetry. And Wynonie Harris and Dinah Washington will make you want to fuck. The gift that keeps on giving for any music lover whose genitalia you cherish. **A**

Rock Stars Kill (Kill Rock Stars '94) 🌑

Roots Rock Guitar Party: Zimbabwe Frontline 3 (Stern's/Earthworks '99) Chimurenga and its vaguely soukous-inflected descendants are liberation music no longer. Mugabe's the new boss, and though he isn't the same as the old boss—they never are, and at least he's not white—he is certainly a tyrant, dividing-and-plundering along tribal and sexual lines. But where Afropop surrendered lilt and intraband debate for escapist desperation and automatic virtuosity as nationhood bore down on the material lives of the people, these 12 tracks, all but one recent, maintain an illusion of communal jollity and balanced progress. Past kisses future as guitars articulate thumb-piano scales into a language all their own, an endeavor spiritually engrossing enough to keep everybody involved occupied. When you read the translated lyrical snippets, you can infer how much the all-male Shona choruses aren't saying. When you listen to the music, you give everybody involved credit for tending their bit of human space. **A–**

Ruffhouse Records Greatest Hits (Ruffhouse '99) The *Miseducation, Score,* and *Cypress Hill* lifts have their own lives. "Insane in the Brain" is worth hearing twice. "Fuck Compton" is history. Kriss Kross weren't always has-beens. Nas wasn't always nasty. John Forte and Pace Won have their own futures. Few labels have done '90s hip hop so proud. **A–**

RZA: The RZA Hits (Razor Sharp/Epic '99) If *Enter the Wu-Tang* is a block party mythologized into a masterwork, its endless spinoffs are soirees in smoke-filled rooms, where intimates tender messages and crack jokes newcomers can only pretend to understand. So this public work is a public service. Never mind that it pulls three tracks from the source and two each from the most obvious solo exceptions, by ODB and Ghostface Killah. Just be grateful that for once they're celebrating the obvious—the anthemic, the obscene, the braggadocious. In this context, even Raekwon sounds like a regular guy. Says the produceur: "That's enough information right there to get you involved, get you inside the system." Whereupon he sets off a three-minute Wu Wear ad. **A–**

S

Robin S: "Show Me Love," "Love for Love," "Back It Up" (*Show Me Love*, Atlantic '93) 🍬

The Sabri Brothers: *Ya Mustapha* (Xenophile '96) Nusrat is Nusrat, these guys straight qawwali, and more fun with saxophones by me ("Ya Mustapha") ★

The Sabri Brothers: *The Greatest Hits* (Shanachie '97) stolider than touristic ecstatics would prefer, but the great track is godlike ("Hazir Hain Hazir Hain") ★★★

Sade: *Love Deluxe* (Epic '92) I'm unable to find fault with her more memorable songs—keep falling asleep before I've finished the sentence. But I swear on a stack of *Billboards* that half these nine fail to qualify. That's nine, eight with words, in four years. Would you say she's honing her art to the bone? Or would you say she's a nice person with a million-dollar scam? And how come her Somalian woman "hurts like brand-new shoes"? Is that, er, "metaphorical distance"? Are we supposed to clap now? **B-** 🦃

Sade: "Please Send Me Someone to Love" (*Philadelphia* [ST], Epic Soundtrax '93) 🍬

Sade: *The Best of Sade* (Epic '94) another loungecore alternative ("Hang On to Your Love," "No Ordinary Love") ★

Saffire: *The Uppity Blues Women* (Alligator '90) Instrumentally and vocally, these three Virginia over-40s are folkies. Ann Rabson's woogie piano and Gaye Adegbalola's unamplified guitar are high-

generic only—their originality is in their feminist redefinition of blues-circuit raunch. Never again do they get as lewd or as fine as "Middle Aged Blues Boogie," in which Adegbalola stakes her claim on that good young cock (and tongue) as if it was her right as a fully sexed human being, but there's a matter-of-fact candor to "Fess Up When You Mess Up" and "School Teacher's Blues" that's rare among younger guitar poets. And if Rabson has decided in her considerable wisdom never to take care of another man, only an MCP could blame her. **B+**

Saffire—The Uppity Blues Women: *Hot Flash* (Alligator '91) talking dirty and saying something ("Two in the Bush Is Better Than One in the Hand," "[Mr. Insurance Man] Take Out That Thing for Me") ★★

Sagat: "Why Is It?" (*Max Mix U.S.A.* [comp], Max '94) 🍬

Saint Etienne: *Foxbase Alpha* (Warner Bros. '92) 💣

Saint Etienne: *So Tough* (Warner Bros. '93) Although their roots in the pretechno dance movement render their pop strictly futuristic, classic English not-rock with pretensions to not being pretentious, I stuck around when the first song evoked the female fanworld and the second cut was a niece of Brian Eno's "Sky Saw." Add the foregrounded textures and hidden tunes of two male pop intellectuals languidly manipulating synths and samplers to Sarah Cracknell's subdued lyricism and you have an educational

---

★★★, ★★, ★ Honorable Mention   🍬 Choice Cut   Ⓝ Neither   💣 Dud   🦃 Turkey

argument for the impressionistic pastiche that's one British pop dream. Cracknell's all-purpose pomo receptivity projects no persona. She's a chameleon, a willing mouthpiece, an aural presence whispering "Close your eyes/Kiss the future/Junk the morgue." **A–**

Saint Etienne: *Tiger Bay* (Warner Bros. '94) 💣

Saint Etienne: *Good Humor* (Sub Pop '98) modern love for the postmodern English—sad, kind, contained ("Mr Donut," "Been So Long") ★★

Saint Etienne: *Places to Visit* (Sub Pop '99) 💣

Dédé Saint-Prix: *Best of* (Déclic/Blue Silver import '93) flute zouk fluke ("Roulé," "Soldat papillon") ★

Ryuichi Sakamoto: *Beauty* (Virgin '90) Ⓝ

Salt: *Ausculcate* (Island '96) 💣

Salt-n-Pepa: *Blacks' Magic* (Next Plateau '90) Though I wish these Hurby Luv Bug graduates were as gimmicky as their preceptor, the beats grab and the lyrics hold. They're too centered, too grounded to cop any attitude; some of their best moments are snatches of fabricated ordinary conversation, like the embarrassed 10-second should-we-or-shouldn't-we that leads into "Let's Talk About Sex" (some remixer should sample Salt's "C'mon, why not?" for everything it's worth). Their you-can't-dog-me threat doesn't sound like they want to turn around and dog him, though they may. They're "Independent" because they'd better be. **A–**

Salt-n-Pepa: *Very Necessary* (Next Plateau/London '93) they go their own way, they know whereof they speak, they sample Whitney's mama ("Shoop," "What a Man," "I've Got AIDS") ★★★

Salt-n-Pepa: "I'm Ready (Remix)" (*Brand New*, London/Red Ant '97) 💣

Samiam: *Clumsy* (Atlantic '94) 💣

Samite: *Silana Musango* (Xenophile '96) It's hard to argue with the life choices of a Ugandan who lost a brother to Idi Amin. But when he opened for the gently ecstatic Samba Mapangala and the eternally vigorous Mahlathini at S.O.B.'s, he was a tragedy of "world music." Mapangala and Mahlathini, whose lives haven't been easy either, do what Afropop masters have always done: import American materials for their own uses. Samite is an exporter who treats music like a cash crop, adapting to the master culture rather than from it. On record you don't have to watch his drummer expressing her spirituality, and Bakithi Khumalo can flat-out play bass. But in any context Samite is soft-headed as a matter of principle—and by now, as a marketing strategy too. **C+** 🦃

Sammy: *Tales of Great Neck Glory* (DGC '96) Rather than hiding their privilege behind obscure witticisms, these alt-rock everyboys tell it like it is for their cultural class—bright, affluent kids who still have more options than they know what to do with. "History hounds" and "encyclopedi-ites," they write mash notes to their own characters and detail manageable traumas like bankruptcy and agoraphobia over hooky post-Pavement dissonances. They're about hedonism not idealism, choice not necessity. Puritans will ostracize them unless and until they succeed. Then they'll try and burn them at the stake. **A–**

Pharoah Sanders: *Message from Home* (Verve '96) Where Sanders's serviceable if eerie new collection of Coltrane replicas is pure middlebrow market ploy, this putatively commercial move ventures into the unknown. With his fabulous sound, un-American activities, and grandly simple musical ideas, the man was made for Bill Laswell's world-jazz stratagems. Lacking an "Upper Egypt" or "The Creator Has a Master Plan," he establishes his leisurely command, then immerses in an "Ocean Song" that is more former than latter before going out on the two friendliest, wildest, and most African of the six cuts. These highlight old Laswell hands Foday Musa Suso and Aiyb Dieng, and by the time they're over, you'll forget whether you remember the tunes. **A–**

The San Francisco Seals: *See SF Seals*

Oumou Sangare: *Moussolou* (World Circuit '91) Cut in Côte d'Ivoire the week of this Wassoulou woman's 21st birthday, it's a crucial quantum more pop than Stern's's far from folkloric *Women of Mali* collection, where Sangare's "Diaraby Nene" stands out even more proudly than it does here. But it's also a crucial quantum less pop than copyright holder Ibrahim Sylla's usual Gallic West African-isms, not to mention those of such world travelers as Salif Keita or Youssou N'Dour. No archivist, Sangare nevertheless avoids horns, synthesizers, and Afrodisco over-drive for the deliberate rhythms and acoustic hooks of her own tradition. Call it a Sahel version of early Dolly Parton—with a deeper groove. **A–**

Oumou Sangare: *Ko Sira* (World Circuit '94) Established now, she stretches out, which in general is more fun for her than it is for us. Note, however, the almost giddy re-sponse her plummy, plangent call gets from her delightedly girlish backup followers by the end of the seven-minute title workout. Regal yet outgoing, this is the model of a woman who could lead a movement. **B+**

Oumou Sangare: *Worotan* (World Cir-cuit '97) Traditional? Folkloric? Malian? "World"? Fusion? Pop? Ignoring such petty distinctions, this sexy sister and rad-ical queen is all these things and none. Its interlock Malian, its forward motion as im-bued with possibility as the message it carries, her music has never been more confident or distinct. She's proud to be a griot, an earth mother, a modern woman, a star—an effective progressive in music as well as politics, up to and including some Pee Wee Ellis horn charts to freshen her funk. She exploits possibilities she finds in Europe and America, and she gives new possibilities back. **A–**

Ñico Saquito: *Good-bye Mr. Cat* (World Circuit '94) Born in 1901, he was a master of *canto popular* rather than folk song—the acoustic but at least semipro-fessional sons, guarachas, and guajiras that were entertaining Oriente province before Castro, Batista, Martí, San Juan Hill. He was 81 when he cut these eight oldies with a shifting cast of skilled revival-ists, most auspiciously the Cuarteto Pa-tria, who are nowhere near as sprightly and tuneful on their own *A Una Coqueta.* The reason is mostly the high-spirited Saquito, an exceptionally wry and flexible vocalist in what must have been some dotage. Spanish and English texts pro-vided, so give it an 87—it's got a sweet beat, and you can read along to it. **A–**

Sarge: *Charcoal* (Mud '96) **Ⓝ**
Sarge: *The Glass Intact* (Mud '98) Roughly pop and crisply punky, this is one of the rare good albums to land tunes-first these days, indubitably fresh despite its verse-chorus-verse and guitar-bass-drums. Partly it's the voice of young Eliza-beth Elmore—unassuming but never retiring, thoughtful but never moony. Read the lyrics—so much happens so fast that they make a difference, and note that they're printed across the booklet, com-pelling you to follow word for word instead of scanning down—and you'll encounter not just a sensible girl but a born writer whose subject is love or relationships de-pending how you look at it. Dissecting one attraction after another, she's still try-ing to figure that out herself. My advice, fat chance she'll take it: male or female, maybe you should rule out people in bands, dear. **A–**

Savage Garden: *Savage Garden* (Co-lumbia '97) twisted tuneful love songs for fruity electronic baritone and jaded late-teen females ("I Want You," "Truly Madly Deeply") ★★
Savage Garden: "Affirmation" (*Affir-mation,* Columbia '99) 🖝

Scarface of the Geto Boys: "I'm Dead" (*Mr. Scarface Is Back,* Rap-A-Lot '91) 🖝
Scarface: "I Seen a Man Die" (*The Di-ary,* Rap-A-Lot/Noo Trybe '94) 🖝

The Scene Is Now: *Shotgun Wedding* (Lost '91) ⓝ

Peter Scherer: *Very Neon Pet* (Metro Blue '95) *Fourth World Vol. V: Possible Technopangaea* ("Blur," "Anonymous Shark") ★

Fred Schneider: *Just Fred* (Reprise '96) 💣

Mimi Schneider: *The Extended Outlook* (Indelible '90) NPR stalwart, EP folkie, student of Donne ("The Party Line," "Urban Friends") ★

Mimi Schneider: *Catasterpiece* (Indelible '91) ⓝ

Schoolly D: *Welcome to America* (Columbia/Ruffhouse '94) 💣

John Scofield: *The Best of John Scofield: Liquid Fire* (Gramavision '94) ⓝ

Scots Pirates: *Revolutionary Means* (Schoolkids' '95) the Allmans join the White Panthers ("88," "Marijuana Wine") ★★

Gil Scott-Heron: *Spirits* (TVT '94) ⓝ

Scrawl: *Travel On, Rider* (Elektra '96) their grim, unpretentious, personal best ("Good Under Pressure," "The Garden Path") ★

Scrawl: *Nature Film* (Elektra '98) With a realism other alt vets should have the modesty to imitate, these likable journeywomen cannibalize obscure old records only their cult will ever hear and come away with six songs they figure will top most of their new ones. Having learned to sing like godmothers Grace Slick and Joan Jett, they pump up "Charles," for the lucky sex partner who waits up after rehearsal, and "11:30 (It's January)," the saddest New Year's Eve song ever told. And thus they help you hear the new "Don't We Always Get There," about the perilous drive to the next gig, or orgasm. **A–**

Screaming Trees: *Sweet Oblivion* (Epic '92) Despite lyrics beholden to Mark Lanegan's attention-grabbing baritone, a big spooky aspiring commodity fetish that puts quantity before quality in the feeling department, these Northwest veterans have started roiling and hooking and knocking 'em dead at the very moment they seemed ready to expire of corporate torpor—not Kurt & Co., but definitely good for a fix. It isn't just songs, which are in evidence on their SST best-of and discernible on their Epic product, and before you credit the production, which must help some, ask yourself why Don Fleming can't do the same for Gumball. My theory: they got a new drummer, just like Kurt & Co. Hey, you never know. **B+**

Screaming Trees: *Dust* (Epic '96) a good old-fashioned cry ("Dying Days," "Traveler") ★

The Scruffs: *Midtown* (Northern Heights '98) it's Memphis, it's the '80s, and darn it, Big Star lives ("Machiavellian Eyes," "Judy [She Put the Devil in Me]") ★★★

Scud Mountain Boys: *Massachusetts* (Sub Pop '96) 💣

Seal: "Crazy" (*Seal,* Sire/Warner Bros. '91) 👁

Seal: *Seal* (ZTT/Sire/Warner Bros. '94) 💣

Dan Seals: "Love on Arrival" (*Greatest Hits,* Capitol '91) 👁

Son Seals: *Living in the Danger Zone* (Alligator '91) ⓝ

Sebadoh: *The Freed Weed* (Homestead '90) What do we know about a subculture where a CD of two bedroom tapes becomes a consumer durable? Who besides talent scouts (and tolerant ones at that) would lay out rent money for a succession of fragments-segued-into-fragments described by one admirer as "mostly written while they're being recorded and rarely played again"? Assuming they've ever paid the rent in their lives, I mean? Maybe kids who crave intimacy as much as amateur sociologists claim—so much that they turn musical doodles into love objects, attributing to them the imaginary smarts and cutes long-distance crushes so often impart.

Those of us who prefer talent will make out maybe four tunes amid the strum and clatter, including the autodestructing "Soul Mate" and the thematic "Temporary Dream." Inspirational Verse (literally, it's recited): "But if you see what you need in me/Then you can't have what you need." **D**

Sebadoh: *Sebadoh III* (Homestead '91) their girlfriends would be very proud if they weren't so pissed off ("Freed Pig," "Truly Great Thing") ★

Sebadoh: *Smash Your Head on the Punk Rock* (Sub Pop '92) 💣

Sebadoh: *Bubble and Scrape* (Sub Pop '93) angry three-headed wimp on the long hard road to love ("Soul and Fire," "Sister") ★

Sebadoh: *Bakesale* (Sub Pop '94) Two decades ago, Lou Barlow might have been Eric Justin Kaz, which I hope cheers anyone who thinks progress has gone out of style. And who recognizes Kaz's name, of course—confessional songpoet, acoustic guitar buried in El Lay clichés when he tried to get his songs out there himself. Believe me, indie-rock irony improves the type. Whether or not this sensitive young man Can Love, at least now the mooniness is under control, and access to technology enables him to make his own noise. Barlow's labyrinthine welter of demos-for-sale includes five previous so-called albums. In 1990, with Eric Gaffney sowing chaos every track he got and Jason Loewenstein's civilizing influence an alternative eon away, he was heard to derogate "the 'repeat the chorus three times' deal." Yet here, four years later, there are refrains, reiterations, hook riffs galore. I doubt I'll hear a catchier indie album all year—or a more visionary Unable to Love song than "Together and Alone." **A**

Sebadoh: *Harmacy* (Sub Pop '96) Pry the black plastic backing from the jewel box and decipher the credits on the nether side of the rear insert—a perfect metaphor for how public these coy alternastars are willing to go. Note that Lou Barlow's tuneful songs focus on his achy breaky voice, while Jason Loewenstein's rockin' ones lead with his sloppy riffs. Figure that Barlow needs Loewenstein because by itself his material would be indigestible—the indie-rock version of a peanut butter and jelly diet. But admit that Loewenstein would be a loud cipher without Barlow, who I only wish did like Ann Powers says he does and paraded his faults to prove his honesty. As with all self-made wimps, the hustle is more insidious—his honesty is supposed to justify his faults. It doesn't. The tunes do. **A–**

Sebadoh: *The Sebadoh* (Sub Pop/Sire '99) Apropos of I don't know, and for whatever good it will do whomever, they remain, on this recorded evidence, as good a band as they ever were, and a better one than back when they were epitomizing indie's recondite reticence. Yes, Lou's songs are, on average, better than Jason's. But Jason's songs are, in general, a relief from Lou's, plus that's his Gang of 4 intro—not gonna hear one of those from the Folk Implosion, are you? Maybe they'll say bye-bye and go home, or maybe they'll make records like this until they have grandchildren. Nobody knows, including them. **A–**

Jon Secada: *Heart Soul and Voice* (SBK/ERG '94) Cute, right. Not offensive like Michael Bolton or Celine Dion, of course. But also less fun than his buddy Gloria Estefan. In fact, the most unlistenable recent exponent of the "soul"-inflected American variant on the international pop ballad style. Just in case you're keeping track. **C–** 🦃

Thione Seck: *Daaly* (Stern's Africa '97) Ⓝ

Sedhiou Band: *Africa Kambeng* (Africassette '98) rolling Mandinka beats from agricultural and above all non-Wolof Senegal ("Nyancho," "Dimbaayaa") ★★

Seefeel: *Quique* (Astralwerks '94) Ⓝ

Mike Seeger: *Solo—Oldtime Country Music* (Rounder '91) 18 salty tunes, 11 acoustic instruments, no overdubs ("Ground Hog," "Tennessee Dog") ★★

Mike, Barbara & Penny Seeger: *Animal Folk Songs for Children* (Rounder '92) ⓝ

Mike Seeger: *Third Annual Farewell Reunion* (Rounder '94) old-timey all-stars ("Shaking Off the Acorns," "Brown's Ferry Blues") ★★

Compay Segundo: *Lo Mejor De La Vida* (Nonesuch '98) ⓝ

Compay Segundo: *Calle Salud* (Nonesuch '99) ⓝ

Sid Selvidge: "Keep It Clean," "Tell Me Why You Like Roosevelt" (*Twice Told Tales,* Elektra Nonesuch '93) 🌑

Semisonic: *Feeling Strangely Fine* (MCA '98) 💣

Yandé Codou Sène: "Gainde" (*Night Sky in Sine Saloum,* Shanachie '97) 🌑

Septeto Nacional & Guests: *Mas Cuba Libres* (Network import '99) high-generic son, pretty much like you-know-who, except I'll take rough-voiced eightysomething P'o Leva (four tracks) over Compay Segundo or Enrico Ferrer ("Oye Como Suena," "Llore Como Lloré") ★

Sepultura: *Roots* (RoadRunner '96) 💣

Sergent Garcia: *Un poquito quema'o* (Higher Octave '99) frantic salsa con reggae from, er, Paris—*auténtico* no, *convincente* yes ("Jumpi," "Si yo llego, yo llego") ★

Erick Sermon: *No Pressure* (Def Jam/RAL/Chaos/Columbia '94) ⓞ

Erick Sermon: *Double or Nothing* (RAL '95) ⓝ

The Setters: "Let's Take Some Drugs and Drive Around," "Hook in My Lip," "Don't Love Me Wisely" (*The Setters,* Watermelon '94) 🌑

The Brian Setzer Orchestra: *The Dirty Boogie* (Interscope '98) Big bands still can't rock, Setzer still can't sing, and that's only the beginning. There is for instance chief arranger Ray Herrmann, Bernard's black-sheep grandnephew, whose dad was 86'd by Stan Kenton because he didn't have any soul. There's the hyperactive desecration visited upon Rosemary Clooney's perky "This Ole House," the croakin' belt an' croon of "Since I Don't Have You," Leiber & Stoller's obscure "You're the Boss" retouched so heavy-handedly you'd think Setzer wrote the thing himself. But no, that was—dig these titles!—"This Cat's on a Hot Tin Roof," "Hollywood Nocturne," the Elmer Bernstein–influenced "Switchblade 372." With its Doc Severinsen blare and Paul Shaffer beats, its gross secondhand nostalgia and showoff guitar, the most preeningly stupid record to mount SoundScan all year. C– 🦃

7 Year Bitch: *Viva Zapata!* (C/Z '94) ⓝ

7 Year Bitch: *Gato Negro* (Atlantic '96) tough broads, hard rock ("Miss Understood," "The History of My Future") ★

Sex Pistols: *Filthy Lucre Live* (Virgin '96) Even though it reprises all 12 songs on *Never Mind the Bollocks* (plus five familiar outtakes and B sides) with their tempos and arrangements intact, this is that rare thing, a live album with a life of its own. Its strength is that its historical moment is so definitively over. Thus it compels us to rehear Steve Jones's immense bluesless riffs, Paul Cook's stone simple beats, and Glen Matlock's melodic glue as pure sound, and to confront how John Rotten-Lydon's hilariously ill-humored gutter-prophet howl, broadened but not softened with age and a decade-plus of paid acting lessons in Public Image Ltd., defined both a new rock voice and a new rock attitude. A–

The Sex Pistols: *Raw* (Music Club '97) live boot (Burton Upon Trent, 9/24/76) as budget-priced history—crude, kinda slow, a few rare titles, four demos added ("Substitute," "No Fun") ★★

Ron Sexsmith: *Ron Sexsmith* (Interscope '95) 💣

Ron Sexsmith: *Other Songs* (Interscope '97) ⓝ

SF Seals: *Baseball Trilogy* (Matador '93) .667 ("Joltin' Joe DiMaggio," "The Ballad of Denny McLain") ★

The San Francisco Seals: *Now Here* (Matador '94) ℕ

S.F. Seals: *Truth Walks in Sleepy Shadows* (Matador '95) postpunk cute, folk-rock homely, dream-pop barely there ("S.F. Sorrow," "Ipecac") ★

Shack: *H.M.S. Fable* (London '99) 🎸

Shadow: "Columbus Lied" (*Columbus Lied,* Shanachie '91) 👁

Shaggy: *Pure Pleasure* (Virgin '93) ℕ

Simon Shaheen: *The Music of Mohamed Abdel Wahab* (Axiom '90) I couldn't tell you how "profound, prolonged, and widespread" Wahab's influence on Middle Eastern music has been, though as a singer and film star as well as Om Kalsoum's arranger, he clearly played a huge role in the secularization and Europeanization of the Koranic repertoire. This great-sounding tribute by a Palestinian Christian oud/violin virtuoso, scholar, and orchestra leader has the apposite high-middlebrow tone. But unlike so many brainy projects, it pushes my pleasure buttons as well as my duty buttons. Some people get off on Ennio Morricone. I like my soundtracks more exotic. **A–**

Shai: *. . . If I Ever Fall in Love* (Gasoline Alley '92) Why are these putative paragons of sexual vulnerability so much more irritating than the rainbow-hued Color Me Badd, the blandly stylish Boyz II Men, or the utterly forgotten Ready for the World? It's not their indifferent singing and rapping, which are only to be expected. It's that they have no class and less sense of humor; they're too smarmy and too slow; they're big phonies. They epitomize the difference between seduction and betrayal—between shared lie and imposed illusion, rascal and bounder, rogue and complete asshole. There's not a winning wink on the entire album. And only "Waiting for the Day" ("When you can spend the night") offers up a fantasy with any educational potential for the fine females who lap up their shit. **B–** 🦃

The Shams: "Watching the Grass Grow" (*Quilt,* Matador '91) 👁

The Shams: *Sedusia* (Matador '93) Women will have no trouble with these three quiet, simple, exquisite songs about love. But what about if you're male? Well, if you're an alternative kinda guy, the sexually explicit "Love Me with Your Mind" will score first—your specialty, right? But if you're a truly alternative kinda guy, the ones about absence and doubt will fill your scheming organ with thoughts of paying attention, settling down. **A–**

Mem Shannon: *A Cab Driver's Blues* (Rykodisc '95) This semipro is an accomplished musician and a better writer. Otherwise, couldn't no concept lift him out of the generic welter of New Orleans bluesmen plying their trade in an entertainment center with scanter historical claim on blues—as opposed to jazz, funk, rock and roll, and countless pianistic celebrations of the second line—than Memphis or Houston, Clarksdale or Chicago. But what distinguishes Shannon's songs about his love life and his work life, Oprah Winfrey and his right to sing the blues, is their context—taped conversations from the back of his cab with locals who've seen their pleasures ruined by the pleasure industry and out-of-towners who got their idea of revelry from old tit magazines. Makes one wonder how much joy can be left in a city fogged in by the rosy mirage of a tourist economy. And gives Mem Shannon the right to sing the blues. **B+**

Mem Shannon: *Mem Shannon's 2nd Blues Album* (Hannibal '98) the saddest sound he ever heard ("Old Men," "One Thin Dime") ★

Shanté: *The Bitch Is Back* (Livin' Large '92) As politically incorrect as the dickheads she disses, Shanté scorns "bitches" and "hos" (and "hookers" and "sluts" and "bull daggers") who think they can rap—that is, every female rival you can think of, many of whom she calls out by name in the scabrous "Big Mama." She claims to rhyme her own, but she had her name on only three tracks last album, which was four years ago, and this one doesn't bother with writing credits. So if in her world the original is still the greatest, that world exists mostly in her own mind. The thing is, it also exists on her records. Because she still *is* the greatest—she just is. Her tone and attack and enunciation vie with Ice-T and Chuck D and Rakim. Her material is full of outrageous insults and filthy internal rhymes. And perhaps because hard is all there is where she comes from, her tough, jazz-tinged music is as fresh as the stuff gets these days. She's of limited use showing off a slow groove or going dancehall, and I'm not going to claim she's got redeeming social value. But I'm also not going to tell you "Brothers Ain't Shit" has nothing to say. **A–**

Sonny Sharrock Band: *Highlife* (Enemy import '91) As with classic Pharoah Sanders, Sharrock's devotion to cacophony turns out to be the obverse of his devotion to tune—his thematic statements are respectfully stately, his variations more sonic than harmonic. So where Ronald Shannon Jackson is a jazz composer exploring rock colors (and sometimes rhythms), Sharrock has the priorities of a genius son of Jimi and Jimmy. An atmospheric Kate Bush tribute that eventually gains momentum is as arty as this gorgeously straightforward guitar record gets, and though no one will mistake the Sanders cover for "Eight Miles High," it's in the tradition. **A**

Sonny Sharrock: *Ask the Ages* (Axiom '91) Bill and Elvin's excellent jazz record ("Little Rock") ★★★

Sonny Sharrock + Ricky Skopelitis: *Faith Moves* (CMP import '91) atmospherics for an oxygen-depleted biosphere ("Uncle Herbie's Dance," "Who Are You") ★★★

Sonny Sharrock: *Space Ghost: Coast to Coast* (Cartoon Network promo '94) a little skronk, a little tune, some weird vocal overlay, and voilà—cable soundtrack fusion ("Hit Single," "Ghost Planet National Anthem") ★

Shaver: *Tramp on Your Street* (Praxis International/Zoo '93) 🎵

Shazzy: *Attitude: A Hip-Hop Rapsody* (Elektra '90) "You nigger-nappin', corny-snappin', booger-pickin', butt-be-kickin', no-tooth big-lip-breathin', night-funk-lovin', mother-starvin' marvin eatin' out o' garbage cans wearin' holey drawers and a bra strap tryin' to call yourself a man." And also: "Black's the race 50 per cent of my blood flow/The other flows white or what society won't show." This never gets catchier than "Giggahoe"'s freestyle dissing and soul-grown piano-and-horns hook. But the music is deep, subtle, and audacious throughout, claiming its turf with a radio-sample intro that includes FDR and Molly Goldberg as well as MLK and Muhammad Ali. You may think she's consorting with the enemy. You may think she's too middle-class, too judgmental. And you may think she's not earth mother enough to talk so sisterly. But she ain't playing—especially with you. **A–**

Shedaisy: *The Whole Shebang* (Lyric Street '99) Here's something you don't know how much you don't need—Dixie Chicks imitators. I do, because I also played the Lace album. The best-selling Osborn sisters have more jam. But although they swear they "won't wear stiletto heels" (unlike all those hussies at the Wal-Mart?), they definitely make nicer to men than Dolly and Loretta if not Tammy and Reba. Nothing in "Still Holding Out for You," cowritten by none other than Richard Marx, suggests that smart sister Kristyn wouldn't dress like a slut to get him back. Somebody send that lovelorn lass a Victoria's Secret catalogue. **C+** 🦃

Duncan Sheik: *Duncan Sheik* (Atlantic '96) Why do I suspect that only a whiner foolish enough to fall for the depressed wacko now suffocating him all over the airwaves would be foolish enough to blame it on her? Because no one ever went broke underestimating the intelligence of guys who program the drums but consider it tasteful to hire out the strings to certified human beings. However desperate the biz may be for matinee idols, anybody who figures this neosensitive can fill Bryan Adams's shoes would have bet on Robbie Nevil back when these things mattered. **C** 🦃

Ricky Van Shelton: *Greatest Hits Plus* (Columbia '92) just handsome and mellifluous enough to snag more top-drawer songs than he deserves ("Life Turned Her That Way," "Somebody Lied," "Rockin' Years") ★★★

She Mob: *Cancel the Wedding* (Spinster Playground '99) three women in wigs shout their shouts and tell their weird, unassuming tales ("Teacher," "Prozac") ★★

Kenny Wayne Shepherd: *Ledbetter Heights* (Giant '96) plays better blues readymades than he writes, writes better blues readymades than his front man sings ("Born with a Broken Heart," "I'm Leaving You [Commit a Crime]") ★

Shinehead: *The Real Rock* (Elektra '90) striver's rap, JA-U.S. style ("Cigarette Breath") ★★
Shinehead: *Praises* (VP '99) 💣

Michelle Shocked: *Arkansas Traveler* (Mercury '92) Personally, I'm sorry she chickened out of doing the cover in blackface, because it would have added yet another fucked-up twist to her impossibly confused attempt to sort out American music's racial debts. After all, her confusion is no more impossible than anybody else's, just further out there, and at least the opacity of her pontifications on minstrelsy illustrates how deep the mysteries run. As someone who knows a fair amount about minstrelsy, I'd point out that most of its tunes were written by whites, albeit whites who aped and/or stole from blacks, or anyway (speaking of confusion), claimed to—after 1860, 'twas oft complained that newer minstrels weren't faux-darkie *enough*. And as someone who'd like to know more, I wish Shocked had said damn the copyright lawyers and detailed the sources of all her new songs, which—except for the gnomic "Arkansas Traveler" on the up side

and the preachy "Strawberry Jam" on the down—are at their best when they seem influenced but not imitated. "Prodigal Daughter" out of "Cotton-Eyed Joe" is a coup—hooray. But is there a sense in which the equally praiseworthy "Come a Long Way" is also a rewrite? Or did those notes just float in from the ether? **B+**
Michelle Shocked: *Kind Hearted Woman* (Private Music '96) 💣

Shonen Knife: *Shonen Knife* (Gasatanka/Giant '90) The problem with the Japanese is that they don't know the difference between a Ramones song and a Wrigley commercial. But we do, or should, and these are Wrigley commercials, in which three lookee-no-touchee geishas do a good job of half implying that the supercatchy "Banana Fish" is a J. D. Salinger reference—in other words, that they condescend to American culture as much as American counterculture condescends to them. Unfortunately, the only thing that might make this ambiguity interesting would be musical dimensions they have no time, use, or aptitude for. **C+** 🦃

Jane Siberry: *When I Was a Boy* (Reprise '93) Interesting music is the perfect cover for mediocre literature. Many serious pop fans, especially genteel ones, are so hungry for tokens of intelligence that they'll cut slack for anyone who transcends the quatrain, pondering sung imagery they wouldn't glance at in a slim volume. If you skip "Sweet Incarnadine" ("edited down from a 20 min. improvisation," God help us), this isn't altogether horrible. Siberry has a sense of shape and texture; there are clever glints of informality in her presentation; her passion shows more smarts and decency than most. But her settings are only settings. And her words are only intelligent. **B–** 🦃

Bobby Sichran: "From a Sympathetical Hurricane," "Don't Break My Heart Kid" (*From a Sympathetical Hurricane*, Columbia '94) 🐢

Silk: *Lose Control* (Elektra '92) 💣

Silkk the Shocker: *Charge It 2 Da Game* (No Limit '97) 💣

The Silos: *Susan Across the Ocean* (Watermelon '94) listen to the originals, keep the covers ("Let's Take Some Drugs and Drive Around," "I'm Straight") ★

Silverchair: *Frogstomp* (Murmur/Epic '95) All respect to Frankie Lymon and Roxanne Shanté, but every once in a while in this business you catch yourself thinking that teenagers don't know dick. These Aussie adolescents admire Nirvana and Pearl Jam, which is cute, and sound like Pearl Jam, which is natural—*almost exactly* like Pearl Jam except no good, which is useless. Since their tastes are constantly maturing, next time they can take Tool or if we're lucky Rancid to Kinko's. Inspirational Verse You May Have Noticed Even if You Never Remember Who It's By: "There's no bathroom/ And there is no sink/The water out of the tap/Is very hard"—[dramatic power chords]—"to drink." **C** 🦃

Silverchair: "London's Burning" (*Burning London: The Clash Tribute* [comp], Epic '99) 🐝

Silverfish: *Organ Fan* (Creation/Chaos/ Columbia '93) Ⓝ

Silver Jews: *Arizona Record* (Drag City '93) 💣

Silver Jews: *The Natural Bridge* (Drag City '96) Ⓝ

Silver Jews: *American Water* (Drag City '98) noise-tune simplified for baritone monotone ("Random Rules," "Night Society") ★

Paul Simon: *The Rhythm of the Saints* (Warner Bros. '90) his life in the bush of a fully formed middle-class music scene more sophisticated than he'll ever be ("The Obvious Child," "The Coast") ★

Paul Simon: *The Concert in the Park—August 15th, 1991* (Warner Bros. '91) 💣

Paul Simon: *Songs from* The Capeman (Warner Bros. '97) Ⓝ

Nina Simone: *A Single Woman* (Elektra '93) 💣

Simply Red: *Greatest Hits* (EastWest '96) while they merely lionized the obliging Mick Hucknall, we fell for the odious Michael Bolton, which ought to scare the Anglophobia out of anyone ("Money's Too Tight to Mention," "So Beautiful") ★

Kym Sims: "Take My Advice" (*Too Blind to See It,* Atco '92) 🐝

Frank Sinatra: *Sinatra and Sextet: Live in Paris* (Reprise '93) 💣

Frank Sinatra: *Duets* (Capitol '93) He creaks, he cracks, he croaks, he clinks, yet that's not quite the point—older guys with worse voices have sung better anyway. Champion Jack Dupree, for instance, prevailed in his eighties because he never staked his manhood on the technical impeccability of his physical instrument. For decades Sinatra's sound was magnificent—not just beautiful, meaningful. But now, though he still outclasses the likes of Bono and Carly Simon, Liza Minnelli takes him to acting school and Luther Vandross sings pretty rings around him. He who lives by the larynx shall die by the larynx. **C** 🦃

Frank Sinatra: *Everything Happens to Me* (Reprise '96) The Chairman on Reprise is a study in why artists shouldn't own record companies. My researches into a catalogue that runs to some 100 LPs have yet to uncover a single title that comes near the great Capitols, and the compilations are not to be trusted. So rather than spending $60 for the choppy 81-song box, try this 20-song oddity, supposedly programmed by Frank himself at age 79 and duplicating only seven box selections. It anoints more Don Costas than Nelson Riddles and surprisingly scant on the Tin Pan Alley pantheon, the defining factor is tempo, almost always moderate or less, accentuating the autumnally ruminative mood of the songs and the old man who looked back on them so fondly. It ain't, to choose the Capitol remaster I've just glommed onto, *Songs for Young Lovers/Swing Easy!* But from the "suddenly you're a lot older" of the 1981 lead track, there's character here no callow 40-year-old would stoop to. **A**

Frank Sinatra with the Red Norvo Quintet: *Live in Australia, 1959* (Blue Note '97) With an official live corpus comprising little beyond Vegas dates, statuesque concert stuff, and an insensate 1962 small-group session, this cleanly remastered version of a tape legendary among the bootleggers he's served so well belongs in a canon that's already as outsized as his FBI file. True, it does sample his sense of humor, and although the economy of crack bandleader Norvo offers relief from his usual arrangers, even the greatest vibes players do inevitably play the vibraphone. Nevertheless, there's no authorized Sinatra like this. Its light, relaxed, groove-powered phrasing may not mean as much as the endless timbral subtlety of his studio work, but it gives up the fun his patter misses, as well as the spontaneous musicality those who think him "merely" pop claim isn't there. In the ebullient "Night and Day" that tops things off, he even risks undermining the lyric. He knows no more heinous sin, and the transgression becomes him. **A–**

Frank Sinatra: *Sinatra '57—In Concert* (DCC '99) The big deal about the new George Jones record is supposed to be that, due to his near-death experience, he didn't get to overdub the vocals. He should have. One of the few better singers in this century was also a perfectionist cautious about preserving his live shows. Of those officially released so far, this is the most impressive, its lighter and less precise attack good for a grace that isn't so prominent in the studio work. The audio is exquisite, the repertoire is choice, the excellent Nelson Riddle arrangements are mixed way below the voice, CD technology lets you zap his monologue, and just to affirm our common humanity, he hits a clinker on "My Funny Valentine." **A–**

Siouxsie and the Banshees: *Twice upon a Time—The Singles* (Geffen '92) 💣

Sir Douglas Quintet: *Day Dreaming at Midnight* (Elektra '94) hippiedom as folklore ("She Would If She Could, She Can't So She Won't," "Romance Is All Screwed Up") ★★

Sir Mix-a-Lot: *Mack Daddy* (Def American '92) ⓝ

Sir Mix-a-Lot: *Chief Boot Knocka* (Rhyme Cartel '94) ⓝ

Sir Mix-a-Lot: *Return of the Bumpasaurus* (American '96) stupid, funky ("Jump on It," "Bark Like You Want It") ★

Sisqo: "Thong Song" (*Unleash the Dragon,* Dragon/Def Soul '99) 🔊

The Sisters of Mercy: "Vision Thing" (*Vision Thing,* Elektra '90) 🔊

Jonah Sithole: *Sabhaku* (Zimbob '95) gentle generic Zimpop, masterful mbira guitar ("Chakafukidza Dzimba," "Vakomano Vehondo") ★★

Sixpence None the Richer: *Sixpence None the Richer* (Squint Entertainment '98) If you hold your breath and are very good, maybe "Kiss Me" will prove a fluke. Maybe in the end it'll only be the innocent invitation to making out a deserving teen subdemographic craved. But don't tell yourself stories about biz or fundamentalist plots. Christians not proselytizers, they're an indie-rock success story who come by their limpid sound more organically than the Sundays or the Innocence Mission, both of whom they sincerely admire. Leigh Nash's clear little voice, like a young Natalie Merchant without the neurotic undertow? Her own. Matt Slocum's classed-up minor-key arrangements, like an acoustic Radiohead without the existential foofaraw? His own. They hope to create pretty, well-meaning stuff like this in perpetuity, for the sheer joy of it. Which means they could be nauseating urban skeptics for years. **C+** 🦃

The 6ths: *Wasps' Nests* (London '95) cavalcade of drips ("San Diego Zoo," "Pillow Fight," "Heaven in a Black Leather Jacket") ★★

Roni Size/Reprazent: *New Forms* (Talkin' Loud/Mercury '97) in the mildly overrated tradition of Massive Attack and Soul II Soul ("Digital," "Electricks") ★★

Skatenigs: "Chemical Imbalance" (*Stupid People Shouldn't Breed,* Megaforce '92) 👁️‍🗨️

Skeleton Key: *Fantastic Spike Through Balloon* (Capitol '97) steam-driven dissonance down a blooze-based groove ("Nod Off," "The World's Most Famous Undertaker") ★★

The Skeletons: *Nothing to Lose* (High-Tone '97) **N**

Skid Row: *Slave to the Grind* (Atlantic '91) 💣

Skunk Anansie: *Paranoid and Sunburnt* (Epic/One Little Indian '96) **N**
Skunk Anansie: *Stoosh* (One Little Indian/Epic '97) **N**

Slant 6: *Soda Pop Rip Off* (Dischord '94) 💣
Slant 6: *Inzombia* (Dischord '95) 💣

Slaughter: *Stick It to Ya* (Chrysalis '90) Schlockier than Tesla, stupider than Queensryche, simpler than Extreme, these sluts win the Consumer Guide Lead Dildo for the most godawful new metal band to go platinum since the last time I checked. They're not even overly offensive—Mark Slaughter slaughters no one, and despite the bimbo-with-knives cover limits the misogyny to one gold digger and one sex predator. She's got "notches in her belt," and by then I was so bored I was aggrieved to learn it wasn't "nachos in her bed." **D** 🐛

Slayer: *Live: Decade of Aggression* (Def American '91) praise the Lord—I can hardly understand a word they're singing ("Hell Awaits") ★

Sleater-Kinney: *Sleater-Kinney* (Chainsaw '95) Heavens to Betsy's warbly wailer Corin Tucker joins Excuse 17's solemn screamer Carrie Brownstein for 10 songs in 22 minutes, and voice-on-voice and guitar-on-guitar they figure out love by learning to hate. Three different lyrics reject the penis *soi-même* with a fervor that could pass for disgust, and while their same-sex one-on-ones aren't exactly odes to joy, they convey a depth of feeling that could pass for passion. In these times of principled irony and shallowness for its own sake, that's enough to make them heroines and outsiders simultaneously. A–

Sleater-Kinney: *Call the Doctor* (Chainsaw '96) Like the blues, punk is a template that shapes young misfits' sense of themselves, and like the blues it takes many forms. This is a new one, and it's damn blueslike. Powered by riffs that seem unstoppable even though they're not very fast, riding melodies whose irresistibility renders them barely less harsh, Corin Tucker's enormous voice never struggles more inspirationally against the world outside than when it's facing down the dilemmas of the interpersonal—dilemmas neither eased nor defined by her gender preferences, dilemmas as bound up with family as they are with sex. As partner/rival/Other Carrie Brownstein puts it in an eloquently tongue-tied moment: "It's just my stuff." Few if any have played rock's tension-and-release game for such high stakes—revolution as existentialism, electric roar as acne remedy. They wanna be our Joey Ramone, who can resist that one? But squint at the booklet and you'll see they also want to be our Thurston Moore. They want it both ways, every which way. And most of the time they get it. **A**

Sleater-Kinney: *Dig Me Out* (Kill Rock Stars '97) One reason you know they're young is that they obviously believe they can rock and roll at this pitch forever. Whatever the verbal message of their intricate, deeply uptempo simplicity—less sexual angst, more rock-as-romance—it's overrun by their excited mastery and runaway glee. Like a new good lover the second or third time, they're so confident of their ability to please that they just can't stop. And this confidence is collective: Corin and Carrie chorus-trade like the two-headed girl, dashing and high-stepping around on Janet Weiss's shoulders. What a ride. **A**

Sleater-Kinney: *The Hot Rock* (Kill Rock Stars '99) What's hard to get used to here, and what's also freshest and perhaps best, is how Corin and Carrie's voices intertwine—even reading the booklet it's hard to keep track of who's saying what to whom about what, as if they'd fallen in love with (or to) the Velvets' "Murder Mystery." Not that meanings would be crystalline in any case, or that they should be. With Cadallaca an outlet for Corin's girlish ways, S-K emerges as a diary of adulthood in all its encroaching intricacy. I mean, the guitars don't crunch like they used to either, and that's the very reason "Get Up" sounds like death and desire at the same time. The reason "The Size of Our Love" sounds like death, on the other hand, is that sometimes love is death. Nobody ever said maturity would be fun and games. **A**

Percy Sledge: *Blue Night* (Sky Ranch/Pointblank '95) out of left field ("You Got Away with Love," "Why Did You Stop") ★★

Sleeper: *Smart* (Arista '95) as sexy as their last song ("Delicious," "Inbetweener") ★

Slick Rick: *The Ruler's Back* (Def Jam/Columbia '91) Cut in a hurry on bail, this widely reviled record will go nowhere, but I hear it as a work of mad avant-garde genius. I'm not kidding—nothing has ever sounded like this. Bass and drums tumbling forward atop submerged hook effects in a trademark groove that never stops, every track checks in fast. And though Rick's bad dreams are almost as full of niggas and bitches as N.W.A's kiddie porn, his quick, preoccupied singsong drawl makes it gratifyingly impossible to pin down the details. In short, it's genuinely surreal, as befits the product of a sick mind. **A–**

Slick Rick: "All Alone (A Love That's True)," "Behind Bars" (*Behind Bars*, Def Jam '94) 👁

Slick Rick: *The Art of Storytelling* (Def Jam '99) The music on this unflappably deft comeback is unlayered, highlighting spare beats with simple scratches or vocal sound effects to showcase the feyly effeminate king's-honeydrip singsong that's been identifiable at 50 yards since "La-Di-Da-Di." Mostly he boasts about how pretty he is and how good he raps, proving the latter with cameos from such modern-day flowmasters as Raekwon, Nas, Snoop, and Big Boi. He plays his prison card by trumping the two-line auditions from the wannabes who serenade him as he walks to freedom with "Kill Niggaz," which describes a fictional crime spree far deadlier than the attack he got sent up for. And he writes about fucking with the detailed relish of someone who's read a lot of pornography. **A–**

Slick Sixty: *Nibs and Nabs* (Mute '99) lounge r&b for the age of techno constructivism and Moog retro ("Hilary, Last of the Pool Sharks," "Dun Deal [Wrestler's Rematch]") ★★★

Slint: *Spiderland* (Touch and Go '91) Out of Squirrel Bait by Hunglikealbini, a Trojan horse. Extolled for their multipartite songforms and, da-da, *dynamic shifts from soft-to-loud,* as well as their intimate knowledge of mental illness, these guys look like unassuming alternative types and in real life may be same. Their sadsack affect fits right in. But musically—structurally, as one might say—they're art-rockers without the courage of their pretensions. And if you promise not to mention their lyrics they promise to keep the volume down. **C+** 🦃

Sloan: *Smeared* (DGC '93) As Nova Scotian as lox and bagels, it's orthodox North American neohip. The specifics of the Halifax "scene" are irrelevant; dissonant, guitar-decentered pop has become the province of anyone within reach of a culturally correct college radio station—anyone "Left of Centre," a title that refers in so many words to "pop culture" rather than politics. The most meaningful song is the opener, about a cool coed whose grade-point average is higher than the singer's even though "her spelling's atrocious." Everywhere else, the ugly beauty of the guitars sustains. **B+**

Sloan: *Twice Removed* (DGC '94) Their popward shift doesn't change their specific gravity because they're all surface either way. Where before their noise was an intrinsically intriguing sonic signpost sweetened by their tunes, now their tunes gain savor from their noise. Talented boys, absolutely, often with something thoughtful to say about feelings the average college graduate has already thought through, and since I've got nothing against surfaces, I look forward to their romantic maturity. I also advise the Algerian and Norwegian pen pals they crib from to demand points. **B+**

Sloan: *One Chord to Another* (The Enclave '97) 🎣

Sloan: "C'Mon C'Mon (Gonna Get It Started)" (*Navy Blues*, Murderecords '98) 👁

Sloan: *Between the Bridges* (Murderecords '99) Ⓝ

Drink Small: *Round Two* (Ichiban '91) "You know I've made a lot of albums/Trying to get national attention/But what it seem like now I'm gonna be a old man/Living off a pension" ("I'm Tired Now," "Widow Woman") ★★

Smash Mouth: *Fush Yu Mang* (Interscope '97) By calculation or osmosis, this unrad agglomeration of semiprofessional entertainers puts bells on the humorous humanism of ska-twice-removed. As you'd figure, the key is songs, most of them by late-arriving guitarist Greg Camp, whose hardcore links are even more theoretical than his bandmates'. His fondly ignorant take on the hippie moment could be Bertrand Russell by pop standards, and how about the album-opening "Flo"? I couldn't swear radio is ready for a cheerful ditty begging the title lesbian to take the singer's girlfriend back. But the world is. **A–**

Smash Mouth: "Can't Get Enough of You Baby" (*Can't Hardly Wait* [ST], Elektra '98) 👁

Smash Mouth: *Astro Lounge* (Interscope '99) surveying the world from a temporary star ("Then the Morning Comes," "I Just Wanna See") ★★★

Smashing Pumpkins: *Lull* (Caroline '91) Ⓝ

Smashing Pumpkins: *Gish* (Caroline '91) if you can dig art-rock fantasia—and hey, why not?—this has a nice witchy wail to it ("Rhinoceros") ★

Smashing Pumpkins: *Siamese Dream* (Virgin '93) hooked on sonics ("Geek U.S.A.," "Today") ★★★

Smashing Pumpkins: "1979" (*Melon Collie and the Infinite Sadness*, Virgin '95) 👁

Smashing Pumpkins: *Adore* (Virgin '98) Ⓝ

Elliott Smith: *Either/Or* (Kill Rock Stars '97) he could too be popular—he just doesn't want to be, that's all ("Rose Parade," "Say Yes") ★

Elliott Smith: *XO* (DreamWorks '98) high tune, low affect ("Waltz #2 [XO]," "Everybody Cares, Everybody Understands") ★

Kendra Smith: *Five Ways of Disappearing* (4AD '95) With the pump organ and all she does have Her Own Sound, especially if you don't remember Nico too clearly—and unlike Nico, she also has a sense of humor. But antiurban survivalists rarely like people much. And quiet as it's kept, agape is a richer musical wellspring than nonconformity. **B–** 🦃

Patti Smith: "Memorial Tribute" (*No Alternative* [comp], Arista '93) 👁

Patti Smith: *Gone Again* (Arista '96) pure as death and taxes ("Summer Cannibals," "Wicked Messenger") ★★★

Patti Smith: *Peace and Noise* (Arista '97) good thing she's still a little nuts, because funny's beyond or beneath her ("Whirl Away," "Memento Mori") ★

Stephan Smith: *Now's the Time* (Rounder '99) Ⓝ

Will Smith: "Gettin' Jiggy wid It," "Just the Two of Us," "Miami" (*Big Willie Style*, Columbia '97) 👁

Will Smith: *Willenniun* (Columbia '99) ⓝ

Chris Smither: *Another Way to Find You* (Flying Fish '91) The second release this recovering alcoholic and stagefright victim has managed since 1972—just him, his blue guitar, and a studio full of fans—redoes most of his two early-'70s albums, both out of print since the early '70s were over, and leaves 1985's *It Ain't Easy* alone. A Cambridge folkie from New Orleans, Smither is an easy taste to acquire: he strums as to the second line born, sings in a lazy, roughly luxuriant baritone, writes when he's got something to say, and understands o.p.'s from the inside out. I know Randy Newman's "Have You Seen My Baby" so well I was sorry he'd covered it, only to be struck like never before by its final lines: "She say I'll talk to strangers if I want to/I'm a stranger too." Next day I recalled the title of his first album: *I'm a Stranger Too.* **A-**

Chris Smither: *Happier Blue* (Flying Fish '93) expansive new songs, congenial new band, and the stompingest foot this side of John Lee Hooker ("Happier Blue," "Honeysuckle Bone") ★★

Chris Smither: *Up on the Lowdown* (HighTone '95) ⓝ

Chris Smither: *Small Revelations* (HighTone '97) blues his religion, his therapy, his metier ("Winsome Smile," "Dust My Broom") ★★★

Chris Smither: *Drive You Home Again* (HighTone '99) Between his somnolent baritone, his blurred melodies, and his big easy guitar, Smither does fade into the background—hear him at a distance and you'd never suspect he was a moral philosopher. But in fact he is that even rarer thing, a moral philosopher with good values, and here his songwriting takes over a career marked by killer covers. From the title manifesto—"These are not petty pleasures/It's a dance that slowly glides/In very complicated measures/That can't be simplified"—to "Tell Me *Why* [italics mine] You Love Me," he thinks on his butt while keeping the beat with his foot. He's worth attending even if you think blues are history. **A-**

Smog: *The Doctor Came at Dawn* (Drag City '96) 💣

Smoking Popes: *Born to Quit* (Capitol '95) 💣

Snakefarm: *Songs from My Funeral* (RCA '99) 💣

Snap: *World Power* (Arista '90) Hip house from London, or maybe Germany, where rough-hewn Cincinnati rapper Turbo B was introduced to European culture as a GI. And in the great transcultural Technotronic tradition, it's crazy and radio-ready at the same time. Also funny. Why else introduce the love rap with a piano hook out of *Music for Airports,* or go out on a B-boy whining like a wino, or call one "Believe the Hype"? **A-**

Snap: *Welcome to Tomorrow* (Arista '95) 💣

Sneaker Pimps: "Low Place Like Home" (*Becoming X,* Virgin '97) 👁

Todd Snider: "Easy Money," "Alright Guy" (*Songs for the Daily Planet,* MCA/Margaritaville '94) 👁

Snoop Doggy Dogg: *Doggystyle* (Death Row/Interscope '93) 💣

Snoop Dogg: *Da Game Is to Be Sold, Not to Be Told* (No Limit '98) It would be a pleasure to dismiss Calvin Broadus's evocatively entitled No Limit debut as another piece of lowballing funk off the N.O. Bounce assembly line. But the lead "Snoop World" is the kind of track that can make an album, playing a synth-bass hook over a real bassline and under triangles and other high elements that never hint at G-funk keyb tweedle, and over the next few songs, cameos from No Limit's two best rappers, Mystikal and Mia X, clear the way for the unoriginal gangsta bullroar of Master P and his brothers. Despite considerable input from Mystikal—whose deep-Delta bellow tenses against Snoop's honey-tongued indifference, adding moral weight to the usual professions of "ex–drug dealer" rectitude—the music soon runs down, however. And though Snoop is surely just a rapper now, he'd no more risk alienating his market than help a Blood's grandma across the street. Da game he's selling is sociopathic violence, and so he commits metaphorical murder, invites thugs to wave their gats in the air, cuts a biyutch improvident enough to suck his dick, and so forth. In short, he proves himself a born liar, showing all the imagination of an ATM in the process. Anyone who counts him a major artist because he can drawl and pronounce consonants at the same time should give equal time to Mariah Carey's high notes and George Winston's magic fingers. **C+** 🦃

Jill Sobule: "I Kissed a Girl" (*Jill Sobule,* Lava '95) 🍤

Social Distortion: *Social Distortion* (Epic '90) the anger of the long-distance runner ("Story of My Life," "Ring of Fire") ★ **Social Distortion:** *Somewhere Between Heaven and Hell* (Epic '92) Like their sceneboys Bad Religion, these hardcore holdouts get over on a saving touch of trad: where Greg Graffin and Brett Gurewitz break into anthem, Mike Ness gives new meaning to hard honky tonk. And where Graffin and Gurewitz ponder the fate of humanity, Ness universalizes his personal problems like millions of unhappy male chauvinists before him. Me, I'd rather the other guys had made a career album. But as all four of us know, life is unfair. **B+** **Social Distortion:** *White Light White Heat White Trash* (550 Music/Epic '96) Ⓝ

Soho: *Goddess* (Atco '90) 💣

Dave Soldier: *The Kropotkins* (Koch '97) postmodern preblues ("Good Cheap Transportation," "Cold Wet Steel") ★★

Solex: *Solex Vs. the Hitmeister* (Matador '98) 💣

Sol y Canto: *Sendero Del Sol* (Rounder '97) 💣

Jimmy Somerville: *The Singles Collection* (London '91) As he fills out his technologically appointed hour and a quarter, the drag has nothing to do with mascara, pulling the educational "There's More to Love Than Boy Meets Girl" down toward the zipless Communards-period electrodance that surrounds it. But punch a few buttons and you get a 10- or 12-track tribute to great divas male and female. The predisco Bee Gees cover defines Somerville's context the way his thin, rapt, ethereal, sexy-by-fiat falsetto defines his devotional passion. Not only is the homoerotic the political—the high tenor is the political. **B+** **Jimmy Somerville:** *Dare to Love* (London '95) 💣

Some Velvet Sidewalk: *Avalanche* (K '92) Ⓝ

Son 14 with Tiburon: *Cubania* (Candela '97) Ⓝ

Sonic's Rendezvous: "Sweet Nothing" (Mack Aborn Rhythmic Arts '98) Ⓝ

Sonic Youth: *Goo* (DGC '90) Their first true major-label album and first true song album stars the bassist, who has always been this paradigm-shifting guitar band's secret weapon. Maybe Kim Gordon overrates Karen Carpenter and undervalues Chuck D. But it's "Tunic" and "Kool Thing" you'll sing along with, not Thurston Moore's pseudo/macho ZZ Top homage. Her friend Goo is your friend and my friend and the reason this music exists. In a world where songs are still counted girly, we need Goo. And it's her big sister's in-my-room ethereality, direct and spaced out at the same time, that gives her a voice. **A–** **Sonic Youth:** *Dirty* (DGC '92) With the help of their first real producer, they stop flirting with progress and concentrate on remaining the world's greatest rock and roll band—if Butch Vig snuck in a "Smells Like Teen Spirit," it's known only to David Geffen's bagmen, who understand things about airplay that you and I don't. "Youth Against Fascism" is catchy indeed, but fun as it would be to hear "I believe Anita Hill" roaring from a passing boombox, I don't think it'll fly. And elsewhere it's gonna be tough extricating the hooks, which are more plentiful than ever, from the noise, which makes a comeback. Aurally as well as lyrically, this album earns its title. Thurston never could carry a tune, but he can surround one. And when Kim warns you not to touch her breasts, the possibility that she's an uptight chick never crosses your mind. **A**

Sonic Youth: *Experimental Jet Set, Trash and No Star* (DGC '94) Instead of distilling their weakness for experimental trash into noise-rock that sounds like a million bucks, they apply their skill at major-label compromise to their eternal propensity for experimental trash. After all this time they know what they're doing when they fuck around, and their long-evolving rock and roll groove breaks down only when they have something better to do—there's nothing aleatory, accidental, or incompetent about it. Anyway, usually the groove holds; this is no *Sister* because it moves when it means to. Its unexpected noises are the marks of flesh-and-blood creatures thinking and feeling things neither you nor they have ever thought or felt before. If they can't quite put those things into words, that's what unexpected noises are for. **A**

Sonic Youth: *Screaming Fields of Sonic Love* (DGC '95) Would have been funny to start with *Daydream Nation* and concoct a perfect *Goo*-style song album in reverse chronological order from their pre-Geffen catalogue. Only they didn't have the material. So instead they concoct a meaningfully imperfect song-and-mess album out of several near-perfect ones and several meaningless ones. This is less funny. **A−**

Sonic Youth: *Washing Machine* (DGC '95) With nothing to prove except that they can do it forever without going gold, they do it again. Recalling their roots, they stretch the title cut past its songful limits and build the finale into a 20-minute improvisation not altogether unreminiscent of the Grateful Dead. But at the same time they stick to the theoretically radio-ready songwriting that is now an aesthetic commitment, even trying their hand at a folk

tune and a Shangri-Las tribute. As it happens, the latter owes the Fleetwoods. But needless to say, both ultimately sound like Sonic Youth, an institution whose guitars are often emulated and never replicated. As does everything else on a record that will startle no one and sound fresh in 2002. **A−**

Sonic Youth: *Anagrama/Improvisation Ajoutée/Tremens/Mieux: De Corrosion* (SYR '97) Nine-minute intro to a song that never begins, stroll through an artificial rain forest, and two improvised explosions, the longer and more playful of which comes in jet-engine stereo. Not rock and roll, although the intro comes close. But not avant-bullshit either. **B+**

Sonic Youth/Jim O'Rourke: *Invito Al Cielo/Hungara Vivo/Radio-Amatoroj* (SYR '97) gongs, factories, and radio transmissions, on the moon and under the sea. ★

Sonic Youth: *Slappkamers Met Slagroom/Still/Herinneringen* (SYR '97) Ⓝ

Sonic Youth: *A Thousand Leaves* (DGC '98) This record is what it seems—mature, leisurely, rather beautiful, perhaps content. But it's neither complacent nor same-old, and after it's settled into their, I'm sorry, oeuvre, it will rank toward the top for everybody except permanent revolutionaries, a noncombatant category if ever there was one. Awash in connubial ardor and childhood bliss, undergirded by the strength-through-strangeness of angry tunings grown familiar, it's the music of a daydream nation old enough to treasure whatever time it finds on its hands. Where a decade ago they plunged and plodded, drunk on the forward notion of the van they were stuck in, here they wander at will, dazzled by sunshine, greenery, hoarfrost, and machines that go squish in the night. The melodies aren't the foci of the 11-tracks-in-74-minutes—more like resting places. But even when the band is punk-rocking le sexisme or pondering the trippy fate of Karen Koltrane, the anxiety the tunes alleviate is never life-threatening. Motto, and they quote: "'We'll know where when we get there.'" **A+**

Sonic Youth: *Goodbye 20th Century* (SYR '99) Ⓝ

Son Volt: *Trace* (Warner Bros. '95) Finally the answer to a question that's plagued me for years. I'd pound my pillow at night, drift into reverie at convocations on fun, plumb forget how my dick got into my hand, wondering why, why, why I could never give two shits about Uncle Tupelo. But the answer, my friends, was blowing in . . . no, I mean hopes "the wind takes your troubles away." Name's Jay Farrar, never met a detail he couldn't fuzz over with his achy breaky drawl and, er, evocative country-rock—and needn't trouble with the concrete at all now that that smart-ass Jeff Tweedy is Wilco over-and-out. In the unfathomable Tupelo, Tweedy whiled away the hours writing actual songs, leaving Farrar the drudgery of mourning an American past too atmospheric to translate into mere words. As sentimental as Darius Rucker himself, Farrar is only a set of pipes and a big fat heart away from convincing millions of sensitive guys that he evokes for them. **C+** 🐫

Son Volt: *Straightaways* (Warner Bros. '97) 🎸

Soul Asylum: *And the Horse They Rode In On* (A&M '90) 🎸

Soul Asylum: *Grave Dancers Union* (Columbia '92) great tunes, corny songs ("Without a Trace," "Somebody to Shove") ★

Soul Asylum: *Let Your Dim Light Shine* (Columbia '95) Welcome evidence that Dave Pirner may not be the Bob Seger of his generation—because where in the late '70s temptation came in the form of classic rock, in the mid-'90s it lies along pop's primrose path, a development that should offend only grunge nostalgiacs. The tunes of these neatly crafted songs are up top, their "roots" submerged the way roots usually are. And the often funny, sometimes fantastic lyrics almost make you think a rather less gruffly soulful Pirner knows how cheap he got away last time. After lingering over idioms like "don't get my hopes up" and "left to my own devices," he moves on to vignettes in which his pervasive depression connects to something less collegiate than existential angst—the hard, sad lives of other people, several of them women seen not as objects of sex or romance, just struggling humans like him and me. **B+**

Soul Asylum: *Candy from a Stranger* (Columbia '98) 🎸

The Soul Brothers: *Soul Mbaqanga* (Riverboat import '94) Ⓝ

The Soul Brothers: *Jump and Jive* (Stern's/Earthworks '95) old pros in control ("Abantu") ★★

The Soul Brothers: *Born to Jive* (Stern's/Earthworks '97) Ⓝ

Soul Coughing: *Ruby Vroom* (Slash/Warner Bros. '94) If it was down to M. Doughty's hipster cynicism and summer-stock declaiming, this would be a novelty act not unlike Tonio K., whose shouted studio speed-rock provided a nonpunk corrective to Jackson Browne. But the music isn't just second-rate poetry-with-fusion backup. Stand-up bassist Sebastian Steinberg (dig his "Misterioso" under "Casiotone Nation") and chopswise drummer Yuval Gabay (hear him threaten to fly off the track on "Blueeyed Devil") remain up front, while keyb man M'ark De Gli Antoni (that's what it says) orchestrates synthesizer and sampler for atmosphere, commentary, and plain old cheap thrills. Not that the music isn't more compelling when Doughty hits his satiric targets, the easy ones included. **A**

Soul Coughing: *Irresistible Bliss* (Warner Bros. '96) the five percent nation of let's-slow-it-down-a-little-right-now ("Disseminated," "4 out of 5") ★★★

Soul Coughing: *El Oso* (Slash/Warner Bros. '98) They wish they could call it *Il Oso,* counterposing parallel verticals against circle-squiggle-circle palindrome in a visualization of their true passion: abstraction. They can't, of course, Spanish is Spanish just like groove is groove, and because these fundamental things apply, their abstractions still hit you in the gut.

Voice-keyb-bass up top are distinct and autonomous constituents, a cable not a gumbo, with the upright romanticism of Sebastian Steinberg and try-anything soundplay of Mark De Gli Antoni providing human touch—as they'd better, because rather than anchoring or signposting, M. Doughty's words establish his intelligence and then bounce us back into the aural construct for emotion and such. You may say you pine for his sarcasm. But he'll just wonder if you thought he'd be corny forever. **A–**

Souls of Mischief: *93 'Til Infinity* (Jive '93) More than the Pharcyde, the Freestyle Fellowship, or the unaffiliated Funkytown Pros, this young Oakland foursome stay aloft on the spiderweb of ideas all West Coast Native Tongues types try to swing from: playful rhyme sounds, metaphorical rhyme violence, spare jazz-intricate beats, and an aversion to all things gangsta, including hooks. They even eschew dirty words: "D.C. got schemes/And we ain't got spit." They won't necessarily stay in your head after the record's over. But while they're there, you won't believe how much life they've got. **A–**

Soul II Soul: *Vol II–1990: A New Decade* (Virgin '90) Jazzie B. is the victim of his own pretensions, and his fickle fans are victims of theirs—anybody so groovy as to mistake a kitschy little dance band from London U.K. for the next phase of world culture is sure to suffer mightily when the truth gets out. But as someone whose chakras weren't realigned by the house album that ate top 40, I must insist—not only is the emperor still wearing clothes, the new ones fit better. You won't find a "Keep On Movin'" here—that honor falls to Snap this year. But the lead cuts are daring and irresistible in their kitschy way, and the boring stretches are all but eliminated—even Fab Five Freddy and Courtney Pine gain the flat-out pop credibility that is Jazzie's true calling. **A–**

Soul II Soul: *Volume III Just Right* (Virgin '92) 💣

Soundgarden: *Badmotorfinger* (A&M '91) OK, OK, I admit it. This is a credible metal album, and not because it leads with the credible "Rusty Cage." You can tell from the guitar noise, the main if not only point of contact between metal albums and what most of us want from rock and roll. While Chris Cornell howls on about "lookin for the paradigm" and "your Jesus Christ pose" (I swear, that's the good stuff), Kim Thayil finishes off "Slaves and Bulldozers" with an electrical storm and erects so much razor wire around "Jesus Christ Pose" (right, same song) you might almost want to interview him. Then he writes a lyric himself. It seems to hinge on the word "begat." **B–**

Soundgarden: *Superunknown* (A&M '94) Having mocked this group's conceptual pretensions for years, I'd best point out that Chris Cornell still isn't Robert Plant, Kim Thayil still isn't Jimmy Page, and so forth, before cheerfully acknowledging that (1) they're all closer than they used to be and (2) it no longer matters. This is easily the best—the most galvanizing, kinetic, sensational, *catchy*—Zep rip in history. And though there may be a philosophical or interpersonal dimension, to me the trick sounds like it was done with songwriting, arrangement, and production. At 70 minutes, it's what used to be called a double album, not quite as long as *Physical Graffiti* but a lot more consistent. And though their apocalyptic pessimism is almost as content-free as Zep's apocalyptic mystagogy, Zep never reached out like Cornell in "My Wave": "Cry, if you want to cry/If it helps you see/If it clears your eyes/Hate, if you want to hate/If it keeps you safe/If it makes you brave." **A–**

Soundgarden: *Down on the Upside* (A&M '96) brutal depression simplified ("Ty Cobb," "Applebite") ★

Soundgarden: *A-Sides* (A&M '97) hear them earn their miserabilism ("Ty Cobb," "Jesus Christ Pose") ★★★

Source Direct: *Controlled Developments* (Astralwerks '97) they can score my horror movie anytime ("Two Masks," "Call & Response") ★★★

Source Direct: *Exorcise the Demons* (Astralwerks '99) I make no pretense to caring what the junglists think they're up to at this late date. But maybe my fellow dabblers will enjoy this particular U.K. concoction. You will hear: beats developed in perceptible patterns, prudently minimalist middle registers, fun vrooms and slams as musical content. You will not hear: strings, jazz, extreme lassitude, the ocean's murky depths, continental drift, Conlon Nancarrow homages. Light instrumental music at its diverting best—which is just good enough. A–

Space: "Judas Priest" (*Sonic Screwdriver,* Sub Bass import '93) 💣

Spacemen 3: *Recurring* (Dedicated '91) Stooges for airports ("Big City") ★

Space Surfers: *Pretty Damn Cool* (Fridge '96) Italian girlpunk with two boys, mucho irony, and a drum machine ("Magilla Godzilla," "Cadillac and Dinosaurs") ★★

Spacetime Continuum: *Double Fine Zone* (Astralwerks '99) 💣

Spanish Fly: *Fly by Night* (Accurate '96) trumpet-tuba-guitar-(drums) improvise ballet score and other variations on "My Bonnie" ("Movement 3: Sisters," "Movement 5: End of the Night") ★★

Sparklehorse: *Good Morning Spider* (Capitol '99) Ⓝ

Spearhead: *Home* (Capitol '94) recyclable Michael Franti—he's black, he's grooveful, he's Gil Scott-Heron ("Crime to Be Broke in America," "People in the Middle") ★

Spearhead: *Chocolate Supa Highway* (Capitol '97) Reinforcing my belief that Michael Franti's musical instincts signify more meaningfully than his knowledge of Frantz Fanon, the brother shrouds his funk in so much murk and smoke there are times you could mistake it for *Maxinquaye* or *There's a Riot Goin' On.* And after the impression passes, the depressive intractability of the sonics continues to add heft to the political clichés, most unforgettably on the tale of an ordinary day that begins bad and gradually goes all the way to hell. A–

Britney Spears: *. . . Baby One More Time* (Jive '99) Madonna next door (". . . Baby One More Time," "Soda Pop") ★

The Specials: *Today's Specials* (Virgin '96) 💣

Ronnie Spector: *She Talks to Rainbows* (Kill Rock Stars '99) pop queen or punk symbol, she comes direct from the land of dreams ("You Can't Put Your Arms Around a Memory," "She Talks to Rainbows") ★

Speech: *Hoopla* (TVT '99) Lauryn wannabe unearths folk-rock tunelets ("Slave to It All," "The Hey Song") ★★

Spell: *Mississippi* (Island '94) Sonic Youth as Ramones from a Denver married-couple-plus-dynamite-drummer who figure somebody might as well go pop with those tricks. Even if they succeed, it won't last—where their models had too much principle to break through, they don't have enough to hang on. But song junkies with dual citizenship in their contiguous aural universes have been taken for much duller rides. B+

Joseph Spence and the Pinder Family: *The Spring of Sixty-Five* (Rounder '94) On most of his records, the Bahamaian Ry-&-Taj influence is one more reason to never trust a guitar cult. Sure he's an original, a self-taught virtuoso, etc.—so much so that his poky vocal gestalt fails to signify for those who believe accompaniment ought to be just that. But with his unfettered in-laws slinging song around, these spirituals, shanties, and other cultural riches are all the way live—felt, gorgeous, jocose, reveled in for what they are and what can be made of them. A–

The Jon Spencer Blues Explosion: *Orange* (Matador '94) For Jon Spencer to make fun not of old black bluesmen but of the white hippies who emulated them so crudely just makes him an asshole coming and going. Given his cultural-chronological advantages, what right does he have to dog, oh, Bob Hite, who did scour the South for lost artists and recordings as well as conceiving Canned Heat, a pretty decent band in the end even if they were less heply dissonant than Jon's? And do you really believe he doesn't relish the excuse to playact a racist stereotype that increases his sex appeal? Irony—an excuse for anything and a reason for nothing. **B-** 🦃

Spice Girls: "Wannabe" (*Spice*, Virgin '97) 🐚
Spice Girls: "Stop" (*Spiceworld*, Virgin '97) 🐚

The Spinanes: *Manos* (Sub Pop '93) 🐚
The Spinanes: *Archers and Aisles* (Sub Pop '98) ❶

Spin Doctors: *Pocket Full of Kryptonite* (Epic Associated '91) "hippies," as in "En Why doing for funk syncopation what San Fran did for blues shuffle" ("Jimmy Olsen's Blues," "Two Princes") ★
Spin Doctors: *Turn It Upside Down* (Epic '94) what's not to like? ("Hungry Hamed's," "Cleopatra's Cat") ★

Spiritualized: *Ladies and Gentlemen We Are Floating in Space* (Arista '97) even druggies deserve a fair hearing ("All of My Thoughts," "Cop Shoot Cop") ★

Spleen: *T. S. Eliot Reads The Waste Land and The Hollow Men* (Skoda '94) what it says—loathes better than Uncle Bill, recites better than Dr. Dre, ace beat tracks, five bucks ★

Sponge: *Rotting Piñata* (Chaos/Columbia '94) 🐚

Sportsguitar: *Happy Already* (Matador '98) "And you're wrong if you think/I am unhappy/Just because I wanna stay/Alone in my house/And sing my Swiss tunes/In a doleful English monotone" ("Youth," "Chasing Bugs") ★

Dusty Springfield: *A Very Fine Love* (Columbia '95) ❶

Spring Heel Jack: "Lee Perry Part One," "Day of the Dead" (*There Are Strings,* Rough Trade import '95) 🐚
Spring Heel Jack: *68 Million Shades . . .* (Island '97) Betty Boo producer cum Spiritualized guitarist John Coxon joins contemporary-classical buff cum hardcore raver Ashley Wales to re-contextualize drum 'n' bass's redolent lingo—its triple-time superdrum pitta-pat, its impossible deep tremblors that modulate whole power plants in repose—by subsuming densely frenetic techno cum dancehall in a witting synthesis of electronic composition and another of Wales's passions, *On the Corner*–era Miles Davis. Where most jungle grooves roll on into a theoretical African eternity, Spring Heel Jack's begin and end even when they stutter or fade. The keyb scale that IDs "Take 1," the sax riff that leads into the brief keyb-and-sax tune of "60 Seconds," the sidelong three-note guitar hook that stops you every time the 75-minute CD reaches "Bar" halfway through—all recur thematically enough to lend a sense of cohesion, closure, even content. Just what the world needed—prog jungle. **A**
Spring Heel Jack: *Busy Curious Thirsty* (Island '97) What direct connection John Coxon and Ashley Wales retain to dance music is as obscure to me as their precise relationship to contemporary composition. But they mine both modes productively enough to cover over the pitfalls that are always tripping up nonbelievers. I love the way "Galapagos 3"'s slowly accreted minimalist detail is blown away by a brief blast of ersatz symphony, the way "The Wrong Guide" opens up a piece of small-group jazz for simulated drums and simulated . . . bassoon (?) to (simulated) pizzicato percussion, soundtrack orchestra, and antiaircraft artillery—all of which continue the improvisation for a while. They're visceral where composition is cerebral and ambient is unmoored. They never fall for rock-techno's arena-scale

gestures or art-techno's fatal conflation of thinking and mooning about. If any competitors out there can make such claims, their identities are obscure indeed. **A**

Spring Heel Jack: *Treader* (Tugboat import '99) Its U.S. release a casualty of the UniMoth merger, this colors in the techno-classical duo's sonic territory without putting any bells on it—except for the chimes and carillons that alternate with drunken brass sections, expensive faucets, and plain old synthesizers on the eight-minute "Winter," which breaks into tradder drum 'n' bass, which gives way to a scary soundtrack explosion. Et cetera. Tops is "More Stuff No One Saw," a rocky one. Its marchlike drum looping under a few phrases of noir saxophone, it crescendos in grand faux brass-organ-triangle swells before scattering into the tail end of a gun battle. If you like these guys, you'll love it all. If you've never heard (of) them, there's no special reason to start here. **A–**

Bruce Springsteen: *Human Touch* (Columbia '92) windbag in love ("Cross My Heart," "The Long Goodbye") ★
Bruce Springsteen: *Lucky Town* (Columbia '92) Ⓝ
Bruce Springsteen: "Streets of Philadelphia" (*Philadelphia* [ST], Epic Soundtrax '93) 🐟
Bruce Springsteen: *The Ghost of Tom Joad* (Columbia '95) his gift for social realist literature exceeds his gift for political music ("The Ghost of Tom Joad," "Across the Border") ★
Bruce Springsteen: "Pink Cadillac," "The Honeymooners," "The Wish," "Leavin' Train," "Gave It a Name" (*Tracks,* Columbia '98) 🐟

Squirrel Nut Zippers: *Hot* (Mammoth '97) They cut their second album live to a single mike because they don't just love old jazz—they love old jazz records, which is also why Katharine Whalen thinks the way to channel Billie Holiday and Betty Boop is to scrunch up your tonsils. However sincerely they disavow nostalgia, they're not good enough to escape it—striving for the life they hear on those records, they're neither acute enough musically nor blessed enough culturally to get closer than a clumsy imitation. Mix in a soupçon of eleganza and you end up with a band that's damn lucky to have written a couple of dandy songs. And if they purloined that calypso novelty hit they put their name on, I hope the teeth that get extruded are their own. **B–** 🦃

Squirrel Nut Zippers: *Perennial Favorites* (Mammoth '98) 🎺

Staind: *Dysfunction* (Flip/Elektra '99) 🎺

Chris Stamey: *Fireworks* (RNA '91) 🎺

Peter Stampfel: *You Must Remember This . . .* (Gert Town '95) Stampfel has never known the meaning of the word respect, which is OK because he's never known the meaning of the word disrespect either. And if this made him a misfit among folkies, that was OK too—he was a misfit everywhere else. For his entire three-decade "career," the last half of which has had a distinctly not-for-profit aura, his own lyrics have celebrated the normality of his misfit life while his intense, eccentric, comic, loud, sincere vocal interpretations imparted to the widest range of pop songs ever negotiated by a single performer the beauty and wonder he originally discerned in Charlie Poole, Charlie Patton, and other icons of authenticity. Stampfel's enthusiasm is so unquenchable you figure he's got to be making fun of such understandably forgotten copyrights as "Haunted Heart" and "Cry of the Wild Goose," and for sure he's not above it. But he is above belittling a song—any fun he may fashion from one is just another facet of its mystery. Stampfel the inveterate fakebook collector says he loves the chords of the impossible favorites he resuscitates here, and I believe him. I also believe he's such a sucker for music that once he falls for a progression he wants to tie the knot for life. **A**
Peter Stampfel: "His Tapes Roll On" (*The Harry Smith Connection: A Live Tribute* [comp], Smithsonian Folkways '98) 🐟

Lisa Stansfield: *Affection* (Arista '90) Like few of her predecessors—Martha Reeves comes to mind, and also, odd though it may seem, Teddy Pendergrass—Stansfield's style is virtually devoid of trademark, display, or drama; all she wants to do with these songs she helped write is sing them. The songs themselves are as attractive and unassuming as her voice, a fine instrument that provides more than the expected quota of aural pleasure without drowning you in its bounty. She loves, she hurts, she has her limits. She's going to be around. **A−**

Lisa Stansfield: "All Woman" (Real Love, Arista '92) 🌺

Lisa Stansfield: *Lisa Stansfield* (Arista '97) 💣

Tammy Faye Starlite and the Angels of Mercy: *On My Knees* (Ephesians 2:28 '99) dotty comedy, country parody, blasphemous obscenity, running incest joke ("God Has Lodged a Tenant in My Uterus," "Did I Shave . . .") ★

Starpoint Electric: "Let My Brother Lie," "Bitter Happiness" (*Bad Directions*, Plastique '99) 🌺

Starship: *Greatest Hits (Ten Years and Change 1979–1991)* (RCA '91) 💣

Static-X: *Wisconsin Death Trip* (Warner Bros. '99) horrorshow abuse in living stereo—they mean it, man ("I'm with Stupid," "Wisconsin Death Trip") ★

The Andy Statman Quartet: *The Hidden Light* (Sony Classical '98) To devotees of machine-age tempos, old-time klezmer often sounds more devotional than celebratory, and rather than being coy about this commercial inconvenience, the mandolin master turned clarinet pro embraces it. The bio's "spiritual jazz" IDs the result aptly enough, except that any Jew who feels like one will recognize its provenance at 50 paces, one way it avoids the New Age vagueness you rightly fear. Those who don't feel like Jews will be impressed enough that something so solemn can be so light—and glad that Statman isn't above reprising traditional tunes or picking up his sharpest axe. **A−**

Steely Dan: *Live in America* (Giant '95) a piece of Mr. Fagen's band ("Bodhisattva," "Peg") ★★

Stereolab: *Transient Random-Noise Bursts with Announcements* (Elektra '93) almost hooky enough to reconcile me to a world that needs Marxist background music ("Tone Burst," "I'm Going Out of My Way") ★★★

Stereolab: *Mars Audiac Quintet* (Elektra '94) not quite hooky enough to reconcile me to a world that needs Marxist background music ("Wow and Flutter," "Fiery Yellow") ★★

Stereolab: *Emperor Tomato Ketchup* (Elektra '96) So it isn't just silly punk songs—yet other people want to fill the world with silly *Marxist* songs, and what's wrong with that? Academia being the main place Marxism remains a cultural fact in Anglo-American culture, I say watered-down *théorie* is as valid as the watered-down surrealism we've always made allowances for. I also say the band's ideological tastes commit it to a measure of musical realism, preventing their postdance from doodling off into the ether. So although the obvious tunes, playful sound effects, pretty counterpoints, and mysterioso textures may—no, do—add up to pop, what they don't add up to, despite the vaunted Tortoise connection, is anything fools can pigeonhole as postrock. Songful, hence no longer cool, this band will finally repay your undivided attention. **A−**

Stereolab: *Dots and Loops* (Elektra '97) From folkie soprano to synthesizer tweedle, many young people are down with the revalidation of high and clean—"Let There Be Flutes," as Bentley Rhythm Ace put it. And on a pretty good track, too, just like *Emperor Tomato Ketchup* is a fine album. Where us down and dirty types say sayonara is after the high artist peaks. Exploring rather than apotheosizing personal secrets, the high artist is like any other formalist, especially since he, she, or they probably suffered from formalist tendencies to begin with. On this album the tunes fall off and the wacky smarts lose the charm of surprise. There's still plenty of agile bass and clever sonic garbage. But only the high and clean will notice. **B** 🦃

Stereolab: Cobra and Phases Group Play Voltage in the Milky Night (Elektra '99) yeah! appropriate that vibraphone! and definitely that Glasstinato! ("Blue Milk," "Blips Drips and Strips") ★★★

Stereo MC's: Connected (Gee Street '92) Rap with an international face. Techno with a human face. Disco with a postmodern face. Techno-rap disco with a pop face. Pleasant. Beatwise. So multifaceted its functionality is fungible and forgettable. **B-** 🦃

Stereo Total: "Get Down Tonight" (*Stereo Total*, Bobsled '98) 🍫

Stetsasonic: "Walkin' in the Rain" (*Blood, Sweat, and No Tears,* Tommy Boy '91) 🍫

Dave Stewart: Greetings from the Gutter (EastWest '94) Bowie lives! ("Heart of Stone," "Oh No, Not You Again") ★

Gary Stewart: Battleground (HighTone '90) As with so many country albums, one's faith fluctuates from listen to listen: the songwriting isn't always absolutely choice, at times the voice lurches back toward the gulps and hollers that swamped his attempted comeback, and his guilt sounds more emotionally whole than his rowdy ways, which is why he's always been a country singer with r&r affinities rather than vice versa. But this is his best in 13 years (just lucky, I guess). His r&r groove is sharp-witted where Steve Earle's is muscle-headed and the average Nashville cat's just mechanical. And whether he's pledging desperate devotion or spitting out the perfect pun-trope "Seeing's believing/So I'll be leaving today," you know damn well it's his fault. Whatever it is. **B+**

Gary Stewart: Gary's Greatest (HighTone '91) Because the label has already reissued 1975's *Out of Hand,* this leans harder on his gradual decline than would seem advisable, and ends up dispelling doubts as a result—he didn't write the 1981 45-only "She's Got a Drinking Problem" ("and it's me"), but it belongs to him anyway. Stewart is obsessed with the fucked-up intersections of booze, sex, and the honest life. He's so far outside Nashville's not inelastic limits that he ended up on a blues indie. And strong song for strong song, he's the equal of any postoutlaw you care to name except maybe John Anderson. So what are you waiting for? **A**

Rod Stewart: Vagabond Heart (Warner Bros. '91) 💣

Rod Stewart: Unplugged . . . and Seated (Warner Bros. '93) "We haven't done this together since we recorded it 22 years ago—most of the band weren't born—me wife was only one—" ("Reason to Believe," "Handbags and Gladrags") ★★★

Stinky Puffs: Songs and Advice for Kids Who Have Been Left Behind (Elemental '96) Ⓝ

The Stone Roses: Second Coming (Geffen '95) Ⓝ

Stone Temple Pilots: Core (Atlantic '92) Once you learn to tell them from the Stoned Tempo Pirates, the Stolen Pesto Pinenuts, the Gray-Templed Prelates, Temple of the Dog, Pearl Jam, and Wishbone Ash, you may decide they're a halfway decent hard rock act. Unfortunately, sometime after they've set you up with their best power chords, you figure out the title is "Sex Type Thing" because it's attached to a rape threat. They claim this was intended as a critique, kind of like "Naked Sunday"'s sarcastic handshake with authority. But at best that means they should reconceive their aesthetic strategy—critiquewise, irony has no teeth when the will to sexual power still powers your power chords. And if it's merely the excuse MTV fans have reason to suspect, the whole band should catch AIDS and die. **B-** 🦃

Stone Temple Pilots: *Purple* (Atlantic '94) 💣

Stone Temple Pilots: *No. 4* (Atlantic '99) Ⓝ

George Strait: *Ten Strait Hits* (MCA '91) Ⓝ

Syd Straw: *War and Peace* (Virgin '96) 💣

Angela Strehli: *Blonde and Blue* (Rounder '93) Ⓝ

Joe Strummer and the Mescaleros: *Rock Art and the X-Ray Style* (Hepcat '99) Ⓝ

Marty Stuart: *The Marty Party Hit Pack* (MCA '95) Ⓝ

Marty Stuart: "The Mississippi Mudcat and Sister Sheryl Crow" (*Honky Tonkin's What I Do Best,* MCA '96) 🍫

Stumpy Joe: *One Way Rocket Ride to Kicksville* (Popllama '92) good old same-old excellent, drinking and girl problems high generic ("Proverbial Straw," "Drunk Idea") ★★

Ned Sublette: *Cowboy Rumba* (Palm Pictures '99) 💣

Sublime: *Sublime* (Gasoline Alley/MCA '96) If you've resisted, I understand. They're surf punks *and* ska boys *and* heroin addicts, each a reasonable ground for summary dismissal. Their indie albums are nothing special. Not only that, one of them is dead. The prognosis is so dismal that it takes time to hear that this ska is evolving toward sinuous skank rather than reverting to zit-popping thrash, to ascertain that the tunes are simple rather than pro forma, to believe that Brad Nowell writes like he's got a life even if he ended up wasting it. Junkies who retain enough soul to create music at all are generally driven to put their brilliance and stupidity in your face. Nowell is altogether more loving, unassuming, good-humored, and down-to-earth—or so he pretends, which when you're good is all it takes. **A–**

Sublime: *Second-Hand Smoke* (Gasoline Alley/MCA '97) Ⓝ

Sublime: *Live: Stand by Your Van* (Gasoline Alley/MCA '99) 💣

Suede: See the London Suede

Sugar: *Copper Blue* (Rykodisc '92) The surprise isn't that Bob Mould has progressed, thank God. It's that he's picked up where he left off. After six years spent straining over *Warehouse: Songs and Stories* and two overarranged records with his name on the cover (why do you think they call them solo efforts?), he not only fabricates a Hüsker Dü album but makes it sound as if it just rushed out of him, like a great Hüsker Dü album should. Never mind who takes Grant Hart's place, because it isn't the new drummer. Fashioning the popwise tunes that were always Hart's specialty and taking on all the vocals himself, the new musician is Mould. Maybe he has progressed after all. **A–**

Sugar: *Beaster* (Rykodisc '93) immanence not transcendence, sonics not songs ("Tilted," "JC Auto") ★★

Sugar: *File Under: Easy Listening* (Rykodisc '94) Loud electric guitar metaphors fall into two basic categories: attack and transport. The buzzsaw, the jackhammer, and the machine gun versus the V-8, the midnight special, and the jet airliner. Bob Mould has always been a barrage man, but here he's in takeoff mode—whether embracing girl-group doo-doo-doos and blues readymades or simply lifting heavenward, his exhilaration doesn't show much downside. The blissful "Your Favorite Thing" (see below) suggests he's running on love sweet love, suffusing even side two's breakups and putdowns with kindness and good humor. It's that impossible dream, an interesting album about happy romance. Remember power pop, all those benighted Byrdsmaniacs and tintinnabulating Rickenbackers? Now imagine it with brains and muscles. **A**

Sugar: *Your Favorite Thing* (Rykodisc '94) Skinflints and formalists both, indie guys resist the digital bloat that sends most releases ballooning toward an hour, and I say good for them. The three otherwise unreleased tracks on this EP would have fit physically onto the new album but undercut it conceptually, and all the worse if few listeners would have noticed. More powerful than *Beaster*, less revealing than *Copper Blue,* this is Mould Inc. in "dark" mode. Fans will be content to pay extra for it. Admirers won't suffer if they pass it by. **B+**

Sugarcubes: *The A Collection* (Elektra '98) a striking voice does not a pop band make—a striking band, maybe ("Birthday," "Vitamin") ★★

Sugar Ray: *Floored* (Lava/Atlantic '97) Crude for sure, without anything to say or much to say it with, they nevertheless have some punky life to them, which I say is enhanced by their blatant ska and hip hop rips. What's most depressing is that their success makes sense—they're the nearest thing to a fresh young rock band the market or the "underground" has kicked up this year. Not counting Radish, of course. **B–** 🐝

Sugar Ray: "Every Morning" (*14:59,* Lava/Atlantic '99) 🐟

Suicidal Tendencies: "You Can't Bring Me Down" (*Lights . . . Camera . . . Revolution,* Epic '90) 🐟

Cree Summer: *Street Faerie* (Work '99) 💣

Andy Summers: *Synaesthesia* (CMP '96) 💣

The Sundays: *Blind* (DGC '92) 💣

Sunscreem: *O₃* (Columbia '93) Ⓝ

Sunz of Man: *(The Last Shall Be First)* (Red Ant '98) "This rap game ain't what it seems/Artists get creamed turn fiend sellin' people a dream," observe these "intellectuals, rhymin' professionals" ("there go the ladies in our directional"), and this bothers them. Pronouncing it cog-knack, exploring their Maccabee heritage in secondhand Yiddish, singsonging a disarmingly tuneless "tryin' to free our minds of all the drugs and crime," Sunz of Man are

poor righteous teachers, street but not hard. And though their Wu-schooled musical religion is more Bernard Herrmann than James Brown, they're deeply proud to share a studio with Earth, Wind & Fire. **A–**

Super Cat: *Don Dada* (Columbia '92) Ⓝ
Super Cat: *The Struggle Continues* (Columbia '95) Ⓝ

Superchunk: "Slack Motherfucker," "Sick to Move" (*Superchunk,* Matador '90) 🐟
Superchunk: *Foolish* (Merge '94) Ⓝ

Supergrass: *I Should Coco* (Capitol '95) 💣
Supergrass: "Sex" (*In It for the Money,* Capitol '97) 🐟

The Superjesus: *Sumo* (Warner Bros. '98) 💣

Supersnazz: *Superstupid!* (Sub Pop '93) Ⓝ

Super Sweet Talks International: See Sweet Talks

Surface: *The Best of Surface . . . A Nice Time 4 Lovin'* (Columbia '91) 💣

Foday Musa Suso: *The Dreamtime* (CMP import '90) Ⓝ

Keith Sweat: *I'll Give All My Love to You* (Vintertainment/Elektra '90) 💣
Keith Sweat: *Get Up on It* (Elektra '94) 💣

Joey Sweeney: "My Name Is Rich" (*The Book of Life Soundtrack* [ST], Echostatic '99) 🐟

Matthew Sweet: *Girlfriend* (Zoo '91) Sweet's turn of phrase and tone of voice don't add much to the store of human knowledge about romantic love, and he's not much better on God or war. So he lets guitars define the ineffables for him—his stormy acoustic, Lloyd Cole's workaday electric chunka, and Greg Leisz's choked steel provide a forum where Richard Lloyd and Robert Quine can testify. And though Lloyd shouldn't be forgotten—his slash and roll jump-start the record—it's Quine's aural kabala, longer on syntheses of ache and soar than on terrible beauty or abstract calm in this context, that contains the wisdom Sweet needs. Just don't expect a translation. **A–**

Matthew Sweet: *Altered Beast* (Zoo '93) he's so great with the help he should hire some lyricists ("Dinosaur Act," "Knowing People") ★★★

Matthew Sweet: "Superdeformed" (*No Alternative* [comp], Arista '93) 💣

Matthew Sweet: *Son of Altered Beast* (Zoo '94) Interim, tour-keyed EP product—one remix, one B side, one live Neil Young cover, four live remakes and outtakes from the decidedly subepochal *Altered Beast* album. Happens to include his contribution to the even more subepochal *No Alternative* comp, which it blew away the way it would have blown *Altered Beast* away if only Sweet had taken the risk. Except on the remix, no Robert Quine—Richard Lloyd is the guitar hero, and he'll do. Because even though the whole record is basically an accident, this is the way live rock and roll is supposed to sound these days—inspiration on the edge of chaos. **A–**

Matthew Sweet: *100% Fun* (Zoo '95) Frustrated because I couldn't grok Bluroraimeemann even after isolating their tunes and turns of phrase, I turned to another pop album I'd never gotten and had a revelation. Not a new idea—what a difference a band makes is old theory by now. Just an experience—this particular band at the moment of this recording, two or three or four guitars layered into densely striated sludge with shiny ribbons of metal sticking out. Perfect for accustoming confused young adults to his sensible truisms about romantic commitment. **B+**

Matthew Sweet: *Blue Sky on Mars* (Zoo '97) Ⓝ

Sweet Talks/A. B. Crentsil: *Sweet Talks—Hollywood Highlife Party + A. B. Crentsil—Moses* (ADC import '92) Two complete albums, both considered classics, both featuring the colorful character who saved Ghanaian music from James Brown—and Osibisa, who were so impressed they bankrolled a band for him when his luck went bad. How Ghanaian Crentsil's music is I couldn't say, since highlife was Westernized to begin with, but at least he brought in palm-wine guitar and African narrative strategies, as the translation of "Moses" makes as clear as is appropriate. The seven earlier cuts, recorded on a 1978 U.S. visit, fall in the five-minute range and will charm if you give them a chance. The two later ones, recorded in 1983, fall in the 16-minute range and will recede unless you read along. **A–**

Super Sweet Talks International: *The Lord's Prayer* (Stern's Africa '95) A. B. Crentsil wanted to be liked, and he was ready to sweet-talk anyone who got in his way. The least of these six circa-1979 highlife tunes is subtly ingratiating, and the charm of the three English-language numbers subsumes the Christian politesse they promote. Then again, "Adjoa"'s quiet 10 minutes of dazzling polyrhythm probably wouldn't be as nice if you could understand the words, in which Ghanaian women are advised to service whatever soldiers are walking around Accra like they own it. **A–**

Swirl 360: *Ask Anybody* (Triune/Mercury '98) 💣

Swollen Members: *Balance* (Battle Axe '99) hip hop interlopers from Vancouver with more technique than content, which falls back on that old reliable, horror comics ("Front Street," "Horrified Nights") ★★

SWV—Sisters With Voices: *It's About Time* (RCA '92) Ⓝ

Sylk Smoov: *Sylk Smoov* (PWA America '91) Ⓝ

System 01: "Drugs Work" (*Berlin 1992—A Tresor Compilation—The Techno Sound of Berlin* [comp], NovaMute '92) 💣

S/COMPILATIONS

The Secret Museum of Mankind Vol. 1 (Yazoo '95) marginally more authentic, marginally less fun (Raderman-Beckerman Orchestra, "A Europaische Kolomyka"; Fonseka, and Party, "Kapirigna") ★★★

The Secret Museum of Mankind Vol. 2 (Yazoo '96) Hopping from Macedonia to the Society Islands, from Ukraine to Trinidad to Crete, Pat Conte has sequenced his "Ethnic Music Classics: 1925–48" for attentive listeners. A fun parlor game would be guessing cultures of origin, with Tower gift certificates awarded anyone who gets the likes of "Paghjelle" (Corsica, tell me about it—I'd have said Mozambique first, even Society Islands). The point of the programming, if there is one, is to showcase a bewildering splatter of incongruent local styles captured by a machine designed to destroy the musical isolation that makes local styles possible. By all means open up to the diversity— these historic moments do break down into pretty airs, lively dances, dark laments, and other familiar categories. But that doesn't mean you won't find many of them merely educational. In fact, if you like them all (feh on Corsican chorales, I say), I bet you don't love any of them the way I do "Yari Mohi Gatai Dehi Mai Shaim," a virtuoso vocal turn by a professor from India. Since you get to choose, try this disc first. It's hookier and—unlike volume one, which picks up about the time the average listener is done looking at yesterday's *Times*—it begins strong. But either way, be prepared to concentrate. **B+**

The Secret Museum of Mankind Vol. 3 (Yazoo '96) Spaniards and Greeks who sound like Arabs, Tuvans and Albanians who sound like each other, Russians who sound like hillbillies, Africans who sound like folks (Thayelo Kapiye Trio, "Mai Wanga Anadiuza"; Grupo Dominicano, "Buen Humor") ★

The Secret Museum of Mankind: East Africa (Yazoo '98) half Kenyan, spanning a mere 24 years up to 1948, these old 78s could almost be said to hold together (Frank and His Sisters, "Mwanangu Lala"; Francis Baloye & Shangaan Band, "Kumbe Siyengetile"; Zoutpansberg Brothers, "Hosi Yehina Masia") ★

Set It Off (EastWest '96) hard r&b epitomized (Queen Latifah, "Name Callin"; En Vogue, "Don't Let Go [Love]"; Organized Noize [Featuring Queen Latifah], "Set It Off") ★★

Sif Safaa: New Music from the Middle East (Hemisphere '95) their hit parade, intense whether hybrid or in the tradition (Mohamed Fouad, "Hawad"; Saleh Khairy, "Agulak") ★★★

Singing in an Open Space: Zulu Rhythm and Harmony 1962–1982 (Rounder '90) John Bhengu and his country cousins (Frans Msomi, "Zinsiza Zase Makhabeleni") ★

Singles (Epic '92) Seattle sampler plus ringer (Paul Westerberg, "Dyslexic Heart," "Waiting for Somebody"; Mudhoney, "Overblown"; Jimi Hendrix, "May This Be Love") ★★

Ska Beats 1 (ROIR '90) So here we are "in the age of sample," and who should come diddybopping out of hip house but Prince Buster and the Skatalites? Evoking history without quoting it on any but the most obvious or abstract levels, the upstart mixers and rappers who mastermind the permutation make the old-timers sound livelier and more righteous than the dancehall competition. Is it pride in a black tradition untainted by the U.S.A. that keeps Brits coming back to ska, or just the all-purpose quickstep of the beat? Irrepressible either way. **A–**

Songs from Chippy (Hollywood '94) generics implanted in the Texas history that produced them (Wayne Hancock, "Thunderstorms and Neon Signs"; Joe Ely and Jo Harvey Allen, "Cup of Tea"; Robert Earl Keen and Butch Hancock, "Morning Goodness") ★★★

The Songs of Jimmie Rodgers—A Tribute Album (Columbia/Egyptian '97) Something about the spiritual proximity of country music's TB-racked founder-hero—plus, perhaps, Bob Dylan's grizzled guidance—moved these lovefesters to sing like the lowly mortals they are. Neatniks David Ball and Mary Chapin Carpenter must have been warming up when somebody rolled the tape; even Bono comes off his high horse a little, although his failure to get his feet out of the stirrups compels him to sing with his head up his ass anyway. As for Jerry Garcia, he just laid down his track yesterday with his new old-timey group, Dead and In the Way. Meanwhile, the great ones—Nelson, DeMent, Earle, and, in this context, Mellencamp, with Dylan topping them all—roll around in their cracks and crannies. Set off by loose-jointed arrangements that move naturally from Dixieland horns to I-for-Indiana fiddle, they reimagine these old songs as if the man who wrote them had had a chance to get old himself. Which in a sense he now has. **A**

The Songs of West Side Story (RCA Victor '96) bet they couldn't organize soul-pop meistersingers behind *Hair* (All-4-One, "Something's Coming"; Aretha Franklin, "Somewhere") ★★

Soul Food (LaFace '97) Babyface for boys—his genius, his fallibility (Total, "What About Us"; Milestone, "I Care 'Bout You") ★★

Soundbombing (Rawkus '97) "You record label people gonna die and your family gonna die too motherfuckers." Far more eager than the militantly joyless Company Flow, far more songful than the secretly ambient Lyricist Lounge, this singles-plus showcase is "underground" hip hop's most convincing advertisement for itself. Reflection Eternal, aka Black Star plus Mr. Man, add crowd samples and a chorus about Medina to an echoing guitar-piano hook and top anything on Black Star's secretly smooth debut. Mos Def and Kweli freestyle with feeling. Company Flow give up their catchiest album track and devolve into the more complex Indelible MCs, who "keep tabs like Timothy Leary and/or ASCAP." And Ra the Rugged Man ("all information concerning Ra is currently unknown"), who swears he'll be into "this rap shit" "Till My Heart Stops," admits that actually he's "not succeedin'": "They turn my mind state into evil 'cause I want everyone dead on this fuckin' earth/It really hurts/'Cause if music doesn't work I got nothing left to live for except dyin' in the poorhouse." Pray he returns on volume two. **A−**

Soundbombing See also *Rawkus Presents Soundbombing*

South African Rhythm Riot: The Indestructible Beat of Soweto Volume 6 (Stern's/Earthworks '99) Trevor Herman knows better than anyone that compilations suffer when they sneak in artists the compiler has a weakness for, but here he gets a little sentimental anyway. Kwaito is the biggest musical fad of postapartheid South Africa, and the smashes he wanted to include—notably Arthur's "Oyi Oyi," one of those dance hits that sweep all parochialism before them—make the choicest township jive seem more received than it used to. Put it all together you get patchwork rather than seamlessness: pop stars like Chicco and Brenda Fassie cambering the old rhythms, the so-calike single-mindedness of Aba Shante's Arthur-produced "Girls," even a visit from the tireless Papa Wemba. Fairly terrific track by track—I've tried hard enough with Fassie to admire how skillfully Herman flatters her, and I'd rather hear "Oyi Oyi" here than on the megahit album of the same name. But a sampler nevertheless. **A−**

South Central (Hollywood Basic '92) six timeless "Good Times" rips, five mortal pieces of hard, one pledge of eternal devotion (Vaughan Mason, "Bounce, Rock, Skate, Roll"; Ronnie Hudson, "West Coast Poplock"; Spectrum City, "Check Out the Radio") ★★

South Park: Bigger, Longer & Uncut (Atlantic '99) In which a cartoonist and a soundtrack hack compose classic post-modern musical-comedy songs, so indiscriminate in their incorrectness that they keep sneaking up on you. Since Eric Cartman can outsing Saddam Hussein and Big Gay Al through a glory hole, only the full-chorus versions of "Mountain Town" can compete with "Kyle's Mom's a B**ch." But the all-around quality of the movie performances is brought into relief by the CD-only "interpretations," where only Joe C. and the Violent Femmes do the material justice; as a writer, Isaac Hayes doesn't get it, and Trey Parker has trouble finding certified gangsta rappers willing to utter the words "uncle fucka." In short, the original cast's greatest hits, undercut by the kind of stoned, wouldn't-it-be-funny-if? fizzles that make the show so dumb sometimes. **A–**

Space Jam (Warner Sunset/Atlantic '96) black pop '97, with more tunes (Seal, "Fly Like an Eagle"; R. Kelly, "I Believe I Can Fly"; Coolio, "The Winner") ★★

The Spirit of Cape Verde (Tinder '99) Heard in the background, as quiet world music comps usually are, the saudade here can be vaguely annoying, like somebody unburdening her troubles out of earshot across the room. Listen close, however, and the melancholy seems so deeply imbued it's as if 300,000 islanders had been lulled to sleep by Billie Holiday before they learned to speak. Though it lapses into the genteel sentimentality that mushes up too much samba, there's a little more muscle to the music's technical intricacy and sensual pulse. And if your attention flags, be sure to come back for the farewell instrumental, cut 30 years before sadness became the nation's cash crop. At two minutes and 12 seconds, it's primal. **B+**

Spirit of the Eagle: Zimbabwe Frontline (Vol. 2) (Virgin '90) Chimurenga godfather Thomas Mapfumo's producer also oversaw the quieter Robinson Banda opener and the more percussive Nyami Nyami Sounds entry, while someone named A. K. Mapfumo produced the other Banda song as well as two by old favorites the Four Brothers. Everywhere the ripple of mbira guitar buoys music whose varied details are mere decoration for a tourist like me—a tourist who sits grinning foolishly, amazed yet again that such a wonderful world could thrive independent of his sustained personal attention. **A–**

The Carl Stalling Project: Music from Warner Bros. Cartoons 1936–1958 (Warner Bros. '90) low on continuity, will keep you alert on the interstate ("Various Cues from Bugs Bunny Films [1943–1956]") ★★★

Steely & Clevie Play Studio One Vintage (Heartbeat '92) Maybe it's mouldy-fig of me to prefer this to the dancehall *Steely & Clevie Present Soundboy Clash*. But having trudged through the Studio One reissues, I ought to recognize something here besides "Fatty Fatty," so you can't convince me "vintage" means sure shot. And with Leroy Sibbles, Alton Ellis, and Marcia Griffiths the big names, the singers are pretty anonymous as well. Rhythm tricks that can't carry any old toast by themselves plus songs that cried out for more juice than Sir Coxsone and his minions had in them. **A–**

Street Jams: Hip Hop from the Top—Part 4 (Rhino '94) circa-'85 novelty comp that tops out on three nasty-girl rarities (Super Nature, "The Show Stoppa [Is Stupid Fresh]"; Roxanne Shanté, "Bite This"; Symbolic Three, Featuring D.J. Dr. Shock, "No Show") ★★

Street Music of Java (Original Music '93) love that girl-group dangdut, appreciate the rest ("Asoi," "Kuda Lumping," "Hai Cuim Dong") ★★★

Streets of Dakar: Generation Boul Falé (Stern's Africa '99) Under the rubric of a new piece of slang whose meaning is surrounded by "carefree," "fed up," and "whatever," young singers in a land where horns are no longer cost-effective make do with synthesizers. Though they use them well, there's a loss not just in color but in punch and ruckus, and though there are plenty of guitars and enough guitar hooks, the few solos never bust out. Leaving us with tama drums that don't-stop-and-they-don't-stop and a profusion of voices, tremendously varied within their penetrating West African attack—girl group and rap crew share space with blues growlers, trumpetless Gabriels, and other secular muezzins. These voices convey resoluteness, spirituality, spunk, moralism, humor—personality. They also convey good-to-great melodies. So, whatever. **A–**

Strength Magazine Presents Subtext (London/Strength '99) W.C.U.W.A (Aceyalone, "Rappers, Rappers, Rappers 12 for 10"; Del the Funkee Homosapien, "Cyberpunks") ★

Strip Jointz (Robbins Music '97) Long convinced that the sexiest soundtrack to coitus and its kissing cousins is provided by the participants, I have no use for slow jams and assume this would suit that purpose even worse. I'm not even positive anyone splits beaver to such stuff. But as an antidote to subtlety, you couldn't beat these soft-core r&b cartoons with a fistful of Vaseline. They flag a little in the middle, you know how it is, but from R. Kelly's pre-Christian "Bump n' Grind" to Clarence Carter's do-it-with-his-eyes-closed "Strokin'," it fairly represents the great middle ground between Li'l Kim and Peabo Bryson where most carnality actually situates itself. **A–**

Suburbia (DGC '97) alternative as new wave, its lost moment a movie nobody noticed (Elastica with Stephen Malkmus, "Unheard Music"; Boss Hog, "I'm Not Like Everybody Else") ★★

Sugar and Poison (Virgin import '96) Two CDs of David Toop–selected musical foreplay that bear the same relation to the quiet-storm makeout comps where labels now recycle late-soul also-rans that Toop's *Ocean of Sound* does to ambient house—the come-ons are edgier in the psychological sense, beset by an anxiety smoover grooves muffle, and thus more actually sexlike than the smarm of Freddie Jackson or the sincerity of Otis Redding. The locus is soul as Northern pop, a '70s sensibility whose roots in gospel and country are twice removed, although the material stretches into the '80s (Loose Ends, Meli'sa Morgan, Tashan's drum 'n' bass-ish 1986 "Chasin' a Dream") and even '90s. Whether it's stuff you love (Sly's "Just Like a Baby," Bootsy's "Vanish in My Sleep," Chic's climactically inevitable "At Last I Am Free") or artists, even songs, you don't care for (O. V. Wright, "Southern Nights"), you've never heard them like this before. Only my wife has ever made me a better mix tape. **A**

Sweet Relief: A Tribute to Victoria Williams (Thirsty Ear/Chaos '93) ⓝ
Sweet Relief II: Gravity of the Situation (Columbia '96) with Vic Chesnutt accounted for, they should move on to Butch Hancock, who I hope is healthy as a horse (Garbage, "Kick My Ass"; Joe Henry and Madonna, "Guilty by Association") ★★

Rachid Taha: *Diwân* (Island '98) On his U.S. debut, the Oran-born Eurodance phenom was so ethnotechno that few Anglophones guessed his politics were tougher than his beats. Lucky for us, here he elects to catch his breath, retreating from message disco into an Algerian equivalent of Bowie's *Pin Ups* or GN'R's *Spaghetti Incident*. An instant touchstone of Arab song and a Taha-composed tour of rai history pitch the collection higher than it can remain if it's gonna be as trad as the artist thinks decent. Throughout, however, the tunes, choruses, instrumental parts, and raw vocals invoke a cultural identity that any moderately adventurous tourist will find more entrancing than ethnotechno. **A–**

Tail Dragger: "American People" (*American People*, Delmark '99) 🐚

Talking Heads: *Stop Making Sense (Special New Edition)* (Sire/Warner Bros. '99) 🎣
Talking Heads: See also the Heads

James Talley: *Woody Guthrie and Songs of My Oklahoma Home* (Cimarron '99) 20 Woody songs done calmly and faithfully, as a spiritual resource ("Belle Starr," "Talkin' Dust Bowl Blues") ★

Taraf de Haïdouks: *Taraf de Haïdouks* (Nonesuch '99) Look, I got no use for Gypsy music, nor for the Balkan stuff to which it is geographically related. Gypsy's too demonstrative in its passion and longing, and as for Balkan, I've tried and failed and gone on with my life. So here's Band of Brigands, three generations of *lautari* from southwestern Romania it says in the notes, the elders not above improvising about the fall of Ceaușesau, the young ones imbued with the old ways even if they love the music of the cities where they dream of performing—and where they now enjoy a presence, this being a best of from three albums on a Belgian label. I love the tongue-twisting "Dumbala dumba," the deep cellar-door creak of "Rustem"'s large cymbalum, and the heartbroke melody of "Sabarelu," which seems to be about rivers. I dunno, maybe the other guys work up that floridity for the tourist trade. Or maybe this is a special band—fast, intense, tuneful, yet always frayed around the edges. **A–**

Tarnation: *Gentle Creatures* (4AD '95) With the Cowboy Junkies gone the way of regular junkies (who either disappear or sign with Geffen, right?), along come these San Francisco country-mopers. Not that it couldn't be worse—I mean, Joan Baez stripped of her chops is more amusing than Joan Baez clinging to them. **C** 🦃

Skatemaster Tate and the Concrete Crew: *Do the Skate* (4th & B'way '91) rap so swinging it takes its bass upright ("Irv's," "Hey Wooley") ★

James Taylor: *New Moon Shine* (Columbia '91) 🎣
James Taylor: "Line 'Em Up," "Walking My Baby Back Home" (*Hourglass*, Columbia '97) 🐚

★★★, ★★, ★ Honorable Mention   🐚 Choice Cut   Ⓝ Neither   🎣 Dud   🦃 Turkey

TBTBT: "One Track Mind" (*Too Bad to Be True*, Cold Chillin' '93) 🔊

Team Dresch: "Fagetarian and Dyke" (*Personal Best*, Chainsaw/Lesbionic Candy-Ass '94) 🔊

Team Dresch: *Captain My Captain* (Chainsaw/Candyass '96) the everything-clashing model of passionate cooperation ("Uncle Phranc," "Don't Try Suicide") ★★

Technotronic: *Recall* (SBK/EMI '94) Jo Bogaert and Patrick De Meyer prove Eurodisco is a producer's music on "2 U X," an instrumental that sets me strutting every time it sneaks up—which it can do because I tune out all the guy singer's exhortations until Ya Kid K (Daisy D.?) picks him up midway through "I Want You by My Side." So if the guy's cuts fade and the girls' take me to techno church, maybe the secret of this spiritual uplift for secular people isn't Bogaert and De Meyer after all. Maybe it's the girls. **A−**

Teenage Fanclub: *God Knows It's True* (Matador '90) Title tune's the only time they've yoked melody/noise/sound and sense/nonsense/paradox at optimum archness without undercutting either or both. The other one with words comes close. The two instrumentals only partly fulfill their modest mission in life, which is fusing strum and skronk. **B+**

Teenage Fanclub: *Bandwagonesque* (DGC '91) a singa with attitude might put some there there ("Metal Baby," "Is This Music?") ★★★

Teenage Fanclub: *Thirteen* (DGC '93) ⓝ

Television: *Television* (Capitol '92) I prefer the more rocking, songful old Television, but it's a tribute to Tom Verlaine's conceptual restlessness and force of personality that in a world where alternative guitar means making noise or mixing and matching from the used bins, these four veterans have regrouped with a distinct new sonic identity. Droll, warmhearted, sophisticated, cryptic, jazzy yet unjazzlike, they sound like nothing else—except, just a little, old Television, mainly because Ver-

laine has ignored the Lloyd Cole jokes and refused to alter his voiceprint. **B+**

Television Personalities: *Yes Darling, but Is It Art? (Early Singles and Rarities)* (Seed '95) part-time punks and how ("Part Time Punks," "Arthur the Gardener") ★

Tenor Saw: "Ring the Alarm" (*The Best of Reggae Dancehall Music Volume 2*, Profile '90) 🔊

Terminator X: *Terminator X & the Valley of the Jeep Beats* (P.R.O. Division/RAL/Columbia '91) ⓝ

Terror Fabulous: "Action" (*Yaga Yaga*, EastWest '94) 🔊

Texas Tornados: *Texas Tornados* (Warner Bros. '90) On record they're a little too country for a honky-tonk conjunto rocking that Western swing. Freddy Fender especially is more ragged and glorious entertaining fellow graybeards in person. But when Augie Meyers gets real silly or Doug Sahm gets real gone now, it doesn't matter at all. And the rest of the time it doesn't matter much. **B+**

Texas Tornados: *Best of Texas Tornados* (Reprise '93) The debut was rougher than tough and sweeter than shit, but as a genre band they're made for this selective, wide-ranging format. Mad rocker Doug Sahm is no longer a legend outside his place and time and *vato* vibrato Freddy Fender is now remembered as a have-a-nice-day one-shot with a novelty artist's name, but not only were they both major in the bilingual, panstylistic Tex-Mex universe, they ain't oldies now. As for Augie Meyers and Flaco Jimenez, they're born sidemen whose solo albums stand up. In short, any young person who loves good rock and roll, good country, good conjunto, maybe even good polka has a supergroup out there waiting. Try "Guacamole," a great sex metaphor. Or "Who Were You Thinkin' Of," a classic country song. Or "Wasted Days and Wasted Nights," no one-shot. **A−**

That Dog: *Totally Crushed Out!* (DGC '95) Biz babies who get too much shade for it, they come through with a sublime, honest little mock-concept album about teen love among the psychologically nondisabled. Their simple noise-pop tunes are actually melodic, their ugly-pretty contrasts actually generate tension, their sophisticated harmonies actually massage one's ears. And "He's Kissing Christian" is the best triangle song since "When You Were Mine." A–

That Dog: *Retreat from the Sun* (DGC '97) For a pop adept, Anna Waronker skimps on the surefire. On no more than half these tracks does the chorus come around and grab the ring; on no more than a couple does the verse leave you waiting for the chorus to make its move. But I think that's because she realizes that we're so inured to tunefulness that the surefire backfires. Waronker's deep hooks are a flatly winsome voice, an unsenti-mental guitar, and a flirty adventurism that promises loving sex without offering much hope she'll be there six months from now—even if she's indulging one of her domestic fantasies at your expense. A–

Thelonious Monster: *Beautiful Mess* (Capitol '92) As always, Bob Forrest is beset by bad feelings he can't compre-hend—about an unjust society, a dys-functional family, a feminist girlfriend who runs off with "some faggot from the Posies," above all about himself. Crawling around the nice house he secured with his advance or gazing awestruck at the nice girlfriend he doubts he deserves, covering Joan Armatrading or dueting with Tom Waits, sleeping eight to a room in Vegas with his equally confused friends, he always seems to end up doing what he does best—whining. He whines tune-fully, loudly, childishly, revoltingly, nakedly, sweetly, intelligently, and though he prob-ably doesn't deserve that girlfriend, you can tell why she doesn't think so. With a jerk like Forrest, this constitutes a major artistic achievement. A–

Therapy?: *Nurse* (A&M '93) enthusiasts (in the religious sense) of despair (ditto) ("Accelerator," "Gone") ★★★

They Might Be Giants: *Flood* (Elektra '90) tunes, aarghh, tunes—please not more tunes ("Dead," "Your Racist Friend") ★★

They Might Be Giants: "We're the Re-placements," "Hey Mr. DJ, I Thought We Had a Deal" (*Miscellaneous T,* Bar/None/Restless '91) 👁

They Might Be Giants: *Apollo 18* (Elektra '92) For a stunning five-song run toward the start, they replicate the brittle brilliance that tricked their old fans into ex-pecting a tour de force every time. The packed pop-pomo pastiches make the redolent meaninglessness of near-literal lyrics signify and sing, softening you up for the more scattered experiments that follow. Which include the XTC-does-Bo-Diddley "Hypnotist of Ladies," the 22-part "Fingertips" ("I'm having a heart attack/I'm having a heart attack"), the brit-tlely brilliant "Dinner Bell," and "Narrow Your Eyes," which if I'm not mistaken is about the actual dissolution of an actual relationship. A–

They Might Be Giants: *Why Does the Sun Shine?* (Elektra '93) ⓝ

They Might Be Giants: "I Should Be Allowed to Think," "Meet James En-sor" (*John Henry,* Elektra '94) 👁

They Might Be Giants: *Factory Showroom* (Elektra '96) to quote the ever clever Ian Dury, there ain't half been some clever bastards ("How Can I Sing Like a Girl?," "I Can Hear You," "James K. Polk," "XTC Vs. Adam Ant") ★★★

They Might Be Giants: *Severe Tire Damage* (Restless '98) Billed as greatest hits but actually just live, and not espe-cially well chosen by my no-more-or-less-idiosyncratic-than-theirs lights—where's "How Can I Sing Like a Girl?"? And of course there are bait cuts, new songs their wee fan base presumably can't live without. What I wouldn't have figured is that "Doctor Worm" ("I'm not a real doctor but I am a real worm") and "They Got

Lost" (on their way to a radio station so low-watt it fades out no matter how they turn) are my favorite things on a record that includes "XTC Vs. Adam Ant" and "Meet James Ensor," reflexively clever titles I include as a guarantee that the songs live up to them. "Meet They Might Be Giants/Brooklyn's cultish songmen/ Set on random and skim their book/ Watch out for falling hooks." **B+**

They Might Be Giants: *Long Tall Weekend* (www.emusic.com '99) The biggest problem with Net-music utopianism is that no matter how fast and convenient downloads get, music itself will continue to exist in, if you'll pardon the expression, real time. That's its very essence. If 1441 minutes of music go up on the Web today, that's a minute more than anyone can hear in that period, period. Might the Net be a useful way for consumers to sample their musical options? Sure. Might it help strapped artists get by? Conceivably. Are there good things there that are unavailable elsewhere? Certainly not as many as in the sum total of specialty shops in our metropolis, although the same may not hold in Wichita. This, however, is one of them. Human song generators whose metier is the miscellany, they're ideally suited to construct a download-only album that isn't an out file taking on airs. Although "They Got Lost" is on last year's live album and patrons of their club gigs and dial-a-song service may recognize other tunes, this is as enjoyable a CD as they've released in the '90s. With love to the literal "Operators Are Standing By," it peaks with "Older," which is about real time. **A–**

Thingy: *To the Innocent* (Absolutely Kosher '99) **Ⓝ**

Thinking Fellers Union Local 282: *Lovelyville* (Matador '91) Although it's possible to imagine these musicians powering a rock and roll band that means a damn thing, this cross between Frisco antiheroes the Residents and Dixie dregs Love Tractor is too avant-garde to serve

up anyone's money's worth. Nothing lasts, that's the message, whether it's the dense riffage of "2X4S" or the orchestrated guffaws and seal barks that finish "More Glee" with a flourish. Lyrics? How vulgar. We should be thankful when they make with the private jokes doted on by performance artists everywhere. **B–** 🦃

3rd Bass: *Derelicts of Dialect* (Def Jam/Columbia '91) 💣

Third Eye Blind: *Third Eye Blind* (Elektra '97) **Ⓝ**

Third Rail: *South Delta Space Age* (Antilles '97) 💣

The Third Sex: *Card Carryin'* (Chainsaw '96) **Ⓝ**

Chris Thomas: *Cry of the Prophets* (Warner Bros. '90) 💣

David Thomas: *Mirror Man* (Thirsty Ear '99) 💣

Thomas Jefferson Slave Apartments: *Bait and Switch* (Onion/American '95) Formerly leader of the slovenly folk-rockers Great Plains, among whose achievements was the best song ever written about Rutherford B. Hayes, Columbus lifer Ron House demonstrates on this $800 debut album that punk and youth need have nothing to do with each other anymore. First five tracks rush by in a perfect furious tunefest, climaxing with a bar song called "Loser's Heaven" that's ripe for total rearrangement by anybody in Nashville with some guts left. After that recognition is less instantaneous except on "RnR Hall of Fame," which comes with liner notes to match: "TJSA proudly accept the honor of being indicted by the Rock and Roll Hall of Fame . . . " If indie scenes are so full of wordwise ne'er-do-wells like this, how come they never put it on tape? **A–**

Thomas Jefferson Slave Apartments: *Straight to Video* (Anyway '97) Ron House makes the sex life of an aging punk in an overgrown college town sound active, raunchy, and not without spiritual rewards—in addition to the professional shank shaker and the prostitute with her leg half chewed off, he fucks several women with truly enormous libraries. He also bids an unsentimental farewell to Lester Bangs and complains about the age of the spectacle. **A–**

Butch Thompson: *Yulestride* (Daring '94) hymns laced with standards and bent quietly into cocktail-piano wassail ("Silent Night," "Jingle Bells") ★★★

Butch Thompson: *Thompson Plays Joplin* (Daring '98) One reason Scott Joplin's rhythmic revolution comes through so faintly on record is that it was swallowed whole by the tempo of 20th-century life. Though it's true enough, as anyone who's ventured near *Treemonisha* knows, that Joplin craved respect, that's no reason to forgive all the concert pianists who've arted up and toned down his beat since Joshua Rifkin. With a firm hand, the man from Lake Wobegon sets them straight. His Joplin doesn't rock, swing, or anything like it. But at their most liltingly delicate these rags are set in motion, as he says, by "the same driving pulse that underlies all of America's truly original music." Marvin Hamlisch go back where you came from. **A–**

Richard Thompson: *Rumor and Sigh* (Capitol '91) From his vintage bike to his veiled belief that Salman Rushdie had it coming, the innate conservatism of this policeman's son is manifest, and at times his prejudices about artistic substance produce meaningful threnodies of no immediate artistic interest. But even the boring stuff goes somewhere, and nobody throws a meaner party. His tales of sex education and old 78s are so cranked up and cranky you wonder how you ever could have thought fun would be easy, and he gets almost as much mileage out of not understanding women as George Jones. Wonder whether George could get through the changes of "I Misunderstood." Or add a little zing to "You Dream Too Much." **B+**

Richard Thompson: "Can't Win," "Tear Stained Letter," "Bogie's Bonnie Belle," "Crash the Party," "From Galway to Graceland" (*Watching the Dark: The History of Richard Thompson,* Hannibal '93) 🌑

Richard Thompson: *Mirror Blue* (Capitol '94) I thought she loved me but she didn't—why does this keep happening? ("Shane and Dixie," "For the Sake of Mary") ★

Richard Thompson: *You? Me? Us?* (Capitol '96) **Ⓝ**

Richard Thompson: *Mock Tudor* (Capitol '99) **Ⓝ**

Thompson & Thompson: *Industry* (Rykodisc '97) The second Thompson is bassist Danny, the instrumental interludes of whose North of England jazz-march unit Whatever set off Richard's six songs in the manner of Charlie Haden or Kurt Weill—with music that intensifies meaning as well as sustaining mood. The songs themselves, all of which attend closely to the title concept, were researched in dying coal mines and the Karl Marx library, among other places, and let's hope they convince Richard that art is 90 percent perspiration. It does him a world of good to get out of himself. **A–**

Teri Thornton: *I'll Be Easy to Find* (Verve '99) A veteran of polio, cancer, incarceration, and cabdriving whose perfect pitch and three-octave range were getting raves when she was in her twenties, Thornton transfigures the showboating artiness that puts pop fans off jazz singers. Since I've lived happily without Sarah Vaughan and Abbey Lincoln, at first I didn't trust my pleasure in the soulful concentration, harmonic subtlety, and deliciously curdled timbre of Thornton's first record since 1963. But from her self-composed blues to her rearranged "Lord's Prayer," her occasional piano to her consistent standards, this woman knows how to serve a song her way. If she's making something of "It Ain't Necessarily So" and "Nature Boy" at this late date, it's only because she's waited a long, long time. **A–**

3Ds: *Hellzapoppin* (First Warning '92) down dirges and squeaky-fast dissonance for the insatiable pomo tunehound ("Hellzapoppin," "Outer Space") ★

Throw That Beat in the Garbage-can!: *Cool* (Spin Art '93) the EP, not *The Cool Album,* which ain't ("Cool," "Little Red Go-Cart") ★

Johnny Thunders: *Have Faith* (Mutiny '96) despite nondescript backup and much solo acoustic, his best crappy live tape yet ("Blame It on Mom," "Too Much Junkie Business") ★

Tiger: "No Wanga Man" (*Mash Up the Place! The Best of Reggae Dancehall* [comp], Rhino '95) 💿

Tiger: *Shining in the Wood* (Bar/None '97) One young U.K. rave cites "The Stooges, The Ramones, Stereolab, Suicide and The Fall"; a middle-aged friend eavesdrops from the kitchen and asks who that is that sounds like the Beatles. In short, this EP evokes everyone and no one, except maybe pop fans who get just plain excited making songs out of Moogy drones and distaff football choruses and bang-crash drums and fab guitars and everything else they like. Not just ebullient, which is rare enough, but ebulliently anything-goes, without any neoprimitivist/neominimalist guardrails keeping them out of the abyss. Plus the kind of obscurely goofy lyrics that are so irritating in ordinary theoretical pop. Goofy—I love it. B-52's? **A**

Tiger Trap: *Tiger Trap* (K '93) ⓝ

Pam Tillis: *Homeward Looking Angel* (Arista '92) 🎩

Timbaland and Magoo: *Welcome to Our World* (Blackground/Atlantic '97) Tim is as simple and deep as his unsampled bass-beats. In fact, he's so uncompromising about being laid-back that he finds himself charged with no less a responsibility than redefining reality, which in his unorthodox view is benign, within limits: "I got my man Big D./Rodney/In case some-body wanna rob me." Magoo does the Flavor Flav thing, leaving Tim free to keep the self-referential rhymes as clean as they wanna be: "I'm on my last verse/As you can see I did not curse/I wanna make it radio-friendly/So people in America can hear me." He's woman-friendly too—won't call you a ho, just lick on your toes. **A−**

Timbaland: *Tim's Bio* (Blackground/Atlantic '98) ⓝ

Timbuk 3: *A Hundred Lovers* (High Street '95) ⓝ

The Time: *Pandemonium* (Paisley Park '90) not enough concept/too much band ("Skillet," "Chocolate," "Pandemonium") ★★

Sally Timms: "Homburg," "Junk Barge" (*To the Land of Milk and Honey,* Feels Good All Over '94) 💿

Sally Timms: *Cowboy Sally* (Bloodshot '97) Piecing together an EP that looks (and probably is) every bit as casual as the rest of her solo noncareer, the old Mekon and new kid-TV star surveys fake authenticity at its weedlike best, from John Anderson's comeback-album title song to "Long Black Veil," which may just be the greatest phony folk song of all time—with Nashville punsters, No Depression punters, and "Tennessee Waltz" betwixt and between. Wryer than your professional country thrush. Kinder, too. **A−**

Sally Timms: *Cowboy Sally's Twilight Laments . . . for Lost Buckaroos* (Bloodshot '99) alt-country songbook ("Cry Cry Cry," "Rock Me to Sleep") ★★

Tin Huey: *Disinformation* (Future Fossil '99) lost postpunk album, more pop and less art than anyone knew at the time ("Seeing," "Cheap Machines") ★

Tiny Tim: "Another Brick in the Wall (Part Two)" (*I Love Me,* Seeland/Ponk '95) 💿

Tiny Tim with Brave Combo: *Girl* (Rounder '95) respect for a lover of popular song ("Stairway to Heaven," "Sly Cigarette," "Fourteen," "Bye Bye Blackbird") ★★★

Aaron Tippin: *Greatest Hits . . . and Then Some* (RCA '97) as prole as Music Row gets ("Ain't Nothing Wrong with the Radio," "Cold Gray Kentucky Morning") ★

TLC: *Oooooooohhh . . . On the TLC Tip* (Arista '92) ◐

TLC: *CrazySexyCool* (LaFace '94) Three great songs here: in ascending order, the cheater's whisper "Creep," the sisters' sermon "Waterfalls," and the wet dream's statement of principle "Red Light Special." The filler sustains, the skits are funnysexycool, the male rappers rock. But other wet dreams end badly—a guy would have to be pretty hard up to sustain four minutes' interest in "Let's Do It Again"'s vow of lifelong intromission—and the project's caution is summed up by the Prince cover. Really, ladies, the brilliance of "If I Was Your Girlfriend" was that a *guy* was singing it. **B+**

TLC: *Fan Mail* (LaFace '99) just like you they are lonely too ("Silly Ho," "Unpretty") ★★★

Tom Tom Club: "Who Wants an Ugly Girl?" (*Dark Sneak Love Action,* Sire/Reprise '92) 👁‍🗨

Tone Loc: "Old Mother Hubbard" (*Rap Rhymes! Mother Goose on the Loose* [comp], Epic '93) 👁‍🗨

Tony! Toni! Toné!: *The Revival* (Wing '90) who says a love band can't play funk music? ("Feels Good," "Oakland Stroke") ★★

Tony! Toni! Toné!: *Sons of Soul* (Wing '93) sexy liars of the year ("If I Had No Loot," "Anniversary") ★

Tony Toni Toné: *House of Music* (Mercury '96) Launched by a hilariously gutsy Al Green homage that knows the great man's every moue and off-beat, Raphael Saadiq and his henchmen give the r&b revival what for, constructing a generous original style from a varied history they know inside out—Tempts, Sly, Blue Magic, Kurtis Blow. And for almost every sound they provide a sharp song, which is more than Holland-Dozier-Holland and Gamble-Huff could manage when they were compelled to stick to one. Defeating second-half trail-off and a CD-age windiness the band isn't beatwise enough to beat, Saadiq's flexible, sensitive, slightly nasal tenor, spelled by the grain of D'Wayne Wiggins's workaday baritone, recasts the tradition in its image. Wasn't sampling supposed to strangle this sort of virtuosity at the root? **A**

Tony Toni Toné: *Hits* (Mercury '97) In the tradition of the Everlys and the Alvins, the Wiggins brothers can't stand each other anymore. So this may be it for them, which is too bad, because only with *House of Music* did they become true sons of the soul revival, the most accomplished r&b act of the '90s. That's still the album to remember them by. This one merely creates the illusion that they always had it in them to match easy pop funk like "Feels Good" and "Little Walter" with come-ons like the opportunistic "Thinking of You" and the steadfast—a whole year, gosh—"Anniversary." **A–**

Tool: *Aenima* (Zoo '96) 🎸

Too Much Joy: *Cereal Killers* (Giant '91) After a year of sleeping on floors, stealing wives, and expressing solidarity with 2 Live Crew, their music is thicker, tougher, hookier, sometimes even a tad overproduced. And their lyrics are still what it's there for. So smart they have dumb people sniffing about the Dead Milkmen, they have their moments of empathy, social responsibility, self-knowledge, and so forth. But as a sucker for a cheap laugh, I prefer "King of Beers" ("Na na na na na na sorrow") and "Long Haired Guys from England" ("I bet in London I could get a date/'cause I'm a short haired guy from the United States"). Both of which are longer on self-knowledge than most dumb people I meet. **A–**

Too Much Joy: *Mutiny* (Giant '92) ◐

David Toop: *Screen Ceremonies* (The Wire import '95) music for a postmodern sex ritual ("The Psychic," "The Darkened Room") ★

David Toop: *Pink Noir* (Virgin import '96) "improvisation" goes trad ambient—

usually with a pulse, which usually makes all the difference ("Mixed Blood," "Slow Loris Versus Poison Snail") ★

Too Short: "The Ghetto" (*Short Dog's in the House,* Jive '90) 🐝

Too Short: *Shorty the Pimp* (Jive '92) In his fourth book, Iceberg Slim—who invented Short Dog's shtick as surely as Dr. Funkenstein—boasted about escaping "the terrible emptiness of the pimp game." He considered old pimps "contemptible," "pathetic." On his seventh album, Too Short boasts that he's "a player for life." Who you believe? **C+** 🐝

Toots and the Maytals: *Time Tough: The Anthology* (Island Jamaica '96) This rocksteady diehard's 1968 "Do the Reggay" named a groove he was too constitutionally uptempo ever to get into; this unspoiled journeyman's soul affinities endeared him to hippie diehards and failed to touch young African Americans, who by the mid-'70s figured the soul that was passé when it came from the South must be pure shuck-and-jive if it came from the islands. So eager to please that only 1988's patently nostalgic *Toots in Memphis* ever showed the courage of his conceptions, he was also too songful ever to come up dry. I can think of things I miss, such as the heartily discomfiting "Famine." But this is the testament of Otis Redding's love child. His eagerness is a natural force. And his pleasures abide. **A−**

Liz Torres: *The Queen Is in the House* (Jive '90) house as in disco, house as in a home ("Loca," "Payback Is a Bitch [What Goes Around Comes Around]") ★

Tortoise: *Millions Now Living Will Never Die* (Thrill Jockey '96) Obviously not stupid, which I can understand means a lot to them after their troubled childhoods, these guys are the class of the American postrock cough cough hack hack movement ptooey ptooey. But I would direct their attention to the British band Mark-Almond, a now forgotten jamming unit that achieved real sales and a measure of hip around the time they were

born. Not that I necessarily think these "eclectic," consciously unspacy, all too unhurried soundscape improvisations are destined for the same degree of obscurity. Patterns of culture have changed, and in a boutique economy, this shit, like all other shit, is probably here to stay. Still, there are surer roads to posterity. Best moment: the lead bassline, lifted directly from "Pop Tones" (by PiL, kids). **B−** 🐝

Tortoise: *TNT* (Thrill Jockey '98) ⓝ

Total: *Kima, Keisha & Pam* (Bad Boy '98) bad girls ("Do Something," "There Will Be No #!*@ Tonight") ★

Ali Farka Toure: *The River* (World Circuit import '90) As a self-taught guitarist who's rarely reviewed without reference to John Lee Hooker, Toure is conflicted about Afro-American music—does he owe it or does it owe him? And although he always displays the guitar style that occasions the comparison (which I'm betting is part influence, part tradition, and part invention), his recordings drift into the folkloric. So it's a relief that unlike Mango's *Ali Farka Toure* or Shanachie's *African Blues,* this one means to cross over a bit. Not only does it make room for a second human being (Amadou Cisse on calabash, the percussion device that Toure overdubs on his Mango release), but tracks colored with harmonica, saxophone, fiddle and bodhran, and the single-stringed njarka that Toure picks up for the finale—not to mention an extra edge of vocal command. I don't know what Malians will think. But I say the result is variety, not compromise. And I say it's what he's always needed. **A−**

Ali Farka Toure: *The Source* (Hannibal/World Circuit '92) in a ruminative mood, with a band cogitating in ("Goye Kur," "Dofana") ★★

Ali Farka Toure with Ry Cooder: *Talking Timbuktu* (Hannibal '94) ⓝ

Ali Farka Toure: *Niafunké* (Hannibal '99) In Mali a little goes a long way, so after his harrowing experience with Ry Cooder's sense of rhythm the artfully primeval guitarist-vocalist took his mod-

est winnings back to the well-named title village, where he devoted himself to making green things grow. Finally, after five years, he surrounds himself entirely with homeboys and reemerges with a record "full of important messages for Africans." Over here he doesn't "expect people to understand," and of course we don't. But when it comes to evoking a sun-baked place where a little goes a long way, you couldn't beat these hymns, homilies, wedding songs, dance tunes, and we-are-what-we-are apostrophes with a trap set. **A–**
Ali Farka Toure: *Radio Mali* (World Circuit/Nonesuch '99) **Ⓝ**

Sidi Touré: *Hoga* (Stern's Africa '96) Adept of the trance-prone voodoo called "holley," inventor of a trad-to-the-future band music where guitars vie wildly with calabashes over a swirling drone of African viol, this Songhai, whose day job is with Mali's big official Bambara band, is not to be confused with fellow Songhai Ali Farka Touré. He's weirder, and more active. It's a Gao thing, you wouldn't understand—until you listen, once. **A–**

Allen Toussaint: "Computer Lady" (*Connected,* NYNO '96) **☜**

Pete Townshend: *Psychoderelict* (Atlantic '93) **☛**
Pete Townshend: *Psychoderelict (Music Only)* (Atlantic '93) Shorn of the voice-overs and bad dialogue designed to make the "dramatic" version as explicit as multileveled self-referentiality can be, what I'd dreamed might be his sparest, strongest, sweetest set of songs in years turns out to have needed all the camouflage it could get. It's long been evident that what turned Townshend on about pop art was the art rather than the pop—he didn't want to drag opera down to rock's level, he wanted to raise rock to opera's. In practice, this means he has a fatal weakness for long synth intros. After the jagged surprises of the lead "English Boy," there are far fewer intelligent moments than a guy this intelligent ought to keep in his back pocket. If he's so damn

worried about the postinformation age, it's because he's in the information business and is afraid of getting left behind. As he damn well should be. **C+** 🦃

T.P O.K Jazz: *Somo!* (TMS import '90) With the leader already too near death to fulfill his commitments, I checked out Franco's band sans Franco a few years ago, and while it wasn't as transcendent as Franco's band avec Franco, which I'd been lucky enough to catch a few years before that, I could barely drag myself away at 2:45 from a set that began around midnight. Honoring the gentle rumbas of the storied past, this seven-track, 55-minute feast doesn't peak like live or get hype like modern. But even at its malest it's sweet, so sweet. **A–**

Traffic: *Far from Home* (Virgin '94) Leave those silly Rolling Stones be, children—you're an old-fart virgin until you've done the deed with this slab of eternal life, created in a mere eight months by two well-heeled boys farting around the Irish countryside. Jim Capaldi's drums are mixed like a tribute to the disco of yesteryear, but Stevie, I mean Steve, enters the CD age on his own terms—where ordinary old farts jack their releases up to an hour by unloading 14 or 15 songs, he stops at 10. Title tune takes a full two-and-a-half minutes of overdubbed overture to get to the lyric. Which begins . . . oh, you don't want to know. **C–** 🦃

Trailer Bride: "Quit That Jealousy" (*Smelling Salts,* Bloodshot '98) **☜**
Trailer Bride: *Whine de Lune* (Bloodshot '99) Melissa Swingle's "got two long arms, and they're as strong as they are thin," but the boxcars are locked. So if you don't let her work on the railroad she may just lay down on the tracks. Cursing snakes, crashing windshields, poking around for a minor chord, that's her way—depressed but determined, with just enough guitar, banjo, and mandolin to make something of it. Slack-jawed mountain dolor in the age of Valium—a hyperconsciously eerie tour de force. **A–**

Tranquility Bass: "La La La" (*Let the Freak Flag Fly*, Astralwerks '97) 🦑

Transvision Vamp: "Down on My Knees Again" (*Little Magnets Versus the Bubble of Babble*, MCA '91) 🦑

Boubacar Traoré: *Mariana* (Stern's Africa '90) Guitar and vocals from a Malian (and Parisian) schoolteacher turned singer-songwriter, who declaims like Ali Farka Toure (only Traoré's lovingly preserved Khassonke guitar has no Hook in it) or the Baaba Maal of *Djam Leelii* (and he accompanies himself). Pealing forth his precepts and laments with a resonant gravity rendered doubly mesmeric by the quiet, implacable instrumentation, Traoré brings me up short every time. If he says everything comes in its own time, then by gum I believe him. And will leave Maal's nice new *Baayo* to the specialists. **A–**

Lobi Traoré: *Segou* (Cobalt import '96) Like his benefactor and cameo sideman Ali Farka Toure, Traoré is a Malian John Lee Hooker fan. Only he's faster and tighter. And he works with three drummers all the time. And he lets in several second guitarists, none of them Ry Cooder. And although I don't find them in the credits, I swear there are birds backing him on one cut. Supposedly he has something to do with blues. I hear Wassoulou circle games myself. **A–**

Lobi Traoré: *Duga* (Cobalt import '99) Mali's eternal round, described with the help of French blues harmonica ("Sogow," "Wolodennu," "Lala") ★★

Traveling Wilburys: *Vol. 3* (Wilbury/ Warner Bros. '90) A genre piece without a genre, this plays down the masquerade— Tom Petty's superstar equipment-storage problems coexist naturally with toxic golfers, blood-yellow skies, uppity wimmin, elusive wimmin, greedy wimmin, and of course beautiful wimmin. From the gal who's "got a body for business, got a head for sin" to riffs that date to when they were pups, it shows off just enough of the colloquial command of the old masters they hype themselves as. Inspirational

Verse: "Lift your other foot up/Fall on your ass/Get back up/Put your teeth in a glass." **B+**

Randy Travis: *Heroes and Friends* (Warner Bros. '90) Ⓝ

Randy Travis: "Better Class of Loser" (*High Lonesome*, Warner Bros. '91) 🦑

Randy Travis: *Greatest Hits Volume One* (Warner Bros. '92) The consumer fraud does his rep an injustice: put all 22 tracks from his two separately sold best-ofs on one CD, where they belong, and there'd be no doubting who's the preeminent country singer of our era. As laid-back as Lefty or Merle with more voice than either, he reaches down to muse in a bass every bit as conversational as the high baritone he beseeches with, and his hits never force an emotion or waste a word. He's a homebody rather than a honky tonker, and he flirts with genre exercise—Lefty didn't need to explain, "I come from the country," or peddle an antialienation homily like "Heroes and Friends." Nevertheless, his style is so consistent that the jumbled chronology will be inaudible to listeners who didn't date their lives by these songs. Not only will it convince you that the genre is his life, but that it has something to do with yours. **A**

Randy Travis: *Greatest Hits Volume Two* (Warner Bros. '92) One sign of how seriously Travis took his commercially chancy separate-disc best-of ploy is that he didn't stint with the bait cuts. Rather than bringing the collection down the way they usually do, four of the five previously unreleased songs on the two records are as classic and made-to-order as his style itself. Note, however, that on this less consistent volume the new ones are highlights. And that new title number five is a Travis-penned greeting card that brings the package to a close—and down. **A–**

Randy Travis: *Wind in the Wire* (Warner Bros. '93) Ⓝ

Randy Travis: *This Is Me* (Warner Bros. '94) give him decent material and let the poor guy be ("Small Y'All," "Gonna Walk That Line") ★

The Treacherous Three: *Old School Flava* (Wrap/Easylee '94) Their would-be comeback has the inconvenient and probably fatal peculiarity of gathering strength as it goes along. Cassette buyers should fast-forward to side two, which excites from "Ain't Nothin' Changed"'s hype beat to "Feel the New Heartbeat"'s eternal hook. And cultural nationalists should ponder "A True Story," in which ordinary show violence is made to seem both memorable and contemptible. Sure somethin"'s changed, and they know what it is. But they refuse to let it suck them in. **B+**

A Tribe Called Quest: *People's Instinctive Travels and the Paths of Rhythm* (Jive '90) Not Afrocentric enough to hear this indubitably progressive pastiche as a groove album, I cut-by-cutted it, and I'm glad I did. Though most of the second "side" remains subtler than is by any means necessary, it has more good songs on it than any neutral observer will believe without trying: the Afrogallic "Luck of Lucien," the slumming "After Hours," the cholesterol-conscious "Ham 'n' Eggs," the lustful "Bonita Applebum," the safe-sex "Pubic Enemy." Which latter, let me cavil, adheres to rap convention by sticking to gonorrhea, thus rendering AIDS Other-by-omission once again. Onward. **B+**

A Tribe Called Quest: *The Low End Theory* (Jive '91) dope jazzbeats and goofball rhymes from the well-meaning middle class ("Check the Rhime," "Buggin' Out") ★★★

A Tribe Called Quest: *Midnight Marauders* (Jive '93) Like so many "beats," *Low End Theory*'s Ron Carter bass was really a glorified sound effect—what excited its admirers wasn't its thrust, or even the thrill of the sound itself, so much as the classiness it signified. Kicking off with a disembodied computer voice promising "presentation precise, bass-heavy, and just right," this follow-up makes that bass rock the house, literally, and never contents itself with concept. Right, they "kick more game than a crackhead from Hempstead." But rather than "kick a

rhyme over ill drumrolls," as I don't doubt they can, they construct horn hooks I love better than I understand. **A–**

A Tribe Called Quest: *Beats, Rhymes and Life* (Jive '96) fighting sensationalist obscurity with philosophic subtlety, which I wish could work ("Jam," "Crew," "The Hop") ★★★

A Tribe Called Quest: "Rock Rock Y'All" (*The Love Movement,* Jive '98) 👁

A Tribe Called Quest: *Anthology* (Jive '99) "They provided the soundtrack for your life," annotator Selwyn Seyfu Hinds reminds the collegiate hip hoppers for whom Quest was the great crew of the '90s, politely failing to mention that for just that reason they don't need this record except to reconceive a catalogue they know by heart. But then there's the rest of us, for whom they've always been background music two ways—as the atmospheric stuff so many hip hoppers make of jazz and as the soundtrack to someone else's life. For us, these nonstop highlights are a godsend. Quest's swinging conversation unifies a sequence subtler and more musical than strict chronology would allow—the way two horny debut cuts poke in toward the end, say. Having added jazz bass to funky drum programmers to quiet flow to hooks-to-go to matter-of-fact realism-not-"reality," they convince our viscera what our brains allowed—that Quest was a great band. So if they want Roy Ayers, they can have him too. **A**

Tribe 8: *By the Time We Get to Colorado* (Outpunk '93) 🄽

Tribe 8: *Fist City* (Alternative Tentacles '95) lay back and trust the band, gal—also your own lyrics ("Freedom," "Barnyard Poontang") ★

Tribe 8: *Snarkism* (Alternative Tentacles '96) 🄽

Tricky: *Maxinquaye* (Island '95) From Soul II Soul to Massive Attack to Tricky is a straight line leading straight down to a bad place you should take a chance and visit. Depressive, constricted, phantasmagoric, industrial, yet warmly beatwise and swathed in a gauzy glow that promises untold creature comforts, these are the audioramas of someone who signed on to work for the wages of sin and lived to cash the check. Determinedly Lo-NRG, he's a sad sack with attitude, a complicated malcontent whose cynicism can't quash his capacity for euphoria or rebellion. And though he long ago saw through the willed optimism of black-Brit dance music, he's here to tell you that a dystopia with Martine singing in it has some serious rewards. **A+**

Tricky: *Pre-Millennium Tension* (Island '96) Far from an anomaly, "Tricky Kid" is definitive here, exploiting two moderately odious clichés—the woes of stardom and I'm-Tricky-and-you're-not—as if they're OK because he's Tricky and you're not. Rubbing our face in shit is his specialty, after all, and since everything else depresses him, why shouldn't that extend to his own success and his own arrogance? Whether you go along depends on how compelling you find his decon job on a hip hop soundscape that's discernibly rawer and starker here than on *Maxinquaye*. I say his music comprehends and inhabits the dystopia of everyday life more radically than Wu-Tang could conceive. And acknowledge that on this evidence, his trick requires Martine and can't work forever. **A–**

Tricky: *Angels with Dirty Faces* (Island '98) "Mellow" might have been recorded in a shipyard—augmenting Scott Ian's nagging if fetching guitar and Greg Lake's steady if seething drums is a rhythm element that suggests a boat whistle heard across a moonless harbor. Next track the artist makes his pop bid with a catchy femme-chorus refrain and a guest star: Polly Jean Harvey, what a draw! For another three songs a decent level of musical amenity is maintained: Martine's crooning tale of woe underpinned by low-register guitar/keyb riffs of unspecified origin and Calvin Weston's free drumming, three-note distorto hook beneath Tricky's speed-mumble, xylophonish tinkle countered by a keyb belch like an engine that won't catch. Thereafter the residues of grimy technologies settle into permanent low-level disorder: foghorns lowing, brakes complaining, clocks sounding across windswept nights, locomotives struggling uphill. He's a hater not a fighter, and the devil is in his details. So give that man a set of horns—he's earned them. **A–**

Tricky with DJ Muggs and Grease: *Juxtapose* (Island '99) As always with Tricky, the right idea for pop isn't necessarily just right for him. Beats, of course; songs, sure; a band, who could say no? And right, individual tracks connect pretty good—hot lesbian porn, you devil you. Yet though his soundscapes be obscure and forbidding, they're what he's great at; his rap affinities and rock dreams are off the point, especially in the studio. So the best thing about these shapely selections is that they remain obscure and forbidding as they stand up and announce themselves. Second-best is their scorn for criminal pretensions, always a boon from a borderline nihilist. **A–**

Travis Tritt: *T-R-O-U-B-L-E* (Warner Bros. '92) 🦅

Travis Tritt: *A Travis Tritt Christmas— Loving Time of the Year* (Warner Bros. '92) "'Free Bird'!" ("Silver Bells") ★

Trotsky Icepick: "Venus de Milo" (*The Ultraviolet Catastrophe*, SST '91) 🌀

Tru: *Tru 2 da Game* (No Limit '97) 🦅

The Derek Trucks Band: *The Derek Trucks Band* (Landslide '97) 🅝

The Derek Trucks Band: *Out of the Madness* (House of Blues '98) Butch's boy can play—also think ("Preachin' Blues," "Young Funk") ★★

John Trudell: *AKA Grafitti Man* (Rykodisc '92) Stubbornly utopian in the face of continuing defeat, hip to the way idealism succumbs to neurosis, his remixed compilation is a counterculture throwback that never seems dated. The settings, sharp studio-rock readymades keyed to the very '60s guitar of the late Jesse Ed Davis and spiced occasionally by Native American chants or drumbeats, can get you going, and Trudell takes them as his due. Making no attempt to sing, he bounces his recitations off their backboard like a beatnik discovering poetry-with-jazz, his timing and inflection devoid of hesitation or bad faith even though Kris Kristofferson's laconically off-key backup sounds harmonically sophisticated by comparison. It's as if nothing of musical moment has happened since *Highway 61 Revisited.* **A−**

John Trudell: *Johnny Damas and Me* (Rykodisc '94) 💣

Jennifer Trynin: *Cockamamie* (Squint/ Warner Bros. '94) Ⓝ

Tubuai Choir: *Polynesian Odyssey* (Shanachie '93) Ⓝ

Moe Tucker: *I Spent a Week There the Other Night* (Sky '94) Tucker's genius as the found drummer in the greatest of all bohemian bands was knowing the shortest distance between two points, and she maintained the knack as a divorced mother of five who couldn't make ends meet working for a Wal-Mart in Douglas, Georgia. It's rare enough for any artist to give this American archetype its due; when the archetype turns artist, it's a gift from the pop muse. Backed by a claque that includes John Cale and two Violent Femmes on these 1991 sessions, the self-taught rhythm guitarist lays down a crude, almost skeletal rock and roll that never suggests anything so highfalutin as minimalism and says what she has to say about poverty, sloth, shyness, and the idiocy of provincial life. There's also a love song to a daughter who has trouble loving back. And an "I'm Waiting for the Man" that's pure found minimalism. **A−**

Moe Tucker: *Dogs Under Stress* (Sky '94) saying less with more ("I Wanna," "Crackin Up") ★

Tina Turner: *Simply the Best* (Capitol '91) With its hyperstylized soul and dominatrix shtick, Tina's pop-queen phase is recommended to Madonna fans who fancy a more serious grade of schlock.

Except on straight love songs, which are rare, her production values will titillate your sensorium even if you're not in the mood—the dream hooker of Mark Knopfler's sexist fantasies come "true." **A−**

Tina Turner: *What's Love Got to Do With It* (Virgin '93) This respects literal chronology even less than the movie, which has her doing "Proud Mary" before Creedence released it. But there's a logic to the willy-nilly segues—in which, for instance, two glossily intelligent new products of her pop-diva phase, the thematic "I Don't Wanna Fight" and the pneumatic "Why Must We Wait Until Tonight?," flank B. B. King's 1964 "Rock Me Baby" and the Trammps' 1978 "Disco Inferno," neither of which has ever had her name on it before. In essence, she's reenacting her career as timeless myth, submitting every brilliant exploit and humiliating compromise to the unmatched lust and lustre of her 54-year-old pipes. She's never sounded more beautiful or more alive. Or more enigmatic—it's as impossible as ever to glimpse what she might be like in "real life," or even to pin down an artistic appeal that at this point seems to inhere in the raw fact of her survival. As for the sex, it's more abstract and calculated than ever. And right—love has nothing to do with it. **A−**

Tina Turner: *Wildest Dreams* (Virgin '96) Ⓝ

Tuscadero: *Step into My Wiggle Room* (Teenbeat '95) Ⓝ
Tuscadero: *The Pink Album* (Elektra/ Teenbeat '96) they want you to know they were gurls, leaving the grrrl question open ("Latex Dominatrix," "Dime-a-Dozen") ★★★
Tuscadero: *My Way or the Highway* (Elektra '98) songcraft as end-in-itself for as long as this contract shall remain in effect ("Not My Johnny," "Queen for a Day") ★

Shania Twain: *"God Ain't Gonna Getcha for That"* (*Shania Twain*, Mercury '93) 🐝

Shania Twain: *The Woman in Me* (Mercury '95) New Nashville's sexually liberated woman—proud, hot, and, especially, male-identified ("[If You're Not in It for Love] I'm Outta Here!" "Home Ain't Where His Heart Is [Anymore]") ★

Shania Twain: *Come On Over* (Mercury '97) Aside from its quota of musical sound effects, Twain's latest incarnation obviously has nothing to do with country. Setting out into the vast unexplored territory separating Garth from Madonna, she and husband-producer-cowriter Mutt Lange glance over at Gwen Stefani and take a few tips from Lange's old charges the Cars before arriving at a new pop formula that's all flirtatious ebullience and lively hooks. And miraculously, this discovery proves more exhilarating than a barrel of orgasms—the happy kind, none of your soul-shaking groaners. Not while this incarnation has juice, anyway. **A−**

21st Century Dub: "Beggars Suite Pt. I, II, III" (*Towering Dub Inferno* [comp], Rykodisc '90) 🐚

20 Toes: "Short Dick Man" (*Max Mix U.S.A.* [comp], Max '94) 🐚

22-Pisterpirkko: *Bare Bone Nest* (Spirit import '90) they have garages in Finland—speak English sometimes too ("Don't Play Cello") ★

Twinz: *Conversation* (Def Jam/RAL '95) 💣

2 Black 2 Strong MMG: *Doin' Hard Time on Planet Earth* (Relativity/Clappers '91) Hard, harder, hardest—fuck America, fuck daisy age, fuck you. The music of this Harlem crew is loud beats anchored to spare guitar, the hip hop obverse of death metal if death metal didn't always strain for drama. In between the bleakest, strongest crack track ever and realest, losingest prison track this side of the Lifers Group comes the autobiography of some Nino Brown or other, only the last we see of him he's still counting his money; fuck Bensonhurst, he says, but that doesn't stop him from enslaving his own people, and the rappers append no warning, no moral. Without reveling in brutality for its own sake, they state the amoral facts as they understand them—or misunderstand them, if it makes any difference. **B+**

2 in a Room: "El Trago" (*Max Mix U.S.A.* [comp], Max '94) 🐚

Two Kings and a Cipher: *From Pyramids to Projects* (Bahia '91) old-school beats, Egyptian mythology, looney tunes ("Daffy Wuz a Black Man") ★

2 Live Crew: *Banned in the U.S.A.* (Luke/Atlantic '90) 💣

Two Nice Girls: *Like a Version* (Rough Trade '90) I'm pleased to report that Karen Carpenter, Kim Gordon, Donna Summer, and—who's this?—Paul Rodgers provide fit company for the rowdy dyke anthem that threatens to swallow every other song they ever write. I'm impressed that I have have no idea where the other two covers come from. I'm disappointed that I don't much care. **B+**

Two Nice Girls: "The Queer Song," "Princess of Power" (*Chloe Liked Olivia*, Rough Trade '91) 🐚

II Unorthodox: "Just a Little Flava" (*The D&D Project* [comp], Arista '95) 🐚

2Pac: "Keep Ya Head Up" (*Strictly 4 My N.I.G.G.A.Z.*, Interscope '91) 🐚

2Pac: *Me Against the World* (Interscope '95) Tough-guy sentimentality is an old story in American culture, but self-pity this rank is usually reserved for teen romances and tales of brave avant-gardists callously rejected by the mass media. His I-love-Mom rings true because Mom was no saint, and his respect for old G's seems genuine, probably because they told him how smart he was. But whether the metaphor be dead homies or suicide threat, the subtext of his persecution complex is his self-regard. What's doubly galling is that these are essential hip hop themes—as Ice Cube and B.I.G. have made all too vivid, it is persecution that induces young black men to kill each other and themselves. That such themes should rise to the top of the charts with this witless exponent of famous-for-being-famous is why pop fans decry the mass media. **C+** 🕊️

2Pac: Greatest Hits (Death Row/Interscope '98) or anyway, greatest myths ("God Bless the Dead," "Keep Ya Head Up") ★

Type O Negative: "Unsuccessfully Coping with the Natural Beauty of Infidelity" (*Slow, Deep and Hard,* RoadRunner '91) 💣

Type O Negative: "Day Tripper (Medley)" (*World Coming Down,* RoadRunner '99) 💣

T/COMPILATIONS

Tapestry Revisited (Lava/Atlantic '95) 💣

A Taste of the Indestructible Beat of Soweto (Earthworks '94) Knowing it would be a waste to raid the seminal mbaganga compilation of the title, which is why his market niche might buy this one (and also why he has a market niche to begin with), Trevor Herman aims to match it out of the half dozen or so less perfect ones that followed. This is self-actualized and public-spirited, and damned if he doesn't come reasonably close. Steve Kekana and the Soul Brothers sweeten the mix, the Tiyimeleni Young Sisters show the Mahotella Queens how Shangaan women call their lover boy, and Mzwakhe Mbuli has the last word. **A**

Technosonic Volume 3 (Sonic '93) Only maniacs and ecstatics track techno subgenres, but since this comp is subtitled "A Journey into Trance," figure it's in "ambient" territory—that is, "boring." It's from Antler Subway Records in Belgium, a famous label for what that's worth, and the reason it isn't "boring" is that this trance seems designed to bring blood to the erectile tissues: "Drive My Body," "Sensual Motion," "Just Can't Get Enough," done mostly with rhythm and texture

rather than porny spoken-word come-ons. With a little poetic license you could call the first half the build to a relaxed orgasm. Relaxed by techno standards, anyway—in real-time measure, only maniacs and ecstatics fuck this fast for more than 30 seconds. The rest is more traditionally trancelike, with occasional forays into afterplay. Brian Eno could do a lot worse, and has. **A–**

Telephone Lobi/Telepone Love (Original Music '95) medium-statured persons of Ghanaian danceband highlife (Red Spots, "Oya Kae Me"; Professional Beach Melodians "Uhuru No. 2," "Akwantu") ★★★

This Is Ska! (Music Club '97) Ska compilations are a puzzlement—once you get the ramshackle groove, the supply of likable stuff you'd never heard expands toward infinity while the roll call of undeniable classics remains as brief as ever. Island instigated the confusion with *Intensified!* and *More Intensified!* almost two decades ago, and finally solved it with the first volume of the four-CD reggae overview *Tougher than Tough*. But this $10, 16-track, 44-minute alternative also strikes just the right mix of funky popsters (two Desmond Dekkers, one Jimmy Cliff) and loose-limbed groovemasters (their pace set by the Skatalites' "Guns of Navarone"). Prime MIAs: the unrepresented Prince Buster's "Al Capone" and Eric Morris's "Solomon Gundie," the latter available on Island's semiobscurantist new *Ska's the Limit,* which does unearth the archetypally out-of-tune sax solo of Lord Creator's "Independent Jamaica." Then there's Music Club's *This Is Ska Too!,* specializing (it says) in third-wave cover faves. Skank on. **A**

Tokyo Invasion, Volume I: Cosmic Hurushi Monsters (Virgin Import '96) Not counting the Boredoms, my knowledge of the 22 Japanese bands on this uproariously thrilling two-CD import is confined to the track listings. Disc two is too arty for anybody this side of the Boredoms, who in context sound weirdly middle-of-the-road and seriously funny, and yet the quiet stuff grew on me. "Martzmer" is almost pretty until the guitar kicks in at around 5:00, and on "Blood Stained Blossoms" even the guitar is pretty. But those are exceptions on a showcase for more ugly guitar than sane people think they want to hear—plus yelling and ranting and crooning and torture, funk song and distorto-metal and funeral march and noise experiments and riffs ad infinitum. Where other comps annoy by jumping from artist to artist, here the bands are so hard to take that each change comes as a relief—which instantly plunges the listener into yet another maelstrom of sensationalism. These carefully selected doses are probably all of this 'orrible stuff us rock and roll normals need. But need it we do. My thanks to Tony Herrington of *The Wire* for doing the dirty work. **A–**

Totally Hits (Arista '99) Of course it cheats—every compilation cheats. Inferior Sugar Ray, Monica, and Madonna, ringer from the hapless Five, awful hit from the imitable Sarah McLachlan. But given its BMG-WEA limitations, this is premier radio fodder. It rescues Cher and LFO from their meaningless albums as it repackages ace Whitney Houston and Deborah Cox remixes, and from "No Scrubs" to "Bawitdaba" it establishes a flow that sets off "Smooth" and "Ray of Light" and the formerly execrable "(God Must Have Spent) A Little More Time on You" as the touchstones they are. The mood is hiply happy and humane—the exceptions, a would-be suicide and some heavy yearning, mean only to prove that this is the real world, troubling at times but always manageable. The stylistic signature is keyb/electric guitar as acoustic guitar, rippling its quiet riffs over the intricate rhythms of a body at peace with itself. As composition, I find it as convincing, if not as elegant or organic, as Steve Reich's *Music for 18 Musicians* or Franco & Rochereau's *Omona Wapi*. Note, however, that the only energy rushes come from Cher's Eurodisco and the show-topping Kid

Rock, who's also the only true rapper here. It's a relief to know Arista needs him to put its lovely lies over the top. **A–**

Tougher Than Tough: The Story of Jamaican Music (Mango '93) Only residents and aficionados have heard half the 95 songs on this four-CD set, and I'm not going to tell you every one is an instant masterpiece. But I will tell you it doesn't much matter, because what's captured besides epiphanies, which are plentiful, are the homespun texture and limitless spirit of a musical culture that now stretches back 35 years. Lovingly or generously or just hegemonically, Island resists the temptation to overplay its own catalogue. Artists who were names on a page are brought to life by their moments in the sun, their place in the world of "Guns of Navarone" and "The Harder They Come" and "Police and Thieves" natural and secure, which in the end lends the classics a historical grandeur the label's earlier compilations don't suggest. What a miracle that one fucked-over little island should prove such a treasure house. And what a lesson. **A**

Township Jazz 'n' Jive (Music Club '97) Before mbaqanga's stomping bumpkin intensity swept the townships, small jazz-style ensembles played indigenous tunes with a South African beat you could jitterbug to. This is that music, the same urbane mode cherry-picked so infectiously on the *Mandela* soundtrack: the swinging jive of the '50s, when social dancing was a passion in every slapped-together apartheid ghetto. Far suaver than mbaqanga or kwela yet no less African, far simpler than Count Basie or the Mills Brothers yet no less artful, it implied an indoor space even if it couldn't always find one big enough for its spiritual ambitions. Its matchless buoyancy is mostly a matter of two learned rhythms coming together. But it evinces an unsinkability nobody would ever puncture. **A**

Trance 2 (Ellipsis Arts . . . '95) Moroccan Gnawas, Turkestanian Sufis, and Balinese

Hindus, none carrying Discmen or coming down from human-made drugs (Halimi Chedli Ensemble, "Touhami Dikr") ★★

Tresor II: Berlin-Detroit . . . A Techno Alliance (NovaMute '93) 🍒

Trespass (Sire/Warner Bros. '92) why hard dies hard (AMG, "Don't Be a 304"; Ice-T and Ice Cube, "Trespass") ★

A Tribute to Curtis Mayfield (Warner Bros. '94) all eyes stay on the prize (Bruce Springsteen, "Gypsy Woman"; Tevin Campbell, "Keep On Pushin'"; Narada Michael Walden, "[Don't Worry] If There's a Hell Below, We're All Going to Go") ★★

A Tribute to Stevie Ray Vaughan (Epic '96) he's dead, his band isn't (Jimmie Vaughan, Eric Clapton, Bonnie Raitt, Robert Cray, B. B. King, Buddy Guy, Dr. John, Art Neville, "SRV Shuffle"; Bonnie Raitt, "Pride and Joy"; Robert Cray, "Lovestruck Baby") ★★★

Tricky Presents Grassroots (Payday/FFRR '96) respect his way with the rappers, love his way with the ladies (Tricky & Laveda Davis, "Devils Helper"; Stephanie Cooke, "Live w/ Yo Self") ★★★

Tropicália Essentials (Hip-O '99) Relics of a cultural revolution—14 1967–1969 songs, all but the Tom Zé written by Caetano Veloso or/and Gilberto Gil and most performed by them. Although these songs outraged their world merely because they weren't Brazilian enough, what's striking at this distance is the Brit specifics of their internationalism, idealizing not the hippie '60s of spaced-out pastoral but the mod '60s of trippy pop. For all the deep rhythms and avant-garde sounds, the guitars are drunk on *Revolver* and *Out of Our Heads*, the orchestrations full of *Blow-Up* and *Modesty Blaise*. Decades later, we can hear how Brazilian their cheese and lyricism remained. But these particular Brazilians were the premier melodists of their generation, and they considered it trippy to juxtapose bright, rebellious music against grim anti-junta fables. Translations provided—read them. **A–**

Turntable Tastemakers Issue No. 1: The Sound of Cleveland City Recordings (Moonshine Music '94) Rarely if ever has steady-state techno sustained so unfailingly for the length of a compilation. Jungle-ish in its body-friendly moderation if not its unexotic sonic range, a single U.K. label's telling hooks, medium-fast mean tempo, and simple, humane, faintly Caribbean beats pull in the impartial listener rather than beating the hesitant dancer over the tympanum. Let the fogies snort when I say it kind of reminds me of Booker T. & the M.G.'s. **A–**

Two Rooms—Celebrating the Songs of Elton John & Bernie Taupin (Polydor '91) Where most tribute albums hitch second-raters to the famous fans who've been sweet-talked into signing on, this superstar showcase aims to turn the tributees into de facto titans, minting much moolah in the process. Sinéad O'Connor was born to cover, and Rod Stewart is reborn for a day. But the material proves less than titanic—it's just plastic, inspiring or enabling Eric Clapton, Tina Turner, Joe Cocker, even the Beach Boys and the Who to construct simulacra of their better selves. As for Sting, Hall & Oates, Bruce Hornsby, Jon Bon Jovi, Wilson Phillips, Phil Collins, and even George Michael, they don't have better selves—they have accidents, none of which happen here. **B–** 🦃

UV

UB40: *Promises and Lies* (Virgin '93) 🎸
UB40: *The Best of UB40 Volume 1* (Virgin '95) what shall it profit a great white reggae band if it should gain the world and sell its own soul? ("One in Ten," "Rat in Mi Kitchen") ★★★

U-God: *Golden Arms Redemption* (Wu-Tang '99) nothing special as a rapper, so sometimes he sings even worse—but unflappably, which is the point ("Hungry," "Night the City Cried") ★★

James Blood Ulmer: *Blues Preacher* (DIW/Columbia '94) Ⓝ
The James "Blood" Ulmer Blues Experience: *Live* (In + Out import '94) The advantage of this live album over Ulmer's studio blues isn't choice material but excess guitar. He's a more proficient (jazz) composer than (r&b) songwriter and a more exciting player than either. His funky rhythm section has slipped into blues-rock, and that he was one of the first jazzmen to understand why Hendrix treated his axe as a noisemaker doesn't mean he commands Hendrix's palette—although he's gotten louder with the years, he still reverts to single-string lines. But with Sonny Sharrock dead, he smokes the competition. Guitar diehards should get hip to this wild, solid cross-section of a seminal genre buster. **B+**
The James "Blood" Ulmer Blues Experience: *Blues Allnight* (In + Out import '96) Ⓝ

James "Blood" Ulmer: See also Music Revelation Ensemble, Odyssey Band, Third Rail, Calvin Grant Weston

Ultramarine: *United Kingdoms* (Sire/Giant '93) 🎸

Uncle Tupelo: *No Depression* (Rockville '90) 🎸
Uncle Tupelo: *Anodyne* (Sire/Reprise '93) Ⓝ
Uncle Tupelo: "Effigy" (*No Alternative* [comp], Arista '93) 💣

Underworld: *Second Toughest in the Infants* (TVT '96) Americans enticed by talk of "rock"-dance fusion should bear in mind the cultural deprivation of our siblings across the sea. Befuddled by the useless "rock"-"pop" distinction, they believe "rock" is something that happened in the '70s. The more inquisitive among them are aware of Pearl Jam and Nirvana, but if they've ever heard of Los Lobos or Hüsker Dü they probably think they're "pop." So check out these comparisons from *admirers* of this inflated trio, spawned by the famously bad new-romantic band Freur and an "art collective" others might call an advertising agency: "pre-stadium Simple Minds," "way beyond the length of a Frank Zappa guitar solo," "J. J. Cale on an ecstasy comedown," "a warm bath." Plus their proper predecessors Pink Floyd "with bigger bass sounds and better drum patterns." Here and there—eight minutes into "Kiteless," for instance—they do work up a

---

★★★, ★★, ★ Honorable Mention   💀 Choice Cut   Ⓝ Neither   🎸 Dud   🦃 Turkey

dangerously off-kilter groove. But the lyrics of *Animals* were more than "insane ramblings" or "the colours of cars going past a friend's house." And *Ummagumma* had more purity of purpose. **C+** 🐛

Underworld: *Beaucoup Fish* (JBO/V2 '99) 💣

Unkle: *Psyence Fiction* (Mo Wax/London '98) not beautiful (or weird) enough for its own beats ("Celestial Annihilation," "Guns Blazing [Drums of Death Part 1]") ★

Unrest: *Imperial f.f.r.r.* (TeenBeat '92) You read it here first: the scattered actual "pop" songs on this 11-cut album—the one about eating pussy is the most enthusiastic—tend to break down into long, repetitive, self-consciously inept codas, which blend in the mind's ear with the scattered instrumentals per se. It would be wrong to call such passages drones, because drones propel, and propulsion would be catering to the hoi polloi—"patterns" is quite kind enough. Cool people whose hobby is inept bands seem to think these whatchamacallems apotheosize self-consciously amateurish charm. If you're among them, call me when you get a life. **C** 🦃

Urge Overkill: *The Supersonic Storybook* (Touch and Go '91) Mix-and-match bohemian one-upsmanship brings us . . . what is this, anyhow? Fashion-plate metal? Lothar-EOAOR? I'm obviously no judge of their . . . what are those, designer leisure suits? Indeed, the Chicago mafia may believe I'm no judge of their metal/AOR either. But bohemian one-upsmanship I know, and these guys are so deep in hype Maurice Starr is lucky they're too old to be new kids. With their sludgy hooks, whiner groans, and arrogant exoticism, they're about as "subversive" as a spirochete—a social disease waiting to happen. **C** 🦃
Urge Overkill: "Sister Havana" (*Saturation,* Geffen '93) 💿

Usher: *My Way* (LaFace '97) the sweetest nonvirgin a mama could ask ("Just Like Me," "You Make Me Wanna . . . ") ★

Usher: *Usher Live* (LaFace '99) 💣

US3: "Cantaloop (Flip Fantasia)" (*Hand on the Torch,* Blue Note '93) 💿
US3: *Broadway & 52nd* (Blue Note '97) they got the beats ("Come On Everybody [Get Down]," "Sheep") ★

Utah Saints: *Utah Saints* (London '92) The first single-artist techno album you can take home to your stereo swallows the *Something Good* EP and spits out the bones, cannibalizing it the way it cannibalizes everything else. Grounded in DJ Tim Garbutt's factitious funk and the low-register, high-energy synth blare of Belgian new beat, it marshals aural images of mass excitement—football match, soul concert, symphonic crescendo—into a bold-faced synthesis of two kinds of phony grandeur: disco's and arena-rock's. Its trance-dance strategy is to transform Philip Glass into a raver, the perfect pomo extension of techno's sometimes irritating, often hilarious fondness for the classical tradition. The most exciting thing to happen to Annie Lennox since childbirth. More fun than a batch file of monkeys. **A–**

U2: *Achtung Baby* (Island '91) 💣
U2: *Zooropa* (Island '93) I've never seen the point of hating U2. Their sound was their own from the git, and for a very famous person, Bono has always seemed thoughtful and good-hearted. I liked what I read about their pop irony too. Problem was, I couldn't hear it—after many, many tries, *Achtung Baby* still sounded like a damnably diffuse U2 album to me, and I put it in the hall unable to describe a single song. But having processed this blatant cool move, I'm ready to wax theoretical. *Achtung Baby* was produced by Daniel Lanois, and Daniel Lanois isn't Brian Eno—he's Eno's pet romantic, too soft to undercut U2's grandiosity, although I admittedly enjoy a few of its anthems-in-disguise now. *Zooropa,* on the other hand, is half an Eno album the way *Low* and *"Heroes"* were. The difference is that Bowie and Eno were fresher in 1977

than Bono and Eno are today. Each must have hoped that the other's strength would patch over his own weakness—that Eno's oft-wearisome affectlessness would be mitigated by Bono's oft-wearisome expressionism and vice versa. But tics ain't strengths, and although these pomo paradoxes have their moments, when I'm feeling snippy the whole project seems a disastrously affected pastiche of relinquished principle. B– 🦃

U2: *Pop* (Island '97) 💣

U2: *The Best of 1980–1990* (Island '98) hit hooks that live off the guitarist's mysterioso lyricism, B sides that fall back on the singer's humanist egotism ("I Will Follow," "Pride [In the Name of Love]") ★

Vandals: *Peace Thru Vandalism/When in Rome Do as the Vandals* (Time Bomb '95) Ⓝ

Luther Vandross: *Love Power* (Epic '91) Ⓝ

Luther Vandross: *Never Let Me Go* (Epic '93) Ⓝ

Luther Vandross: *Greatest Hits* (Epic '99) Ⓝ

Van Halen: *For Unlawful Carnal Knowledge* (Warner Bros. '91) 💣

Van Halen: *Best of Volume I* (Warner Bros. '96) preening for the spotlight, they can be funny and spectacular—until Sammy Hagar horns in ("Jump," "Runnin' with the Devil") ★

Van Halen: *Van Halen 3* (Warner Bros. '98) 💣

Vanilla Ice: *To the Extreme* (SBK '90) You idealist you—you thought rap couldn't get blander than Hammer. Fact Is, It can get blander than this "mediagenic" white man, but for now he's mugger one. His suave sexism, fashionably male supremacist rather than dangerously obscene, is no worse than his suave beats, Hollywood Florida going Hollywood USA. At least Hammer's simple samples are fun sometimes. C– 🦃

Dave Van Ronk: *Going Back to Brooklyn* (Gazell '91) the most steadfast of the original folkies—and the funniest ("Another Time and Place," "Garden State Stomp") ★

Dave Van Ronk: *To All My Friends in Far-Flung Places* (Gazell '94) Ⓝ

Dave Van Ronk: "Garden State Stomp" (*Christine Lavin Presents Laugh Tracks Volume 2* [comp], Shanachie '96) 🐚

The Vaselines: *The Way of the Vaselines: A Complete History* (Sub Pop '92) Sloppy, silly, barely on the four much less the one, the 19-song studio output of Kurt Cobain's favorite obscure pub band is one of those punk revelations that makes you think anyone can do it just when you were convinced nobody ever would again. The pro in potentia is Eugene Kelly, now of Eugenius; the genius is his then-girlfriend Frances McKee. Toon topics include an acid trip, a dead cat, Catholicism, and coitus, which undergoes an array of ironically far-out genderfuck jokes that bespeak detailed experience of actual fucking. Kelly says the group broke up over "sexual differences." I'm sure he deserved no better. A–

Stevie Ray Vaughan and Double Trouble: *The Sky Is Crying* (Epic '91): Elmore James with chops—too many sometimes ("Boot Hill," "Close to You") ★★★

Stevie Ray Vaughan and Double Trouble: *In the Beginning* (Epic '92) live and unfledged, 4/1/81—blues as a barely controllable torrent of electric sound ("Shake for Me," "Tin Pan Alley") ★★★

Stevie Ray Vaughan and Double Trouble: *Greatest Hits* (Epic '95) Vaughan was the greatest traditional guitarist of his generation, his true mentor Jimi Hendrix even if Johnny Copeland and Albert King were hands-on. Like Hendrix he put sound before notes and playing before writing. Hence *Live Alive,* the perfect place to go with the torrent. But like Hendrix he could do the other stuff too. Here's believing. A–

Stevie Ray Vaughan and Double Trouble: *Live at Carnegie Hall* (Epic '97) Ⓝ

Stevie Ray Vaughan and Double Trouble: *The Real Deal: Greatest Hits Volume 2* (Epic/Legacy '99) shameless reshuffle though it is, it maintains a caught-in-the-act feel for a good hour ("Love Struck Baby," "Leave My Girl Alone [Live]") ★

Stevie Ray Vaughan: See also Albert King

The Vaughan Brothers: *Family Style* (Epic Associated '90) dance music from Jimmy and Nile ("White Boots," "Hard to Be") ★★★

Alan Vega/Alex Chilton/Ben Vaughan: *Cubist Blues* (2 13 61 '96) 💣

Suzanne Vega: *Days of Open Hand* (A&M '90) Right off she declares for the new realism: "Oh mom/The dreams are not so bad/It's just that there's so much to do/And I'm tired of sleeping." About time, too—only she can't take it. She's politically alienated and not too thrilled about that abortion. She throws up her hands at the future. She's decorous, tuneful, art-directed. And she gets her title, whatever it means, from the one called "Book of Dreams." **B–** 🐛

The Veldt: *Afrodisiac* (Mercury '94) 💣

Velocity Girl: *Copacetic* (Sub Pop '93) Ⓝ

Caetano Veloso e Gilberto Gil: *Tropicália 2* (Elektra Nonesuch '94) Playful, pretentious, political, speculative, and above all gorgeous, this collaboration is enough to make me stop carping about kitsch and wonder whether samba isn't the pop avant-garde after all. Gil gains a beguilingly arty patina as he grounds Veloso's precious lyricism, and if the translations reduce primal beauty to intelligence, that's what we get for never studying Portuguese. Not only do the airy tunes and shimmering beats promise an endless summer, they prove heat needn't addle the brain. **A–**

The Velvet Underground: *Live MCMXCIII* (Sire/Warner Bros. '93) PSA: booklet notwithstanding, deprogram 4–6 to avoid John Cale singing "All Tomorrow's Parties" and "The Gift" ("Some Kinda Love") ★

Vengaboys: *The Party Album!* (Groovilicious '99) 💣

Tom Verlaine: *Warm and Cool* (Rykodisc '92) Ⓝ

Veruca Salt: *American Thighs* (Minty Fresh/DGC '94) Who cares whether it's "real" or not? However much Nina Gordon, Louise Post, and their bepenised rhythm section sound like the Breeders, you could tell the two apart in a blindfold test (probably). But the confluences overpower the divergences anyway, and good. Commercial calculation is as irrelevant here as they're-just-a-band gender-has-nothing-to-do-with-it crapola. Whatever their motives and existential reality, they're less coy, less goofy, clearer melodically, and surer of their rhythmic turf at least in part because the Breeders got over, thus diminishing (but not eliminating) their felt need for diversionary tactics in a continuing project of aesthetic reconceptualization—creating a pop-rock style that steers between male-identified canons of manipulative pseudocertainty and female-identified canons of pseudoconfessional sensitivity. At present, what they say with that style means less than how coherently and attractively they configure it. If and when they become (even) better artists, it won't. **A–**

Veruca Salt: *Blow It Out Your Ass It's Veruca Salt* (DGC '96) two catchy-not-poppy A's, two sludgy-not-grungy B's ("Shimmer Like a Girl," "I'm Taking Europe with Me") ★★★

Veruca Salt: *Eight Arms to Hold You* (Outpost '97) striving toward bar band to be born ("Straight," "Benjamin") ★

The Verve: "The Drugs Don't Work" (*Urban Hymns,* Vernon Yard '97) 🕭

The Verve Pipe: *Villains* (RCA '96) Although bands like this still offend idealists, you can't call them pseudoalternative anymore, because they don't bother pretending. They're just rockers who crash the album chart, where the money is, from the singles chart, where they're supposedly no longer welcome—in other words, pop bands who can play their axes. There's San Francisco's gold-certified Third Eye Blind, whose little sex kinks are too catchy to get het up about. There's Orlando's double-platinum Matchbox 20, whose breakthrough hit some mistakenly (as is always claimed) believe promotes spousal abuse. Much worse than either is this near-pseudoalternative one, grown men from Michigan who released two indie albums before their major-label debut catapulted to platinum on a soggy prowoman morality tale aimed at frat rats, who are urged not to drive girls to suicide by dumping them. When Brian Vander Ark finally emotes the chorus, it's like, I dunno, grunge lives. **C** 🐸

The Vindictives: *The Many Moods of the Vindictives* (Lookout '95) ⓝ

Vio-lence: *Torture Tactics* (Megaforce/Caroline '91) Corporate-censored off the Atlantic-backed *Oppressing the Masses,* the title track reflects thrash-metal's chronic confusion between politics and horror comics. "Gutterslut" ("Gonna make this bitch bleed") and "Dicks of Death" ("Suck it, whore") reveal the lighter side of earnest nihilists who have hormones after all. Plus a live remake equals an EP. I prefer the major-label version. **C–**

Violent Femmes: *Add It Up (1981–1993)* (Slash/Reprise '93) No deep thinker and probably a jerk, Gordon Gano is the good-looking cad in a collegiate picaresque, putting himself across on feckless charm and endless libido. Most will grant the Femmes' 1983 debut its cult status and leave it at that, but the 19 titles otherwise unaccounted for on this typically irresponsible compilation suggest that they stayed young through the '80s. They get away with countless variations on the hoary "America is the home of the hypocrite"—"I Hate the TV," "Old Mother Reagan," "Lies," it goes on—and sell a lyric that

begins and ends "Dance, motherfucker, dance!" They score with obscure erotic escapades like "Gimme the Car" and "Out the Window." And having rendered the titillating faux-folk gothic of "Country Death Song" and the rank jungle fever of "Black Girls" doubly offensive with bad-boy cuteness, they then somehow make them illustrate a shallow postfolkie primitivism they transcend by exploiting. Their demiacoustic sound the essence of inspired amateurism even when surrounded by horns, sitars, Jerry Harrison, Michael Beinhorn, they remain funny, sexy, sloppy, irreverent, unpredictable, and above all lively—still unconvinced they'll ever have to worry about their permanent record. **A–**
Violent Femmes: **"Don't Start Me on the Liquor"** (*New Times,* Elektra '94) 😎

Virunga: *Feet on Fire* (Stern's Africa '91) Samba Mapangala is no titan—just a persistent pro with studio smarts whose career path took him to East Africa instead of France. A women's wedding song retrofitted with male chauvinist lyrics provides a stolen high. There are telling touches from English session men playing sax and accordion. And the record is definitely his kind of soukous anyway. **B+**
Virunga: See also Samba Mapangala

Viva la Musica & Papa Wemba: See Papa Wemba

Volebeats: *Sky and the Ocean* (Safe House '97) neotraditionalism across the pop guitar-band spectrum ("Two Seconds," "Don't I Wish") ★

The Voluptuous Horror of Karen Black: *The Anti-Naturalists* (Triple X '95) ⓝ

Voodoo Child: *The End of Everything* (Trophy import '96) 💣

Vova Nova: *Vova Nova* (Chameleon '92) ⓝ

Voyager: **"Rhythm Dream"** (*Zoo Rave 1* [comp], Zoo '92) 😎

The Vulgar Boatmen: *Please Panic.* (Safe House/Caroline '92) as if one of those shapeless arguments where you just can't concentrate on your partner's complaint were love, sweet love ("You're the One," "You Don't Love Me Yet") ★★

UV/COMPILATIONS

Ultimate Christmas (Arista '98) chestnuts roasting on an open fire plus surprise gifts—but who invited Kenny, Carly, Sarah, Luciano? (Aretha Franklin, "Winter Wonderland"; Luther Vandross, "O Come All Ye Faithful") ★★★

United Kingdom of Punk: The Hardcore Years (Music Club '98) "Perhaps I'm not too clever, perhaps I'm not too bright," yowls Mensi on the debut single from the Angelic Upstarts, who at least I've heard before. Four of these circa-1980 bands are on *Oi!—The Album,* two are on *Carry on Oi!,* here's the good ol' Anti-Nowhere League, and that's it—Stateside, these yobs were lucky to see the inside of an import store. None are clever and none bright, at least not so's they'll tell you about it, because where in American hardcore the us-against-them is about age, in Britain it flouts class in all its manifestations—not just money but manners, education, culture. So above all they're rude—the Pistols, the Clash, and Generation X are limp-wristed art wankers by comparison. The rant can get tedious—a song called "Free Speech for the Dumb" ought to be smarter. But 20 years after we sussed that British fascism looks more like a middle-aged housewife than a boot boy downing pints at a football match, these antieverything anthems prove that anyone who pegged them as a menace was neither clever nor bright. **A–**

United Kingdom of Punk 2 (Music Club '99) live tracks, demos, and now-obscure gems from the first golden era (999, "Homicide"; the Lurkers, "Cyanide") ★

Uptown Lounge (The Right Stuff '99) Rarely have more black singers I dislike been gathered in one place. Billy Eckstine and Arthur Prysock, Lena Horne and Carmen McRae, Nina Simone and Sarah Vaughan, Lou Rawls and Nancy Wilson, Bobby Short and Sammy Davis Jr.—the grand and the genteel, the expressionistic and the arty, the smarmy and the pop pop pop. But after dozens upon dozens of hi-fi "lounge" comps, at least three of which I tried my damnedest to get through, they all do justice to old songs worth hearing. It's a credible, likable, enjoyable rendering of the pseudosophistication ginheads have been promoting since the second coming of Esquivel. The secret is that for once even Short and Horne sound comfortable in their bodies. This is not something I'd say about Esquivel or most ginheads. And comfort, ladies and gents, is supposed to be what lounging is about **A–**

Uptown MTV Unplugged (Uptown/MCA '93) 💣

URBMix Vol. 1: Flammable Liquid (Planet Earth '94) L.A. DJ Doc Martin's steady bass roll (Paperclip People, "Throw"; Freaky Chakra, "Transcendental Funk Bump") ★★

Vibrant Zimbabwe (Zimbob '94) Ⓝ

The Waco Brothers: *... To the Last Dead Cowboy* (Bloodshot '95)
The Waco Brothers: *Cowboy in Flames* (Bloodshot '97) Buck and Ringo notwithstanding, country music doesn't come naturally—not to city slickers, or city neoprimitivists either, especially Brits. So of course transplanted Chicagoan Jon Langford grasps it more palpably now than he did in 1985. And if this can't very well make us forget *Fear and Whiskey,* at least now we know the W. Bros.' debut was only a run-through. "White Lightning" and "Big River" will obviously impress anyone innocent of Jones and Cash. But Langford's remakes add a last-chance soul both songs put to use, and eventually, many of the originals surpass them. Leaving a radical postcountry record that begins in a "suburb of Babylon" and ends snorting the ground-up bones of "the Jones and the Caashizz." A–
Waco Brothers: *Do You Think About Me?* (Bloodshot '97) their "militant honky tonk" could stand some "Nashville songcraft" ("Hard Times," "Revolution Blues") ★★
Waco Brothers: *WacoWorld* (Bloodshot '99) The more you listen to Jon Langford—or see him live, where he'll spout wisecracks for hours—the more impressive his verbal facility seems. But Deano is an equal partner in this particular metaphor system, which defines country music as the great lost conduit of white male working-class desperation. Langford tends toward the grimly matter-of-

fact: "That's why they're called bars, 'cos they keep me inside," "But I'll paint myself back out/Of this corner everytime." Deano is more visionary, as in "Pigsville," where you wake up next to your own chalk outline, or "Hello to Everybody," where aliens abduct you to "a warmer planet/Where there is no consequence." Both sing so lustily that the band's indifference to the niceties of country as it exists in history is of no consequence. When the milder-voiced mandolinist Mr. Tracey Dear takes the mike, however, the illusion pales. A–

Bunny Wailer: *Gumption* (Shanachie '90)
Bunny Wailer: *Just Be Nice* (RAS '93)

The Wailers: *The Never Ending Wailers* (Tuff Gong '93)

Loudon Wainwright III: *History* (Charisma '92) at its best, why he needs the men's movement; at its worst, why you don't ("Talking New Bob Dylan," "Hitting You") ★
Loudon Wainwright III: *Career Moves* (Virgin '93) Wainwright has aged no better than most likable bad boys, maybe worse. His promising-to-excellent young songs turned gamy in the '80s—how many rueful immaturity jokes can one over-30 sing?—and though some claim he grew up with *History,* its *Iron John* sensitivity was a cover for the same old self-involvement. But by sampling the highs of his over-30 output while eliding its numer-

---

★★★, ★★, ★ Honorable Mention   🐚 Choice Cut    Neither   💣 Dud   🦃 Turkey

ous flubs, this constitutes a summing up. Framed by two unembittered accounts of how he makes his living and dotted with illustrative patter, it has its heart-tuggers ("Your Mother and I," written to explain the inevitable breakup to his and Suzzy Roche's daughter), but mostly it presents him as what he is—a talented wag who came in his cummerbund, dropped clown acid, and never became a star. It should cheer any over-30 bad boy who can forget that his spotty sex life and pathetic adventures in substance abuse will never be as entertaining as this born entertainer's. It may also convince the bad boy's squeeze that things could be worse. **A**

Loudon Wainwright III: *Grown Man* (Virgin '96) In a music where scions of the upper-middle class are supposed to camouflage their cultural impoverishment, one of the many irritating things about L-III is that he's never bothered. Another is his great subject, which boils down to divorce whether the metaphor is his kids or his mom or his waitress. Here, however, the metaphor surpasses itself on at least four songs—about a jerk doing the women's-lib hustle after the porch door has closed, a philandering father and his faithless son, who then becomes a father who meets his daughter on her first birthday, and an older daughter who gets the last word because her father scripts it for her. "That Hospital," which is about life and death, is where his belated maturity comes from. Don't bet it lasts. **A–**

Loudon Wainwright III: *Little Ship* (Charisma Records America, Inc. '98) jape, jape against the dying of the light ("Four Mirrors," "So Damn Happy") ★★★

Loudon Wainwright III: *Social Studies* (Hannibal '99) commentary not protest, and usually worse for it ("Tonya's Twirls," "Pretty Good Day") ★

Rufus Wainwright: *Rufus Wainwright* (DreamWorks '98) Just like the daddy he so much doesn't want to grow up like, this mother's son is a born clown who hits the racks awash in poetry. Since he's also a mind-boggling original, however, next-

big-thingers are sure to fib about the pleasures of his debut. He can write, and he'll write better; his voice has no obvious precedents, and he'll learn to define it. But for the nonce what he has to offer depends mostly on his piano, played to suggest amateur lieder or the accompaniment at rehearsals of *Oklahoma!,* and the compositional gift of a melodist whose songs seldom snap shut on a sure-shot refrain and incur no discernible debt to blues materials. Especially as embellished by Van Dyke Parks, whose nutball Americana has been waiting for Wainwright since Brian Wilson vacated the premises, his talent is too big to let pass. And if that doesn't make his hyperromanticism easier to take, there's no point being narrow-minded. *Kate & Anna McGarrigle* it ain't. But a hell of a lot more actualized than *Loudon Wainwright III.* **B+**

Tom Waits: *The Early Years* (Rhino '91) Ⓝ

Tom Waits: *Bone Machine* (Island '92) ace arranger in thrall to four-flushing singer-songwriter ("Goin' Out West," "All Stripped Down," "I Don't Wanna Grow Up") ★★

Tom Waits: *The Black Rider* (Island '93) prime collaborators, could use a libretto ("Russian Dance," "Crossroads," "That's the Way," "I'll Shoot the Moon") ★★★

Tom Waits: *Beautiful Maladies: The Island Years* (Island '98) Whereas my favorite moments on Waits's many inconsistent albums—the pop parody-throwaway "I'll Shoot the Moon," the rawly elegant "All Stripped Down"—avoid the American grotesquerie he's overrated for, these 23 self-selections do not. As your designated bean counter I note that 10 of them come from *Swordfishtrombones* and *Rain Dogs,* which hold up as totalities. Yet even when I program around those 10, this also holds up as a totality, persuading me that the main reason Waits is overrated is that he's never given up on himself. Over more years than most reprobates have in them he's covered more ground than most boho-lowlife shtick has room for—in a cockeyed, wildly varied body of songs that find form in a music nobody dares call lounge-rock because Kurt Weill and Leadbelly will come back and feed them to the fishes if they do. This is a sound with no interest whatsoever in glamour, even as something to make fun of. When it meshes, who can niggle about the literary and vocal affectations of such a hell of a bandleader? **A–**

Tom Waits: *Mule Variations* (Epitaph '99) Between 1985 and 1993 Waits managed to seem prolific while generating exactly one album that wasn't tied to a film or theater piece. Between 1993 and 1998 he managed to remain mythic while generating occasional occasional songs and a rumor that he'd split with his wife. So it's a pleasure to report that his best record since *Swordfishtrombones* has Ms. Kathleen Brennan all over it, which he's proud to testify is why it's also his kindest record ever: "She puts the heart into all the things. She's my true love." Together they humanize the percussion-battered *Bone Machine* sound, reconstituting his '80s alienation effects into a Delta harshness with more give to it—enough to accommodate a tenderness that's never soft. Sure "Eyeball Kid" is a sick joke about a freak show; sure "Big in Japan" is a send-up about a failure. But by the blues-drenched reconciliation hymn "Come On Up to the House," he knows how lucky he is: "Come down off the cross/We can use the wood/Come on up to the house." **A–**

Rick Wakeman: *The Art in Music Trilogy* (Music Fusion import '99) You thought he'd died and gone to his reward, and so did the All-Music Guide, where his timeline ends in the '80s, but his discography tells a different tale: easily the most prolific "rock" artist of the '90s, manufacturing "instrumental new world ambient music" and God knows what else at a staggering clip. *Night Airs, Aspirant Sunrise, Aspirant Sunset, Black Knights in the Court of Ferdinand IV, Phantom Power, Softsword: King John and the Magna Charter* (sic), *A World of Wisdom,* and *2000 A.D. into the Future* get us only to the end of 1991, and he's kept it up—by my count, 35 albums in the decade, including this recent set, all three discs of which I swear I listened to while awake. Brief pieces suffused with the twixt-strings-and-keyboard echoes that are the special curse of synthesizers on today's auriculum, they favor harpsichord over piano and will dabble in anything a synth can, including drums and voices. The first disc "The Sculptor," is the most soporific, which isn't a dis—"The Writer" gave me insomnia, and not because I blamed myself. **D** 🦃

The Walkabouts: "Stir the Ashes" (*Scavenger*, Sub Pop '91) 👁

Joe Louis Walker: *Preacher and the President* (Verve '98) Ⓝ

Scott Walker: *It's Raining Today: The Scott Walker Story (1967–70)* (Razor & Tie '96) Nothing I'd read about this L.A. wannabe turned moody Brit teenthrob—going back to Nik Cohn's *Rock from the Beginning,* which pegged him as "top-heavy and maudlin" in 1968—prepared me for how purely godawful he'd be. We're talking Anthony Newley without the voice muscles, "MacArthur Park" as light-programme boilerplate, a male Vera Lynn for late bloomers who found Paul McCartney too r&b. Go ahead, believe Nick Cave, Oasis, Foetus, and, I cannot tell a lie, compiler Marshall Crenshaw. But I'm warning you—when I gave him the benefit of the doubt, all I got was this lousy review. **C–** 🦃

The Wallflowers: *The Wallflowers* (Virgin '92) 💣
The Wallflowers: *Bringing Down the Horse* (Interscope '95) Ⓝ

Don Walser: *Rolling Stone from Texas* (Watermelon '95) 💣

Robert Ward and the Black Top All-Stars: *Fear No Evil* (Black Top '90) He played guitar on the Falcons, "I Found a Love." He started the band that became the Ohio Players. He hired on with Norman Whitfield. All of which could add up to not much when he's carrying an artist's load, except that he's a better-than-average writer, a hooky arranger, and a sneaky soloist you remember for the wobbly sound of his Magnatone amp alone—a sound that's seeped into his singing. Add the Neville Brothers' label of last resort and you have the black-trad trinity attempting the comeback of a lifetime—soul, blues, and New Orleans in one person. Also, he loves his wife and knows how to say so. **A–**

Robert Ward: *Rhythm of the People* (Black Top '93) 💣

Warda: *Lebanon/Algeria* (Metro Blue '97) The Parisian-born daughter of an Algerian nightclub owner who fled with her family to Lebanon in 1956, she shed most of her Algerian accent before hitting the Egyptian studios in 1960 and is now tabbed by an informed source as "one of the Arab world's great musical hacks." But for most Americans, this CD ain't really about Warda. Rather, her richly generic pan-Arab emotionality provides a way into Cairo's pop mysteries. Hyped up by the beats modern taste demands, the string sections of what used to be called ughniyah sound a lot fresher than TSOP's or Goldie's. And the beats have more uses than the belly-dancing websites her lyrics show up on. **A–**

David S. Ware: *Flight of i* (DIW/Columbia '93) eso blowing sessions and pop beatdowns from the grandest, breathiest sax ever to come out of a loft ("Aquarian Sound," "There Will Never Be Another You," "Infi-Rhythms #1") ★★

Justin Warfield: *My Field Trip to Planet 9* (Qwest/Reprise '93) just the kind of "beatnik," "B-boy on acid," "black Jew," and "drugstore cowboy" rap as a form is ripe for ("Dip Dip Divin'," "Drugstore Cowboy") ★★

Warrant: "Cherry Pie" (*Cherry Pie*, Columbia '90) 🗑

Wartime: *Fast Food for Thought* (Chrysalis '91) Black Flag goes electrofunk ("Right to Life") ★

Was (Not Was): *Are You Okay?* (Chrysalis '90) With soulful Sweet Pea Atkinson fulfilling their authenticity quota and sarcastic David Was rapping like he thinks Stanard Ridgway is Kool Moe Dee, they diddybop nasty as they wanna diddybop along the edge of racial presumption, certain of their right to give "Papa Was a Rolling Stone" to Papa's number-one son and to feel "better than James Brown" (whatever that means in 1990) even though they know they're gonna sideswipe his sexism two tracks later. Sure they're shallower than they wanna be half the time, in the geopolitics especially. But even then they're sort of funny. **A–**

Crystal Waters: "Gypsy Woman (She's Homeless)" (*Surprise*, Mercury '91) 👁
Crystal Waters: *Storyteller* (Mercury '94) Ⓝ

Muddy Waters: *Blues Sky* (Epic Associated/Legacy '92) He hasn't quite been reduced to an industry, but the profusion of product since the three-CD *Chess Box* is transforming oeuvre into catalogue. The luxurious and intimate *Folk Singer* remaster, the seminal and historic *Complete Plantation Recordings* dig, even the rare and unexceptional *One More Mile* vault-scrape are worthy addenda to said catalogue. But although this selection from his four post-Chess LPs with Johnny Winter may be on the wrong label, it's the one Mud to buy if you're buying more than one. Beat way big, slide and harp all over the place, it reasserts his virility as it establishes his droit du seigneur. In 1983, just after he turned 68, McKinley Morganfield died. In 1980, he was a 65-year-old mother fuyer. **A–**

Muddy Waters & Friends: *Goin' Way Back* (Just a Memory import '97) Ⓝ
Muddy Waters: *Paris, 1972* (Pablo '97) Ⓝ

Muddy Waters: *The Lost Tapes* (Blind Pig '99) Live Muddys are flooding the market on multiple labels, with differences in quality slighter than they want you to know, but real nonetheless. What makes this well-recorded two-venue combo the choicest has more to do with sound, repertoire, and intangibles of commitment than with changing casts of axeslingers and harmonicats—the big man's basic slide is always what stands out in his bands anyway. Here he is in 1970, reasserting his distance from the just-deceased Leonard Chess's rock dreams—an old-fashioned artist returning to his legendary strengths. By Pablo's 1972 Paris disc he's gotten just slightly complacent; by Just a Memory's 1977 Montreal gig, which has better but more familiar songs, he's relaxed into a seigneurial blues entertainer. Here he still has something to prove—or find out. **B+**

Muddy Waters: *Hoochie Coochie Man* (Just a Memory import '99) Montreal 1977—the old man shows off his second drawer and takes some standards to school ("Kansas City," "Nine Below Zero") ★★★

Norma Waterson: *Norma Waterson* (Hannibal '96) **Ⓝ**

Mike Watt: *Contemplating the Engine Room* (Columbia '97) Credwise, Watt's got it all. He was the fulcrum of a great band, he's serious with a sense of humor about it, he's got not just politics but class consciousness, he talks a great game, and, oh yeah, he networks like crazy. The only thing he isn't is a compelling artist. He can't sing at all, can't write much, and still pretends the bass solo is a viable musical form. Like fIREHOSE, like his name-dropping solo debut, this "punk rock opera" ("I just hate the words 'concept record.' That's fucking tired-ass, where opera's funny") looks great on paper and hasn't been played for a year by anyone it impressed. It will prove a valuable resource for the numerous forthcoming doctoral dissertations on the alternative rock subculture. **C+** 🦃

We: *As Is* (Asphodel '97) Attentive repose their prerequisite, ambient and jungle their coordinates, these heady New York futurists construct tracks from just two or three elements—always a keyb riff/figure/drone/moo, decked out with drum 'n' bass speedbeat, slurping electrosuck, old-fashioned stereo phasing, bird tweets, even the occasional human voice. Making up for flavorless stretches like the well-named "Dyed Camel Skins," the decorations gather mystery with rhythmwise repetition. Sit back and enjoy a cool one. **A–**

We: *Square Root of Negative One* (Asphodel '99) sounds from the dark side ("Diablos," "Gaya's Kids") ★

Ween: *Pure Guava* (Elektra '92) It's to the half-credit of these Bucks County wise guys that the studio amenities of their major-label debut impel them toward fucked-up sounds, which come hard, rather than fucked-up songs, which they write without thinking (and how). But I don't buy the claim that they'll do anything for a laugh. Ever since they went on about pussy for nine minutes (good idea) in a Princey blues-minstrel drawl (bad one), I've assumed they were the kind of rec-room gigglefritzes who enjoy a good nigger joke when they're sure their audience is sophisticated enough to enjoy it. And to be perfectly honest, I don't hear one of those here. **C+** 🦃

Ween: "Spinal Meningitis (Got Me Down)" (*Chocolate and Cheese*, Elektra '94) 🍭

Weezer: *Weezer* (DGC '94) **Ⓝ**

Scott Weiland: *12 Bar Blues* (Atlantic '98) 💣

Gillian Welch: *Revival* (Almo Sounds '96) Who cares if her polka-dot dress is a costume rather than a heritage? She's got as much right to be a folkie as 10,000 mediocrities and a few dozen geniuses before her. Iris DeMent is a custodian's daughter, Lucinda Williams a poet's daughter, Bonnie Raitt a musical comedy star's daughter, yet from their differing authenticities each has said something unique about the rural South and everyday people. Welch is a songwriting team's daughter who, as is more common, hasn't—not yet, probably not ever. She just doesn't have the voice, eye, or way with words to bring her simulation off. Unless you're highly susceptible to good intentions, a malady some refer to as folkie's disease, that should be that. **B–** 🦃

Gillian Welch: *Hell Among the Yearlings* (Almo Sounds '98) **N**

Kevin Welch: *Beneath My Wheels* (Dead Reckoning '99) **N**

Paul Weller: *Heavy Soul* (Island '97) Forget the dance comps clogging the top 10 of a land that now believes 1988 was 1977. Never mind who the Lighthouse Family might be. If you want to know how little U.S. and U.K. share anymore, pull out your cherished copy of Weller's acclaimed 1993 comeback (wha?) *Wild Wood* and note that in its roots-AOR wake the artist to whom this minor punk is now compared is Neil Young. **C** 🦃

Papa Wemba: *Le Voyageur* (EarthBeat! '92) **N**

Papa Wemba et Viva la Musica: *Papa Wemba et Viva la Musica* (Sonodisc import '94) *fromage Afropop à la mode Parisienne* ("Oldies Are Goodies," "Moyi") ★★

Papa Wemba: *Emotion* (RealWorld '95) Ominously, this made-for-export enlists Jean-Philippe Rykiel, whose strange keyb technique—suggesting a cross between eternal transcendence and drowning grilled asparagus in Velveeta melt—already permeates Keita's *Soro* and N'Dour's *Wommat*. But with the neofolkloric Lokua Kanza also on hand, its 11-tunes-in-38-minutes constitute the most appealing crossover Wemba has yet devised for the voice his hopes come down to. Piercing and penetrating without a hint of muezzin, he also commands a "natural," "conversational" timbre richer and rangier than that of his more soft-sung Zairean colleagues. A singer you should hear in a showcase you can find. **A–**

Viva la Musica & Papa Wemba: *Pole Position* (Sonodisc import '95) As an excellent soukous record, this is indeed a return to form for the most excellent of active soukous artists. "Endena (Unfukutanu)" is one of those grooves so eternal that it seems to (a) go on longer than its near-seven minutes and (b) approach eternal life rather than endless tedium in the process. And for sure the accordion beats any synthesizer not counting the one that generates it. But whether all of this would so excite the Afropop faithful if Wemba hadn't just compromised himself credibly for Peter Gabriel I honestly can't fucking tell. **A–**

Papa Wemba: *M'zée Fula-Ngege* (Sonodisc import '99) At his New York dates of the past few years, the soukous sapeur seemed both enervated and inflated by the labor of Anglophone crossover, and he puts out so many records in Paris that some doubt he can remember one from the other. But here, at greater length than on any '80s album, he rings in his 50th year with superabundant pizzazz. The new touch—there's generally a new touch—is a xylophone. The old touches are the now sweet, now rich, now cutting leads, the varisized choruses, the assured shifts of tempo and mood, the synths emulating flutes and horns and innerspring mattresses. In the right frame of mind, *il reste toujours magnifique.* **A–**

Wenge Musica: *Bouger Bouger* (Africassette '94) indigenous, understated neoclassic 1988 soukous, replete with tasty-not-speedy guitar ("Bakolo Budget," "La Fille du Roi") ★★

Paul Westerberg: *14 Songs* (Sire/Reprise '93) Like most know-nothings—"Knowledge is power/Got your books, go read 'em"—he equates freedom with individualism and wisdom with unbridled sentiment. But the Replacements were a monument to bad faith by the end, and being as it's time for him to shit or get off the pot, he shits. "Things," to a woman who deserves better than the guy who wrote this song, will tempt you to forgive the songpoems about junkyard flowers and runaway winds. "Down Love" and "A Few Minutes of Silence" are new ways to say shut up. You'll want to hear that riff again—that one too. Because his official solo debut is considerably more raucous than *Don't Tell a Soul* or *All Shook Down.* **B+**

Paul Westerberg: *Eventually* (Reprise '96) too mean because he's not as important as he thinks he is, too irrelevant because he's not as important as he should be ("These Are the Days," "MamaDaddyDid") ★★

Paul Westerberg: *Suicaine Gratification* (Capitol '99) what gives this fool the right to ruminate all over your earhole is his trick cocktail piano ("Whatever Makes You Happy," "Final Hurrah") ★

Calvin Grant Weston: *Dance Romance* (In + Out '96) Blood's strongest studio blues, in part because he's not the leader ("Preview," "Chocolate Rock") ★★

Westside Connection: *Bow Down* (Priority '96) If you think East Coast Illuminati fantasies are silly, wait till you hear the "*gangsta rap* in its highest form" that Ice Cube and two like-minded liars counter with. Not only that, they threaten to cut off the scrotum of "All the Critics in New York." Gosh, I sure hope they don't mean mine. **D+** 🦃

Whale: *We Care* (Virgin '95) In which three media pros—a female VJ, a hot producer, and the hip host of a tongue-in-cheek talk show—buy into the new international pop hegemony, in which neatness not only doesn't count but marks you a square. Could come out a prefab pseudomess, except they're Swedish, far enough away from it all that they still mean their we-don't-care. They have fun as they "just have fun." Their jolly insults are indistinguishable from their jolly fucks, their candy tunes from their skronk guitar. They're so good you have to think

twice to remember which two tracks Tricky helped out on. **A–**

Whale: *All Disco Must End in Broken Bones* (Virgin '98) 💣

Catherine Whalen's Jazz Squad: *Catherine Whalen's Jazz Squad* (Mammoth '99) Ⓝ

Wheat: *Hope and Adams* (Sugar Free '99) falling-apart love songs for a broken world ("Body Talk [Part 2]," "Slow Fade") ★★★

Caron Wheeler: *U.K. Blak* (Capitol '91) 💣

Cheryl Wheeler: "I Know This Town" (*Circles and Arrows,* Capitol '90) 🐚

Whiskeytown: *Strangers Almanac* (Outpost '97) Ⓝ

Barry White: *The Icon Is Love* (A&M '94) "You know time has played a very important role in our relationship/It was time that first brought us together and/It's time that we separate and leave each other" ("Practice What You Preach," "Whatever We Had, We Had") ★

Dr. Michael White: *Live at the Village Vanguard* (Antilles '92) if not Dixieland without corn, then Dixieland with spirit, smarts, chops, and a sense of the present ("Lord, Lord, Lord") ★

Don White: *Live at the Somerville Theatre* (Lyric Moon '95) Of the 11 cuts on this debut CD, only six are songs, because this 37-year-old Massachusetts home alarm system installer is my favorite kind of folksinger—a comedian. His laugh lines wear down like anybody else's, but not before he's poked holes in both the working-stiffs-if-they're-lucky of Lynn, where he comes from, and the folkies-if-anything of . . . what's that fancy name they call Harvard? Macadamia? . . . for whom an employee of America's largest marshmallow·fluff factory is as exotic as a native of Fiji. And not before he's convinced me his 16-year marriage has a reasonable shot at 60. **A–**

Don White: *Rascal* (Lyric Moon '97) two cans of Niblets beyond the great song-poet of the actually existing lower-middle class he's too modest to be ("Po' Po' Baby," "Great Day," "Nowhere Tornado") ★★★

Don White: *Brown Eyes Shine* (Lumperboy '99) White gigs every weekend, mostly tiny folk venues and "private shows"—gather some friends in your rec room and he'll make it worth everybody's while. Yet though he lives just 220 miles away, he hasn't hit Manhattan since 1996, because his wife says he has to come home with more money in his pocket than when he left. And come home he does. Thus he stands as the only folkie I can think of who's never footloose or romantically bereft—his subject matter, most of it autobiographical, is domestic, focusing here on parent-teen relationships. The monologue where his brain explodes after a homework discussion with his 14-year-old can only be understood by someone who's been there, and anyone who's been there will immediately play it again. With or without his band he's a strained singer with an unmediated New England accent and barely a guitarist at all, and when he isn't funny he's corny. But usually he's original enough to turn corny into a virtue. **A–**

Michael White: "One of My Near Mrs." (*Familiar Ground,* Warner Bros. '92) 🐟

White Zombie: *Astro-Creep: 2000* (Geffen '95) 🎣

Barrence Whitfield with Tom Russell: *Cowboy Mambo* (EDC '93) Ⓝ

Chris Whitley: *Living with the Law* (Columbia '91) Ⓝ

Chris Whitley: *Din of Ecstasy* (Columbia '95) 🎣

Keith Whitley: *Greatest Hits* (RCA '90) His best came last, and only those who already love the ingrained sorrow and liquored-up ease of *I Wonder Do You Think of Me,* which provides the four finest performances on this record, should invest in the glimmers it compiles: the way his brave front breaks through such Nashville formula as the cute longing of "Miami, My Amy," the lust at first sight of "Ten Feet Away," the terse lovewords of "When You Say Nothing at All." And in "Tell Lorrie I Love Her," recorded in his living room two years before he died, a voice from beyond the grave tells us he could have sung his best any time the smart boys were ready to package him that way. **B+**

Keith Whitley: *Kentucky Bluebird* (RCA '91) postproduced (which is good) outtakes (which isn't) ("Backbone Job," "I Never Go Around Mirrors") ★★

Keith Whitley: "Light at the End of the Tunnel" (*Wherever You Are Tonight,* BNA '95) 🐟

Keith Whitley: "Don't Our Love Look Natural" (*The Essential Keith Whitley,* BNA '96) 🐟

The Who: *Live at the Isle of Wight Festival 1970* (Columbia/Legacy '96) Commemorating a signal moment in rock history—the day Sony got a piece of the Who. **C+** 🦃

Whoopi and the Sisters: "Ball of Confusion (That's What the World Is Today" (*Sister Act 2* [ST], Hollywood '93) 🐟

Wilco with Syd Straw: "The T.B. Is Whipping Me" (*Red Hot + Country* [comp], Mercury '94) 🐟

Wilco: *A.M.* (Sire/Reprise '95) realist defiance grinding sadly down into realist bathos ("Casino Queen," "Box Full of Letters") ★★★

Wilco: *Being There* (Reprise '96) Is a two-CD package that could fit onto one conning consumers, taking on airs, or wallowing in nostalgia for a lost time when songs were songs and double albums were double albums? All three. Yet there's no point denying Jeff Tweedy's achievement as long as you recognize its insularity. His simple melodies, felt vocals, and easy stylistic sweep all evoke a past when roots music came naturally, from bluegrass to the Rolling Stones—a past he preserves by removing it to the privacy of his head and your sound system. There's no dynamism to his music—the rockers are slackers, the hooks essentially atmospheric. Yet as objects of contemplation both have their power and charm. **B+**

Wilco: *Summerteeth* (Reprise '99) old-fashioned tunecraft lacking not pedal steel, who cares, but the concreteness modern popcraft eschews ("Summer Teeth," "She's a Jar") ★★

Bo Dollis & the Wild Magnolias: *I'm Back* (Rounder '90) 💣

The Wild Magnolias: *The Wild Magnolias* (Polydor '93) Like *The Wild Tchoupitoulas,* where Allen Toussaint hung vocals on the Meters, *The Wild Magnolias* is a producer's record. What's made it legendary isn't its documentation of Mardi Gras Indians but the myth Willie Tee hangs on his guitaristic funk. It jams on and on, a pseudofolkloric *Get on the Good Foot,* yet it's as taut as the Magnolias' faux field recording with Ron Levy is slack. This digital version adds five tracks for 11 in all, including carnival songs the Tchoups took over and the astonishing nine-minute call-and-response Monk Boudreaux builds off "Shoo fly, don't bother me." In 1974 I might have found it repetitive. Now I think it jams on and on and on. **A–**

The Wild Magnolias: *Life Is a Carnival* (Metro Blue '99) the New Orleans Funk Repertory Orchestra ("Pocket Change," "Pock-a-Nae") ★

Dar Williams: *Mortal City* (Razor & Tie '96) 💣

Dar William: *End of the Summer* (Razor & Tie '97) ◐

Hank Williams Jr.: *America (The Way I See It)* (Curb '90) Even known assholes don't come up with concept albums slavering to send our "top guns" after Saddam (sounds like "Satan"), complaining to Lincoln about "nuisance suits," and advocating the freelance murder of miscreants who beat the rap (he claims). Take it as proof that Monday night football is a right-wing plot. And ask the RIAA why his guns 'n' vengeance don't rate a warning sticker. **C–** 🐢

Hank Williams III: *Risin' Outlaw* (Curb '99) Unlike so many musical scions, he's got the equipment—songs he wrote, songs he didn't write, lonesome whine, pissed-off groove, rebel drawl, rebel attitude. But except when it comes to devil's daughters, he lacks the power to convince anyone that he's reinventing rather than reclaiming—that this is expression as well as art. "I plan on livin' long," he boasts, and that's something to brag about. But sometimes there's a cost. **B+**

Lucinda Williams: *Sweet Old World* (Chameleon '92) On two songs as lived in as their titles, "Lines Around Your Eyes" and "Something About What Happens When We Talk," a star-crossed poet of the everyday grows into middle-aged love. The fetishized tire iron and casserole of "Hot Blood" romanticize attraction and commitment with a lit major's passion. And then there's death. The most powerful track on this Springsteen-meticulous work of songcraft is the raw, bare, strophic threnody "Pineola," where the truest poetic stroke is the bereftly banal "And they went to call someone." So, do the boys who inspired "He Never Got Enough Love" and "Little Angel, Little Brother" actually die, by which I mean fictionally die? Maybe not, but it sounds like they do. Death is how she knows the world is sweet. Music is how she tries to convince the rest of us. **A**

Lucinda Williams: *Car Wheels on a Gravel Road* (Mercury '98) Williams hasn't just perfected a style, she's mastered a subject. She doesn't just write realistically and music traditionally, she describes and evokes Southerners for whom realism and traditionalism are epistemological givens. She writes *for* them too—not exclusively, she hopes, but in the first instance. They are her people and her neighbors, with damn few media-savvy professionals among them. So reassuring shows of hip come no more naturally to her finely worked, cannily roughed-up songs than pop universality. Situated in a subculture far removed from both Manhattan and Alternia, these indelible melodies and well-turned lyrics constitute a dazzling proof of the viability of her world and a robust argument for its values. Emotion makes you smirk? Local color has no place in your global mall? Well, you have Lucinda Williams to answer to. Because this is where she establishes herself as the most accomplished record-maker of the age. **A+**

Robbie Williams: *The Ego Has Landed* (Capitol '99) Ⓝ

Vanessa Williams: *Greatest Hits: The First Ten Years* (Mercury '99) 💣

Victoria Williams: "Summer of Drugs," (*Swing the Statue!,* Rough Trade '90) 🗲

Victoria Williams: *Loose* (Mammoth '94) Whimsy's not a pose or an aesthetic decision with this woman, it's who she is, and there's no use blaming her for it. Instead, gauge how far you can tolerate her quirks and proceed accordingly, because she's finally transformed her folksy positivism into a worldview worthy of her talent—or maybe honed her talent into a winning vehicle for her worldview. Either way I suspect the reason is less that she's seen the flip side of eternity than that she can no longer doubt how many people love her. It's a responsibility, that much affection—makes you track down those inspirations, finish those songs, get up and go to the studio no matter how scared you are. Makes you not just love back but say why. **A–**

Victoria Williams & the Loose Band: *This Moment in Toronto* (Mammoth/Atlantic '95) Ⓝ

Victoria Williams: *Musings of a Creekdipper* (Atlantic '98) There's eccentric and then there's loopy, and this fragile, well-named follow-up is loopy; *Loose* could be a Peter Asher record by comparison. Williams ruminates around with

trap washes and a tentative piano fanfare before delivering a discursive, indirect opener, and is moved to recollect the entrancing "Kashmir's Corn" before settling into more declarative material, as in: "I'd like to take this time to complain about the train!" Give it time and you could fall hard. Bucolic dreamers aren't my cup of branch water either. **A–**

Sonny Boy Williamson: *Keep It to Ourselves* (Alligator '90) With his unerring slur and direct wit, Sonny Boy II, born Rice Miller circa 1897 and dead some 68 years later, is Chicago's third W: his great Chess albums stand with Wolf or Muddy. These 1963 recordings, culled from two much sparer purist LPs on a Danish label, are late-night visits to the Delta where he saw the light and kicked the bucket, and what they show off above all is his sexy, long-suffering harmonica cry. Where fools like his star pupil James Cotton strain against the dynamic limitations of that little piece of steel, Sonny Boy plays it ike he sings it like he talks it—slyly, lethally, whispering complaints, secrets, existential questions, and promises made to be broken to anyone who ventures within earshot. Guitarist Matt Murphy on most cuts and pianist-vocalist Memphis Slim on a few are all the friends he needs. **A–**

Sonny Boy Williamson/Willie Love: *Clownin' with the World* (Alligator '93) Ⓝ

Kelly Willis: *Well Travelled Love* (MCA '90) in love with her own voice, which deserves it, and him for listening, which is a mistake ("My Heart's in Trouble Tonight," "River of Love") ★★

Kelly Willis: *Bang Bang* (MCA '91) Up till the Joe Ely conceit she goes out on, this 22-year-old doesn't get a single lyric worthy of her lusty-voiced appetite for decent love. She claims she'll wrap her pipes around any original her drummer husband hands her, but since the five on the debut are down to two here, there's reason to hope that next time her Nashville handlers will put her in touch with an actual female songwriter. Would

Lucinda Williams be asking too much? **B+**

Kelly Willis: *Kelly Willis* (MCA '93) Willis loves singing like George Jones loves singing, like Rosanne Cash loves singing, and once a fella notices how hard she tries and how strong she feels, he'll want to hug and kiss her till that smile is back on her pretty little face. But though the tunes are her solidest yet, Don Was's Billy Bremner guitar and Jellyfish harmonies don't set them off any more clearly than Tony Brown's neoclassical taste did. That's mostly because Willis's idea of a good lyric is a simple lyric. No wordplay, no narrative, no trenchant details—just the musical statement, alive and direct. OK honey, if you say so. But I still think maybe you should join that T-group with K.T. and Mary Chapin. **B+**

Kelly Willis: *Fading Fast* (A&M '96) at four tracks in three years, she's not gonna pick a title song called "Going Strong" ("Fading Fast," "Aren't I True") ★★★

Kelly Willis: *What I Deserve* (Rykodisc '99) Still has that enormous voice. Still has big-time man problems. Still tries too hard to feel. Will never reveal how scared she is inside. Will never sweep all before her. Still tries to do the right thing. Still sounds better the closer you listen. Still has that enormous voice. **B+**

Will to Power: *Journey Home* (Epic '90) Auteur-fuehrer-rapper Bob Rosenberg's unprecedented meld of disco cheese and heavy pop-rock proves yet again that originality and fatuity aren't mutually exclusive—especially if you don't take originality too far. Of the 10 songs here, Rosenberg wrote eight. These do not include (10cc's) "I'm Not in Love," the highly belated follow-up to his 1988 Skynyrd-Frampton medley, or "Boogie Nights," to which he adds the moving if redundant confession, "It took some remakes to get your attention." They do, however, include the six-minute spoken-word-cheesy-pop-heavy-disco-rock "Koyaanisqatsi," a political manifesto as daring and thoughtful as anything dreamed by Jello Bangladesh or Minions of Dull Chords. Quoting Jefferson, Whitman, Emerson, Wilde, his man Nietzsche, Solzhenitsyn, and the National Rifle Association, Rosenberg declares free speech useless and sweet reason all, while coming out in favor of animal rights, the Second Amendment, and robbing the rich—an exemplary melange of the one-stop individualism that's long passed for politics in every wing of the rock counterculture. Words to live by: "Death before dishonor, as it were." **C** 🐛

Brian Wilson: *I Just Wasn't Made for These Times* (MCA '95) Ⓝ
Brian Wilson and Van Dyke Parks: *Orange Crate Art* (Warner Bros. '95) Ⓝ
Brian Wilson: *Imagination* (Giant '98) Wilson's genius has never been as indelible or universal as worshipers believe. Generating illusions of eternal sunlight or crafting frames for crackpot solipsism, he was magical; stripped by Don Was or cambered by Van Dyke Parks, he was at least interesting. Submitting to adult-contempo tycoon Joe Thomas, however, he's just what you'd fear: a middle-aged pop pro who's proud he's no longer nuts and knows even less about the world than when he was. The lead cut has a happy tune, the dark finale some dysfunctional intimations. In between, he makes too much of attendant hacks and gestures at old glories from a failing high end. **C** 🐛

Cassandra Wilson: *Blue Light 'Til Dawn* (Blue Note '93) respects her texts at long last ("Come on in My Kitchen," "Sankoma") ★
Cassandra Wilson: *New Moon Daughter* (Blue Note '96) Compelled to pretend they're superior to the pop text as well as the pop tune, encouraged to express rather than interpret but forbidden to ignore the words, too many jazz singers have trouble figuring out what to make of their material. And however admirable Wilson's independence of so-called classic pop, most of these songs escape her attentions without a mark on them. Which isn't to mention the "Strange

Fruit" that establishes the surpassing weirdness of Billie's original, or the disastrous Monkees cover, designed to prove she has a sense of humor I'm now convinced isn't there. **B–** 🦃

Cassandra Wilson: *Traveling Miles* (Blue Note '99) Ⓝ

Wilson Phillips: *Wilson Phillips* (SBK '90) Genealogically, Chynna's group—the elaborately arranged professional folk-rock of her mama and papa, rather than the obsessively reworked private surf-rock of Carnie and Wendy's boyish dad, is where their (and the world's) polished pop comes from, and their fashion sense is Laurel Canyon a land grab later. Finicky and well manicured though it is, it's not without its intricately minor pleasures, notably on compositions untouched by the singers' hands—"Impulsive," or (Gunnar and Matthew, why didn't you think of this?) "Eyes Like Twins." The '60s myth "The Dream Is Still Alive" they claim as their own. **C** 🦃

Winger: *In the Heart of the Young* (Atlantic '90) The pall pop metal casts upon 1990's horrendous Hot 100 is a triumph of mass narrowcasting. By downplaying anything blatant in the music, marketers minimize tuneouts based on accidents of gender or subgeneration—potentially, any passive Caucasian under age 25 should be willing to consume (in descending order of marginal differentiation) Poison or Warrant or Jon Bon or Heart or Cheap Trick or David Goddamn Cassidy. So let the nadir stand in for all of them. Swallowing hooks from blooze to prog, masking their will to power in fake vulnerability and youthcult rote, Winger is Whitesnake with the sexism muted and the face-lifts down the road. They may last a while, they may not. They're so bad that they're not even completely terrible. **C–** 🦃

Wingless Angels: *Wingless Angels* (Mindless/Island Jamaica '97) Ⓝ

Wipers and Greg Sage: *The Best of Wipers and Greg Sage* (Restless '90) Gun Club Meets Suicide—Guitars Win ("Romeo," "Nothing Left to Lose") ★

Wir: *The First Letter* (Mute/Elektra '91) The idea that asking a small tier of machines to stand in for drummer Robert Gotobed jolted them back to their original vision doesn't hold up against their original sound, which was starker and drier than this even after they'd gone art-rock. But vision and sound aren't the same, and here everything decentered and acerbic in the eerie, fluent electrodisco they fashioned upon returning—everything that kept their fans hoping they'd return for real—is upped a notch. Now let's hope they devolve. **A–**

Wire: *The Drill* (Mute '91) 💣

Wire: *1985–1990: The A List* (Mute '93) Those who disdain Wire's second coming don't understand how the Sex Pistols and ABC could have been born of the same impulse. First freeze-drying punk, then rendering neodisco slick into Teflon sausage casing, this band knew. And by now they've recorded more memorable music than the Pistols and ABC put together—while maintaining an aesthetic distance so severe they make Sham 69 and Frankie Goes to Hollywood seem archetypal by comparison. To program this summum they invited supporters to vote on their finest recent moments, then laid the highest finishers end to end until the CD was full. Number 16 does drag. **A**

Wire: *Behind the Curtain* (EMI import '95) For *Pink Flag* as opposed to Wire cultists, and of course there's a difference. We prefer them at their punkest, fastest, and shortest, as with the many titles on this 1977–78 outtakes comp that didn't make any of their first three albums or the *On Returning* best-of, all 17 of which fit easily on one side of a C-60. These include the five live songs not on *Roxy London WC2*—"Mary Is a Dyke"! "New York City"! "After Midnight"! (Eric Clapton's!)—as well as preliminary settings for riffs that will resurface in other guises. The other 14 tracks are punker, faster, shorter, louder, and/or rougher versions of songs Wire cultists have never forgotten and never mind hearing again. **B+**

Witchdoctor: *. . . A S.W.A.T. Healin' Ritual* (Organized Noize/Interscope '98) 💣

Howlin' Wolf: *Ain't Gonna Be Your Dog* (Chess '94) Muddy's marginalia slip past when you're not listening. Wolf's always register—two hour-long discs containing 42 U.S.-uncollected tracks (including a mere smattering of acoustic versions and alternate takes), and not a song just makes nice and lies there. Even when he's only stretching his lungs, his voice fills the room, and from jump blues to pop soul, all attempts at commercial affability are swamped by his huge natural sound. Plus a bunch of horn arrangements that somebody up there probably thought were too bizarre or raggedy or something. The thing about Wolf is, he can never be too anything. **A–**

Peter Wolf: *Up to No Good* (MCA '90) 💣

Lee Ann Womack: *Lee Ann Womack* (Deeca '97) Ⓝ
Lee Ann Womack: *Some Things I Know* (Decca '98) reclaiming female feistiness, which is as close as Nashville gets to feminism ("I'll Think of a Reason Later," "The Man Who Made My Mama Cry") ★

Womack & Womack: *Family Spirit* (RCA '91) Ⓝ

Stevie Wonder: *Music from the Movie "Jungle Fever"* (Motown '91) a genius even when that's all he's selling ("Jungle Fever," "Fun Day") ★★★
Stevie Wonder: *Conversation Peace* (Motown '95) Sure you can take him for granted. He's as set in his ways as Neil Young or John Updike, his lyrics complacent mush even when he's preaching against handguns or "man's inhumanity to man." But overlaying track after track alone in his studio, he's a font of melody, a wellspring of rhythm, a major modern

composer. So if at some level you've heard all this before, that doesn't mean it's worn out its welcome. And the seven-minute groove-sound workout "Cold Chill" will make you check back to make sure he's ever been better. **A–**
Stevie Wonder: *Song Review: A Greatest Hits Collection* (Motown '96) if comp you must, *Original Musiquarium* is on CD, and the good rarities here you can somehow do without ("Hold on to Your Dream," "Redemption Song") ★

Worl-a-Girl: "No Gunshot (Put Down the Gun)," "Ten Commandments" (*Worl-a-Girl,* Chaos/Columbia '94) 💿

The World Famous Beat Junkies: *Vol. 2* (Blackberry '98) Ⓝ

World Party: *Goodbye Jumbo* (Chrysalis '90) 💣

World Saxophone Quartet and African Drums: *Metamorphosis* (Elektra Nonesuch '91) most prefer their Africa less hectic, their jazz more straight-ahead ("The Holy Man," "Metamorphosis") ★★

Wreckx-N-Effect: "Rump Shaker," "New Jack Swing II" (*Hard or Smooth,* MCA '92) 💿

Wu-Tang Clan: *Enter the Wu-Tang (36 Chambers)* (RCA/Loud '93) They are or have been, if not "gangstas," at the very least dealers. But note that the slice of life where they doctor their wares with baking soda is decisively jokier than the tragic-sounding hit where they sell them on the corner. They aren't just grander than their West Coast opposite numbers, they're also goofier, and both are improvements. Expect the masterwork this album's reputation suggests and you'll probably be disappointed—it will speak directly only to indigenous hip hoppers. Expect a glorious human mess, as opposed to the ominous platinum product of their opposite numbers, and you'll realize the dope game isn't everyone's dead-end street. **A–**
Wu-Tang Clan: "America" (*America Is Dying Slowly* [comp], Red Hot '96) 💿

Wu-Tang Clan: *Wu-Tang Forever* (Loud '97) the five percent nation of Oscar aspirations ("The M.G.M.," "For Heavens Sake") ★★

Wu-Tang Clan: "Sucker MC's" (*In tha Beginning . . . There Was Rap* [comp], Priority '97) 🍩

Wu-Tang Killa Bees: *The Swarm* (Wu-Tang '98) miscellaneous battle cries and war stories ("Never Again," "Cobra Clutch")

Robert Wyatt: *Dondestan* (Gramavision '91) 🎯

Robert Wyatt: *Shleep* (Hannibal '98) Ⓝ

Tammy Wynette: "Unwed Fathers" (*Best Loved Hits,* Epic '91) 🍩

Tammy Wynette: See also George Jones & Tammy Wynette, Loretta/Dolly/Tammy

Steve Wynn: *Kerosene Man* (Rhino '90) 🎯

Wynonna: See Wynonna Judd

W/COMPILATIONS

Waiting to Exhale (Arista '95) With the shining exception of Aretha Franklin and the dim one of Chaka Khan, none of this amazing array of divas has proven funny, honest, introspective, or original enough to sustain entire albums—not matriarch Patti LaBelle or B-girl Mary J. Blige or new jills SWV or sexpots TLC, not Toni or Brandy or Whitney herself. And since producer-songwriter Babyface has always been kind of soft as well, it's not as if they suddenly equal Billie Holiday, singly or collectively. But because they're enough like each other to flow and enough unlike each other to put the music through some changes, this stands as a stirring showcase for a sensibility. Proudly pliant, mucous membranes at the ready, the one woman they fuse into isn't quite a virtuoso even when she has the chops, because that would distract from her business, which is pleasure. Anyway, it's her skills that count, not her chops. **A–**

Welcome to the Future (Epic '93) squiggly when it's generic, transcendent when it isn't (Jaydee, "Plastic Dreams [Original Version]"; Out of the Ordinary, "Da Da Da") ★★

What a Bam Bam!: Dancehall Queens (Shanachie '96) errs on the side of conscious, which beats erring on the side of slack (Shelly Thunders, "Kuff"; JC Lodge, "Telephone Love") ★★

Where the Pyramid Meets the Eye: A Tribute to Roky Erickson (Sire/Warner Bros. '90) acid damage as consistency—meaning formal wisdom (R.E.M., "I Walked with a Zombie"; Thin White Rope, "Burn the Flames") ★

White Country Blues (1926–1938): A Lighter Shade of Blue (Columbia/Legacy '94) Columbia has mined its blues catalogue with an assiduousness that verges on exploitation—the thematic albums are dully inconsistent, the single-artist jobs find deathless art in every $20 take. But this one is fascinating and fun. By now the sound of half-remembered crackers co-opting, emulating, and creating 12-bar laments and 16-bar romps is more provocative than the sound of black "originals" that are often only versions themselves. It fleshes out our dim awareness that Sam Phillips's white-rebels-singing-the-blues had a long history in the South (and you thought Carl Perkins wrote "Matchbox" like the Beatles said he did). Breaching the borders of the status quo, these hillbilly troubadours hewed to the innocent escapism of small-time show business—they stole only the catchiest tunes, and when the jokes fell flat they pumped in their own. In the course of two hour-long discs, there's still the occasional irritating sense that three generations later, ordinary subcultural entertainment music has been declared good for you. But mostly it's just ribald rhymes and wrecked romance—sometimes pained, but imbued with a droll detachment that epitomizes rural cool. If late minstrelsy was anything like this, I'm sorry we haven't heard more. **A–**

Wild About My Lovin': Beale Street Blues 1928–1930 (RCA '91) I don't know about Frank Stokes or Jim Jackson—acoustic-guitar songsters can fade to gray when their material isn't on the money. But as a longtime addict of Yazoo's Memphis Jug Band double-LP, I happily mainline Cannon's Jug Stompers' quarter-CD. Immersed in pop and vaudeville and minstrelsy because that was the competition, slick enough for slickers and downhome enough for traveling men, this stuff is a music of back alleys and medicine shows. Eventually it will spawn jump blues—and rock and roll. **A**

Wind Your Waist (Shanachie '91) **Ⓝ**

Wipeout XL (Astralwerks '96) so what if it's a little early for a Chemical Brothers tribute? (Fluke, "Atom Bomb"; the Future Sound of London, "We Have Explosive"; Orbital, "Petrol") ★★★

Woodstock 94 (A&M '94) **Ⓝ**

A World out of Time (Shanachie '92) Pomo folklorists Henry Kaiser and David Lindley stick their fretboards into these 18 Malagasy songs at will because despite their thing for Madagascar's isolation (you'd never guess from title or music that hundreds of thousands of strikers filled the capital's streets during their two-week visit), they understand that this Indian Ocean island is as multicultural as it gets—an Asian/Malaysian/Polynesian part of Africa that's been fucked over by Europe like everywhere else. The 13 artists represent a profusion of mostly commercialized styles, yet between their euphonious language and the indigenous timbres of their lutes and flutes, they blend gracefully together. Fittingly, the gentle Japanese pop tune the foreigners feed them melds better than "I Fought the Law." From lullaby to jamboree, melody is clearly treasured in this place. **A–**

A World out of Time Vol. 2 (Shanachie '93) outtakes from a field trip (Tarika Ramilson, "The Welcome Party"; Roger Georges, "Tsaiky Mboly Hely"; Rammy & the Indri, "Lemur Rap") ★

A World out of Time Vol, 3 (Shanachie '96) **Ⓝ**

Wu-Chronicles (Wu-Tang '99) **Ⓝ**

X: *Hey Zeus!* (Big Life/Mercury '93) Stripped of the vicious tensions that made them great—between good and evil, John and Exene, Billy Zoom and Skunk Baxter—they return as the reason young bohos are afraid to grow up. This isn't folk-rock in disguise; Tony Gilkyson's hooks evoke a machine shop, not a barn raising. But they leave going 120 to a bad old black-and-white—even with their seat belts on, the kids in the back would get hurt real bad in a crash. And save hostility for the warmongers—ensconced in separate but functional marriages, John and Exene have nothing to fight about anymore. Which in the usual tragic contradiction leaves the emotion so abstract that the songs are tough to grab hold of. Only the spiteful putdowns—Exene's "Everybody," John's "Baby You Lied"—sound like old times. Not to mention new ones. **B-** 🦃

X: *Unclogged* (Infidelity '95) 🎯

X: *Beyond & Back: The X Anthology* (Elektra '97) the "mostly unreleased x-cellence" comprises mostly known songs—an honorable, listenable live/demo/etc. fans-only collectorama ("The World's a Mess/It's in My Kiss," "How I [Learned My Lesson]") ★★

Mia X: *Unlady Like* (No Limit '97) Her mackstress bona fides are predictably generic despite the gender-bent pimp routine, and even after she progresses to the womanisms that dominate the second half of a typically excessive 80-minute No Limit disc, she can't very well avoid clichés: adoring her kids, mourning her G, fending off her current knucklehead, she's role-playing straight up. But especially after she expresses her love for a dead homegirl, her declarations of leather-skinned cynicism and wit's-end vulnerability take on a retrospective weight that counterbalances their surface contradictions. A ghetto story, real as fiction. **B+**

Mia X: "Put It Down," "Daddy" (*Mama-Drama*, No Limit '98) 🐚

X-Clan: *To the East, Blackwards* (4th & B'way '90) As message rap achieves the glut of gangster rap, party rap, and crossover rap, prophets and demagogues of every description join the myriad of wannabes, enabling lugs like these avowedly non-"humanist" Brooklynites to make their subcultural dent. Hallmarks: obscure Egyptological insults and flowing funk beats. Keywords: "vanglorious," which is vainglorious, and "sissy," a cross between the deep euphemism of "sucker" and the shameless bigotry of "faggot." Osiris is getting sick of this shit. **C** 🦃

Xscape: *Hummin' Comin' at 'Cha* (So So Def/Columbia '93) En Vogue? Mary J. Blige? Phooey—they're not even TLC, much less Kris Kross. Their hit weak, their album a guaranteed cutout, they're noteworthy only because they may convince Jerome Dupri he can repeat "Jump" whenever he wants. Don't encourage this antisocial delusion. **C** 🦃

★★★, ★★, ★ Honorable Mention   🐚 Choice Cut   Ⓝ Neither   🎯 Dud   🦃 Turkey

X-Statik: "Rapture" (*Kickin Mental Detergent Vol. 2* [comp], Vol. 2, Instinct '93) 🐞

XTC: *Rag and Bone Buffet* (Geffen '91) 💣

XTC: *Nonsuch* (Geffen '92) 💣

XTC: *Upsy Daisy Assortment* (Geffen '97) the best songs come from the best albums, an inconvenience ("Grass," "Making Plans for Nigel," "Dear God") ★★★

XTC: *Apple Venus Volume 1* (TVT '99) Since their outtakes weren't even rags or bones and their idea of a class pop arranger was the same as Elton John's, I figured that if they were feuding with their record company their record company was right. But after years of orchestral fops à la Eric Matthews and Duncan Sheik, I'm ready for McCartney fans who can festoon their famous tunes with something resembling wit and grace. Studio rats being studio rats, the lyrics aren't as deep as Andy and Colin think they are, but at least irrelevant doesn't equal obscure, humorless, or lachrymose. The next rock and roller dull-witted enough to embark on one of those de facto Sinatra tributes should give Partridge a call. **B+**

Yaggfu Front: "My Dick Is So Large" ("*Action Packed Adventure,*" Mercury '94) 🐞

Ya Kid K: "Move This," "You Told Me Sex" (*One World Nation*, SBK '93) 🐞

Yall So Stupid: *Van Full of Pakistanis* (Rowdy '93) Ⓝ

Yanni: *Yanni Live at the Acroplis* (Private Music '94) Affluent spirituality cum cornball romanticism from a florid New Age keyb maestro, his guitarless yet oddly rockish band (dig those drum solos), and one of those symphony orchestras that'll hook up with anyone who leaves enough cash on the night table. Given the august location of this "event of a lifetime," it seems only appropriate to cite pseudo-Plutarch, the Roman protomusicologist who summed up the Greek "new wave" composers of the fifth century B.C.: "Crexus, Timotheus and Philoxenus . . .

displayed more vulgarity and a passion for novelty, and pursued the style nowadays called 'popular' or 'profiteering.' The result was that music limited to a few strings, and simple and dignified in character, went quite out of fashion." Whether you're a diehard punk or a self-actualized higher being who got lost on the way to the futon ads, there's much to ponder in this ancient wisdom. And f.y.i.: Timotheus was the premier composer of his age, kind of a cross between Chopin, Wagner, and Andrew Lloyd Webber. If Yanni had any idea who he was, even Yanni would acknowledge that he had more to say to his time than Yanni does to his. I think. **D+** 🦃

Eva Ybarra y Su Conjunto: *A Mi San Antonio* (Rounder '94) Ⓝ

Trisha Yearwood: "Walkaway Joe" (*Hearts in Armor,* MCA '92) 🐞

Trisha Yearwood: "XXXs and OOOs (An American Girl)" (*Thinkin' About You,* MCA '95) 🐞

Trisha Yearwood: *Everybody Knows* (MCA '96) Trisha had a dream, and by 1985 she was in Nashville pursuing it—studying "music business," as her bio says, at Belmont College. An internship and some demo singing later, she had signed with MCA, where she now epitomizes the blandness of today's quality country. Not that she's bad or anything. Her voice is big and precise, and she ends up with a good song or two on every album—including this one, where she doesn't ruin strong titles by Kevin Welch and Steve Goodman and brings off a terrific Matraca Berg line about chocolate and magazines. But if songwriters love her so much, it must be because she brings nothing to their work but what they put there. The same cannot be said of Willie Nelson, George Jones, Reba McEntire, Garth Brooks—even Shania Twain. In pop music, good taste isn't timeless. It's boring. **B** 🦃

Trisha Yearwood: *Songbook (A Collection of Hits)* (MCA '97) precisely as good as her material, which gets stuffier all the time ("Walkaway Joe," "She's in Love with the Boy") ★

Stephen Yerkey: "Cocksucking Blonde" (*Confidence Man,* Heyday '94) 🍮

Yothu Yindi: *Tribal Voice* (Hollywood '92) 💣

Dwight Yoakam: *If There Was a Way* (Reprise '90) a honky tonker with a grudge, not a stud with the rhythm and blues ("The Heart That You Own," "The Distance Between You and Me") ★★★

Dwight Yoakam: *This Time* (Reprise '93) neotraditionalism as neoclassicism, which he knows; cold son of a bitch as victim, which he doesn't ("This Time," "A Thousand Miles from Nowhere") ★★

Dwight Yoakam: *Gone* (Warner Bros. '95) Ⓝ

Dwight Yoakam: *Under the Covers* (Warner Bros. '97) 💣

Dwight Yoakam: *A Long Way Home* (Reprise '98) Ⓝ

Dwight Yoakam: *Last Chance for a Thousand Years: Dwight Yoakam's Greatest Hits from the 90's* (Reprise '99) Whenever I ponder this multithreat singer-songwriter, honky-tonk ideologue, Hollywood role player, published author, and hunk-if-you-like-your-meat-lean, I remember what Sharon Stone said about the prospects for their reunion: "I'd rather eat a dirt sandwich." Normally with country music you swallow the male chauvinism and figure guys feeling sorry for themselves is what makes it go; with Yoakam, so talented and so conscious, you expect a little movement within the paradigm, and conclude that he chose neotrad because movement was the last thing on his mind. But even if his most romantic moment is the Waylon cover where he goes back to his old lady because his new lady was playing games, he's sung and written his way into the male chauvinist canon. His best song of the '90s, for its heart-broke melody: 1990's "The Heart That You Own." Latest rock cover: the finale, Queen's "Crazy Little Thing Called Love." He "just can't handle it," "must get 'round

to it," etc. Right, Dwight. Or is that just Dirtbag? **A–**

Yo La Tengo: "Speeding Motorcycle," "The Summer," "Emulsified" (*Fakebook,* Restless/Bar/None '90) 🍮

Yo La Tengo: *May I Sing with Me* (Alias '92) hey Mr. and Mrs. Tambourine Man, play that feedback for me ("Some Kinda Fatigue," "Upside-Down") ★★★

Yo La Tengo: *Painful* (Matador '93) Correcting for off-and-on songwriting by declining to write full-fledged ones, they turn into Hoboken's answer to My Bloody Valentine on this expansive collection of riffs to jam on. The difference is that even at their most aleatory, which in a close contest is probably the Hammond B-3 workout "Sudden Organ," they're always friendly. This is not the forbidding experimentation of an aspiring vanguard. This is the fooling around of folks who like to go out on Saturday night and make some noise—and then go home humming it. **A–**

Yo La Tengo: *Electr-O-Pura* (Matador '95) *Altern-A-Pura* would be more like it. Brimful of punk, fuzz, feedback, noise, and the lovingly amped squelches of fingers sliding off strings, their seventh album is a subcultural tour de force, luxuriating so sybaritically in guitar sound that I'm reluctant to mention that the tunes are pretty good. That's why it's the best record they've ever made, though. Singing's breathy as usual, with Ira yelling when the time is right. As for the lyrics, you know—murmured, gnomic, pop culture references, that kind of thing. **A**

Yo La Tengo: "Can't Seem to Make You Mine" (*Camp Yo La Tengo,* Matador '95) 🍮

Yo La Tengo: *Genius + Love = Yo La Tengo* (Matador '96) Ⓝ

Yo La Tengo: *I Can Hear the Heart Beating as One* (Matador '97) No one has made more of bohemian easy-listening—cocktail samba, trance-skronk, good old-fashioned slow ones—than Ira Kaplan and Georgia Hubley, boho dream couple and cultural miniaturists. From the misshapen piano figure that trumps "Moby Octopad"'s Peter Townshend guitar swell to "Deeper into Movies"'s raveup workout, from Georgia's simulated Astrud Gilberto cover to James McNew's simulated Neil Young ballad, this is a band that has figured out what makes its faves tick and its tickers beat as one. The very peak is "Autumn Sweater," which with its "We could slip away" refrain comes on like (gulp!) a cheating song, only to reveal itself as Ira's diffident, lovestruck tribute to Georgia's companionable support. Modest rather than narrow, their joy and sadness are no less sweet or intense for the larger life they know nothing of. **A**

Yondo Sister: *Dernière Minute* (TJR import '94) **Ⓝ**

Neil Young & Crazy Horse: *Ragged Glory* (Reprise '90) "It's three o'clock in the fucking morning, will you turn that thing down? All I hear down here all night is thump-thump-thump-thump thump-thump-thump-thump—same fucking tempo, same fucking beat on permanent repeat, you don't even have to walk over to the amplifier to start it up again, just galumph up and down in that stupid hippie pogo. Of course I love him too. I know the guitar is great. So what? This isn't the Beacon, goddamn it. It's my apartment." **A–**

Neil Young and Crazy Horse: *Weld* (Reprise '91) File the 35 minutes of orchestrated amplifier overrun that is *Arc.* Snicker as 1980–88 gets schneidered. Grouse that he reprises all six songs on the rock half of the 1979 summum *Live Rust,* several of which he defined then and none of which he redefines now. But don't dare forget that except for Saint Jimi there's no live-er rock and roller than Mr. Time Fades Away—not because he's an ace improviser, though he can amaze you, but because his edges cut conceptually, rough where blooze and punk and garage jokers settle for ragged. And remember too that in 1979 he was half a folkie, as he will be again. This live double is all rock

and roll. Anyway, repeating yourself a dozen years later is a concept in itself. **A–**

Neil Young: *Harvest Moon* (Reprise '92) mean length of *Harvest* track not counting six-minute opus: 3:14; mean length of *Harvest Moon* track not counting 10-minute opus: 4:37 ("Old King," "Harvest Moon") ★★★

Neil Young: *Lucky Thirteen* (Geffen '93) As David Geffen himself would concur, though perhaps not in a legal brief, Neil's non-Reprise period was a mess even for him—Reagan, techno, horn sections, rockabilly takeoffs. But despite the arrangements and the unavoidably jarring segues, just about every one of these 13 selections therefrom (only four available in this precise form, only two totally unfamiliar) is a Good Song. And this is all we have a right to ask—except that *Trans* be reissued as a CD. **A–**

Neil Young, "Philadelphia" (*Philadelphia* [ST], Epic Soundtrax '93) 🕭

Neil Young: *Unplugged* (Reprise '93) folkie and proud, he's earned one of these things if anyone has ("World on a String," "Like a Hurricane") ★★★

Neil Young and Crazy Horse: *Sleeps with Angels* (Reprise '94) Although I'd love to hear him throw something together with Dave Grohl and Chris Novoselic, the Cobain connection is a ringer—dozens of young bands could scare up a Nirvana tribute more wrenching and dynamic. Instead think Johnny Rotten revisited and *Rust Never Sleeps.* The 14-minute "Change Your Mind" is not now and never will be "Like a Hurricane." But this caps five years of trying with lyrical will-o'-the-wisps, weird road tales, sociological crazy mirrors, rock and roll's first great middle-age anthem, and the ecology edition of "Welfare Mothers." Now let's hope he doesn't go for *Hawks and Doves.* **A–**

Neil Young: *Mirror Ball* (Reprise '95) baby he was born to lumber—and Pearl Jam wasn't ("Downtown") ★

Neil Young & Crazy Horse: *Broken Arrow* (Reprise '96) undeniable yes, irresistible no ("Music Arcade," "Big Time") ★★

Neil Young: *Dead Man* (Vapor '96) 🍢
Neil Young With Crazy Horse: *Year of the Horse* (Reprise '97) Largest word on package: LIVE. A dozen songs, mostly at the usual midtempo stomp, more than half dating to the '70s (or '60s). Also three off last year's barely noticed *Broken Arrow*—one terrific then too, one improving as it gets (even) longer, one a permanent drag. The climax is *Life*'s long-lost "Prisoners" (formerly "of Rock 'n' Roll"), which climaxes with the deathless "That's why we don't want to be good." Men of their word, they're great sometimes and good never. And then the CD version—on *Broken Arrow, vinyl* was the bonus-cut format—climaxes again with a wilder "Sedan Delivery" than the one they thrashed out on *Live Rust* 18 years ago. Guy never gives up, does he? That's why his completists have more fun. **B+**
Neil Young: "War of Man (Live)" (*No Boundaries: A Benefit for the Kosovar Refugees,* Epic '99) 🎩

Young Black Teenagers: *Young Black Teenagers* (SOUL '91) 🍢

The Young Gods: "Feu," "Did You Miss Me" (*The Young Gods,* Wax Trax '90) 🎩

Yo-Yo: *Make Way for the Motherlode* (EastWest '91) By loosing Roxanne Shanté's tough talk on Queen Latifah's leadership seminar, Ice Cube's no-shit sister doubles her chance of teaching "intelligent black women" how one respects onself. Her most salient theme is an ass she's not inclined to give up on the first date, and when she succumbs she lives to regret it at speeds that'll set you on yours. Sir Jinx's soul-thick, jazz-inflected production suits her gritty drawl and wayward mouth. And if they should split she'll figure out another way to get over. **A–**
Yo Yo: *Black Pearl* (EastWest '92) Foreshortening Stax-Volt or Zapp or "Strawberry Letter 23," the nervous propulsion and unreleased tension of her funk agitates mind-body-spirit, only to be put right by a voice that's gotten kinder without

even thinking about going soft. Advising the downpessed or dissing fools, her lyrics are smarter throughout and stunning on one that makes a battered wife's bizness its own. But yo, Yo—the title cut and the love ballad are not "East Coast." They're nowhere. **A–**
Yo Yo: *You Better Ask Somebody* (EastWest '93) Her voice has always suggested the honeyed grit of an Irma Thomas or a Jackie Moore. Here it gets richer as her timing gets sharper, and the beats could make you squeal. Eschewing soul steals, her latest production crew samples straight-up funk and other rap records, as in the corkscrew funk of "Givin' It Up," built off a reconstructed Mtume riff, and the easygoing sing-along of "Pass It On," which credits Cypress Hill and "Poison" as well an obscure Webster Lewis track: five Intelligent Black Women pass a blunt and a mic, boasting about how fucked up they get in the kind of morally retrograde one-off that's given sin good word-of-mouth since snakes could talk. And then there's a Yo Yo lyric Ice Cube couldn't come near. "Letter to the Pen," in which a loyal gangsta bitch risks her neck keeping her imprisoned "soldier"'s "pockets fat" as his buddies outside play him and his buddies inside swear she's fucking him over, is as touching as love songs get. It's not "reality"; it may not even be realistic, though I doubt it. But it evokes a reality, one that remains poorly documented after five solid years of hardcore—a reality in which even the hardcore faithful somehow live through the shit. **A–**
Yo Yo: *Total Control* (EastWest '96) As distasteful as I find Lil' Kim, who conveys even less pleasure in sex than that tragic sensualist Eazy-E, and Foxy Brown, who isn't subtle enough to shroud her vicious fantasies in an aura of mystery, at least they break new ground in candor and aggression. And Yo Yo's East Coast counterpart Lyte has grown in wisdom and principle, while the self-appointed Intelligent Black Woman has gone soft. The beats are a case study in the banality of

G-funk, and where once she was a proud, tough-minded observer, here her only winning moments come when she pledges allegiance to her ordinary G and fantasizes momentarily about having babies. These dreams die, she don't know why, and soon it ain't nuthin' but a party where she can find her dream guy—"nice and thick with more dollars than sense." Hey, didn't she steal that line from Julie Brown or somebody? L.A., what a town. **B–**

Yuri Yunakov Ensemble: *New Colors in Bulgarian Wedding Music* (Traditional Crossroads '97) Unable to resist such an enticing title, I couldn't deny the frenetic high spirits it came with either. Soon I learned that "wedding music" is an insurgent genre favored by Gypsies and feared by Commies—and that the sax-wielding leader is a retired prizefighter who now makes his home in the Bronx. Do Muzsikás have beats like this? Ivo Papasov, even? Not that I've been able to notice. **A–**

Zaiko Langa Langa: *Nkolo Mboka/ Avis de Recherche* (Stern's Africa '95) **Ⓝ**

Zap Mama: *Adventures in Afropea 1* (Luaka Bop/Warner Bros. '93) Like most a cappella, this ethnomusicological pop move—melodies lifted from all over Africa as well as Spain and Cuba and Syria, with Zairian tunes and Pygmy chants foregrounded—requires concentration. In the background it can fade or annoy, but on the Walkman, or a good sound system with the street noise under control, it's pure joy of timbre—female timbre, plus clicks and gutturals and percussion sounds and camel-driver impressions. And unless you fancy ethnomusicology lectures, which tend to be prissy, don't worry about the words. **A–**

Zap Mama: *Sabsylma* (Luaka Bop/ Warner Bros. '94) splitting the difference between sound effects and multilingualism ("De la Vie a la Mort," "Mr. Brown") ★

Zap Mama: *Seven* (Luaka Bop/Warner Bros. '97) world beat at its all too all-embracing best ("Baba Hooker," "Beigo Zairoise") ★★

Zap Mama: *A Ma Zone* (Luaka Bop '99) 💣

Hukwe Zawose: *Chibite* (RealWorld '96) thumb-piano extravaganza from an appointed guardian of Tanzanian tradition ("Nyangawuya," "Munyamaye") ★★★

Tom Zé: *Brazil Classics 4: The Best of Tom Zé* (Luaka Bop/Warner Bros. '90) These '73–'75 songs catch a poor Brazilian (albeit a Brazilian who says his dad won the lottery) on his way from pop tropicália to leftist jingles and instruments constructed from household appliances, only unlike his buddy Caetano Veloso, he puts the rebellion and satire out there in the music for benighted English speakers to hear. Zé delivers his portion of lulling lyricism, but it's his jarring rhythm hooks that you've never heard before—and will notice so fast you'll make sure you get to notice them again. The overtly pop-avant moves would have garnered desperate if imprecise Beefheart comparisons in their time, and the Arto Lindsay translations have the makings of international legend. Paul Simon should be so smart. Not to mention postmodern. **A+**

Tom Zé: *Brazil 5: The Return of Tom Zé: The Hips of Tradition* (Luaka Bop/Warner Bros. '92) Zé is the kind of artist you think could be your leader if only he worked in English—your Dylan, your Weill, your David Byrne, some failed or dead hero like that. But if he'd been brought up Anglophone his lyrics would reach for the sky and never get out of the library, and his atonal songcraft wouldn't be so staccato yet grooveful, so acrid yet sweet—in just the right proportions for us, but maybe not for Brazil, where it took none other than David Byrne to rescue him from avant-obscurity. I couldn't swear that the fractured synthesis of sentiment and sarcasm these mementos of his down time convey in translation is any more viable, here or there, than the triumphant fusions of his U.S. debut. But they radiate hope and hilarity nevertheless. **A**

Tom Zé: *Fabrication Defect/Com Defeito de Fabrição* (Luaka Bop '98) With a little practice, I heard so far past Zé's experimentalism that his two collections ended up among my most played records of the '90s. On Puerto Rican vacations they provided just the Latin-flavored reality prinicple I needed while speeding bedward from Boqueron or navigating the crammed strip malls and barrios of Ponce. So it's a tribute to Zé's avant-garde principles that it took me forever to access this album-as-album. Although the songs are no less tuneful/grooveful for their latest batch of odd rhythms and found harmonies, I was distracted by the amelodic spareness of three or four, all of which I now savor, especially the one with the (is that?) forro accordion. In a world where the poor are rationalized into "civilized trash," "androids" reduced to their economic functions and dysfunctions, Zé insists on the vitality of the technological. Among the defects he celebrates in so many words are politics, curiosity, genes, and the waltz. **A–**

Johnny Zee: "Yaar Nach La" (*What Is Bhangra?* [comp], I.R.S. '94) 🐷

Warren Zevon: *Mr. Bad Example* (Giant '91) Ⓝ

Warren Zevon: *Learning to Flinch* (Giant '93) 💣

Warren Zevon: *Mutineer* (Giant '95) putting the mean fun back in being unrepentant and existentially pissed ("Seminole Bingo," "Rottweiler Blues") ★★★

Warren Zevon: *I'll Sleep When I'm Dead (An Anthology)* (Rhino '96) His limitations are manifest and probably permanent. A gonzo drunk who thinks pounding is rocking and considers it the secret of his charm when his bassist observes, "He's just as crazy now as he was then, only now he knows it," he specializes in what his buddy Jackson Browne (who's such a wheel his best-of CD is on his *real label*) calls "song noir," which means he's overimpressed with Raymond Chandler and occasionally matches his buddy Carl

Hiaasen. As a tough-guy neoclassicist he cultivates his mawkish side (what *is* "sentimental hygiene," anyway?), preserved in all its lovingly worked poetry on this, his interim will and testament. His gifts have faded slowly. And if he's good enough that I'd replace a third of the 44 selections here, that means he's also good enough to roll his own. **A–**

Zimbabwe Legit: *Zimbabwe Legit* (Hollywood Basic '92) 💣

ZZ Top: *Recycler* (Warner Bros. '90) title of the year ("Concrete and Steel," "Decision or Collision") ★

ZZ Top: *Greatest Hits* (Warner Bros. '92) With their fairly major guitarist and fairly ferocious groove, they're the class of arena blues, and they also write songs. So here are 18, a dozen choice. For nonarena types the revelation is the show-stopping "Got Me Under Pressure"—its groove brooks no modifiers. But from "Legs" to "Tush," from "Sharp Dressed Man" to "Cheap Sunglasses," only one blues standard emerges: "I'm Bad, I'm Nationwide," which could have been stolen off some black genius's porch, and if it really was I apologize. But this makes me wonder. I mean, just suppose Billy Gibbons or Dusty Hill sang as good as he plays. Could I still say this? **A–**

ZZ Top: *Antenna* (RCA '94) Ⓝ

ZZ Top: *XXX* (RCA '99) meaning of title: very, very dirty (sounding) ("Fearless Boogie," "Beatbox") ★★

XYZ/COMPILATIONS

Yalla: Hitlist Egypt (Mango '90) One reason rock and rollers don't get Cairo pop is that it's pop in the pre-Warhol, pre-Elvis sense: a middle-class music hemmed in by classical and liturgical conservativism and half-acknowledged Europe envy. Both working-class shaabi and student-class al jeel rebel against these strictures—they're faster, snazzier, and (when they can get away with it) ruder than the ughniyah competition. The ear-catching arrangements and fuck-you spirit of the signature cuts transcend bothersome details of language and mode—their audacity is in the grooves, and you won't want to resist. Delving deeper takes more time, but eventually the rock glitz and Bedouin grit on the al jeel side sound both inventive and inevitable. The shaabi side just sounds gritty and glitzy. **A–**

Yo! MTV Raps (Def Jam '97) to paraphrase the eminent RZA: "This ain't true hip hop you listenin' to right here, in the pure form; this is some r&b with the wack nigga takin' the loop, be loopin' that shit and stickin' in choruses thinkin' it's gonna be the sound of the culture"—and it has its uses (Bone Thugs-n-Harmony, "Tha Crossroads"; L.L. Cool J, "Loungin' [Who Ya Love Remix]") ★★

Y2K: **Beat the Clock** (Columbia '99) Starts out blatant—it don't get blatanter than "Rockafeller Skank"—and then, generously, remains that way for half its allotted 73 minutes: quality Prodigy, that Wildchild song everyone loved last summer, Crystal Method's reason for existence. Second half's less enlightened if equally obvious: "Lost in Space," "Born Slippy," Björk remix, Orb edit, spanking-new remake of Sparks' prophetically annoying and exciting title song. In short, all the big beat an adherent of the first big beat need own. **A–**

Zouk Attack (Rounder '92) **Ⓝ**

HOW TO USE THESE APPENDICES

In a dogged stab at completism, I had some fun with the back matter in my '70s and '80s books, where I divided artists who hadn't made the text proper into three categories: honorable Subjects for Further Research, laughable Distinctions Not Cost-Effective, and unspeakable Meltdown. For the '80s I added a classification designated New Wave, which listed in order of preference precisely 200 bands vaguely deserving of that cheap, dated badge of rock coolness. Partly because new methods expand my coverage, and partly because new glut renders expansion futile, I've cut back on these stratagems—completism isn't even a good joke anymore. Distinctions and Meltdown are gone, and Subjects for Further Research is shortened. With four artists—Steve Coleman, Fugazi, Huun-Huur-Tu, and Uz Jsme Doma—I've kept the album that got me interested (meaning the one I'm sure of) in the appropriate A List; with one—Jimi Hendrix, the exception to every rule—I stopped reviewing mid-decade and explained why in the appendix.

The A Lists, which add best-ofs to revised versions of the Dean's Lists I publish in the *Voice*'s Pazz & Jop Critics' Poll every February, continue unchanged: registers of every A record released in a given year. As always, these are arranged in order of preference, with some caveats. Let me be clear: I have *not* relistened to all 870-odd A and A minus records to find out how well they held up. Listening to each one just once would take roughly eight 14-hour seven-day weeks—or, please mister, 20 work weeks as conceived by any self-respecting American union member. As part of my ongoing criticism-can-be-fun program, I have checked out titles whose positioning looked way wrong; I've also relistened to albums newly reviewed or revised for this book, and moved other titles up and down according to the use, pleasure, and stimulation they've been good for over the years. This can be tricky, especially with best-ofs pitting whole careers and genres against single albums; committed grader, rater, and quantifier though I am, I almost had an anxiety attack comparing *Anthology of American Folk Music* and *ESPN Slam Jams Vol. 1,* some pair, to my favorite true 1997 releases, Arto Lindsay's *Mundo Civilizado* and Sleater-Kinney's *Dig Me Out.* I expect my final order—*Mundo-Anthology-ESPN-Dig*—will seem esoteric if not bananas to part-timers who believe, sanely, that even if these are all "rock" records in my expansive sense, they're also incommensurably different. So what would you think were I then to claim that the ringer of the four is the six-CD *Anthology,* whose many dull moments are toned up considerably by their positioning in the monument?

Those critics who don't consider 10-best lists a betrayal of their august calling fall into three schools, two of which I belong to. Nuts to the one-from-group-A approach, in which crits pay tribute to pop's broad palette—and also prove what nonracist/nonsexist/nonrockist fellows they are—by reserving slots for rap (the Arrested Development Memorial Set-Aside) or country (didn't Dolly Parton do a bluegrass thing?) or women (not Dolly, we already counted her for country) or . . . Music doesn't break down so neatly, especially when predivided into arbitrary 12-month chunks. But I refuse to choose between the fun school, in which you vote for the records you've played the most, and the art school, in which you vote for the records you adjudge "best."

Fun is a value, in pop music a big one; not only that, quantity is a quality. Problem is, quality is a quality too. My favorite album of all time, since you ask, is either *The Clash* or *New York Dolls* (actually, that would be *rock* album—for reasons I'm not professionally required to go into, thank God, my all-music fave is Thelonious Monk's *Misterioso*). Both are "fun," as it happens. But they're also loud and harsh, and don't fit very neatly into my middle-aged, nuke-fam leisure schedule. On the rare occasions when I play them, however, they still amaze from beginning to end with their power and subtlety, their never-ending freshness and in-your-face wit. That's aesthetic quality as I define it—an important species of it, anyway. I play *Guitar Paradise of East Africa* much more these days, *Mundo Civilizado* and *Latin Playboys* and *Have Moicy!* too. They're all high on my life list as well. But *The Clash* and *New York Dolls* beat them out. The A Lists were constructed by balancing many psychic scales—balancing fun against art, pondering how any slam jam could enrich my life more than Rabbit Brown's "James Alley Blues," comparing the greatest disco survey/party anyone will ever compile to a fluke career album by a deservedly cultish New Zealand pop band. The ones toward the top I heartily recommend to almost anyone; the ones toward the bottom I simply guarantee to be good records, whatever that means (only we both know, don't we?).

Between Subjects for Further Research and the A Lists fall two additional sections. As you might expect in a decade when the record biz made its margin repackaging history, Compilations is twice as long as it was in the '80s. Even with multiple-artist collections separated out in the text, trying to remember the title of that good African comp is bad for your mental health. The Compilations register sorts them by genre; scan down, page back to the review, and the answer will come to you. And speaking of repackaging history, who better to do the job than those who made it, if only in their own minds? Hence the cavalcade of elsewhere unaccounted-for has-beens in Everything Rocks and Nothing Ever Dies, which replaces Distinctions Not Cost-Effective, Meltdown, and even, all things must pass, New Wave.

The title originated as my colleague Eric Weisbard's all-purpose review for the venerable rock artists who would mysteriously rematerialize every summer—sometimes on big-ticket tours, sometimes on free gigs sponsored by the Parks Department and other well-meaning institutions. In less cosmopolitan areas, many hit the county fairs, where rock dinosaurs now vie with aging country stars as favored perennials. And hey, that's entertainment. Let the people have their fun and the old-timers collect their checks—no one should have to live on social security. But in a decade when everybody else made records, it would be unrealistic in the extreme to expect these lifers to abstain. So all the human beings and brand names listed in what I'll nickname Everything ventured albums of new studio material in the '90s. Some had lost it, some had never had it, some were proud to be skilled labor. Many were attempting comebacks, others had stuck at it, and one was Sting. None of the individuals were clones so far as I know, but too many of the groups were—the oldies circuit is rife with undistinguishable doowop brands featuring second tenors who put in three months in 1958, and, to choose one instance, the version of the Guess Who that recorded features neither of the band's leads.

Of course, were Burton Cummings and Randy Bachman to rejoin bassist Jim Kale in a fully reconstituted band (they could open for *Tal* Bachman, that would be heartwarming), there still wouldn't be any reason to check out the ensuing product. For every Percy Sledge reemerging on a pretty damn good album there are dozens of Boz Scaggses and Solomon Burkes birthing barely OK or utterly DOA ones. And not only were all three of the just-named more gifted than the Guess Who to begin with, they weren't groups. Group dynamics are of the essence in rock and roll, a living metaphor and prime energy source. But they wear down a lot faster than individual metabolisms. Pere Ubu rejelled in the late '80s, and the Holy Modal Rounders have been reuniting periodically since something like 1964. But the vast majority of reunions are stillborn, bald plays for name recognition. So let us take a moment to silently honor the following groups for not making new records in the '90s: Humble Pie, Gentle Giant, Iron Butterfly, Slade, the Sweet, the Four Seasons, the Five Satins, Poco, Pavlov's Dog, Dexy's Midnight Runners, Skafish, Klaatu, the Everly Brothers, the Boswell Sisters, Mott the Hoople, Cream, and Blind Faith.

I like old people, especially old people who love music—I'm one myself. As I've been arguing since I was a wizened 33 or so, the claim that rock and roll is exclusively for the young is a big fat lie. So it's possible that one or two or even five of the precisely 200 acts specially selected for this category came up with something new. No more, though. I'm sure because I've heard nearly half of them. In fact, a great many of their contemporaries sang and played their way into the text, with more than a few—Bonnie Raitt, Randy Newman, George Clinton, Peter Stampfel, Willie Nelson, Loudon Wainwright III, Neil Young of course, why not mention Ladysmith Black Mambazo, more—coasting onto the A Lists. The downside is that I initially dispensed with several albums by Everything artists as Duds or Neithers, only to conclude that they weren't worth that much book space. War's eponymous 1994 comeback isn't half bad. But it isn't half good either. So while it's fine with me if it recharged their Keoghs and their cardiovascular systems, I can't in good conscience advise a neutral music lover to give it a second thought.

What the Everything list might look like in 2010 I can't imagine. I can't even swear I'm looking forward to finding out. Then again, I can't really imagine what'll be on the A Lists either. But I'll bet the Keogh on this: If the artists on this decade's A Lists can be said to span a 40-year age spread, 10 years from now it'll be 50. What more can I ask?

SUBJECTS FOR FURTHER RESEARCH

Barenaked Ladies   Humorous Canadian folk-rock group with name suggesting fascination/discomfort with s-e-x—oh great. But in a wide-open singles market where any hooky novelty had a shot, they scored a few. By the time I heard that 1996's *Rock Spectacle* doubled as a de facto best-of, however, I'd skipped it (*live album* by humorous Canadian folk-rock group with name suggesting fascination/discomfort with s-e-x—oh really great). While indeed hooky, "One Week" wasn't humorous enough to change my ways. Maybe someday there'll be a real best-of. And maybe there won't.

Frank Black   As the face of the Pixies, the former Black Francis was dandyishly to devilishly arch, epitomizing what people who can't stand "college rock" can't stand about college rock. So though the Pixies had more slash and burn than any art band between Hüsker Dü and Nirvana, Fran sorely needed the fierce musicianship of Joey Santiago and, I like to think, the sweet humanizing gravity of Kim Deal. On his own he's generated plenty of tune, plenty of 'tude, yet seemed silly anyway. If you were to start with 1998's *Frank Black and the Catholics* you might think better of him. The pseudo-Pixies comp lurking in his catalogue includes *Frank Black*'s "Fu Manchu" and *Pistolero*'s "So. Bay."

Bongwater   This collaboration between performance artist Ann Magnuson and guitarist-entrepreneur Kramer had its moments—the acid "Kisses Sweeter Than Wine" was pretty mean. But Magnuson was never as funny as she was supposed to be, and the rock settings Kramer tossed off were trapped in the genericism they postmodernized, which is what he gets for thinking rock and roll is easy. The pair released four albums on Kramer's Shimmy-Disc label before learning to hate each other. In 1998 Shimmy-Disc vouchsafed us the four-CD *A Box of Bongwater.* Very conceptual.

Boredoms   Never trust a band beholden to *Metal Machine Music.* Never trust a band who dare you to take their horrible name literally either. I checked out random albums and concluded that this drone-prone Osaka avant-rock collective wasn't for me. I mean, if "ambient hardcore" and a concept where all titles include the word "Anal" are your kind of thing, maybe you should be consulting some other expert. But I liked their track on the *Cosmic Hurushi Monsters* comp, and, rechecking, I agree that 1990's *Soul Discharge* is kinda funny—and that 1998's *Super AE* has a ritualistic vibe. This must mean they're mellowing.

Calypso   Most of the music had been collected before, but three Dick Spottswood-compiled '90s releases on Rounder—*Calypso Pioneers 1912–1937* (strongest), *Calypso Breakaway 1927–1941* (strangest), and *Calypso Carnival 1936–1941* (happiest)—provide a fetching introduction to world-pop's most logocentric genre. For those suspicious of soca's unslackening drive and calypso's weakness for stock melody, the goofy dance bands that cavort by here are a carnivalesque surprise. The New York-based Gerald Clark and His Caribbean Serenaders feature guitar, trumpet, violin, clarinet, piano, bass, and usually cuatro, the Port-of-Spain units more or different wind instruments, sometimes percussion. All share a loose, off-the-cuff, polyphonic sound/groove that evokes both klezmer and competing Latin American dance musics, but is without Stateside parallel. Melodies repeat, oh yes they do. The most fetching adorns Sam Manning's "Lieutenant Julian," Wilmoth Houdini's "War Declaration," the Executor's "My Reply to Houdini," Lord Executor's "Seven Skeletons in the Yard," Lord Executor's "How I Spent My Time at the Hospital," Codallo's Top Hat Orchestra's "I Want to Build a Bungalow," Lion's "I Am Going to Buy a Bungalow," Lion's "Vitalogy," Lion and Atilla the Hun's "Guests of Rudy Vallee," King Radio's "Neighbor," King Radio's "Old Men Come Back Again," and King Radio's "It's the Rhythm We Want," among others. But as in the great blues tune families, tempo and phrasing provide decisive variety and arrangement counts for a lot. Then the lyrics begin to signify: "Lieutenant Julian" was a black aviator, "Neighbor" fingers a sex offender, "Seven Skeletons in the Yard" lists Christmas horrors, "Vitalogy" takes off on Latinate medical lingo. But since none is as well turned as Cole Porter, Johnny Mercer, *Beyond a Boundary,* or *Miguel Street,* at this distance their main job is atmospheric: concreteness, morality, and wit to ground the bacchanal.

Steve Coleman   In his pop-friendly Afrocentric brass, the M-Base altoist is like a younger version of tenor man David Murray, except that Murray is all of one year his senior—and also a great player where Coleman is a very good one, so common a breed in jazz these days that only specialists bother telling them apart. But with his multitude of bands—Five Elements, Metrics, Mystic Rhythm Society, Council of Balance—Coleman works up more convincing funk and Afropercussive grooves than anyone else working this turf (Greg Osby, to be specific), as in 1990's *Rhythm People (The Resurrection of Creative Black Civilization).* Predictably, the jazz loyalists "bored" by his propulsion prefer *Black Science,* Cassandra Wilson lyrics and all. In 1995, Coleman released four live albums simultaneously and knocked me for a loop—there were pleasures aplenty there, but I never sorted them out. I've also enjoyed 1996's Afro-Cuban *The Sign and the Seal,* 1998's big-band *Genesis,* and 1999's syncretic *The Sonic Language of Myth.* But as a nonspecialist I'll make my fine distinctions elsewhere.

Kevin Coyne   When this name showed up in a listing one week, I was delighted to announce that the long-lost '70s gravel-voice, first the leader of the prophetically pubbish Siren and then a solo act whose three albums reached America mainly on Elektra's release schedule, had reemerged from what I had feared was a literal bout of the insanity he'd mimicked so convincingly. And though it turned out the Coyne who came to New York was actually some Irish folk musician, I soon received word that the English Coyne had conquered alcoholism and found a good woman in Germany, where he was painting, writing, churning out CDs, and cross-promoting himself like he's in it for life. With most failed old rocker and rollers, survivalist careerism is a species of mortality-in-denial. But Coyne had always played the old codger anyway. And while his mature worldview was rife with roots-rock humanism, he put his back, mind, and voice into it. His most notable German album is the narrative/conceptual *Adventures of Crazy Frank.* Best U.S. address: c/o Glenn Hirsch, P.O. Box 650326, Fresh Meadows, NY 11365.

Everything but the Girl   Tracey Thorn has always been one of those singers who sounded dandy on other people's records, notably Massive Attack's. Her diffident quietude is designed for new sophisticates, meaning not me, and linked to Ben Watt's lounge jazz once removed she always seemed to warrant that all-purpose what-me-worry dis, boring. Nor did things improve when Watt took cues from Massive Attack and went techno; although he was always understated about it, his affinities were clearly with jungle's soundtrack and fusion tendencies. I decided to get down to cases with these two over 1999's well-regarded *Temperamental.* But having duly noted that after multiple plays I still had no idea what the songs were about, I sat down with the lyric sheet and realized I'd been missing something—on *Temperamental,* at least, Thorn's alienated single woman of no special status alone in the city is chillingly and compassionately observed (or is that experienced?). I shouldn't have needed the print, of course—it's the singer's job to make you notice such stuff. Nevertheless, I'm officially sorry I once called her pseudo-Sade. She's realer than Sade.

Fugazi   The most principled band of the '90s declined to send out promos, a decision I would have respected even if they hadn't been so stalwart in minimizing ticket prices, staging all-ages shows, and otherwise putting punk's D.C.-based straight-edge ethos into practice. Since their Dischord label remained solvent as other indies went mainstream or under, I'm sure they understood venture capital better than I do. I bought three early-'90s albums: *13 Songs, Repeater,* and *Steady Diet of Nothing.* These were enough to convince me that from the strictures of Minor Threat's razor-sharp hardcore to the confrontational formalism of Fugazi's surgical AOR, Ian MacKaye has always been a musical puritan as well as all the other kinds. Obsessed with corruption, he figured out that words and voices don't excise it as efficiently as a well-honed guitar—specifically Guy Picciotto's precise, rock-solid distorto riffs. On *Repeater,* Picciotto offered something like pleasure. On the other two the resemblance was more abstract. I'm not any kind of puritan. So I stopped buying their records.

Hedningarna   As a true American, I relate more naturally to African music than European, which is how I explain my indifference to the Balkan, Irish, Breton, Irish, Basque, Irish, Italian, and Irish folk music I've passed by. The same goes for the "Nordic" stuff released in such abundance on Minneapolis's NorthSide label. But these pan-Scandinavian

Swedish and Finnish guys, whose name means the Heathens, are intense—fast, sexual, even sometimes that great snow-country sham, shamanistic. *Trä* is where to begin; the *Hippjokk* wolfsong "Návdi/Fasa" is pretty scary; the borderland tribute *Karelia Visa* imports two female Finns who immediately start making nice—too nice.

Jimi Hendrix   Hendrix is the John Coltrane of rock discography—a revered improviser cut down so young that every taped leaving is treasured by his acolytes. And where, for better and worse, Coltrane's legacy has always been controlled by his widow, it took 25 years for Hendrix's family to get what they deserved. This resulted in many wondrous late-'90s rerereleases. Because Hendrix's art was preeminently sonic, the vibrant digitalized sound on the three studio albums he put out while alive is reason enough to buy them again. The reconstructed *First Rays of the New Rising Sun* is a worthy replacement for 1971's *The Cry of Love* and its confusion of successors. But like Alice Coltrane, the Hendrix family has completist tendencies reflecting their uncritical regard for the artist they're charged with rendering unto history. This means that twice so far they've replaced excellent Eddie Kramer–overseen reconstructions with longer, less excellent Eddie Kramer–overseen reconstructions: *Live at Woodstock* for *Woodstock* (MCA 1999, MCA 1994), *BBC Sessions* for *Radio One* (MCA 1998, Rykodisc 1988). For what it's worth, which may not be much, I actually like the lo-fi authorized bootleg *Live at the Oakland Coliseum* (MCA 1998). But unless you're an acolyte, I'd suggest that to supplement the '60s basics you pick up MCA's 1994 *Blues* before it's deleted, or shop around for the out-of-print MCA *Woodstock* and Rykodisc *BBC Sessions* and *Live at Winterland* before they disappear. All are available at www.secondspin.com as I write.

Huun-Huur-Tu   These stagewise Tuvans tour too much to be cowboys at heart. They're entertainers—cowboys who wish they could quit their day jobs. Around 1993 they ignited a brief vogue for Tuvan throat singing, in which a single vocalist produces two or three harmonics simultaneously. Far more than Smithsonian's culture-specific ethnographic CDs or Shu-De's half-assed RealWorld pop move, Shanachie's 1993 *60 Horses in My Herd—Old Songs and Tunes of Tuva* is where to sample this exotic sound. Rather than weirdness that fetishizes its own alienation, like yours and mine, this is weirdness at home with itself, a cheerful and awesome thing. Songs and tunes are so slow they sound thoughtfully devotional even when they aren't, which is usually, and traditional fiddle and percussion accompaniment admit a guitar now and then. But it remains so weird that I never developed any sense of their later Shanachie releases. Those who want more should catch their show, which comes with a traveling ethnomusicologist and a shamanistic minidrama featuring animal noises. Or rent the film *Tuva Blues,* starring folkie bluesman Paul Pena, who taught himself throat singing from records. Or check out Baby Gramps, who learned from Popeye.

K. D. Lang   As an out lesbian singing putative country music she galvanized an audience ready to take her seriously—mostly gay, but including me. Conceiving pop as jazz à la Lyle Lovett rather than schlock à la Garth Brooks, she piled on the cred. And she definitely has a voice—calm yet bereft, cool yet kind. But how you respond to a voice is always deeply idiosyncratic, and Lang's continued cult status suggests that not getting hers is nothing to feel guilty about. Or maybe it's just that in a decade when technically accomplished singing made a major pop comeback—which it did, I ambivalently insist, despite what rap haters feared—good singers writing mediocre songs got more play than they deserved. I listened hard to every one of her albums and stuck every one in my Neither file. Her claque cheers loudest for 1992's *Ingénue*.

Astor Piazzolla   The New York-born tango revolutionary made some 40 albums before escaping his niche with 1986's severe, white-hot *Tango: Zero Hour,* and once he died in 1992, there seemed a chance every one of them would be repackaged along with 12 miles of concert tape—as I write, one Web retailer lists 79 consumables. Stick with the Kip Hanrahan-enabled *Zero Hour,* then seek out its follow-up, *The Rough Dancer and the Cyclical Night;* avoid classical ensembles, jazz vibraphonists, and the Milan label. Back when I was trying, I rather liked Tropical Storm's *Love Tanguedia.* But if you crave a dose of avant-garde romanticism con bandoneon, why not just spring for the three-CD *Tangamente 1968–1973?* That ought to hold you for a while.

The Promise Ring   Sometime in the '90s hardcore punk spawned the catchword "emo"—short for emotional, more than that don't ask me, including when if ever this Milwaukee quartet epitomized it. But I know this—"emo" and "Promise Ring" are often seen on the same page. Dragged to a 1999 gig, I found them transcendentally dull, only to discover later that album number three, *Very Emergency,* was indeed a tuneful little number. The special poetry in pitch-challenged lead dork Davey vanBohlen's well-meaning search for love is that nowadays most punks are well-meaning dorks going through a phase. I suspect *Very Emergency* represented a great leap forward. Old fans, already on the train for two or even three years, claim the opposite.

Rock en español   You know I'm desperate when I confess spiritual ignorance not of an artist but a whole genre—hell, a whole musical world. I lived two months in Honduras while adopting my daughter, spend more time in Puerto Rico than I do in New Jersey, adore selected Márquez and Carpentier. But although I enjoy the older Cuban genres, Colombian cumbia, and Mexican son, I'm allergic to Iberian melodrama—loathe international balladry (cf. *Hot Latin Hits*), cringe at flamenco, have never even been a salsa fan. And when it comes to Mexican rock and all its offshoots, well, if I were actually arrogant I'd just say I can't stand any of it—not Los Fabulosos Cadillacs, not Café Tacuba, not Maldita Vecindad, all of whom have occupied many hours of my ear time. Each is different, of course, but all share a kitchen-sink stop-and-go that I associate with the bright, cheap, found jumble of Mexico's visual folk culture. As a look, I love it. As music, I think it's art-rock, except when it's *really* arted up (and grooved down) by my beloved and very L.A. Latin Playboys. Maybe someday I'll retire to Coamo, learn Spanish, and get it. More likely I'll never do any of these things.

Santana   It has long been the habit of artists on Arista Records to thank for their success God and Clive Davis, in that order, and if anybody has a right to put God first, it's Haight-Ashbury's longest-running hippie mystic. But though Carlos Santana released plenty of honorable albums in the '90s, including several shows of multicultural piety and some typically just-better-than-average archival digs, 1999's star-studded *Supernatural* was Clive's miracle: a tribute album owned solely by the tributee (and his corporate sponsor, natch), complete with the hit songs Davis always insists on and quite often gets. Hook him up with Matchbox 20? I ask you, does God have that kind of chutzpah?

Jimmy Scott A jazz balladeer who took the tempo as slowly as any pop stylist of the past 50 years, Scott is as pure as lounge singing gets, yet his 1991 comeback at age 66 preceded and then eluded alt-rock's lounge pseuds. Not only was he African-American, which couldn't have helped, he had too much character—that ethereal croon is so deeply immiserated it seems to detach itself from its own pain and rise from the body that produces it. This style is so recondite that I get suspicious when his admirers marvel over his phrasing while brushing by what's obviously the most interesting thing about the guy—his sexuality or asexuality as the case may be. With his soft soprano and timid cool, he's a strikingly hermaphroditic figure—not campy in the slightest, and if anybody knows whether he's gay it isn't me, but almost eunuchlike. Scott's impassive challenge to conventional gender roles makes him a living counterpart to Billy Tipton. The album I recommend isn't Tommy LiPuma's or Cassandra Wilson's, certified jazzbos though both may be. It's *Dream,* produced by Mitchell Froom of Richard Thompson/Suzanne Vega/Latin Playboys fame, which swings a little if you listen close. Usually, however, I find him, well, slow.

Tarika Sammy Over and above their fine Afro-Asian tunes and sonorities, the secret of Madagascar's most successful export was female vocalist Hanitra. At her ebullient best she's a pep pill for the soul, but at her chirpy worst she can leave you so nauseous with memories of Peter, Paul & Mary you start to suspect that all these lively rhythms and lovely melodies are nothing more than the market-ready "folk music" of the planet's largest one-world theme park. Shortly after making their mark with 1992's *Fanafody,* the group split, with Hanitra and her confederates forming the efficiently dubbed Tarika (Malagasy for "band") while musical maestro Sammy held on to the Tarika Sammy brand. Tarika Sammy Mach II is tasteful if not too tasteful—modernist by the standards of their multicultural petri dish of an island homeland, they sound like folkies from here. Tarika, meanwhile, continue bright if not too bright. I enjoyed 1997's *Son Egal* but, as usual, got first dizzy and then depressed deciding whether it was chirpy or ebullient.

Uz Jsme Doma Given the debts these Czechs owe the Residents and Uriah Heep, Chris Norris's jape made me giggle—Prague-rock. Slavic bands are almost always prog one way or the other—cf. Skoda's *Czeching In* comp. Yet on this one's '93 Europe/'96 U.S. *Hollywood,* the tempo shifts and horn lines and sudden bursts of ugly were as funny as they should have been, more than on the theatrical '91 Europe/'97 U.S. *Unloved World.* And did these guys have catalogue. I played the '90 Europe/'98 U.S. *Fairytales from Needland* all the way through several times, I swear it, then mislaid the thing. As for the two-CD Europe '90/U.S. '99 *In the Middle of Words,* well, I gave it my usual three cuts and never returned. Sorry—I'm just not a prog kind of guy.

Caetano Veloso   I only gained respect for the Kurt-Weill-X-Bing-Crosby of tropicália artsong in the '90s, especially admiring 1999's Bahiabeat-cum-jungle (as in techno, not the Amazon) *Livro* and the irrepressible Gilberto Gil collaboration *Tropicália 2* (see UV inside). But the latter record belongs to Gil, the only Brazilian musician save the avant-unique Tom Zé striking enough to carry an Anglophone provincial past his or her Portuguese. I really don't understand how non-Lusophones can wax ecstatic over a songpoet whose words they know from a trot—which, let me add, may not be as poetic as one dreams. So if some polyglot wanted to call him the greatest popular musician of our era, I wouldn't be inclined to argue. I'd just shrug.

EVERYTHING ROCKS AND
NOTHING EVER DIES

AC/DC

Air Supply

America

Eric Andersen

Asia

Asleep at the Wheel

Average White Band

Bad Company

Joan Baez

Barclay James Harvest

Bauhaus

The Beach Boys

Pat Benatar

Tony Bennett

Big Country

Black Sabbath

Blue Magic

The Blue Nile

Boston

David Bromberg

Arthur Brown

Dennis Brown

Gatemouth Brown

Ruth Brown

Peabo Bryson

Solomon Burke

Canned Heat

Cheap Trick

Chicago

Judy Collins

Phil Collins

Alice Cooper

James Cotton

The Cramps

Christopher Cross

The Damned

Deep Purple

The Delfonics

Rick Derringer

Dire Straits

Dr. Feelgood

Dokken

Donovan

The Doobie Brothers

The Drifters

Duran Duran

Earth, Wind & Fire

Echo and the Bunnymen

Emerson, Lake & Palmer

Fairport Convention

Flamin' Groovies

A Flock of Seagulls

The Flying Burrito Brothers

Foghat

Foreigner

The Four Tops

Peter Frampton

Rory Gallagher

Bob Geldof

Genesis

Gary Glitter

Golden Earring

Gong

The Guess Who

Sammy Hagar

Nina Hagen

Hawkwind

The Headhunters

Heart

Steve Hillage

Hot Tuna

The Human League

Joe Jackson

Millie Jackson

Japan

Jefferson Starship

Jethro Tull

Journey

Judas Priest

Tonio K.

Kansas

KC and the Sunshine Band

King Crimson

The Kinks

Kiss

The Knack

Krokus

Julian Lennon

Lindisfarne

Little Feat

Little River Band

Lobo

Lulu

Lynyrd Skynyrd

Magma

The Manhattan Transfer

Manfred Mann

Phil Manzanara

The Marshall Tucker Band

John Martyn

Country Joe McDonald

Freddie McGregor

The Monkees

The Moody Blues

Giorgio Moroder

Mountain

Nazareth

Bill Nelson

Night Ranger

Nitty Gritty Dirt Band

Ted Nugent

Gary Numan

OMD

Robert Palmer

Graham Parker

Alan Parsons

Tom Paxton

The Pentangle

Carl Perkins

Peter, Paul & Mary

Pink Floyd

Player

The Pointer Sisters

Jean-Luc Ponty

The Pretty Things

Procol Harum

Queensryche	Steel Pulse
Quicksilver Messenger Service	Steppenwolf
Quiet Riot	Al Stewart
Kenny Rankin	John Stewart
Chris Rea	Stiff Little Fingers
Helen Reddy	Sting
Terry Reid	The Stranglers
Renaissance	The Strawbs
REO Speedwagon	Suicide
The Residents	Supertramp
Cliff Richard	Tangerine Dream
Lionel Richie	Johnnie Taylor
Paul Rodgers	The Temptations
Mick Ronson	10cc.
Linda Ronstadt	The The
Tim Rose	Third World
Diana Ross	.38 Special
Todd Rundgren	Irma Thomas
Rush	Toto
Leon Russell	Pat Travers
The Rutles	Robin Trower
Savoy Brown	UFO
Saxon	Ultravox
Boz Scaggs	Uriah Heep
Scorpions	The Ventures
The Searchers	Joe Walsh
John Sebastian	War
Carly Simon	Roger Waters
Slave	Jimmy Webb
The Smithereens	Paul Williams
Sparks	Edgar Winter
Spyro Gyra	Johnny Winter
Squeeze	Steve Winwood
Michael Stanley	Wishbone Ash
Ringo Starr	Link Wray
Status Quo	Yellowman
Steeleye Span	Yes

COMPILATIONS

Hip Hop

Bad Boy Greatest Hits Volume 1 (Bad Boy '98)

Beats & Rhymes: Hip Hop of the '90s Part I (Rhino '97)

Beats & Rhymes: Hip Hop of the '90s Part II (Rhino '97)

Beats & Rhymes: Hip Hop of the '90s Part III (Rhino '97)

Big Phat Ones of Hip-Hop Volume 1 (BOXtunes '95)

Bulworth: The Soundtrack (Interscope '98)

CB4 (MCA '93)

The Corruptor (Jive '99)

Chuck D Presents Louder Than a Bomb (Rhino '99)

Diggin' in the Crates: Profile Rap Classics Volume One (Profile '94)

DJ Red Alert's Propmaster Dancehall Show (Epic Street '93)

'80s Underground Rap: Can I Kick It? (Rhino '98)

'80s Underground Rap: Can You Feel It? (Rhino '98)

'80s Underground Rap: Don't Believe the Hype (Rhino '98)

The Funky Precedent (Loosegroove/No Mayo '99)

Girls Town (Mercury '96)

Hip Hop Greats: Classic Raps (Rhino '90)

Judgment Night (Immortal/Epic Soundtrax '93)

Juice (SOUL '92)

Lyricist Lounge Volume 1 (Rawkus '98)

M-Boogie: Laid in Full (Blackberry '99)

Millennium Hip Hop Party (Rhino '99)

MTV Party to Go Volume 2 (Tommy Boy '92)

MTV Party to Go Vol. 4 (Tommy Boy '93)

MTV Party to Go Volume 6 (Tommy Boy '94)

Muggs Presents . . . The Soul Assassins Chapter 1 (Columbia '97)

New Jack City (Giant '91)

No More Prisons (Raptivism '99)

Pass the Mic: The Posse Album (Priority '96)

Phat Rap Flava (Cold Front '95)

Profilin': The Hits (Arista '99)

Quannum Spectrum (Quannum Projects '99)

Rawkus Presents Soundbombing II (Rawkup '99)

The Real Hip-Hop: Best of D&D Studios Vol. 1 (Cold Front '99)

Ruffhouse Records Greatest Hits (Ruffhouse '99)

The RZA Hits (Razor Sharp/Epic '99)

Soundbombing (Rawkus '97)

South Central (Hollywood Basic '92)

Street Jams: Hip Hop from the Top—Part 4 (Rhino '94)

Strength Magazine Presents Subtext (London/Strength '99)

Trespass (Sire/Warner Bros. '92)

Tricky Presents Grassroots (Payday/FFRR '96)

Wu-Chronicles (Wu-Tang '99)

Yo! MTV Raps (Def Jam '97)

Dance/Techno

Amp (Astralwerks '97)

Aural Ecstasy: The Best of Techno (Relativity '93)

The Best of Reggae Dancehall Vol. 1 (Profile '90)

Big Rock'n Beats (Wax Trax!/TVT '97)

Big Beat Conspiracy: BBC 1 (Pagan '98)

Brother's Gonna Work It Out: A DJ Mix Album by the Chemical Brothers (Astralwerks '98)

City of Industry (Quango '97)

Concept in Dance: The Digital Alchemy of Goa Trance Dance (Moonshine Music '94)

Dancehall Stylee: The Best of Reggae Dancehall Music Vol. 4 (Profile '93)

Dance Hits U.K. (Moonshine Music '94)

Detroit: Beyond the Third Wave (Astralwerks '96)

The Disco Years, Vol, 1: Turn the Beat Around (1974–1978) (Rhino '90)

The Disco Years, Vol. 2: On the Beat (1978–1982) (Rhino '90)

The Disco Years, Vol. 4: Lost in Music (Rhino '92)

Ethnotechno (TVT '93)

Excursions in Ambience (Caroline '93)

Future House: Best of House Music Volume 4 (Profile '93)

Futurhythms (Medicine '93)

Handraizer (Moonshine Music '94)

History of House Music Vol. 2: New York Garage Style (Cold Front '97)

A History of Our World Part 1: Breakbeat & Jungle Ultramix by DJ DB (Profile '94)

Hot Luv: The Ultimate Dance Songs Collection (EMI '96)

Incursions in Illbient (Asphodel '96)

The Jackal (MCA '97)

Journeys by DJ: Billy Nasty Mix (Moonshine Music '93)

Kickin Mental Detergent (Kickin USA '92)

Live at the Social Volume 1 (Heavenly import '96)

Make 'Em Mokum Crazy (Mokum '96)

MTV's Amp 2 (MTV/Astralwerks '98)

New Groove 3: Déconstruire Le Groove Esoterique (REV '99)

The Night Shift (C&S '96)

Ocean of Sound (Virgin import '96)

Only for the Headstrong: The Ultimate Rave Compilation (FFRR '92)

Pop Fiction (Quango '96)

Prodigy Present the Dirtside Recordings Volume One (Beggars Banquet '99)

Technosonic Volume 3 (Sonic '93)

Trance 2 (Ellipsis Arts . . . '95)

Tresor II; Berlin-Detroit . . . A Techno Alliance (NovaMute '93)

Turntable Tastemakers Issue No. 1: The Sound of Cleveland City Recordings (Moonshine Music '94)

URBMix Vol. 1: Flammable Liquid (Planet Earth '94)

Welcome to the Future (Epic '93)

What a Bam Bam!: Dancehall Queens (Shanachie '96)

Wipeout XL (Astralwerks '96)

Y2K: Beat the Clock (Columbia '99)

R&B

Bad Boy Greatest Hits Volume 1 (Bad Boy '98)

Boomerang (LaFace '92)

Crooklyn (MCA '94)

Get Shorty (Antilles '95)

Move to Groove: The Best of 1970s Jazz-Funk (Verve '95)

MTV Party to Go Volume 2 (Tommy Boy '92)

MTV Party to Go Vol. 4 (Tommy Boy '93)

MTV Party to Go Volume 6 (Tommy Boy '94)

MTV: The First Thousand Years: R&B (Rhino '99)

1-800-NEW-FUNK (NPG '94)

Pimps, Players and Private Eyes (Sire/Warner Bros. '92)

The Preacher's Wife (Arista '96)

Risqué Rhythm: Nasty '50s R&B (Rhino '91)

Set It Off (EastWest '96)

Soul Food (LaFace '97)

South Central (Hollywood Basic '92)

Space Jam (Warner Sunset/Atlantic '96)

Sugar and Poison (Virgin import '96)

Uptown Lounge (The Right Stuff '99)

Uptown MTV Unplugged (Uptown/MCA '93)

Waiting to Exhale (Arista '95)

African

African Ambience (Shanachie '99)

A*F*R*I*C*A*N E*L*E*G*A*N*T (Original Sound '92)

Adventures in Afropea 3: Telling Stories to the Sea (Luaka Bop/Warner Bros. '95)

African Salsa (Stern's/Earthworks '98)

Afro-Latino (Putumayo World Music '98)

Azagas and Archibogs (Original Music '91)

Before Benga Vol. 2: The Nairobi Sound (Original Music '93)

Bergville Stories (Columbia import '97)

Cape Verde (Putumayo World Music '99)

Dada Kidawa/Sister Kidawa (Original Music '95)

Divas of Mali (Shanachie '96)

Éthiopiques 1 (Buda Musique import '98)

Éthiopiques 2 (Buda Musique import '98)

Éthiopiques 3 (Buda Musique import '98)

Éthiopiques 4 (Buda Musique import '98)

Freedom Fire—The Indestructible Beat of Soweto (Vol. 3) (Virgin '90)

Gnawa Music of Marrakesh: Night Spirit Masters (Axiom '90)

The Gospel According to Earthworks (Stern's/Earthworks '98)

Guitar Paradise of East Africa (Earthworks '91)

Heart of the Forest (Hannibal '93)

Heavy on the Highlife! (Original Music '90)

Hi-Jivin' (Kijima import '90)

Holding Up Half the Sky: Voices of African Women (Shanachie '97)

I've Found My Love: 1960's Guitar Band Highlife of Ghana (Original Music '93)

Jit—The Movie (Earthworks '91)

Jive Nation: The Indestructible Beat of Soweto Vol. 5 (Stern's/Earthworks '95)

Jive Soweto: The Indestructible Beat of Soweto Vol. 4 (Earthworks '93)

Kenya Dance Mania (Earthworks '91)

Kerestina: Guitar Songs of Southern Mozambigue 1955–1957 (Original Music '95)

The Kings and Queens of Township Jive: Modern Roots of the Indestructible Beat of Soweto (Earthworks '91)

Kings of African Music (Music Club '97)

Lightning over the River (Music Club '99)

Mandela (Mango '97)

Mbuki Mvuki (Original Music '93)

The Music in My Head (Stern's Africa '98)

Muziki Wa Dansi (Afrocassette '95)

No Easy Walk to Freedom (Music Club '98)

Only the Poorman Feel It: South Africa (Hemisphere '95)

Oujda-Casablanca Introspections Vol. 1 (Barbarity import '94)

Pop-Rai and Rachid Style (Earthworks '90)

Queens of African Music (Music Club '97)

Roots Rock Guitar Party: Zimbabwe Frontline 3 (Stern's/Earthworks '99)

The Secret Museum of Mankind: East Africa (Yazoo '98)

Singing in an Open Space: Zulu Rhythm and Harmony 1962–1982 (Rounder '90)

South African Rhythm Riot: The Indestructible Beat of Soweto Volume 6 (Stern's/ Earthworks '99)

The Spirit of Cape Verde (Tinder '99)

Spirit of the Eagle: Zimbabwe Frontline (Vol. 2) (Virgin '90)

Streets of Dakar: Generation Boul Falé (Stern's Africa '99)

A Taste of the Indestructible Beat of Soweto (Earthworks '94)

Telephone Lobi/Telephone Love (Original Music '95)

Township Jazz 'n' Jive (Music Club '97)

Vibrant Zimbabwe (Zimbob '94)

A World out of Time (Shanachie '92)

A World out of Time Vol. 2 (Shanachie '93)

A World out of Time Vol. 3 (Shanachie '96)

Yalla: Hitlist Egypt (Mango '90)

Latin American

Afro-Latino (Putumayo World Music '98)

Afro-Peruvian Classics: The Soul of Black Peru (Luaka Bop/Warner Bros. '95)

Casa de la Trova (Detour '99)

Cuba Classics 2: Dancing with the Enemy (Luaka Bop/Warner Bros. '91)

Cuba: Fully Charged (Earthworks/Caroline '92)

Cuban Dance Party: Routes of Rhythm Volume 2 (Rounder '90)

Cuba Now (Hemisphere '98)

Cumbia Cumbia (World Circuit import '91)

Cumbia Cumbia 2 (World Circuit '94)

El Caimán: Sones Huastecos (Corason '96)

Hot Latin Hits/Exitos Latinos Calientes: The '90s (Rhino '98)

La Iguana: Sones Jarochos (Corason '96)

Nova Bossa: Red Hot on Verve (Verve '96)

Nuyorican Soul (Giant Step/Blue Thumb '97)

Tropicália Essentials (Hip-O '99)

Reggae

The Best of Reggae Dancehall Vol. 1 (Profile '90)

Dancehall Stylee: The Best of Reggae Dancehall Music Vol. 4 (Profile '93)

Reggae for Kids (RAS '92)

Ska Beats 1 (ROIR cassette '90)

Steely & Clevie Play Studio One Vintage (Heartbeat '92)

This Is Ska! (Music Club '97)

Tougher than Tough: The Story of Jamaican Music (Mango '93)

What a Bam Bam!: Dancehall Queens (Shanachie '96)

World

Anokha: Soundz of the Asian Underground (Quango '97)

Bombay the Hard Way (Motel '99)

Buddhist Liturgy of Tibet (World Music Library import '93)

Dublin to Dakar: A Celtic Odyssey (Putumayo World Music '99)

Ethnotechno (TVT '93)

Kalesijski Svuci: Bosnian Breakdown: The Unpronounceable Beat of Sarajevo (GlobeStyle import '92)

Kneelin' Down Inside the Gate: The Great Rhyming Singers of the Bahamas (Rounder '95)

Kwanzaa Music (Rounder '94)

Mbuki Mvuki (Original Music '93)

Money No Be Sand (Original Music '95)

Music of Indonesia 2: Indonesian Popular Music: Kroncong, Dangdut, and Langgam Jawa (Smithsonian/Folkways '91)

The Mystic Fiddle of the Proto-Gypsies (Shanachie '97)

Oujda-Casablanca Introspections Vol. 1 (Barbarity import '94)

Pop-Rai and Rachid Style (Earthworks '90)

Putumayo Presents the Best of World Music: Volume 1: World Vocal (Rhino '93)

Putumayo Presents the Best of World Music: Volume 2: Instrumental (Rhino '93)

The Secret Museum of Mankind Vol. 1 (Yazoo '95)

The Secret Museum of Mankind Vol. 2 (Yazoo '96)

The Secret Museum of Mankind Vol. 3 (Yazoo '96)

Sif Safaa: New Music from the Middle East (Hemisphere '95)

Street Music of Java (Original Music '93)

Tokyo Invasion, Volume I: Cosmic Hurushi Monsters (Virgin Import '96)

Wind Your Waist (Shanachie '91)

Yalla: Hitlist Egypt (Mango '90)

Zouk Attack (Rounder '92)

Rock/Alternative

Backbeat (Virgin '94)

The Best Punk Album in the World . . . Ever! (Virgin import '95)

Born to Choose (Rykodisc '93)

The Commitments (MCA '91)

Dangerhouse: Volume One (Frontier '91)

Dazed and Confused (Medicine '93)

Drive Me Crazy (Jive '99)

ESPN Presents Slam Jams Vol. 1 (Tommy Boy '97)

The Flintstones: Music from Bedrock (MCA '94)

Gabba Gabba Hey (Triple X '91)

Hard Rock Café: Party Rock (Hard Rock/Rhino '98)

Hedwig and the Angry Inch (Atlantic '99)

Honeymoon in Vegas (Epic '92)

Hype! (Sub Pop '96)

Judgment Night (Immortal/Epic Soundtrax '93)

Lipstick Traces (Rough Trade import '93)

The King's Record Collection (Hip-O '98)

Monsters, Robots and Bug Men (Virgin import '96)

Red Hot + Blue (Chrysalis '90)

Rock Stars Kill (Kill Rock Stars '94)

Suburbia (DGC '97)

Tokyo Invasion, Volume 1: Cosmic Hurushi Monsters (Virgin import '96)

Totally Hits (Arista '99)

United Kingdom of Punk: The Hardcore Years (Music Club '98)

United Kingdom of Punk 2 (Music Club '99)

Soundtrack

The Adventures of Priscilla: Queen of the Desert (Mother '94)

Asia Classics 1: The South Indian Film Music of Vijaya Anand: Dance Raja Dance (Luaka Bop/Warner Bros. '92)

Austin Powers—The Spy Who Shagged Me (Maverick '99)

Backbeat (Virgin '94)

Batman Forever (Atlantic '95)

The Beavis and Butt-head Experience (Geffen '93)

Bombay the Hard Way (Motel '99)

Boomerang (LaFace '92)

Bulworth: The Soundtrack (Interscope '98)

CB4 (MCA '93)

The Commitments (MCA '91)

The Corruptor (Jive '99)

Crooklyn (MCA '94)

Dazed and Confused (Medicine '93)

Dead Man Walking (Columbia '95)

Drive Me Crazy (Jive '99)

Excess Baggage (Prophecy '98)

The Flintstones: Music from Bedrock (MCA '94)

Get Shorty (Antilles '95)

Girls Town (Mercury '96)

Honeymoon in Vegas (Epic '92)

Hype! (Sub Pop '96)

The Jackal (MCA '97)

Jit—The Movie (Earthworks '91)

Judgment Night (Immortal/Epic Soundtrax '93)

Juice (SOUL '92)

The Lion King (Walt Disney '94)

Magnolia (Reprise '99)

Mandela (Mango '97)

Naked Lunch (Milan '92)

New Jack City (Giant '91)

Passengers: Original Soundtracks I (Island '95)

Pimps, Players and Private Eyes (Sire/Warner Bros. '92)

The Preacher's Wife (Arista '96)

Set It Off (EastWest '96)

Singles (Epic '92)

Soul Food (LaFace '97)

South Central (Hollywood Basic '92)

South Park: Bigger, Longer & Uncut (Atlantic '99)

Space Jam (Warner Sunset/Atlantic '96)

Suburbia (DGC '97)

Trespass (Sire/Warner Bros. '92)

Waiting to Exhale (Arista '95)

Tribute

All the King's Men: Scotty Moore & D. J. Fontana (Sweetwater '97)

Beat the Retreat: Songs by Richard Thompson (Capitol '94)

Cole Porter: A Centennial Celebration (RCA '91)

Deadicated (Arista '91)

For the Love of Harry: Everybody Sings Nilsson (MusicMasters '95)

Honeymoon in Vegas (Epic '92)

Hound Dog Taylor: A Tribute (Alligator '98)

The King's Record Collection (Hip-O '98)

The Look of Love: The Burt Bacharach Collection (Rhino '98)

No Prima Donna: The Songs of Van Morrison (Polydor '94)

Real: The Tom T. Hall Project (Sire/Delmore/Kickstand '98)

Red Hot + Blue (Chrysalis '90)

Return of the Grievous Angel: A Tribute to Gram Parsons (Almo Sounds '99)

The Songs of Jimmie Rodgers—A Tribute Album (Columbia/Egyptian '97)

The Songs of West Side Story (RCA Victor '96)

Sweet Relief: A Tribute to Victoria Williams (Thirsty Ear/Chaos '93)

Sweet Relief II: Gravity of the Situation (Columbia '96)

Tapestry Revisited (Lava/Atlantic '95)

A Tribute to Curtis Mayfield (Warner Bros. '94)

A Tribute to Stevie Ray Vaughan (Epic '96)

Two Rooms—Celebrating the Songs of Elton John & Bernie Taupin (Polydor '91)

Where the Pyramid Meets the Eye: A Tribute to Roky Erickson (Sire/Warner Bros. '90)

Historical

American Pop: An Audio History (West Hill Audio Archives '98)

Anthology of American Folk Music (Smithsonian Folkways '97)

The Civil War (Elektra Nonesuch '90)

Closer Than a Kiss: Crooner Classics (Rhino '97)

Heritage (Six Degrees/Island '97)

The Jazz Age (Bluebird '91)

Mama Don't Allow No Easy Riders Here (Yazoo '98)

Risqué Rhythm: Nasty '50s R&B (Rhino '91)

White Country Blues (1926–1938): A Lighter Shade of Blue (Columbia/Legacy '94)

Wild About My Lovin': Beale Street Blues 1928–1930 (RCA '91)

Miscellaneous

Ain't Nuthin' but a She Thing (London '95)

Antone's Women (Antone's '92)

Baby Sounds (Kid Rhino '98)

Bring in 'Da Noize, Bring in 'Da Funk (RCA Victor '96)

Christmas Party with Eddie G. (Strikin' It Rich/Columbia '90)

Closer Than a Kiss: Crooner Classics (Rhino '97)

Deep Blues (Atlantic '92)

Every Road I Take: The Best of Acoustic Blues (Shanachie '99)

Floyd Collins (Nonesuch '96)

Great Divorce Songs for Her (Warner Bros. '94)

Guys and Dolls (RCA Victor '92)

Hedwig and the Angry Inch (Atlantic '99)

Help (London '95)

Hempilation (Capricorn '95)

Incredibly Strange Music (Caroline '94)

The Jazz Age (Bluebird '91)

Jazz Satellites—Volume 1: Electrification (Virgin import '96)

Knitting on the Roof (Knitting Factory '99)

Lach's Antihoot: Live from the Fort at Sidewalk Café (Shanachie '96)

Christine Lavin Presents Laugh Tracks Volume 1 (Shanachie '96)

Lesbian Favorites (Rhino '98)

Lipstick Traces (Rough Trade import '93)

The Look of Love: The Burt Bacharach Collection (Rhino '98)

Mama Don't Allow No Easy Riders Here (Yazoo '98)

The Most Beautiful Christmas Carols (Milan '91)

Love to Groove: The Best of 1970s Jazz-Funk (Verve '95)

Nova Bossa: Red Hot on Verve (Verve '96)

Ocean of Sound (Virgin import '96)

Red Hot + Blue (Chrysalis '90)

Rent (DreamWorks '96)

Songs from Chippy (Hollywood '94)

The Carl Stalling Project: Music from Warner Bros. Cartoons 1936–1958 (Warner Bros. '90)

Strip Jointz (Robbins Music '97)

Totally Hits (Arista '99)

Ultimate Christmas (Arista '98)

Uptown Lounge (The Right Stuff '99)

White Country Blues (1926–1938): A Lighter Shade of Blue (Columbia/Legacy '94)

Wild About My Lovin': Beale Street Blues 1928–1930 (RCA '91)

Woodstock 94 (A&M '94)

THE A LISTS

1990 (87)

Tom Zé: *Brazil Classics 4: The Best of Tom Zé* (Luaka Bop/Warner Bros.)

The Go-Betweens: *1978–1990* (Capitol)

The Disco Years, Vol. 1: Turn the Beat Around (1974–1978) (Rhino)

Madonna: *The Immaculate Collection* (Sire)

Public Enemy: *Fear of a Black Planet* (Def Jam)

The Chills: *Submarine Bells* (Slash/Warner Bros.)

L.L. Cool J: *Mama Said Knock You Out* (Def Jam)

Heavy on the Highlife! (Original Music)

Red Hot + Blue (Chrysalis)

Go-Go's: *Greatest* (I.R.S.)

Hip Hop Greats: Classic Raps (Rhino)

Pixies: *Bossanova* (4AD/Elektra)

L7: *Smell the Magic* (Sub Pop)

Meat Puppets: *No Strings Attached* (SST)

Madonna: *I'm Breathless* (Sire/Warner Bros.)

Alpha Blondy: *The Best of Alpha Blondy* (Shanachie)

Gang of Four: *A Brief History of the Twentieth Century* (Warner Bros.)

Ladysmith Black Mambazo: *Classic Tracks* (Shanachie)

Beats International: *Let Them Eat Bingo* (Elektra)

Ice Cube: *Kill at Will* (Priority)

Macka-B: *Natural Suntan* (Ariwa)

The Beautiful South: *Welcome to the Beautiful South* (Elektra)

Bob Dylan: *Under the Red Sky* (Columbia)

Rosanne Cash: *Interiors* (Columbia)

Ladysmith Black Mambazo: *Two Worlds One Heart* (Warner Bros.)

The Civil War (Elektra Nonesuch)

Sonic Youth: *Goo* (DGC)

The Deighton Family: *Mama Was Right* (Philo)

Nick Lowe: *Party of One* (Warner Bros.)

Living Colour: *Time's Up* (Epic)

Ministry: *In Case You Didn't Feel Like Showing Up (Live)* (Sire/Warner Bros.)

Samba Mapangala & Orchestre Virunga: *Virunga Volcano* (Virgin)

Jewel Ackah: *Me Dear* (Highlife World import)

Eno/Cale: *Wrong Way Up* (Opal/Warner Bros.)

Bangles: *Greatest Hits* (Columbia)

Eric B. & Rakim: *Let the Rhythm Hit 'Em* (MCA)

Snap: *World Power* (Arista)

The Ousmane Kouyate Band: *Domba* (Mango)

Pretenders: *Packed!* (Sire/Warner Bros.)

Yalla: Hitlist Egypt (Mango)

Pépé Kallé: *Pépé Kallé* (Gefraco)

Ska Beats 1 (ROIR)

Brand Nubian: *One for All* (Elektra)

The Fall: *458489 A Sides* (Beggars Banquet)

Cuban Dance Party: Routes of Rhythm Volume 2 (Rounder)

Pylon: *Chain* (Sky)

The Pooh Sticks: *Formula One Generation* (Sympathy for the Record Industry)

Freedom Fire—The Indestructible Beat of Soweto (Vol. 3) (Virgin)

Neil Young & Crazy Horse: *Ragged Glory* (Reprise)

Evan Lurie: *Selling Water by the Side of the River* (Island)

Lou Reed/John Cale: *Songs for Drella* (Sire/Warner Bros.)

Steve Coleman and Five Elements: *Rhythm People (The Resurrection of Creative Black Civilization)* (Novus)

Fugazi: *Repeater* (Dischord)

Spirit of the Eagle: Zimbabwe Frontline (Vol. 2) (Virgin)

Loketo: *Soukous Trouble* (Shanachie)

The Flatlanders: *More a Legend Than a Band* (Rounder)

Boubacar Traoré: *Mariana* (Stern's Africa)

Was (Not Was): *Are You Okay?* (Chrysalis)

Sonny Boy Williamson: *Keep It to Ourselves* (Alligator)

Blake Babies: *Sunburn* (Mammoth)

Ali Farka Toure: *The River* (World Circuit import)

Devo: *Greatest Hits* (Warner Bros.)

The Perfect Disaster: *Up* (Fire)

Mekons: *F.U.N. '90* (A&M)

Hi-Jivin' (Kijima)

Guy: *The Future* (MCA)

Salt-n-Pepa: *Blacks' Magic* (Next Plateau)

Macka-B: *Looks Are Deceiving* (Ariwa)

Lisa Stansfield: *Affection* (Arista)

Abed Azrié: *Aromates* (Elektra Nonesuch)

The Clean: *Vehicle* (Rough Trade)

The Disco Years, Vol. 2: On the Beat (1978–1982) (Rhino)

Jali Musa Jawara: *Yasimika* (Hannibal)

Simon Shaheen: *The Music of Mohamed Abdel Wahab* (Axiom)

The Fugs: *Songs from a Portable Forest* (Gazell)

Monie Love: *Down to Earth* (Warner Bros.)

Dreams Come True: *Dreams Come True* (Antone's)

Shazzy: *Attitude: A Hip-Hop Rapsody* (Elektra)

The Best of Reggae Dancehall Vol. 1 (Profile)

Soul II Soul: *Vol II–1990: A New Decade* (Virgin)

Fela: *Black Man's Cry* (Eurobond import)

K. T. Oslin: *Love in a Small Town* (RCA Victor)

Jerry Lee Lewis: *Rockin' My Life Away* (Tomato)

Thomas Anderson: *"Alright It Was Frank . . . And He's Risen from the Dead and Gone Off with His Truck"* (Out There)

Meat Beat Manifesto: *99%* (Mute)

My Bloody Valentine: *Glide* (Sire/Warner Bros.)

Youssou N'Dour: *Set* (Virgin)

1991 (79)

James Brown: *Star Time* (Polydor)

Guitar Paradise of East Africa (Earthworks)

Nirvana: *Nevermind* (DGC)

Linton Kwesi Johnson: *Tings an' Times* (Shanachie)

Wild About My Lovin': Beale Street Blues 1928–1930 (RCA)

Public Enemy: *Apocalypse '91: The Empire Strikes Black* (Def Jam)

Pet Shop Boys: *Discography* (EMI)

Loketo: *Extra Ball* (Shanachie)

The Jazz Age (Bluebird)

Sonny Sharrock Band: *Highlife* (Enemy)

R.E.M.: *Out of Time* (Warner Bros.)

Risqué Rhythm: Nasty '50s R&B (Rhino)

Bonnie Raitt: *Luck of the Draw* (Capitol)

The Feelies: *Time for a Witness* (A&M)

P.M. Dawn: *Of the Heart, of the Soul and of the Cross: The Utopian Experience* (Gee Street)

Run-D.M.C.: *Together Forever: Greatest Hits 1983–1991* (Profile)

Al Green: *One in a Million* (Word/Epic)

Ice-T: *O.G.: Original Gangster* (Sire/Warner Bros.)

Gary Stewart: *Gary's Greatest* (HighTone)

Pulnoc: *City of Hysteria* (Arista)

Tshala Muana: *Soukous Siren* (Shanachie)

The Kings and Queens of Township Jive: Modern Roots of the Indestructible Beat of Soweto (Earthworks)

John Prine: *The Missing Years* (Oh Boy)

Cumbia Cumbia (World Circuit Import)

Digital Underground: *This Is an EP Release* (Tommy Boy)

Dorothy Masuka: *Pata Pata* (Mango)

Pixies: *Trompe le Monde* (Elektra/4AD)

The Leaving Trains: *Loser Illusion Pt. 0.* (SST)

Slick Rick: *The Ruler's Back* (Def Jam/Columbia)

Michael Jackson: *Dangerous* (Epic)

The Blasters: *The Blasters Collection* (Slash/Warner Bros.)

Matthew Sweet: *Girlfriend* (Zoo)

Jimmie Dale Gilmore: *"After Awhile"* (Nonesuch)

Cypress Hill: *Cypress Hill* (Ruffhouse/Columbia)

The Pooh Sticks: *The Great White Wonder* (Sweet Virginia)

Bob Marley & the Wailers: *Talkin' Blues* (Tuff Gong)

The Bats: *Compiletely Bats* (Communion)

Eleventh Dream Day: *Lived to Tell* (Atlantic)

My Bloody Valentine: *Loveless* (Sire/Warner Bros.)

Mekons: *Curse of the Mekons* (Blast First import)

Black Stalin: *Roots Rock Soca* (Rounder)

Yo-Yo: *Make Way for the Motherlode* (East West)

Motorhead: *1916* (WTG)

Jit—The Movie (Earthworks)

The Only Ones: *The Peel Sessions* (Strange Fruit)

John Lee Hooker: *Mr. Lucky* (Charisma/Pointblank)

Tabu Ley Rochereau: *Man from Kinshasa* (Shanachie)

Pulnoc: *Pulnoc* (Globus International import)

Linda Gail Lewis: *International Affair* (New Rose import)

G. W. McLennan: *Watershed* (Beggars Banquet)

Kenya Dance Mania (Earthworks)

The Most Beautiful Christmas Carols (Milan)

Lee "Scratch" Perry: *Lord God Muzick* (Heartbeat)

Eurythmics: *Greatest Hits* (Arista)

Too Much Joy: *Cereal Killers* (Giant)

Downtown Science: *Downtown Science* (Def Jam/Columbia)

Charlie Feathers: *Charlie Feathers* (Nonesuch)

New Jack City (Giant)

The La's: *The La's* (London)

Alex Chilton: *19 Years: A Collection of Alex Chilton* (Rhino)

Tina Turner: *Simply the Best* (Capitol)

Neil Young and Crazy Horse: *Weld* (Reprise)

Chris Smither: *Another Way to Find You* (Flying Fish)

Wir: *The First Letter* (Mute/Elektra)

Dennis Alcapone: *Forever Version* (Heartbeat)

Oumou Sangare: *Moussolou* (World Circuit)

Champion Jack Dupree: *Forever and Ever* (Bullseye Blues)

The Go-Betweens: *The Peel Sessions* (Strange Fruit)

Roky Erickson: *You're Gonna Miss Me: The Best of Roky Erickson* (Restless)

Garth Brooks: *Ropin' the Wind* (Capitol)

Robert Ward and the Black Top All-Stars: *Fear No Evil* (Black Top)

The KLF: *The White Room* (Arista)

Ali Hassan Kuban: From Nubia to Cairo (Shanachie)

Lifers Group: *Lifers Group* (Hollywood Basic)

My Bloody Valentine: *Tremolo* (Sire/Warner Bros.)

Kid Creole and the Coconuts: *You Shoulda Told Me You Were . . .* (Columbia)

King Missile: *The Way to Salvation* (Atlantic)

I.K. Dairo M.B.E. and His Blue Spots: *I Remember* (Music of the World)

Pavement: *Perfect Sound Forever* (Drag City)

1992 (82)

Freedy Johnston: *Can You Fly* (Bar/None)

Ya Ntesa Dalienst & Le Maquisard: *Belalo* (Sango Music import)

Mzwakhe Mbuli: *Resistance Is Defence* (Earthworks)

David Murray: *Shakill's Warrior* (DIW/Columbia)

Lucinda Williams: *Sweet Old World* (Chameleon)

Taj Mahal: *Taj's Blues* (Columbia/Legacy)

L7: *Bricks Are Heavy* (Slash)

Coupé Cloué: *Maximum Compas from Haiti* (Earthworks)

Tom Zé: *Brazil 5: The Return of Tom Zé: The Hips of Tradition* (Luaka Bop/Warner Bros.)

Madonna: *Erotica* (Maverick/Reprise)

Sonic Youth: *Dirty* (DGC)

Pavement: *Slanted and Enchanted* (Matador)

Yoko Ono: *Walking on Thin Ice* (Rykodisc)

The Roches: *A Dove* (MCA)

The Goats: *Tricks of the Shade* (Ruffhouse/Columbia)

Randy Travis: *Greatest Hits Volume One* (Warner Bros.)

Shanté: *The Bitch Is Back* (Livin' Large)

Popinjays: *Flying Down to Mono Valley* (Epic/One Little Indian)

Utah Saints: *Utah Saints* (London)

Gregory Isaacs: *Best of Volumes One and Two* (Heartbeat)

Giant Sand: *Ramp* (Restless)

Orchestra Baobab: *On Verra Ça* (World Circuit)

E. T. Mensah: *Day by Day* (Retroafric)

Thelonious Monster: *Beautiful Mess* (Capitol)

The Robert Cray Band: *I Was Warned* (Mercury)

Asia Classics 1: The South Indian Film Music of Vijaya Anand: Dance Raja Dance (Luaka Bop/Warner Bros.)

Les Ambassadeurs Internationales Featuring Salif Keita: *Les Ambassadeurs Internationales Featuring Salif Keita* (Rounder)

John Lee Hooker: *The Ultimate Collection 1948–1990* (Rhino)

Bikini Kill: *Bikini Kill* (Kill Rock Stars)

The Disposable Heroes of Hiphoprisy: *Hypocrisy Is the Greatest Luxury* (4th & B'way)

T.P O.K Jazz: *Somo!* (TMS import)

Prince and the New Power Generation: *[File Under Prince]* (Paisley Park/Warner Bros.)

A World out of Time (Shanachie)

Stacy Dean Campbell: *Lonesome Wins Again* (Columbia)

The Disco Years, Vol. 4: Lost in Music (Rhino)

The Vaselines: *The Way of the Vaselines: A Complete History* (Sub Pop)

PJ Harvey: *Dry* (Indigo)

Kickin Mental Detergent (Kickin USA)

Pete Johnson: *King of Boogie* (Milan)

Eric B. & Rakim: *Don't Sweat the Technique* (MCA)

Th Faith Healers: *Lido* (Elektra)

Eric Agyeman: *Highlife Safari* (Stern's Africa)

Only for the Headstrong: The Ultimate Rave Compilation (FFRR)

Ministry: *Psalm 69: The Way to Succeed and the Way to Suck Eggs* (Sire/Reprise)

Luna^2: *Lunapark* (Elektra)

Body Count: *Body Count* (Sire/Warner Bros.)

Kris Kross: *Totally Krossed Out* (Ruffhouse/Columbia)

Randy Travis: *Greatest Hits Volume Two* (Warner Bros.)

Joe Houston: *Cornbread and Cabbage Greens* (Specialty)

Grateful Dead: *Two from the Vault* (Grateful Dead)

Nirvana: *Incesticide* (DGC)

Sugar: *Copper Blue* (Rykodisc)

John Trudell: *AKA Grafitti Man* (Rykodisc)

Chris Bell: *I Am the Cosmos* (Rykodisc)

Yo Yo: *Black Pearl* (EastWest)

The Chills: *Soft Bomb* (Warner Bros.)

Master Musicians of Jajouka: *Apocalypse Across the Sky* (Axiom)

Guys and Dolls (RCA Victor)

Orchestra Marrabenta Star de Moçambique: *Independance* (Piranha import)

George Jones: *Walls Can Fall* (MCA)

Morrissey: *Your Arsenal* (Sire)

Leonard Cohen: *The Future* (Columbia)

Hoosier Hot Shots: *Rural Rhythm 1935–1942* (Columbia/Legacy)

Sweet Talks/A. B. Crentsil: *Sweet Talks—Hollywood Highlife Party + A. B. Crentsil—Moses* (ADC import)

FU-Schnickens: *F.U.—Don't Take It Personal* (Jive)

Azagas and Archibogs (Original Music)

They Might Be Giants: *Apollo 18* (Elektra)

ZZ Top: *Greatest Hits* (Warner Bros.)

Steely & Clevie: *Steely & Clevie Play Studio One Vintage* (Heartbeat)

Gilberto Gil/Jorge Ben: *Gil e Jorge* (Verve)

Ladysmith Black Mambazo: *Greatest Hits* (Shanachie)

Monty Python: *Monty Python Sings* (Virgin)

The Beautiful South: *0898 Beautiful South* (Elektra)

Dennis Robbins: *Man with a Plan* (Giant)

Nirvana: *Hormoaning* (DGC import)

Ramones: *Mondo Bizarro* (Radioactive)

Ani DiFranco: *Imperfectly* (Righteous Babe)

The Breeders: *Safari* (4AD/Elektra)

Pavement: *Watery, Domestic* (Matador)

Diblo Dibala & Matchatcha: *Laissez Passer* (Afric Music import)

Rosie Flores: *After the Farm* (HighTone)

Boogie Down Productions: *Sex and Violence* (Jive)

1993 (89)

Elmore James: *The Sky Is Crying: The History of Elmore James* (Rhino)

Tougher than Tough: *The Story of Jamaican Music* (Mango)

John Prine: *The John Prine Anthology: Great Days* (Rhino)

Janis Joplin: *Janis* (Columbia/Legacy)

Liz Phair: *Exile in Guyville* (Matador)

Liliput: *LiLiPUT* (Off Course import)

Etoile de Dakar: *Volume 1—Absa Gueye* (Stern's Africa)

Nirvana: *In Utero* (DGC)

Mighty Sparrow: *Volume One* (Ice)

Loudon Wainwright III: *Career Moves* (Charisma)

Pet Shop Boys: *Very* (EMI)

Wire: *1985–1990: The A List* (Mute)

Archers of Loaf: *Icky Mettle* (Alias)

PJ Harvey: *Rid of Me* (Island)

De La Soul: *Buhloone Mindstate* (Tommy Boy)

Mbuki Mvuki (Original Music)

Digable Planets: *Reachin' (A New Refutation of Time and Space)* (Pendulum)

Before Benga Vol. 2: The Nairobi Sound (Original Music)

P.M. Dawn: *The Bliss Album . . . ?* (Gee Street)

Jimmie Dale Gilmore: *Spinning Around the Sun* (Elektra)

Yo Yo: *You Better Ask Somebody* (EastWest)

Dazed and Confused (Medicine)

Moby: *Move* (Elektra)

The Wild Magnolias: *The Wild Magnolias* (Polydor)

Tom Petty & the Heartbreakers: *Greatest Hits* (MCA)

Dramarama: *Hi-Fi Sci-Fi* (Chameleon)

The Afghan Whigs: *Gentlemen* (Elektra)

Digital Underground: *The Body-Hat Syndrome* (Tommy Boy)

Guns N' Roses: *"The Spaghetti Incident?"* (Geffen)

MTV Party to Go Vol. 4 (Tommy Boy)

A Tribe Called Quest: *Midnight Marauders* (Jive)

Yo La Tengo: *Painful* (Matador)

Fellow Travellers: *Things and Time* (OKra import)

Heart of the Forest (Rykodisc)

Wu-Tang Clan: *Enter the Wu-Tang (36 Chambers)* (RCA/Loud)

The Auteurs: *New Wave* (Caroline)

The London Suede: *Suede* (Columbia)

Joan Jett and the Blackhearts: *Flashback* (Blackheart)

Bobbie Cryner: *Bobbie Cryner* (Epic)

The Shams: *Sedusia* (Matador)

Tina Turner: *What's Love Got to Do with It* (Virgin)

Pablo Lubadika: *Okominiokolo* (Stern's Africa)

Van Morrison: *Too Long in Exile* (Polydor)

Biz Markie: *All Samples Cleared* (Cold Chillin'/Warner Bros.)

Bikini Kill: *Pussy Whipped* (Kill Rock Stars)

Janet Jackson: *janet.* (Virgin)

Gavin Bryars: *Jesus' Blood Never Failed Me Yet* (Point Music)

The Cranberries: *Everybody Else Is Doing It, So Why Can't We?* (Island)

Zap Mama: *Adventures in Afropea 1* (Luaka Bop/Warner Bros.)

KRS-One: *Return of the Boom Bap* (Jive)

Bob Dylan: *World Gone Wrong* (Columbia)

Technosonic Volume 3 (Sonic)

Huun-Huur-Tu: *60 Horses in My Herd—Old Songs and Tunes of Tuva* (Shanachie)

Jive Soweto: The Indestructible Beat of Soweto Vol. 4 (Earthworks)

George Gershwin: *Gershwin Plays Gershwin: The Piano Rolls* (Elektra Nonesuch)

Saint Etienne: *So Tough* (Warner Bros.)

The Breeders: *Last Splash* (4AD/Elektra)

Texas Tornados: *Best of Texas Tornados* (Reprise)

Blake Babies: *Innocence and Experience* (Mammoth)

The Killer Shrews: *The Killer Shrews* (Enemy)

Orchestra Baobab: *Bamba* (Stern's Africa)

Living Colour: *Stain* (Epic)

Born to Choose (Rykodisc)

Big Star: *Columbia: Live at Missouri University 4/25/93* (Zoo)

Judgment Night (Immortal/Epic Soundtrax)

Heavenly: *P.U.N.K. Girl* (K)

Rosanne Cash: *The Wheel* (Columbia)

Ghorwal: *Majurugenta* (RealWorld)

Mahlathini: *King of the Groaners* (Earthworks)

Garth Brooks: *In Pieces* (Liberty)

Mighty Sparrow: *Volume Two* (Ice)

Pavement: *Westing (By Musket and Sextant)* (Drag City)

Dancehall Stylee: The Best of Reggae Dancehall Music Vol. 4 (Profile)

Kanda Bongo Man: *Soukous in Central Park* (Hannibal)

MC Lyte: *Ain't No Other* (First Priority)

George Clinton: *Hey Man . . . Smell My Finger (Paisley Park)*

The Robert Cray Band: *Shame and a Sin* (Mercury)

Souls of Mischief: *93 'til Infinity* (Jive)

Neil Young: *Lucky Thirteen* (Geffen)

Butthole Surfers: *Independent Worm Saloon* (Capitol)

Sue Foley: *Without a Warning* (Antone's)

Violent Femmes: *Add It Up (1981–1993)* (Slash/Reprise)

En Vogue: *Runaway Love* (EastWest)

His Name Is Alive: *Mouth by Mouth* (4AD)

K. T. Oslin: *Greatest Hits: Songs from an Aging Sex Bomb* (RCA)

Journeys by DJ: Billy Nasty Mix (Moonshine Music)

The David Johansen Group: *The David Johansen Group Live* (Epic Associated/Legacy)

Thomas Anderson: *Blues for the Flying Dutchman* (LSR)

Aerosmith: *Get a Grip* (Geffen)

Luna: *Slide* (Elektra)

1994 (73)

Latin Playboys: *Latin Playboys* (Slash/Warner Bros.)

Iris DeMent: *My Life* (Warner Bros.)

Sonic Youth: *Experimental Jet Set, Trash and No Star* (DGC)

Nirvana: *MTV Unplugged in New York* (DGC)

Beck: *Mellow Gold* (Bong Load/DGC)

A Taste of the Indestructible Beat of Soweto (Earthworks)

Aretha Franklin: *Greatest Hits (1980–1994)* (Arista)

Hole: *Live Through This* (DGC)

Garth Brooks: *The Hits* (Liberty)

Pavement: *Crooked Rain, Crooked Rain* (Matador)

M People: *Elegant Slumming* (Epic)

Soul Coughing: *Ruby Vroom* (Slash/Warner Bros.)

Sebadoh: *Bakesale* (Sub Pop)

Grandmaster Flash and the Furious Five: *Message from Beat Street: The Best of Grandmaster Flash and the Furious Five* (Rhino)

Khaled: *N'ssi N'ssi* (Mango)

Handraizer (Moonshine Music)

Sugar: *File Under: Easy Listening* (Rykodisc)

The Bottle Rockets: *The Brooklyn Side* (ESD)

L7: *Hungry for Stink* (Slash/Reprise)

Howlin' Wolf: *Ain't Gonna Be Your Dog* (Chess)

Moe Tucker: *I Spent a Week There the Other Night* (Sky)

Public Enemy: *Muse Sick-N-Hour Mess Age* (Def Jam)

Heavens to Betsy: *Calculated* (Kill Rock Stars)

Archers of Loaf: *Archers of Loaf vs The Greatest of All Time* (Alias)

The Notorious B.I.G.: *Ready to Die* (Bad Boy)

Cachao: *Master Sessions Volume 1* (Crescent Moon/Epic)

Green Day: *Dookie* (Reprise)

White Country Blues (1926–1938): A Lighter Shade of Blue (Columbia/Legacy)

Jon Hassell and Bluescreen: *Dressing for Pleasure* (Warner Bros.)

R.E.M.: *Monster* (Warner Bros.)

Kwanzaa Music (Rounder)

Marianne Faithfull: *Faithfull* (Island)

Jimi Hendrix: *Woodstock* (MCA)

NOFX: *Punk in Drublic* (Epitaph)

Veruca Salt: *American Thighs* (Minty Fresh/DGC)

Cumbia Cumbia 2 (World Circuit)

Caetano Veloso e Gilberto Gil: *Tropicália 2* (Elektra Nonesuch)

John Fahey: *Return of the Repressed: The John Fahey Anthology* (Rhino)

FU-Schnickens: *Nervous Breakdown* (Jive)

El DeBarge: *Heart, Mind and Soul* (Reprise)

Dark City Sisters/Flying Jazz Queens: *Dark City Sisters and Flying Jazz Queens* (Earthworks)

Soundgarden: *Superunknown* (A&M)

Neil Young and Crazy Horse: *Sleeps with Angels* (Reprise)

Dave Alvin: *King of California* (HighTone)

Ass Ponys: *Electric Rock Music* (A&M)

Victoria Williams: *Loose* (Mammoth)

Bill Frisell: *This Land* (Elektra Nonesuch)

Michael Hall: *Adequate Desire* (DejaDisc)

Oujda-Casablanca Introspections Vol. 1 (Barbarity import)

House of Pain: *Same As It Ever Was* (Tommy Boy)

Hüsker Dü: *The Living End* (Warner Bros.)

Jimi Hendrix: *Blues* (MCA)

Marshall Crenshaw: *Marshall Crenshaw Live . . . My Truck Is My Home* (Razor & Tie)

Digable Planets: *Blowout Comb* (Pendulum/EMI)

Joseph Spence and the Pinder Family: *The Spring of Sixty-Five* (Rounder)

Roaring Lion: *Sacred 78's* (Ice)

Technotronic: *Recall* (SBK)

Dance Hits U.K. (Moonshine Music)

Built to Spill: *There's Nothing Wrong with Love* (Up)

Ñico Saquito: *Good-bye Mr Cat* (World Circuit)

Backbeat (Virgin)

Sam Mangwana: *Rumba Music* (Stern's Africa)

Etta James: *Mystery Lady: Songs of Billie Holiday* (Private Music)

Henri Bowane: *Double Take—Tala Kaka* (RetroAfric)

Ladysmith Black Mambazo: *Liph' Iquinso* (Shanachie)

Salif Keita: *The Mansa of Mali . . . A Retrospective* (Mango)

Beat the Retreat: Songs by Richard Thompson (Capitol)

Matthew Sweet: *Son of Altered Beast* (Zoo)

Ahmad: *Ahmad* (Giant)

Turntable Tastemakers Vol. 1: The Sound of Cleveland City Recordings (Moonshine Music)

Skip James: *She Lyin'* (Genes)

Pearl Jam: *Vitalogy* (Epic)

Beastie Boys: *Ill Communication* (Grand Royal)

1995 (90)

Tricky: *Maxinquaye* (Island)

Luna: *Penthouse* (Elektra)

Orüj Guvenc & Tumata: *Ocean of Remembrance* (Interworld)

Archers of Loaf: *Vee Vee* (Alias)

Peter Stampfel: *You Must Remember This . . .* (Gert Town)

Pavement: *Wowee Zowee* (Matador)

New Order: *(The Best of) New Order* (Qwest/Warner Bros.)

James Carter: *The Real Quietstorm* (Atlantic)

Yo La Tengo: *Electr-O-Pura* (Matador)

Randy Newman's Faust (Reprise)

PJ Harvey: *To Bring You My Love* (Island)

The Best Punk Album in the World . . . Ever! (Virgin import)

John Prine: *Lost Dogs and Mixed Blessings* (Oh Boy)

[File Under Prince]: *The Gold Experience* (Warner Bros.)

The Prodigy: *Music for the Jilted Generation* (Muse)

Ornette Coleman: *Tone Dialing* (Verve)

Coolio: *Gangsta's Paradise* (Tommy Boy)

Janet Jackson: *Design of a Decade 1986/1996* (A&M)

Sonic Youth: *Washing Machine* (DGC)

Whale: *We Care* (Virgin)

Adventures in Afropea 3: Telling Stories to the Sea (Luaka Bop/Warner Bros.)

Bad Religion: *All Ages* (Epitaph)

Jive Nation: The Indestructible Beat of Soweto Vol. 5 (Stern's/Earthworks)

Grant McLennan: *Horsebreaker Star* (Atlantic)

Elastica: *Elastica* (DGC)

That Dog: *Totally Crushed Out* (DGC)

Half Japanese: *Greatest Hits* (Safe House)

Barry Black: *Barry Black* (Alias)

The Beautiful South: *Carry on Up the Charts: The Best of the Beautiful South* (Mercury)

Swamp Dogg: *Best of 25 Years of Swamp Dogg . . . Or F*** the Bomb, Stop the Drugs* (Pointblank)

Jo Carol Pierce: *Bad Girls Upset by the Truth* (Monkey Hill)

Godwin Kabaka Opara's Oriental Brothers International: *Do Better If You Can/Onve Ikekwere Mekeya* (Original Music)

Everclear: *Sparkle and Fade* (Capitol)

Alison Krauss: *Now That I've Found You: A Collection* (Rounder)

Yoko Ono/IMA: *Rising* (Capitol)

Shane MacGowan and the Popes: *The Snake* (Warner Bros.)

Buju Banton: *'Til Shiloh* (Loose Cannon)

The Highwaymen: *The Road Goes on Forever* (Liberty)

Thomas Jefferson Slave Apartments: *Bait and Switch* (Onion/American)

Sleater-Kinney: *Sleater-Kinney* (Chainsaw)

The Klezmatics: *Jews with Horns* (Xenophile)

Stevie Wonder: *Conversation Peace* (Motown)

Super Sweet Talks International: *The Lord's Prayer* (Stern's Africa)

The Chemical Brothers: *Exit Planet Dust* (Astralwerks) ·

Mose Fan Fan & Somo Somo Ngobila: *Hello Hello* (Stern's Africa)

Ramones: *It's Alive* (Sire/Warner Archives)

Rancid: *. . . And Out Come the Wolves* (Epitaph)

Ruby Braff and Ellis Larkins: *Calling Berlin, Vol. 1* (Arbors)

Little Charlie and the Nightcats: *Straight Up!* (Alligator)

Massive Attack: *Protection* (Virgin)

Sam Mangwana: *Maria Tebbo* (Stern's African Classics)

Sonic Youth: *Screaming Fields of Sonic Love* (DGC)

Music Revelation Ensemble: *In the Name of . . .* (DIW/Columbia)

Moby: *Everything Is Wrong* (Elektra)

brute.: *Nine High with a Bullet* (Capricorn)

R. Kelly: *R. Kelly* (Jive)

Kirsty MacColl: *Galore* (I.R.S)

Lord Melody: *Precious Melodies* (Ice)

Al Green: *Don't Look Back* (BMG import)

M People: *Forbidden Fruit* (Epic)

Ol' Dirty Bastard: *Return to the 36 Chambers* (Elektra)

Thomas Mapfumo: *Chimurenga Forever: The Best of Thomas Mapfumo* (Hemisphere)

Naughty by Nature: *Poverty's Paradise* (Tommy Boy)

Rolling Stones: *Stripped* (Virgin)

Cornershop: *Woman's Gotta Have It* (Luaka Bop/Warner Bros.)

Mighty Sparrow: *Volume Four* (Ice)

Waiting to Exhale (Arista)

Cachao: *Dos* (Salsoul)

Ani DiFranco: *Not a Pretty Girl* (Righteous Babe)

Marshall Chapman: *It's About Time . . . Recorded Live at the Tennessee State Prison for Women* (Margaritaville)

Steve Earle: *Train a Comin'* (Winter Harvest)

Super Sweet Talks International: *The Lord's Prayer* (Stern's Africa)

Muziki Wa Dansi (Africassette)

Raekwon: *Only Built 4 Cuban Linx . . .* (Loud/RCA)

Stevie Ray Vaughan: Greatest Hits (Epic)

Mu-Ziq: *In Pine Effect* (Astralwerks)

Bonnie Raitt: *Road Tested* (Capitol)

Cachao: *Master Sessions Volume II* (Crescent/Epic)

Belly: *King* (Sire/Reprise)

Green Day: *Insomniac* (Reprise)

New York's Ensemble for Early Music: *Istanpitta Vol. 1* (Lyrichord)

Viva La Musica & Papa Wemba: *Pole Position* (Sonodisc import)

Real McCoy: *Another Night* (Arista)

The Magnetic Fields: *Get Lost* (Merge)

Mark Chesnutt: *Greatest Hits* (Decca)

Only the Poorman Feel It: South Africa (Hemisphere)

Don White: *Live at the Somerville Thgatre* (Lyric Moon)

Liz Phair: *Juvenilia* (Matador)

Animaniacs: *The Animaniacs Faboo! Collection* (Kid Rhino)

Papa Wemba: *Emotion* (RealWorld)

David Murray: *Jug-a-Lug* (DIW import)

1996 (88)

DJ Shadow: *Endtroducing . . . DJ Shadow* (Mo' Wax/FFRR)

Fluffy: *Black Eye* (The Enclave)

Fugees: *The Score* (Ruffhouse/Columbia)

Sleater-Kinney: *Call the Doctor* (Chainsaw)

Frank Sinatra: *Everything Happens to Me* (Reprise)

Amy Rigby: *Diary of a Mod Housewife* (Koch)

The Go-Betweens: *Spring Hill Fair* (Beggars Banquet)

Iris DeMent: *The Way I Should* (Warner Bros.)

Ocean of Sound (Virgin import)

Hot Luv: The Ultimate Dance Songs Collection (EMI-Capitol Music Group)

L.L. Cool J: *All World* (Def Jam)

Los Lobos: *Colossal Head* (Warner Bros.)

Mutabaruka: *The Ultimate Collection* (Shanachie)

Ghostface Killah: *Ironman* (Razor Sharp/Epic Street)

Nirvana: *From the Muddy Banks of the Wishkah* (DGC)

James Carter: *Conversin' with the Elders* (Atlantic)

Toni Tony Toné: *House of Music* (Mercury)

Imperial Teen: *Seasick* (Slash/London)

Willie Nelson: *Spirit* (Island)

Etoile 2000: *Etoile 2000* (Dakar Sound import)

Los Guanches: *The Corpse Went Dancing Rumba* (Corason)

El Caimán: Sones Huastecos (Corason)

Nusrat Fateh Ali Khan & Party: *Intoxicated Spirit* (Shanachie)

Sublime: *Sublime* (MCA/Gasoline Alley)

Youssou N'Dour: *Lii!* (Jololi import)

George Clinton: *Greatest Funkin' Hits* (Capitol)

Joni Mitchell: *Hits* (Reprise)

Fine Young Cannibals: *The Finest* (London/MCA)

Pet Shop Boys: *Bilingual* (Atlantic)

Warren Zevon: *I'll Sleep When I'm Dead (An Anthology)* (Rhino)

Sam Chege: *Kickin' Kikuyu-Style* (Original Music)

Loudon Wainwright III: *Grown Man* (Virgin)

Beck: *Odelay* (DGC)

Kwanzaa Party! (Rounder)

Pulp: *Different Class* (Island)

Sammy: *Tales of Great Neck Glory* (DGC)

Graham Haynes: *Transition* (Antilles)

Tokyo Invasion, Volume 1: Cosmic Hurushi Monsters (Virgin import)

Stereolab: *Emperor Tomato Ketchup* (Elektra)

Pop Fiction (Quango)

Bikini Kill: *Reject All American* (Kill Rock Stars)

Babyface: *The Day* (Epic)

Chaka Khan: *Epiphany: The Best of Chaka Kahn Volume One* (Reprise)

Arto Lindsay: *O Corpo Sutil/The Subtle Body* (Bar/None)

Djeli Moussa Diawara: *Sobindo* (Mélodie import)

Tricky: *Pre-Millennium Tension* (Island)

Fluffy: *5 Live* (The Enclave)

R.E.M.: *New Adventures in Hi-Fi* (Warner Bros.)

Chuck D: *Autobiography of Mistachuck* (Mercury)

Sidi Touré: *Hoga* (Stern's Africa)

Local H: *As Good as Dead* (Island)

Sebadoh: *Harmacy* (Sub Pop)

Ani DiFranco: *Dilate* (Righteous Babe)

Prince Paul: *Psychoanalysis (What Is it?)* (WordSound)

Tshala Muana: *Mutuashi* (Stern's Africa)

Lobi Traoré: *Ségou* (Cobalt import)

Chief Stephen Osita Osadebe: *Kedu America* (Xenophile)

Girls Against Boys: *House of GvsB* (Touch & Go)

[File Under Prince]: *Chaos and Disorder* (Warner Bros.)

Pharoah Sanders: *Message from Home* (Verve)

Kate & Anna McGarrigle: *Matapedia* (Rykodisc)

Sugar and Poison (Virgin import)

Pass the Mic: The Posse Album (Priority)

Ray Condo and His Ricochets: *Swing Brother Swing!* (Joaquin)

Latyrx (Lateef & Lyrics Born): *The Album* (SoleSides)

Archers of Loaf: *All the Nations Airports* (Alias)

Tabu Ley Rochereau: *Africa Worldwide* (Rounder)

Etoile De Dakar: *Volume 3: Lay Suma Lay* (Stern's Africa)

Lou Reed: *Set the Twilight Reeling* (Warner Bros.)

Al Jolson: *Let Me Sing and I'm Happy: Al Jolson at Warner Bros. 1926–1936* (Turner Classic Movies/Rhino)

Make 'Em Mokum Crazy (Mokum)

FU-Schnickens: *Greatest Hits* (Jive)

Dramarama: *The Best of Dramarama: 18 Big Ones* (Elektra Traditions)

Sex Pistols: *Filthy Lucre Live* (Virgin)

[File Under Prince]: *Emancipation* (NRG)

Leon Parker: *Belief* (Columbia)

Thomas Mapfumo: *The Singles Collection 1977–1986* (Zimbob)

Toni Braxton: *Secrets* (LaFace)

Modest Mouse: *This Is a Long Drive for Someone with Nothing to Think About* (Up)

Grandmaster Flash, Melle Mel & the Furious Five: *More of the Best* (Rhino)

His Name Is Alive: *Stars on E.S.P.* (4AD)

Morcheeba: *Who Can You Trust?* (Discovery)

Archers of Loaf: *The Speed of Cattle* (Alias)

Bobbie Cryner: *Girl of Your Dreams* (MCA)

Rage Against the Machine: *Evil Empire* (Elektra)

Grateful Dead: *Dozin' at the Knick* (Grateful Dead)

Uz Jsme Doma: *Hollywood* (Skoda)

Massive Attack V Mad Professor: *No Protection* (Gyroscope)

1997 (102)

Arto Lindsay: *Mundo Civilizado* (Bar/None)

Anthology of American Folk Music (Smithsonian Folkways)

ESPN Presents Slam Jams Vol. 1 (Tommy Boy)

Sleater-Kinney: *Dig Me Out* (Kill Rock Stars)

Pavement: *Brighten the Corners* (Matador)

Yo La Tengo: *I Can Hear the Heart Beating as One* (Matador)

Joan Jett and the Blackhearts: *Fit to Be Tied: Great Hits by Joan Jett and the Blackhearts* (Blackheart/Mercury)

Township Jazz 'n' Jive (Music Club)

Spring Heel Jack: *Busy Curious Thirsty* (Island)

The Notorious B.I.G.: *Life After Death* (Bad Boy)

Sinéad O'Connor: *So Far . . . The Best of Sinéad O'Connor* (Chrysalis/EMI-Capitol)

Closer than a Kiss: Crooner Classics (Rhino)

Tiger: *Shining in the Wood* (Bar/None)

Cornershop: *When I Was Born for the 7th Time* (Luaka Bop/Warner Bros.)

This Is Ska! (Music Club)

Miles Davis: *Dark Magus* (Columbia/Legacy)

The Beautiful South: *Blue Is the Colour* (Ark 21)

Doc Cheatham & Nicholas Payton: *Doc Cheatham & Nicholas Payton* (Verve)

The Songs of Jimmie Rodgers—A Tribute Album (Columbia/Egyptian)

The Klezmatics: *Possessed* (Xenophile)

Toots and the Maytals: *Time Tough: The Anthology* (Island Jamaica)

Jazz Passengers Featuring Deborah Harry: *Individually Twisted* (32)

Sublime: *Sublime* (Gasoline Alley/MCA)

Spring Heel Jack: *68 Million Shades . . . (Island)*

Badar Ali Khan: *Lost in Qawwali* (Worldly/Triloka)

Belle and Sebastian: *If You're Feeling Sinister* (The Enclave)

Oumou Sangare: *Worotan* (World Circuit)

Iggy and the Stooges: *Raw Power* (Columbia/Legacy)

Wyclef Jean: *Wyclef Jean Presents the Carnival Featuring Refugees Allstars* (Ruffhouse/Columbia)

Bob Dylan: *Time Out of Mind* (Columbia)

Jeb Loy Nichols: *Lovers Knot* (Capitol)

Missy "Misdemeanor" Elliott: *Supa Dupa Fly* (The Gold Mind, Inc./EastWest)

Amp (Astralwerks)

The Waco Brothers: *Cowboy in Flames* (Bloodshot)

Mary J. Blige: *Share My World* (MCA)

That Dog: *Retreat from the Sun* (DGC)

Luna: *Pup Tent* (Elektra)

Nusrat Fateh Ali Khan: *Greatest Hits Vol. 1* (Shanachie)

Timbaland and Magoo: *Welcome to Our World* (Blackground/Atlantic)

Modest Mouse: *The Lonesome Crowded West* (Up)

Rubén González: *Introducing . . . Rubén González* (World Circuit)

Shania Twain: *Come on Over* (Mercury)

Mase: *Harlem World* (Bad Boy)

Smash Mouth: *Fush Yu Mang* (Interscope)

John Anderson: *Takin' the Country Back* (Mercury)

Corey Harris: *Fish Ain't Bitin'* (Alligator)

Jazz Satellites—Volume 1: Electrification (Virgin import)

Freedy Johnston: *Never Home* (Elektra)

Kinleys: *Just Between You and Me* (Epic)

Thompson & Thompson: *Industry* (Rykodisc)

Bergville Stories (Columbia import)

Arcana: *Arc of the Testimony* (Axiom/Island)

David Murray: *Fo deuk Revue* (Justin Time import)

Mystikal: *Unpredictable* (Jive/No Limit)

Bis: *The New Transistor Heroes* (Grand Royal)

The Bottle Rockets: *24 Hours a Day* (Atlantic)

Janet Jackson: *The Velvet Rope* (Virgin)

Muggs Presents . . . The Soul Assassins Chapter 1 (Columbia)

Cesaria Evora: *Cabo Verde* (Nonesuch)

Tony Toni Toné: *Hits* (Mercury)

Wayne Kramer: *Citizen Wayne* (Epitaph)

Chemical Brothers: *Dig Your Own Hole* (Astralwerks)

Soundbombing (Rawkus)

Nusrat Fateh Ali Khan: *Rapture* (Music Club)

Dan Bern: *Dan Bern* (Work)

The Murmurs: *Pristine Smut* (MCA)

Apples in Stereo: *Tone Soul Evolution* (SpinArt/Sire)

Oruç Guvenc and Tumata: *Rivers of One* (Interworld)

Big Rock'n Beats (Wax Trax!/TVT)

Kings of African Music (Music Club)

Los Van Van: *Best of Los Van Van* (Milan Latino)

Mandela (Mango)

Beats & Rhymes: Hip Hop of the '90s, Part II (Rhino)

Frank Sinatra and the Red Norvo Quintet: *Live in Australia, 1959* (Blue Note)

Ani DiFranco: *Living in Clip* (Righteous Babe)

Patsy Cline: *Live at the Cimarron Ballroom* (MCA)

Willie Nelson: *I Let My Mind Wander* (Kingfisher)

History of House Music Vol. 2: New York Garage Style (Cold Front)

Blondie: *Essential Blondie: Picture This Live* (EMI/Capitol)

Ornette + Joachim Kühn: *Colors* (Harmolodic/Verve)

Steve Earle: *El Corazón* (Warner Bros.)

L7: *The Beauty Process: Triple Platinum* (Slash/Reprise)

Spearhead: *Chocolate Supa Highway* (Capitol)

Bobby Brown, Bell Biv Devoe, Ralph Tresvant: *New Edition Solo Hits* (MCA)

Backstreet Boys: *Backstreet Boys* (Jive)

Buju Banton: *Inna Heights* (VP)

Pavement: *Shady Lane* (Matador)

Strip Jointz (Robbins Music)

Thomas Jefferson Slave Apartments: *Straight to Video* (Anyway)

Replacements: *All for Nothing/Nothing for All* (Reprise)

Yuri Yunakov Ensemble: *New Colors in Bulgarian Wedding Music* (Traditional Crossroads)

Miles Davis: *Black Beauty* (Columbia/Legacy)

Beats & Rhymes: Hip Hop of the '90s, Part III (Rhino)

All the King's Men (Sweetfish)

The Neckbones: *Souls on Fire* (Fat Possum/Epitaph)

Forest for the Trees: *Forest for the Trees* (DreamWorks)

Sally Timms: *Cowboy Sally* (Bloodshot)

Foo Fighters: *The Colour and the Shape* (Roswell)

Warda: *Lebanon/Algeria* (Metro Blue)

We: *As Is* (Asphodel)

Moby: *Animal Rights* (Elektra)

1998 (85)

Lucinda Williams: *Car Wheels on a Gravel Road* (Mercury)

The Music in My Head (Stern's Africa)

Sonic Youth: *A Thousand Leaves* (DGC)

Billy Bragg & Wilco: *Mermaid Avenue* (Elektra)

American Pop: An Audio History (West Hill Audio Archives)

Liz Phair: *Whitechocolatespacegg* (Matador/Capitol)

Miles Davis: *Panthalassa: The Music of Miles Davis 1969–1974* (Columbia)

The Plastic People of the Universe: *1997* (Globus International import)

Public Enemy: *He Got Game* (Def Jam)

Aretha Franklin: *A Rose Is Still a Rose* (Arista)

Hard Rock Café: Party Rock (Hard Rock/Rhino)

George Clinton & the P-Funk All Stars: *Dope Dogs* (Dogone)

The B-52's: *Time Capsule: Songs for a Future Generation* (Warner Bros.)

The Coup: *Steal This Album* (Dogday)

Gang of Four: *100 Flowers Bloom* (Rhino)

Beastie Boys: *Hello Nasty* (Grand Royal)

Cadallaca: *Introducing Cadallaca* (K)

Los Van Van: *La Colección Cubana* (Music Club)

Canibus: *Can-I-Bus* (Universal)

Bonnie Raitt: *Fundamental* (Capital)

James Carter: *In Carterian Fashion* (Atlantic)

Local H: *Pack Up the Cats* (Island)

Mary J. Blige: *The Tour* (MCA)

Pulnoc: *Live in New York* (Globus International import)

Grandaddy: *Under the Western Freeway* (V2)

Marc Ribot y Los Cubanos Postizos (The Prosthetic Cubans): *Marc Ribot y Los Cubanos Postizos (The Prosthetic Cubans)* (Atlantic)

Sarge: *The Glass Intact* (Mud)

Kid Rock: *Devil Without a Cause* (Atlantic/Lava)

P.M. Dawn: *Dearest Christian, I'm So Very Sorry for Bringing You Here. Love, Dad* (Gee Street/V2)

PJ Harvey: *Is This Desire?* (Island)

John Lennon: *Wonsaponatime* (Capitol)

Alanis Morissette: *Supposed Former Infatuation Junkie* (Maverick/Reprise)

Mama Don't Allow No Easy Riders Here (Yazoo)

Bang on a Can: *Music for Airports: Brian Eno* (Point Music)

Rancid: *Life Won't Wait* (Epitaph)

OutKast: *Aquemini* (LaFace)

Butch Thompson: *Thompson Plays Joplin* (Daring)

Air: *Moon Safari* (Source/Caroline)

Tom Waits: *Beautiful Maladies: The Island Years* (Island)

Chumbawamba: *Uneasy Listening* (EMI import)

Fat Beats & Brastraps: Classics (Rhino)

Tom Zé: *Fabrication Defect/Com Defeito De Fabricão.* (Luaka Bop)

Alvin Youngblood Hart: *Territory* (Rykodisc)

Archers of Loaf: *White Trash Heroes* (Alias)

Amy Rigby: *Middlescence* (Koch)

Soul Coughing: *El Oso* (Slash/Warner Bros.)

Beck: *Mutations* (DGC)

James Brown: *Say It Live and Loud: Live in Dallas 08.26.68* (Polydor)

The King's Record Collection (Hip-O)

Tricky: *Angels with Dirty Faces* (Island)

Sunz of Man: *(The Last Shall Be First)* (Red Ant)

New Radicals: *Maybe You've Been Brainwashed Too* (MCA)

Kate & Anna McGarrigle: *The McGarrigle Hour* (Hannibal)

Black Star: *Mos Def & Talib Kweli Are Black Star* (Rawkus)

Jon Langford: *Skull Orchard* (Sugar Free)

United Kingdom of Punk: *The Hardcore Years* (Music Club)

Redman: *Doc's da Name 2000* (Def Jam)

Bran Van 3000: *Glee* (Capitol)

The Andy Statman Quartet: *The Hidden Light* (Sony Classical)

Belle and Sebastian: *The Boy with the Arab Strap* (Matador)

Killah Priest: *Heavy Mental* (Geffen)

Chris Knight: *Chris Knight* (Decca)

Bikini Kill: *The Singles* (Kill Rock Stars)

Badar Ali Khan: *Lost in Qawwali II* (Worldly/Triloka)

King Sunny Ade: *Odú* (Atlantic/Mesa)

John Lee Hooker: *The Best of Friends* (Pointblank)

Ani DiFranco: *Little Plastic Castle* (Righteous Babe)

Youssou N'Dour: *Best of 80's* (Celluloid import)

Afro-Latino (Putumayo World Music)

MTV's Amp 2 (MTV/Astralwerks)

Buddy Guy and Junior Wells: *Last Time Around* (Silvertone)

The Offspring: *Americana* (Columbia)

Odyssey the Band: *Reunion* (Knitting Factory Works)

Red Hot + Rhapsody (Antilles)

Paolo Conte: *The Best of Paolo Conte* (Nonesuch)

Hound Dog Taylor: A Tribute (Alligator)

Rachid Taha: *Diwan* (Island)

Pearl Jam: *Yield* (Epic)

Mary Lou Lord: *Got No Shadow* (Work)

Scrawl: *Nature Film* (Elektra)

Henri Dikongué: *C'Est La Vie* (Tinder)

Quasi: *Featuring "Birds"* (Up)

Garbage: *Version 2.0* (Almo Sounds)

Cuba Now (Metro Blue)

Ali: *Crucial* (Island Black Music)

Victoria Williams: *Musings of a Creekdipper* (Atlantic)

1999 (102)

The Magnetic Fields: *69 Love Songs* (Merge)

Moby: *Play* (V2)

A Tribe Called Quest: *Anthology* (Jive)

Le Tigre: *Le Tigre* (Mr. Lady)

John Prine: *In Spite of Ourselves* (Oh Boy)

Holy Modal Rounders: *Too Much Fun* (Rounder)

Latin Playboys: *Dose* (Atlantic)

Sleater-Kinney: *The Hot Rock* (Kill Rock Stars)

MTV: The First Thousand Years: R&B (Rhino)

Handsome Boy Modeling School: *So . . . How's Your Girl?* (Tommy Boy)

Willie Nelson: *Night and Day* (Pedernales/FreeFalls)

Prince Paul: *Prince Paul Presents A Prince Among Thieves* (Tommy Boy)

Q-Tip: *Amplified* (Arista)

Jay-Z: *Vol 2 . . . Life and Times of S. Carter* (Roc-A-Fella)

Old 97's: *Fight Songs* (Elektra)

Steve Earle and the Del McCoury Band: *The Mountain* (E Squared)

Randy Newman: *Bad Love* (DreamWorks)

Goodie Mob: *World Party* (LaFace)

RZA: *The RZA Hits* (Razor Sharp/Epic)

Eminem: *The Slim Shady LP* (Aftermath/Interscope)

Mandy Barnett: *I've Got a Right to Cry* (Sire)

Imperial Teen: *What Is Not to Love* (London)

The Handsome Family: *Down in the Valley* (Independent import)

Taj Mahal and Toumani Diabate: *Kulanjan* (Hannibal)

Mary J. Blige: *Mary* (MCA)

Trailer Bride: *Whine de Lune* (Bloodshot)

Tropicàlia Essentials (Hip-O)

Tom Waits: *Mule Variations* (Epitaph)

Papa Wemba: *M'zée Fula-Ngenge* (Sonodisc import)

Gang Starr: *Full Clip: A Decade of Gang Starr* (Virgin)

The Dismemberment Plan: *Emergency and I* (DeSoto)

Blink 182: *Enema of the State* (MCA)

Pretenders: *Viva el Amor* (Warner Bros.)

South Park: Bigger, Longer & Uncut (Atlantic)

Spring Heel Jack: *Treader* (Tugboat import)

Totally Hits (Arista)

Y2K: Beat the Clock (Columbia)

Pet Shop Boys: *Nightlife* (Parlophone/Sire)

Drive-by Truckers: *Pizza Deliverance* (Soul Dump)

Salif Keita: *Papa* (Metro Blue)

Pavement: *Terror Twilight* (Matador)

Cesaria Evora: *Café Atlantico* (Lusafrica/RCA Victor/BMG Classics)

Dr. Dooom: *First Come, First Served* (Funky Ass)

Charlie Burton: *One Man's Trash: The Charlie Burton Story: '77–'99* (Bulldog)

Waco Brothers: *WacoWorld* (Bloodshot)

The Beastie Boys: *Beastie Boys Anthology: The Sound of Science* (Grand Royal/Capitol)

Ladysmith Black Mambazo: *Live at the Royal Albert Hall* (Shanachie)

Ali Farka Toure: *Niafunké* (Hannibal)

Dream Warriors: *Anthology: A Decade of Hits 1988–1998* (Priority)

Baby Gramps: *Same Ol' Timeously* (Grampophone)

Dee Dee Bridgewater: *Live at Yoshi's* (Verve)

Sebadoh: *The Sebadoh* (Sub Pop/Sire)

Slick Rick: *The Art of Storytelling* (Def Jam)

Blondie: *No Exit* (Beyond)

Albert King with Stevie Ray Vaughan: *In Session* (Stax)

Ani DiFranco: *Up Up Up Up Up Up* (Righteous Babe)

Chris Smither: *Drive You Home Again* (HighTone)

Estrellas de Arieto: *Los Heroes* (World Circuit/Nonesuch)

Genaside II: *Ad Finite* (Durban Poison)

The Del-Lords: *Get Tough: The Best of the Del-Lords* (Restless)

Taraf de Haïdouks: *Taraf de Haïdouks* (Nonesuch)

The Real Hip-Hop: Best of D&D Studios Vol. 1 (Cold Front)

Baaba Maal: *Live at the Royal Festival Hall* (Palm Pictures)

Cape Verde (Putumayo World Music)

Liquid Todd: *Action* (Ultra)

Mos Def: *Black on Both Sides* (Rawkus)

Rawkus Presents Soundbombing II (Rawkus)

South African Rhythm Riot: The Indestructible Beat of Soweto Volume 6 (Stern's/Earthworks)

Black Box Recorder: *England Made Me* (Jetset)

Uptown Lounge (The Right Stuff)

They Might Be Giants: *Long Tall Weekend* (www.emusic.com)

Arto Lindsay: *Pride* (Righteous Babe)

Paul McCartney: *Run Devil Run* (Capitol)

Streets of Dakar: Generation Boul Falé (Stern's Africa)

Natacha Atlas: *Gedida* (Beggars Banquet)

Baobab: *N'Wolof* (Dakar Sound import)

Casa de la Trova (Detour)

The Donnas: *Get Skintight* (Lookout!)

Continental Drifters: *Vermilion* (Razor & Tie)

The Robert Cray Band: *Heavy Picks—The Robert Cray Band Collection* (Mercury)

Frank Sinatra: *Sinatra '57—In Concert* (DCC)

Uptown Lounge (The Right Stuff)

Millennium Hip Hop Party (Rhino)

Teri Thornton: *I'll Be Easy to Find* (Blue Note)

Pere Ubu: *Apocalypse Now* (Thirsty Ear)

Fiona Apple: *When the Pawn . . .* (Clean Slate/Epic)

Roots Rock Guitar Party: Zimbabwe Frontline 3 (Stern's/Earthworks)

Ruffhouse Records Greatest Hits (Ruffhouse)

Dwight Yoakam: *Last Chance for a Thousand Years: Dwight Yoakam's Greatest Hits from the 90's* (Reprise)

Idlewild: *Hope Is Important* (Odeon)

Mekons: *I Have Been to Heaven and Back: Hen's Teeth and Other Fragments of Unpopular Culture Vol. 1* (Quarterstick)

Return of the Grievous Angel: A Tribute to Gram Parsons (Almo Sounds)

Tricky with DJ Muggs and Grease: *Juxtapose* (Island)

Lightning over the River (Music Club)

Marshall Crenshaw: *Number 447* (Razor & Tie)

Belle and Sebastian: *Tigermilk* (Matador)

Kelis: *Kaleidoscope* (Virgin)

Source Direct: *Exorcise the Demons* (Astralwerks)

Alpha Yaya Diallo: *The Message* (Wicklow)

Sheryl Crow and Friends: *Live from Central Park* (A&M)

The Comedian Harmonists: *The Comedian Harmonists* (Hannibal)

Don White: *Brown Eyes Shine* (Lumperboy)